# Contents

Acknowledgments                                    xix
Foreword by John B. Hattendorf                     xxi
Introduction                                       xxiii
Editorial Note                                     xxix
Abbreviations                                      xxxi
List of Maps and Charts                            xxxiii

## *Part I*

# The War of the French Revolution

*Chapter numbers correspond to sites on maps, pp. xvi and xviii.*

### 1.  In the King's Service, 1793–1794                3

With only a silver watch and one rupee to his name, William Richardson is pressed
into service while in India. He describes life on board the 48-gun frigate *Minerva*
and how a mutiny was avoided; from *A Mariner of England: An Account of William
Richardson from Cabin Boy in the Merchant Service to Warrant Officer in the Royal Navy
[1780 to 1819] as Told by Himself,* edited by Colonel Spencer Childers, C.B., R.E.

### 2.  Commence the Work of Destruction:
### The Glorious First of June, 1794                   12

On board Gambier's speedy 74-gun HMS *Defence*, fourteen-year-old William Dillon
experiences the heat of the Glorious First of June in the hellish lower deck; from *A*

*Narrative of My Adventures (1790–1839),* by Sir William Henry Dillon, K.C.H., Vice-Admiral of the Red, edited by Michael A. Lewis, C.B.E., M.A., F.S.A., F.R.Hist.S.

### 3. The Noted Pimp of Lisbon and an Unwanted Promotion in Bull Bay, 1794                                                              33

Sailing homeward on board the *Gorgon*, 44 guns, James Gardner reports on ship life and shore leave in Gibraltar, Cadiz, and Lisbon. Along the way, French prisoners nearly revolt upon hearing the "Marseillese," American sailors invite a brawl over a beef pie, and a deserter gets an undesirable promotion from a chamber pot; from *Recollections of James Anthony Gardner, Commander R.N. (1775–1814)*, edited by Sir R. Vesey Hamilton, G.C.B., Admiral, and John Knox Laughton, M.A., D.Litt.

### 4. For the Good of My Own Soul, 1795                                 45

An itinerant merchant and naval seaman dodges the press gangs in England and describes a brief stay in London before meeting his inevitable fate; from *The Nagle Journal: Diary of the Life of Jacob Nagle, Sailor, from the Year 1775 to 1841*, edited by John C. Dann.

### 5. They Would as Soon Have Faced the Devil Himself as Nelson, 1796                                                                   54

Nelson and his shipmate Archibald Menzies, better known as the "Scotch Hercules," oversee the evacuation of Bastia, Corsica, after Spain enters the war against Britain; from "Nelson at Bastia," by M.C., An Old Agamemnon, *United Service Journal*, February 1841, no. 147.

### 6. The Battle of Cape St. Vincent, 1797                              64

In an inspired moment, Nelson deviates from the battle plan and produces one of the most unlikely triumphs of the war; from *A Narrative of the Battle of St. Vincent; with Anecdotes of Nelson, Before and After that Battle*, by John Drinkwater Bethune, F.S.A.

### 7. Mad Dickey's Amusement, 1798–1800                                 88

At last, Jacob Nagle finds his niche in the Royal Navy. On board the sloop *Netley*, he is a very busy prizemaster; from *The Nagle Journal*, edited by John C. Dann.

### 8. The Fortune of War, 1799                                         108

In the Bay of Bengal, a captive merchant captain experiences a fierce battle between two powerful frigates, the French *La Forte*, 50 guns, and HMS *La Sybille*, 44 guns; from *A Master Mariner: Being the Life and Adventures of Captain Robert William Eastwick*, edited by Herbert Compton.

**9.  The Audacious Cruise of the *Speedy*, 1800–1801**     **120**

Captain Thomas Cochrane, later the tenth earl of Dundonald, and the fifty-four-man crew of the *Speedy*, 14 guns, have the gall to engage and board the Spanish xebec frigate *El Gamo*, 32 guns, 319 men; from *The Autobiography of a Seaman*, by Thomas, Tenth Earl of Dundonald, G.C.B., Admiral of the Red, Rear-Admiral of the fleet, Marquess of Maranham, etc.

# Part II

# Peace

**10.  Bermuda in the Peace, 1802–1803**     **139**

A midshipman recounts the loss of a shipmate during a gale and horseplay in Bermuda during a lull in the action; from *The Midshipman: Being the Autobiographical Sketches of His Own Early Career, from Fragments of Voyages and Travels*, by Captain Basil Hall, R.N., F.R.S.

# Part III

# The Napoleonic War

**11.  The Battle of Trafalgar, 1805**     **159**

Nelson's greatest triumph as seen by William Robinson from the lower deck; from *Jack Nastyface: Memoirs of a Seaman*, by William Robinson.

**12.  The Death of Lord Nelson, 1805**     **169**

Dr. Beatty observes Admiral Nelson throughout his ultimate battle and reports here his words with Captain Hardy and others, including his last words; from *The Death of Lord Nelson, 21 Oct. 1805*, by William Beatty, M.D., edited by Edward Arber, F.S.A.

**13.  An Unequal Match, 1807–1808**     **185**

Given an unworthy command, Captain William Dillon makes the best of an ugly situation in northern waters. In command of the brig *Childers*, against the much heavier Danish brig *Lügum*, Dillon shows his heart of oak; from *A Narrative of My Adventures (1790–1839)*, by Sir William Henry Dillon, K.C.H., Vice-Admiral of the Red, edited by Michael A. Lewis.

14.    With Stopford in the Basque Roads, 1808–1809                    213

Fifteen years after being impressed into the Royal Navy, William Richardson, now a warrant officer, participates in one of the most storied naval actions of the Napoleonic wars; from *A Mariner of England*, edited by Colonel Spencer Childers.

15.    When I Beheld These Men Spring from the Ground, 1809        234

When first heard from in *Every Man Will Do His Duty*, Midshipman Hall was avenging the death of Shakings, a cur, on board the *Leander* in the waters off Bermuda. Five years later, having recently passed for lieutenant, Hall witnesses an awesome sight, the Battle of Corunna, and assists in the embarkation of retreating British troops; from *The Midshipman*, by Captain Basil Hall.

16.    "Damn 'em, Jackson, They've Spoilt My Dancing,"
       1809–1812                                                              255

Beset by four French ships, HMS *Junon*, 38 guns, fights courageously and her captain is fatally wounded. But for the *Junon*'s Lieutenant Jackson, this is just the beginning of a wild odyssey through the French prisons of Verdun and Bitche and back home again; from *The Perilous Adventures and Vicissitudes of a Naval Officer, 1801–1812; Being Part of the Memoirs of Admiral George Vernon Jackson (1787–1876)*, edited by Harold Burrows, C.B.E., F.R.C.S.

17.    The Woodwind Is Mightier than the Sword, 1809–1812           290

A former U.S. Navy seaman, James Durand is impressed by the British, is wounded in battle, and discovers a novel way to ease the burden of service; from *James Durand: An Able Seaman of 1812, His Adventures on "Old Ironsides" and as an Impressed Sailor in the British Navy*, edited by George S. Brooks.

## Part IV

# The Napoleonic War, Continued, and the War of 1812

18.    HMS *Macedonian* vs. USS *United States*, 1812                   303

During the bloody battle between the *Macedonian* and the *United States*, Samuel Leech fights the *Macedonian*'s fifth gun on the main deck and loses some of his mess; from *Thirty Years from Home or A Voice from the Main Deck*, by Samuel Leech.

19.    An Unjustifiable and Outrageous Pursuit, 1812–1813             320

Down on his luck, George Little, an American seaman, turns to privateering and his luck grows worse. A story of fighting, cannibals, and prison; from *Life on the Ocean; or, Twenty Years at Sea: Being the Personal Adventures of the Author*, by George Little.

**20.   A Yankee Cruiser in the South Pacific, 1813**                    345

Sent to the South Pacific to protect American whalers and to wreak havoc upon British shipping and whaling interests, Captain David Porter runs up the coast of Chile and Peru to the Galapagos Islands in his mighty little frigate *Essex;* from *Journal of a Cruise Made to the Pacific Ocean by Captain David Porter in the United States Frigate Essex, in the Years 1812, 1813, and 1814.*

**21.   Showdown at Valparaiso, 1814**                                  367

The *Phoebe's* Captain Hillyar is a friend of Captain Porter's. In earlier days, Porter spent many pleasant hours with the Hillyar family in Gibraltar. Yet Hillyar's mission is to destroy Porter's frigate, the *Essex.* Far from home waters, the tension mounts as the two frigates lie anchored in a neutral port; from *Journal of a Cruise Made to the Pacific Ocean by Captain David Porter.*

**22.   We Discussed a Bottle of Chateau Margot Together, 1812–1815**                                                        395

Lieutenant William Bowers cruises off southwestern England and then takes a land tour on the other side of the Channel; from *Naval Adventures During Thirty-Five Years' Service,* by Lieutenant W. Bowers, R.N.

Notes on the Texts                                            407
Selected Bibliography                                         413
Index                                                        415

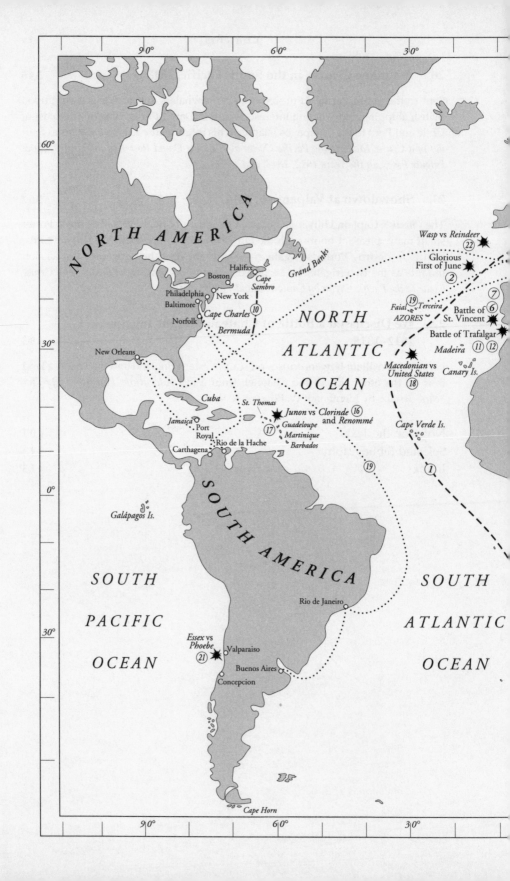

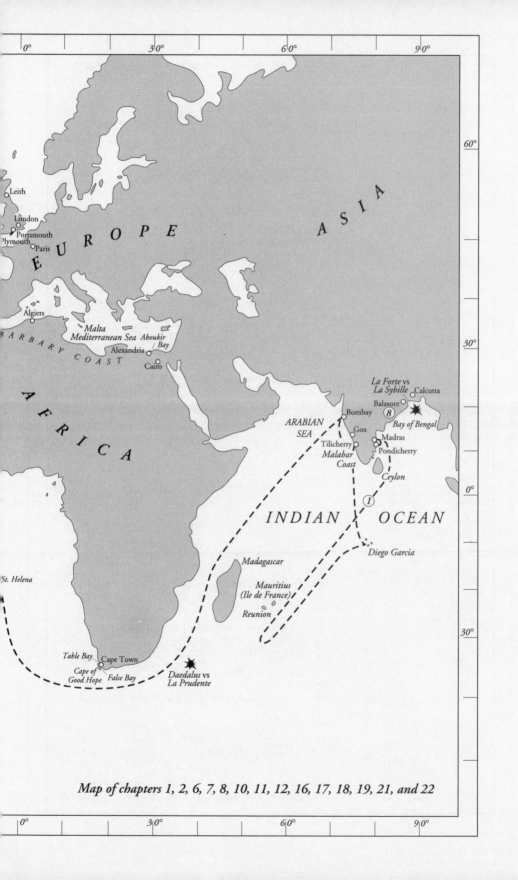

Map of chapters 1, 2, 6, 7, 8, 10, 11, 12, 16, 17, 18, 19, 21, and 22

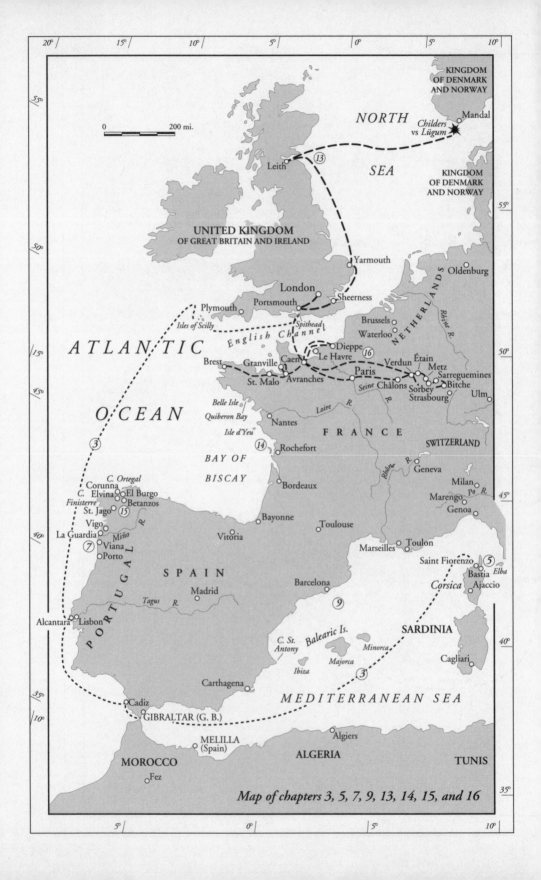

*Map of chapters 3, 5, 7, 9, 13, 14, 15, and 16*

# Acknowledgments

The editors wish to express their gratitude to Jessica King for her editorial input, to J. Worth Estes for his suggestions for works to be included, and to Adam Merton Cooper for his excellent maps and battle charts. They would also like to thank John C. Dann for permission to use material from *The Nagle Journal* and the Navy Records Society for permission to reprint selections from *Recollections of James Anthony Gardner* and Dillon's *Narrative of My Adventures*. The Henry E. Eccles Library of the Naval War College and the library of the New York Yacht Club generously made available the books from which many of the selections in this volume are excerpted. Once again, our sincerest thanks to David Sobel and Jonathan Swain Landreth at the Victualling and Ordnance Board and Jody Rein, our prize agent.

# Foreword

$T$HE EDITORS OF THIS VOLUME started out with a shared interest in the historical novels of Patrick O'Brian, particularly his series of eighteen Aubrey-Maturin books dealing with the Royal Navy in the wars of the French Revolution and Empire, 1793–1815. O'Brian's work, like all the best historical fiction, both draws strength from and sheds light on its chosen era. It has a well-researched historical framework around which the author develops his characters and builds his plot, slipping seamlessly between fact and fiction. Ideally, the work raises curiosity and deeper interest in the historical period in which the novels are set. With that in mind, we produced *A Sea of Words*, a general guide to the historical background and the technical language used in the novels. Then we went on to produce *Harbors and High Seas*, a geographical companion to the series with new and period maps. Both works were designed to help readers better understand the historical setting and technical references that O'Brian uses in his novels.

In *Every Man Will Do His Duty*, we took a further step in this direction. This time we hoped to draw the dedicated readers of novels about the Royal Navy in this period to some of the remarkable nonfiction accounts written by the men who were actually there. To that end, we selected works of the period that describe events that have inspired not only Patrick O'Brian, but also C. S. Forester, Alexander Kent, C. Northcote Parkinson, Dudley Pope, et al.

We chose a series of cohesive, short essays that we think are well-written examples of the literature and that touch on many of the highlights of the wars. These passages have certainly been pored over by historians of maritime affairs, although some are rather obscure. We presented our collection in a way that leads the reader chronologically through the course of the period. Our purpose was to create a readable and interesting book that brings readers one step closer to original materials.

We excerpted from previously published memoirs, diaries, and accounts in an attempt to represent the true voices of the age. All the pieces in this volume are evocative of life in the navy during the age of sail, and, in this respect, all are good sources. While we can be certain that most of these pieces were actually written by the seamen who participated in the events, a few raise doubts in the historian's mind. In these cases, the documentary evidence has not yet been found that would allow researchers to subject these works to the closest scrutiny. The pieces we selected have been convincing enough to satisfy earlier generations, even those who lived at the time; in one or two cases, however, they still may not have been written by the sailors themselves, from their own experience. They may have been ghostwritten or incomplete; some have surely been retouched by overzealous publishers. Nevertheless, they are evocative of the era and persuasive as nonfiction descriptions, if not testimonies of actual experience.

The works collected here are the predecessors of, and even the direct sources for, historical novelists. Any serious examination of the maritime literature for this period must start with published pieces such as these. Historians will eventually compare them to other forms of evidence that they find. In the meantime, modern readers can see these pieces on a variety of levels, learn from them, begin to ask questions about them, and, above all, enjoy reading them.

JOHN B. HATTENDORF

# Introduction

*P*RIOR TO THE BATTLE OF TRAFALGAR, Admiral Lord Nelson issued to the captains of his fleet one of the lines for which he was so revered: "In case signals can neither be seen nor perfectly understood, no captain can do very wrong if he places his ship alongside that of an enemy." Nelson was an expert at distilling naval tactics down to a level readily understood by individual captains, their officers, and men: Be flexible and responsive to the immediate tactical situation by looking for and making the most of opportunities; get each ship and its guns into effective action against the enemy; and maintain that action as long as possible, optimally until the enemy ship strikes or is sunk. The key was getting all of the ships into action, something that had been a recurring problem in naval tactics since the seventeenth century. At the same time, Nelson appealed directly to their sense of courage, a virtue of which he was the paragon.

Just before the battle actually began on October 21, 1805, Nelson had another message to deliver, this time to the seamen of his fleet. The sentiment he chose, "England expects that every man will do his duty," was singularly brilliant. Nelson was clearly out for glory that day, in the form of French and Spanish blood. This understated message swept away the pall of grievances held by the seamen of the British fleet in a resounding battle cry. Nelson was in touch with these men, many of whom were conscripted against their will and were subsequently governed by captains who had little choice but swift and merciless punishment to keep order.

As William Robinson, one lower-deck hand who was present that day and who deeply resented the arbitrary and excessive use of the cat-o'-nine-tails, later wrote in his memoirs:

How happy must that officer be, who has the consolation to know that he was beloved by his ship's company. . . . Out of a fleet of nine sail of the line I was with, there were only two captains thus distinguished. . . . Those two ships beat us in reefing and furling; for they were not in fear and dread, well knowing they would not be punished without a real and just cause. Those men would have stormed a battery, or have engaged an enemy at sea, with more vigour and effect than the other seven; for the crews of those seven felt themselves so degraded at being wantonly and unmanly beaten about, that their spirits were partly broken; and in going to battle, the only thing that could stimulate, cheer, and inspire them, was not veneration for their commanders, but the recollection of the land that gave them birth, OLD ENGLAND. (pp. 136–37)

Clearly, Robinson—better known by his publishing pseudonym Jack Nastyface—had an ax to grind, and he may have overstated his case. A fighting captain and a friend of the foremast jack, Nelson was much esteemed by his seamen as well as his country. Still, he was well aware that, given the harsh nature of life on board a man-of-war and the dubious and often cruel means of naval recruitment, the undivided loyalty of the men of his fleet lay primarily in one place—their country. He knew that this loyalty was so strong and so deeply felt that, in the face of the enemy, it would overcome all else.

*Every Man Will Do His Duty* presents some of the voices of the seamen and officers who fought and lived at sea during the French Revolutionary War (1793–1802), the Napoleonic War (1803–1815), and the War of 1812 (1812–15), which were interrupted only by a brief period of peace, the roughly year-long Peace of Amiens beginning on March 25, 1802. Notwithstanding an often rapacious desire for the pecuniary rewards of victory, the seamen who tell their stories here, whether British or American, were, generally speaking, motivated by national and personal pride, as well as for the love and respect of their shipmates.

Many of the great and historically important moments of the Napoleonic wars are captured in this reader, among them the Glorious First of June (1794), the Battle of Cape St. Vincent (1797), the Battle of Trafalgar (1805), the (land) Battle of Corunna (1809), and the frigate action between HMS *Macedonian* and USS *United States* (1812). In that sense, this book serves as a selective history of these wars, as told by eye-witnesses.

To cover all of the great fleet actions and the most significant frigate actions would consume far more space than one volume allows. Instead this book tries to capture the nature of life and war at sea in square-rigged ships—not just the heroic moments but the deprivations, the monotony, the pleasures, the pain, the justice and injustice. Cochrane's cruise of the Mediterranean in 1801 and Porter's cruise of the South Pacific in 1812, 1813, and 1814, while not as historically significant as the previously mentioned actions, perhaps better capture the mystique of life at sea and the political nature and psychological effects of life on board a man-of-war.

Jacob Nagle's two narratives and James Gardner's account are especially strong at evoking the personalities of man-of-war men and their daily lives, on land as well as at sea. The accounts of Robert Eastwick and George Little, both merchantmen, reveal the effects of the wars on men outside the navy. Eastwick experiences, in the Bay of Bengal, the frigate action between the French *La Forte* and HMS *La Sybille* while prisoner on board the enemy, and Little turns to privateering as a means of making a living, only to be captured by cannibals on the former Spanish Main and then imprisoned in England.

IN THE CASE of the lower-deck seamen, these passages are akin to oral histories, frequently told in rough diction and jumping from one episode to another with little transition. These seamen wear their grievances in scars across their backs and frequently expound on the injustice and arbitrariness of the Royal Navy's strict disciplinarians. If Studs Terkel had been there to document this "good war," these are the accounts that he would have heard. In other cases, such as Drinkwater Bethune's description of the Battle of Cape St. Vincent and Captain David Porter's account of the action between USS *Essex* and HMS *Phoebe,* the presentation is more studied, often with a sense of creating or correcting history—the former wrote to glorify Nelson, the latter partly to document the violations of the rules of war by his opponent—and certainly from a more polished hand.

Whether well educated or less so, the writers have frequently borrowed from historians of the day to help set their experiences in place. Basil Hall, for example, frequently cites General Sir William Francis Patrick Napier's history of the Peninsular War when setting the scene for the Battle of Corunna, which he witnessed.

In some cases the seamen are working from journals or writing shortly after the events occurred. William Henry Dillon recorded the events of his career, which included a stint in the Impress Service and several years in French prisons, in a series of letters to his first cousin and good friend Sir John Joseph Dillon. Later he used these letters in creating his seven-notebook, twenty-six-hundred-page manuscript. Bethune's account of the Battle of Cape St. Vincent was originally written as a letter to his father.

Other stories, such as George Little's, were written well after the event by aging and often financially strapped seamen. Many of these state in apologetic prefaces that they were compelled to write by friends and family, who so desired the authors to record their lives at sea that their humble natures were forcibly overcome. Little was, in fact, blind, and so dictated his story.

The degree of detail and flow of events correspond to the amount of time between the action and the writing, and whether or not the writer has kept any sort of diary. Each type of account has its own intrinsic merits and demerits that must be borne in mind during the reading. Accounts written very near the time of the event often contain fairly accurate dialogue and crisp details. But too much detail can be tedious, and enthusiasm combined with lack of perspective can cloud the author's judgment. More distantly scribed sea accounts are frequently well seasoned from the retellings and should be taken with a grain of salt. The minutiae that indicate accuracy have been washed away by the sea of years. The gauntlet of time that has buried lesser accounts has also frequently rounded the surviving narrative, like it has King Offa's dyke, into a beautiful, mythic form.

SINCE THESE ARE by and large the accounts of the men who fought the battles, their vantage points were frequently limited. Midshipman Dillon describes the Glorious First of June from the lower deck of HMS *Defence*, the first ship into action. Locked in a cabin on board the French frigate *La Forte*, merchant captain Eastwick describes a battle—between two powerful frigates, *La Forte*, 50 guns, and HMS *La Sybille*, 44 guns—that he didn't see. He did, however, have to duck friendly shot that pierced the cabin. Together these portraits of war tell not just what happened but what it actually was like to be there.

Some of these accounts, like Beatty's, Cochrane's, Gardner's, and Robinson's, are considered classics. As Christopher Lloyd writes in his 1955 introduction to James Anthony Gardner's comparatively "racy and colourful" memoirs, "These recollections have been the favourite reading of members of the Navy Record Society since they were first printed for the Society in 1906." Others here are less well known but equally as powerful. Jacob Nagle's was only recently discovered by Professor John Dann and published for the first time in 1988.

While the viewpoint is primarily British, there are several Americans represented here. Some of the Americans fought in the Royal Navy by choice—Nagle fought against the British during the American Revolution and for them during the French Revolutionary War—and some were coerced. While the rest of his shipmates frolicked on land just prior to embarking on a cruise, James Durand slept on board his ship to avoid any risk of falling prey to the hot press in Plymouth. They escaped it; he didn't, and he bitterly resented the treatment he and other Yankee sailors received on board a British man-of-war. Samuel Leech, on the other hand, fought for the British, was taken in a bloody frigate action by the USS *United States,* and later shipped in the U.S. Navy. Such were the vagaries of war.

ONE FINAL NOTE on the episodes that follow: you will notice that some authors appear more than once. For instance, William Richardson, who tells of his early service after being impressed in India in 1793, later narrates the interesting action at Basque Roads, where, he complains, those who performed the dangerous work—rigging fire-ships with explosives—received no recognition for it. William Dillon, who wrote one of the most extensive and detailed diaries of the wars, gives two accounts, one of the Glorious First of June and another of a much-honored single-ship action in which he fought against great odds. And Basil Hall narrates two episodes in *Every Man Will Do His Duty,* only one of which is a battle on land, where he is merely an observer. But Hall's accounts vividly capture life in the Royal Navy during the time. Being present with him at the Battle of Corunna is truly thrilling.

I hope that the time lapse between the stories of these writers, and several others who appear more than once in this book, sheds some light on how the authors' lives and naval careers progressed and how they become more interesting as people. Ultimately this war, like any war, was fought by individuals, and they had to make very personal decisions, often under great duress.

IN ANY EVENT, I hope this collection presents an informative cross-section of the firsthand accounts that exist from the great Age of Nelson, that it is evocative of the many varied experiences of naval life during this period, and that it catches many of the highlights of the period's memoirs. Above all, I hope that these accounts provide today's readers, as they have those of previous generations, splendid reading.

DEAN KING

# Editorial Note

The texts for this book were previously published, not taken from original manuscripts. They were edited minimally to conform to modern grammatical standards (for example, quotation marks, capitalization, the italicizing of ship names, and the use of numbers and numerals have been standardized, in most cases). Occasionally the punctuation has been altered for clarity, and, in some places, paragraph breaks were added for readability. Spellings have not been altered, except in a very few cases where it was necessary to prevent confusion. All bracketed material and footnotes that have been added by the editors of this book are italicized. All other notes are those of the original editor, though they were altered in places to conform to the style for this edition. For additional bibliographical information, see the Notes on the Texts section, beginning on page 407.

By request of the original editor, no changes were made to the two passages written by Jacob Nagle.

# Abbreviations

Some variation of the following abbreviations will be seen after the names of many of the editors and authors of the histories in this book.

C.B. = Commander of the Order of the Bath

C.B.E. = Commander of the Order of the British Empire

D.Litt. = Doctor of Literature

F.R.C.S. = Fellow of the Royal College of Surgeons

F.R.Hist.S. = Fellow of the Royal Historical Society

F.R.S. = Fellow of the Royal Society

F.S.A. = Fellow of the Society of Antiquaries

G.C.B. = Knight Grand Cross of the Order of the Bath

K.C.H. = Knight Commander of the Order of Hanover

K.H. = Knight of Hanover

M.A. = Master of Arts

R.E. = Royal Engineers

R.N. = Royal Navy

# List of Maps and Charts

Map of the Actions: World . . . . . . . . . . . . . . . . . . xvi

Map of the Actions: Europe . . . . . . . . . . . . . . . . xviii

The Battle of the Glorious First of June . . . . . . . . 23

The Battle of Cape St. Vincent . . . . . . . . . . . . . . 74

The Audacious Cruise of the *Speedy* . . . . . . . . 124

The Battle of Trafalgar . . . . . . . . . . . . . . . . . . . . 163

The Battle in the Aix Roads . . . . . . . . . . . . . . . . 227

A Yankee Cruiser in the South Pacific . . . . . . . . 348

His Lordship came to me on the poop, and, after ordering certain Signals to be made, about a quarter to noon, said, "Mr. Pasco, I want to say to the fleet, 'England confides that every man will do his duty.' " He added, "You must be quick, for I have one more to add, which is for 'Close Action.' " I replied, "If your Lordship will permit me to substitute expects for confides, the Signal will soon be completed, because the word expects is in the vocabulary, and confides must be spelt." His Lordship replied in haste, and with seeming satisfaction, "that will do, Pasco, make it directly."

As the last hoist was hauled down, Nelson turned to Captain Blackwood, who was standing by him, with, "Now I can do no more. We must trust to the great Disposer of all events, and the justice of our cause. I thank God for this great opportunity of doing my duty."

When Lord Nelson's message had been answered by a few ships in the van, he ordered me to make the signal for "Close Action" and keep it up. Accordingly I hoisted No. 16 at the top-gallant masthead, and there it remained until shot away.

—Pasco, the *Victory*'s signal lieutenant

# Gratuities to the Relations of Officers and Others Killed in Action

1. To a widow, her husband's full pay for a year.
2. Orphans, each the one-third proportion of a widow; posthumous children are esteemed orphans.
3. Orphans married are not entitled to any bounty.
4. If there is no widow, a mother, if a widow and above fifty years of age, is entitled to a widow's share.
5. The relations of officers of fire-ships are entitled to the same bounty as those of officers of like rank in fourth rates.
6. Captains are to set down the names of the killed at the end of the muster book, and on what occasion.
7. This bounty extends to those who are killed in tenders, in boats, or on shore, as well as to those on board the ships; also to those who are killed in action with pirates, or in engaging British ships through mistake. They who die of their wounds after battle are all equally entitled with those killed in action.

—*The Naval Chronicle*, 1799

# Part I

## The War of the French Revolution

# WILLIAM RICHARDSON

*⌁*

# In the King's Service
## 1793-1794

*A t the outbreak of the war King George's fleet numbered some 115 ves-
sels, including seventy-five ships of the line. France's fleet numbered
only seventy-six, but her dockyards were operating at full tilt. Both nations
took stock of their naval forces around the globe and rushed to augment
them. In the East Indies, the British possessed three frigates, the most powerful of which was the* Minerva, *and two smaller craft. Among the Royal
Navy's new recruits was William Richardson.*

*After thirteen perilous years in the merchant service, Richardson was
picked up by the press gang in Calcutta to face even more hardships in the
Royal Navy. In this passage, the Navy turns a batch of raw recruits into a
taut crew. Richardson, expecting the war to be short-lived, opts not to
desert, and later regrets it.*

THE *MINERVA* WAS a fine large frigate, with a poop lately erected on
her for the convenience of the admiral and captain, and mounting 48
guns. I was stationed to do any duty in the maintop; all my clothes were
on my back, and with an old silver watch and one rupee, which constituted my all, I had now, as it were, the world to begin again; and a poor
prospect I had before me. I had no bed, neither did I care for any, for
my bones had got so hardened since I came to sea that I could sleep as
comfortable on a chest lid or on the deck as on the best bed in the
ship; and having only one shirt, I went without when I had to wash and
dry it.

The *Bien Aimé* was bought into H.M.'s Service, and Lieutenant King (since Sir Richard King) was appointed to her as master and commander; she was officered and manned totally from the *Minerva* and the *Minerva*'s crew (filled up by pressing out of the East Indiamen as they arrived from Europe), and a great many able seamen we got out of them.

Soon after this Lord Cornwallis[1] came on board, and we got under way; he was brother to our admiral [*Sir William Cornwallis, 1744–1819*], and we proceeded to Pondicherry. A day or two after we came to anchor off that place, and his lordship went on shore to view the works: it was at one time in contemplation to blow them up, but that was not done. He returned on board again, we got under way, returned to Madras Roads, and landed his lordship again.

One of these evenings, as I was sitting on the coamings of the after-hatchway pondering my hard fate, Mr. Robinson, our first lieutenant, a worthy and good man, observed me, and sent for me to his cabin; and then, taking a sheet from off his bed, gave it to me and told me to get some clothes made from it, and said that when his dabash (a gentoo [*a gentile, or non-Mohammedan*] agent) came on board he would give me a good rig-out of clothing; but the ship sailed before he came, and so disappointed us. However, I got a light jacket and two pairs of trousers made from the sheet, and was very thankful for his kindness to me, a stranger.

There were no slops at this time on board the *Minerva*; the purser at stated periods served out to the ship's company so many yards of dungaree as were required to each man for jackets, shirts and trousers, with needles and thread for them; and my messmates, being a set of good fellows and accustomed to the work, soon taught me to cut out and make them, by which means I soon got a good rig-out and a new straw hat, which I made by their instructions; as for shoes and stockings, they were not worn by sailors in this hot country.

Shortly after this Lord Cornwallis embarked on board the *Swallow* packet for a passage to England, and we, with the *Bien Aimé,* got under way and convoyed her clear of the Mauritius, where the French had several ships of force lying. We then proceeded to the Island of Diego Garcia, one of the Mauritius Islands, and having been told that a French frigate and brig were lying there, and as it was thought there might be an occasion for landing, 150 of our crew were picked out to be trained to the use of small arms, and I was one of the number. Nothing could be more diverting than to see the blunders we made at the first beginning: we were arranged in

---

[1] *Charles Cornwallis, 1st Marquis Cornwallis (1738–1805), served as governor and commander in India from 1786 to 1793.*

two lines along the quarterdeck, with the captain and fugleman[2] in our front, and the booms full of people laughing and grinning at us; some put their muskets on the wrong shoulder, some let the butt fall on their next neighbour's toes, some could not stand with their backs straight up, and were threatened in having a cross-bar lashed to it, and some had their shoulders chalked by the captain that they might know the right from the left, which only bothered them the more; in short, there was nothing but blunders for a week or two, and then we began to mend.

This exercise was performed twice every day, and for our encouragement when over we were marched, with drum and fife playing before us, round the quarterdeck gangway and forecastle, and in the evening had an extra pint of grog each; but the awkward squad had to stand on one side with their muskets presented to us as we marched past them, and not allowed extra grog. We improved so in the course of a few weeks that it was said we fired a better volley than the marines.

When we arrived off Diego Garcia we hoisted French colours, and, though the wind was against us, worked the ship into the harbour and there came to anchor. We saw no frigate, but discovered a brig lying at the upper end of the harbour, and immediately sent our boats manned and armed to take possession of her, which they soon did, as the crew and few inhabitants, who are turtle catchers, fled into the woods for safety.

This is a noted place for catching turtle, and we found a pen with two hundred in it. The island is low and very woody, and the harbour a good-sized one; and, as we were in want of fresh water, we digged holes deep enough for each cask bung deep, and, putting them down in the evening, we found them full in the morning; but it was rather brackish, and only served for cooking. Our people caught several wild pigs here, which were good eating. In the course of their rambles several lascars who were hidden in the woods, hearing our people speak English, came and delivered themselves up to them: they said they had been wrecked here in an English ship belonging to Bombay several months ago, and, being afraid to deliver themselves up to the French for fear they would have sent them to the Mauritius and sold them for slaves, they had hid themselves in the woods and lived on cocoanuts and what else they could find there; so we took them all on board, and, when we arrived at Bombay, discharged them, to their great satisfaction.

Having nothing more to do to draw our attention here, we loaded the brig with turtles, and got near fifty on board the *Minerva* and the *Bien Aimé*, being as many as we could conveniently stow on the main deck between

[2] *See footnote 1, page 28.*

the guns; then, setting fire to the poor Frenchmen's huts (which happened to be on Guy Fawkes' day, November 5th, 1793), we got under way, and stood out to sea.

We shaped our course for one day, and each day lived like aldermen on turtle soup: every evening for near six weeks, a turtle was hung up to the skids by its two hind fins and the head cut off to let it bleed; and although each one was large enough to serve a day for our crew of three hundred men, scarcely half a pint of blood came from it. Next morning it was cut up and put into coppers, and when boiled, served out to all hands with two or three bucketsful of eggs into the bargain.

About midway on our passage we parted company one dark night with the *Bien Aimé* and brig, and when we got on the Malabar coast came to anchor off Tilicherry, where our admiral went on shore, but soon returned again with intelligence of a large frigate and a brig having passed that way, steering to the northward; and as we made sure they must be enemies, we got under way immediately and steered our course after them. On the following night, as we were going along with a fine breeze from the east, and a fore topmast steering sail set, we saw a large frigate and a brig pass us to windward, but on the other tack; and instead of putting our ship about to follow her, Captain Whitby ordered the hammocks to be piped up and the drummer to beat to quarters, and then gave his chief attention to us at the quarterdeck guns, in seeing that we primed them in a proper manner. Although I was a young man-of-war's man, I had my thoughts, and was surprised that he did not put the ship about and stand after the enemy.

At last the old admiral came up in his nightdress, and asked what direction the enemy was in; and I, being nearest to him, said she was going from us on the other tack. He immediately sent for Captain Whitby, who was then on the forecastle, and, when he came, told him to haul down the steering sail, put the ship about, then steer after the enemy, and he would have sufficient time to get the guns ready; so accordingly this was done, or we should not have met each other till we had got to the Antipodes.

We came up with them early in the morning, our people all eager for battle; but when daylight appeared (which was waited for, knowing they could not escape our superior sailing), we were much disappointed in seeing them hoist Portuguese colours; so we sent a boat to board the frigate, and found they were from Goa, and bound to another port in the Portuguese settlements on this coast; so we let them proceed, but could not help laughing to see their seamen going aloft dressed with stuffed clothes, cocked hats, and some with boots on.

The *Minerva* was under good discipline, and, had we had an experienced captain to carry on the duty, should have been more comfortable; but he was too young—had come out with the admiral on this station a mid-shipman, and in the course of three or four years had got made a post captain when only nineteen years of age; he could work the ship very well, and that was all. Not a word was to be spoken in wearing or tacking the ship except from the commanding officer; everything was done as silently as possible, and the boatswain's pipe just loud enough to be heard, the admiral not allowing the side to be piped for him or any other officer; they were not to be whistled in like dogs.

Not an oath was allowed to be spoken, but as there were so many new pressed men in the ship it was almost impossible to avoid it, and when any was heard to swear their names were put on a list, and at seven next morning were punished, though not severely, few getting more than seven or eight lashes; yet it was galling, and how I escaped God only knows, for my name had been put on the list several times, and I suppose it must have been through the kindness of my good friend Mr. Robinson, the first lieutenant.

Though the punishment was light, it displeased the men very much, who had not had time to divest themselves of this new crime they had been so long accustomed to, and was nearly attended with serious consequence. Every evening, weather permitting, it was customary for the people to have a dance, and one of these evenings the lanthorns were lighted as usual, and hung on each side of the launch, which was stowed in those days on the main deck under the booms, and the fiddler on the topsail sheet bits began to play away on his violin; but nobody came to dance.

By-and-by the gunners' wads began to fly about in all directions, the lights were extinguished, the lanthorns knocked to pieces, and a wad rolled into the admiral's cabin as he walked there. The old boy soon saw that something was the matter and sent for Captain Whitby; but when Captain Whitby came he pretended that he knew nothing was the matter with the ship's company. The admiral's steward came into the cabin at the time, and being asked if he knew what was the matter with the people, replied that he heard the men say that there was too much dancing at the gangway in the morning to keep them dancing in the evening; so the admiral, seeing through it immediately, instead of using severe means (as many a tyrant would have done, and perhaps caused a real mutiny), adopted a better way, and that was in cautioning Captain Whitby not to use the cat on such light occasions, and never to flog a man again without his permission.

When the people heard of this they were greatly satisfied, and did their duty more cheerfully and better, and not a man was flogged after this but one, and he richly deserved it—it was for striking an officer when on shore on duty. But in all my experience at sea I have found seamen grateful for good usage, and yet they like to see subordination kept up, as they know the duty could not be carried on without it; but whenever I hear of a mutiny in a ship, I am much of the opinion of Admiral Lord Collingwood, who said it must assuredly be the fault of the captain or his officers.

Our ship being leaky, we went to Bombay and there docked her, and during this time the *Bien Aimé* and prize arrived; but the turtle had all lately died from the cold weather at nights. The prize was immediately sold, and I received three rupees and a quarter for my share.

My little prize money was soon expended, together with my watch, which I sold to pay my part of the expenses of the mess; and the most of it went for gin, though I was averse to ardent spirits. But some of them were as wild as March hares, and among them a little Welshman named Emmet, whom we had sometimes to lay on a chest and tie his hands and feet to the handles till he was sober. One day when he was on shore on liberty, and of course tipsy, in passing a shop in Bombay he saw a large glass globe hanging in it, with gold fish swimming and live birds in it; he stopped and stared at it with astonishment, and muttered to himself, "What, birds swimming and fish flying!—impossible"; and in order to be satisfied, he threw a stone which hit the globe and knocked it all to pieces about the shop.

He was soon arrested and sent to jail, and a report was sent on board next morning that one of our people was there. An officer was sent to see who it was and there found poor Tom Emmet very much cast-down in the mouth. He was released and brought on board, but the globe was to be paid for; therefore the ship's company subscribed eight hundred rupees (a great sum for the value of the globe) and paid the owner for it!

One day a Gentoo, who spoke a little English, came on board, and said he was from Dongaree and sent by one of our men for his leg, as he could not return on board without it. This demand seemed so strange that they took no notice of it at first, but the Gentoo in his bad English insisted that he was right, and, after a deal of puzzling, one of the people recollected that Bandy (the ship's cook) was on shore, and inquiring among his messmates, found that one of them who had been on shore with Bandy, and slept in the same house, had brought away Bandy's wooden leg by way of frolic—and no wonder the man could not return without his leg, which was soon sent to him, and he returned on board.

The *Minerva*, having got her leak stopped, and new coppered, was brought out of dock, and the *Bien Aimé* went in; but she was found so rotten that they broke her up, after being only a few months in the service (she mounted 20 guns). We then began to rig the *Minerva* with all speed; and I could easily have deserted here, but we had such accounts from England that the war could not last six months, as almost all Europe were at war against the French Republic, that I fixed my mind on returning to England in the *Minerva*, in order, when paid off, to visit my remaining friends and relations, then bid them a long farewell, return to Calcutta, and there remain until I could do something to better my situation.

The *Minerva* being rigged and stored, we sailed from Bombay on January 12, 1794, none of us knowing (except the admiral) where we were bound for, for he always kept the ship's destination a secret to himself. Some said we could not be bound for England, as we had left several casks of water behind on the Bunder Head, and that no ship had come out to relieve us; however, when we got a little distance out we shaped a homeward-bound course, which made us rejoice.

Near the entrance of the British Channel we came up with and passed two homeward-bound Indiamen, but as they hoisted Dutch colours we did not stop to examine them, as we were then at peace with that nation; but we heard afterwards that they were French, and were captured soon afterwards and carried into Plymouth by one of our frigates.

In proceeding up Channel we were chased a whole day by a line-of-battle ship, which in the dusk got within hail of us; we were all ready to fight her, as our admiral hoped to succeed by manoeuvring, though she was of such superior force. They hailed to know from whence we came, and our reply was "His Britannic Majesty's ship *Minerva*"; they then asked if it was not the *Minerva* out of Havre de Grace, and were very suspicious of us; we answered that it was H.M. Ship *Minerva*, Rear-Admiral Cornwallis, from India, and this satisfied them; they shortened sail, hove to, and their captain came on board to pay his respects, and we found her to be the *Intrepid* (64 guns). One of their boat's crew, an Irishman, when alongside was hardly satisfied that we were English, for, said he, what right had we to have a poop, being only a frigate? One of our wags told him it was to keep our prize-money in, and Pat believed him!

Next morning we saw four frigates ahead standing across our bows, little thinking they were enemies; fortunately a fog came on, and we passed them. Next morning we saw four more, who would not let us escape. The first that came up was the *Arethusa*, Sir Edward Pellew (since Lord Exmouth), who, seeing our flag, brought to and came on board, and told us the other three frigates were the *Flora, Concord,* and *Melampus*, all under the command of Sir John Borlase Warren. When he was told we had passed four English frigates yesterday (he very near committed himself for swearing), he said, with an oath, that there were not four British frigates together in the Channel but themselves, therefore the others must be French; so hastening to his ship he gave us a salute, then bore down to his commodore, gave him news, and off they all set in search of the other four frigates, and the next day, being April 23, 1794, they overtook them. A smart action ensued, and ended with the capture of the *Pomone* (44 guns), the *Engageant* (56 guns), and *Babet* (28 guns); the other escaped, having run on shore on the French coast, being chased by the *Concord*, Sir Richard Strachan.

That same day we came to anchor at St. Helens, after a fine passage from Bombay of three months and seventeen days; but instead of finding the war over, found it only beginning—a sad drawback to many of our hopes. Next morning, the Channel fleet, under Lord Howe, weighed from Spithead and anchored here, previous to the glorious battle of June 1, and we got under way went to Spithead, and there moored ship.

As the admiral was dressing to go on shore, he saw out of the cabin windows two wherries pulling up to the ship full of girls; he came out much agitated, and sending for Captain Whitby, desired him not to allow any such creatures to come near the ship, so they were hailed to keep off; but as soon as the admiral got on shore they were permitted to come on board, and the ship was soon full of them.

It was very strange that the admiral—a religious and good man—could not bear the sight of a female; and yet he had been very much among them in his youthful days, and called a wild fellow. It was reported on board here as a fact that he once went on shore to dine with the Governor at Madras, and, as some ladies began to take their seats at the table while he was there, he arose, took up his hat, and left the company, to the astonishment of them all, and came on board!

I now began to weigh matters and ponder on my situation, and found that since I had left England the balance was much against me: then I had a chest of clothes and bedding, and my liberty; now I have little clothing, no shoes or stockings, and no liberty, and much decayed in my condition; my gums were swelled over my teeth by the scurvy so that I could not chew my victuals without them being covered with blood. I and several others ought to have been sent to the hospital, but instead of that were not allowed to set our feet on the land!

The admiral struck his flag and went to London; the *Minerva* went into Portsmouth Harbour to be paid off; and after being a week in there (the ship stripped and nearly cleared of her stores), without having a moment's liberty on shore, after being so long abroad in unhealthy climates, thirty-seven of us were drafted on board the *Royal William* at Spithead, and the same day drafted again into the *Prompte*, a frigate of twenty-eight guns (Captain Taylor), and ready for sea. Here was encouragement for seamen to fight for their king and country! A coolie in India was better off! This took place on May 2, 1794. However, by getting good, fresh provisions the scurvy began to abate, thank God! and my gums broke away bit by bit at a time, and without any pain as the new ones came.

• • •

*Had the* Minerva *arrived at Portsmouth any earlier, Richardson probably would have been drafted by one of the ships of the Channel fleet under Admiral Lord Howe, soon to see action at the Glorious First of June. As it turned out, Richardson would see some significant action later in his career (another episode from his narrative, "With Stopford in the Basque Roads, 1808–1809," begins on page 213). But for the time being he was relegated to convoy duty in and around home waters.*

*A month after Richardson entered the crew of the* Prompte, *the first major fleet action of the war took place—without him—some four hundred sea miles west of Ushant, France. There, Howe, with twenty-five ships of the line, battled a French fleet of twenty-six ships of the line commanded by Rear-Admiral Villaret-Joyeuse. The French fleet was protecting a convoy of 125 merchantmen loaded with badly needed grain from America. Lord Howe's job was to stop the grain from getting to France.*

# WILLIAM HENRY DILLON

*◢*

# Commence the Work
# of Destruction:
# The Glorious First of June
## 1794

*A diminutive fourteen-year-old and already a four-year veteran of the Royal Navy, Midshipman William Henry Dillon rushes wide-eyed into one of the great fleet actions of the era. HMS* Defence, *74 guns, under Captain Gambier, is the first British ship into battle this day and remains in the thick of the action throughout. Dillon's perspective on the great battle of the first of June is through the lower-deck ports of the* Defence, *where he commands three of the great guns. Despite this limited vantage point, his account of what transpires on the smoky lower deck does much to illuminate the furious nature of the battle. But first he recounts the tense days at sea immediately preceding the Glorious First of June.*

A NAVAL PROMOTION of flag officers and captains having taken place, our whole thoughts were turned to the fleet. On April 23 the first division of it under Admiral Graves[1] (in which the *Defence* was included) proceeded to St. Helens. During our stay at this anchorage several Indiamen and merchantships of all descriptions assembled here, to be escorted down Channel by the Grand fleet under Lord Howe. By May 2, all being ready, we weighed and made sail by divisions. We had delightful weather, and the sight was a splendid one—so many fine ships coming out in succession

---

[1] Thomas (later Lord) Graves, Capt. 8/7/55; R-Ad. 19/5/79; commanded the British fleet in the unsuccessful action off the Chesapeake, 5/9/1781; V-Ad. 24/9/87; Ad. 12/4/94; Second-in-Command on the First of June, being awarded an Irish peerage for his services on that occasion. [*Dictionary of National Biography.*]

and forming into order. There were the East India, West India and Newfoundland convoys, with men of war appointed to take charge of each of
them. On the 5th, we had cleared the Channel. Lord Howe then made the
signal for the convoys to separate, and to his fleet to form the order of sailing, in two lines. By degrees these operations were executed with beautiful
precision. Seven sail of the line left us—Rear Admiral Montagu[1] with six
two-deckers—to cruize on a detached station. The *Suffolk*, 74, under Commodore Rainier,[2] in which was my friend Jekyll, had charge of the Indiamen. So soon as we were clear of all the convoys, a course was shaped for
the Island of Ushant, which we saw the next day. Our fleet consisted of 26
sail of the line, three of 100 guns, four of 98 and two of 80: all the rest 74's
with 7 frigates, one fire ship and an hospital ship. All these were in an
excellent state of discipline, anxious to meet the enemy.[3]

Lord Howe was the favourite of that day. He had been allowed, not
only to select the ships to be placed under his command, but also the officers commanding them. There were a great many 64's in our Navy, but his
Lordship, as if aware of the general inferiority of our line of battle ships to
those of the French, would not have any of that description with him, so
that the 74 was the smallest ship in his fleet.

On the 14th, we recaptured and sent into port the brig *Argo*, under charge
of one of our mids and seven seamen. Several more of our merchant vessels
were recaptured daily. From these we learned that an enemy's squadron had
taken the *Castor*,[4] 32 guns, and her convoy from Guernsey and Jersey bound
for Newfoundland. On the 18th we chased a strange squadron of ships of
war, which proved to be Rear-Admiral McBride. Shortly afterwards, the fleet
returned to the Island of Ushant, not far from Brest. Two sail of the line, with
two frigates, were sent in-shore to reconnoitre that port. On the evening of
that day, the 20th, when they rejoined us, they brought intelligence of the
enemy's fleet being at sea. This news caused the greatest excitement on
board our ships, and nothing was heard but bringing the French to action. A
course was now shaped to meet the enemy, and the signal was made to prepare for battle. Many more merchant ships fell in with us that had been taken
by the enemy, but Lord Howe could not spare any more seamen from his
fleet. Consequently they were burned. The ship that we were ordered to set

[1] George Montagu, Capt. 15/4/74; R-Ad. 12/4/94; V-Ad. 1/6/95; Ad. 1/1/1801.
[2] Peter Rainier, Capt. 29/10/78; R-Ad. 1/6/95; V-Ad. 14/2/99; Ad. 9/11/1805.
[3] In consequence of Lord Howe's failure in capturing the enemy's ships in the previous
November, he had established on this occasion a flying squadron of four sail of the line, constantly stationed on the weather bow of the fleet.
[4] Captain T. Troubridge, taken off Cape Clear, 9/5/94; recaptured later in the same month by
the *Carysfort*, Captain F. Laforey, off the Lizard.

on fire proved to be the *Demourisque*, belonging to Guernsey, a very fine vessel indeed of her class, taken by the French frigate *la Seine*. It made my heart ache when I saw the flames spreading over her; in fact hurling her to destruction. From these vessels we took out the Frenchmen, who did not fail to boast famously of the powers of their fleet.

One of our first duties whilst in quest of the enemy was to fill an ample quantity of powder for the use of our guns. This service is generally performed at night, when all the fires and lights are out. On that occasion, when the gunner's crew were at work in the magazine, I could not rest, having, while asleep in my hammock, had three different dreams that the ship would be blown up. I therefore turned out, and requested the officer of the watch to allow me to go and take charge of the lightroom.[1] This was readily granted. I hastened to the place, and relieved the mid stationed there. He was very glad at my appearance, cordially thanking me for taking his place. When he was gone, I called out to the gunner through the horn of the lantern to inquire if all was going on right with the powder. He assured me that all was in good order, and no danger. However, my anxiety on this account was so intense that I could not help repeating my question so often that the old gunner would not make any further reply. At last he told me to mind my own business, and that I was sent there to mind the candles. "Mind," said he, "that you snuff them properly, or I will report you for neglect of duty." By 6 o'clock in the morning the magazine duties were over, and my mind relieved from an oppression that I could not control, the recollection of which is still fresh in my memory to this day.

In our pursuit of the enemy strange vessels were seen daily. One of the number, a French line of battle ship, took our fleet for hers; but, being a superior sailer, she escaped from being captured. It was a touch and go affair with her. However, two of the enemy's sloops of war stood close into the rear of our fleet one evening, and by daylight they were in our centre. They had not made any signals, or taken the usual precautions on such occasions. Consequently, when they found out their mistake, they attempted to make off: in vain, as they were instantly captured.

Some of the officers from these vessels were sent to the *Defence*. They became my messmates. One of them, a gentleman of fortune, had been ruined by the Revolution, and taken to the naval service of his country as his last resource. He related to me many of the horrors of that unfortunate period. He spoke in very high terms of the discipline of the French fleet, making quite sure that we should be beaten when we brought them to

[1] A small enclosed space adjoining each magazine and separated from it by a window fitted with two thicknesses of horn or glass, through which the lantern light could be thrown into the magazine. This obviated the risk of having the light in the room itself.

action. Nevertheless he could not help expressing his astonishment at the cleanliness and good order of the *Defence*, which led him at times to let slip some remarks indicating apprehensions and doubts of the final success of his countrymen on the day of trial. He watched all the motions of our fleet with extreme anxiety, and the maneuver which seemed to attract his attention most was the rapidity with which our ships were tacked; often within five minutes, whereas the French ships, he told us, were always a ¼ of an hour under that evolution.

Meeting so many vessels led us to believe that we were not far from the enemy, and it became evident that reinforcements were on their way to him. I may mention here the critical state of France at that period. From the failure of the harvest, that country was on the brink of a famine, and the National Convention had contracted with America for ample supplies of corn and flour. They had sent some ships of war to convoy them home from the States.[1] Another squadron[2] was ordered to look out for those ships—upwards of 300 sail of them—and assist in escorting them into the French ports. We on our side had detached a squadron to intercept and capture such a valuable convoy.[3]

On the morning of May 28, having strong breezes and hazy weather, the fleet being on the starboard tack, about 8 o'clock the signal was made from the flying squadron that a strange fleet was in sight, some distance to windward, which proved to be the enemy we had been so anxiously looking for. His ships were not, by appearance, in any regular order of sailing. Lord Howe made the signal to prepare for battle, and for the flying squadron to chace and engage the enemy. So soon as those signals were displayed to our ships, a state of excitement was manifested totally beyond my powers of description. No one thought of anything else than to exert himself to his utmost ability in overcoming the enemy. It was also very satisfactory to observe the change of disposition in the ship's company of the *Defence*. All animation and alacrity pervaded these men: no more sulky looks. The enemy was near, and all hands were determined to support their captain. The ships when near each other were cheered by their crews in succession. Death or Victory was evidently the prevailing feeling.

The enemy's fleet did not alter its course upon seeing us: therefore it neared. But unluckily the wind, increasing to a gale, obliged us to reef the topsails, and our progress was in consequence much delayed. Our Captain exerted himself in a wonderful manner, determined to set a noble example to all under his command. Whilst we were in chace, a splinter netting was

---

[1] Five ships—two "of the line"—sent from Brest under Rear-Admiral Van Stabel, 26/12/1793.
[2] Five of the line, under Rear-Admiral Nielly, which left Rochefort, 6/5/1794.
[3] *I.e.* Rear-Admiral Montagu's squadron mentioned [*previously*].

fitted over the quarter deck to receive the blocks that might be shot away aloft, and a cask of water was hoisted into the main top, to be prepared for fire. The enemy, having closed us to about eight miles, hauled to the wind (in the western quarter). The whole of our fleet being in chace, the order of sailing was no longer an object. About 4 o'clock in the afternoon the wind moderated a little. Just at this time we noticed one of the advanced squadron, under Rear Admiral Pasley,[1] firing upon the enemy's rear. Some of our sails were split, but luckily held on. At 7 o'clock our ships were closing, and brought the French to action about 8 o'clock. The engagement was followed up with great spirit, but moderated, and finally ceased, as night came on. The wind had lulled, and as total darkness prevailed, all further operations were at an end. Every ship in the British fleet carried distinguishing lights, to prevent mistakes with the enemy's, and the night was passed in watching each other's motions, as well as it could be done.

At daylight on the 29th, the two fleets were on opposite tacks, and the leading ship of our van, the *Caesar* of 80 guns, exchanged shots with the rear of the French. But our opponents had contrived to keep the weather gage. We soon tacked, to place ourselves upon a line with our adversaries. We now missed the *Audacious*, 74. It was evident she had parted from us during the night. Her absence reduced our number to 25 sail of the line. In counting the enemy's fleet, we made out 26 of the line. It was afterwards ascertained that the *Audacious* had parted company in attempting to take possession of the *Revolutionnaire*,[2] a French three decker that had been disabled by the fire of our ships on the previous evening; but, failing to do so, fell in the next morning with a squadron of enemy, and was obliged to run off to prevent being captured: and, finally, instead of trying to rejoin our fleet, put into Plymouth.

We had a commanding breeze this day, but as our opponents kept well to windward, we could not close with them. However, about 10 o'clock, the enemy's van gradually edged down towards ours, and they began a distant engagement before 11 o'clock. Lord Howe then made the signal for the *Caesar*, the leading ship, to tack and cut through the French rear. But this signal not being obeyed disconcerted his Lordship, who was completely at a loss in not having his plan of attack carried into effect. Meanwhile the firing on both sides was kept up with determined spirit. The signal mentioned was repeated several times, but the *Caesar* kept on her course. At length Lord Howe tacked, in the *Queen Charlotte*, and those ships near followed the example. When he thought that he should succeed in the desired object, he made the signal for a general chace. That signal left every captain

---

[1] "Pasely" in MS.
[2] Which ship had actually struck to the *Audacious*, but escaped.

at liberty to follow his own plan in bringing his ship into action, and the line of battle was no longer in force. Consequently every ship was trying to attack the enemy in the best way that offered. However, this signal was entirely annulled by the sudden visitation of a violent squall of wind, accompanied by a thick mist with rain, during which no object could be distinguished at 100 yards' distance. Such an unexpected event brought the English fleet into a state of disorder. When the mist cleared away, scarcely any two ships were on the same tack, and many were near running on board each other. Nothing but confusion was visible in our fleet, whilst the enemy's line was in perfect order. Had the enemy availed himself of the opportunity thus offered, not intentionally, of attacking our broken line, who knows what might have been the result?

Every British officer was aware of our critical position: therefore no time was lost in forming the line as well as it could be done. Lord Howe had cut through the enemy's line at the 5th ship from his rear. Many ships had followed, and, at last, it came to our turn. At the opening that had been made in the enemy's line lay a large French 80-gun ship, l'Indomptable. All her topmasts had been shot away, and she was motionless. But she kept up a most spirited fire as we passed her. The Orion, 74, had taken a position on her lee quarter, and we concluded that she would be taken. However, whilst all these operations were going on, the French admiral noticed the dangerous situation of the ship mentioned, as well as of another, le Tyrannicide, also disabled. He wore his fleet, and by that means rescued them.

So soon as we had passed through the French rear, we attempted to tack, but failed; then were obliged to wear. In performing that evolution we nearly ran on board of another ship, as several of ours were rather crowded, and too close together to admit of forming the line without risk. Nevertheless, with care and good management we extricated ourselves from all these difficulties; and, having finally brought to the wind on the starboard tack, we became exposed to the attack of a large French three decker. The shot from him flew about us like hailstones. As yet we had not any man hurt, but our sails and rigging were much injured. At this critical moment the Defence lay over so much that our quarter deck was open to the enemy's fire, our opponents pelting away without intermission. Presently one of his shot struck the upper part of the quarter deck bulwark, on the larboard side, killed one man and wounded nine. One or two shots passed so close to the captain that I thought he was hit. He clapped both hands upon his thighs with some emotion: then, recovering himself, he took out of his pocket a piece of biscuit and began eating it as if nothing had happened. He had evidently been shook by the wind of the shot. He had on a cocked hat, and kept walking the deck, cheering up the seamen with the greatest coolness.

I had never seen a man killed before. It was a most trying scene. A splinter struck him in the crown of the head, and when he fell the blood and brains came out, flowing over the deck. The captain went over, and, taking the poor fellow by the hand, pronounced him dead. The others, who were wounded, were taken below to the Surgeon. Just at that moment, a volley of shot assailed the poop, cut away the main brace, and made sad havoc there. Some of the men could not help showing symptoms of alarm: which the captain noticing, he instantly went up, and, calling the seamen together, led them to set the brace to rights. At this instant [Lieut.] Twysden made his appearance, and explained to the captain that our guns from the main deck had no effect upon the three decker. To prove this, he waited till the smoke had cleared away, then went down and, giving one of the guns the utmost elevation, fired it. The shot only reached halfway to the Frenchman. Consequently our firing was useless. Under these circumstances our guns were kept quiet. We were in a most trying situation, receiving the enemy's fire without being able to return the compliment. But, luckily, one of our three deckers, the *Glory*, noticing the danger to which we were exposed, closed upon us and, directing his broadsides upon our adversary, drew off his attention. This act of the *Glory*'s gave us a little breathing time, by which we were enabled to set the ship to rights.

I was quartered on the lower deck under Lieut. Beecher. He had the command of the seven foremost guns, and three of them in the bow were under mine. As we could not use the guns below, I availed myself of that circumstance to attend on the quarter deck, to witness all that was passing. Never having been before present in an action of the kind, my curiosity and anxiety were beyond all bounds. The danger to which I exposed myself had not the slightest influence over me. Owing to that desire I saw more than most of the mids, who kept to their stations, and I can now relate what I really did see. The result of this action, which had fallen sharply upon a few of our ships, was the obtaining of the weather gage: an advantage of considerable importance, as it enabled the British admiral to direct his attack upon the enemy when it suited his convenience.[1] The two ships that suffered most in our fleet were the *Royal George*, 100 guns, Admiral Sir Alexander Hood,[2] and the *Queen*, 98, Sir Alan Gardner.[3] The sails of both those ships were literally torn into shreds. There they lay, perfectly motion-

---

[1] W.H.D. is quite right; this was by far the most important result of the day's fighting.

[2] The younger of the famous brothers Hood; then Vice-Admiral of the Red, and 3rd in command under Lord Howe; created Baron Bridport for his services in this campaign.

[3] Capt. 19/5/66; R-Ad. 1/2/93; V-Ad. 4/7/94; Ad. 14/2/99. Created baronet for services at First of June; and baron, December 1800. Commanded Grand fleet (instead of Cornwallis, who was sick) during part of the Trafalgar campaign (March–June 1805). Died, 1/1/1809.

less, the eyes of the whole fleet turned upon them, whilst their crews were occupied in unbending and replacing their useless sails. *L'Indomptable* and *le Tyrannicide*, two deckers, bore the brunt of the action on the side of France, as those ships lay exactly in that part of their line where ours cut through. In due time both fleets were formed in the order of battle, and, about 5 o'clock, all again in as complete a condition as circumstances would permit. The French ships appeared to have suffered more than ours, as several had lost topmasts and yards, whereas on our side nothing of the kind was discernible.

At this season of the year we could reckon upon daylight till past 8 o'clock. We had, therefore, plenty of time to renew the action. Why that was not done astonished all hands on board the English fleet. Lord Howe had obtained, by clever tactics, the position most desirable for his operations, and we all expected the signal would be made to renew the battle. But this was not the case. It was the custom with the French to wait the attack, instead of being the aggressors. They were under easy sail to leeward of us, on the larboard tack, evidently anticipating our closing upon them. Lord Howe, it seems, was not satisfied that the enemy had shown a resolution to fight, and not evade us. Under that impression, he determined to take his time. By that decision we had two or three days of more anxiety, previous to our having an opportunity of bringing affairs to a conclusion. The night was passed in tolerable quietness.

On the morning of the 30th we had foggy weather. Our fleet not being in very good order, the signals were made from Lord Howe's ship to form in line of battle. The *Caesar* happened at that moment to be close to us, pumping out quantities of water, the effect of the shot she had received below. We heard that one of her guns had burst on the previous day, by which 18 men were killed and wounded. The fog partially clearing away, the enemy was seen to leeward. The admiral instantly made the signal to prepare for action, upon which the *Caesar* threw out the signal of inability to do so. Our fleet formed in line of battle as well as circumstances would allow, but the hazy weather rendered our evolutions uncertain, and there did not appear any probability, that day, of any more fighting. Finally, the fog becoming thicker, we lost sight of the French, so that we could not close upon the enemy.

The morning of the 31st was still misty, with favourable symptoms of its clearing away, the wind in the S.W. quarter. In the afternoon, the fog disappearing, we beheld the enemy some distance to leeward. We prepared for action, and made sail to close upon him. By 7 o'clock we had reached within five miles of the French fleet. The weather became fine, and we enjoyed one of the most splendid sights ever witnessed—the two fleets

close to each other in line of battle, only waiting for the signal to commence
the work of destruction, the repeating frigates of the two nations within
gunshot. However, all passed off in quietness. Lord Howe, having placed
his fleet in an exact line with that of the enemy, he drew off for the night,
which we passed in extreme anxiety. We could not reckon on more than six
hours of darkness, and therefore concluded that we should commence
operations with the dawn. Very few of the *Defences* took off any clothing,
and the hammocks were not piped down. Our whole thoughts hung upon
the approaching event. As to your humble servant, being rather fatigued, I
preferred, it being a beautiful starlight night, to remain on deck. I selected
one of the topsail halyard[1] tubs on the forecastle, and coiled myself as well
as I could inside of it, where I took a snooze which I enjoyed, and felt more
refreshed when awoke by the tars than I should have done had I gone to
bed: at least I thought so. I felt an elasticity beyond expression.

RISING THEN from my tub, I beheld the enemy about 10 miles off to leeward, on the starboard tack. There was a fine breeze and lovely weather. It
was Sunday, and I thought the Captain would not have much time for
prayers, as the work in hand would be of a very different nature. Lord
Howe drew up the fleet in capital order. He made several changes in the
disposition of the ships, to render every part of his line equal. The *Defence*
was the seventh ship in the van. When his Lordship had completed his
arrangements for attacking the enemy, he made the signal for the different
divisions, that is the van, centre and rear, to engage the opposite divisions
of the French: then for each ship in the English line to pass through the
enemy and attack his opponent to leeward. Next, the fleet was hove to,
that the crews might have their breakfasts. This was going to work in a
regular methodical manner. His Lordship knew that John Bull did not like
fighting with an empty stomach; but it was a sorry meal, scarcely deserving the name. We had not had much time for a fire in the range for cooking since the 28th of last month. All the tables and conveniences were
stowed below; all the partitions taken down; nothing to be seen on the
decks but powder, shot, ramrods and instruments of destruction. Whilst
the ship's Company were making the best of the time allowed for refreshment, the Captain collected most of his officers in the cabin, where a short
prayer suitable to the occasion was offered to the Almighty for protection
against the impending event. The half hour having elapsed, up went the
signal for the fleet to bear down and bring the enemy to action, it being

[1] "Haulyard" in MS.

then near 9 o'clock. What an awful moment! How shall I describe it? A scene of magnificence and importance, not of common occurrence, and not often equalled on the ocean—upwards of 50 sail of the line viewing each other, and preparing to pour out their thunder destructive of the human species, which would decide the fate of either fleet, and probably that of the nation.

Our Captain went round the ship and spoke to all the men at their guns in terms of encouragement, to fight for their country. The replies he received were gratifying in the highest degree. The noblest feelings of patriotism were proclaimed, with expressions of the warmest enthusiasm: in short, a determination to conquer prevailed throughout the ship—and, I may as well say, throughout the British fleet. As we neared the French up went our colours—

> *"High o'er the poop the flattering winds unfurl'd*
> *Th' imperial Flag that rules the watery world."*

The *Defence*, being a good sailer, made rapid speed through the waves, going under double reefed topsails with a commanding breeze. Twysden, noticing that we had advanced too far beyond our line, hastened on to the quarter deck to point out to his Captain, with becoming respect, that he was exposing his ship to the utmost danger by going on singlehanded without support, and that he ran the risk of being either sunk or totally disabled. The maintopgallant sail had been set by us, the only ship in the line to have done so. In fact, when the signal had been made to bear down, the ship came before the wind, and the Captain, anxious to obey orders, was striving to commence the action as soon as he could. Lord Howe had observed this action of Capt. Gambier's, and mentioned it to the officers near him, saying, "Look at the *Defence*. See how nobly she is going into action!" His Lordship then turning round and casting his eyes over the fleet, said, "I believe I cannot make any more signals. Every ship has had instructions what to do"; then, shutting his signal book, left the poop to take his chance on the quarter deck. Lieut. Twysden prevailed on his Captain to take in the maintopgallant sail, but the ship still proceeded, and extended her distance beyond the British line. Then the mizen topsail was braced aback, by which more wind filled the maintopsail. Therefore, instead of retarding her motion, it was accelerated. The lieutenant mentioned this, but the Captain would not make any more reduction of sail. He said, "I am acting in obedience to the admiral's signal. Fill the mizen topsail again. It may probably be thought that I have no wish to do so if I shorten sail." This last reply quieted Twysden. As I happened to be present at that particular moment, I heard every word that passed. The mizen topsail was braced round to receive the wind, and our whole attention was then directed to the ship in the enemy's line— the 7th—that we were to engage.

The French fleet had their maintopsails to the mast, and were waiting for our attack. Shortly after 9 o'clock we were getting very near to our opponents. Up went their lower deck ports, out came the guns, and the fire on us commenced from several of the enemy's van ships. Twysden then went to his quarters on the main deck, and your humble servant went below to his station. We retained our fire till in the act of passing under the Frenchman's stern, then, throwing all our topsails aback, luffed up and poured in a most destructive broadside. We heard most distinctly our shot striking the hull of the enemy. The carved work over his stern was shattered to pieces. Then, ranging up alongside of him within half pistol shot distance, our fire was kept up with the most determined spirit. When we had measured our length with that of our adversary, we backed the maintopsail. In that position the action was maintained for some time. We had instructions below to lower the ports whilst loading the guns,[1] that the enemy's musketry might not tell upon our men, and also to fire with a slight elevation, as the upper deck guns would be depressed a few degrees, thus making a cross fire upon the Frenchman. After the two or three first broadsides, I became anxious to have a good view of the ship we were engaging. To effect this object, I requested the men at the foremost gun to allow me a few seconds, when the port was hauled up, to look out from it. They complied with my wishes. The gun being loaded, I took my station in the centre of the port; which being held up, I beheld our antagonist firing away at us in quick succession. The ship was painted a dark red, as most of the enemy's fleet were, to denote (as previously mentioned) their sanguinary feelings against their adversaries. I had not enjoyed the sight long—only a few seconds—when a rolling sea came in and completely covered me. The tars, noticing this, instantly let down the port, but I got a regular soaking for my curiosity. The men cheered me, and laughingly said, "We hope, Sir, you will not receive further injury. It is rather warm work here below: the salt water will keep you cool."

One of these, John Polly, of very short stature, remarked that he was so small the shot would all pass over him. The words had not been long out of

---

[1] A most valuable innovation, used by the British but not by the French, and made possible only by the recent introduction into our service of spoons, sponges, rammers and worms with flexible handles. Upon recoil, the guns' muzzles never came very far inboard, so that the old, rigid-handled loading instruments not only compelled their users to expose their persons, even to climbing half-way out of the ports, but also made it impossible to lower the ports between broadsides. This was a great casualty-preventer, and proved a source of considerable advantage to the British.

# The Battle of the Glorious First of June

## June 1, 1794

### (Ushant 450 miles to east)

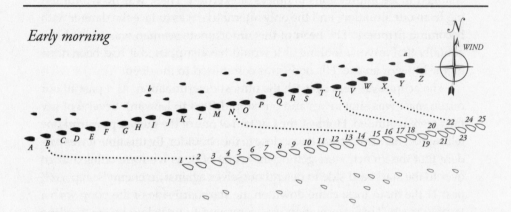

*Early morning*

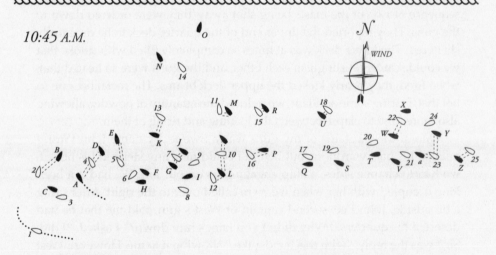

*10:45 A.M.*

### BRITISH FLEET

1. *Caesar*
2. *Bellerophon*
3. *Leviathan*
4. *Russell*
5. *Royal Sovereign*
6. *Marlborough*
7. *Defence*
8. *Impregnable*
9. *Tremendous*
10. *Barfleur*
11. *Invincible*
12. *Culloden*
13. *Gibraltar*
14. *Queen Charlotte*
15. *Brunswick*
16. *Valiant*
17. *Orion*
18. *Queen*
19. *Ramillies*
20. *Alfred*
21. *Montagu*
22. *Royal George*
23. *Majestic*
24. *Glory*
25. *Thunderer*

### FRENCH FLEET

A. *Convention*
B. *Gasparin*
C. *America*
D. *Téméraire*
E. *Terrible*
F. *Impétueux*
G. *Eole*
H. *Mucius*
I. *Tourville*
J. *Trajan*
K. *Trente-et-un Mai*
L. *Audacieux*
M. *Juste*
N. *Montagne*
O. *Jacobin*
P. *Achille*
Q. *Patriote*
R. *Vengeur du Peuple*
S. *Northumberland*
T. *Jemmapes*
U. *Entreprenant*
V. *Neptune*
W. *Républicain*
X. *Sans Pareil*
Y. *Scipion*
Z. *Pelletier*
a. *Mont Blanc*
b. *Tyrannicide*

\* Sources vary for the order
of the French battle line

his mouth when a shot cut his head right in two, leaving the tip of each ear remaining on the lower part of the cheek. His sudden death created a sensation among his comrades, but the excitement of the moment soon changed those impressions to others of exertion. There was no withdrawing from our situation, and the only alternative was to face the danger with becoming firmness. The head of this unfortunate seaman was cut so horizontally that anyone looking at it would have supposed it had been done by the blow of an axe. His body was committed to the deep.

The action was kept up with the utmost determination. At ½ past 10 our mizen mast was shot away, and our ship drifted to leeward. Several of my men were wounded. Holmes, the Captain of one of the guns, a powerful fine fellow, had his arm carried away close to the shoulder. By this time it was evident that the French were getting the worst of it, as we were obliged to go over to the starboard side to defend ourselves against an enemy's ship. At ½ past 11 the main mast came down on the starboard side of the poop with a terrible crash. This information was conveyed to us below by some of the seamen who had been in the tops. As they could no longer be useful in consequence of two of the masts being shot away, they were ordered down to the guns. They reported the upper end of the quarter deck to be dreadfully shattered. The lower deck was at times so completely filled with smoke that we could scarcely distinguish each other, and the guns were so heated that, when fired, they nearly kicked the upper deck beams. The metal became so hot that, fearing some accident, we reduced the quantity of powder, allowing also more time to elapse between the loading and firing of them.

One of the Captains of my guns was a Swede, by name John West. I noticed his backwardness, but before I could take any steps in his behalf, we had to change sides, a ship engaging us on our left. We had not been long occupied with her when we were called over to the right. After firing a broadside, John Lee, second captain of West's gun, told me that he had deserted his quarters. "Why didn't you knock him down?" I asked. "I did, Sir," was the reply, "with this handspike," showing it to me. However, West had absconded, and I was too much taken up with the pressing events of the moment to look after him. The ship we were engaging was very close, and the shot from him did us considerable injury. One of my guns was dismounted. This disaster created some confusion, more especially as the ship, from the loss of her masts, was rolling deeply; and we had considerable difficulty in securing the gun. Whilst we were occupied about this job, Lieut. Beecher thought that he observed a disinclination on the part of the seamen to exert themselves. All of a sudden he drew his sword from the scabbard, and began flourishing it about with threats that he would cut the first man down that did not do his duty. The tars were rather astonished at this proceeding of their officer as, hitherto, he had approved of their conduct. They had been fighting hard for upwards of two hours, and naturally were fatigued. They explained their anxiety to do their best. This pacified the heroic lieutenant. He sheathed his sword, and the men went on at the guns as before.

Just as this scene terminated, two of the men were blown down from the wind of a shot from the ship we were engaging, and I was carried away with them by the shock. I thought myself killed, as I became senseless, being jammed between these men. So soon as the smoke cleared away, our companions noticed my situation. They came, lugged me out, and began rubbing my limbs. This brought me to my senses. They lifted me up, enquiring if I felt myself hurt. I called out for water to drink. They handed to me a bowl with water. When I drank of it, it was quite salt. There were some salt bags hanging up close by, belonging to the men of that particular mess. These had been shot down, and had impregnated the water placed there to be used as required by those that were thirsty. Recovering myself, I felt considerable pain in my head and shoulders. My left cheek was cut by a splinter and bled profusely. I then examined the two men with whom I had been knocked down. In outward appearance they were dead; but as I did not consider myself a sufficient judge of these matters, I desired a couple of seamen to take them below to the surgeon. Whilst I was giving these directions, we were called over to the larboard side to repel the attack of an enemy. After a few broadsides he passed us. From him we received no injury at my quarters. Not long after, another Frenchman ranged up on the starboard side. Away we turned to, and pelted him as hard as we could. In crossing over I beheld the two wounded men still lying in the same position I had left them. Then, calling upon those to whom I had given orders to take the disabled men below, I insisted upon their immediately complying with my directions. They were then conveyed to the cockpit. After a few broadsides exchanged with our opponent, he made sail to leeward, and we had a few minutes' rest. This gave me an opportunity of looking out of the ports, but there was not much to be seen from that low situation. All that we could make out, in our conjectures, led us to believe that the action was nearly over. We could plainly at times distinguish the French ships sailing off and forming to leeward, engaging our ships as they passed by.

We had not long been quiet, when we received orders from the quarter deck for all hands to lie down, as an enemy three decker was coming to rake us. This ship closed gradually upon us with only her foremast standing, the sail of which enabled him to make way at a very slow pace. This was, to me, the most awful part of the battle. We could not defend ourselves from the stern, and here was an immense overpowering ship of upwards of 100 guns going to pour in her broadside into the weakest and most exposed part of our ship. It was a moment of extreme anxiety, as there was a chance of our being sunk. As he neared us there was an appearance of intending to board, and the boarders were called to repulse the attempt. But when he altered his course to rake, we were again ordered to lie down. We waited the coming event with a silent suspense not easily described. At length the enemy in passing across our stern, to our astonishment, only fired a few random shot, which brought down our disabled foremast. We were now completely dismasted and quite unmanageable. The three decker, ranging up on our larboard side, gave us an opportunity of sending some well directed shot into him. In watching the motions of this ship, I noticed that the Frenchmen, in many instances, loaded their guns from the outside. One man I distinctly saw riding upon a lower deck gun, loading it. He was stripped from the waist upwards, and had we been sufficiently near, our marines could have picked him off with their muskets. This three decker soon got out of range, leaving us free of further molestation.

It was past 12 o'clock, and I concluded the fighting part of our duty to be at an end. My clothes were still damp: my shoes, to which I had small buckles, were covered with blood; my face and hands smutched with powder and blood. At my quarters I had 14 men killed and wounded (if I included myself I should say 15); and a gun. I now ascertained that no part of the lower deck had suffered so much as mine. On my way aft I shook hands with other mids who had escaped. Of these I shall never forget Ritchie. He was in his shirt upwards, with a bandage round his head. These were all bloody, and I thought he had been hurt. On my inquiring of him if it were the case, he gave me a hearty shake by the hand, telling me he was strong and hearty, and ready to continue the action when required. The bloody spots on his linen were occasioned by his having assisted some wounded men below. He gave the strongest symptoms of a bold and daring spirit, and had it not been for the bloody marks upon him, one might have supposed he had been at a merry and jovial party instead of a destructive battle. The next person I came in contact with was one of my messmates, Consitt. He also had taken off his coat and waistcoat, and his linen too was all bloody, which led me to suppose that he had been injured. However, upon enquiry, I found that he was safe and sound. In a few words he gave me an interesting account of what had been going on upon the quarter deck, as he was one of the Captain's aides-de-camp. He had been sent down to the lower deck to ascertain its state and condition. Among the informations received from him, he stated that the *Royal Sovereign*, one of our three deckers, had fired into us and wounded some of our men. Upon further inquiry his assertion turned out to be true.

I now hastened up to the quarter deck. In attempting to do so I was prevented by the splinter netting which, from its lying across the quarter deck
under the mainmast, had turned the place into a sort of cage. There was no
getting on it until the netting had been cut away. Whilst on the ladder, Mr.
Hawtayne, the clergyman, came to me. From my appearance he thought
that I had been seriously injured, but I soon set his mind at rest on that subject. Leaving him, I at length reached the poop, where I met my Captain. He
noticed me very kindly, and in replying to his questions I related to him
what had happened at my quarters. Whilst in conversation with him, the
second lieutenant, Mr. Dickson,[1] began firing some of the starboard main
deck guns. He was drunk. By this rash act he set the ship on fire, as the fore-
topsail was lying over the side. But in due time the fire was extinguished,
and our alarms at an end.

The cannonade of the hostile fleets had lulled the wind, but the swell of
the sea was still paramount, and our ship, without sails or masts to balance
her motion, laboured in a most annoying manner. The first object that
attracted my notice on the quarter deck was the immense quantity of the
enemy's musket shot lying there. On the starboard side, which had at the
commencement of the action been the lee one, they were at least three or
four tier deep, and the rest of the deck completely covered with them.[2]
How could it be possible, thought I, for anyone to escape being hit where
so many thousand instruments of death had fallen? But so it was; and the
Captain, with many of those around him, came off without injury. The only
officers of the ship that were killed were the master, Webster, and the
boatswain, Mr. Fitzpatrick. Lieut. Boycott of the 2nd Regiment, Queen's,
was severely wounded. He was a remarkably fine young man. The effect of
his wounds obliged him to quit the ship upon our arrival at Spithead, to the
regret of all who knew him. Looking around me, I saw the *Queen*, 98, some
distance to leeward of us, still engaged with the enemy's ships which had
formed a line on the starboard tack. That ship had lost her main mast, but
it soon became evident that she would rejoin us, and there was no apprehension on her account. But the *Brunswick*, 74, was to leeward of the
French, and we were uneasy about her fate.[3] She had lost her mizen mast.
By one o'clock all firing was at an end.

The next thing to be done was to attend to the disabled ships. We made
the signal for assistance from the stump of our mizen mast. In clearing
away the lumber on the poop, a marine was found stowed away under the

[1] Probably John Dixon, Lt. 10/9/81; not promoted.
[2] Surely an exaggeration; not elsewhere corroborated.
[3] Though much damaged in her famous duel with the *Vengeur*, she arrived safely at Spithead
on June 12.

hen coops. Those who lugged him out thought him dead. However, he soon came to life. This was the Fugleman[1] of that Corps, one of the finest limbed men I ever beheld, and the most perfect in his exercise. All hands laughed at him when they saw he had not been hurt. He was, also, like my friend West, a foreigner.

There was no walking the quarter deck till the small shot had been cleared away. The next object of consequence was to get rid of the main mast, which with some difficulty was finally rolled overboard. The quantity of damaged spars, with rigging, that was floating about gave proofs of the severity of the contest in which we had been engaged. The *Queen Charlotte,* Lord Howe's flagship, passed close to leeward of us. She had lost all her topmasts, which prevented his following the French admiral. We gave his Lordship three hearty cheers, at which moment, we were afterwards told, Lord Howe observed, "If every ship of the fleet had followed Capt. Gambier's example, the result of this action would have been very different from what it is." The flagship having stood on a little while longer, signals were made to form on the starboard tack. While these things were passing, an opinion existed on board of us that the action would be renewed, as it became clear that the French were fairly beaten.

But that signal was not made. There were 14 sail of the line dismasted, 12 French and two English—ourselves and the *Marlborough,* 74, Capt. the Hon. George Berkeley.[2] Capt. Gambier, giving me his spy glass (which had been hit by a shot) desired me to let him know the number of ships in the British fleet with topgallant yards across; and as Mr. Twysden overheard that order, he said he would assist me in the counting. We accordingly set to work, and after a strict examination, twice repeated, we made out 18 sail of the line in our fleet with topgallant yards across, and in appearance fit to go into battle. We had 7 disabled ships; the French more than 12. What astonished us most at this critical moment was the want of instructions. No signal had as yet been made to take possession of the enemy's disabled ships. Capt. Troubridge,[3] who had been captured in the *Castor,* already mentioned, was a prisoner of war on board the *Sanspareil,* 80. He was quite lost at this apparent inactivity. Had that signal been made at the close of the action, we might with ease have captured their 12 disabled ships; instead of which upwards of an hour was allowed to elapse before such a signal was thrown out. In that hour

[1] "Fugal man" in MS. "Soldier placed in front of regiment etc. while drilling to show the motions and time." *Concise Oxford Dictionary.*
[2] (Admiral) the Hon. (Sir) George Cranfield Berkeley (G.C.B.), Capt. 12/9/80; R-Ad. 14/2/99; V-Ad. 9/11/1805; Ad. 31/7/10. Lord High Admiral of Portugal, 1810. Died, 1818.
[3] (Sir) Thomas Troubridge (Bart.), Capt. 1/1/83; R-Ad. 23/4/1804. Lost in the *Blenheim* off Madagascar in February 1807 when en route from India to take up the command at the Cape.

5 French ships contrived to slip through our line under their spritsails, and join their own to leeward, leaving 7 with us, which were then taken possession of. I hardly know how to restrain my feelings on this subject even now, 26 years after the event.[1] Had Lord Howe been a younger man, there is every probability—I ought to say *no* doubt—but the action would have been renewed. We were 200 miles away from the land, with plenty of sea room for evolutions. His Lordship was clever at naval tactics: therefore, had the French been brought to action that afternoon, the result would have been the most splendid victory ever achieved on the ocean over our enemy. On our way into port, the many officers that visited the *Defence* expressed the same opinions as I have herewith written down.

Many years afterwards, I heard from the best authority that the Captain of the fleet, Sir Roger Curtis,[2] who had been selected by Lord Howe to assist him in his naval duties, when consulted by his Lordship after the action, replied, "You have gained a victory. Now make sure of it. If you renew the action, who knows what may be the result? Make sure of what you have got. Your Lordship is tired. You had better take some rest, and I will manage the other matters for you." Lord Howe accordingly went below, to bed I believe, leaving the Captain of the fleet to make signals as he thought necessary.[3]

To return to the *Defence:* whilst we were hard at work in clearing the wreck, the *Invincible,* 74, the Hon. Capt. Thomas Pakenham,[4] came up and hailed us. These two Captains were very intimate. "Jemmy," said Capt. Pakenham, "whom the Lord loveth He chasteneth"—in allusion to the shattered condition we were in. Our Captain made a suitable reply, then asked if he had lost many men: to which question he answered, "Damn me if I know. They won't tell me, for fear I should stop their grog." A few more words passed, when Capt. Pakenham sent an officer on board to inquire if any help was required. I shall never forget that gentleman. When he came alongside he was dressed in a Guernsey jacket with a welch wig, and had not the slightest appearance of an officer, as all the boat's crew were similarly attired. When he reached the quarter deck, we ascertained by the buttons on his

---

[1] *I.e.* in 1820, when these letters were written.

[2] Lt. 19/1/71; Cdr. 11/7/76; Capt. 30/4/77; in command of naval forces in Gibraltar during the famous siege; R-Ad. 4/7/94; created baronet for services at First of June; V-Ad. 14/2/99; Ad. 23/4/1804. Died, 14/11/16.

[3] One of several versions of the conversation on the quarter deck of the flagship. The precise truth will probably never be known. What is certain is that it was very widely held in naval circles that Lord Howe erred seriously on the side of overprudence and that his Captain of the fleet exerted his influence in making him do so. That Curtis himself was often prudent to the verge of defeatism seems clear. *Cf. Life of Sir Edward Codrington,* I, 28 *et seq.*

[4] Capt. 2/3/80; R-Ad. 14/2/99; V-Ad. 13/4/1804; Ad. 31/7/10. Died, 2/2/36.

smalls that he was a lieutenant—McGuire. He was presented to the Captain, to whom he said he had been sent to offer us assistance. Capt. Gambier naturally put many questions to him relating to the action. His replies were delivered with many oaths, which so disgusted our chief that he turned his back and left him. The lieutenant then, very quietly folding his arms, seated himself on the stump of the main mast; but as none of the *Defences* seemed inclined to take further notice of him after his rudeness, he left the ship. Capt. Pakenham, it seems, had given directions that his officers and Ship's Company, all Irish, should all be dressed alike: of which Mr. McGuire was a specimen. The Hon. Thos. Pakenham, brother to Lord Longford, was a regular character, and established a discipline on board the *Invincible* in direct opposition to the established rules of the Navy. But as I shall have to bring him again into notice, I take my leave of the Honourable Captain for the present.

We had scarcely done with the *Invincible* when the *Phaeton* Frigate, Capt. George Bentinck,[1] came to take us in tow. This ship had been commanded by Sir Andrew Douglas. Several of my messmates of the *Alcide* were on board her, from whom I received many hearty congratulations at having escaped with my life. I little thought then that I should command that frigate. It is not many months since I paid her off.[2] She was, without exception, one of the best sea boats I have ever had my foot on board. Whilst the frigate was taking us in tow, up came another line of battle ship, the *Valiant* (I believe Capt. Pringle).[3] Her Captain overloaded ours with compliments upon the noble example he had shown to the whole fleet: and among other sayings he insisted that we had sunk an enemy's ship. This we could not make out. However, it was for a long time the general opinion that we had sent a French 74 to the bottom. But time set this matter at rest. The ship we engaged in breaking the line was called *l'Eole*. She arrived safe at Brest: consequently, she could not have been sunk by us.

So soon as the Surgeon could make his report, it appeared that we had 91 men killed and wounded on this day: altogether, in the two actions of May 29 and June 1, twenty killed and eighty wounded.[4] One of our Mates, Mr. Elliot,[5] was severely wounded in the thigh by a grape shot. He was in the first instance moved into the Captain's cabin, where I saw him resting on a sofa in great agony, until he could be taken below to the doctor. He had served in the American War, and was a very superior young man. The havoc

---

[1] Should be *William* Bentinck, Capt. 15/9/83; R-Ad. 9/11/1805.
[2] *I.e.* in 1820.
[3] Yes. Thomas Pringle; Capt. 25/11/76; R-Ad. 4/7/94.
[4] These figures tally closely with those of other accounts with regard to the "killed"; but, here, the "wounded" are put a good deal higher; Consitt gives 56, Brenton 39. James 36.
[5] Never promoted; died soon after.

on board us was terrific. Two of the ports on the larboard side of the main deck were knocked into one by the shot. Only one shot penetrated between wind and water. It came into the bread room on the larboard side and smashed some of the lanterns there, without any serious injury to the ship. The spars upon our booms were sadly cut up. One of our boats, smashed to atoms, was thrown overboard, and, I am sorry to say, many other things were cast into the sea that might have been turned to account. My duty, I thought, was to obey orders, and not to point out the acts of wastefulness I witnessed. No doubt there were many similar ones on board of the other ships. The expense in refitting the fleet must have been immense.

The number of men thrown overboard that were killed, without ceremony, and the sad wrecks around us taught those who, like myself, had not before witnessed similar scenes that war was the greatest scourge of mankind. The first leisure I had, I went to see the Captain of my gun, who had lost his arm. He was in good spirits, and when I told him we had gained the victory, he replied, "Then I don't mind the loss of my arm. I am satisfied." Leaving him, I met a young man who had lost a part of his arm. When I spoke to him he was quite cheerful, not seeming to mind his misfortune. He was eating a piece of buttered biscuit as if nothing had happened. It was a very gratifying circumstance to witness so many acts of heroic bravery that were displayed on board our ship. Patriotic sentences were uttered that would have done honour to the noblest minds: yet these were expressed by the humblest class of men.

Many of our ships that had slightly suffered in their yards, sails and rigging were all to rights in the afternoon. But the ship that astonished us all by her extraordinary exertions was the *Queen*. She had lost her main mast. This was replaced in a most able manner before the evening of this day: all her sides were scrubbed, her paintwork looking as clean as if nothing had happened—a good proof of what can be done with good discipline and management. In the evening, boats were sent to remove the crew from the French prize *le Vengeur*,[1] 74. She was in a sinking state, and went to the bottom about 10 o'clock. 250 of her men were saved.[2]

---

[1] This, of course, is the true story, ignoring the well-known "propaganda" version of Barrère in the National Convention. [*On July 10, 1794, Barrère de Vieuzac told the Convention that three British vessels had been sunk and that the* Vengeur *had gone down firing at the enemy with her colors bravely flying. Implying that the ship had never surrendered, he asserted that the officers and men had preferred death to captivity, cheering for the Republic, for Liberty, and for France as they went to their deaths. Many historians have repeated this story but it was proved false when* Vengeur's *captain, Renaudin, and many of his men returned with the true story.*]

[2] Certainly not less. Most accounts give considerably more—up to 400. Mahan's estimate, reached by subtracting the lost from the original complement, is 367. He also gives the relevant part of Barrère's speech in full. (*Fr. Rev. and Empire*, I, 144.)

So soon as I could get hold of the surgeon, I enquired the fate of the two men I had sent him from my quarters. He told me they were both killed! One of them was without the slightest mark of a wound on any part of his body: the other had a bruise across his loins, supposed to have been occasioned by his having come in contact with the bitts[1] in his fall. It is therefore clear that they were killed by the wind of a shot. Few persons will believe that the wind of a shot can take away life. But here was proof that it could, and the surgeon was a witness to its having happened. My next question to the doctor was whether he recollected anything of West: if such a person had been to him. He replied that he had; and, upon examining him, he noticed a bruise on the neck. "Yes," said I, "that was a blow he received from the second captain of his gun with a handspike, for deserting his quarters." So the Swede told a good story to the surgeon, and remained snug in the cockpit for the remainder of the action.

* * *

*Despite the fact that Howe did not prevent the grain-bearing merchant fleet from reaching France, the battle of June 1, 1794, was hailed as "Glorious." The victory could have been more complete, but it was sound enough to provide a needed morale boost in England. Both houses of Parliament voted their thanks to Howe, his officers, and seamen. On board his ship at Spithead, the king presented Howe with a diamond-hilted sword. June 1 was a highlight of Dillon's career. Later, events beyond his control would conspire to stall his rise as an officer. But when a much delayed and somewhat dubious opportunity arrived, he grabbed it with zeal (see "An Unequal Match, 1807–1808," page 185).*

*Meanwhile, in July of 1794, Midshipman Gardner, a man of much lighter temperament than Dillon, joined HMS* Gorgon *in the Mediterranean. For every great sea battle waged by the Royal Navy, there were many more thousands of sea miles logged. Gardner, a sort of seaman's Chaucer, extracts some very amusing, somewhat ribald, tales from his journey back to England.*

---

[1] Two stout timbers to which the cables are secured on the lower deck.

# JAMES ANTHONY GARDNER

# The Noted Pimp of Lisbon and an Unwanted Promotion in Bull Bay

## 1794

*The son and grandson of navy men, James Gardner's name was carried on the books of various ships from the time he reached five years old. He was at sea by the age of twelve, but with the death of his father at St. Lucia, West Indies, in 1780 and some imprudent demands upon his naval benefactors, his advancement through the ranks was slow. At the time of this passage, which begins off Corsica in the Gulf of St. Florent (San Fiorenzo), he is a twenty-four-year-old midshipman.*

IN JULY 1794 I joined the *Gorgon*, Captain James Wallis, at St. Fiorenzo, and after considerable delay sailed for Gibraltar with the convoy bound for England under Vice-Admiral P. Cosby, who had his flag on board the *Alcide*, 74. The following men of war, to the best of my recollection, in company: *Alcide*, 74 (Vice-Admiral Cosby); *Commerce de Marseilles*,[1] 136; *Gorgon*, 44; *Pearl*,[1] 36; *Topaze*,[1] 36; *St. Fiorenzo*, 36; *Modeste*, 32.

At the time we left Corsica we had forty-seven French prisoners on board. One of them could play the violin remarkably well. One morning on the forecastle, this man was reading to some of his comrades, and having

---

[1] French ships brought from Toulon. *Cf.* Schomberg, *Naval Chronology*, iv. 471. It will be seen that the lists of these squadrons differ from Schomberg's, which are probably the more correct. The *Alert [which Gardner mentions on page 38]*, for instance, had been captured on the coast of Ireland, in May.—James, i. 439. *[A strong royalist,]* Rear-Admiral *[the comte de]* Trogoff, with his flag in the *Commerce de Marseille*, left Toulon in company with the English *[Toulon was evacuated December 17, 1793]* but he died within a few months.—Chevalier, *op. cit.* pp. 90, 91.

33

his violin with him, Mr. Duncan (our late master in the *Berwick*) requested him to play *Ça Ira*, which he for some time refused, being fearful of giving offence.[1] At last he struck up the Marseilles hymn accompanied by his voice, which was very good, and when he came to that part "*Aux armes, Citoyens, formez vos bataillons,*" etc., he seemed inspired; he threw up his violin half way up the foremast, caught it again, pressed it to his breast, and sung out "*Bon, Ça Ira,*" in which he was joined by his comrades.

> *Fired with the song the French grew vain,*
> *Fought all their battles o'er again,*
> *And thrice they routed all their foes; and thrice they slew the slain;*

and seemed ready and willing for any mischief. But our soldiers were called up and the French were sent below, and not so many allowed to be on deck at a time.

On the passage we were frequently sent as a whipper-in among the convoy. On one occasion, a master of a merchantman was rather slack in obeying the signal and gave tongue when hailed; upon which Captain Wallis sent the first lieutenant and myself to take charge of his vessel. It was in the evening, blowing fresh, with a heavy sea, and we had great difficulty in getting on board; our boat cut as many capers as a swing at a fair, and in returning got stove alongside. We remained all night on board and had to prick for the softest plank. When Edgar, the first lieutenant, awoke in the morning, it was laughable to hear him exclaim, "God bass 'e" (for he could not say "blast ye," and for this he was nicknamed little Bassey) "What's got hold of me?" The fact was the night was hot, and the pitch in the seams waxed warm, and when he attempted to rise, he found his hair fastened to the deck and his nankin trowsers also. He put me in mind of Gulliver when fastened to the ground by the Liliputians. Captain Wallis having sent for us, we took this chap in tow. It blew very fresh, and the wind being fair, we towed him, under double reefed topsails and foresail, nine knots through the water, so that his topsails were wet with the spray. The master would sometimes run forward and hail, saying, "I'll cut the hawser"; and Captain Wallis would reply, "If you do, I'm damned if I don't sink you, you skulking son of a bitch; I mean to tow you until I work some buckets of tar out of the hawser."

---

[1] "*Ça Ira!,*" literally *"That will succeed!"* in French, is an *often repeated phrase in a revolutionary song that was sung at many events during the Terror. "Ça Ira" was later named the official song of the Revolution.*

Our admiral (Cosby) was a glorious fellow for keeping the convoy in order, and if they did not immediately obey the signal, he would fire at them without further ceremony.

We had a very pleasant passage to Gibraltar, where we remained some time in the New Mole, and then started for Cadiz to take in money and to join the convoy assembling there for England. While lying at Gibraltar a Portuguese frigate arrived, and one of our midshipmen (Jennings, a wag) was sent on board with a message from Captain Wallis. Having stayed a long time, the signal was made for the boat, and when she returned the captain asked Jennings what detained him. "Why, sir, to tell you the truth, saving your presence" (for Jennings was a shrewd Irishman), "the commanding officer of the frigate was so busy lousing himself on the hen-coop that I could not get an answer before."

⌐⌐

ON THE PASSAGE we got on shore a few leagues to the southward of Cadiz, and had very near taken up our quarters on the shoals, and, what was remarkable, a frigate had been sent before us for the same purpose, but got on shore in this place, and was obliged to return, and we (being clever) after laughing at the circumstance, were sent to repair her errors and went bump on shore on the very spot.

When we arrived at Cadiz to join the convoy and to bring home dollars, the merchants used to smuggle the money off to the ship to avoid paying the duty; and for every hundred taken on board, they would give as a premium two dollars and sometimes two and a half. It was a dangerous traffic, but very tempting; and some of our officers while lying there made sixty and others eighty pounds. On one occasion, my old shipmate, Lieutenant Chantrell, fell down in the street with six hundred dollars at his back—a moderate load—and sung out to some of the Spaniards who were looking on, "Come here, you sons of ———, and help me up." Had they known what he had at his back they would have helped him up to some purpose; imprisonment and slavery would have been the punishment. The manner they carried the dollars was this. A double piece of canvas made to contain them in rows, fixed to the back inside the waistcoat, and tied before. It was to an English hotel where they were sent to be shipped. This house was kept by Mr., or rather Mrs., Young, an infernal vixen, who would make nothing of knocking her husband down with a leg of mutton or any other joint she had in the larder, and he fool enough to put up with it. She used to charge us very high for our entertainment, which is the case in all English houses abroad; and if you have a mind to be treated fairly you must go to a house kept by a native, who will never impose on you. Having got a load of dollars to take off, we found our boat had left the landing place; so we hired a shore boat, and it appeared their custom house officers had suspicions, for they gave chase, and it was by uncommon exertion that we escaped, as they were nearly up with us when we got alongside. And yet those very men who would have seized us used to smuggle. I saw one of them come alongside and throw into the lower-deck port a bag of dollars containing, as I understood, a thousand, with a label on the bag, and then shove off his boat to row guard and prevent smuggling!

At Cadiz there is a beautiful walk with trees, called the Alameda, much frequented, particularly on a Sunday. It has three walks for the different grades of people. I happened to be on shore with some of our officers on the above day, and taking a stroll through the Alameda, we observed several well-dressed women in a balcony of one of the large houses that overlooked the walks. When they caught sight of us, they beckoned, and we went, as we thought, into the house. On going up two pairs of stairs without seeing any one, we imagined it was a trick, when casting my eye to a door that was partly open, I saw a fellow with a drawn stilletto ready to make a stab; upon which I called to the rest to make their retreat as fast as possible. One of them (a Mr. Crump) was deaf, and I was obliged to push him downstairs as I could not make him understand. This was a warning not lost upon us.

The *America*, 64, having arrived at Cadiz to take charge of the convoy, we were put under her orders, and having got on board the money, sailed with the convoy for Lisbon.

> *Farewell and adieu, ye fair Spanish Ladies,*
> *Farewell and adieu, ye Ladies of Spain;*
> *For we've received orders to sail for old England,*
> *In hopes in short time for to see you again.*—Old Song.

After a passage of near three weeks we arrived in the Tagus, fortunately the day before a tremendous hurricane, which blew dead upon the shore, came on and lasted a considerable time.

A droll circumstance happened while at Lisbon. A party of us had been to see the famous aqueduct over the valley of Alcantara, and on coming back, one of them (Tomlinson, of the *Berwick*) to show his dexterity jumped on the back of a donkey. He had on a round jacket and light nankin pantaloons; the latter he split from clue to earing, and was obliged to walk to the boat in that situation, and by way of helping a lame dog over a stile, we took the longest way, where we had to pass by several ladies, with his shirt sticking out and every one laughing at him. He declared to me it was the most miserable time he ever experienced in the whole course of his life.

We were one day accosted while walking in Black-Horse Square, by a genteel-looking young man who, in broken English, said he would be happy to show us about the city, which offer was accepted, though much against my will. As we were walking through the streets, I observed the people as they passed us to laugh and point to others and then at us. At last we met an officer belonging to our squadron, who asked if we knew the person we had in company, because, says he, "If you don't I'll tell you. He is the noted pimp of Lisbon, and makes a trade of showing, not only the city, but all the ladies of easy virtue from the lowest brothel in Bull Bay to the highest in the upper town." This was quite enough, and we told the fellow to be off, but he had the impudence to follow us to the boat for payment, and even got upon the gang board and was coming in, when Jennings, in his dry way, said to the bowman, "Don't you see the gentleman is dusty? Have you no way of rubbing it off?" winking at the time. Upon this the bowman without any ceremony pitched him overboard up to his neck and then shoved off. We met the fellow several times after, but he took good care to steer clear.

I went with Lieutenant Chantrell to dinner at an ordinary at Lisbon. Among the company were several Americans. One of the dishes at the bottom of the table occasioned a dispute that had nearly terminated in a battle. A Yankee from the head of the table came and snatched up a beef-steak pie that an English master of a transport (one of our convoy) was serving out, and carried it off to his companions; upon which the Englishman stood up and harangued his countrymen as follows: "I say, if you stand this you ought to be damned, and may as well take a purser's shirt out of the rigging.[1] Now, I move that all you that are Englishmen shall rise from the table and throw the Yankees out of the window." This speech had the same effect as that of Nestor's to the Greeks, and the Yankees would for a certainty have been thrown into the street, had not Lieutenant Chantrell requested them to forbear, observing that abuse was innocent where men were worthless. This had the desired effect; and the pie being restored to its place in rather a diminished state, and the Yankee who took it away saying he only meant it in Har-mo-ny, the war was put an end to, and the dinner ended in peace.

One of our men having deserted, I was sent with Ducker, the boatswain, and a couple of marines to hunt in Bull Bay, which is the Wapping of Lisbon,

---

[1] A shirt in the rigging was the recognised signal from a merchantman for a man-of-war boat to be sent on board.

and after a long search we found him and were returning to the boat. In passing through one of their dirty streets, something which shall be nameless was hove out of a window and fell upon the shoulder of Ducker, about the size of a large epaulette. I wished him joy of his promotion and told him that he looked extremely well in his new uniform. A piece of the same material fell on his nose and stuck out like the horn of a rhinoceros. I never saw a fellow so vexed. He was going to break the windows, but I told him to consider, as Bull Bay was not to be attacked too hastily. I had hardly made the observation when his foot slipped, and he fell back in the gutter, where he lay cursing the whole race of Portuguese. Then

> *Vigorous he rose; and from the effluvia strong*
> *Imbibed new strength, and scoured and stunk along.*[1]

I thought I should have died a-laughing, while he was cursing every native he met with until he got to the boat.

We remained several weeks at Lisbon collecting the convoy. At last when everything was ready we got under way, I think the latter end of September, the following men of war in company: *America*, 64 (Hon. John Rodney, commodore, having charge of the convoy); *Gorgon*, 44 (Captain Wallis); *Pearl*, 36; *Topaze*, 36; *St. Fiorenzo*, 36 (Capt. Sir C. Hamilton (?)); *Modeste*, 32 (Captain [Byam Martin]); *Alert*, 18.

We had a most dreadful passage home, blowing a gale of wind the whole time with seldom more sail set than a close-reefed main topsail. The French squadron that captured the *Alexander*, 74, had been on the look-out for us. We had several French officers (emigrants) who had left Toulon at the evacuation. They were in the greatest tribulation all the passage for fear of being taken. We had also many invalids from the fleet, of very little service had we met with an enemy; and our effective complement I think mustered under a hundred, so that we should have stood but a poor chance had we met with the squadron. The forty-seven French prisoners that we had with us were left at Gibraltar, which was a great relief to the emigrants we had on board, as they were in constant fear of their taking the ship from us. Fortunately for them and for us the Jacobin squadron got on the wrong scent.

I don't know how it happened, but some people kept an odd kind of reckoning, and we had some idea of making the banks of Newfoundland instead of the British Channel. However, at last we got to the northward

---

[1] *The Dunciad*, ii. 105. A reference to the original—of which only the tense is here altered—will show the strict appositeness of the quotation.

and westward of Scilly, with the wind at SW; but it must be understood, to give the devil his due, that we had not an observation for a long time, and our dead reckoning was not to be trusted; but at last we found out by instinct or soundings that we were not in the right place. Now it so happened that we were lying to on the larboard tack, the wind, as I have stated, at SW, under a close-reefed main topsail and storm staysails, when in a thundering squall it shifted to NNW and took us slap aback. Over she went, with the upper dead-eyes on the lower rigging in the water, and we thought she never would right, but the old ship came to herself again. She was a noble sea-boat; it would have been worth any man's while to leave the feast, the dance, or even his wife, to have been on board this ship in a gale of wind to witness her glorious qualities.

I must now speak of Jerry Hacker, the purser. He was a man, take him all in all, ye ne'er will see his like again. He messed by himself in the cockpit, and would sit in his cabin in the dark with a long stick in his hand, calling out to everyone that came down the cockpit ladder, "What strange man is that?" He was in constant fear of being robbed or cheated, and lived in the most miserable manner. I have known him to corn meat in his hand-basin and in something else. He was suspicious to a degree and always saying he should be ruined, though there was little fear of that, as Jerry took good care to trust no one; and what he was only charged two shillings a gallon for, he kindly offered to let me have for five shillings, paying ready money; but I was not to be taken in so easy. He could not bear the sight of a midshipman in the cockpit, and did everything in his power to annoy them, and before I joined the ship, he used to sing a verse of an old song reflecting on the midshipmen. One morning while I was in the cockpit, he was quarrelling with some of them, and then struck up his favourite air, not thinking that any person knew the song but himself. However, in this he was mistaken, and when he had finished the following verse, I struck up another that settled him.

Tune, The Black Joke.
*Ye salt beef squires and quarter deck beaus,*
*Who formerly lived upon blacking of shoes:*
*With your anchors a-weigh and your topsails a-trip.*
*If they call us by name and we don't answer, Sir!*
*They start us about till not able to stir;*
*A lusty one and lay it well on.*
*If you spare them an inch you ought to be damn'd;*
*With your anchors a-weigh and your topsails a-trip.*
*Our b——— of a purser, he is very handy,*
*He mixes the water along with the brandy;*

> *Your anchors a-weigh and your topsails a-trip*
> *The bloody old thief he is very cruel;*
> *Instead of burgoo he gives us water gruel;*
> *    A lusty one and lay it well on.*
> *If you spare him an inch you ought to be damn'd,*
> *With your anchors a-weigh and your topsails a-trip.*

After hearing the last verse Jerry's "heavenly voice was heard no more to sing," and he looked with an evil eye upon me ever after.

In the gale of wind near the Channel, when we were taken aback in the squall that I have mentioned, every article we had was broken with the exception of the cover of a very large mess teapot. This we handed round as a measure to one another with wine from a black jack. I remember being at supper soon after the squall, in the midship berth in the cockpit, the ship rolling gunwale under, when we heard a noise in the after-hold like the rush of many waters, and it struck everyone that a butt end had started and that we should founder in a few minutes. The alarm was given immediately. The sick and lame left their hammocks; the latter forgot his crutch, and leaped—not exulting—like the bounding roe. Down came the captain and a whole posse of officers and men. The gratings were instantly unshipped, and in rushed the carpenter and his crew, horror-struck, with hair standing on end, like quills on the fretful porcupine; when, behold, it was a large cask of peas that had the head knocked out, and the peas as the ship rolled rushed along with a noise exactly like that of water.[1]

After looking at one another for some time the following ludicrous scene took place, which I was an eye-witness to:—

The captain shook his head, took snuff, and went upon deck.

Old Edgar, first lieutenant, followed, and said, "God bass 'e all."

Billy Chantrell gave a grin, and damn'd his eyes.

The parson exclaimed, "In the midst of life we are in death."

The carpenter said, "Damn and b——— the peas."

Old Jerry Hacker, the purser, swore he was ruined, as no allowance would be made him; and cursed the field the peas grew in; and the French emigrant captain (Dubosc) said, "it was as vel for him to stay at de Toulon and be guillotined, as to come to dis place and be drowned in de vater."

---

[1] At this time peas were issued whole. Split peas were not issued till about 1856—after the Russian war.

I never shall forget this scene as long as I live. I dined with Captain Wallis the next day, and he asked me, in a very knowing manner, if he should help me to some peas soup.

AFTER STANDING to the southward for some time until we thought we had got into 49°30′ by our dead reckoning, which is the latitude of mid-channel, we then altered our course to SEbE½E. I had a presentiment that something bad was hanging over us, and I went on the fore topsail yard (I think about nine at night) to look out ahead, the ship scudding at the rate of eleven knots, which brought to my mind the following lines:

> The fatal sisters on the surge before
> Yoked their infernal horses to the prow.—Falconer.

But in this instance they were outwitted, for lo and behold, after running some time I saw a light right ahead, which I instantly knew to be Scilly light, and I called to Captain Wallis, who immediately hauled the ship off to the southward. If the weather had not cleared after the squall before mentioned we should certainly have made the port where Sir Clowdsiley Shovell[1] took in his last moorings.

The gale separated the convoy, and in standing up Channel we had near run on the Bolt Head, but hauled off just in time. At last we arrived at Spithead, where a large fleet of men of war were assembled. Before we came to an anchor we had nearly run foul of several ships, and I remember the *Invincible*, 74, hailing us, saying, "You have cut my cable, sir." This was not all, for we shaved off the old *Royal William*'s quarter gallery, which some shipwrights were repairing—who had barely time to save themselves. We were not allowed to anchor at Spithead, but to proceed to the Motherbank to perform quarantine on December 4, 1794, after the most extraordinary voyage that ever took place since the expedition of the Argonauts. Here I left the *Gorgon* and joined the *Victory*, who I found to my astonishment at Spithead.

BEFORE I QUIT the *Gorgon* I must relate a few things. . . . As I have stated before, every ship has strange characters, and the *Gorgon* had her full share. I shall begin with the captain, who was a very good seaman and had many

---

[1] *Admiral Sir Clowdisley Shovel had commanded the Mediterranean fleet during the War of the Spanish Succession in 1707. On his passage home, in one of the great disasters in British naval history, his flagship and several others struck the rocks off the Scilly Isles, where he and many others drowned.*

good qualities, but at times he appeared half mad. He once said to me, pointing to Ducker, the boatswain, on the forecastle, "I'll hang that fellow; and you go down directly and take an inventory of his stores." I could hardly keep my countenance, but went forward, and as the captain turned his back I said to Ducker, "You are going to be hanged, and I am sent for a piece of white line to tuck you up genteelly." On my reporting progress, he seemed to have forgot that he gave such an order, and, taking a pinch of snuff, merely said, "Let the fellow go to hell, and say no more about him."

The first lieutenant, Edgar, was another strange and unaccountable being. He had sailed round the world with Cook, and was master of the ship Captain Clerke commanded. He was a good sailor and navigator, or rather had been, for he drank very hard, so as to entirely ruin his constitution. He and the captain often quarrelled, particularly at night. I have heard the captain say, "Edgar, I shall get another first lieutenant." The other would answer, "Ye-ye-ye-yes, sir, another first lieutenant." The captain again, "Edgar, you are drunk." "No, sir, bass me if I am." A day or two before we left Corsica, the captain ordered the sails to be bent and went on shore to St. Fiorenzo. On coming on board late at night he asked Edgar if the sails were bent. This question Edgar could not answer, his memory having failed him; and on the captain asking him again, he said, "Bass me if I know, but I'll look up," forgetting it was dark. "You need not do that," says the other, "for damn me if you can see a hole through a grating." Then taking a pinch of snuff, part of which blew into Edgar's eye, he asked him down to supper. This the other readily agreed to, but said, Bass him, if he could see the way.

Our gunner was one of the drollest fellows I ever met with—it was his delight to come on the forecastle in the first watch and sing comic songs to amuse the midshipmen assembled there. "Arthur O'Bradley" was one that he used to sing with a great deal of humour. I believe it contained forty verses. "Bryan O'Lynn" was another which I shall relate, leaving out the lines that may not be liked by those endued with fine feelings.

> *Bryan O'Lynn and his wife, and wife's mother,*
> *They all hid under a hedge together;*
> *But the rain came so fast they got wet to the skin—*
> *We shall catch a damned cold, says Bryan O'Lynn.*

> *Bryan O'Lynn and his wife, and wife's mother,*
> *They went in a boat to catch sprats together;*
> *A butt end got stove and the water rushed in—*
> *We're drowned, by the holy, says Bryan O'Lynn.*

*Bryan O'Lynn and his wife, and wife's mother,*
*They all went on a bridge together;*
*The bridge it broke and they all fell in—*
*Strike out and be damned, says Bryan O'Lynn.*

*Bryan O'Lynn and his wife, and wife's mother,*
*They all went out to chapel together;*
*The door it was shut and they could not get in—*
*It's a hell of a misfortune, says Bryan O'Lynn.*

*Bryan O'Lynn and his wife, and wife's mother,*
*They went with the priest to a wake together,*
*Where they all got drunk and thought it no sin—*
*It keeps out the cold, says Bryan O'Lynn.*

*Bryan O'Lynn and his wife, and wife's mother,*
*They went to the grave with the corpse together;*
*The earth being loose they all fell in—*
*Bear a hand and jump out, says Bryan O'Lynn.*

*Bryan O'Lynn and his wife, and wife's mother,*
*When the berring was over went home together;*
*In crossing a bog they got up to the chin—*
*I'm damned but we're smothered, says Bryan O'Lynn.*

*Bryan O'Lynn and his wife, and wife's mother,*
*By good luck got out of the bog together;*
*Then went to confess to Father O'Flinn—*
*We're damnation sinners, says Bryan O'Lynn.*

*Bryan O'Lynn and his wife, and wife's mother,*
*Resolved to lead a new life together;*
*And from that day to this have committed no sin—*
*In the calendar stands SAINT BRYAN O'LYNN.*

I have left out four verses as being rather out of order. I have heard the old gunner sing this when the sea has been beating over the forecastle and the ship rolling gunwale under. We used to get a tarpaulin in the weather fore rigging as a screen, and many a pleasant hour have I passed under its lee, with a glass of grog and hearing long-winded stories. Alas! how dead are times now. Captain Wallis behaved very kindly to me. I used to dine with him two or three times a week. He had, as I have stated, strange whims and few men are without them, but his many good qualities threw them in the background, and I have, with grateful remembrance and respect for his memory, to be thankful for his kindness, and particularly for the certificate he gave me on leaving the ship.

• • •

*Gardner's ample sense of humor would later come in handy. No doubt it was help-ful in passing the tedious hours when he commanded the signal station at Fairlight, three miles from Hastings, from 1806 to 1814. A half-pay lieutenant from 1814, Gardner was retired as a commander in 1830.*

*Back in England in 1795, a hot press was on. The government of the newly formed Batavian Republic (French-occupied Netherlands) formally allied with France in the month of May, and peace between Spain and France was signed in July. Also in July, Britain's attempt, at Quiberon Bay, to open a front on French soil, using French Royalist forces supported by British soldiers, failed miserably. New recruits were needed for a planned second attempt. Jacob Nagle, the lower-deck sea-man whose account follows, describes an almost feudal atmosphere, with the Army, the Navy, and the East India Company struggling for recruits. A seaman needed some sort of protection to secure any sort of power over his own destiny.*

# JACOB NAGLE

~

# For the Good
# of My Own Soul
## 1795

*Returning from a fifteen-month voyage to India on board the merchant ship* Rose, *Jacob Nagle, an able and wily American seaman, arrives in England during a recruiting feeding frenzy by both the Army and the Navy. At thirty-three years old, Nagle, who has served in both the United States Navy during the American Revolution and in the Royal Navy, from which he has already deserted once, is a prime target for the press gangs of both services. Despite being a deserter, which was punishable by death, Nagle seems remarkably cool. Once in the city of London, he is safe from the Army but not the Navy. He seeks the help of Mr. Goodall, who he has described as a "capt'n of troops belonging [to] the East India Company" (The Nagle Journal, p. 152). Nagle's frank presentation of life on shore is one of the most enlightening to emerge from the period.*

AT LENGTH [10 May 1795] we sailed for England with a prosperous and pleasent breese. When we got on the coast of Ingland, we stood well to the westward and made Ireland, meaning to put in there, but making the land we saw seven sail bearing down upon us [17 July 1795]. We took them to be a French squadron as we had intilegence they ware on the lookout for us. Immediately the oldest capt[ain] belonging to the Company ships in the fleet made a signal to form the line, which was done and that so close under each others sterns that the line could not be broken without they run on board of our ships, but we hoisting the Companies colours, they hoisted English. They came down and spoke the Commedore and inform'd they

45

ware cruising to protect us and likewise to prevent us from going into Ireland to smugel. They pressed 4 men out of each ship.[1]

We then made sail for the Channel of England and having a fine moderate breeze from the westward we fetched round Cilly Roks and bore up
Channel. When we passed the Isle of White [Wight], runing for the Downs,
we ware brought too [22 July 1795] by the *Dimond* Frigate and boarded us
and pressed 23 men out of us, the rest being stowed away amongst the
cargo. Coming into the Downs we had to come to an anchor, and 27 of us
which the capt[ain] and chief mate wished to save from the press we ware
put down amongst the cargo. The men of war sent all their boats along side
to press all they could find, but they dare not open the hatches, and all the
rest were pressed excepting us 27.

The pilot coming on board with 45 ticket men after dark, they begin to
heave up the anchor, but those landlubers new so little about it that they
could not get under way. We having some inveleads soldiers on board, the
chief mate came down to us to come up and get the ship under way. We put
on the soldiers jackets and hats, run up aloft, and cleared away the riging,
sheated home, and hoisted the topsails and got hur underway in sailing
trim, then went below. The ticket men seeing the activity of us swore we
ware not soldiers, and we being shy of them for fear they would give information. While in the whole [hold] we ware supplyed with provisions and
grog by our officers.

When we got up to the Lower Hope [25 July 1795], the capt[ain] seeing
two large men of war laying farther up, the capt[ain] sent the chief mate to
let us know how to act. They lowered the boat down and hall'd hur along
side. Likewise he borrowed a boat from another vessel.

Amediately the signal was given, the 27 of us jumped up on the quarter
deck and laid holt of a crow bar and pretended to brake open the arm chest
which was left open for that purpose, the capt[ain] and mate crying out,
"Men, what are you about?" We made no answer, but took a brace of pistols with 24 rounds of catrages and a cutlash each of us and went into the
boats and pulled away for the shore. A revenew cutter purceiving us
stoped us to overhall for smugled goods. They took chiefly what we had,
but did not get all. The capt[ain] hailed the officer and beged he would let
us go, as there was three men of wars boats after us. He let us go and we
pulled for life. By the time we landed and got on the bank, we paraded in

[1] The ships that bore down on the *Rose* on July 17 included the "*Poliphemus* 64, *Apollo, Cerberus*
& *Margretta* frigates & *Hazard* under Capt. Manly." Log of Alexander Gray, *Rose*, L/MAR/59D,
India Office Library, London.

the medow. They ware close to the shore by this time and seeing we did not run but determened to fight, they lay on their oars and looked at us for awhile, then returned to their ships again. We got on the road for London. In a half an hour after we fell in with 10 sailors armed with harpoons, and we joined company.

We coming to a small village, we ware informed that 30,000 regular troops ware incamped at the Lower Hope within three miles of us, and the light horse being on the road had orders to take all sailors that they came a cross, and one of them undertook to pilate [pilot] us a cross the country clear of the high roads.

After refreshing our selves we started. When about half way we had to take part of the main road, but before we got out of it again we fell in with about fourteen light horse beside the capt[ain]. We immediately paraded close a long the fence with our pistols cocked in each hand. When they came abrest of us, they stoped. The harpeners hove there harpoons over there heads, shining like silver. The capt[ain] enquired from whence we came. We informed him. He discours'd with us a considerable time. The solders vewed the harpoons over their heads as they sat on there horses, and seeing us so well armed, 47 in number, he told us he did not wish to trouble us and rode off.

When getting within a mile of Popler, we fell into the main road again and met a general going to camp with six or seven servents attending him. He stoped us to enquire what news from India and what ships had arived. He very genteelly wished us safe to London.

We, ariving at Popler, we gave our pilot a silk hankerchief a peace, which was 27, worth 5 shillings sterling each. He was well pleased and said he had made a great days work. We refreshed our selves at the first public house. We ware informed there was four press gangs in Popler. We sent for two coaches and started for London with the harpeners on the top of the coaches, and going through Popler we kep a continuel firing till we came to the subburbs of London, then discharged all our arms before we entered the citty, as the press gangs are not allowed to press within the citty. At this time it was expected that Bonepart would invade England.[1]

---

[1] A general history of the Quiberon Bay invasion fiasco, and the political and diplomatic background, can be found in John Ehrman, *The Younger Pitt: The Reluctant Transition* (London, 1983), 567–79. The troops that had assembled in the area were not raised to repel a French invasion but to be part of the French invasion themselves. Nagle's group avoided the main roads until they got to Poplar. Although he notes that there were reportedly four press gangs in the village, it was essentially an East India Company town at this period, and the men felt relatively safe beyond this point.

We delivered up our arms to the Company at the East India House. In a short time the capt[ain] got us our wages. I remained at the White Swan for a few days, not daring to go out of the citty without a protection.[1]

I sent a few lines to Mr. Goodall on Tower Hill. He came to me and took me to his house. He being aquainted with the press master, went to him. It was agre'd I should come over in the evening and he would be there. Accordingly I went into the public house which was only three dores from my boarding house. The gang sitting there, I enquired for the capt[ain] of the press gang. They stared at me, seeing a sailor dressed in India gingams and sattin enquiring for their capt[ain]. They directed me to the stair case, and the landlady showed me up with a light. When I entered, he knowing my business, he told me it would be necessary for me to hail for some man a war in the river that I enter'd for. He said the *Gorgeon* [*Gorgon*] 44 was laying at Woolage [Woolwich] fitting out and would not be ready for see under two month as a Kings storeship. Therefore he gave me a protection as belonging to the *Gorgeon*. I thank'd him and went down stairs.

There was two livers of the place playing a game of draughts. I stood looking on and one beat the other till he gave it up, a pot of beer a game. The winer asked me if I would take a game. I told him I had no objections. For the good of the house we plaid. I beat him. The gang standing round, I told them to drink as it came in. The other trades man wished to try me. I beat him. The gang then begin, and I beat the whole gang which in the whole in the barroom was 12 and had all the bear [beer] in. "Wel," said I, "as I have not been beat, I will have my pot in," which made a purty hearty laugh amongst them all, but the gang thought that would not excuse me, expecting I might have no protection, but not being alowed to over hall me in the house, but when I bid them all good night, they follow'd me and wish'd to [k]now weather I had a protection. I went in again and showed it. They had no more to say. I went home. I then could go wherever I pleased. The gangs [k]nowing me, they seldom overhall'd me.

One evening, going up Ratlif [Ratcliffe] high way, I sept'd [stepped] into a public house and caled for something to drink, and sitting at the same table where two young girls were sitting, supposing they belonged to the house, I fell in discourse with one of them I supposed could not be more than thirteen. I asked hur if she was the landlords daughter. She said, "No,

---

[1] The White Swan tavern was apparently very near the East India Company headquarters on Leadenhall Street, and from Nagle's comments concerning arrangements for his voyages of 1795 and 1805–7, it appears that the company had an official or unofficial arrangement with the tavern for recruiting men. While the company had to be careful about the methods it used, the tavern and its landlord could and apparently did resort to whatever practices would raise men for the company and make money for themselves.

Sir, but I live close by." I had drink'd my beer and was going out. She asked me if I would see hur home. I was surprised, but I told hur I would if she would show me the way. She got up and we went out.

She took me up a lane and entered a house where there was an elderly woman sitting a mending some cloking. They asked me to sit down. I observed the old woman was droping a tear. I asked hur what troubled hur mind. She said she had lost hur husband about two months ago and she had no one to help hur but hur daughter and was comp[elle]d to do what could not be helped. I felt for hur and expected they ware in want.

I pretended I wanted something to drink and I felt hungry. I asked hur daughter if she would fetch me some. She said by all means. I gave hur a seven shilling peace and told hur to go to a cook shop and get some cook'd victuals. I told hur to bring a half pint of rum and a quart of beer and the rest in provisions. She took a cloth and some materiels with hur. In hur absence I had some conversation with the old lady in respect of London being so great and popular a city why there was not assistance given to the poor. She said there was in some cases, but it requird friends, and then there was many hundreds in London pereshing for want. By this time hur daughter return'd with all that was required. I took a glass of grog and eat a little, and gave me pleasure to see them eat.

After supper I ment to bid them good night, but the daughter would not purmit me, and likewise hur mother wish'd me to stop as it was late. We went up stairs and I laid down, when she pulled hur gown'd off, which was clean and deasent, but hur shift was nothing but rags. It hurt me to see so lovely a young girl so much in distress for the want of some assistance, and I found by discourse it was to support hur poor mother.

In the morning when rising, I gave hur a half a guinea and told hur to get a couple of shifts. She cried and took me round the neck. I went down stairs and the old ladie was there. I bid hur good morning and she return'd the complement with chearfulness. I presented hur a guinea and told hur it might be of service to hur. She seemed stagnated, and I told hur purhaps you may never see me any more and bid them both good morning. I always thought I never done a better job in my life for the good of my own soul.

When in London before, I got acquainted with a family [that] lived near Stepney Church, though they came from the Isle of White [Wight] abreast of Portsmouth Harbour. I took a liking to a daughter of Mr. Pitmuns, a lively hansome girl in my eye, and maried hur. She had three brothers that I was acquainted with before.

Being at her fathers house, we took a walk down street. Then I proposed walking up to Tower Hill to Mr. Goodalls. Coming along towards St.

Catherine, we saw the gang in chase of a sailor. Passing us in the dusk of
the evening, the last of the gang purceiving me, came up to me, and asked
me who I was and wanted to [k]now whether I had a protection. I told him
I belonged to the *Gorgeon* at Woolage and my ticket was where I was going
to on Tower Hill. He begin to make free with my wife and I nock'd him
down, and a nother coming up, I made him stager, but a number gathering
round me and a midshipman of the gang, I told him I would go where he
pleased but not to allow his vagabons to insult my wife. He said they
should not. Then I walked on with them, and my wife with me.

They took me to Iron Gate where the randevoos was.[1] As soon as I
entered I sent my wife up to Mr. Goodalls to bring him down, as I hail for
the *Gorgeon*. I was then brought up stairs before the pressmaster. There was
several capt[ains] there and a number of ladies. The capt[ain] of the *Gorgeon*
[Edward Tyrrell] being one of the company, desired the pressmaster to let
him overhall me, as I hail'd for his ship, before I was brought up. I was well
dressed in silk jacket, waiscoat, and India gingums. When I apeared they
all took there vew of me, both ladies and officers.

"Well," said the capt[ain] of the *Gorgeon*, "what ship do you hail for?"

"The *Gorgeon*, Sir, laying at Wollige."

"Are you aquainted with the capt[ain]?"

"No, Sir, I would not know him if I met him in my dish." There was a
loud laugh with the ladies and gentlemen.

"Well, how came you to enter for the *Gorgeon* particularly, not [k]now-
ing the capt[ain]?"

"I can inform you, Sir. Mr. Goodall, I believe, is a friend to me, and I
board in his house since I new London, and Mr. Burley, belonging to the
*Gorgeon*, which boards there and I believe is pusser [purser] of the ship,
inform'd me the capt[ain] was a fine man and by going in hur I could
remain with me wife for a short time as she is not ready for see."

By this time my wife return'd and told me Mr. Goodall was up in the
citty. "Well," said the capt[ain], "you must content yourself for the night on
board the tender. I am capt[ain] of the *Gorgeon* and I will come and see you
in the morning."

---

[1] Although the eastern, riverside gate to the Tower of London was eliminated in the late eigh-
teenth century, Irongate Stairs, giving access to the Thames, remained in Nagle's day. The
name was apparently used by a nearby tavern, where Captain Edward Tyrrell established the
"rendezvous" for his press gang. Tyrrell was an interesting, resourceful man, and his correspondence to the Admiralty concerning the problems associated with impressment is interesting to read. Captain's Correspondence "T," ADM/1/2596 (1795) and ADM/1/2597
(1796–97), PRO; John Charlton, *The Tower of London* (London, 1978), 112–13.

"Sir," said I, "will you tear me away from my wife no sooner than I am maried to hur, and she is here now, and if you send me on board the tender this night I wont go in your ship, I will go aboard the largest ship in the navy first."

The ladies endeavoured to interceed for me, but the capt[ain] said he was afraid to trust me without security and Mr. Goodall not being at home. I desired my wife to go and stay with Mrs. Goodall for to night and come on b[oar]d the tender after breckfast.

Going down into the barroom, the gang being all there, I asked the landlady for a pint of beer. "No," said the gang, "we cant wait, you must come a long. Dont bring any beer."

I gumped on a table in a box next to a window fronting the street and drew my knife. "The first raskel that comes in reach of me I will be his death." Some run out and bared the windows, came and locked the dore.

The midshipman run up stairs to the officers. Down came Capt[ain] Terrel. "What's the matter?"

"These raskels," said I, "wont allow me a pint of beer, and I am famishing with drought."

"Madam, fetch him some beer. You raskels, how dare you refuse him that privilage!" The beer was brought.

I sat down and drank my beer. "Now I will go with you."

After going out of the house towards Iron Gate Steps, there was one of each side of me, some a head and some behind me. The two that was a long side of me, I nocked them both backwards, but the fellow behind hit me with a club which stagerd me. The capt[ain], hearing the noise, hollowed out of the window, "You raskels, if you hurt that man I will flog every man of you."

By this time they had all got close round me and got into the very [wherry], which is a boat in common in crossing the river or elsewhere. They placed themselves all a round me. My intention was to jump over board and dive a mongst the ships in a strong tide. They could not have found me, but they kept fast holt of me till they got me on board.

The steward demanded me to give him somthing to put my days allowance in. I had nothing. He took my hat and put bisquit and chees into my hat, then on locked the bars and put me on a stair case that led me into the hole [hold]. Coming to the bottom there was a demand for a shilling to drink. There was about 14 prest men. They had a candle burning, and the liquor was soon got by a halling line from the upper deck. I discovered an old shipmate that had run away from the *Brumswick* and was pressed again. I put my bisquit and cheese on a platform that was made to lay on, having no apetite for eating, but in less than five minutes there was not a crum to be foun, and when I laid down to take a nap, they would be draging at my close [clothes], which were large Norway rats that ware so numerous and ravenous you could get no rest for them.[1]

The next morning Capt[ain] Terrel came on board, and I was call'd up on the quarter deck. He asked me if I would go on board his ship. I told him through the treatment I had received I did not care where I went to, and I was American. He new he could not get me, as I was pressed on board the tender, unless I entered particularly for his ship, being a Kings transport, and I would be sent on board some line a battle ship. He told me he took a great liking to me, and if I would go on board his ship he would let me come up to London till the ship was ready for see. Likewise he would get me the large bounty which was then allowed for seeman. I new if I did not except of that offer, my portion was a three decker at the Nore, therefore I agreed. The whole sum amounted to 35 Ld. sterling.

The next day I went down in the tender that took all the prest men down to the Nore, but I was not put below as the rest ware. Coming to Wollige [Woolwich], we hail'd the *Gorgon* and a jolly boat was sent, and I came aboard and went on the quarter deck and enquired for the commanding officer. He came up and told me he had just received a litter from the capt[ain] to let me come up to London amediately. I received a ticket.

My wife being with me, the boatswain, being a Merican and his wife being on board, they invited us to dinner, and after dinner the leutenant maned the boat and took us on shore. Took stage and arrived in London, went to my boarding house, and from thence to hur fathers. Hur father was about moving to Portsmouth. His son being a ship carpenter, and he a boat builder, he thought he would do better there with his son.[2]

By the time my liberty ticket was out, the capt[ain] send for me, and Mr. Goodall went with me, he boarding on Little Tower Hill. When we arived we ware introduc'd up stairs and a great number of capt[ains] in the navy ware there. My capt[ain] was much pleased with me and asked for my ticket. I gave it to him, and he backe my ticket, week after week, till I did

---

[1] There may have been an unusual infestation of rats on shipping at this time. The log of George Chatterton, Master on the *Gorgon*, to which Nagle was assigned, contemporaneously noted that the crew was "pointing the Foresail and repairing the Damaged Mainsail which had been eat by the Rats in several Places." HMS *Gorgon*, Master's Log, ADM/52/3057, PRO.

[2] According to George Rude in *Hanoverian London, 1714–1808* (Berkeley, Cal., 1971), 228–29, shipbuilding was the most depressed of the major industries of Britain in the 1790s, particularly along the Thames. Nagle's in-laws, the Pitmans, were a family of boat and shipbuilders who apparently had migrated from their home on the Isle of Wight in the 1780s or at the beginning of the French Wars. As of 1795, they were thinking of going back, and by 1796, it would seem that the Pitmans were at Portsmouth.

not wish to remain any longer, and every time he sent for me, he treated me very hansomely in whatever I chused to drink.

During this time Mr. Smith, that I came home with in the Indiaman, sent the pusser [purser] after me, he going capt[ain] of the same ship, that if I would desert, he would send me into the country till the ship was ready for sea and give me 10 Lb. sterling pr. month. I told the pusser I new the danger and death would be my portion if caught again, therefore I would not atempt it.[1] After being a month in London, I returned on board.

. . .

*Nagle's service on board the* Gorgon *would not be happy, nor would his subsequent service on board the frigate* Blanche, *which was commanded first by Captain Charles Sawyer, a homosexual who lost effective control of his crew, and later by Henry Hotham, an officer whose reputation for harsh discipline caused the crew to rebel when he came on board. It was apparently Nelson himself who appealed to the good senses of the crew of the* Blanche *and brokered their reluctant acceptance of Hotham. Nagle's career eventually took a turn for the better aboard an experimental sloop that proved quite successful—despite its innovation; see "Mad Dickey's Amusement, 1798–1800," on page 88.*

[1] Presumably John Greatrise Smyth, who had been first mate on the *Rose* under Captain Gray on the previous voyage. *Rose,* "Ledger" and "Receipt Book," L/MAR/B/59V, L/MAR/59 V-2, India Office Library, London.

# They Would as Soon
# Have Faced the Devil Himself
# as Nelson

## 1796

*In 1796, with Napoleon on the move in Italy, and Spain entering the war against Britain, the Royal Navy was on the retreat in the Mediterranean. Much to the chagrin of the more hard-nosed naval officers, like Sir John Jervis, commander in chief in the Mediterranean, and Captain Horatio Nelson, the theater would have to be abandoned altogether. On October 19, the French invaded Corsica, a British possession from 1793 to 1796. By November 2, Nelson, on board the* Captain, 74, *and in company with the* Egmont, 74, *had evacuated Bastia, capital of the island of Corsica, including the viceroy, Sir Gilbert Elliot. The author of this passage, An Old Agamemnon who signed the piece "M.C.," describes the scene.*

IN THE YEAR 1796 [*actually, 1795*] Captain Nelson had charge of a small squadron, under Admiral [*of the Blue William*] Hotham, which was sent to co-operate with the Austrian general, in order to drive the French from the Riviera de Genoa. It was during the night that the admiral got under weigh, but did not get sight of the enemy for several days, when a partial action took place [*on July 13, 1795*]. L'*Alcide* (74) struck, but the rest of the fleet got a wind, which blowing right on the land, enabled them to get close in shore, while the English fleet, at seven miles distance, were completely becalmed. About half an hour after L'*Alcide* struck, a box of combustibles, which were stowed in her foretop, accidentally caught fire, and, despite of all exertions to extinguish it, the flames spread so quickly that the ship was soon an entire mass of flame. The crew were seen running to and fro in a state of distraction. Our fleet lost no time in manning their boats, and we succeeded in rescuing upwards of 200 of the crew. Our boats were the last that left the vessel, and had not got a mile from her ere she blew up, with a tremendous explosion, scattering in the air those of her unfortunate crew that remained on board, and who could not have been less than 300 souls. Our ship, the *Agamemnon*, had none killed, and not more than one or two wounded. But we got a number of shots under water, and we had sharp work at the pumps to keep her dry. We anchored only a few hours at St. Fiorenzo, and then Captain Nelson was again despatched in the *Agamemnon*.

Nelson at this time was made colonel of Marines, which he had long wished for, but little expected. It was pretty well known that great changes were about to take place in the fleet, and Nelson expressed an ardent hope that he should be commissioned for some ship. His health, however, had been much impaired, and until this promotion occurred he had harboured a wish to return to England, and rest awhile; but the events that intervened effectually prevented it. Admiral Jervis was appointed to the command of the Mediterranean fleet early in November *[1795]* and his penetration soon discovered that Nelson possessed a combination of resources and abilities rarely to be met with, and he determined to give him immediate opportunities of signalizing himself.

The *Agamemnon*, having been severely cut to pieces by shot in the late engagement, had been brought into Leghorn to refit, and it was expected she would be sent home; and Captain Nelson intended to return in her to England. But Admiral Jervis did not feel inclined to part with him; he therefore offered him the *St. George*, 90 guns, or the *Zealous*, 74, which he, however, declined, but at the same time expressed a great wish to serve under the admiral, should the war continue.

The candid manner in which Nelson expressed himself made a most favourable impression on Admiral Jervis, and they soon became mutually attached. Jervis quickly fathomed the disposition of Nelson; he saw that his great aim was command, and that he yearned to try his fortune as a Commander. He, therefore, convinced Nelson that it would be folly to think of going to England at a moment when every chance of rapid promotion offered itself; and finding that Nelson's resolution wavered, he at once promoted him to the rank of temporary commodore. The lure was too tempting to be evaded, and Nelson at once resolving to forego his intended trip to England, hoisted his pendant on board his old ship, the *Agamemnon*. There was little or nothing to be done; Buonaparte was then the great meteor of France, and affairs were undergoing a rapid change. Nelson was now established in permanent rank, and appointed to the *Captain*, 74; having a Captain appointed to command under him.

We gained intelligence that six vessels, laden with ordnance and ammunition, had sailed from Toulon, for the siege of Mantua. Nelson, having the aid of Captain Cockburn, in the *Meleager*, went in pursuit, and drove them under a battery, which kept up a sharp cannonade; but we soon silenced it, and, pursuing the flying enemy, succeeded in capturing the whole of them. In addition to the ordnance and warlike stores on board, we found military books, plans and maps of Italy, and many very useful papers, intended for Buonaparte's use. The consequence of this victory was disastrous to the French, who, being deprived of their expected supply of ammunition, were obliged to raise the siege of Mantua, and if the Allied Powers had taken more active measures on land, they would doubtless have improved this success, and prevented Buonaparte from taking possession of Leghorn [*Livorno*], which he did soon after; but Nelson was on the alert, and closely blockaded him in Leghorn, while, at the same time, he landed a British force on the island of Elba.

In consequence of the war with Spain,[1] orders were received that Corsica was immediately to be given up, and the fleet were to quit the Mediterranean. Nelson was paralyzed. This intelligence was so contrary to the orders he had received from Admiral Jervis that he knew not how to act. He immediately sent a despatch to the admiral, and loudly lamented the present orders, which he openly characterized as disgraceful to the honour of England. His chagrin was too great to be concealed from his officers or crew, and in the bitterness of his disappointment he remarked, "The Ministers at home do not seem to know the capabilities of our fleet. I frankly declare I never beheld one in point of officers and men equal to that under Sir John Jervis, who is a commander-in-chief fully capable of increasing the glory of England."

Sir John Jervis was as much chagrined as Nelson, and although the bluff sailor concealed his feelings from those around him, yet the whole fleet were well aware that he was prepared to act very differently. However, much as we all regretted it, there was no help. The orders had arrived, and must be obeyed.

On the 13th of October, Captain Nelson was close in with Bastia by daylight, in the *Diadem*, Captain Towry; and, before it came to anchor, Nelson, accompanied by his boat's crew, went on shore to visit the viceroy, who was rejoiced to see him, and requested that his valuable papers might immediately be sent on board by our boat, for it was impossible to foresee how long they might be safe on shore at Bastia.[2]

---

[1] *Spain declared war on October 8, 1796.*
[2] *Sir Gilbert Elliot (1751–1814) was viceroy of Corsica from 1794 to 1796.*

We went to the viceroy's house, and got all the valuables safe into the boat, which we took on board ship, and then returned with a further supply of boats and men. It now appeared that the Corsicans had taken up arms, and that a committee of thirty had seized and detained all the property of the English, and that a plan had been laid to seize the person of the viceroy. General de Burgh also reported to Captain Nelson, that, from the number of armed Corsicans, there was little or no prospect of saving either stores, cannon, or provisions. But Nelson, whose decision was promptitude itself, ordered the citadel gate to be shut, in order to prevent any more armed Corsicans from entering, and gave immediate orders to moor his ships opposite the town. The merchants and owners likewise informed him that even their trunks of clothes were refused them, and that they would be complete beggars unless he could help them. A privateer had been moored across the mole-head by the Corsicans, which would not even allow a transport boat to pass. Nelson requested them to remain easy, and assured them that he would soon find means to relieve them.

At this time, while our boat's crew were waiting on shore, we observed several armed Corsicans making towards the citadel, who seemed struck with surprise when they found the gate closed upon them. We could not refrain from laughing at their disappointment; which provoked them to such a degree, that one fellow had the temerity to present his piece at us, exclaiming, "Brigands Anglais!" (rascally Englishmen!) intending to fire amongst us: but, unfortunately for him, Archibald Menzies, our stroke-oar (whom we nicknamed "Scotch Hercules" on account of his immense strength), who was taking his cutty, or short pipe, comfortably near the gate, caught sight of this maneuver, and, rushing up to the dastard Corsican, gave him such a severe blow under the ear with his iron fist that he fell and completely rolled over in the dust with the force of the blow. His companions paused for a moment in surprise, as they eyed the tall gaunt figure of Archibald, but suddenly rushed in a body upon him; but Archibald, having torn up a wooden rail that ran along the road-side, laid about him with such fury that the cowardly Corsicans threw down their arms and ran for their lives; and before we could reach the spot, although we ran as quickly as we could, to assist our messmate, Archibald was master of the field, his assailants having all decamped except two unfortunate fellows whom he held fast in his iron gripe.

"Deil tak you!" exclaimed Archy,—"d'ye ken me? Never show your ugly walnut-coloured faces to a Briton again, unless you can behave like cannie men, or, by Saint Andrew! I'll batter your faces against each ither till ye shallna ken whether you be yourselves or no. Get awa wi' ye, ye cursed black-nebs! I dinna like to swear, but I'll be d——d if I don't mak haggis-meat o' ye, if I catch you here again."

Having let them loose, which he did with a kick behind, the fellows made swift work of it, and were soon out of sight. We collected the arms they had left, and stowed them safely in the boat.

Nelson having returned from the citadel, we quickly got on board in order to commence operations. The *Egmont*, Captain *[John]* Sutton, had now arrived, and was ordered to moor the same as the *Diadem*. At noon, Captain Nelson made the signal for the boats manned and armed, and Captain *[George Henry]* Towry *[of HMS* Diadem*]* proceeded into the mole with them, in order to open the passage for all vessels which might choose to come out. Captain Towry had also received instructions from Nelson to take the first English vessel in tow which he met with; and, if the slightest molestation was offered, he was to send to the municipality in his (Nelson's) name, to tell them that if any obstruction was thrown in the way of getting any vessel out of the mole, or removing any of the property belonging to the English, he would instantly batter the town about their ears.

Now it has always been said, that the great John Duke of Marlborough created such terror and dismay among the enemies of England, by his rapid and surprising succession of victories, that he was in France held up as a bugbear[1]; and nurses were accustomed to frighten refractory children into submission by telling them *Malbrouk would come and take them away*. The name of Nelson was not without its terrors among the Corsicans, and they never heard it without a feeling of fear; and I believe they would as soon have faced the devil himself as Nelson, as the sequel will show.

Captain Towry proceeded to the mole, when the privateer, which was moored across it, immediately pointed her guns at him, and at least an hundred guns were levelled from the mole-head. On observing this, Capt. Sutton immediately sent Nelson's message on shore, which threatened to batter down the town if a single shot was fired, and, taking out his watch, said he would give them a quarter-of-an-hour for a reply, which if not fully satisfactory the ships would instantly open their fire.

Nelson's name was enough, and more so when the Corsicans found that Towry and Sutton were not to be trifled with. The message acted like magic, for in a few minutes the people quitted the privateer; and those at the mole-head, even to the Corsican sentries, quitted the spot with the utmost precipitation, leaving the vessels to come out of the mole entirely unmolested.

[1] *John, Duke of Marlborough, was the victor of the battles of Blenheim (1704), Ramilles (1706), Oudenarde, (1708) and Malplaquet (1709) during the War of the Spanish succession.*

We were now occasionally on shore as well as on board, according to circumstances; for it appeared the municipality were still bent on committing depredations whenever they could do so with impunity. Captain Nelson, therefore, made it his custom to remain where he could be easiest of access, in order that all persons who had complaints to make might do so with facility.

In the course of the day, the owner of a privateer came to complain that he had forty hogsheads of tobacco and other goods in the custom-house, which the municipality refused to deliver to him; whereupon Captain Nelson told him to go to the Committee of Thirty, and say that he (Nelson) had sent for the goods, which, if not instantly delivered, he would fire upon the town. The owner not liking to go alone, Nelson sent a midshipman, with half-a-dozen men as a kind of convoy, among whom was Archibald Menzies. The owner delivered the message, and the Committee seemed to hint at requiring time to consider; but the midshipman said he could brook no delay; whereupon Archibald, who could contain himself no longer, burst out with, "Hoot awa' wi' ye, and your dally dirty ways; ye ken this gentleman is our officer, and we canna stand here waiting for your decision. Ye ken, if ye dinna give up the goods this instant, our Captain will give your dirty town such a belabouring, that he'll nae leave one stane upon the t'other. So come awa' wi' ye, mister merchant." Archy's speech decided the controversy; the Corsicans did not like the threats of Captain Nelson, nor did they like the looks of the man that uttered them. They all turned as pale as death; and, without uttering a single word, delivered up the keys to the merchant, who returned with the boat's crew to Nelson, and acquainted him with the result of his errand; who took immediate means to put the owner in possession of his property.

One would have supposed that the Corsicans had received sufficient proofs that the English would not be trifled with; but they still obstinately clung to their desire to annoy the British merchants, for, in the evening, they made an attempt to get duty paid for some wine which was about to be embarked by a British merchant. However, Captain Nelson sent a message to them, declaring, that if any more complaints were made to him, however slight their nature, he should, without any further notice, pay them such a visit as they would have cause to repent. This was conclusive; the Committee saw that further attempts at opposition would be likely to draw down destruction on them, and they therefore gave up their system of annoyance; and from that moment not an armed man was to be seen in the streets of Bastia.

The viceroy was taken on board our ship that night, and was consequently placed out of danger. Nelson landed his troops on the 15th, early in the morning; who took post at the viceroy's house, which covered the spot where the embarkation took place. General de Burgh also furnished another hundred men for the same purpose, part of which kept post in the citadel. One hundred seamen were also sent on shore to complete the embarkation. One of our men met with a strange adventure. John Thompson, while ashore, heard the wailings of a female, and other persons' voices speaking peremptorily. Jack, conceiving he had a right to interfere if anything was going wrong, listened awhile, and soon found that his assistance would be required. The door opened, and four rough-looking fellows pulled a couple of chests into the street.

"Avast! you saffron-faced swabs," cried Jack, as he placed himself in front of them; "What are you going to be after with the lady's cargo, eh?" "*Contrabande! contrabande! choses prohibées*[1]*!*" exclaimed the Corsicans. "Chose be d——d," cried Jack; "none of your nonsense with me. Let the lady have her goods, or by the honour of my Commander, I'll spoil your daylights!" "*Non intendo, non intendo!*" exclaimed the Corsicans, (meaning, we don't understand you.) But Jack mistook the meaning of the word, and exclaimed, "Not intend it! Yes, but you *did* intend it, you lying swab, and you would have DONE it too, if I had not been here to prevent you." The Corsicans paused a little; but seeing that Thompson was quite alone, and they were four in number, they determined on attacking and overpowering him; consequently two of them advanced, but Jack Thompson knocked them down with his fists; the others then advanced, but at this moment an unexpected reinforcement arrived; for the hostess observing the unequal attack of the cowardly Corsicans, rushed to the spot, followed by her stable-boy, and seizing a broomstick, while the stable-boy presented a pitchfork, they laid about them with such spirit that they proved a powerful reinforcement to Jack Thompson. Others of the Corsican breed joined their rascally companions, and Jack Thompson and his two auxiliaries would doubtless have been defeated; but the timely arrival of half-a-dozen of our crew struck the Corsicans with such terror that they made a precipitate retreat, and left Jack Thompson and his confederates in possession of the prize. The husband of the hostess wore a wooden leg, and therefore could not join in the active part of the fray; he, however, proved of signal service, and acted occasionally as a flanking battery; for, having seated himself on one of the tubs, he pulled off his wooden leg, and every Corsican who happened to come within his reach during the scuffle, received a hearty thump with it from the old gentleman, who, at every blow, roared out, "*Viva Inglesi—Bono Inglesi!*" The hostess and her *caro marito* (as she termed her

[1] Smuggled goods.

husband) insisted on our partaking of some refreshment; and so pleased were they with our presence, that I believe, if we could have emptied one of their brandy casks, we should have been welcome. Having regaled ourselves, we assisted them to remove their property to a place of safety.

We now went heartily to work in removing provisions, cannon, gunpowder, and various stores, besides a vast quantity of baggage and household articles; for the poor emigrants could not afford to leave any things behind them. There were many novel scenes exhibited in Bastia at this time. Whole families might be seen moving along with their little stock of goods under the protection of British sailors or soldiers, while their enemies could do no more than look on with envy and vexation, and see themselves deprived of their intended plunder.

Our sailors had plenty of opportunities of displaying their gallantry; for it was nothing uncommon to see two or three of our ship's crew marching along with a female under each arm, convoying them safely to the place of embarkation. Here you might see a group of men conveying a lot of furniture, while the family were carrying the lighter articles, such as bandboxes, bundles, and such-like gear. Our carpenter's second mate was an Irishman, and a merry fellow he was; but he was rather ill-favoured in his appearance. He had somewhat of a squint about his eyes, rather a flat nose, and a wide mouth, and he passed by the cognomen of the "Munster Beauty." Poor Pat Macguire! he was as able a seaman as ever sailed in the fleet; and whenever he committed a blunder it was on the right side: he lived long enough to see much service, for I think it was in the battle of Trafalgar that a grape-shot signed his death-warrant.

Pat Macguire had charge of the removal of the domestic part of the goods, and proud enough he was of the berth, and well pleased into the bargain; for Pat was always fond of being in ladies' company, and here he was surrounded by all ranks. Old and young, rich and poor—all came to consult Pat as to the manner in which they were to proceed.

Some of our strongest men, who were employed in removing the cannon and other cumbersome materials, took good care to jeer Pat Macguire in his enviable employment. One would say, "There's Mister Macguire, the lady's man—pretty, delicate creature—he's obliged to be stationed here to look after the gowns and petticoats, because our work is too hard for him."

Old Jack Townsend (the grumbler) would say, "What can you expect of an Irishman?—They never were able seamen; they're of no use on board, unless it be to act as washerwomen."

"A bull—a bull!" cried Pat Macguire; "who ever heard of a man-washerwoman? Now, look you, Master Townsend, it's no use your jibing and jeering after that fashion, because ye see the Captain has picked me out for this especial service, because I was one of the most polite and best-behaved of the crew. And let me tell you that there's neither man, woman, nor child, that sails on the salt sea, that knows how to accommodate the ladies better, or half so well, as an Irishman. So, roll that up as a quid and chew it, Master Townsend, if you plase."

"Ugh!" said old Townsend, "that's all you're good for. I dare say the Captain will give you a new berth aboard—he'll make you head nurse to the women." "Och, good luck to him!" cried Pat; "I wish he may. Hurrah, old Jack! Pat Macguire's just the boy for a nursery-maid."

Had our time not been too much occupied, we should have derived much amusement by setting old Townsend and Pat Macguire on the high ropes, but our duty was rather hard, and time was running short, and, therefore, there was no other jeering except a little occasional shy fighting between these two, whose opinions differed as widely as the east and west winds.

Pat Macguire was also a bit of a politician and occasionally made some very shrewd remarks. When the despatch arrived which ordered us to evacuate Corsica, it caused much murmuring in the fleet, particularly among those who had seen good service under Sir John Jervis; and this gave Pat Macguire an opportunity of giving his opinion on the state of parties. One of the sailors having asked who it was that caused such orders to be given, Pat replied, "Sure, it was the Parliament."

"Then," said one of the topmen, "the Parliament never sailed under Admiral Jervis, nor fought as we have done." Whereupon Pat Macguire, with a look of the most signal contempt, exclaimed—

"'Sblood, man, d'ye take the Parliament for a man or a woman? The Parliament, I'd have you to know, is a great many people mustered together, and they settle the affairs of the nation by talking to each other."

"Talking to each other!" echoed the topman.

"Yes," continued Pat; "they talk till they talk the breath out of each other, and then it's put to the vote as to who spoke the longest and loudest, and that's the one as gains the day."

"And is that all they do?" inquired the topman.

"Yes, honey," replied Pat; "they talk and we execute."

Pat's logic was too learned to allow the topman to argue any further; and the Boatswain having piped to quarters put an end to the debate.

We had now worked without intermission till sunset on the 19th, and must have saved about two hundred thousand pounds' worth of stores, and other effects belonging to the emigrants.

The French had landed their troops at Cape Corse on the 18th, and on the following day they sent to the municipality to know if they intended to receive them as friends, because, if so, they required that the English should be prevented from embarking. Time would not allow us to save anything more, and, therefore, after having spiked all the guns, we quitted the citadel at midnight; but, from the wind blowing a gale, it was dawn of day before we all got on board. All the time these transactions were going on, we were observed by a mob of Corsicans, who lined the shore, and who had the mortification to witness every soul embark who chose to leave the island, without their daring to offer the least molestation.

Captain Nelson and General de Burgh were the last who left the spot; and as Nelson stepped into the boat, he coolly turned to the mob and said, "Now, John Corse, follow the natural bent of your detestable character—plunder and revenge!" We were soon on board, and in less than half an hour we showed our sterns to the island of Corsica.

•   •   •

*Toward the end of 1796 and in early 1797, France intended to land a force in Ireland. A first attempt, under Vice-Admiral Morard de Galles and General Hoche, in December of 1796, went awry due primarily to severe weather and confusion among the French Brest fleet, some seventeen ships of the line, thirteen frigates, and twenty transports. In 1797 a second plan called for fleets from Batavia and Spain to join the Brest fleet. In the following passage, it is Admiral Don José de Cordova's Spanish fleet of twenty-seven ships of the line, en route from Cartagena to Brest to join the invasion force, that Commodore Nelson—carrying Sir Gilbert Elliot, the former viceroy of Corsica now bound for England—encounters off the Straits of Gibraltar.*

JOHN DRINKWATER BETHUNE

# The Battle of
# Cape St. Vincent
## 1797

*A*s a passenger on board first the frigate Minerve, 40, then the Lively,
32, Colonel John Drinkwater Bethune witnesses and describes not only
the Battle of Cape St. Vincent, February 14, 1797, but also the battle's pream-
ble and aftermath. An aide to Sir Gilbert Elliot in Corsica, Drinkwater's self-
importance stands in clear contrast to matter-of-fact seamen's accounts, but
there is no greater enthusiast of Nelson, whom he has gotten to know in the
line of duty and during travels across the Mediterranean to Gibraltar after
Nelson evacuated Corsica and Elba. Before the colossal battle off Cape St. Vincent, Drinkwater sees one of Nelson's more singular moments, when he
refuses to lose Lieutenant Hardy, again, despite great danger.

ON THE FORENOON of the 11th of February, the *Minerve* got under
weigh. She had scarcely cast round from her anchorage, when two of the
three Spanish line-of-battle ships in the upper part of Gibraltar Bay were
observed to be also in motion. It was soon evident that they had been
watching the commodore's movements, and were prepared to pursue him
as soon as the *Minerve* should take her departure from Gibraltar.

As the Spanish ships had a steady wind from the eastward over the
Isthmus, whilst the *Minerve* was embarrassed with the eddies and baffling flaws, that usually prevail in an easterly wind, near the Rock, the
Spaniards had for some time the advantage in pushing forwards in the
bay. The *Minerve* was not, however, long in getting the steady breeze, and
soon after got into the Straits, when the chace of the enemy became, as

we afterwards heard, a most interesting "spectacle" to our friends of the garrison.

The *Minerve* was a captured ship from the French—taken in the Mediterranean in 1795, and considered to be a tolerably good sailer, particularly with the wind on her quarter. The Spanish ships were not equally good goers; one of them, the *Terrible*, was a first-rate sailer, well known to the British officers, Culverhouse and Hardy, who had been exchanged from her only the day before. Her consort was a dull sailing ship. Advancing into the Straits, the *Minerve* had the wind abaft, and after marking her progress with that of the enemy, it was evident that the headmost ship of the chace gained on the British frigate. No sooner was this point ascertained, than directions were given by Sir Gilbert Elliot to have certain parts of his public papers ready to be sunk, if necessary, at a moment's notice. The ship was cleared for action, and the position of the *Minerve* was now becoming every moment more and more interesting. At this period I was walking with Commodore Nelson, conversing on the probability of the enemy's engaging the *Minerve*, and his words, and manner of uttering them, made a strong impression on me. He said that he thought an engagement was very possible, as the headmost ship appeared to be a good sailer; but, continued he (looking up at his broad pendant), "before the Dons get hold of that bit of bunting I will have a struggle with them, and sooner than give up the frigate, I'll run her ashore."

Captain Cockburn, who had been taking a view of the chacing enemy, now joined the commodore, and observed that there was no doubt of the headmost ship gaining on the *Minerve*. At this moment dinner was announced, but before Nelson and his guests left the deck, orders were given to set the studding sails. At table I found myself seated next to Lieutenant Hardy, and was congratulating him on his late exchange from being a prisoner of war, when the sudden cry of a "man overboard," threw the dinner party into some disorder. The officers of the ship ran on deck: I, with others, ran to the stern windows to see if any thing could be observed of the unfortunate man; we had scarcely reached them before we noticed the lowering of the jolly boat, in which was my late neighbour Hardy, with a party of sailors; and before many seconds had elapsed, the current of the Straits (which runs strongly to the eastward) had carried the jolly boat far astern of the frigate, towards the Spanish ships. Of course the first object was to recover, if possible, the fallen man, but he was never seen again. Hardy soon made a signal to that effect, and the man was given up as lost. The attention of every person was now turned to the safety of Hardy and his boat's crew; their situation was extremely perilous, and their danger was every instant increasing from the fast sailing of the headmost ship of the chace, which, by this time had approached nearly within gun-shot of the *Minerve.* The jolly boat's crew pulled "might and main" to regain the frigate, but apparently made little progress against the current of the Straits. At this crisis, Nelson, casting an anxious look at the hazardous situation of Hardy and his companions, exclaimed, "By G—— I'll not lose Hardy! Back the mizen top-sail." No sooner said than done; the *Minerve's* progress was retarded, leaving the current to carry her down towards Hardy and his party, who seeing this spirited manoeuvre to save them from returning to their old quarters on board the *Terrible,* naturally redoubled their exertions to rejoin the frigate. To the landsmen on board the *Minerve* an action now appeared to be inevitable; and so, it would appear, thought the enemy, who surprised and confounded by this daring manoeuvre of the commodore (being ignorant of the accident that led to it,) must have construed it into a direct challenge. Not conceiving, however, a Spanish ship of the line to be an equal match for a British frigate, with Nelson on board of her, the Captain of the *Terrible* suddenly shortened sail, in order to allow his consort to join him, and thus afforded time for the *Minerve* to drop down to the jolly-boat to take out Hardy and the crew; and the moment they were on board the frigate, orders were given again to make sail.

Being now under studding sails, and the widening of the Straits allowing the wind to be brought more on the *Minerve's* quarter, the frigate soon regained the lost distance; and, in a short time, we had the satisfaction to observe, that the dastardly Don was left far in our wake; and at sunset; by steering further to the southward, we lost sight of him and his consort altogether.

What course the *Minerve* pursued after nightfall, I did not remark. The interesting incidents of the preceding day had afforded matter to occupy our attention; and we landsmen retired to rest, congratulating ourselves on what we could not but feel to have been a fortunate escape.

On the removal of the passengers from the *Romulus* into the *Minerve,* at Gibraltar, the crowded state of the latter frigate would not allow of other arrangements than of my having a cot slung alongside of that of the viceroy, in the after cabin. So situated, I was awakened in the night, by the opening of our cabin door, through which I saw, by the light burning in the fore cabin, some person enter, and on raising myself, I observed that it was Nelson. Seeing me awake, he enquired if Sir Gilbert was asleep, to which I replied in the affirmative. To my enquiry if any thing new had occurred, the commodore approached my cot, and told me that he had every reason to believe that the *Minerve* was at that very moment in the midst of the Spanish fleet. From their signals, he said that he knew it was not that of Sir John Jervis; that the night was foggy; that the *Minerve* was then between two very large ships within hail of each of them, and others were near on all sides; that he and Captain Cockburn had little doubt of the strangers being Spanish; that Captain Cockburn and his officers were all on the alert; and every cautionary direction given, particularly to watch the movements of the strange ships, and do as they did, &c., &c.

When Nelson had finished these details, I could not help observing that this was a verifying of the old adage, "out of the frying-pan into the fire," alluding to our escape of the day before. The commodore allowed that we had got into something like a scrape, but added that it was quite unavoidable, on account of the night and fog; nevertheless, he thought that, with address, we might extricate ourselves.

He remained for some time, making various observations on these strange ships, and then continued to the following effect:—If they did not belong to the Spanish grand fleet, he thought they must be a convoy, or detached squadron, proceeding to the West Indies (of which, it appears, he had received some previous information), and that, if the latter were the fact, they must be destined to strengthen the Spanish naval force in that quarter; in which case, it would be of the first moment that the British commander on the West India station should be early apprised of these movements of the enemy; a duty, he conceived he was called upon to undertake, instead of joining Sir John Jervis.

On hearing Nelson express these opinions, I could not avoid saying, "But what will you do with Sir Gilbert Elliot? it is of the greatest importance, owing to his recent interviews with the Italian states, that he should not only see Sir John Jervis, but reach England with the least possible delay."—The commodore admitted the force of these remarks; but the other point, in his judgment, outweighed every other consideration: "but," said he, breaking off, "I'll go on deck, and see how things are going on." To awake Sir Gilbert in our present uncertainty could answer no good purpose; I therefore did not disturb him, but ruminated on this new and unlooked for occurrence, in the hope of devising some means of avoiding a trip to the West Indies, which, I thought would be at least an untoward conclusion of our Mediterranean campaign.

It soon occurred to me, that as we must pass near Madeira, in our way to the West Indies, the viceroy and his party might be landed on that island; or, if any neutral ship crossed our track, we might equally avail ourselves of a transfer to her, and obtain a passage to Lisbon, or perhaps to England.

This plan I had settled to my own satisfaction, when Nelson again appeared, and observed that the strange ships having been seen to tack, or wear, I forget which, the *Minerve* had followed their example; and that after having so done, directions were given for the frigate's edging away insensibly, and that Captain Cockburn and himself were inclined to think the

*Minerve* was getting out of the thick of the fleet, and would soon cease to be embarrassed with them. After this gratifying communication, Nelson repeated his former opinions and intentions, and we were earnestly discussing the subject, when Sir G. Elliot was awakened by our conversation. He was then made acquainted with all that had been passing, with the commodore's suspicions regarding the strange ships, and with his conditional plan, to proceed immediately to the West Indies. After some general observations, and repeating his determination, if necessary, of carrying us to the West Indies, the commodore left the cabin again, and soon returned with the agreeable intelligence that the *Minerve* had, he trusted, got quit of the strange fleet. "We propose," added Nelson, "to stand on our present course during the night: at daybreak, we shall take another direction, which will enable us to fall in with the strange ships again, should they be on their way to the westward. I shall then ascertain the force of the convoy, or of the squadron, if it consist only of men-of-war; and should it then appear advisable, I shall start for the West Indies. Should we not fall in with any strange ships in the course which the *Minerve* will steer after daybreak, my conclusion is, that the fleet we have fallen in with must be the grand fleet of Spain; it will be then of the first importance that I join Sir John Jervis as soon as possible, in order that he may be informed of the enemy's fleet not having been yet able to get into Cadiz, and of their state on quitting Carthagena, of which Lieutenants Culverhouse and Hardy are able to give the latest and most minute accounts."

The commodore then left Sir Gilbert Elliot and me to our repose, if that were possible. After he had left the cabin, I asked Sir Gilbert what he thought of this new occurrence, and of the prospect of a trip to the West Indies. "It was another escape," he replied, "and as to the voyage to the West Indies, if the commodore considered the public service required that proceeding, he must submit to circumstances; he was only a passenger." This cool way of receiving and considering our present situation and prospects did not surprise me, well acquainted as I was with the viceroy's character. However, I made known to him the plan I had devised to avoid a visit to a tropical climate, of which he approved. Nothing further occurred until we all met at breakfast, when the incidents of the last twenty-four hours became the subject of conversation, and were fully discussed. I then learned that the *Minerve* was at that instant standing on the course which would soon confirm one of the two suspicions entertained by Nelson, regarding the strange ships seen during the past night. A good look out was naturally kept during the whole of the 12th of February, but no ships of any sort appearing, Nelson felt assured that the fleet with which the *Minerve* had been entangled the night before, was the Spanish grand fleet; and being more confirmed in this idea as the day advanced, he became very anxious to join Sir John Jervis's fleet, whose rendezvous, as fixed with the commodore, was not far from the place where we then were.

At daybreak, on the 13th of February, the weather was hazy, and as the *Minerve* was approaching the place of rendezvous, orders were given for keeping a good look out. In the forenoon a brig and cutter hove in sight, and soon after a larger sail, which, as the frigate neared, was discovered to be a ship of war. She proved to be the British frigate, the *Lively*, of thirty-two guns, an out-skirter of Sir John Jervis's fleet, which in a very short time the *Minerve* joined, not a little to the gratification of all parties.

On joining Sir John Jervis's fleet, the commodore, accompanied by the viceroy, repaired on board the flag-ship the *Victory*—the latter to confer with the admiral on political matters, the former to report in what manner he had executed his last orders, and to communicate all the naval intelligence he had gleaned in his late cruize, particularly of his being chaced by the enemy on leaving Gibraltar, and of his very recent nightly rencontre with the Spanish grand fleet. It was at this period that the capture of Lieutenants Culverhouse and Hardy, so much regretted at the time it took place, proved to be of the highest importance. The recaptured Spanish frigate, *Santa Sabina*, in which the above officers had been made prisoners, had returned to Carthagena, where the greatest part of the Spanish grand fleet was equipping for sea. These English officers had thus many favorable opportunities of noticing their state and condition, and having also sailed with the fleet when it left Carthagena for Cadiz, they had ample means of obtaining accurate knowledge of their numbers, equipment, and discipline. The information collected by Lieutenants Culverhouse and Hardy was of the greatest value, and being made known to the British admiral, was found to corroborate much of what he had learned from other quarters. Being also assured, not only by Nelson's intelligence, but by additional information brought by the *Bonne Citoyenne*, that the Spanish fleet was close at hand, Sir John Jervis, with that decision which was a prominent trait in his character, determined, notwithstanding the enemy's very superior force, to bring the Spaniards, if possible, to action.

No sooner was this decision taken, than the admiral's intentions were promulgated to his squadron, by throwing out the signal to prepare for action. Nelson, on rejoining the fleet, quitted the *Minerve*, and resumed the command of his regular ship, the *Captain*. Sir Gilbert Elliot and his party also left the *Minerve*, and were directed to repair on board the *Lively* frigate, commanded by Lord Garlies, who had orders to proceed with them immediately to England. But the viceroy could not bear the idea of leaving the British fleet at so critical and interesting a juncture. His Excellency's first request of Sir John Jervis was to be allowed to remain with the admiral as a volunteer on board of the *Victory,* until the issue of the approaching contest was known, which proposal Sir John positively refused; and all that the viceroy could obtain, was the admiral's assent that the *Lively* should not leave the British fleet until she could carry with her the despatches conveying the result of the expected engagement.

This enabled me to be an eye-witness of the action of the 14th of February, 1797, and the following letter to my father contains the Narrative of that battle, which, as already mentioned, I published, on my arrival in England, in the spring of that year.

ON BOARD THE LIVELY FRIGATE, OFF THE ISLAND OF SCILLY,
*February 27, 1797.*

ONCE MORE, MY DEAR SIR, *I am in sight of Old England, the land of rational liberty; and the pleasure of revisiting my native country, after an absence of six years, is not a little increased by the satisfaction of being on board a frigate that is the messenger of great and important news—a splendid and decisive victory—a victory unparalleled in the annals of our naval history.*

*Admiral Sir John Jervis, with fifteen sail of the line and four frigates, has defeated the Spanish Grand fleet, consisting of twenty-seven ships of the line and ten frigates, and captured four sail of the line, two of which are of three decks.*

*This brilliant affair took place off Cape St. Vincent on the 14th of February, the anniversary of St. Valentine, who by this glorious event has almost eclipsed his brother Crispian; and henceforth we must say, with the poet:*

> *"He that's outliv'd this day, and comes safe home,*
> *Will stand a tiptoe when the day is nam'd,*
> *And rouse him at the name of Valentine."*

*Captain Calder, Captain of the fleet under the command of Sir John Jervis, bears home the admiral's dispatches and is now on board the Lively. It is expected that he will land to-morrow; and I purpose to avail myself of that opportunity, to transmit you such an account of this splendid action, as I have been able to arrange in the time that has elapsed since we separated from the British fleet in Lagos Bay.*

*Before I enter on the detail of the proceedings of the important day which will certainly immortalize the name of Jervis, and of his brave seconds, it is proper to state the relative force of the British and Spanish fleets.*

*The British fleet, or to use, I believe, a more correct term, the British squadron, consisted of fifteen sail of the line, four frigates, a sloop of war, and a cutter; viz., two of 100 guns, two of 98 guns, two of 90 guns—total, six three-deckers, eight of 74 guns, and one of 64 guns.*

*The Spanish fleet was composed of twenty-seven sail of the line, ten frigates, and one brig; viz., one of four decks, carrying 136 guns; six of three decks, each of 112 guns; two of 84 guns, and eighteen of 74 guns each.*

*The Spanish admiral had sailed from Carthagena the 4th February. On the 5th, he passed Gibraltar, leaving in that Bay three line-of-battle ships, supposed to be laden with military stores for the Spanish troops stationed before that garrison; two of which ships afterwards chaced Commodore Nelson, in the* Minerve. *The strong easterly gale that had been friendly for their getting out of the Mediterranean was, however, unpropitious to their gaining the Port of Cadiz.*

*On the night of the 11th, as I have before mentioned, they were fallen in with, off the mouth of the Straits, by the* Minerve. *And the evening of the day on which Commodore Nelson joined Sir John Jervis off Cape St. Vincent, we find their fleet driven farther to the westward; for a part of them were not only seen by the* Min-erve, *before she joined the British fleet, but* La Bonne Citoyenne, *a British sloop of war, commanded by Captain Lindsay, arrived in the fleet the same evening with intelligence that not two hours before she had exchanged shots with one of the enemy's frigates, and that the enemy's fleet was not far distant.*

*Before sun-set in the evening of the 13th, the signal had been made for the British squadron to prepare for battle, and the ships were also directed to keep in close order during the night.*

*At daybreak on the 14th (St. Valentine's day) the British fleet was in complete order, formed in two divisions standing on a wind to the SSW. The morning was hazy. About half-past six o'clock,* A.M., *the* Culloden *made the signal for five sail in the SW by S quarter, which was soon after confirmed by the* Lively *and* Niger *frigates, and that the strange sail were by the wind on the starboard tack. The* Bonne Citoyenne *sloop of war, Captain Lindsay, was therefore directed to recon-noitre. At a quarter past eight o'clock, the squadron was ordered, by signal, to form in a close order; and in a few minutes afterwards the signal was repeated to prepare for battle.*

*About half-past nine o'clock, the* Culloden, Blenheim, *and* Prince George *were ordered to chace in the S by W quarter; which, upon the* Bonne Citoyenne's *making a signal that she saw eight sail in that quarter, was afterwards strength-ened by the* Irresistible, Colossus, *and* Orion.

*A little past ten o'clock, the* Minerve *frigate made the signal for twenty sail in the SW quarter, and a few minutes after, of eight sail in the S by W. Half an hour afterwards the* Bonne Citoyenne *made the signal that she could distinguish six-teen, and immediately afterwards twenty-five of the strange ships, to be of the line. The enemy's fleet were indeed become now visible to all the British squadron.*

*The ships first discovered by the* Culloden *were separated from their main body, which being to windward, were bearing down in some confusion, with a view of joining their separated ships. It appeared to have been the British admiral's intention, upon discovering the separated ships of the enemy's fleet, to have cut them off, if possible, before their main body could arrive to their assistance; and, with this view, the fast sailing ships of his squadron were ordered to chace.*

*Assured now of the near position of their main body, he probably judged it most advisable to form his fleet into the line of battle, and the signal was made for their forming the line of battle a-head and a-stern as most convenient. A signal was made directing the squadron to steer SSW.*

*About twenty minutes past eleven o'clock, the admiral pointed out that the* Victory *(his flag-ship) would take her station next to the* Colossus. *Some variation in steering was afterwards directed, in order to let the rear ships close up. At twenty-six minutes past eleven o'clock, the admiral communicated his intention to pass through the enemy's line, hoisting his large flag and ensign, and soon after the signal was made to engage.*

*The British van by this time had approached the enemy; and the distinction of leading the British line into action fell to the lot of the* Culloden, *commanded by Captain Troubridge. About half-past eleven o'clock, the firing commenced from the* Culloden *against the enemy's headmost ships to windward.*

*As the British squadron advanced, the action became more general; and it was soon apparent that the British admiral had accomplished his design of passing through the enemy's line.*

*The animated and regular fire of the British squadron was but feebly returned by the enemy's ships to windward, which, being frustrated in their attempts to join the separated ships, had been obliged to haul their wind on the larboard tack: those to leeward, and which were most effectually cut off from their main body, attempted also to form on their larboard tack, apparently with a determination of either passing through, or to leeward, of our line and joining their friends; but the warm reception they met with from the centre ships of our squadron soon obliged them to put about; and excepting one, the whole sought safety in flight, and did not again appear in the action until the close of the day.*

*The single ship just mentioned persevered in passing to leeward of the British line but was so covered with smoke that her intention was not discovered until she had reached the rear, when she was not permitted to pass without notice, but received the fire of our sternmost ships; and as she luffed round the rear, the* Lively *and other frigates had also the honor of exchanging with this two-decker several broadsides.*

*Sir John Jervis, having effected his first purpose, now directed his whole attention to the enemy's main body to windward, consisting at this time of eighteen sail of the line. At eight minutes past twelve, the signal therefore was made for the*

*British fleet to tack in succession, and soon after he made the signal for again pass-
ing the enemy's line.*

*The Spanish admiral's plan seemed to be to join his ships to leeward, by wear-
ing round the rear of our line; and the ships which had passed and exchanged shots
with our squadron had actually borne up with this view.*

*This design, however, was frustrated by the timely opposition of Commodore
Nelson, whose place in the rear of the British line afforded him an opportunity of
observing this maneuver, and of penetrating the Spanish admiral's intention. His
ship, the* Captain, *had no sooner passed the rear of the enemy's ships that were
to windward, than he ordered her to wear, and stood on the other tack towards
the enemy.*

*In executing this bold and decisive maneuver, the commodore reached the sixth
ship from the enemy's rear, which was the Spanish admiral's own ship, the* Santissima Trinidad, *of 136 guns, a ship of four decks, and said to be the largest in the
world. Notwithstanding the inequality of force, the commodore instantly engaged
this colossal opponent, and for a considerable time had to contend not only with her,
but with her seconds a-head and a-stern, of three decks each. While he maintained
this unequal combat, which we viewed with admiration mixed with anxiety, his
friends were flying to his support; and the enemy's attention was soon directed to
the* Culloden, *Captain Troubridge, and in a short time after to the* Blenheim, *of 90
guns, Captain Frederick, who opportunely came to their assistance.*

*The intrepid conduct of the commodore staggered the Spanish admiral, who
already appeared to waver in pursuing his intention of joining the ships cut off by
the British fleet, when the* Culloden's *arrival, and Captain Troubridge's spirited
support of the* Captain, *together with the approach of the* Blenheim, *followed by
Rear-Admiral Parker, with the* Prince George, Orion, Irresistible, *and* Diadem,
*not far distant, determined the Spanish admiral to change his design altogether,
and to make the signal for the ships of his main body to haul their wind, and make
sail on the larboard tack.*

*Advantage was now apparent in favor of the British squadron, and not a
moment was lost in improving it. As the ships of Rear-Admiral Parker's division
approached the enemy's ships, in support of the* Captain *and her gallant seconds,
the* Blenheim *and* Culloden, *the cannonade became more animated and impressive. The superiority of the British fire over that of the enemy, and its effects on the
enemy's hulls and sails, were so evident that we in the frigate no longer hesitated
to pronounce a glorious termination of the contest.*

*The British squadron at this time was formed in two divisions, both on the
larboard tack; their situation was as follows: Rear-Admiral Parker, with the*
Blenheim, Culloden, Prince George, *the rear-admiral's ship,* Captain, Orion,
Irresistible, *composed one division, which was engaged with the enemy's rear. Sir
John Jervis, with the other division, consisting of the* Excellent, Victory, Barfleur,

# The Battle of Cape St. Vincent

*February 14, 1797*

British    Spanish

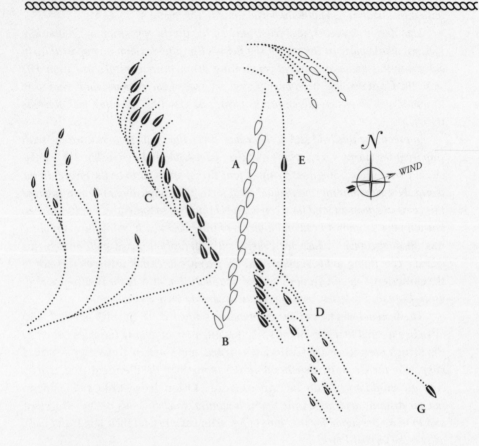

## Stage 1: Just after 12:00 noon

**A** British fleet passing through the enemy's line.

**B** *Culloden* tacking to engage the enemy's main body to windward.

**C** Main body of the Spanish fleet, which, after passing the British fleet on the larboard tack, bore up with an apparent design of joining their ships to leeward.

**D** Spanish ships cut off from their main body, attempting to join their friends, but obliged to wear and sheer off by the superior force of the British fire.

**E** A Spanish line-of-battle ship, which succeeded in joining the main body.

**F** The British frigates exchanging fire with the Spanish two-decker as she passed the rear of the British line.

**G** A large ship, which at the commencement of the action set all sail and soon disappeared to leeward.

## Stage 2: About 12:45 P.M.

**A** The main body of Spanish fleet hauling wind on larboard tack and making sail in consequence of spirited attack of Nelson, in *Captain*, 74, supported by *Culloden*, 74, Captain Troubridge.

**B** *Captain* engaged with *Santissima Trinidad*, 136, and two other three-decked ships, which were seconds to the Spanish Admiral.

**C** *Culloden*, engaged with the rear ships of the enemy's main body.

**D** *Blenheim*, a three-decker of 90 guns, commanded by T. L. Frederick, advancing to the assistance of *Captain* and *Culloden*.

**E** Rear-Admiral W. Parker, in *Prince George*, 98; with *Orion*, 74; *Irresistible*, 74; and *Diadem*, 64; approaching to support attack on center and rear of the enemy's fleet.

**F** *Colossus*, 74, Captain G. Murray, disabled by the loss of her fore-yard and fore-topsail-yard.

**G** Spanish ships that tried to rejoin fleet but were obliged to sheer off and made all sail to south.

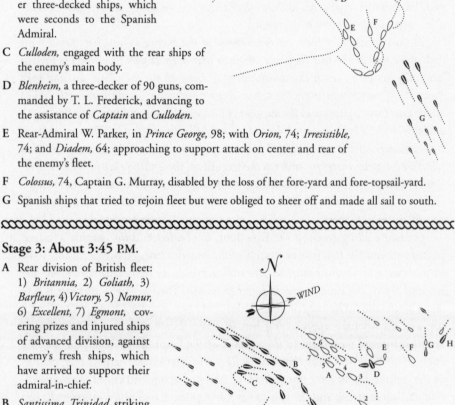

## Stage 3: About 3:45 P.M.

**A** Rear division of British fleet: 1) *Britannia*, 2) *Goliath*, 3) *Barfleur*, 4) *Victory*, 5) *Namur*, 6) *Excellent*, 7) *Egmont*, covering prizes and injured ships of advanced division, against enemy's fresh ships, which have arrived to support their admiral-in-chief.

**B** *Santissima Trinidad* striking or about to.

**C** Two line-of-battle ships wearing, on the arrival of fresh ships, to support their Chief.

**D** *Captain*, entangled with her two prizes, *San Nicolas* and *San Josef*.

**E** *Diadem*, 64, and *Minerva* frigate assisting *Captain*, to disengage her from her prizes.

**F** *Colossus*.

**G** *Lively* frigate towing *San Ysidro*, the first Spanish ship that struck.

**H** *Salvador del Mondo* attended by *Bonne Citoyenne*.

Namur, Egmont, Goliath, *and* Britannia, *was pressing forward in support of his advanced squadron, but had not yet approached the real scene of action.*

*The* Colossus *having, in the early part of the day, unfortunately lost her fore-yard and fore-top-sail-yard, was obliged, in consequence of these losses, to fall to leeward, and the* Minerve's *signal was made to take her in tow, which was, however, handsomely declined by Captain Murray when the* Minerve *had come within hail in execution of her orders.*

*While the British advanced division warmly pressed the enemy's centre and rear, the admiral meditated, with his division, a co-operation, which must effectually compel some of them to surrender.*

*In the confusion of their retreat, several of the enemy's ships had doubled on each other, and in the rear they were three or four deep. It was therefore the British admiral's design to reach the weathermost of these ships, then bear up, and rake them all in succession with the seven ships composing his division. His object afterwards was to pass on to the support of his van division, which, from the length of time they had been engaged, he judged might be in want of it. The casual position, however, of the rear ships of his van division, prevented his executing this plan: the admiral, therefore, ordered the* Excellent, *the leading ship of his own division, to bear up; and, with the* Victory, *he himself passed to leeward of the enemy's rearmost and leewardmost ships, which, though almost silenced in their fire, continued obstinately to resist the animated attacks of all their opponents.*

*Captain Collingwood, in the* Excellent, *in obedience to the admiral's orders, passed between the two rearmost ships of the enemy's line, giving to the one most to windward, a seventy-four, so effectual a broadside that, with what she had received before, her captain was induced to submit. The* Excellent *afterwards bore down on the ship to leeward, a three-decker; but observing the* Orion *engaged with her, and the* Victory *approaching her, he threw into her only a few discharges of musketry and passed on to the support of the* Captain, *at that time warmly engaged with a three-decker carrying a flag. His interference here was opportune, as the continual and long fire of the* Captain *had almost expended the ammunition she had at hand, and the loss of her fore-top-mast, and other injuries she had received in her rigging, had rendered her nearly ungovernable.*

*The Spanish three-decker had lost her mizenmast; and before the* Excellent *arrived in her proper station to open on this ship, the three-decker dropped astern aboard of, and became entangled with, a Spanish two-decker that was her second: thus doubled on each other, the* Excellent *gave the two ships her fire, and then moved forwards to assist the headmost ships in their attack on the Spanish admiral and the other ships of the enemy's centre.*

*Meanwhile, Sir John Jervis, disappointed in his plan of raking the enemy's rear ships, and having directed, as before observed, the* Excellent *to bear up, ordered the* Victory *to be placed on the lee-quarter of the rearmost ship of the enemy, a three-*

*decker, and having, by signal, ordered the* Irresistible *and* Diadem *to suspend their firing, threw into the three-decker so powerful a discharge that her commander, seeing the* Barfleur, *carrying Vice-Admiral the Hon. W. Waldegrave's flag, ready to second the* Victory, *thought proper to strike to the British chief. Two of the enemy's ships had now surrendered, and the* Lively *frigate and* Diadem *had orders to secure the prizes. The next that fell were the two with which Commodore Nelson was engaged.*

*While Captain Collingwood so nobly stepped in to his assistance, as has been mentioned before, Captain R. W. Miller, the commodore's captain, was enabled to replenish his lockers with shot and prepare for a renewal of the fight: no sooner, therefore, had the* Excellent *passed on than the gallant commodore renewed the battle.*

*The three-decker with which he was before engaged having fallen aboard her second, that ship, of 84 guns, became now the Captain's opponent. To her Commodore Nelson directed a vigorous fire; nor was it feebly returned, as the loss of the* Captain *evinced, near twenty men being killed and wounded in a very few minutes. It was now that the various damages already sustained by that ship through the long and arduous conflict which she had maintained, appearing to render a continuance of the contest in the usual way precarious, or perhaps impossible; and the commodore not bearing to part with an enemy of whom he had assured himself, he instantly resolved on a bold and decisive measure, and determined, whatever might be the event, to attempt his opponent sword in hand. The boarders were summoned and orders given to lay the* Captain *on board the enemy.*

*Fortune favors the brave; nor on this occasion was she unmindful of her favorite. Captain Miller so judiciously directed the course of the* Captain *that she was laid aboard the starboard quarter of the eighty-four gun ship, her spritsail yard passing over the enemy's poop, and hooking her mizen shrouds; and the word to board being given, the officers and seamen destined for this duty, headed by Lieutenant Berry, together with the detachment of the 69th regiment, commanded by Lieutenant Pearson, then doing duty as Marines on board the* Captain, *passed with rapidity on board the enemy's ship; and in a short time the* San Nicolas *was in the possession of her intrepid assailants. The commodore's impatience would not permit him to remain an inactive spectator of this event. He knew the attempt was hazardous; and his presence, he thought, might contribute to its success. He therefore accompanied the party in this attack, passing from the fore chains of his own ship into the enemy's quarter gallery, and thence through the cabin to the quarterdeck, where he arrived in time to receive the sword of the dying commander, who was mortally wounded by the boarders. For a few minutes after the officers had submitted, the crew below were firing their lower-deck guns: this irregularity, however, was soon corrected, and measures taken for the security of the conquest. But this labor was no sooner achieved, than he found himself engaged in another and more arduous one. The stern of the three-decker, his former opponent, was directly amidships on the weather-beam of the* San Nicolas; *and, from her poop and galleries, the enemy sorely annoyed, with musketry, the British on board the* San Nicolas. *The commodore was not long in resolving on the conduct to be observed upon this momentous occasion. The alternative that presented itself, was to quit the prize, or advance. Confident in the bravery of his seamen, he determined on the latter. Directing therefore an additional number of men to be sent from the* Captain, *on board the* San Nicolas, *the undaunted commodore headed himself the assailants in this new attack, and success crowned the enterprise. Such, indeed, was the panic occasioned by his preceding conduct that the British no sooner appeared on the quarter-deck of their new opponent than the Commandant advanced, and asking for the British commanding officer, dropped on one knee and presented to him his sword; making, at the same time, an excuse for the Spanish admiral's not appearing, as he was dangerously wounded. For a moment Commodore Nelson could scarcely persuade himself of this second instance of good fortune; he therefore ordered the Spanish Commandant, who had the rank of a brigadier, to assemble the officers on the quarter-deck, and direct steps to be taken instantly for communicating to the crew the surrender of the ship. All the officers immediately appeared, and the commodore found the surrender of the* San Josef *ascertained, by each of them delivering to him his sword.*

*The coxswain of Nelson's barge had attended him throughout this perilous adventure. To his charge the commodore gave the swords of the Spanish officers as he received them; and the jolly tar, as they were delivered to him, tucked these honorable trophies under his arm, with all the* sang-froid *imaginable.*

*It was at this moment also that an honest Jack Tar, an old acquaintance of Nelson's, came up to him in the fullness of his heart, and excusing the liberty he was taking, asked to shake him by the hand, to congratulate him upon seeing him safe on the quarter-deck of a Spanish three-decker.*

*This new conquest had scarcely submitted, and the commodore returned on board the* San Nicolas, *when the latter ship was discovered to be on fire in two places. At the first moment appearances were alarming; but presence of mind and resources were not wanting to the British officers in this emergency. The firemen were immediately ordered from the* Captain; *and proper means being taken, the fires were soon got under.*

*A signal was now made by the* Captain *for boats to assist in separating her from her prizes; and as the* Captain *was incapable of further service until refitted, the commodore hoisted his pendant, for the moment, on board the* Minerve *frigate, and in the evening removed it to the* Irresistible, *Captain Martin.*

*Four of the enemy's ships were now in [the] possession of the British squadron (two of three decks, the* Salvador del Mondo *and the* San Josef, *of 112 guns each; one of 84, the* San Nicolas; *and the* San Ysidro, *of 74 guns;) and the van of the*

British line still continued to press hard the Santissima Trinidad and others in the rear of the enemy's flying fleet. The approach, however, of the enemy's ships which had been separated from their main body in the morning, two new ships also bearing down from to windward, and two of the enemy's flying ships wearing to support their chief, at that time severely pressed, add to which, the closing of the day—these circumstances, but more particularly the lateness of the hour, while the prizes were not yet properly secured, determined the British admiral to bring to. The headmost of the enemy's approaching ships (in all nine in number, two of which were of three decks) had indeed advanced to fire on the Britannia, in which Vice-Admiral Thompson carried his flag, and the sternmost ships of the rear-division, which were fortunately, at this period, in a situation to keep the enemy in check. The Victory likewise, with the Barfleur and Namur, had formed to cover the prizes. The British admiral, therefore, a little before four o'clock, P.M., made the preparative, and soon after the signal for the British fleet to bring to. The enemy's fresh ships, on approaching, opened a fire on our covering ships; but, though both fresh, and so superior in numbers, they contented themselves with the noise of a few irregular broadsides, leaving their captured friends, and seeming too happy to be allowed to escape with their discomfited chief, and his disabled companions, to think of molesting our squadron in bringing to on the starboard tack.

The frigates having orders to take in charge the prizes not already taken possession of, the four were soon secured as well as circumstances permitted; and the Captain having suffered very considerably in her masts and rigging, the Minerve was ordered to take her in tow.

At the close of the evening, the British fleet was again formed in most admirable line of battle, on a wind with their heads to the southward, and the Niger frigate ordered to look out during the night.

The close of the day, before the four prizes were secured, undoubtedly saved the Spanish admiral's flag from falling into the hands of the victors. The Santissima Trinidad, in which he carried it, had been so much the object of attention that the ship was a perfect wreck when the action ceased. Many indeed aver that she actually struck both her flag and ensign, hoisting a flag as a signal of submission; but as she continued her course, and afterwards hoisted a Spanish jack, others doubt this circumstance. It is however, a truth that her fire had been silent for some time before this event is reported to have occurred.

The loss of the enemy in this engagement must have been very considerable. The fire of the British squadron was, throughout the action, superior in the proportion of five or six to one; and if we were to judge from the number of killed and wounded found on board the prizes, their casualties must greatly exceed the numbers that have been usually computed. Almost all their wounded that had lost limbs died for want of assistance; and many others, who were wounded in other parts, were found dead in the holds.

*The loss of the British squadron, in killed and wounded, amounted to exactly three hundred: moderate indeed, when compared with that of the enemy, and considering the duration of the action! But the expenditure of ammunition was, I am told, beyond any recent example. The* Culloden *expended, it is said, one hundred and seventy barrels of powder; the* Captain, *one hundred and forty-six; and the* Blenheim, *one hundred and eighty; other ships expended in the same proportion. It is not unworthy of remark also that not a single gun in the British squadron burst in this action.*

*The* Captain *fired more shot than are usually given to a ship of her rate, at her first equipment in England; and it was observed, that when shot or grape were wanting on board this ship for the carronades, the tars substituted in their place nine-pounds shot, seven of which were frequently discharged at one time, and then at so short a distance that every shot of the seven must have had effect.*

*If I may be permitted to hazard an opinion, the whole squadron have gained immortal honor; for the victory of the 14th of February stands, in all its circumstances, first and unparalleled in naval history.*

*Thus, my dear Sir, you have the most interesting particulars of this brilliant affair. I have other anecdotes in store; which I reserve until we meet to talk over this, as well as other occurrences, that have happened since we parted. I cannot, however, conclude my letter without remarking, for your satisfaction, knowing you to be a particular man, that the time mentioned in the narrative is taken from the minutes kept on board the* VICTORY. *Some difference occurs between them and those kept on board other ships; but I have thought proper to follow the former, conceiving them to be the most correct. In the hope of our meeting in a few days, I remain,*

MY DEAR SIR, &C.
J. DRINKWATER.

## A MEETING WITH NELSON

On the morning of the 15th, Sir Gilbert Elliot proceeded to offer to the British admiral his congratulations on the success of the previous day. Lord Garlies of course accompanied him.[1] I was to have been of this party, and was actually descending the side ladder, when, being in uniform, it was discovered that I was without side-arms, for which I returned; but, when I got back to the gangway, the place destined for me was occupied by

---

[1] *George, Viscount Garlies, was the Scottish captain of HMS* Lively. *In 1806, he succeeded his father as Earl of Galloway and was promoted to rear admiral in 1810.*

another person. My friends kindly offered to make room for me, but as this could not be done without occasioning great inconvenience to the whole party, I reluctantly gave up the intention of accompanying them.

My disappointment, however, was amply made up by what took place immediately after the *Lively*'s barge had left the frigate. A boat was seen approaching the *Lively* on the opposite side, and I heard with surprise, and no little pleasure, that Nelson was on board of her. Seeing me on the quarter-deck, the commodore immediately approached me, offering his hand, which I seized with a most cordial grasp, expressing, at the same time, my high admiration of the gallant conduct of the *Captain* on the preceding day, and my warmest congratulations on the success of the battle.

"Where is Sir Gilbert?" was his first inquiry. "Gone with Lord Garlies to the *Victory*," was my reply.—"I hoped," he rejoined, "to have caught him before he saw the admiral, but come below with me," and he led the way to the cabin.

Seated alone with the commodore, I renewed in the most expressive terms, my congratulations on his safety from the perils of such a fight, and on the very distinguished part he had personally taken in the action, of which many particulars had by this time reached the *Lively*. He received my compliments with great modesty, though evidently with great satisfaction. I then remarked that, as the *Lively* would bear the glorious news to England, I should feel much obliged by his giving me as many particulars of the proceedings of his ship, the *Captain*, and of his own conduct in the capture of the two ships, as he was disposed to communicate. Our intimacy was such that I felt no difficulty in drawing from him these details; and this circumstance will be an apology for my making these remarks with such great freedom. I observed to him that the position of the *Captain* appeared to all of us in the *Lively* to be for a long time most extraordinary and unaccountable. We had expected every instant to see the ship annihilated by the overpowering force to which she was singly opposed. In the animation of conversation, I went so far as to ask, "How came you, commodore, to get into that singular and perilous situation?" He good-naturedly replied, "I'll tell you how it happened. The admiral's intention, I saw, was to cut off the detached squadron of eight sail and afterwards attack the main body, weakened by this separation. Observing, however, as our squadron advanced and became engaged with the enemy's ships, that the main body of the enemy were pushing to join their friends to leeward, by passing in the rear of our squadron, I thought, unless by some prompt and extraordinary measure, the main body could be diverted from this course, until Sir John (at that time in action in the *Victory*) could see their plan, his well arranged designs on the enemy would be frustrated. I therefore ordered the *Captain* to wear, and passing the rear of our squadron, directed Captain Miller to steer for the centre of the enemy's fleet, where was their admiral-in-chief, seconded by two three-deckers, hoping by this proceeding to confound them, and, if possible, make them change their course (as he did), and thus afford Sir John Jervis time to see their movements, and take measures to follow up his original intention."—I do not say that Nelson expressed himself in exactly the above words, but his statement was to the same effect.[1]

In compliance with my request, he then gave me the details of his boarding the *St. Nicholas*, and afterwards the *St. Josef*, which are given in the original Narrative, adding the following particulars:—"I saw (and then he spoke with increased animation) that from the disabled state of the *Captain*, and the effective attack of the approaching British ships, I was likely to have my beaten opponent taken from me; I therefore decided to board the *St. Nicholas*, which I had chiefly fought and considered to be my prize. Orders were given to lay the *Captain* aboard of her: the spritsail-yard passed into her mizen rigging. Lieutenant Berry with the ship's boarders, and Captain Pearson with the 69th regiment (acting as marines on board the *Captain*), soon got possession of the enemy's ship. Assisted by one of the sailors, I got from the fore-chains into the quarter-gallery through the window, and thence through the cabin to the quarter-deck, where I found my gallant friends already triumphant." He then gave me the details of the extraordinary circumstances attending his afterwards getting possession of the *St. Josef*. Of course, my high admiration of his conduct was often expressed, as he proceeded, in giving me these very interesting particulars, of which I made pencil notes on a scrap of paper I found at hand; and these communications from my gallant friend were the more valuable from their

---

[1] I have since often heard Commodore Nelson's conduct, in the above transaction, variously commented on. According to the strict rules of discipline, some persons say the *Captain* should not have quitted the British line-of-battle without orders. The strength of Sir John Jervis's squadron lay in its compactness, and the loss of one ship, from any cause, where the numbers opposed to each other were so disproportionate, might have defeated the British admiral's maneuvers, and even have endangered the safety of the whole. Others have remarked, and apparently with good grounds, that when Nelson saw the necessity of some immediate and bold measure to disconcert the enemy, and had decided on the step he took, he should not have gone alone, but have taken with his own seventy-four, all the ships in his rear; and if we may judge from results, and the success of one ship, there can be no doubt that the attack of the *Captain*, supported by two or three others, must have been more effective, and the victory of the day would, in that case, have been more complete. In these comments there seems to be reason and good sense; but in warfare, circumstances must often arise which baffle principles, and customary modes of proceeding. Nelson, no doubt, saw the conduct of the Spanish admiral in its true light: his decision and boldness astonished and confounded the enemy, who were thus taken by surprise, and unprepared for such singular resolution. The measure succeeded, and to this movement, hazardous as it was, may chiefly be attributed the success of the day.

being made before he had seen any other officer of the fleet, except Captain G. Martin, of the *Irresistible,* to which ship he had repaired for refreshment and repose, until the *Captain,* his own ship, almost a wreck in her rigging, &c., could be put into manageable order.

Towards the conclusion of this interesting interview, I repeated my cordial felicitations at his personal safety, after such very perilous achievements. I then adverted to the honors that must attend such distinguished services. "The admiral," I observed, "of course will be made a peer, and his seconds in command noticed accordingly. As for you, commodore," I continued, "they will make you a baronet." The word was scarcely uttered, when placing his hand on my arm, and looking me most expressively in the face, he said, "No, no: if they want to mark my services, it must not be in that manner."—"Oh!" said I, interrupting him, "you wish to be made a Knight of the Bath," for I could not imagine that his ambition, at that time, led him to expect a peerage. My supposition proved to be correct, for he instantly answered me, "Yes; if my services have been of any value, let them be noticed in a way that the public may know me—or them." I cannot distinctly remember which of these terms was used, but, from his manner, I could have no doubt of his meaning, that he wished to bear about his person some honorary distinction, to attract the public eye, and mark his professional services.

This casual discovery of Nelson's peculiar feelings on this subject was not forgotten, or without consequences. As was expected, his Majesty, in reward for Nelson's distinguished conduct, had intended to create him a baronet. Sir Gilbert Elliot, who took a warm interest in Nelson's welfare, called on me in London to impart this news; when I made known to him the purport of my conversation on board the *Lively,* and suggested that it was advisable to make this circumstance known to the government. Sir Gilbert saw the matter in the same light. He lost no time in communicating what had passed on this subject to some member of the cabinet, Lord Spencer, I believe, who was then at the head of the Admiralty Board, and his lordship took steps to meet Nelson's wishes, in the manner most likely to gratify his feelings, by obtaining for him, instead of a baronetcy, the Order of the Bath, although, for that purpose, it was necessary to make him an extra knight.

What I had noticed in the above interview with Nelson, agreed perfectly with the opinion I formed from all I observed during our subsequent acquaintance. The attainment of public honours, and an ambition to be distinguished above his fellows, were his master passions. His conduct was constantly actuated by these predominant feelings. It will account for the personal gratification he invariably evinced at receiving the many decorative honors presented to him by almost every power in Europe in amity with Great Britain; but, in reference to such distinctions, it may be observed, that if such pre-eminent talents as those of this most extraordinary man could be so cheaply purchased, the English nation, and indeed Europe, situated as she then was, had only to approve and applaud his moderation.

When Nelson quitted the *Lively*, he went on board the *Victory* to receive from his gallant Chief, Sir John Jervis, and from his friend, Sir Gilbert Elliot, those congratulations and commendations which he so highly merited.

## HOMECOMING

There being little wind on the 15th of February, both fleets, as has been already remarked, remained almost becalmed in sight of each other. That of the enemy appeared in great disorder; the British squadron was concentrated. On the 16th, the British squadron was still off Cape St. Vincent, which, on account of the adverse wind, and the disabled state of the prizes, the squadron could not weather. If they could have passed to the westward of the Cape, it was thought the admiral would have proceeded to Lisbon.

During the day, some movements of the enemy indicating an intention of approaching the British squadron, Sir John, closely attentive to their proceedings, ordered the frigates to assemble round the *Victory*, to be at hand to act towards the prizes (which, in case of a renewal of hostilities, might embarrass him) in such manner as circumstances might point out.

Various reports were in circulation regarding their disposal in case of another action. Amongst other measures, it was rumoured that it had been suggested to run the four prizes ashore on the coast of Portugal, and to leave the Spanish crews to shift for themselves. All conjecture on this head was, however, removed in the afternoon: finding it not practicable to get round Cape St. Vincent, the admiral made the signal to bear away for Lagos Bay, a few leagues to leeward, where the squadron and the prizes came to anchor in the evening.[1]

---

[1] On the fleet's assembling in Lagos Bay, the admiral communicated, in general orders, his thanks to the admirals and officers of the squadron under his command, in the following terms:—

"VICTORY, LAGOS BAY,
February 16, 1797.

"SIR,

"No language I am possessed of can convey the high sense I entertain of the exemplary conduct of the flag-officers, captains, officers, seamen, marines, and soldiers, embarked on board every ship of the squadron I have the honor to command, present at the vigorous and successful attack made upon the fleet of Spain on the 14th inst. The signal advantage obtained by His Majesty's arms on that day is

On the 17th, despatches were sent off by land to Lisbon, giving information of the late victory. In the course of the day, intelligence reached Sir John, through an American trader, that a large three-decker, supposed to be the *Santissima Trinidad*, had been seen off Cape St. Mary's, in distress, with an English frigate hovering round her. Two frigates were in consequence detached to bring her in, or to destroy her; but although the disabled ship proved to be the ship in question, her crew at length contrived to get her into port.

The 18th of February proved to be calm, but a fine day. The Spanish fleet had now approached Cape St. Vincent, off which they were seen, in number, twenty-two ships of the line, manoeuvring, as well as they were able, to form a line-of-battle.

Arrangements having by this time been made with the Portuguese authorities at Lagos, for the reception of the Spanish prisoners of war, they were landed this day, to the number of about 2,300 men, and commenced their march to the eastward for the Spanish frontier. In the afternoon, a large Spanish frigate that had hugged the shore, under cover of a small headland, forming the western point of the Bay of Lagos, suddenly appeared, almost within shot of the British squadron. The *Lively*'s signal was made to slip and chace, but the enemy no sooner saw his danger, than he hauled his wind, and, crowding all sail, stood for the Spanish fleet, then drawing off from the land, and the *Lively*'s signal was annulled. At night, two of the British frigates were chaced into the anchorage of the fleet by one of the enemy's line-of-battle ships. On Sunday, the 19th of February, Captain Robert Calder, captain of the fleet, came on board the *Lively*, with the admiral's despatches, of which he was to be the bearer to England. About noon, the *Lively* got under way, and the wind having become favorable, and blowing fresh, she soon doubled Cape St. Vincent, seeing nothing of the Spanish fleet, and before night-fall, had left the British squadron far behind.

The *Lively* lay her course towards England until the 23rd of February, when the wind changed to the eastward. On the 25th, she had got into

---

*entirely owing to their determined valor and discipline; and I request you will accept yourself and give my thanks and approbation to those composing the crew of the ship under your command.*

"I AM, SIR,

"YOUR MOST HUMBLE SERVANT,

"J. JERVIS."

"TO ———, CAPTAIN

OF H. M. SHIP ———."

Considering how distinguished had been the services of some of the commanders of the fleet in the action of the 14th, it was thought extraordinary at the time, that not the least notice, by name, was taken of any of these officers in the preceding circular communication to the squadron.

soundings, but the adverse easterly wind prevented her advancing up the Channel. By the 28th, the *Lively* had weathered the Scilly Islands, and passed to the northward, between those islands and the Lands End. There being little prospect of any change of wind, and Captain Calder being very impatient to reach London with his good news, he desired Lord Garlies to put him on shore at St. Ive's, where he landed, giving express orders that no letters, nor any other person except himself and servant should be allowed to land. Some idea was then entertained that the *Lively* might make for Milford Haven, but our good fortune interposed to defeat this project, which, had it been carried into effect, might have brought the frigate into contact with a French flying squadron, then hovering off the coast of South Wales, and which had landed a body of troops near Fish-guard. It was luckily decided to return to the English Channel, where the frigate contrived to contend for some days against a stiff Levanter, until she had got abreast of the Eddystone, when seeing little prospect of any alter-ation in the wind, and anxious to get on shore, Sir Gilbert Elliot requested Lord Garlies to land him and his party at Plymouth; and, in a few hours after our course was changed, I had the satisfaction (which is only to be felt and understood by those who have been absent long on foreign service) of finding myself once more in old England.

We landed on Sunday, the 5th of March. Being the messengers of such glorious news as the defeat of the Spanish grand fleet, the rumour of which, it was concluded, would have already reached Plymouth, we antic-ipated a most joyful reception. We expected, on our reaching the shore, that the *Lively*'s arrival would have been hailed with the customary congratula-tions and rejoicings; but the people who received us, did not even enquire whence she came. Not a word nor a sign of welcome met our landing. Cap-tain Calder had kept his good news so secret, that not a whisper of it had reached Plymouth, where, not a little to our surprise, we saw nothing but long faces and desponding looks in all classes.

We were not, however, long in learning the cause of this appearance and behaviour. Before we could tell them our gratifying intelligence, they announced to us the news (which had reached them that morning from the metropolis) of the shutting up of the National Bank of England, and the gen-eral *suspension of cash payments*. The union of the Spanish with the French fleets, they added, was considered as certain. Some flying squadrons of the latter were then known to be in the Irish channel, and the usual alarm of invasion universally prevailed. Nothing but England's disgrace and down-fall was foretold and talked of throughout the kingdom.

After listening to these discouraging details for some time, we availed ourselves of the first favorable opening to relieve them of some of their apprehensions. Immediate invasion, we said, was not to be looked for. Sir John Jervis had retarded, if not entirely defeated that measure; and we then made known the particulars of the glorious Battle of St. Valentine's day. For some time they would scarcely give our statements credit; and even when at length the fact was forced on their belief, such was the panic then prevailing that we could only collect at Plymouth, from the admiral, the general, and other friends, fifteen guineas in gold, towards enabling the viceroy, and his party of six individuals, and their servants, to pay their travelling expenses to the metropolis.

I cannot better conclude these anecdotes than by recording a conversation which I had with Nelson on the very next occasion of my seeing him. After the battle of St. Vincent, it is well known that he was actively employed in the bombardment of Cadiz, and subsequently detached on a special service to Santa Cruz, in the island of Teneriffe, where he met with the injury which caused him the loss of his right arm. He had returned to England, and was still suffering severely from the effects of the amputation, when I was allowed to see him. This was just before the victory of Camperdown [October 11, 1797] and intelligence of interest was hourly expected to arrive from Admiral Duncan's fleet. One of the first questions which Nelson put to me, was whether I had been at the Admiralty. I told him there was a rumour that the British fleet had been seen engaged with that of Holland. He started up in his peculiar energetic manner, notwithstanding Lady Nelson's attempts to quiet him, and stretching out his unwounded arm—"Drinkwater," said he, "I would give this other arm to be with Duncan at this moment"; so unconquerable was the spirit of the man, and so intense his eagerness to give every instant of his life to the service of his country.

• • •

*The Battle of Cape St. Vincent represented sea warfare on a grand scale. Steel's Naval Chronologist of the War records that the British had 73 men killed and 223 wounded, while the enemy had, in just the four ships taken, 261 killed and 342 wounded, and in all some 5,000 killed, wounded, and captured. Admiral Jervis was created an earl (St. Vincent) and awarded an annual pension of £3,000. Vice-Admiral Thompson and Rear-Admiral Parker were created barronets. Nelson was invested with the Order of the Bath.*

*At the other end of the scale, Jacob Nagle is about to engage in warfare almost of a personal nature. The western coastal waters of Spain and Portugal are virtually lawless, that is until the* Netley, *a happy and somewhat rapacious British schooner commanded by Captain Francis Bond, arrives.*

# JACOB NAGLE

 ~

# Mad Dickey's Amusement
## 1798-1800

*W*hen *we last encountered Jacob Nagle (1795), he had been impressed into service on board the* Gorgon. *From that time he
served on board the* Gorgon *and the* Blanche *as conditions deteriorated in
the Mediterranean for the British fleet. In this passage, the* Blanche *has
returned to Portsmouth for repairs. The unhappy crew petitions to be
drafted by other ships, and Nagle transfers to the unusual sloop* Netley,
*which has an experimental sliding keel that can be retracted in shallow
waters. Following a stint off the Channel coast of France, the* Netley *plies
the Atlantic coast of Spain and Portugal and becomes a very successful
cruiser—with a minimum of scruples. Witness the fact that the author
somehow accumulates a surplus of watches.*

IN ABOUT TEN DAYS AFTER, orders came to draught our ships crew.
The most of them were sent on board the *Le Tigat*, 84 gun ship, and
Capt[ain] Bond came on board, being aquainted with the first leutenant,
and had a pick of choice seamen and their recommendations from the
first leut[enan]t to the number of 45 seamen. She was a new constructed
schooner with fals keels. We ware sent on board [28 July 1798], laying at
Spithead.[1]

[1] HMS *Netley*, a 16-gun schooner with a sliding keel, was designed by General Samuel Bentham and launched in 1798. The ship was 82.6 feet in length, and had a tonnage of 177 and a
mean draft of 9.3. The ship surrendered to the French in the West Indies in 1806. "Rupert Jones
List," National Maritime Museum.

88

When we had received our wages for the *Blanch* we sailed [2 August 1798] for Haverdegrass [Le Havre-de-Grâce], but that evening we came to an anchor at St. Hellena and the capt[ain] having the hands all sent aft to station them, he call'd them all in rotation excepting three of us, which was nearly on the first of the list. When they were all station'd, I said to the cap[tain], "You have forgot us, Sir."

"No, I have not," said he. Pointing to Donalson, "You are to act as boatswain and Covington, you are to act as guner," and as for me, I was chief quartermaster and afterwards prize master and third in command. I kept the first watch, and a beautiful night, the men laying about the decks, the most of them "sowed up," as the sailors terms is, and bottles of liquor between the guns on both sides.

In the morning, washed the decks down and got under way and arived off Haverdegrass to assist in blockading four frigates and four sloops of war that lay in the mold [mole]. We prevented all vessels from going in and took all that attempted to come out.

One morning two gun boats a coming a long shore, they mounted 8 thirty twos and 24 pounders each. We gave chace. They finding we ware coming up with them, they run on shore on a sand bank. We followed them till we got aground, but having fals keels, we drew 16 feet water and when we lifted our keels, they drew 10 feet forward and a leven aft. Therefore after boaring them for a half an hour with our 24 pounders, we lifted our keels, hove a bout, and left them there.

At every spring tide there would be 6 or 7 frigates to joine us, as the French frigates could not come out at any other time. Sir Richard Strawen [Strachan] was the commedore, which the sailors call'd Mad Dickey.

At Haverdegrass there is three forts, one round the town, one large battery on the north side, a good highth from the level of the water, and a four gun battery out side towards the point. The mold [mole] for the shiping is inside of the town, on the River Seane [Seine]. It lays 45 miles west of Rowen [Rouen] and 112 N.W. of Paris upon the English Channel, Log'd. 11°E., Latt'd 42°29′N.

The commedore having a French young gentleman on board of note, which had been taken prisoner, and meaning to send him on shore, lowered the cutter down and sent him to be landed with a flag of truce, but no sooner than the boat got under there guns they opened a heavy fire from the foregun battery on them till they shot all there oars away and lay there like a target, and still continuing there fire, meaning to sink the boat, the commedore then made our signal to go in and fetch the boat out. We run in under the four gun battery and hove two and opened our broad side with our 24 pounders and made the rocks fly over there heads as thick and coming down upon them that they had to leave the battery. We then took the boat in tow and brought hur out.

Shortly after, on a Sunday morning [19 August 1798], Mad Dickey ment to give us some amusement. At 8 o'clock he made the signal to go to breck-fast, at 9 o'clock to go to prayers, and a little before noon, the signal was made to go to dinner. About one o'clock he hoisted a flag for action and our signal to lead the van, and we went a head.

There was 2 frigates, our schooner, and a bum ship, but the other frigate did not come in, as he thought it was not proper to have his men killed and of no service. However we obey'd the signal and the commedore followed us, the bum laid off, and a long the beach, from the town to the large battery, laid 47 gunboats in a range, between us and the fort, and raked them every broadside, and what shot went over the gunboats would go into the fort. The frigate could not come in so far as we ware, and finding our heavey mettal so warm, that they nearly neglected the frigate to fire at us till the water apeared like hail around us with grape and canister, one thirty two pound shot struck the muzel of one of our 24 pounders and disabled the gun and kiled and wounded five men, and the capt[ain] wounded in the thy.

We engage'd two hours and fifteen minutes when Mad Dickey made a signal to put about and stand out, and as soon as we ceased firing, the French quit likewise, though we ware still under their guns. I beleive they liked our room better than our company, though we never fired a shot into the town, as we new there ware none but wimen and children. The men of the town and the seamen ware all in the batiries and gunboats. The frigate received no damage excepting hur riging, the bum ship laying at so great a distance that she received no damage, though she could heave hur shells into the fort.

As soon as we ware from under the enemies guns, the com[modore] sent his docktor on board to assist in dressing the wounded. Our masts being wounded, we had to fish them. The next day we ware ordered to Spithead for repair. We ariving [21 August 1798], run into harbour and our schooner went into dock and the capt[ain] and wounded went to the hospittle.[1]

In about a month we are ready for see with new masts, and Capt[ain] Bond came on b[oar]d from the hospittle. We sailed again [18 September

---

[1] In a letter of 12 September 1798, from Haslar Hospital, Portsmouth, Captain Bond wrote to Evan Nepean, secretary of the Admiralty, that he not only suffered from the wound in the thigh, but also from having received "a violent contusion in my breast, the effect of which is not a little alarming, though the pain, by blistering etc. is something palliated." Health may have been a factor in limiting his active career. Captain's Correspondence, ADM/1/2756, Public Records Office.

1798] for Haver de Grass and remained on that station for two months. During this time we had some French men going backwards and forwards as spies, and we would land them in the night and when they wanted to return they would make a few small fiers according to the signals they would agree on and then send a boat for them when they had the information they required and then send them to England, but the French having some information, a cutter that was with us landing one of them in the night, and the French laying wait took the boats crew as well as the spy, but the spy they hung on the first tree, but the crew and officer ware made prisoners of.

During this station, in the winter was very severe, we came a cross a decked boat which pretended to be a fishing boat, as we did not mislist [molest] them, but overhalling hur we found both men and arms and brought hur with us to Spithead. Laying there awhile and being ready for sea, we receiv'd orders to take a convoy to Porto Port in Portangal [Portugal] and afterwards to remain on that station till further orders from Cape Finister, to the lattitude of Lisbon.

After getting the convoy safe into Porto Port we cruised for one month, chased and spoke a great number of vessels, but all proving to be neutral vessels or English. At length on the 1st day of May, early in the morning, I kept the capt[ain's] watch. The capt[ain] came on deck, and we fell into discourse. I inform'd him it was surprising to me that we should cruise on that coast so long without falling in with privateers or vessels taken by them. When cruising in the *Blanch* Frigate we fell in with a great many, but always being off the land so far in the frigate, they would fetch into the small harbours before we could come up with them. While discoursing, the man at mast head cried out, "Sail ho."

The capt[ain] made answer, "Where abouts?"

"Right to windward." Turn'd the hands up and made sail as close as she would lay. In a short time we ware a longside the brig off of Mount Vigo on the point of the see shore and the entrance of the River Commencia [Miño], which devides Spain and Portangal [Portugal]. She proved to be an English brig [*Black Eyed Susan*] taken by a French privateer.

While putting men on b[oar]d we saw a schooner [*L'Egyptienne*] coming down upon us with all sail set [1 May 1799]. We being riged like a Dutch galyot, deceived them. This was the privateer that took the brig, but when she got so near as to purceive our guns, she hall'd hur wind, but it was of no use, for we could lay closer to the wind than any vessel I ever saw. She then up hellem and clap'd hur before the wind. We ware then alongside in 15 minutes. They stood to there quarters till we gave them 3 or 4 of our 24 pounders. They all run below, leaving the French capt[ain] to hall the colours down.

While getting the prisoners on board we saw a Dutch galyott [*Wohlfort*] to windward, and understanding by the Dutchmen that they ware taken by the privateer, we sent the schooner in chase and took hur. I went on b[oar]d the brig with 5 men and we took them all into Porto Port.

In a few days we put to see again and run off Vigo where the French and Spanish privateers generally made there randevoes. Sometimes we would come to an anchor in side of one of the islands in sight of the priva-teers laying and looking at us and water our vessel and wash our clothes and dry them. There lay at one time a French 24 gun ship and 14 small pri-vateers. We got underway and run in within gun shot and they would not come out to atackt us.

One day we observed a schooner coming a long shore towards the bat-tery, abrest of the town, and we run hur a shore, and got our boat out and got hur off, but finding nothing in hur excepting ballast as we supposed, we tared hur decks and set hur on fire in several places. The boat had not reached the schooner before she blew up, having a number of barrals of powder under the ballast for the fort that we are then laying within gun shot of.

We saw a nother small privateer laying inside of the fort, a front of the town. We maned our boats and sent them on board. The fort opened upon us, and we on them, but our 24 being much heavyer than there mettle, and what went over the fort tore the town down, therefore they stoped firing at us. We then ceased firing but brought the privateer out and took hur with us into Porto Port.

There was such a number of privateers on the coast that we ware falling in with some almost every day. In one day we took a leven priv-eteers and retaken vessels. In that number was three Portegee Brazeal ships, and a Spanish privateer of 16 guns came down to sea what we ware, and we took hur, but having no men to put on board of hur, we had to let hur go. We had then but 17 men on board with the marines. We runing down amongst the fleet, she made sail again and went off, we having at the same time 132 prisoners on board, but they had no way to come on deck, excepting by one scuttle and only one could come up at a time, and a brass 4 pounder pointing down the scuttle loaded with musket balls, and a sentry with match pistols and cutlash, every man being armed with pistols below or aloft.

At length Capt[ain] Bond agreed with the French capt[ai]ns to make a carteel of one of the vessels that was in ballast to take them into Vigo on conditions to purmit hur to return to Portoport, which they did with hon-our. In getting our prises into Lisbon, the master, being in one of the Brazel ships, got inside the Burlins and was lost, but the men were saved.

Coming out again we took a lugger [*L'Esperance*] of 8 guns, 4 swivels, and a long brass 9 pounder off of Vigo [22 December 1798]. I was sent on board to take hur into Porto Port, but while with the *Netley*, a fleet hove in sight to the sotherd. We stood for them, but a heavy frigate stood out from among them and gave us chace. I prepared my large lugs to keep hur before the wind upon one mast so that hur sails would not all be of any use to hur, but the *Netley* being to windward, the frigate luffed up for hur and the frigate being a French bilt ship made us jubus [dubious], but Capt[ain] Bond kept his wind till they gave him a gun, and the *Netley* returned the salute, then hoisting his colours, bore down upon him and ran under his quarter. She proved to be the *Manerva* which had been taken from the French.

I made sail and stood in for Porto, where this convoy was bound to. The frigate spoke me and inform'd me I must take charge of the convoy, which was a bout 40 sail. I inform'd him I had but 5 men onboard. He told me if acasion required to take a seaman out of each ship. Likewise he gave the pilot orders not to take me in till the convoy was all safe over the bar, and then the frigate left us.

The *Netley* was then gone on a cruise. The winds being unfavou[r]able, we lay off and on, day after day. In about a week we saw a lugger standing in for the convoy from the sotherd. I aplyed to the capt[ain] of the convoy for men to go and engage the luger, but there was not a man that would turn out. Therefore I stood out of the convoy and maid sail for the luger, but when they saw me, they up hallom afore the wind. Then I hall'd to the wind for the convoy. In about 10 days they all got in except our selves.

On Chrismas Eve, coming on to blow from the N. West, I stood off the land. In the night, laying too under the mizen lug, I fell in with a schoner. Laying two, hailing hur, I found she was from Lisbon bound to Viana with codfish. They took us to be an enemy by our lug sails and a privateer, but when they found we ware English and belong'd to the *Netley,* or "trees kealus" as the Portegees call'd her, [k]nowing we ware guarding there coast from the privateers, they ware rejoiced, and the capt[ain] told me if I would lay two by him, he would pilot me into Viana in the morning if I would follow him, which I agreed to.

About three A.M., blowing heavy, our mizen lug went overboard, mast and all. We got it on b[oar]d and lay two under a close reef mainsail, we being well to windward of the harbour. At daylight the schooner bore up and I followed him. We entered through the chanal and was in side the reef, standing a long shore with a leading wind, but before we reached the mouth of the harbour, the wind choped round to the N.W. and headed us, and the heavy surf roling over the reef, and not having room to ware, there was no way to escape but to plump them on shore. The schooner [*L'Esper-ance*] run on the beach amediately and I up helem and run under hur lee, it blowing, raining, thundered, and lightened a most tremendious that day and all that night. The English Counsel, Mr. Allen, came with a gard of sol-diers to protect the vessels from being plundered. We pitched tents with our sails and got the guns out and provisions that was not damaged and even the masts we got out of hur, but the schooner was totally lost and went to pieces before morning, and all hur cargo was drifted away and no more to be seen of hur.

When the Counsal had sold what was saved out of the luger it was allowed that there was not one hundred Lbs. lost by the lugger, and by the report of the Counsel to the capt[ain] I receiv'd great praise for my conduct when ariving in Porto Port from the Counsel and likewise from my com-mander when the *Netley* arived off the barr.

Mr. Allen, Vice Counsel, paid every attention both to me and my crew. He had a country seat on the subbords of the town, that we lived in and some more that had been taken in prises and caried into Vigo in Spain and was purmited to travel to Viana by land, and the Counsel put them under my command, being supperior with the rest of the prize masters.[1] While under the Counsels charge, I got aquainted with a genteel family within a few dores of us, and it was his wish that I would come and make his house and family as I would my own. They wished me to sleep in their house. At every evening, if I would not be there, I was sent for unless I was with the Counsel. I could not at that time understand any Portegees, excepting by our motions and behaviour, but I, upon that coast, had the privilage from Capt[ain] Bond to chuse one or two men that I was well assured I could depend on. Therefore I had one, and he understood the Portegee languige perfectly. This gentleman was well a quainted with the Counsel, where we had been several times before in respect of my duty.

This gental[ma]n had two sons, but the eldest was a young officer in the army, about 17 years of age, and bold in his temper. His mother was a lovely woman and of the most kind and afable wimen I ever was in com-pany with, even before hur husband, but he was one of the most kindest, free hearted men I ever met, for the most part of the Portegees dont purmit their wives and daughter to be amongst stranger, unless it is some particu-lar friend that they may introduce you to their family. But this I must say upon oath, though I was not aware of any mistrust or any temptation what-

[1] In a letter of 4 July 1797, Samuel Hood wrote to Admiral Jervis describing his illfated effort to take Vigo. He attributed the failure to "extraordinary" poor intelligence provided by Vice-Consul Allen. Allen's kindness to Nagle may have been, in part, an effort to improve his rep-utation with the Royal Navy.

ever, but that lovely woman gave way to hur own inclinations and was determended to be folse to a true and loving husband, which I loved and respected while I ever new him. Even hur sun, that had no suspicion, if he and me walked out after night, she would give him the greates caution that I should not be hurt by the soldiers taking there rounds in the night, though I caried my side arms and pocket pistols as well as they did, but no sooner than he gave the contersigne they would walk off and leave us.[1]

One day hur sun invited me and my linkister [interpreter] to ride out into the country upon an excurcion. We stop'd at a wine house and took a little refresment. In our return, about two miles from town, he took a small whissel out of his pocket and begin to blow it. I understood before that it was a signal. I begin to be a little doubtful of him, and seeing two men on horse back came riding out a wood towards us, I put myself in a posicion of defence and my comrod likewise. The young officer burst out a laughing and when these men came up he told my linkister they ware friends and I need not be under any apprihension while we ware together. In entering the town we stoped at a very genteel house and introduced me to a hansome young woman and told me that was to be his intended bride. They treated us to some good wine. We then returned home.

We had now been about a month in Viana. By consulting with my linkister, I thought it best to prepare for Porto Port, as I wished to get on b[oar]d. There was 12 men in all, beside myself. The Counsel gave me the money that was allowed for the men, beside money I drew upon my agent in Porto, which was Sq[uire] Cazy. This gentl[eman] and his wife understanding that we ware going away the next morning, he came with us a cross the river and after landing, walking up the road, we came to a church, and who should I see but his wife and a servent girl with two baskets, one with provisions ready dressed and the other with wine, and desired us all to come into a large porch and regale our selves before we went any farther. We then started on the road, and while walking about a mile, she fill'd my pockets with amons [almonds], raeaons [raisins], and different kinds of dried fruit, unpurceiv'd by him. Coming to the foot of a hill, we parted and arived in Porto the day following.

Shortly after the *Netley* came off the barr, and we went on board. Runing off Vigo, we fell in with an English brig taken by a Spanish privateer, but she was in ballast. I was sent on b[oar]d to take hur into Porto, where

[1] Nagle is confusing with regard to his acquaintances at Vigo. The editor's reading of the journal is that the consul, Mr. Allen, arranged for Nagle to board with neighbors. Although Nagle is not clear about how close the relationship became, he suggests that the wife of Allen's friend exceeded the bounds of propriety in her show of affection for him. Nagle may be teasing his reader a bit, or he may be salving a guilty conscience.

she had been bound to for port wine. When I came off the bar and was runing in, the fort fired me off, thinking we ware load'd and not water sufficient for a loaded vessel, but being light there was water sufficient as the
head pilot inform'd me afterwards. The wind being dead on shore from the
westward, I had to hall close to the wind to get off shore as fast as I could.

It conn[ti]n[ue]d on to blow hard from the S.W. I found the ship was
making water fast. I found by three Spaniards, prisoners I had on b[oar]d,
that she had receiv'd some shot between wind and water, and we could not
find out where the leaks was. We kept one pump constantly going. By 12
o'clock in the night it blew a gale with rain. I got hur under close reef topsails and foresail, but carreing away our fore and aft mainsail, I then took
in the foresail and fore topsail and laid hur two under the main topsail. She
then lay two very well, but the ballast in the whole was sand and nothing
to prevent the sand from washing to the pump. It would choke, though we
pumped a great deal on deck, and while lifting the pum[p] to clear it and
put it down again the leak gained on us. We then got both pumps agoing,
but they soon choaked again. In lifting the larboard pump, as we had the
starbourd three of four times, we found it was splised, therefore it was useless. In bending an other mainsail and lifting the one pump so often, that by
daylight she was two thirds full of water, but the gale had luled a good
deal, but the ballace washing about begin to heave hur on hur side, or on
hur beam ends, I found there was no hopes of saving the vessel.

We got a six oard boat out, and in hoisting hur out in a hurry we lost
three oars, but with great difficulty we got hur under the stern. We could
not get either bread or water, being below. I allowed we ware about ten or
a leven leagues from the high lands of Viana. I found it time to leave hur.
They all got over the stern by a rope, excepting a Portegee boy and myself,
which was the last, and he begin to cry. He understood the Spaniards was
going to cut the painter and leave us behind. I having a brace of ships pistols in my belt, I drew one and told them I would kill the first man that let
go the rope till the boy was in the boat. I hove another rope over the stern,
and while they ware receiving the boy, I was down likewise.

I went aft and took charge of the boat. I kept hur before the wind and as
the see fell I edged in for the land. All our crew in the boat was 9 in number: 3 Spanish prisoners, 3 Portegees beside the boy, ware friendly with the
Spanish at that time, the capt[ain's] son which was left on board, being sick,
and myself. We puled with two oars and steared with the other. We continued all day and all night in that situation. In the morning before day light
we ware within 3 or 4 miles of the shore. They became so weary that they
hove the two oars across the boat and fell asleep. I endeavoured to encourage them, but all in vain. I found the boat was nearly as full of water as we

had left the ship, and as I had not before mentioned when we ware about 500 yards she was under water.

The men sitting on the seats asleep, I laid my stearing oar in and turned to bailing till I had got hur nearly clear of water. I then roused up the Portegees and they assisted to clear the boat entierly. They took fresh courage. We got in shore about 4 o'clock P.M. but could not land, the surf being very high. We pulled a long shore till we made the entrance of Comenia River, a Portegee fort being there, and night coming on, I was determened to risk it through the surf, beside I understood by the Portegees that the Spaniards wanted them to land on the north side, under the Spanish fort, beside, for the want of water and nourishment, we ware nearly helpless. I up hellem and away we went. The Portegee soldiers looking at us, they came on the beach to receive us, but the boat struck a rock that lay under water, which we could not see, and stove hur to peaces, and we ware left a floating in the surf, nearly helpless. The soldiers came in to their necks in the water and brougt us out, but they put us into the fort, not [k]nowing weather we ware friends or enemies, but the Portegees that I had with me inform the commander who we ware, and knowing the *Netley* protected there coast, he took me to his own room. I having money, I gave him a half joe and he sent two soldiers to a public house about a mile off and brought a feather bead, wine, and fowls for the capt[ain] of the fort and myself and a good supply for the few soldiers that ware there and the men that ware with me, which refresh'd us very much that night.

In the morning the commander inform'd me that we must go to Commenia to be overhall'd and give information from whence we came, which was four miles out of our road. However we started with a guard, and ariving there, was overhall'd by the Squiers, and all being rectified, they gave me a passport and a small sum of money to take us to Viana, which was 4 leagues. That evening we arived in Viana. Being acquainted with the Counsel, beforementioned, I applyed to him. He informed me there was a capt[ain] of a vessel had been taken by the Spanierds and was then on his way to Portoport, and if I could make it convenient, we could both start in the morning, and he would find mules for us both, and inform'd me where I would find the capt[ain] in the morning.

I took my departure from the Counsel that evening and went to see my old friends, which I have heretofore made mention of. Ariving at there habutation, they ware rejoiced to see me, and supper was provided, but he purceiving my shoes was torn in traveling, without saying anything to me, he went out and brought some new shoes to fit me, he supposing that I had lost everything and moneless [moneyless] (by the acount they had received), which was true excepting money. When the shoes was fited he then went into his bedroom and brought out a bag of money, opened it, and would insist on my taking as much as I thought proper. It was all silver and gold. I refused and told him I had money, but he would not be satisfied till I show'd him nine half joes, beside what I had spent. Then he apeared to be satisfied. He would not receive any money for the shoes and likewise when I was in his house before mentioned would not receive any money from me. I then having two watches about me, I beged he wout give the one I gave him to a watchmaker to clean it, as it had got wet in the boat, and to keep it till I sent for it, being then valued at 25 dollars. He promised he would, but it was not my intention ever to send for it after the kindest treatment I could receive from my greatest friends.

We had an excelent super, but I must confess my felings was hurt by the conduct of his wife. He served my plate upon his left hand and his wife on the right, then serving himself. His wife observing, according to hur opinion that he had taken the preference to himself, she took hur fork and put the prime piece into my plate and put what he had put into my plate into his plate, which would apear very singular in many parts that I had travel'd at that time, however it all pased as kindness to a stranger, which it apeared to me that it pleas'd him in hur so doing.

The young officer, being present at supper, was to escort me before daylight to the place where the capt[ain] was to be ready. We had not went above half way to the main street when two soldiers came up to us drawing there swords. We both drew, but he steped forward and cried out "Leguardo," and they seeing him in officers uniforms, they run and was soon out of sight. We went on and found the capt[ain] preparing. The young officer being aquainted with the family, we remained till daylight, ful of friendship and mirth. We took our departure. The Counsel had a flat and the mules with a man to bring them back. We cross'd the river and arived in Porto about 9 o'clock that night, which is call'd 10 leagues, but cruel, bad roads, rocks, sands, swamps, and rivers, where a horse could not go.

I remained sum time in Porto til the *Netley* arived and then went on board. Laying off Vigo, we fell in with a brig of sixteen guns bound into Vigo, taken by a French cutter mounting 18 long 18 pounders. She proved to be American brig [*Nymph*] from Philadelphia bound up the Straits. This was in the year [26 March] 1800. I was sent on board to take charge, though the capt[ain] when taken was left on board. He told Capt[ain] Bond that the French cutter was crusing for the *Netley* in the latt'd of Lisbon. I was ordered to take the brig into the first port that would be most convenient.

I run off Porto barr, came to an anchor, and having but a light air of wind and the pilots would not atempt to take a vessel in without being high tide and a favouable wind, beside having a boat a head with a ketch anchor, I then begin to lift my anchor, having but 5 men with myself, and the capt[ain] walking the quarter deck. Having no windless or capstan, we had a leading takle to the quarter deck, and when the takle was a block we had to stoper the cable till we fleeted our purchase. In the meantime, being calm, I had my topsails hoisted to the mast head, the fore topsail crased aback to heave hur head off shore, and the main topsail to shiver the wind. We pulling with all our might to get the anchor to the bows, I observed the swell was drawing us in shore.

I said to the capt[ain], "Will you give us a pul till we get the anchor to the bows?"

"No," said he, "but if you get my vessel on shore, I will blow your brains out."

It inraged me. I let go the fall, and the four men held on and took a turn standing, looking on. I run to the armchest and took out a brace that I had loaded myself and steped on the weather side where he was. "Now, Sir, I am ready. Is your pistol loaded?"

"Yes."

"Then lay holt of it, or walk down into the cabin. I will let you [k]now that I command this vessel." He said no more but walked into the cabin. We turned too and got the anchor up, cated [catted], and fish'd, and secured. We ketched a breeze, sprung up from the N.W., and kep away for Lisbon.

In the evening he came on deck and apeared to be very sociable. I overhall'd the guns to see weather they ware in order, as there was a great number of small privateers lurking about the Burlins, a few leagues to the N. of the rock of Lisbon. Laying near the entrance on the north side of the river Tagus, it is a remarkable high mountain, 22 miles west of Lisbon, Long'd 9°35'W., Lat'd 38°42'N., and Porto port lays in 41°15'N. L'd, Long'd 10°W. by account.

On the passage the capt'n was very desirous I would run away and he would take me as his chief mate. When we got into Lisbon I saw his deception and put no trust in him. Whin we came to Bellam Castle we had to come to an anchor till further orders. In lifting our anchor he went and got some more men to help us to take the vessel up. When coming to an anchor, our agent came on b[oar]d. The capt[ain] demanded an order from me to the Counsel to pay those men, thinking he would trick me. The agent told me to give it to him and the Counsel would laugh at him. I gave it to him. He then required me to go with him. I did so and went to the Counsel. When he gave it to him, and he looked at it, the Counsel looked at me, and we both laughed. The Counsel told him if he hired a hundred men he would have to pay them, as one eighth goes to the vessel that retook hur from the enemy. The Counsel laugh'd and I laugh'd and he bit his lips with anger, and I thought I was about square with him for his trickery to me. The brig was delivered up to the capt[ain], and shortly after the *Netley* came into Lisbon. I went on board.

In a few days we put to see and run off Vigo. Cruising, at about 10 o'clock A.M., we ware standing to the south, we discovered a sail standing for us till she could make out that it was the *Netley*. We ware in the rig of a galyot chiefly, but in 20 minutes we could be a schooner, but they had been deceived so often by us that the sight of us was a dred to them, but this was the cutter [*La Légère*] that the French capt[ain] told the Americans he was cruising for the *Netley* and wished he could meet us, but now when she perfectly new what we ware, she halled hur wind, standing to the north to get into Vigo. We put about and stood after hur, but we still kept to leeward betwen hur and the shore. The wind being light, they got their swepes out. We then got our sweeps out and in a dead calm we could pull the *Netley* three mile in an hour. She proved to be the same vessel before mentioned.

We ware prepared and had our (boarding) nettings up, knowing hur force, which was 18 long 18 pounders and one hundred men. Our force was 16–24 pounders and our full compliment was 60 men, but by taking so many vessels we often had more. We sailing faster than the cutter, we came up alongside of hur. They ware for boarding, but our boarding netting being three quarters of an inch and nearly up to the catharpens [catharpins], which made it very difficult, the French got into the riging and netting to cut away, but we being prepared with cutlash, pistols, and boarding pikes, beside we had a brass 4 pounder we could ship fore and aft with musket balls that they dreaded. Being close quarter, our great guns was not used except an oppertunity served. Likewise, we could fier our guns twice to there once, there guns being long.

In the smoke I purceiv'd the French capt[ain] drawing a pistol from his belt to fire at our capt[ain] that was giving command. I drew a pistol at the same time and let him have the contents. At the same time a stout Frenchman made a blow at me with a large hanger, from the netting, but the man behind me saw the blow and covered my head with his boarding pike, which was cut that it fell and the bare pint struck me in the head and I fell, but the man ketch'd up the pike and run it into his body and he fell between the two vessels. I recovered in a few minutes.

They finding they could not board us, and there capt[ain] slain, and our small brass piece made a scattering on their decks, they found it in vain and struck their colours [29 May 1800] in less than 30 minutes. We had no men killed but a good many wounded. What was kiled on b[oar]d the cutter we had no purticular account of, as some went over board, but a great many wounded.

We cleared the decks and repaird the riging and took hur into Lisbon. We refited and refreshed the crew. The cutter was sold into the Portogees service as a man of war.

We put to see again. Runing off Porto we took a Spanish lugger. I went on board, and in going to Lisbon, the *Netley* in company, we took two more, and the *Netley* going on a cruise, left me in charge of them. I took them in, and laying there under the charge of Mr. Lynes & Gill, our agents, Mr. Lynes had bought a privateer schooner that had been taken, and I laying in one of the luggers, close two hur off of Buckeys Stairs, about the center of the town, which is a square where the gentry generally walk and meat [meet] upon acasion on the River Tagos. Mr. Loynes wished I would "give an I," or take charge of the schooner, as well as the rest, having only one old man on board, a Portegee, and all hur powder on board.

One forenoon, being on board my own lugger with the men and one of the prisemasters belonging to one of the luggers, we purceived the flames and smoke coming up the main hatchway. I jumped into the skiff and asked who would follow me. They, knowing the danger, refused, till one man by the name of Wm. Grimes came with me and a bucket. We got on b[oar]d as fast as posseble. The merchant ships that lay all around hur wore away their cables to the klinch, [k]nowing she had a good deal of powder in and expecting she would blow up every moment. We got on board, and the old man was sitting before the fire in the hatchway and the bulkhead all in a blaze. There was the lazareet between the magazeen and the fire, which was not more than 10 or 12 feet.

The oul man, as soon as he saw me, cried out, "O, munta frees," and rubing his hands, which was that he was very cold.

"Yes, dam you," said I, "you will be hot a nuff presently," jumping down the hatchway, with a crowbar in my hand, and stove away the bulk head, as he kept heaving water wherever I stove down the bricks and boards. Some bricks in the fireplace had been broken, therefore the bulk head ketched fire on the opposite side. We got the fire out but could not be certain. I hailed the nearest ship to send there boat to take the powder out of the schooner, but the mate told me he could not get a man to go. I inshured him there was no danger.

At length one of the men came with the mate in the lanch [launch] a long side. I broke open the magazeen scuttle and took out 14 whole and half barrels of powder, several boxes of hand granades, several boxes of muskets catriges, and boxes of glas handgronades, which are to heave by hand, where you see them most numerous for boarding. I took it all on b[oar]d the lugger, which I was in myself and would not allow any fier on b[oar]d while I had charg of it. If she had been blown up there would of been a great distruction both by the houses on shore and the shiping laying roun about hur. I went to the agent and inform'd him, but he had the news before I inform'd him. I and my comrad receiv'd great aplause for our conduct, but I had a new suit of clothing spoilt for my labour. Shortly after the *Netley* came in and Capt[ain] Bond was inform'd by the agent of my conduct in saving his vessel and a number of lives, which gave me a great deal of privilage both on b[oar]d and a shore.

The *Netley* being complete for see we all went on b[oar]d and put to see. After passing Fort Julian, which stands on the north side and west end in entering the Tagos up to Lisbon, we fell in with a Portegee fishing boat. They inform'd us there was a Spanish privateer laying under the fort at an anchor with an English brig they had taken the same day. We run in shore and by this time it was dark. We saw both schooner and brig. We lowered the boat down, armed, and boarded hur as we run under hur stern. When we had possession we lufed up for the schooner. I was order to be ready with 25 men to jump on board as soon as we tutched hur sides. The anchor was let go the moment we tuched hur main chains, head and stern. We jumped on board. Some run below, and some that did not got wounded. We cleared the decks. The officers run down in the cabin. I told them to remain there and they would not be hurt. I claped a sentry on the dore, and we cut the cable and made sail out to see, and the *Netley* hove up hur anchor and followed us.

In the morning we fell in with a fleet of Portegee merchantmen under convoy of an English 24 gun ship man of war and a privateer of 16 guns. The privateer had seen the Spanish schooner the day before and was afraid to engage hur and supposing she and the *Netley* was coming to take the convoy, begin to fire at us by whole broad sides, and we could not fire at hur without damaging or hurting some of the merchat men, till the *Netley* made sail and spoke the commedore. Then they ceased, but there shot was at random and done us no harm, excepting cuting our riging. We went in with them and our prises. The Portegees thought to take them from us, as they ware taken under there forts, but we took the privateer out in the night and sent hur to England. The English privateer lay below Bellom Castle and would not come up to Lisbon for fear of our captain.

We put to see again and run to Porto Port and went in as soon as we came to an anchor. We ware inform'd that a French privateer of 14 guns had come off the barr and had taken an English brig that lay under the fort. Being loaded, and not able to get hur in till the tide served, therefore the Portegees new they would have to pay for hur. Being taken under cover of there guns, they sent out a Kings lugger mounted 12 twelve pounders to retake the brig. Being heavyer mettal than the Frenchman off Viana, she came up with them. The privateer engaged the luger and in a quarter of an hour took the luger. The next day we ariving and hearing of the event, the capt[ain] got under way to go out, but the pilots said it was unpossible, as the wind was due west and right into the harbour, and the channel too narrow to beat out over the barr. The capt[ain] was determend to take hur out himself and he beat hur out. The pilots said there never was the like done before over that bar.

We stood to the nothord, but the wind died away almost calm. The capt[ain] seeing a fishing boat within gunshot, we fired a 24 pounder over them and they came a long side amediately, [k]nowing the *Netley*. We took the men on b[oar]d. The master and myself with 25 men took to the oars and pulled all night to the nothord. We had no other arms but pistols and cutlashes. By daylight we ware off Viana and saw the brig in the offin. The *Netley* had ketched a breze of wind in the night and had got farther to the nothord than we ware. The lugger was close in shore, but the wind was very light. We made for the brig and came up with hur and boarded hur. I rem[aine]d on board with 5 men and 9 Spaniards. The master went to the *Netley* and from thence to the lugger, pulled up a stern and boarded hur, but they could of kill'd every man if they had fired, but they said they new the *Netley* would take them, and if they had fired they expected no quarter from us. The privateer had got off Vigo, and seeing hur prizes taken she was glad to get in hurself. We took the prizes into Porto Port. Capt[ain] Bond and ships company agreed to make the lugger a present to the King again, and I having charge of hur, I received a letter to deliver hur up to the Kings officer when he came on board, which I did according to my orders. We went out again and fell in with a Sweedish ship that had been taken by the Spaniard. I was sent on board and took charge of hur, though the capt[ain] and mate were left on board.

About 10 o'clock the next day, having light winds and fair weather, coming in with the bar off Porto Port, distance about 5 mile, I purceived a French privateer schooner boarding every vessel that was coming into the bar, and an English man of war of 24 guns was laying at an anchor without the bar and took no notice of hur. At the same time a convoy of Portegees vessels was to the sotherd of harbour, distance about 5 or 6 miles. The Frenchman was now coming to board me, but when about half way, they purceived a vessel standing out to the westward from the convoy. The Frenchman new hur and amediately called them back again and got the boat in and made sail. I amediately new hur to be the *Netley*. This French schoon[er] was supposed to out sail anything on the coast, which made hur so daring with the 20 gun ship, but the *Netley* having such a name made them jubus [dubious] of hur. The *Netley* was coming up with hur very fast.

When we ware going over the bar, about 9 o'clock P.M., the *Netley* got with in gun shot, and to the Frenchmans misfortune, shot away the head of hur foremast. Then she was amediately a long side of hur. They struck and was brough[t] into Porto next morning.

In a few days I returned on board, and we put to sea. Cruising off Laguardo we saw a schooner coming down upon us before the wind, and we were then in the rig of a Dutch galyot, which I before mentioned we could be in the rig of a schooner in twenty minutes, and when our ports were closed and caps on the muzels of the guns they could not purceive we had any till they got near us. This schooner had a French sailor on board that had been taken by us twice before. He inform'd the French capt[ain] that we ware the "trees keelus" as they call'd us, having three keels, but the French capt[ain] thought he new better and said we ware a Sweedish galyot, as they ware very comon then on the Portegee coast trading from Hollond. However they came down so close that they could purceive we had guns but not at any great distance with the spy glass. They hall'd their wind. We then made sail. In a short time we ware abrest of them. They up hellem and claped hur before the wind, but all would not do, we ware amediately along side of hur and they struck their colours.

The Frenchman that we had taken before got up on one of the guns and cried out, "Capt[ain], how you do." We all new him.

The capt[ain] asked him why he did not [k]now the *Netley*. He replyed, "Yes, Sir, I [k]now de trees keelus. De capt[ai]n no belief me. I tel him many times. Now he tink so two."

We got the prisoners on b[oar]d and this Frenchman went to the capt[ain] and told him he must stay on board the *Netley*. The capt[ain] asked him if he wanted to enter for the *Netley*. He replyed, "Yes, Sir, I go no more from de trees keelus. He take me tree times, I must stay here." Therefore he remain'd on board. Som tim after, we retook an English ship from Newfound land which had been taken by the Spaniards. She had seven thousand kentals [quintals] of kodfish on board, and in sending hur into Lisbon, this Frenchman was one sent in hur. In going in in a gale of wind the ship was lost and all hands perished excepting this Frenchman. He got on shore and left Lisbon, and we never heard of him afterwards.

The *Netley*, though a man of war, having such excelent yousage on board from Capt[ain] Bond that we could at any time get as many seamen out of the merchant ships as he wanted and would not except of them unless they ware good seaman, I being on shore waiting for the *Netley* to come off the bar at Porto and having orders from the capt[ain] to enter some good seam[en], and when they had intilegence, there ware more came than I would except of, but I took 28 men and a good many of them ware mates and boatswains of merchantmen, and when I came on b[oar]d we had more men than we wanted. Capt[ain] Bond runing into Lisbon in my absence had entered some there. In a few days after we fell in with a gansey [Guernsey] privateer that had all hur men pressed by a sixty four and had not men sufficient to take hur into harbour. Capt[ain] Bond gave him the priviledge of having any of the new hand if they chewsed to go, but all he could get was one Sweed and a boy.

Capt[ain] Bond took a delight in making his ships company comfortable, and when in harbour as much liberty as could be expected. He could not bare to punish men at the gangway, but he contrived a collar of one inch plank to ware round there necks with a large padlock for any certain time, which they dreaded more than floging. Likewise for lighter crimes was a scarlot cap full of black tossels hung all over it. When any strangers came on board, these men that had them on would sneak a way below for shame.

We fell in with a Merican ship that had lost hur masts and hur side stove in, which made hur so leakey they could scarcely keep hur free. We sent men on board and carpenters on board, tared a tarpolan, and ocam [oakum] over it, and nail'd it well over with boards, which stoped the leak considerable, and took hur in tow and caried hur into Lisbon where she was bound to. She belonged to the notherd.

On our cruises there was two privateers hove in sight, a cutter of 18 guns, the schooner of 16 guns, and we gave chase after them. Coming up, we run betwen both of them with our colours hoisted. The cutter fired two broad sides, great guns and small arms, and then made sail. We having the schooner under our lee, when the cutter made sale, he gave hur one 24 p[ounde]r, which dismounted one gun, killed one man, and wounded several more. At the same time the capt[ain] gave me orters to give the schooner a gun, which I did and split hur stem. The men left their quarter and the capt[ain] hall'd the coluurs down. We sent the boat on board and brought the capt[ain] on board. They proved to be English privateers from the Isle of Ganzey [Guernsey]. They new we ware an English man of war, but they expected we would press there men. As luck would have it, they done us no harm excepting cutting some of our riging. We took one man out of the schooner, not as we wanted him, but to certify as a witness. The capt[ain] rought to the Admiralety and there was strict orders sent to Gernsey that the capt[ain] of the cutter was never more to have command of a vessel out of the port, if known.

We then run north as far as Cape Finister and was laying two, close under the Cape, sounding, and the capt[ain] was taking the remarks of the Cape, of a thick foggy morning [13 August 1800]. All of a suddent appeared a verry large ship in the fog. We up hellem before the wind, but coming to vew hur with the spy glass and counting hur port, we found she carried only 24 guns. We hall'd our wind for hur. She hoisted hur Spanish colours. When we got a long side we up English colours and gave hur three or four of our 24 pounders. They finding our mettle so heavy, they run from there quarter and struck there colours.

We boarded hur. She proved to be a fine packet [*La Reyna Luisa*] from South America bound to Spain with a good quantity of Kings money on board. She had two capt[ains] and a Spanish general on b[oar]d. Mr. Buchan, master, took charge, he being my suprior officer, while I took the officers on board. When we ordered the men into the cabin and overhall'd them, we found a good quantity of dollars, half joes, doubleelons, 7 lb. bars and 14 lb. bars of gold. We overhall'd the men twice and found as much with them the last time as we did the first. We found doubleoons sowed in the soles of there stockings, 2 deep, from one end to the other. All the money we found was among the men and officers and some bars they hove overboard. The general got away with 4 gold bars, as the Spanis[h] capt[ain] inform Capt[ain] Bond afterwards. We brought hur into Lisbon. She had a great quantity of curious articles on board such as curious mats, wild fir skins, one of them was so butiful, dimond cut of different colours and not more than three and a half square, it sold for 38 dollars on b[oar]d the *Netley* Schooner. She had on b[oar]d 30,000 neats tongues dried, ostrige feathers in stands, length about two feet and about 40 in one stand, and 45 pigs of tooth and egge, beside a great quantity of goods in boxes which I cannot give an acount of. The ship was a fast sailor. The Spanish capt[ain] inform'd us that two English frigates had chased them three days and could not cetch them. When the prisoners were sent on shore, I remain'd on b[oar]d the Spanish ship with the men I had with me.

Having some business on shore I landed at the lower end of the town [Lisbon] where the ship lay and walked up to town, but being two late to go to the ship, about 10 o'clock at night I went down to Buckleys Stares to go on b[oar]d the *Netley* that lay off in the stream. While standing at the foot of the stairs, next to the water, calling a boat, two men came down the steps behind me. One, raped [wrapped] up in a cloak, clap'd a small sord to my brest. The other, behind me, had a Portegee dirk and put the point of it to my side. I had no arms, neither would they allow me to put my hand into my pocket for fear I had arm. They took my gold watch, a silver chain purse, and about forty five gold dollars and even some copper in my jacket pocket. I had a large gold ring on my finger which they did not observe. They then left me. I went up the steps when they ware at a small distance to see where they went to, but when they see me follow them, they gave chase after me. I took up a large street, [k]nowing if they came up with me they would kill me. I run for life. Coming to a large brick building that was broke down, I run into the back side of it and covered myself with bricks and the dry morter. When they came up, they looked all round, both in side and out and then discoursed together and went off. I lay there till day light, for fear they might be watching me. When day light apeared, I got up and brushed myself as well as I could and went and got some refreshment and went on board. The next day I received two hundred Pounds [sterling], therefore I only regreted the loss of my watch, though I had others at the same time.

We went out, and standing to the nothord we saw a schooner at a long distance off. We made sail and was coming up very fast with hur, when to our surpris she hove two and took in hur sale when she was above two leagues off. Coming up to hur, our capt[ain] asked him what he hove two for.

"O, I [k]now de trees kealus. No can run away, so I stay," which made all hands laugh.

We took hur into Lisbon. Ariving, Capt[ain] Bond received a Letter of Preferment from the Board of war. It was a severe cut to the ships crew. Capt[ain] Bond wished to take me with him, but not having a nother ship apointed, he could not take me with him.

•   •   •

*While the* Netley *wreaked its own peculiar brand of havoc off Spain and Portugal, in the Indian Ocean, several oversize French frigates were creating bad news for British merchants and thus for the Royal Navy. Merchantman and shipowner Robert Eastwick sees his fortunes rise and fall several times over as two heavy frigates duke it out off the coast of India. One of the combatants, the French* La Forte, *launched at Rochefort in 1795, was, at the time, the largest frigate ever built originally as a frigate.*

# ROBERT EASTWICK

~

# The Fortune of War

## 1799

*B*orn in London in 1772, Robert Eastwick went to sea in the merchant
*service at age twelve. After being taken by the press gang and serv-
ing very briefly on board HMS* Inconstant *prior to the Napoleonic wars,
Eastwick returned to the merchant service on board an East Indiaman. He
eventually settled with his wife near Calcutta and hauled freight in the
East Indies, dodging potentially ruinous confrontations with pirates and
the king's enemies. Finally his luck runs out, but not without a few twists
of fate.*

I HAVE MENTIONED how dangerous was the Bay of Bengal in these
days, owing to the French men-of-war, and privateers that were continu-
ally cruising about in search of our merchant ships. It was computed that
within a single twelve-month British shipping to the value of not less than
two millions sterling had been captured or sunk. There were three notorious frigates which every one had learnt to dread, the *Preneuse*, the *La Prudente*, and the *La Forte*. It was from the latter two ships that I had escaped
when returning from Bencoolen in 1797, and by a strange coincidence they
were both captured in the month of February, 1799, though at points many
hundreds of miles apart. The victory over the *La Forte* I shall presently
relate. Her companion ship, the *La Prudente*,[1] on the 16th of the same

---

[1] La Prudente, *30 (pierced for 42): Taken by the* Daedalus, *32, H. L. Ball, after an action of 57 minutes, Cape of Good Hope Station, February 9, 1799.* (Steel's Naval Chronologist of the War, *p. 20)*

month, was sighted early one morning off the south-east coast of Africa by the *Daedalus*, Captain Ball, who immediately gave chase, and by midday brought her into action, and in fifty-seven minutes forced her to strike. She was returning to Europe from the Isle of France, and had three hundred men on board. In the next year the *Preneuse*[1] likewise met her fate off the same coast, being run ashore and burnt by her own captain in order to escape capture at the hands of a British squadron that was in pursuit of her. But before these three frigates were taken their presence had paralyzed our Eastern trade, and the rates asked for insurance were so prohibitive, that at last I was totally unable to afford the premiums demanded, and on the voyage I am now describing I remained uninsured.

During my passage to Bombay I had been most fortunate, not having sighted a single hostile sail, and on my return had arrived as far as the Balasore Roads, close to Juggernauth Pagoda, and in the waters where the Bengal pilots are always cruising, without encountering any of the enemy, so that I was already congratulating myself upon my good fortune, when at the eleventh hour I found myself all undone.

For towards evening, while we were becalmed and on the lookout for a pilot, a large ship was sighted in the offing, which, on a breeze springing up, stood towards us. As she came near I felt sure she was a man-of-war, and the cut of her sails soon indicated a French one. My belief was presently confirmed by seeing her fire a shot to windward at another vessel of my own size that chanced to be passing. As, however, her chase was after me, she did not alter her course, so I crowded on all sail and endeavoured to escape. But I soon found the frigate was faster than I, for she overhauled us rapidly, and after a time brought her bow-chasers to bear, and sent a shot after us. It showed that we were within her range, for the ball went clean through our main and fore sails, making great holes in them, and carrying away some of the rigging. In this extremity I altered my course, and stood in towards a sand-bank in the Balasore Roads, with various soundings from ten to four fathoms, and considered dangerous to large ships. The Frenchman evidently had this feeling and redoubled his fire, his aim being very accurate, and the shot going over our deck, and through our sails and cutting away our rigging. The man at the helm was so alarmed that I was obliged to threaten him to keep him at his duty, but with the effect of making him steer very badly. It now became a stiff breeze, and the enemy having drawn quite close, evidently with a view to ending the matter, made disposition to give me a broadside. As such would have

[1] La Preneuse, *44: Run on-shore near Port Louis, Isle of France, by the* Tremendous, *74, J. Osborn, and* Adamant, *50, W. Hotham, and destroyed by the boats of those ships under Lieut. Gray, of the* Adamant, *December 11.* (Steel's Naval Chronologist of the War, *p.* 22)

sunk me, or at any rate occasioned great loss of life, and it being evident that to hold out longer was only risking the safety of those on board, and that there was no alternative but to strike, I threw my sails aback. And so at 9 p.m. on the last day of February, 1799, I was forced to haul down my colours and surrender my ship.

I cannot describe my feelings of mortification as I saw the boarding party put foot on my deck and heard the officer summon me to give up my vessel. It was the first time I had ever been placed in such a position, and although there was no disgrace in being captured by an enemy so superior, still my spirit rebelled at having to strike my colours to a Frenchman.

Having placed a prize officer and crew on board the *Endeavour*, I and my chief and second mates were taken as prisoners to the frigate, which proved to be the famous *La Forte*. She now put about and proceeded to chase, and soon captured, the vessel at which she had first fired, and which was the *Mornington*, Captain Cooke, with a valuable cargo and sixty thousand dollars specie on board. On this capture they put a prize master and a very considerable body of men, and also a commissary with an additional crew to secure the money. The two prizes were then told to keep within signalling distance until further orders were sent them in the morning, and all the ships were hove to for the night.

Captain Cooke and Mr. Mackerel (a passenger on board the *Mornington*) were brought prisoners on board the frigate, and sent to keep us company on deck, where I had seated myself behind one of the guns. I was previously acquainted with the former, and we were comforted to meet, even under such distressing circumstances. He, like myself, had lost his entire fortune with his ship, and we mutually condoled with each other upon the unlucky fate that had robbed us of our all just as safety seemed within our grasp.

There were several other English prisoners on board the *La Forte*, from whom we learnt the treatment we might expect. Their food was salt beef, boiled in vinegar, to which was added boiled peas as a substitute for bread. Only one quart of water was allowed *per diem*, and not a glass of wine or spirits.

As for the discipline of the ship, it was very slack. It was not at all unusual to see one of the foremast men, with his beef in his hands, eating it while walking the quarter-deck, and claiming an equal right to do it with the commanding officer, thus, I suppose, demonstrating the claims of liberty, equality, and brotherhood. Nor was any scruple made of playing cards on the quarter-deck. The lieutenants generally came on deck with only trousers and an open shirt, often a check one, so that it was almost impossible to distinguish them. The men, however, went through their duty with alacrity and were obedient to orders.

Amongst the prisoners were two officers of the 28th Light Dragoons. They had been in charge of 107 men of their regiment, who were being conveyed on board the *Osterley* from Madras to Calcutta, when that ship was captured, about a week previously to us, by the frigate. An exception had been made in their favour, for they were most courteously treated, especially by Captain Beaulieu La Loup, the second in command on board the *La Forte*. Whilst we were sitting talking about these matters, a message was brought to us that Captain Cooke, Mr. Mackerel, and myself were required aft. We immediately went to the quarter-deck, where we found the admiral [*Rear-Admiral Marquis de Sercey*], a fine old man and a very distinguished officer. He told us that he was sorry for us, as he was informed that we were the owners, as well as the commanders, of the ships he had just taken, but that we must console ourselves by the reflection that it was the fortune of war, and that, seeing what a loss we had already sustained, he would give us our liberty, and also allow the passenger, Mr. Mackerel, to accompany us, and that in the morning a long boat and all our personal property would be placed at our disposal and permission granted us to make our way ashore.

The French admiral's reference to the "fortune of war" was soon to find another illustration; for at the very time he was speaking there was a fine English man-of-war within a few miles. This was the *La Sybille*, of forty-four guns, and commanded by Captain Cook, one of the best officers in his Majesty's service, and a son of the great Captain Cook, whose ships the *Resolution* and the *Discovery* I had once seen when a boy.[1] Captain Cook, of *La Sybille*, had made an extraordinary quick passage from Madras in search of this very Frenchman who had taken us, having been informed that *La Forte* was creating the utmost havoc upon our commerce at the head of the Bay. On arriving at the Sand Heads he had cruised about for three days, but failing to sight *La Forte* had almost given up all hope of meeting her, when the flashes of the bow-chasers fired at me were observed by his sailing master, Mr. Douglas, who at once gave it as his opinion that they proceeded from the firing of cannon, although on account of the great distance no reports were heard. Captain Cook was of a different opinion, considering the flashes were caused by sheet or summer lightning on the horizon; but he yielded to his sailing master's opinion, and stood towards the direction indicated, and soon found that the enemy he was in search of was discovered.

The *La Forte* was a frigate of fifty guns, 24-pounders, and was 170 feet long and 45 feet beam. Her admiral and captain were most distinguished

[1] La Sybille *was commanded by Captain Edward Cooke, no relation to Captain James Cook, the famous explorer. Eastwick seems to have gotten much of his incorrect information from the attached newspaper article, which was printed with his account (see p. 117).*

officers, and their conduct towards us personally was, I must admit, both kind and generous. But they had sent so many men away on board the various prizes they had recently captured (of which there were at least seven or eight) that their crew was very much diminished, and they were left badly manned, having not more than three hundred souls on board, all told.

The English frigate had, on the contrary, more than her full complement of men, there being, in addition to the sailors, a company of the Scotch brigade on board, who had taken the place of marines, the strength of these latter having been much reduced by deaths consequent upon a fever contracted by them when a large force was landed for some time at Calcutta. These soldiers were under the command of Captain Davis, an aide de camp of Lord Mornington, who had volunteered for the service.

In addition to this, the *La Sybille* was commanded by a captain as gallant as any that ever stepped, and, fired by his spirit, the whole crew were determined to wipe away the stain that the many recent naval disasters we had sustained had brought upon the British flag in those seas.

It was a brilliant moonlight night, with light winds and calm sea. Captain Cooke and I, having retired after our interview with the admiral to a corner of the quarter-deck, were sitting talking, and congratulating ourselves upon our promised liberty, when our attention was suddenly drawn to a strange sail making towards us and distinctly visible in the moonlight. She was a large vessel, and there was a curious fact about her, that she did not display a single light, but sailed serenely on with all her canvas spread, and yet without any signs of life on board. The French officers actually mistook her for a merchantman "with the watch asleep," and about to be delivered into their hands. They had enjoyed such a career of good fortune during the last month that they were ready to accept this new ship as only a further installment of the luck that seemed to be theirs.

Nearer and nearer came the strange sail, as calm and stately as if she had the entire ocean to herself and no other vessel in sight. Such confidence amounted to audacity, for the display of lights from the French frigate marked her as a man-of-war. As the approaching ship continued her course and came within range, the Captain of the *La Forte* began to exhibit some doubts about her and ordered a few shots to be fired at her. But these eliciting no response, he commanded the firing to cease, observing in my hearing, "She will prove another *Bon Prix!*" Still, as a matter of precaution, every man was kept at his quarters, though in a careless way, and the guns were all loaded and pointed at the stranger.

We prisoners were now ordered to retire below and were shown into the officers' berth-place, the door of which was locked upon us. This did not, however, altogether prevent us from obtaining a view of what was going on, for there was a small port-hole, through which we peered in turn, and tried to conjecture who or what this vessel might be that came on in such a masterly manner and appeared to anticipate no danger, although she was sailing into the very teeth of one of the strongest frigates afloat, and one which had proved herself to be a terror in those waters.

Suddenly, having got into a proper position, and as the moment of action arrived, all the tarpaulins which had covered the lanterns and hidden the lights on board of the *La Sybille* were removed as if by magic, and an illuminated large English ship exposed to view. She was now within two cables' lengths and luffed to the wind on the starboard tack, and the next instant the whole broadside of a well-directed fire was poured into *La Forte*. Then edging down, after the discharge, before the wind, the *La Sybille* came fairly alongside.

And now occurred such a scene on board the French frigate as I can find no words to describe. Her decks had been raked with the small grape-shot that came like hail from the 24-pounders of her opponent, and in a moment all was shouting and noise and confusion. Whistles were piped, orders were cried out, and the crew were hurried up to serve the guns, urged on by their officers. The admiral was killed early in the action, and the captain fell next, as gallant a man as could be desired. He was cut in half by a chain-shot whilst trying to rally his crew, who, having been fairly caught a napping, were all in alarm and confusion. The execution wrought amongst their ranks by the sudden broadside was dreadful, and the whole ship resounded with the shrieks and groans of the wounded, making a noise that was sickening to hear. Still a gallant fight was kept up, despite the demoralizing effects of that deadly fire. The musketry rattled, and between the thunder of the guns, as broadside after broadside was returned, there came the lesser but constant discharges of the brass swivels mounted on the quarter-deck. There was, however, one great disadvantage that the *La Forte* suffered; owing to her enormous height she could not depress her guns sufficiently to fire with proper effect at her opponent, because of the close quarters at which the action was fought, whilst the *La Sybille*'s shot told with disastrous results at each discharge.

After fifty-five minutes' hot fighting, the Frenchman, finding she was beaten, desired to escape and attempted to make sail. But this the *La Sybille* was determined to prevent, and altering the aim of her guns, the *La Forte*'s shrouds were presently shot away, and soon afterwards her masts went by the board one after another with an awful crash, carrying all the top hamper with them, until the deck became an inextricable mass of tangled rigging, and the frigate lay a helpless cripple upon the water.

Meanwhile we prisoners below had long since resigned our position by the port-hole and sought safer quarters at the further end of the berth-place. When we heard the crash of the falling masts, we thought the *La Forte* was being boarded, although we could not at all understand the situation, being at the time unaware that the ship we were in conflict with was a British man-of-war, but rather believing it to be one of the Company's vessels. Though not engaged, we were most dangerously as well as uncomfortably confined, and being denied the satisfaction of assisting in the fight, could not have been more cruelly situated. The cabin we were imprisoned in was about thirty feet long, and ten feet above water, and during the engagement at least thirty shots passed through it. One of these went so close to us, as we were sitting on a chest together, that we were induced to shift our position, and scarce had we done so than a cannon-ball struck the chest itself and demolished it altogether. There was only one dim lantern burning in the cabin, and the gloom and obscurity seemed to increase the sensation of danger from which, since we had been locked in, there was no apparent escape.

I had rather be in a dozen actions face to face with belching cannon, and exposed to the full fire of the tops, than experience again such another hour as we passed through. The din and noise were awful; the great ship shook and quivered under every discharge of her guns; a suffocating smell of gunpowder smoke pervaded the whole vessel, we being to leeward; and every second or third minute there came a great crash, most startling in the dark, and we heard a shot go rioting through the prison we were confined in, and did not know whether the next might not carry us all off. From overhead came the trampling of feet, the cries of the wounded, the crashing sounds of falling spars and top hamper, heard between the thundering of the cannon and the lesser roar of the small arms. The excitement of action was wanting, which assists men to face fire, and at times hardly to heed it. And added to all was the terrible sense of uncertainty as to what was happening, with whom we were contending, and whether the *La Forte* was winning the day or losing it.

After the tenth or twelfth shot had penetrated the berth-room, Captain Cooke swore he could stand it no longer and that it required more courage than he possessed to sit still and be shot at, like a rat in a hole. He therefore began groping about to find a means of exit and came across an aperture in the bulkhead, made by the starting of the timbers consequent on a shot striking the place. Through this, being exceedingly spare in person, he managed with great difficulty to squeeze his body, and so got further below to a place of comparative safety, from whence he called to us to join him.

The advice was excellent enough in its way, but the thing was to carry it out. Mr. Mackerel attempted the task first, I, at his request, aiding his exertions. But unfortunately he was a very fat man and got fairly wedged when half-way through, so that he called out violently to be hauled back. This was no easy matter, and accomplished with such difficulty that the ludicrous effect of the scene has never passed from my memory, and critical as our situation was, I could not refrain from laughing aloud, when, in my endeavours to pull him back by the legs, his pantaloons first began to peel off, and when I transferred my grip to his feet, one of his boots gave way in my hand and sent me sprawling backwards.

Mr. Mackerel was mightily indignant at my levity and upbraided me for it in solemn and measured language after I had at last managed to extricate him. He then very soberly laid himself down flat on the floor, observing, with a groan, that it was safer than standing; and as this seemed sensible, and I did not like to desert him, I followed his example, jestingly thanking him for the extra protection his ample person afforded me—a joke he was in far too much consternation to relish.

There we lay for half an hour, Mr. Mackerel saying not a word, but breathing very hard, and whenever a crash was heard, turning instantly on his side, so as to present his back to the attack if it should come, and then giving vent to a groan, by way of thanksgiving, when he found himself unhurt.

At last the action began to draw to a close. The discharges of cannon were less frequent, and the *La Forte's* men being all engaged in trying to set sail, the rattle of musketry on the quarter-deck above our heads almost ceased. Very nearly the last shot fired was one which, in penetrating the berth-place, was so checked, that it came rolling slowly towards us; upon which Mr. Mackerel jumped up and made a clean bound over it with an agility that would have done credit to a goat. As I scuttled out of its way, its size showed me it came from a twenty-four pounder, and I knew it must have been fired by a man-of-war. But before I had time to acquaint my companion of this joyful discovery and bid him take heart, a great number of men (the *La Forte* having now struck) came running down below to secure the valuables plundered from the various prizes and tie them round their persons, and one of these unlocked the door of the berth-place with the object, I conceive, of appropriating some of the dead officers' property, and this enabled Mr. Mackerel and myself to get out.

I immediately went on deck, where the second captain, who was quite a lad, caught sight of me. The tears were in his eyes, and he was greatly agitated as he asked me to hail the British frigate and say we had struck. Young though he was, the command had devolved upon him through the death of all the senior officers. Still, if he had been a veteran of a hundred fights, it would not have been in his power to continue the action any longer, nor could he have shown more proper feeling at the unfortunate position in which he was placed.

I ran to the side of the *La Forte* and shouted out that she had hauled down her colours, and then through the thick cloud of smoke that hung over and almost hid the vessels from each other's view, there came back such a ringing English cheer as few are privileged to hear. I have never in my life, before or since, heard any cry like it. It filled the welkin with a glorious sound that recorded the accomplishment of a great deed, and I felt my heart beat faster and my blood go rushing through my veins in pride. Then the firing ceased, and in a short while a boat containing Mr. Vashon, the second lieutenant, and Mr. Major, the third, was lowered from the *La Sybille* and came to take charge of the *La Forte*.

The surrender of the French frigate was soon completed. I then went on board the *La Sybille*, which I found in charge of Lieutenant Hardyman, Captain Cook being dangerously wounded. I at once represented the probability of recapturing the *Endeavour* and the *Mornington*, which were still within sight. It was, however, impracticable to do anything then, since it was necessary to attend to the wounded and temporarily repair the more urgent damages that both ships had sustained. There were many prisoners also to be placed in safety, and these matters occupied the whole night. By morning order was restored on both frigates, and they were brought to anchor off the roads of Ballasore.

At my suggestion the French colours were now hoisted above the English on board the *La Sybille*, and the *Endeavour* lured into a position where her recapture was almost certain. But success depended upon the cant of the frigate: if she canted round one way my ship would have been placed in a situation that would have ensured her being at our mercy; but if the frigate canted the other way, there was then no room without going past the French frigate and afterward hauling up to windward for a long stern chase. Although his sailing master, Mr. Douglas, recommended the course I proposed, Lieutenant Hardyman, who was a very obstinate man, would not listen to it. The prize-master in charge of the *Endeavour* suspected something, and tacked and stood under the French frigate's stern, where he saw enough to inform him of the true position of affairs, and at once sailed off, giving a signal of warning to the *Mornington*, which wore ship and followed. I then begged Mr. Hardyman to sail in pursuit, but he pleaded the damaged condition of the *La Sybille*, saying that the carpenter had reported her mainyard to be too badly wounded to carry sail. Having a great interest at stake, I earnestly pressed him to reconsider his decision, and urged in seamanlike phrase that crowbars or fishes might be lashed on to the yard for a makeshift, and there being a large property to be recovered it was worth the trial, as the frigate with her mainsail set would certainly keep pace with the *Endeavour*. But he would not listen to me, and I had the mortification of seeing my own ship escape before my eyes. It meant a loss to me of £10,000 in property uninsured and certainly an indirect one of double that amount by the capture of my vessel at a time when tonnage was scarce, much work to be done, and no other craft to be obtained. The *Endeavour* was a ship of the best class, suitable for transporting troops and just the kind the government sought for, and there was a certainty, had I recovered her, of my being engaged at a very high freight, for the expedition then being sent to fight Buonaparte in Egypt.

In this celebrated action, according to the returns which I obtained for the navy agent, out of three hundred men on board the *La Forte,* fifty-five were killed, including the fine old admiral, the captain, and the first, second, and third lieutenants, and eighty-five wounded. On board the *La Sybille* there were only fifteen killed and wounded, the fire from the *La Forte* having gone clean over the heads of her crew, and never been brought to bear properly upon the deck. But amongst these were Captain Davis (an aide de camp to Lord Mornington), who was on board as a volunteer in command of the Scotch Brigade, and who died of the wounds he received; and Captain Cook, who also succumbed some months later at Calcutta,[1] and was accorded the honour of a public funeral. The engagement was one of the sharpest and severest that had taken place during the war, and was begun and ended in one hundred minutes.

THE TIMES of August 3, 1799, has the following leading article referring to the incident mentioned in the text:—

"Advices have been received at the India House of the capture of the following country ships in the Bay of Bengal: *Recovery*—McKinley;

---

[1] Captain Edward Cook *[should be Cooke throughout]* died at Calcutta on the 23rd of May following. There is a striking monument in Westminster Abbey erected to his memory by the East India Company. It bears a fine relief representing the *La Forte* and *La Sybille* in close action, surmounted by a bas-relief of Captain Cook, who is depicted as wounded and supported by one of his men. This monument, which is immediately behind one erected to the memory of General Wolfe, the hero of Quebec, bears the following inscription:—"Erected by the Honourable East India Company as a grateful testimony to the valour and the eminent services of Captain Edward Cook, commander of His Majesty's ship *Sybille,* who on the 1st March, 1799, after a long and well-contested engagement, captured *La Forte,* a French frigate of very superior force, in the Bay of Bengal, an event not more splendid in its achievement than important in its results to the British trade in India. He died in consequence of the severe wounds he received in this memorable action, on the 23rd May, 1799, aged 27 years."

*Yarmouth*—Beck; *Earl Mornington*—Cooke; *Chance*—Johnson; *Endeavour*—Eastwick; *Surprize*—Moore; and two others, names unknown. The first has been sent to Madras as a cartel. They were captured by the *La Forte,* frigate.

"We have the satisfaction to state that the *Sybille,* frigate, Captain Cook, afterwards fell in with and captured *La Forte,* after a severe engagement. The French frigate did not strike her colours till after she had lost her captain and all her officers. When the ship struck she was in possession of a boy. *La Forte* mounted fifty guns, and was full of men. We consider her capture to be fully an equivalent for the loss of all the ships she had just before taken.

"The *La Forte* was commanded by the famous Admiral de Serci, a pupil of Suffreins, and certainly the most active and distinguished officer in the French service. Whilst the East India Company have to rejoice at getting rid of so formidable an enemy, every man must lament the fate of a very brave officer. He had the character of great humanity towards those whom the chances of war threw in his path.

"Captain E. Cook, who commanded *La Sybille,* is likewise well known in the service. He is the son of the famous navigator of that name, and the officer who undertook the hazardous negotiation between Lord Hood and the magistrates of Toulon, previous to our fleet taking possession of that town and harbour. We are sorry to learn that he is dangerously wounded in both arms. Our loss is very small as to men."

On the 5th of August, *The Times* gives further particulars of this action:—

"The following are some further particulars respecting the capture of *La Forte* frigate. Captain Cook on arriving at Madras in *La Sybille,* 44 guns, received information that *La Forte* of 55 guns, 24-pounders, had taken several of our ships, and was cruising in the Bay of Bengal. He instantly went in search of her. They met in the night near Ballysore. *La Forte* mistook *La Sybille* for an Indiaman, and fired some random shots to bring her to, one of which unfortunately killed Captain Davis, aid du camp (*sic*) to Lord Mornington. Captain Cook approached without showing any lights, and first undeceived the enemy by a broadside. During an action of an hour and a half, the French officers did everything that was possible to keep their people at their guns, but our fire was tremendous, and the slaughter great. All the French officers were amongst the killed before a lad, who had for some time commanded, finding further opposition fruitless, struck his colours.

"The *La Forte* was laid down for a 74, and is perhaps the largest and finest frigate in the world, carrying her guns four feet higher than the *Victorious.* Admiral De Sercy (*sic*), on returning lately from Batavia, married a Creole lady, with whom he obtained a large fortune."

•  •  •

*Lieutenant Hardyman was given command of the* Forte, *an appointment that was ratified by the Admiralty promoting Hardyman to post-captain.*

*Back in the Mediterranean, in February 1800, a French squadron flying the flag of Rear-Admiral Perrée sailed to relieve the garrison of Valetta, Malta, then besieged by Maltese troops and blockaded by Admiral Nelson. Nelson intercepted the squadron, and Perrée, on board the* Généreux *(74), one of the two French ships of the line to escape Nelson at the Battle of the Nile, was killed in the process. The dubious honor of carrying the much-battered prize safely into Port Mahon, Minorca, fell to a high-spirited lieutenant named Cochrane. After battling fierce storms, Cochrane succeeded. He was promoted by Admiral Keith to the rank of master and commander and was appointed to the command of the brig* Speedy.

# Thomas Cochrane

*~*

# The Audacious Cruise
# of the *Speedy*

## 1800-1801

*A headstrong Scot, Thomas Cochrane entered the Royal Navy at age seventeen as a midshipman on board HMS* Hind, *commanded by his uncle, Captain Alexander Cochrane. Of course, his name had been carried on the books for some years before, which would have guaranteed him early promotion had it not been for his tempestuous nature. In 1798 he served on board HMS* Barfleur, *the flagship of Admiral Lord Keith, and in 1800, after bringing Nelson's recent prize, the* Généreux, *into Port Mahon, was given his own command. It doesn't take Cochrane long to prove himself one of the fightingest captains in the Royal Navy. In fact, his exploits would inspire generations of future novelists. Here is his own account of the legendary David-and-Goliath action between the* Speedy *and the* El Gamo.

THE *SPEEDY* WAS little more than a burlesque on a vessel of war, even sixty years ago. She was about the size of an average coasting brig, her burden being 158 tons. She was crowded, rather than manned, with a crew of eighty-four men and six officers, myself included. Her armament consisted of fourteen 4-*pounders!*, a species of gun little larger than a blunderbuss, and formerly known in the service under the name of "miñion," an appellation which it certainly merited.

Being dissatisfied with her armament, I applied for and obtained a couple of 12-pounders, intending them as bow and stern chasers, but was compelled to return them to the ordnance wharf, there not being room on deck to work them; besides which, the timbers of the little craft were found on trial to be too weak to withstand the concussion of anything heavier than the guns with which she was previously armed.

With her rig I was more fortunate. Having carried away her mainyard, it became necessary to apply for another to the senior officer, who, examining the list of spare spars, ordered the *foretopgallant-yard* of the *Généreux* to be hauled out *as a mainyard for the Speedy!*

The spar was accordingly sent on board and rigged, but even this appearing too large for the vessel, an order was issued to cut off the yard-arms and thus reduce it to its proper dimensions. This order was neutralized by getting down and planing the yard-arms as though they had been cut, an evasion which, with some alteration in the rigging, passed undetected on its being again swayed up; and thus a greater spread of canvas was secured. The fact of the foretopgallant-yard of a second-rate ship being considered too large for the mainyard of my "man-of-war" will give a tolerable idea of her insignificance.

Despite her unformidable character and the personal discomfort to which all on board were subjected, I was very proud of my little vessel, caring nothing for her want of accommodation, though in this respect her cabin merits passing notice. It had not so much as room for a chair, the floor being entirely occupied by a small table surrounded with lockers, answering the double purpose of storechests and seats. The difficulty was to get seated, the ceiling being only five feet high, so that the object could only be accomplished by rolling on the locker, a movement sometimes attended with unpleasant failure. The most singular discomfort, however, was that my only practicable mode of shaving consisted in removing the skylight and putting my head through to make a toilet-table of the quarterdeck.

In the following enumeration of the various cruises in which the *Speedy* was engaged, the boarding and searching innumerable neutral vessels will be passed over, and the narrative will be strictly confined—as in most cases throughout this work—to log extracts, where captures were made, or other occurrences took place worthy of record.

"*May* 10.—Sailed from Cagliari, from which port we had been ordered to convoy fourteen sail of merchantmen to Leghorn. At 9 A.M. observed a strange sail take possession of a Danish brig under our escort. At 11:30 A.M. rescued the brig and captured the assailant. This prize—my first piece of luck—was the *Intrépide*, French privateer of six guns and forty-eight men.

"*May* 14.—Saw five armed boats pulling towards us from Monte Cristo. Out sweeps to protect convoy. At 4 P.M. the boats boarded and took possession of the two sternmost ships. A light breeze springing up, made all sail towards the captured vessels, ordering the remainder of the convoy to make the best of their way to Longona. The breeze freshening we came up with and recaptured the vessels with the prize crews on board, but during the operation the armed boats escaped.

"*May* 21.—At anchor in Leghorn Roads. Convoy all safe. 25.—Off Genoa. Joined Lord Keith's squadron of five sail of the line, four frigates and a brig.

"26, 27, 28.—Ordered by his lordship to cruise in the offing, to intercept supplies destined for the French army under Massena, then in possession of Genoa.

"29.—At Genoa some of the gun-boats bombarded the town for two hours.

"30.—All the gun-boats bombarded the town. A partial bombardment had been going on for an hour a day, during the past fortnight, Lord Keith humanely refraining from continued bombardment, out of consideration for the inhabitants, who were in a state of absolute famine."

This was one of the *crises* of the war. The French, about a month previous, had defeated the Austrians with great slaughter in an attempt, on the part of the latter, to retake Genoa; but the Austrians, being in possession of Savona, were nevertheless able to intercept provisions on the land side, whilst the vigilance of Lord Keith rendered it impossible to obtain supplies by sea.

It having come to Lord Keith's knowledge that the French in Genoa had consumed their last horses and dogs, whilst the Genoese themselves were perishing by famine, and on the eve of revolt against the usurping force—in order to save the carnage which would ensue, his lordship caused it to be intimated to Massena that a defence so heroic would command honourable terms of capitulation. Massena was said to have replied that if the word "capitulation" were mentioned his army should perish with the city; but, as he could no longer defend himself, he had no objection to "treat." Lord Keith, therefore, proposed a treaty, viz., that the army might return to France, but that Massena himself must remain a prisoner in his hands. To this the French general demurred; but Lord Keith insisting—with the complimentary observation to Massena that "he was worth 20,000 men"—the latter reluctantly gave in, and on the 4th of June, 1800, a definite treaty to the above effect was agreed upon, and ratified on the 5th, when the Austrians took possession of the city, and Lord Keith of the harbour, the squadron anchoring within the mole.

This affair being ended, his lordship ordered the *Speedy* to cruise off the Spanish coast, and on the 14th of June we parted company with the squadron.

"*June* 16.—Captured a tartan off Elba. Sent her to Leghorn, in the charge of an officer and four men.

"22.—Off Bastia. Chased a French privateer with a prize in tow. The Frenchman abandoned the prize, a Sardinian vessel laden with oil and wool, and we took possession. Made all sail in chase of the privateer; but on our commencing to fire she ran under the fort of Caprea, where we did not think proper to pursue her. Took prize in tow, and on the following day left her at Leghorn, where we found Lord Nelson, and several ships at anchor.

"25.—Quitted Leghorn, and on the 26th were again off Bastia, in chase of a ship which ran for that place, and anchored under a fort three miles to the southward. Made at and brought her away. Proved to be the Spanish letter of marque *Assuncion*, of ten guns and thirty-three men, bound from Tunis to Barcelona. On taking possession, five gun-boats left Bastia in chase of us; took the prize in tow, and kept up a running fight with the gun-boats till after midnight, when they left us.

"29.—Cast off the prize in chase of a French privateer off Sardinia. On commencing our fire she set all sail and ran off. Returned and took the prize in tow; and the 4th of July anchored with her in Port Mahon.

"*July* 9.—Off Cape Sebastian. Gave chase to two Spanish ships standing along shore. They anchored under the protection of the forts. Saw another vessel lying just within range of the forts;—out boats and cut her out, the forts firing on the boats without inflicting damage.

"*July* 19.—Off Caprea. Several French privateers in sight. Chased, and on the following morning captured one, the *Constitution*, of one gun and nineteen men. Whilst we were securing the privateer, a prize which she had taken made sail in the direction of Gorgona and escaped.

"27.—Off Planosa, in chase of a privateer. On the following morning saw three others lying in a small creek. On making preparations to cut them out, a military force made its appearance, and

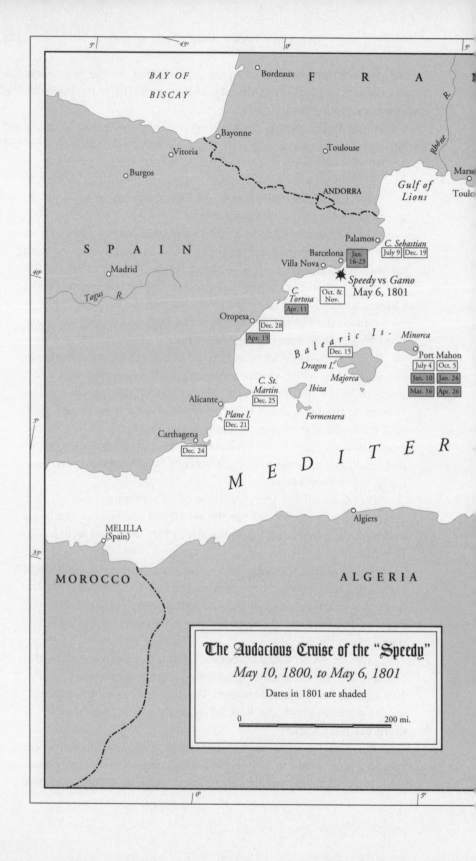

BAY OF
BISCAY

Bordeaux

F  R  A

R.

Bayonne

Vitoria

Toulouse

Rhône

Burgos

ANDORRA

Gulf of
Lions

Marse

Toulo

S  P  A  I  N

Palamos

*C. Sebastian*

Madrid

Barcelona

Villa Nova

Jan.
16-23

July 9

Dec. 19

*Speedy* vs *Gamo*
May 6, 1801

*Tagus R.*

C.
Tortosa

Oct. &
Nov.

Apr. 11

Oropesa

Dec. 28

Apr. 13

*B a l e a r i c   I s .*

Minorca

Port Mahon

Dec. 15

July 4

Oct. 5

*Dragon I.*

Jan. 10

Jan. 24

*Majorca*

Mar. 16

Apr. 26

C. St.
Martin

*Ibiza*

Alicante

Dec. 25

*Plane I.*

*Formentera*

Dec. 21

Carthagena

M  E  D  I  T  E  R

Dec. 24

Algiers

MELILLA
(Spain)

MOROCCO

ALGERIA

# The Audacious Cruise of the "Speedy"

*May 10, 1800, to May 6, 1801*

Dates in 1801 are shaded

0                                    200 mi.

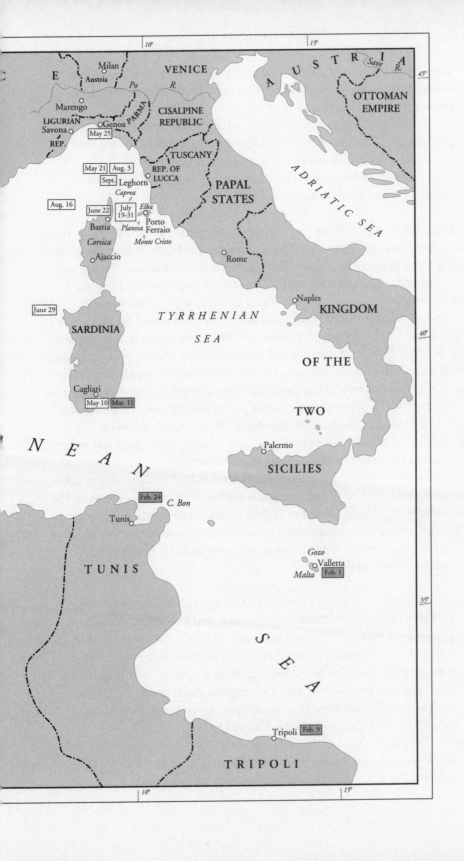

AUSTRIA

Save R.

OTTOMAN
EMPIRE

VENICE

Milan
Austria

Po
PARMA

CISALPINE
REPUBLIC

R.

LIGURIAN
Savona REP.

Marengo

Genoa

May 25

TUSCANY

REP. OF
LUCCA

ADRIATIC SEA

May 21 | Aug. 3

Sept. Leghorn

Caprea

Aug. 16

June 22 | July 19-31 | Elba

Bastia Planosa Porto Ferraio

Corsica Monte Cristo

Ajaccio

PAPAL
STATES

Rome

June 29

SARDINIA

TYRRHENIAN

SEA

Naples

KINGDOM

OF THE

Cagliari

May 10 | Mar. 11

N E A N

E A N

TWO

Palermo

SICILIES

Feb. 24

C. Bon

Tunis

T U N I S

Gozo

Valletta

Malta Feb. 1

S E A

Tripoli Feb. 9

T R I P O L I

commenced a heavy fire of musketry, to which it would have
answered no purpose to reply. Fired several broadsides at one of the
privateers, and sunk her.

"31.—Off Porto Ferraio in chase of a French privateer, with a
prize in tow. The Frenchman abandoned his prize, of which we took
possession, and whilst so doing the privateer got away.

"*August* 3.—Anchored with our prizes in Leghorn Roads, where
we found Lord Keith in the *Minotaur*."

Lord Keith received me very kindly, and directed the *Speedy* to run
down the Spanish coast, pointing out the importance of harassing the
enemy there as much as possible, but cautioning me against engaging anything beyond our capacity. During our stay at Leghorn, his lordship frequently invited me ashore to participate in the gaieties of the place.

Having filled up with provisions and water, we sailed on the 16th of
August, and on the 21st captured a French privateer bound from Corsica to
Toulon. Shortly afterwards we fell in with HMS *Mutine* and *Salamine*,
which, to suit their convenience, gave into our charge a number of French
prisoners, with whom and our prize we consequently returned to Leghorn.

On the 14th of September we again put to sea, the interval being occupied by a thorough overhaul of the sloop. On the 22nd, when off Caprea,
fell in with a Neapolitan vessel having a French prize crew on board.
Recaptured the vessel, and took the crew prisoners.

On the 5th of October, the *Speedy* anchored in Port Mahon, where information was received that the Spaniards had several armed vessels on the
look-out for us, should we again appear on their coast. I therefore applied
to the authorities to exchange our 4-pounders for 6-pounders, but the latter
being too large for the *Speedy*'s ports, we were again compelled to forego
the change as impracticable.

"*October* 12.—Sailed from Port Mahon, cruising for some time
off Cape Sebastian, Villa Nova, Oropesa, and Barcelona; occasionally visiting the enemy's coast for water, of which the *Speedy* carried
only ten tons. Nothing material occurred till November 18th, when
we narrowly escaped being swamped in a gale of wind, the sea
breaking over our quarter, and clearing our deck, spars, &c., otherwise inflicting such damage as to compel our return to Port Mahon,
where we were detained till the 12th of December.

"*December* 15.—Off Majorca. Several strange vessels being in
sight, singled out the largest and made sail in chase; shortly after
which a French bombard bore up, hoisting the national colours. We

now cleared for action, altering our course to meet her, when she bore up between Dragon Island and the Main. Commenced firing at the bombard, which returned our fire; but shortly afterwards getting closer in shore she drove on the rocks. Three other vessels being in the passage, we left her, and captured one of them, the *La Liza* of ten guns and thirty-three men, bound from Alicant to Marseilles. Took nineteen of our prisoners on board the *Speedy*. As it was evident that the bombard would become a wreck, we paid no further attention to her, but made all sail after the others.

"*December* 18.—Suspecting the passage between Dragon Island and the Main to be a lurking-place for privateers, we ran in again, but found nothing. Seeing a number of troops lining the beach, we opened fire and dispersed them, afterwards engaging a tower, which fired upon us. The prisoners we had taken proving an incumbrance, we put them on shore.

"*December* 19.—Stood off and on the harbour of Palamos, where we saw several vessels at anchor. Hoisted Danish colours and made the signal for a pilot. Our real character being evidently known, none came off, and we did not think it prudent to venture in."

It has been said that the *Speedy* had become the marked object of the Spanish naval authorities. Not that there was much danger of being caught, for they confined their search to the coast only, and that in the daytime, when we were usually away in the offing; it being our practice to keep out of sight during the day, and run in before dawn on the next morning.

On the 21st, however, when off Plane Island, we were very near "catching a Tartar." Seeing a large ship in shore, having all the appearance of a well-laden merchantman, we forthwith gave chase. On nearing her she raised her ports, which had been closed to deceive us, the act discovering a heavy broadside, a clear demonstration that we had fallen into the jaws of a formidable Spanish frigate, now crowded with men, who had before remained concealed below.

That the frigate was in search of us there could be no doubt, from the deception practised. To have encountered her with our insignificant armament would have been exceedingly imprudent, whilst escape was out of the question, for she would have outsailed us, and could have run us down by her mere weight. There was, therefore, nothing left but to try the effect of a *ruse*, prepared beforehand for such an emergency. After receiving at Mahon information that unusual measures were about to be taken by the Spaniards for our capture, I had the *Speedy* painted in imitation of the Danish brig *Clomer*; the appearance of this vessel being well known on the

Spanish coast. We also shipped a Danish quartermaster, taking the further precaution of providing him with the uniform of an officer of that nation.

On discovering the real character of our neighbour, the *Speedy* hoisted Danish colours, and spoke her. At first this failed to satisfy the Spaniard, who sent a boat to board us. It was now time to bring the Danish quartermaster into play in his officer's uniform; and to add force to his explanations, we ran the quarantine flag up to the fore, calculating on the Spanish horror of the plague, then prevalent along the Barbary coast.

On the boat coming within hail—for the yellow flag effectually repressed the enemy's desire to board us—our mock officer informed the Spaniards that we were two days from Algiers, where at the time the plague was violently raging. This was enough. The boat returned to the frigate, which, wishing us a good voyage, filled, and made sail, whilst we did the same.

I have noted this circumstance more minutely than it merits, because it has been misrepresented. By some of my officers blame was cast on me for not attacking the frigate after she had been put off her guard by our false colours, as her hands—being then employed at their ordinary avocations in the rigging and elsewhere—presented a prominent mark for our shot. There is no doubt but that we might have poured in a murderous fire before the crew could have recovered from their confusion, and perhaps have taken her, but feeling averse to so cruel a destruction of human life, I chose to refrain from an attack, which might not, even with that advantage in our favour, have been successful.

It has been stated by some naval writers that this frigate was the *Gamo*, which we subsequently captured. To the best of my knowledge this is an error.

"*December* 24.—Off Carthagena. At daylight fell in with a convoy in charge of two Spanish privateers, which came up and fired at us; but being to windward we ran for the convoy, and singling out two, captured the nearest, laden with wine. The other ran in shore under the fort of Port Genoese, where we left her.

"25.—Stood for Cape St. Martin, in hope of intercepting the privateers. At 8 A.M. saw a privateer and one of the convoy under Cape Lanar. Made sail in chase. They parted company; when, on our singling out the nearest privateer, she took refuge under a battery, on which we left off pursuit.

"30.—Off Cape Oropesa. Seeing some vessels in shore, out boats in chase. At noon they returned pursued by two Spanish gunboats, which kept up a smart fire on them. Made sail to intercept the gun-boats, on which they ran in under the batteries.

"*January* 10, 1801.—Anchored in Port Mahon, and having refitted, sailed again on the 12th.

"16.—Off Barcelona. Just before daylight chased two vessels standing towards that port. Seeing themselves pursued, they made for the battery at the entrance. Bore up and set steering sails in chase. The wind falling calm, one of the chase drifted in shore and took the ground under Castel De Ferro. On commencing our fire, the crew abandoned her, and we sent boats with anchors and hawsers to warp her off, in which they succeeded. She proved to be the Genoese ship *Ns. Señora de Gratia*, of ten guns.

"22.—Before daylight, stood in again for Barcelona. Saw several sail close in with the land. Out boats and boarded one, which turned out a Dane. Cruising off the port till 3 A.M., we saw two strange vessels coming from the westward. Made sail to cut them off. At 6 P.M. one of them hoisted Spanish colours and the other French. At 9 P.M. came up with them, when after an engagement of half an hour both struck. The Spaniard was the *Ecce Homo*, of eight guns and nineteen men, the Frenchman, *L'Amitié*, of one gun and thirty-one men. Took all the prisoners on board the *Speedy*.

"23.—Still off Barcelona. Having sent most of our crew to man the prizes, the number of prisoners on board the *Speedy* became dangerous; we therefore put twenty-five of the Frenchmen into one of their own launches and told them to make the best of their way to Barcelona. As the prizes were a good deal cut up about the rigging, repaired their damages and made sail for Port Mahon, where we arrived on the 24th, with our convoy in company.

"28th.—Quitted Port Mahon for Malta, not being able to procure at Minorca various things of which we stood in need; and on the 1st of February, came to an anchor at Valetta, where we obtained anchors and sweeps."

An absurd affair took place during our short stay at Malta, which would not have been worthy of notice, had it not been made the subject of comment.

The officers of a French royalist regiment, then at Malta, patronized a fancy ball, for which I amongst others purchased a ticket. The dress chosen was that of a sailor—in fact, my costume was a tolerable imitation of that of my worthy friend, Jack Larmour,[1] in one of his relaxing moods, and per-

[1] *Jack Larmour, Cochrane's "sea daddy" when he entered the Royal Navy, was one of the rare seamen promoted from the forecastle to the quarterdeck.*

sonated in my estimation as honourable a character as were Greek, Turk-
ish, or other kinds of Oriental disguises in vogue at such reunions. My costume was, however, too much to the life to please French royalist taste, not
even the marlinspike and the lump of grease in the hat being omitted.

On entering the ball-room, further passage was immediately barred,
with an intimation that my presence could not be permitted in such a dress.
Good-humouredly expostulating that, as the choice of costume was left to
the wearer, my own taste—which was decidedly nautical—had selected
that of a British seaman, a character which, though by no means imaginary,
was quite as picturesque as were the habiliments of an Arcadian shepherd;
further insisting that as no rule had been infringed, I must be permitted to
exercise my discretion. Expostulation being of no avail, a brusque answer
was returned that such a dress was not admissible, whereupon I as
brusquely replied that having purchased my ticket, and chosen my own
costume in accordance with the regulations, no one had any right to prevent me from sustaining the character assumed.

Upon this a French officer, who appeared to act as master of the ceremonies, came up, and without waiting for further explanation, rudely
seized me by the collar with the intention of putting me out; in return for
which insult he received a substantial mark of British indignation, and at
the same time an uncomplimentary remark in his own language. In an
instant all was uproar; a French picket was called, which in a short time
overpowered and carried me off to the guard-house of the regiment.

I was, however, promptly freed from detention on announcing my
name, but the officer who had collared me demanded an apology for the
portion of the *fracas* concerning him personally. This being of course
refused, a challenge was the consequence; and on the following morning
we met behind the ramparts and exchanged shots, my ball passing through
the poor fellow's thigh, and dropping him. My escape, too, was a narrow
one—his ball perforating my coat, waistcoat, and shirt, and bruising my
side. Seeing my adversary fall, I stepped up to him—imagining his wound
to be serious—and expressed a hope that he had not been hit in a vital part.
His reply—uttered with all the politeness of his nation—was, that "he was
not materially hurt." I, however, was not at ease, for it was impossible not
to regret this, to him, serious *dénouement* of a trumpery affair, though arising from his own intemperate conduct. It was a lesson to me in future never
to do anything in frolic which might give even unintentional offence.

On the 3rd of February we sailed under orders for Tripoli, to make
arrangements for fresh provisions for the fleet. This being effected, the
*Speedy* returned to Malta, and on the 20th again left port in charge of a convoy for Tunis.

24th.—At the entrance of Tunis Bay we gave chase to a strange sail, which wore and stood in towards the town, anchoring at about the distance of three miles. Suspecting some reason for this movement, I despatched an officer to examine her, when the suspicion was confirmed by his ascertaining her to be *La Belle Caroline*, French brig of four guns, bound for Alexandria with field-pieces, ammunition, and wine for the use of the French army in Egypt.

Our position was one of delicacy, the vessel being in a neutral port, where, if we remained to watch her, she might prolong our stay for an indefinite period or escape in the night; whilst, from the warlike nature of the cargo, it was an object of national importance to effect her capture. The latter appearing the most beneficial course under all circumstances, we neared her so as to prevent escape, and soon after midnight boarded her, and having weighed her anchor, brought her close to the *Speedy*, before she had an opportunity of holding any communication with the shore.

The following day was employed in examining her stores, a portion of her ammunition being transferred to our magazine, to replace some damaged by leakage. Her crew, now on board the *Speedy* as prisoners, becoming clamorous at what they considered an illegal seizure, and being, moreover, in our way, an expedient was adopted to get rid of them, by purposely leaving their own launch within reach during the following night, with a caution to the watch not to prevent their desertion should they attempt it. The hint was taken, for before daylight on the 27th they seized the boat, and pulled out of the bay without molestation, not venturing to go to Tunis lest they should be retaken. We thus got rid of the prisoners, and at the same time of what might have turned out their reasonable complaint to the Tunisian authorities, for that we had exceeded the bounds of neutrality there could be no doubt.

On the 28th we weighed anchor, and proceeded to sea with our prize. After cruising for some days off Cape Bon, we made sail for Cagliari, where we arrived on the 8th of March, and put to sea on the 11th with the prize in tow. On the 16th, anchored in Port Mahon.

On the 18th we again put to sea, and towards evening observed a large frigate in chase of us. As she did not answer the private signal, it was evident that the stranger was one of our Spanish friends on the look-out. To cope with a vessel of her size and armament would have been folly, so we made all sail away from her, but she gave instant chase, and evidently gained upon us. To add to our embarrassment, the *Speedy* sprung her maintopgallant-yard, and lost ground whilst fishing it.

At daylight the following morning the strange frigate was still in chase, though by crowding all sail during the night we had gained a little upon her; but during the day she again recovered her advantage, the more so, as the breeze freshening, we were compelled to take in our royals, whilst she was still carrying on with everything set. After dark, we lowered a tub overboard with a light in it, and altering our course thus fortunately evaded her. On the 1st of April we returned to Port Mahon, and again put to sea on the 6th.

"*April* 11.—Observing a vessel near the shoal of Tortosa, gave chase. On the following morning her crew deserted her, and we took possession. In the evening anchored under the land.

"13.—Saw three vessels at anchor in a bay to the westward of Oropesa. Made sail up to them and anchored on the flank of a ten-gun fort. Whilst the firing was going on, the boats were sent in to board and bring out the vessels, which immediately weighed and got under the fort. At 5:30 P.M. the boats returned with one of them; the other two being hauled close in shore, we did not make any further attempt to capture them. As the prize, the *Ave Maria*, of four guns, was in ballast, we took the sails and spars out of her, and set her on fire.

"On the following morning at daybreak, several vessels appeared to the eastward. Made all sail to intercept them, but before we could come up, they succeeded in anchoring under a fort. On standing towards them, they turned out to be Spanish gun-boats, which commenced firing at us. At 10 A.M. anchored within musket-shot, so as to keep an angle of the tower on our beam, thus neutralising its effect. Commenced firing broadsides alternately at the tower and the gun-boats, with visible advantage. Shortly before noon made preparation to cut out the gun-boats, but a fresh breeze setting in dead on shore, rendered it impossible to get at them without placing ourselves in peril. We thereupon worked out of the bay.

"15.—Two strange sail in sight. Gave chase, and in a couple of hours came up with and captured them. Made sail after a convoy in the offing, but the wind falling light at dusk, lost sight of them.

"On the 26th we anchored in Mahon, remaining a week to refit and procure fresh hands, many having been sent away in prizes. On the 2nd of May put to sea with a reduced crew, some of whom had to be taken out of H.M.'s prison."

We again ran along the Spanish coast, and on the 4th of May were off Barcelona, where the *Speedy* captured a vessel which reported herself as Ragusan, though in reality a Spanish four-gun tartan. Soon after detaining her we heard firing in the WN-W and steering for that quarter fell in with a Spanish privateer, which we also captured, the *San Carlos*, of seven guns. On this a swarm of gun-boats came out of Barcelona, seven of them giving chase to us and the prizes, with which we made off shore, the gun-boats returning to Barcelona.

On the following morning the prizes were sent to Port Mahon, and keeping out of sight for the rest of the day, the *Speedy* returned at midnight off Barcelona, where we found the gun-boats on the watch; but on our approach they ran in shore, firing at us occasionally. Suspecting that the object was to decoy us within reach of some larger vessel, we singled out one of them and made at her, the others, however, supporting her so well that some of our rigging being shot away, we made off shore to repair, the gun-boats following. Having thus got them to some distance, and repaired damages, we set all sail, and again ran in shore, in the hope of getting between them and the land, so as to cut off some of their number. Perceiving our intention, they all made for the port as before, keeping up a smart fight, in which our foretopgallant-yard was so much injured, that we had to shift it, and were thus left astern. The remainder of the day was employed in repairing damages, and the gun-boats not venturing out again, at 9 P.M. we again made off shore.

Convinced that something more than ordinary had actuated the gun-boats to decoy us—just before daylight on the 6th we again ran in for Barcelona, when the trap manifested itself in the form of a large ship, running under the land, and bearing ES-E. On hauling towards her, she changed her course in chase of us, and was shortly made out to be a Spanish xebec frigate.

As some of my officers had expressed dissatisfaction at not having been permitted to attack the frigate fallen in with on the 21st of December, after her suspicions had been lulled by our device of hoisting Danish colours, &c., I told them they should now have a fair fight, notwithstanding that, by manning the two prizes sent to Mahon, our numbers had been reduced to fifty-four, officers and boys included. Orders were then given to pipe all hands, and prepare for action.

Accordingly we made towards the frigate, which was now coming down under steering sails. At 9:30 A.M., she fired a gun and hoisted Spanish colours, which the *Speedy* acknowledged by hoisting American colours, our object being, as we were now exposed to her full broadside, to puzzle her, till we got on the other tack, when we ran up the English ensign, and immediately afterwards encountered her broadside without damage.

Shortly afterwards she gave us another broadside, also without effect. My orders were not to fire a gun till we were close to her; when, running under her lee, we locked our yards amongst her rigging, and in this position returned our broadside, such as it was.

To have fired our popgun 4-pounders at a distance would have been to throw away the ammunition; but the guns being doubly, and, as I afterwards learned, trebly, shotted, and being elevated, they told admirably upon her main deck; the first discharge, as was subsequently ascertained, killing the Spanish captain and the boatswain.

My reason for locking our small craft in the enemy's rigging was the one upon which I mainly relied for victory, viz. that from the height of the frigate out of the water, the whole of her shot must necessarily go over our heads, whilst our guns, being elevated, would blow up her main-deck.

The Spaniards speedily found out the disadvantage under which they were fighting, and gave the order to board the *Speedy*; but as this order was as distinctly heard by us as by them, we avoided it at the moment of execution by sheering off sufficiently to prevent the movement, giving them a volley of musketry and a broadside before they could recover themselves.

Twice was this maneuver repeated, and twice thus averted. The Spaniards finding that they were only punishing themselves, gave up further attempts to board and stood to their guns, which were cutting up our rigging from stem to stern, but doing little farther damage; for after the lapse of an hour the loss to the *Speedy* was only two men killed and four wounded.

This kind of combat, however, could not last. Our rigging being cut up and the *Speedy*'s sails riddled with shot, I told the men that they must either take the frigate or be themselves taken, in which case the Spaniards would give no quarter—whilst a few minutes energetically employed on their part would decide the matter in their own favour.

The doctor, Mr. Guthrie, who, I am happy to say, is still living to peruse this record of his gallantry, volunteered to take the helm; leaving him therefore for the time both commander and crew of the *Speedy*, the order was given to board, and in a few seconds every man was on the enemy's deck—a feat rendered the more easy as the doctor placed the *Speedy* close alongside with admirable skill.

For a moment the Spaniards seemed taken by surprise, as though unwilling to believe that so small a crew would have the audacity to board them; but soon recovering themselves, they made a rush to the waist of the frigate, where the fight was for some minutes gallantly carried on. Observing the enemy's colours still flying, I directed one of our men immediately to haul them down, when the Spanish crew, without pausing to consider by whose orders the colours had been struck, and naturally believing it the act of their own officers, gave in, and we were in possession of the *Gamo* frigate, of thirty-two heavy guns and 319 men, who an hour and a half before had looked upon us as a certain if not an easy prey.

Our loss in boarding was Lieutenant Parker, severely wounded in several places, one seaman killed and three wounded, which with those previously killed and wounded gave a total of three seamen killed, and one officer and seventeen men wounded.

The *Gamo's* loss was Captain de Torres—the boatswain—and thirteen seamen killed, together with forty-one wounded; her casualties thus exceeding the whole number of officers and crew on board the *Speedy*.

Some time after the surrender of the *Gamo,* and when we were in quiet possession, the officer who had succeeded the deceased Captain Don Francisco de Torres, not in command, but in rank, applied to me for a certificate that he had done his duty during the action; whereupon he received from me a certificate that he had "conducted himself like a true Spaniard," with which document he appeared highly gratified, and I had afterwards the satisfaction of learning that it procured him further promotion in the Spanish service.

Shortly before boarding, an incident occurred which, by those who have never been placed in similar circumstances, may be thought too absurd for notice. Knowing that the final struggle would be a desperate one, and calculating on the superstitious wonder which forms an element in the Spanish character, a portion of our crew were ordered to blacken their faces, and what with this and the excitement of combat, more ferocious looking objects could scarcely be imagined. The fellows thus disguised were directed to board by the head, and the effect produced was precisely that calculated on. The greater portion of the Spaniard's crew was prepared to repel boarders in that direction, but stood for a few moments as it were transfixed to the deck by the apparition of so many diabolical looking figures emerging from the white smoke of the bow guns; whilst our other men, who boarded by the waist, rushed on them from behind, before they could recover from their surprise at the unexpected phenomenon.

In difficult or doubtful attacks by sea—and the odds of 50 men to 320 comes within this description—no device can be too minute, even if apparently absurd, provided it have the effect of diverting the enemy's attention whilst you are concentrating your own. In this, and other successes against odds, I have no hesitation in saying that success in no slight degree depended on out-of-the-way devices, which the enemy not suspecting, were in some measure thrown off their guard.

The subjoined tabular view of the respective force of the two vessels will best show the nature of the contest.

| Gamo. | Speedy. |
|---|---|
| Main-deck guns.—Twenty-two long 12-pounders. | Fourteen 4-pounders. |
| Quarter-deck.—Eight long 8-pounders, and two 24-pounder carronades. | None. |
| No. of crew, 319. | No. of crew, 54. |
| Broadside weight of shot, 190 lbs. | Broadside weight of shot, 28 lbs. |
| Tonnage, 600 and upwards. | Tonnage, 158. |

It became a puzzle what to do with 263 unhurt prisoners now we had taken them, the *Speedy* having only forty-two men left. Promptness was however necessary; so driving the prisoners into the hold, with guns pointing down the hatchway, and leaving thirty of our men on board the prize—which was placed under the command of my brother, the Hon. Archibald Cochrane, then a midshipman—we shaped our course to Port Mahon—not Gibraltar, as has been recorded—and arrived there in safety; the Barcelona gun-boats, though spectators of the action, not venturing to rescue the frigate. Had they made the attempt, we should have had some difficulty in evading them and securing the prize, the prisoners manifesting every disposition to rescue themselves, and only being deterred by their own main deck guns loaded with cannister, and pointing down the hatchways, whilst our men stood over them with lighted matches.

· · ·

*Cochrane's daring victory was quickly followed by a daring defeat. On July 3, 1801, while marauding the coast of Spain, the* Speedy *was caught in an impossible predicament. French Admiral Linois, having escaped the blockade at Toulon with three ships of the line, happened to be within viewing distance when the* Speedy *ignited a Spanish vessel carrying oil off Malaga. Linois hove to. Believing them to be merchant vessels, Cochrane positioned himself for a morning attack. At daylight, he found himself in the midst of an overwhelming enemy force. He surrendered, but not before trying to run between two of the 74-gun ships, either of which could have blown the* Speedy *out of the water with one broadside. In short order, Cochrane was paroled, court-martialed for the loss of his ship (a necessary formality), promoted to post-captain, and then brought back to earth again. On October 1, 1801, the preliminaries of the Peace of Amiens were signed. Peace would not be official until March 25, 1802, but the newest addition to the post-captain's list had little prospect of a commission.*

# *Part II*
## Peace

# BASIL HALL

*⌐*

# Bermuda in the Peace
## 1802-1803

*In July 1802, Midshipman Basil Hall sailed for Halifax on board HMS
Leander, the flagship of Sir Andrew Mitchell, commander in chief on
the North American Station. Along the way, Hall suffered from seasickness
and a chronically sore tooth and endured relentless teasing for his Scotch
patois and the unfortunate nickname of "Mr. Justice Gobble" (received
after he complained about not getting his share of suet pudding one day).
After a six-week sail, Hall finds himself in Halifax and—in the midst of the
Peace of Amiens—with little to do other than cause mischief.*

## A WHALE OF AN ADVENTURE

THE *LEANDER*, a fifty-gun ship, is well known to the profession, as having formed one of the sturdiest combatants in the action of the Nile, though
not strictly entitled to a place in line of battle. She afterwards maintained a
glorious, though unsuccessful fight with a large French seventy-four, *le
Généreux*, when on her way to England with Nelson's despatches. To our
eyes she was the prettiest ship of her class; and she became permanently
endeared to us as a practical illustration of the beautiful thought—that our
"march is on the mountain wave, our home is on the deep."

This domestic character gives the Navy of England its peculiar distinction, and mainly contributes to its success,—English naval men, and they
alone, do truly make the sea their home. When afloat, they have no other

thoughts of professional duty but what are connected with their vessel; they take a pride in her looks, and bring up her crew to honourable deeds, as they would wish to instruct their sons. Even the rate of sailing is a subject of never-ending discussion with officers, midshipmen, and crew; every soul of whom considers his own individual honour involved in all that his ship does, or is capable of doing. This is true, almost universally; but it is most striking in our first ship, which, like our first love, is supposed to drink up, from the opening flower of our young feelings, the richest drops of sentiment, never to be equalled by future attachments! I am sure the old *Leander* must ever remain the ship nearest and dearest to my nautical heart. I remember every corner about her—every beam—every cabin—every gun. I can almost look back to the school on board of her, with much of that affectionate sort of interest with which I observe Eton men regard the place of their education. Whenever any of the old Leanders meet, who were shipmates together at the happy time I speak of, every other topic is speedily swept aside, and, for hours together, the boyish adventures, and even the most ordinary events of the dear old ship, form the most delightful subject of conversation, the old stories and jokes, repeated fifty times before, invariably flow back again, recommended by increasing interest, and by that genuine freshness of spirits, so "redolent of joy and youth, which breathes a second spring."

On the 6th of December, we sailed from Halifax, with a fresh north-westerly wind, in a day so bitterly cold that the harbour was covered over with a vapour called "the Barber," a sort of low fog, which clings to the surface of the water, and sweeps along with these fierce winter blasts in such a manner as to cut one to the very bone. The Barber is evidently caused by a condensation of the moisture close to the water in this severe temperature. As the thermometer, when we sailed, stood at eleven degrees below zero, nothing but the violence of the wind, which broke the surface into a sheet of foam, prevented our being frozen up in the harbour, like Parry[1] and his north-western voyagers at Melville Island.

As we dashed by one of the lower wharfs of Halifax, just before coming to the narrow passage between George's Island and the main land on the south side of this magnificent inlet, a boat put off, having a gentleman on board, who, by some accident, had missed his passage, but succeeded in getting alongside the ship. In seizing hold of a rope, thrown to him from the main-chains, one of the boatmen, in his hurry, caught a turn with the line round the after thwart, instead of making it fast forward. The

---

[1] *Sir William Edward Parry (1790–1855) searched for the Northwest Passage between 1819 and 1825 and attempted to reach the North Pole via sledge boat from Spitzbergen in 1827.*

inevitable and immediate consequence was, to raise the stern of the boat quite out of the water, and, of course, to plunge her nose under the surface, for the ship was running at the rate of ten knots.

In the twinkling of an eye, officer, boatmen, and all were floating about grasping at the oars or striking out for the land, distant, fortunately, only a few yards; for the water thereabouts is so deep that a ship in sailing out or in may safely graze the shore. Considering the intensity of the cold, we were quite astonished to see people swimming away so easily; but we afterwards learned that the water being between forty and fifty degrees warmer than the air, they felt, when plunged into it, as if they had been soused into a hot bath. The instant they reached the pier, however, and were lugged out, like half-drowned rats, they became literally enclosed in firm cases of ice from head to foot! This very awkward coat of mail was not removed without considerable difficulty; and one of them told me that he could not move at all till he had been laid for some hours in a well-warmed bed, between two other persons; and, for several months afterwards, he remained too unwell to leave his room.

For us to stop, at such a time and place, was impossible; so away we shot like an arrow past Chebucto Head, Cape Sambro, and sundry other fierce-looking black promontories of naked rock, smoothed off, apparently, by the attrition of some vast current. The breeze, which rose rapidly to a hard gale, split our main-top-sail to shreds, and sent the fragments cracking off to leeward in the storm, in such style, that, to this hour, I can almost fancy I hear the sound in my ears. I know, indeed, few things more impressive than the deep-toned thunder-like sounds caused by the flapping of a wet topsail, in such a fierce squall, when both sheets are carried away, and the unconfined sail is tugging and tearing to get clear of the yard, which bends so fearfully, that even the lower mast sometimes wags about like a reed.

I was standing, where I had no business to be, on the weather side of the quarter-deck, holding on stoutly by one of the belaying-pins; but the admiral looked up to the splitting sail quite composedly, and only desired that the main-top-men should be called down, out of the way of the ropes, which were smacking about their heads. Every now and then, the weather-wise glance of the veteran's eye was directed to windward, in anxious hope that matters would mend. But they only became worse; the foremast bent over like a cane, though the foresail had been reefed. Without waiting for his orders to run through the usual round of etiquette by which an admiral's commands are generally transmitted, he exclaimed, in a voice so loud that it made me start right over to the lee side of the deck:—

"Man the fore-clue garnets!"

In the next minute the sail rose gradually to the yard, and the groaning ship, by this time strained to her innermost timber, seemed to be at once relieved from the pressure of the canvas which had borne her headlong right into the seas, making the old barky tremble from stem to stern, as if she were going to pieces.

The jib-boom was now got in, in order to ease the bowsprit. In effecting this operation, rather troublesome at all times, one of the primest of our seamen fell overboard. He was the second captain of the forecastle; and his steadiness and skill as a steersman had, one day, elicited the complimentary remark from the captain, that he must surely have nailed the compass-card to the binnacle. On this, and other accounts, he was so much esteemed in the ship that more than the usual degree of regret was felt for his melancholy fate. I saw the poor fellow pitch headlong into the water, and watched him as he floated past, buoyant as a cork, and breasting the waves most gallantly, with an imploring look towards us, but in less than a minute he was out of sight. A boat could not have lived in such weather, and no further attempt could be made to save him, than to throw over ropes, which fell short of their mark. This, my first gale, was also one of the fiercest I ever saw. It lasted for three days, totally dispersed our little squadron, well nigh foundered one of them, the *Cambrian,* and sent her hobbling into Bermuda some days after us, with the loss of her main-mast and all three top-masts.

The Bermudas consist of upwards of a hundred little islands, clustered round two or three large ones. The seat of government then lay in St. George's Island, which measures about four or five miles long by two broad, and is very low. The neat little town, which runs across the valley half a mile each way, is built on the south-east side, on a gentle and very pretty declivity which fronts the harbour. None of the houses are more than two stories; they are built of the soft freestone of which all these islands are composed, and most of them own but one chimney. In walking through the streets in hot days, such is the extreme whiteness of the walls that the glare is very painful to the eyes; but as most of these dwellings are surrounded by bananas, calabashes, orange-trees, and various members of the palm tribe, the disagreeable effect of the light is not felt, except in the open streets. It was then mostly inhabited by blacks, a great many of whom were householders, who had gained their freedom by purchase or some other means, most of whom held under them slaves as black as themselves, who were never allowed to have fire-arms in their hands for fear of revolt.

Hardly any birds are to be seen, except the common blue and red birds of the island, the plumage of which is very brilliant. They are about the size of a fieldfare; but neither the one nor the other sings a note. In the midshipmen's berth, accordingly, we had no scruple of conscience about baking them by scores in our pies, and demolishing them, in the absence of more substantial fare.

Besides St. George's, there are numerous lesser islands, and a large district, called the Continent, from its being by far the most spacious in the cluster; no less, I believe, than twelve or fifteen miles from end to end! At the north-western end of the group lies Ireland Island, on which an extensive naval establishment had been erected; close to that spot was the anchorage for ships of war.

There is nothing more remarkable in this singular cluster of islands than the extensive coral reefs which fend off the sea on the northern side, and stretch out in a semicircular belt, at the distance of two or three leagues from the land. If I recollect rightly, only one of these ledges, called the North Rock, shows its head above water. As all the others lie out of sight below the surface, they form one of the most dangerous traps that nature has ever set in the path of mariners. Dangerous though they be, however, there are few things more beautiful to look at than these groves of corallines when viewed through two or three fathoms of clear and still water. It is hardly an exaggeration to assert, that even the bright colours of the rainbow are put to shame, on a sunny day, by what meets the eye on looking into the calm sea in those fairy regions. On the other hand, there are not many things, in the anxious range of navigation, more truly terrific, or, in fact, more dangerous, than these same beautiful submarine flower-beds, raising their treacherous heads, like the fascinating syrens of old, or the fair and false mermaids of a later epoch. If, by sad fortune, the unwary sailor once gets entangled among them, it is too well known that his chance of escape is but small.

They tell a story at Bermuda ("the still vexed Bermoothes" of Shakespeare) of a boatman who, it is said, lived by these disasters, and who once went off to an unlucky vessel, fairly caught, like a fly in a cobweb, amongst the coral reefs, not far from the North Rock. The wrecker, as persons of his trade are called, having boarded the bewildered ship, said to the master,—

"What will you give me now to get you out of this place?"

"Oh, anything you like—name your sum."

"Five hundred dollars?"

"Agreed! agreed!" cried the other. Upon which the treacherous pilot "kept his promise truly to the ear, but broke it to the hope," by taking the vessel out of an abominably bad place, only to fix her in one a great deal more intricate and perilous.

"Now," said the wrecker to the perplexed and doubly-cheated stranger, "there never was a ship in this scrape, that was known to get out again;

and, indeed, there is but one man alive who knows the passages, or could, by any possibility, extricate you—and that's me!"

"I suppose," dryly remarked the captain, "that 'for a consideration' you would be the man to do me that good service. What say you to another five hundred dollars to put me into clear water, beyond your infernal reefs?"

The hard bargain was soon made; and a winding passage, unseen before, being found, just wide enough, and barely deep enough, for the vessel to pass through, with only six inches to spare under her keel, in half an hour she was once more in blue water, out of soundings, and out of danger.

"Now, master rapscallion of a wrecker," cried the disentangled mariner, "tit for tat is fair play all the world over; and, unless you hand me back again my thousand dollars, I'll cut the tow-rope of your thievish-looking boat, and then, instead of returning evil for evil, as I ought to do, I'll be more of a Christian, and do you a very great service, by carrying you away from this infamous place to the finest country imaginable—America; and, as you seem to have a certain touch of black blood in your veins, I may chance to get good interest for my loan of these thousand dollars, by selling you for a slave in Charleston negro-market! What say you, my gay Mudian?"

We lay at Bermuda, moored in Murray's anchorage, for the greater part of the winters of 1802 and 1803. There was no war, and, in the absence of active service, we were fain to catch at anything to amuse and occupy ourselves. The master, and a gang of youngsters who were fond of navigation, set about surveying the coral reefs already mentioned. This party of philosophers, as they were of course dubbed, landed on St. David's Head, and other conspicuous points of land, to ascertain the longitude with more care; to observe the latitude and the variation of the compass; or to measure the perpendicular rise and fall of the tides; or, lastly, and much the most frequently, to have a good hour's swim in the deliciously-warm sea.

At first-sight, many of these pursuits may appear trivial; but it ought to be recollected that, although it is easy enough to make such observations in a rough way, there is hardly any scientific experiment which does not demand much attention and labour. For example, it seems a very simple affair to draw a base or straight line on the ground; but if the measurement is to be very exact, or of a particular length, so as to be neither more nor less, the problem is one of great delicacy, and employs the talents of some of the ablest engineers of the day. In fact, these refinements in surveying and observing are pretty much like the pound-of-flesh question in the *Merchant of Venice*, with one comfortable difference, that the philosopher's neck is not in such danger, even if, in a base of half-a-dozen miles, he should happen to err in the estimation by half-a-dozen hair-breadths! It is well for young officers to recollect, however, that there is a professional tribunal before which a man who undertakes such tasks is apt to be arraigned, and, if found wanting, pretty severely dealt with.

Sailors, like the element upon which they are tossed about, are scarcely ever at rest: the moment a ship arrives at a port, the navigators straightway erect their observatory, fix up their instruments, set their clocks a-going, and commence their attack, like the giants of old.

One of our party of mids, who has since turned out a valuable and enterprising officer, took it in his head to make a trip in a whale-boat belonging to the Bermuda fishery. Having ascertained the time when the whale-boats started, he obtained leave to go on shore, and completely succeeded in his object by being present at the capture of a whale. The monster, however, led them a considerable dance off to sea, and long after the time appointed for his return the youth made his appearance, delightfully perfumed with blubber, and having a glorious tale to tell of his day's adventures.

This was voted by acclamation to be "something like an expedition;" and the youngster, of course, gained great credit for his spirit. I was one of another party, who, I suppose, being a little jealous of our companion's laurels, took the earliest opportunity of trying to signalize ourselves in a similar way. A large whale was seen one morning playing about the *Leander,* in Murray's anchorage, and, of course, far within the belt of reefs already described as fringing the roadstead on its eastern and northern sides. How this great fellow had got into such a scrape, we could not conjecture. Possibly, in placing himself alongside one of the rugged coral ledges, to scrub off the incrustations of shell-fish, which torment these monsters of the deep, he had gradually advanced too far; or, more probably, he may have set out in pursuit of some small fry, and, before he was aware of it, had threaded his way among this labyrinth of rocks, till escape was impossible. At all events, he now found himself in comparatively deep water, from eight to ten fathoms, without any visible means of retreat from his coral trap. All hands crowded into the rigging to see the whale floundering about; till at length some one proposed, rashly enough, certainly, to pay him a visit in one of the ship's boats, with no better implements, offensive or defensive, than the ordinary boat-hooks—light poles, not unlike a shepherd's crook, with a spike and hook at the end; not bad things for fishing up a turtle when caught napping, but slender reeds, in all conscience, against a whale forty or fifty feet long!

Away we went, however, on our wild-goose whale-chase, without any precise idea what we were to do if we should come up with the game. As the great leviathan was approached, his aspect became more and more formidable; and it became necessary to think of some regular plan of attack. As to defence, it may easily be imagined that was never thought of; yet one gentle whisk of his tail might have sent the cutter and her crew, boat-hooks, oars, and all, spinning over the fore yard-arm of the flagship. All eyes being now upon us, it was agreed unanimously, after a pause, that we should run right on board of him and take our chance. So we rowed forward; but the whale, whose back was then showing just above the water, like a ship keel upwards, perhaps not approving of our looks, or possibly not seeing us, slipped down, clean out of sight, leaving only a monstrous whirlpool of oily-looking water, in the vortex of which we continued whirling round for some time, like great ninnies as we were, and gaping about us. At this time, the boat lay not half a ship's length from the *Leander*; so that our disappointment caused considerable amusement on board, and the people came laughing down from the rigging, where they had been perched, to see the grand fight between the whale and the young gentlemen!

While we were lying on our oars, and somewhat puzzled what to do next, we beheld one of the most extraordinary sights in the world; at least, I do not remember to have seen many things which have surprised me more or made a deeper impression on my memory. Our friend the whale, probably finding the water disagreeably shallow (for, as I have said, it was not above fifty or sixty feet deep), or perhaps provoked at not being able to disentangle himself from the sharp coral reefs, or for some other reason of his own, suddenly made a spring out of the sea. So complete was this enormous leap that for an instant he was seen fairly up in the air, in a horizontal position, at a distance from the surface not much short, I should think, of half his own breadth. His back, therefore, must have been at least twenty feet, in perpendicular height, above our heads. While in his progress upwards there really appeared in his spring some touch of the vivacity which belongs to a trout or to a salmon shooting out of the water. The whale, however, fell back again on the sea, like a huge log thrown on its broadside; and with such a thundering crash as made all hands stare in astonishment, making even the "boldest hold his breath for a time." Indeed, total demolition must have been the inevitable fate of our party had the whale taken his leap one minute sooner, for he would then have fallen plump on the boat! The surge of the waves caused by the explosion spread over half the anchorage! nor, if the *Leander* herself had blown up, could the effects have extended much further. As we rolled about in the cutter from side to side, we had time to balance the expediency of further proceedings against the tolerable chance of being smashed to atoms under the whale's belly at his next leap. All idea of capturing him, therefore, was given up; if, indeed, any such frantic notion could ever seriously have entered our heads. But our curiosity was vehemently roused to witness such another feat; and, after lying on our oars for some time, we once more detected the whale's back at a little distance from us.

"Let us poke him up again!" cried one of the party.

"To be sure, let's board him;" roared out the others; and away we dashed, in hopes of producing a repetition of this singular exploit. The whale, however, did not choose to exhibit any more, though we often succeeded in coming very near him. At last he fairly bolted, and took the direction of the North Rock, hoping, perhaps, to make his escape by the narrow passage probably known only to the most experienced denizens of those intricate submarine regions.

It was not until we had entirely lost sight of the chase, and when we had rowed so far that we could just see the top of St. George's Island astern of us, that we had leisure to remark the change of weather which had taken place during this absurd pursuit. The sky had become overcast, and the wind had risen to a smart breeze from the south-west, and when we again put the boat's head towards the island, it was quite as much as we could do to make any headway at all, and sometimes we hardly held our own. Had the wind increased a little more, we must inevitably have been blown to sea; even as it was, it cost us many hours of the severest tugging at the oars to regain the anchorage just before nightfall—the fishing party completely worn out.

## HISTORY OF SHAKINGS, THE MIDDIES' CUR

During the long winters of our slothful residence at Bermuda, the grand resource among the *Leander*'s officers was shooting—that never-ending, still-beginning amusement, which Englishmen carry to the remotest corners of the habitable globe. If Captain Parry had reached the Pole, he would unquestionably have had a shot at the axis of the earth!

In the mean time, the officers and young gentlemen of the flag-ship at Bermuda, I suppose to keep their hands in, were constantly blazing away among the cedar groves and orange plantations of those fairy islands, which appeared more and more beautiful after every such excursion. The midshipmen were contented with knocking down the blue and red birds with the ship's pistols, charged with his Majesty's gunpowder, and, for want of small shot, with slugs formed by cutting up his Majesty's musket bullets. The officers aimed at higher game, and were, of course, better provided with guns and ammunition. Several of them had some fine dogs—high-bred pointers; while the middies, also, not to be outdone, must needs

have a dog of their own: they recked very little of what breed; but some sort
of animal they said they must have.

I forget how we procured the strange-looking beast whose services we
contrived to engage; but, having once obtained him, we were not slow in
giving him our best affections. It is true, he was as ugly as anything could
possibly be. His colour was a dirty, reddish yellow; and while one part of
his hair became knotted and twisted into curls, another portion hung
down, quite straight, almost to the ground. He proved utterly useless for
all the purposes of real sport, but furnished the mids with plenty of fun
when they went on shore—in chasing pigs, barking at old white-headed
negresses, and other amusements, suited to the exalted tastes and habits of
the rising generation of officers.

People differ about the merits of dogs; but we had no doubts as to the
great superiority of ours over all the others on board, though the name we
gave him certainly implied no such confidence on our part. After a full
deliberation it was decided to call him Shakings. Now, be it known, that
"shakings" is the name given to small fragments of rope-yarns, odds and
ends of cordage, bits of oakum, old lanyards—in short, to every kind of
refuse, arising out of the wear and tear of the ropes. This odd name was
perhaps bestowed on our beautiful favourite in consequence of his colour
not being very dissimilar to that of well-tarred Russia-hemp; a resemblance
which was daily increased by many a dab of pitch, which, in the hot
weather, his rough coat imbibed from the seams between the planks of
the deck.

If Shakings was no great beauty, he was at least the most companion-
able of dogs. He dearly loved the midshipmen, and was dearly beloved by
them in return; but he had enough of the animal in his composition to take
a still higher pleasure in the society of his own kind, and when the high-
bred showy pointers belonging to the officers returned on board, after each
shooting excursion, Mr. Shakings lost no time in applying to his fellow-
dogs for the news. The pointers, who liked this sort of familiarity very well,
gave poor Shakings all sorts of encouragement. Not so their masters, the
officers, who could not bear to see "such an abominable cur," as they called
our favourite, at once "so cursedly dirty and so utterly useless," mixing
with their sleek and well-kept animals. At first, their dislike was confined
to such insulting expressions as the above; then it came to an occasional
kick on the stern, or a knock on the nose with the butt end of a fowling-
piece; and lastly to a sound cut across the rump with the hunting-whip.

Shakings, who instinctively knew his place, or, at all events, soon
learned it, took all this in good part, like a sensible fellow, while the mids,
when out of hearing of the higher powers, uttered curses both loud and

deep against the tyranny and oppression exercised towards an animal which, in their fond fancy, was declared to be worth all the showy dogs in the ward-room put together. They were little prepared, however, for the stroke which soon fell upon them, perhaps in consequence of these very murmurs—for bulkheads have ears as well as walls. To their great horror and indignation, one of the lieutenants, provoked at some liberty which Master Shakings had taken with his newly-polished boot, called out, one morning,—

"Man the jolly-boat, there, and land that infernal dirty beast of a dog belonging to the young gentlemen!"

"Where shall I take him to, sir?" asked the strokesman of the boat.

"Oh, anywhere; pull to the nearest part of the shore and pitch him out on the rocks. He'll shift for himself." Such was the threatened fate of poor dear Shakings!

If a stranger had come into the midshipmen's berth at that moment, he might have thought his Majesty's naval service was about to be broken up. All allegiance, discipline, and subordination seemed utterly cancelled by this horrible act. Many were the execrations hurled upwards at the offending "nobs," who, we declared, were combining to make our lives miserable. Some of our party proposed a letter of remonstrance to the admiral against this unheard-of outrage; and one youth swore deeply that he would leave the service, unless justice were obtained: but as he had been known to swear the same thing half-a-dozen times every week since he joined the ship, no great notice was taken of this pledge. Another declared, upon his word of honour, that such an act was enough to make a man turn Turk, and fly his country! At last, by general agreement, it was decided that we should not do duty, or stir from our seats, till we obtained redress for our grievances.

While we were in the very act of vowing mutiny and disobedience, the hands were turned up to "furl sails!" upon which the whole party, forgetting their magnanimous resolution, scudded up the ladders and jumped into their stations with more than usual alacrity, wisely thinking that the moment for actual revolt had not yet arrived.

A better scheme than throwing up the service, or writing to the admiral, or turning Mussulman, was afterwards concocted. The midshipman who went on shore in the next boat easily got hold of poor Shakings, who was howling on the steps of the watering-place. In order to conceal him, he was stuffed neck and crop into the captain's cloak-bag, brought safely on board, and restored once more to the bosom of his friends.

In spite of all we could do, however, to keep Master Shakings below, he presently found his way to the quarter-deck, to receive the congratulations of the other dogs. There he was soon detected by the higher powers, and very shortly afterwards trundled over the gangway, and again tossed on the beach. Upon this occasion he was honoured by the presence of one of his own masters, a middy, sent upon this express duty, who was specially desired "to land the brute, and not to bring him on board again." Of course, this particular youngster did not bring the dog off; but, before night, somehow or other, old Shakings was snoring away in grand chorus with his more fashionable friends the pointers, and dreaming no evil, before the door of the very officer's cabin whose beautifully-polished boots he had brushed by so rudely in the morning.

This second return of our dog was too much. The whole posse of us were sent for to the quarter-deck, and in very distinct terms positively ordered not to bring Shakings on board again. These injunctions having been given, this wretched victim of oppression, as we thought him, was once more landed among the cedar groves. This time he remained a full week on shore; and how or when he found his way off again, no one ever knew—at least, no one chose to divulge. Never was there anything like the mutual joy felt by Shakings and his two dozen masters at this meeting. He careered about the ship, barking and yelling with delight, and, in his raptures, he actually leaped, with his dirty feet, on the milk-white duck trousers of the disgusted officers, who heartily wished him at the bottom of the anchorage! The poor beast unwittingly contributed to accelerate his own hapless fate by this ill-timed show of confidence. If he had only kept his paws to himself, and stayed quietly in the dark recesses of the cockpit, wings, cable-tiers, and other wild regions—the secrets of which were known only to the inhabitants of our submarine world—all might have been well with him.

We had a grand jollification on the night of Shakings' restoration; and his health was in the very act of being drunk, with three times three, when the officer of the watch, hearing an uproar below, the sounds of which were distinctly conveyed up the windsail, sent down to put our lights out; and we were forced to march off, growling, to our hammocks.

Next day, to our surprise and horror, old Shakings was not to be seen or heard of. We searched everywhere, interrogated the coxswains of all the boats, and cross-questioned the marines who had been sentries during the night on the forecastle, gangways, and poop; but all in vain!—no trace of Shakings could be found.

At length the idea began to gain ground among us that the poor beast had been put an end to by some diabolical means, and our ire mounted accordingly. This suspicion seemed the more natural, as the officers said not a word about the matter, nor even asked us what we had done with our dog. While we were in this state of excitement, one of the midshipmen, who had some drollery in his composition, gave a new turn to the expression of our thoughts.

This *young* gentleman, who was more than twice as old as most of us, say about thirty, had won the affections of the whole of our class, by the gentleness of his manners, and the generous part he always took on our side. He bore among us the pet name of Daddy; and certainly he was as a father to those who, like myself, were adrift in the ship without any one to look after them. He was a man of talents and classical education; but he had entered the navy far too late in life ever to take to it cordially. He could not bend to the mortifying kind of discipline, which it is essential every officer should run through, but which only the young and light-hearted can brook; and our worthy friend, accordingly, with all his abilities, taste, and acquirements, never seemed at home on board ship. At all events, our old friend Daddy cared more about his books than about the blocks, and delighted much more in giving us assistance in our literary pursuits, and trying to teach us to be useful, than in rendering himself proficient in professional mysteries. This had secured our confidence. On all cases of difficulty, we never failed to cluster round him, to tell our grievances, great and small, with the certainty of always finding in him that great desideratum in calamity—a patient and friendly listener.

It will easily be supposed, that our kind Daddy took more than usual interest in this affair of Shakings, and that he was applied to by us at every stage of the transaction; like us, he felt sadly perplexed when the dog was finally missing; and, for some days afterwards he could afford us no comfort, nor suggest any mode of revenge which was not too dangerous to be put in practice. He prudently observed, that, as we had no certainty to go upon, it would be foolish to get ourselves into a serious scrape for nothing at all.

"There can be no harm, however," he at last exclaimed, in his dry and slightly sarcastic way, which all who knew him will recollect as well as if they saw him now, drawing his hand slowly across his mouth and chin, "There can be no possible harm, my boys, in putting the other dogs in mourning for Shakings; for, whatever is become of him, he is lost to them as well as to you, and his memory ought to be duly respected by his old masters."

This hint was no sooner given than a cry was raised for crape, and every chest and bag ransacked, to procure badges of mourning. Each of the pointers was speedily rigged out with a large bunch of black crape, tied in a handsome bow upon his left leg just above the knee. The joke took immediately, and even the officers could not help laughing; for, though we considered them little better than fiends at that moment of excitement, they really showed themselves (except in this instance) the best-natured and most indulgent persons I remember to have sailed with. They ordered the crape, however, to be instantly cut off from the dogs' legs; and one of them remarked very seriously, that "as we had now had our piece of fun out, there were to be no more such tricks."

Off we scampered, to consult old Daddy what was to be done next, as we had been positively ordered not to meddle any more with the dogs.

"Put the pigs in mourning!" said he.

All our crape had been expended by this time; but this want was soon supplied by men whose trade it is to discover resources in difficulty. With a generous devotion to the memory of the departed Shakings, one of the juvenile mutineers pulled off his black neckerchief, and, tearing it in pieces, gave a portion to each of the circle; and thus supplied, away we all started to put into practice this new suggestion of our director-general of mischief.

The row which ensued in the pig-sty was prodigious, for in those days hogs were allowed a place on board a man-of-war, a custom most wisely abolished of late years, since nothing can be more out of character with any ship than such nuisances. But these matters of taste and cleanliness were nothing to us; we intermitted not our noisy labour till every one of the grunters wore his armlet of such crape as we had been able to muster; then, watching our opportunity, we opened the door and let out the whole herd of swine on the main-deck just at the moment when a group of the officers were standing on the fore part of the quarter-deck. Of course the liberated pigs, delighted with their freedom, passed in review under the very nose of our superiors, each with his mourning-knot displayed, grunting or squealing along, as if it was their express object to attract attention to their sorrow for the loss of Shakings. The officers now became excessively provoked; for they could not help seeing that these proceedings were affording entertainment, at their expense, to the whole crew. The men, of course, took no part in this touch of insubordination; but they (like the middies) were ready enough, in those idle times of the weary, weary peace, to catch at any species of distraction or devilry, no matter what, to compensate for the loss of their wonted occupation of pommelling their enemies.

The matter, therefore, as a point of discipline, necessarily became rather serious; and the whole gang of young culprits being sent for on the quarter-deck, were ranged in a line, each with his toes at the edge of a plank, according to the orthodox fashion of these gregarious scoldings, technically called "toe-the-line matches." We were then given to understand that our proceedings were impertinent, and, after the orders we had received, highly offensive. It was with much difficulty that either party could keep their countenances during this official lecture, for, while it was going on, the sailors were endeavouring, by the direction of the officers, to remove the bits of silk from the legs of the pigs; but if it be difficult—as most difficult we found it—to put a hog into mourning, it is ten times more troublesome to take him out again. Such at least is the fair inference from these two experiments, the only cases, perhaps, on record; for it cost half the morning to undo what we had effected in less than an hour; to say nothing of the unceasing and outrageous uproar which took place along the decks, especially under the guns, and even under the coppers, forward in the galley, where two or three of the youngest pigs had wedged themselves, apparently resolved to die rather than submit to the degradation of being deprived of their sable badges.

All this was very creditable to the memory of poor Shakings; but, in the course of the day, the real secret of this extraordinary difficulty of taking a pig out of mourning was discovered. Two of the mids were detected in the very fact of tying on a bit of black bunting to the leg of a sow, from which the seamen declared they had already cut off crape and silk enough to have made her a complete suit of black.

On these fresh offences being reported, the whole party of us were ordered to the mast-head as a punishment. Some were sent to sit on the top-mast cross-trees, some on the top-gallant yard-arms, and one small gentleman being perched at the jibboom end, was very properly balanced abaft by another little culprit at the extremity of the gaff. In this predicament we were hung out to dry for six or eight hours, as old Daddy remarked to us with a grin, when we were called down as the night fell.

Our persevering friend, being rather provoked at the punishment of his young flock, set seriously to work to discover the real fate of Shakings. It soon occurred to him, that if the dog had indeed been made away with, as he shrewdly suspected, the ship's butcher, in all probability, must have had a hand in his murder: accordingly, he sent for the man in the evening, when the following dialogue took place:—

"Well, butcher, will you have a glass of grog tonight?"

"Thank you, sir, thank you. Here's your honour's health!" said the other, after smoothing down his hair and pulling an immense quid of tobacco out of his mouth.

Old Daddy observed the peculiar relish with which the rogue took his glass: and mixing another, a good deal more potent, placed it before the fellow. He then continued the conversation in these words:—

"I tell you what it is, Mr. Butcher—you are as humane a man as any in the ship, I dare say; but if required, you know well that you must do your duty, whether it is upon sheep or hogs?"

"Surely, sir."

"Or upon dogs, either?" suddenly asked the inquisitor.

"I don't know about that," stammered the butcher, quite taken by surprise, and thrown all aback.

"Well—well," said Daddy, "here's another glass for you—a stiff northwester. Come! tell us all about it now. How did you get rid of the dog?—of Shakings, I mean."

"Why, sir," said the peaching scoundrel, "I put him in a bag—a breadbag, sir."

"Well!—what then?"

"I tied up the mouth, and put him overboard, out of the midship lowerdeck port, sir."

"Yes—but he would not sink?" said Daddy.

"Oh, sir," cried the fellow, now entering fully into the subject, "I put a four-and-twenty pound shot into the bag along with Shakings."

"Did you?—Then, Master Butcher, all I can say is, you are as precious a rascal as ever went about unhanged. There—drink your grog and be off with you!"

Next morning, when the officers were assembling at breakfast in the ward-room, the door of the captain of marines' cabin was suddenly opened, and that officer, half-shaved, and laughing through a collar of soap-suds, stalked out with a paper in his hand.

"Here," he exclaimed, "is a copy of verses which I found just now in my basin. I can't tell how they got there, nor what they are about; but you shall judge."

So he read aloud the two following stanzas of doggerel:—

> *"When the Northern Confederacy threatened our shores,*
> *And roused Albion's Lion, reclining to sleep,*
> *Preservation was taken of all the King's Stores,*
> *Nor so much as a Rope Yarn was launched in the deep.*
>
> *"But now it is Peace, other hopes are in view,*
> *And all active service as light as a feather,*
> *The Stores may be d——d, and humanity too,*
> *For SHAKINGS and Shot are thrown o'erboard together!"*

I need hardly say in what quarter of the ship this biting morsel of cockpit satire was concocted, nor indeed who wrote it, for there was no one but our good Daddy who was equal to such a flight. About midnight, an urchin—who shall be nameless—was thrust out of one of the after-ports of the lower deck, from which he clambered up to the marine officer's port, and the sash happening to have been lowered down on the gun, the epigram, copied by another of the youngsters, was pitched into the soldier's basin.

The wisest thing would have been for the officers to have said nothing about the matter, and let it blow by; but as angry people are seldom judicious, they made a formal complaint to the captain, who, to do him justice, was not a little puzzled how to settle the affair. The reputed author, however, was called up, and the captain said to him—

"Pray, sir, are you the writer of these lines?"

"I am, sir," he replied, after a little consideration.

"Then, all I can say is," remarked the captain, "they are clever enough, in their way; but take my advice, and write no more such verses."

So the matter ended. The satirist took the captain's hint in good part, and confined his pen to topics less repugnant to discipline.

In the course of a few months the war broke out, and there was no longer time for such nonsense; indeed our generous protector Daddy, some time after this affair of Shakings took place, was sent off to Halifax, in charge of a prize. His orders were, if possible, to rejoin his own ship, the *Leander*, then lying at the entrance of New York harbour, just within Sandy Hook light-house.

Our good old friend, accordingly, having completed his mission, and delivered up his charge to the authorities of Halifax, took his passage in the British packet sailing from thence to the port in which we lay. As this ship sailed past us, on her way to the city of New York, we ascertained, to our great joy, that our excellent Daddy was actually on board of her. Some hours afterwards, the pilot-boat was seen coming to us, and, though it was in the middle of the night, all the younger mids came hastily on deck to welcome their worthy messmate back again to his home.

It was late in October, and the wind blew fresh from the northwestward, so that the ship riding to the ebb, had her head directed towards the Narrows, between Staten Land and Long Island: consequently, the pilot-boat (one of those beautiful vessels so well known to every visitor of the American coast) came flying down upon us with the wind nearly right aft. Our joyous party were all assembled on the quarter-deck, looking anxiously at the boat as she swept past. She then luffed round, in order to sheer alongside, at which moment the main-sail jibed, as was to be expected. It was obvious, however, that something more had taken place than the pilot had anticipated, since the boat, instead of ranging up to the gangway, being brought right round on her heel, went off upon a wind on the other tack. The tide carried her out of sight for a few minutes, but she was soon again alongside; when we learned, to our inexpressible grief and consternation, that on the main-boom of the pilot-boat swinging over, it had accidentally struck our poor friend, and pitched him headlong overboard. Being encumbered with his great-coat, the pockets of which, as we afterwards heard, were loaded with his young companions' letters, brought from England by this packet, he struggled in vain to catch hold of the boat, but sunk to rise no more.

* * *

*Basil Hall remained on board the* Leander *until shortly after the death of Sir Andrew Mitchell in 1806. In 1808 he was promoted to lieutenant, and in 1809 he was sent to Corunna. (See "When I Beheld These Men Spring from the Ground, 1809," on page 234.)*

*The peace through which Hall and his fellow middies so restlessly passed their time at Bermuda was, for them, mercifully short-lived. In March 1803, the French fleet began to prepare for an invasion of England, and on May 16, Britain declared war on France. Britain made aggressive moves in the West Indies, taking St. Lucia and Tobago from France and Demerara and Barbice from the Batavian Republic, and resumed its blockade off key French ports. On December 14, 1804, Spain declared war on Britain.*

*Nelson was stationed in the Mediterranean on the Toulon blockade. In early 1805, he chased Villeneuve to the West Indies and back. Napoleon still held out hope of combining the French and Spanish fleets to invade England, but that would end on October 21, 1805, off Cape Trafalgar, Spain.*

# *Part III*
## The Napoleonic War

~

# The Battle of Trafalgar

## 1805

*W*illiam Robinson *volunteered for the Royal Navy in May of 1805. Serving on board the newly built HMS* Revenge, *a 74-gun ship of the line commanded by Captain Robert Moorsom, Robinson quickly learned how to holy-stone, keep a watch, and drink Scotch coffee (burnt bread boiled in water with sugar). He saw discipline brutally instilled with the cat-o'-nine-tails. "By this regular system of duty," he later wrote, "I became inured to the roughness and hardships of a sailor's life. I had made up my mind to be obedient, however irksome to my feelings, and our ship being on the Channel station, I soon began to pick up a knowledge of seamanship." He would also soon be a battle-hardened man-of-war's man. On October 21, the* Revenge *would suffer twenty-eight men killed and fifty-one wounded. This is the first of two passages recounting the events of one of the Royal Navy's greatest and most tragic days.*

AFTER BEATING about the Channel for some time, we were ordered to proceed along the Spanish coast, to look after the combined fleets of France and Spain. Having heard that Sir Robert Calder had fallen in with them a few days previous, we pursued our course, looking in at Ferrol and other ports, until we arrived off Cadiz, where we found they had got safe in. Here we continued to blockade them, until Lord Nelson joined with us with five sail of the line. In order to decoy the enemy out, stratagem was resorted to, and five sail were sent to Gibraltar to victual and water, whilst Lord Nelson, with his five sail, kept out of sight of the enemy, and thus they

thought we were only twenty-two sail of the line, whilst their fleet consisted of thirty-three sail. With this superior force they put to sea, with the
intention, as we afterwards learned, of taking our fleet; and, if they had
succeeded, possessed of so great a force, they were to occupy the Channel,
and assist in the invasion of England by the troops then encamped along
the French coast, with an immense number of flat-bottomed boats, with
which the French ports swarmed; but here, as in many other instances, they
reckoned without their host. British valour and seamanship frustrated
their design, and destroyed their hopes; for on the memorable 21st of October, 1805, as the day began to dawn, a man at the topmast head called out,
"a sail on the starboard bow," and in two or three minutes more he gave
another call, that there was more than one sail, for indeed they looked like
a forest of masts rising from the ocean; and, as the morning got light, we
could plainly discern them from the deck, and were satisfied it was the
enemy, for the admiral began to telegraph to that effect. They saw us, and
would gladly have got away when they discovered that we counted
twenty-seven sail of the line, but it was too late, situated as they were;
hemmed in by Cape Trafalgar on the one side, and not being able to get
back to Cadiz on the other.

As the enemy was thus driven to risk a battle, they exhibited a specimen of their naval tactics by forming themselves into a crescent, or half-
moon, waiting for our approach; which did not take place until ten minutes
of twelve o'clock, so that there was nearly six hours to prepare for battle;
while we glided down to them under the influence of a gentle breeze,
cheering to every seaman's heart, that Providence took us in tow; and from
a signal made by Lord Nelson, our ships were soon formed into two lines,
weather and lee.

DURING THIS TIME each ship was making the usual preparations, such
as breaking away the captain and officer's cabins and sending all the lumber below—the doctors, parson, purser and loblolly men, were also busy,
getting the medicine chests and bandages out; and sails prepared for the
wounded to be placed on, that they might be dressed in rotation as they
were taken down to the after cock-pit. In such a bustling, and it may be
said, trying as well as serious time, it is curious to notice the different dispositions of the British sailor. Some would be offering a guinea for a glass
of grog, whilst others were making a sort of mutual verbal will, such as, if
one of Johnny Crapeau's shots (a term given to the French), knocks my
head off, you will take all my effects; and if you are killed, and I am not,

why, I will have yours, and this is generally agreed to. During this momentous preparation, the human mind had ample time for meditation and conjecture, for it was evident that the fate of England rested on this battle; therefore well might Lord Nelson make the signal, *"England expects each man will do his duty."*[1]

Here, if I may be indulged the observation, I will say that, could England but have seen her sons about to attack the enemy on his own coast, within sight of the inhabitants of Spain, with an inferior force, our number of men being not quite twenty thousand, whilst theirs was upwards of thirty thousand; from the zeal which animated every man in the fleet, the bosom of every inhabitant of England would have glowed with an indescribable patriotic pride; for such a number of line-of-battle ships have never met together and engaged, either before or since. As we drew near, we discovered the enemy's line was formed with a Spanish ship between two French ones, nearly all through their line; as I suppose, to make them fight better; and it must be admitted that the Dons fought as well as the French in that battle; and, if praise was due for seamanship and valour, they were well entitled to an equal share. We now began to hear the enemy's cannon opening on the *Royal Sovereign,* commanded by Lord Collingwood, who commenced the action; and, a signal being made by the admiral to some of our senior captains to break the enemy's line at different points, it fell to our lot to cut off the five stern-most ships; and, while we were running down to them, of course we were favoured with several shots, and some of our men were wounded. Upon being thus pressed, many of our men thought it hard that the firing should be all on one side and became impatient to return the compliment: but our captain had given

---

[1] It has been the generally received opinion that this memorable Signal was, *"England expects every man to do his duty,"* but an extract from the Log-book of the *Victory,* will shew it correctly. It was made by Telegraph, with the different coloured numerical flags, as follows: *On the 21st October,* 1805. *Note:* For alternative readings, see "Journal of Lieutenant John Barclay" and "The Log of HMS *Orion*" in T. Sturges Jackson, ed., *The Logs of the Great Sea Fights, 1794–1805.* Publications of the Navy Records Society, volume XVIII. (London, 1900), pp. 213, 278.

TELEGRAPH

| | |
|---|---|
| 253—ENGLAND | |
| 269—EXPECTS | |
| 238—EACH | 4 ⎤ D |
| 471—MAN | 21 ⎥ U |
| 958—WILL | 19 ⎥ T |
| 220—DO | 24 ⎦ Y |
| 370—HIS | |

orders not to fire until we got close in with them, so that all our shots might tell; indeed, these were his words: "We shall want all our shot when we get close in: never mind their firing: when I fire a carronade from the quarter-deck, that will be a signal for you to begin, and I know you will do your duty as Englishmen." In a few minutes the gun was fired, and our ship bore in and broke the line, but we paid dear for our temerity, as those ships we had thrown into disorder turned round, and made an attempt to board. A Spanish three-decker ran her bowsprit over our poop, with a number of her crew on it, and, in her fore rigging, two or three hundred men were ready to follow; but they caught a Tartar, for their design was discovered, and our marines with their small arms, and the carronades on the poop, loaded with canister shot, swept them off so fast, some into the water and some on the decks, that they were glad to sheer off. While this was going on aft, we were engaged with a French two-deck ship on our starboard side, and on our larboard bow another, so that many of their shots must have struck their own ships and done severe execution. After being engaged about an hour, two other ships fortunately came up, received some of the fire intended for us, and we were now enabled to get at some of the shot-holes between wind and water and plug them up: this is a duty performed by the carpenter and his crew. We were now unable to work the ship, our yards, sails, and masts being disabled, and the braces completely shot away. In this condition we lay by the side of the enemy, firing away, and now and then we received a good raking from them, passing under our stern. This was a busy time with us, for we had not only to endeavour to repair our damage, but to keep to our duty. Often during the battle we could not see for the smoke whether we were firing at a foe or friend, and as to hearing, the noise of the guns had so completely made us deaf, that we were obliged to look only to the motions that were made. In this manner we continued the battle till nearly five o'clock, when it ceased.

It was shortly after made known by one of our boat's crew, that Lord Nelson had received a fatal shot: had this news been communicated through the fleet before the conflict was over, what effect it might have had on the hearts of our seamen I know not, for he was adored, and in fighting under him, every man thought himself sure of success; a momentary but naturally melancholy pause among the survivors of our brave crew ensued.

We were now called to clear the decks, and here might be witnessed an awful and interesting scene, for as each officer and seaman would meet (oh! what an opportunity for the Christian and man of feeling to meditate on the casualty of fate in this life), they were inquiring for their mess-mates. Orders were now given to fetch the dead bodies from the after cock-pit,

# The Battle of Trafalgar
## October 21, 1805

◔ British ship of the line     *VICTORY* Flagship
◑ Spanish ship of the line     *Aigle* Prize
● French ship of the line     *Achille* Sunk

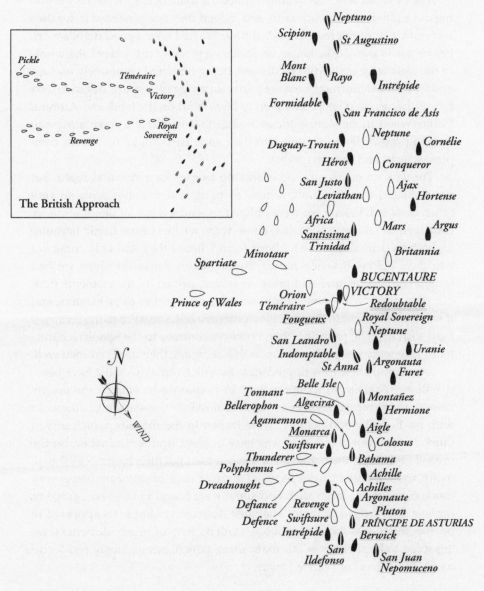

The British Approach

and throw them over-board; these were the bodies of men who were taken down to the doctor during the battle, badly wounded, and who by the time the engagement was ended were dead. Some of these, perhaps, could not have recovered, while others might, had timely assistance been rendered, which was impossible; for the rule is, as order is requisite, that every person shall be dressed in rotation as they are brought down wounded, and in many instances some have bled to death.

The next call was, "all hands to splice the main brace," which is the giving out a gill of rum to each man, and indeed they much needed it, for they had not ate or drank from breakfast time: we had now a good night's work before us; all our yards, masts, and sails were sadly cut, indeed the whole of the sails were obliged to be unbent, being rendered completely useless, and by the next morning we were partly jury-rigged: we now began to look for our prizes, as it was coming on to blow hard on the land, and Admiral Collingwood made signals for each ship that was able to take a prize in tow, to prevent them drifting into their own harbour, as they were complete wrecks and unmanageable.

We took an eighty gun Spanish ship in tow for a day and night, but were obliged to cast her off, it blew so hard, and our ship being so very much disabled, indeed we were obliged to scuttle a few of them; some we contrived to take into Gibralter; some were wrecked near Cadiz harbour; and others drifted into the harbour from whence they had only come out two days before. It was a mortifying sight to witness the ships we had fought so hard for, and had taken as prizes, driven by the elements from our possession, with some of our own men on board as prize masters, and it was a great blight to our victorious success; but, in justice to the enemy, it may with truth be recorded, that, however contrary to the Spanish character as an enemy generally, yet, upon this occasion, they used our men well.

In order to shew the crippled state in which our ships must have been, it will be requisite to mention that, in preparing to engage the enemy closely, and protect ourselves as much as possible, the seamen's hammocks with the bedding and blankets were lashed to the shrouds, which served much to save our rigging, as was very evident from examination on the second night after the battle; for when our men got their hammocks down, many were found to have received a great deal of damage, being very much cut with the large shot, and some were found to have had grape or canister shot lodged in them. The most destructive shot to us appeared to be the thirty-two pounds double-headed; two of these deafeners we observed to be sticking in our main-mast, which, miraculously and fortunately for us, was not carried away.

I will now call the reader's attention to some occurrences during and after the battle, which, although they may not regularly belong to a seaman's log, yet they may be found interesting.

AS WE WERE closely engaged throughout the battle, and the shots were playing their pranks pretty freely, grape as well as canister, with single and double headed thunderers all joining in the frolic; what was termed a *slaughtering one*, came in at one of the lower deck ports, which killed and wounded nearly all at the gun, and amongst them, a very merry little fellow, who was the very life of the ship's company, for he was ever the mirth of his mess, and on whatever duty he might be ordered, his spirits made light the labour. He was the ship's cobbler, and withall a very good dancer; so that when any of his messmates would *sarve* us out a tune, he was sure to trip it on light fantastic toe, and find a step to it. He happened to be stationed at the gun where this messenger of death and destruction entered, and the poor fellow was so completely stunned by the head of another man being knocked against his, that no one doubted but that he was dead. As it is customary to throw overboard those, who, in an engagement are killed outright, the poor cobbler, amongst the rest, was taken to the port-hole to be committed to the deep, without any other ceremony than shoving him through the port: but, just as they were about to let him slip from their hands into the water, the blood began to circulate, and he commenced kicking. Upon this sign of returning life, his shipmates soon hauled the poor snob in again, and, though wonderful to relate, he recovered so speedily, that he actually fought the battle out; and, when he was afterwards joked about it, he would say, "it was well that I learned to dance; for if I had not shown you some of my steps, when you were about to throw me overboard, I should not be here now, but safe enough in *Davy Jones's Locker*."

WHILST WE WERE engaging the combined fleets, a French ship caught fire, the crew of which made every effort to escape from the flames, and as

"Britons fight but to conquer, and conquer to save,"

our frigates and schooners, which had been laying off during the battle, sent their boats to endeavour to save as many lives as possible. Amongst those who were thus preserved from a watery grave was a young French woman, who was brought on board our ship in a state of complete nakedness.

Although it was in the heat of the battle, yet she received every assistance which at that time was in our power; and her distress of mind was soothed as well as we could, until the officers got to their chests, from whence they supplied her with needles and thread, to convert sheets into chemises, and curtains from their cots to make somewhat of a gown and other garments, so that by degrees she was made as comfortable as circumstances would admit; for we all tried who would be most kind to her; and as the history of this adventurer may acquire some interest from the account she gave of it, the following is the statement, as collected from herself;—

"The combined fleets, (she says) were ordered to proceed from Cadiz, where they lay, to make an attack and take that of the British; for, from their superior force they were confident of success and elated at the same time with the idea that it would be but an easy task. That no impediment might be in the way, all the females were ordered to go on shore; she was married, and to quit her husband could not endure the thought; she was therefore resolved to share his glory or his death. No time was lost in carrying her plan into execution; for, having rigged herself out in a suit of sailor's clothes, thus disguised, she entered on board, and went in the same ship with him, as a seaman. In this state she remained, doing duty, during the engagement, when, whilst fighting by the side of her husband, a ball killed him on the spot. On seeing him fall dead, the conflict was too great:— nature displayed itself; she became overwhelmed with grief, and, by it, betrayed her sex.

To add to the distress which this discovery occasioned, an alarm was now spread that the ship was on fire; she seemed to care very little about it; life to her was not desirable, whilst all hands were employed in the endeavour to check the fire's progress. This seemed to be impossible, and it became necessary to think of the means to escape; for the fire raged with great fury, and there was every probability that, in a few minutes, the ship would be blown into the air, as the fire was fast approaching the magazines.

The resolution to take to the water being now unavoidable, the men commenced to undress themselves; and in this dreadful situation she was strongly urged to do the same, that it was a duty to make every effort for self-preservation, and it being the only chance she could possibly have. After much entreaty, persuasion, and remonstrance, she summoned up sufficient resolution, and prepared herself to endure the agonizing alternative, for the only choice which her unfortunate case presented, was, either to strip or perish in the flames. She was then lowered into the ocean by a rope from the taffrail, the lead of which was melting at the time, and, whilst letting her down, some of it dropped, and burned the back of her neck. On reaching the water, one of her shipmates, who was a good swimmer, staid by her side, and supported her until she was picked up by a boat belonging to the *Pickle* schooner, and brought on board the ship she was then in." [Here let the reader pause, and paint to himself, if he can, what were the inward workings and heartfelt sufferings of this extraordinary heroine, and bright instance of conjugal fidelity and attachment.]

Her name was Jeannette, of French Flanders, and she remained with us until our arrival at Gibralter, when a cartel took her to a Spanish port. On leaving our ship, her heart seemed overwhelmed with gratitude; she shed abundance of tears, and could only now and then, with a deep sigh, exclaim, *"les bons Anglois."*

SOME OF OUR MEN were sent on board of the Spanish ship before alluded to, in order to assist at the pumps, for she was much shattered in the hull, between wind and water. The slaughter and havoc our guns had made, rendered the scene of carnage horrid to behold: there were a number of their dead bodies piled up in the hold; many, in a wounded or mutilated state, were found lying amongst them; and those who were so fortunate as to escape our shot were so dejected and crest-fallen that they could not, or would not, work at the pumps, and of course the ship was in a sinking state.

The gale at this time was increasing so rapidly that manning the pumps was of no use, and we were obliged to abandon our prize, taking away with us all our men and as many of the prisoners as we could. On the last boat's load leaving the ship, the Spaniards who were left on board, appeared on the gangway and ship's side, displaying their bags of dollars and doubloons, and eagerly offering them as a reward for saving them from the expected and unavoidable wreck; but, however well inclined we were, it was not in our power to rescue them, or it would have been effected without the proffered bribe.

Here a very distressing and affecting scene took place; it was a struggle between inclination and duty. On quitting the ship, our boats were overloaded in endeavouring to save all the lives we could, that it is a miracle they were not upset. A father and his son came down the ship's side to get on board one of our boats; the father had seated himself, but the men in the boat, thinking, from the load and the boisterous weather, that all their lives would be in peril, could not think of taking the boy; as the boat put off, the lad, as though determined not to quit his father, sprung from the ship into the water and caught hold of the gunwale of the boat; but his attempt was resisted, as it risked all their lives, and some of the men resorted to their cutlasses to cut his fingers off, in order to disentangle the boat from his grasp; at the same time the feelings of the father were so worked upon, that he was about to leap overboard and perish with his son: Britons could face an enemy, but could not witness such a scene of self-devotion; as it were, a simultaneous thought burst forth from the crew, which said "let us save both father and son or die in the attempt." The Almighty aided them in their design; they succeeded, and brought both father and son safe on board of our ship, where they remained, until, with other prisoners, they were exchanged at Gibraltar.

• • •

*Using the pseudonym Jack Nastyface, Robinson published his book* Nautical Economy, *containing the preceding account, in 1836. He fails to mention in it that he deserted in 1811. Much more particular in its detail and far closer to the central plot was the narrative of William Beatty, the surgeon on board Nelson's flagship* Victory *during the bittersweet British triumph at the Battle of Trafalgar.*

# WILLIAM BEATTY

## The Death of Lord Nelson

### 1805

*A*t the age of forty-seven, Admiral Lord Horatio Nelson had already lost his right eye and right arm in the service of his country. His courageous maneuvers had helped win smashing triumphs over the Spanish at the Battle of Cape St. Vincent (1797), over the French at the Battle of the Nile (1798), and over the Danish at the Battle of Copenhagen (1801). But Nelson was as vain as he was courageous. ("I am envious only of glory; for if it be a sin to covet glory, I am the most offending soul alive," he wrote Lady Hamilton in 1800.) He insisted on wearing his honorary medals on his uniform during battle, which made him an obvious target for enemy sharpshooters. In this passage, Surgeon William Beatty delivers his classic account of the Battle of Trafalgar—down to Nelson's last words.

AS THE VICTORY drew near to the enemy, his Lordship, accompanied by Captain Hardy, and the captains of the four frigates (*Euryalus, Naiad, Sirius,* and *Phoebe*) who had been called on board by signal to receive instructions, visited the different decks of the ship. He addressed the crew at their several quarters, admonishing them against firing a single shot without being sure of their object; and expressed himself to the officers highly satisfied with the arrangements made at their respective stations.

It was now plainly perceived by all on board the *Victory,* that from the very compact line which the enemy had formed, they were determined to make one great effort to recover in some measure their long lost naval reputation. They wore in succession about twenty minutes past seven o'clock;

and stood on the larboard tack, with their heads toward Cadiz. They kept
a good deal of sail set; steering about two points from the wind, with top
sails shivering. Their van was particularly closed, having the *Santissima
Trinidada* and the *Bucentaur* the ninth and tenth ships, the latter the flagship
of Admiral Villeneuve: but as the admirals of the Combined fleets declined
shewing their flags till the heat of the battle was over, the former of these
ships was only distinguished from the rest by her having four decks; and
Lord Nelson ordered the *Victory* to be steered for her bow.

Several officers of the ship now communicated to each other their sentiments of anxiety for his Lordship's personal safety, to which every other
consideration seemed to give way. Indeed all were confident of gaining a
glorious victory, but the apprehensions for his Lordship were great and
general; and the surgeon made known to Dr. Scott his fears that his Lordship would be made the object of the enemy's marksmen, and his desire
that he might be entreated by somebody to cover the stars on his coat with
a handkerchief.

Dr. Scott and Mr. Scott (public secretary) both observed, however, that
such a request would have no effect; as they knew his Lordship's sentiments on the subject so well, that they were sure he would be highly displeased with whoever should take the liberty of recommending any
change in his dress on this account; and when the surgeon declared to Mr.
Scott that he would avail himself of the opportunity of making his sick
report for the day, to submit his sentiments to the admiral, Mr. Scott
replied, "Take care, Doctor, what you are about: I would not be the man to
mention such a matter to him."

The surgeon notwithstanding persisted in his design, and remained on
deck to find a proper opportunity for addressing his Lordship; but this
never occurred: as his Lordship continued occupied with the captains of
the frigates (to whom he was explaining his intentions respecting the services they were to perform during the battle) till a short time before the
enemy opened their fire on the *Royal Sovereign*, when Lord Nelson ordered
all persons not stationed on the quarter deck or poop to repair to their
proper quarters; and the surgeon, much concerned at this disappointment,
retired from the deck with several other officers.

The boats on the quarters of the ship, being found in the way of the
guns, were now lowered down and towed astern.

Captain Blackwood, of the *Euryalus*, remained on board the *Victory* till
a few minutes before the enemy began to fire upon her. He represented to
his Lordship that his flagship would be singled out and much pressed by
the enemy; and suggested the propriety therefore of permitting one or two
ships of his line to go ahead of the *Victory*, and lead her into action, which

might be the means of drawing in some measure the enemy's attention from her.

To this Lord Nelson assented, and at half past nine o'clock he ordered the *Téméraire* and *Leviathan* by signal (the former of which ships, being close to the *Victory*, was hailed by his Lordship) to go ahead for that purpose; but from the light breeze that prevailed they were unable, notwithstanding their utmost efforts, to attain their intended stations. Captain Blackwood foresaw that this would be the case; and as the *Victory* still continued to carry all her sail, he wished Captain Hardy to acquaint his Lordship, that unless her sail was in some degree shortened, the two ships just mentioned could not succeed in getting ahead previously to the enemy's line being forced: this, however, Captain Hardy declined doing, as he conceived his Lordship's ardour to get into battle would on no account suffer such a measure.

About half an hour before the enemy opened their fire, the memorable telegraphic signal was made, that "ENGLAND EXPECTS EVERY MAN WILL DO HIS DUTY," which was spread and received throughout the fleet with enthusiasm. It is impossible adequately to describe by any language the lively emotions excited in the crew of the *Victory* when this propitious communication was made known to them: confidence and resolution were strongly pourtrayed in the countenance of all; and the sentiment generally expressed to each other was that they would prove to their country that day how well British seamen *could* "do their duty" when led to battle by their revered admiral.

The signal was afterwards made to "prepare to anchor after the close of the day;" and Union Jacks were hoisted at the foretop mast and topgallant stays of each ship, to serve as a distinction from the enemy's, in conformity with orders previously issued by the commander in chief. By his Lordship's directions also, the different divisions of the fleet hoisted the St. George's or White Ensign, being the colours of the commander in chief: this was done to prevent confusion from occurring during the battle, through a variety of national flags.

The *Royal Sovereign* now made the signal by telegraph, that "the enemy's commander in chief was in a frigate." This mistake arose from one of their frigates making many signals.

Lord Nelson ordered his line to be steered about two points more to the northward than that of his second in command, for the purpose of cutting off the retreat of the enemy's van to the port of Cadiz; which was the reason of the three leading ships of Admiral Collingwood's line being engaged with the enemy previously to those of the commander in chief's line.

The enemy began to fire on the *Royal Sovereign* at thirty minutes past eleven o'clock; in ten minutes after which, she got under the stern of the *St.*

*Anna,* and commenced a fire on her. Lieutenant Pasco, signal officer of the *Victory,* was heard to say while looking through his glass, "There is a topgallant yard gone." His Lordship eagerly asked, "Whose topgallant yard is that gone? Is it the *Royal Sovereign's?*" and on being answered by Lieutenant Pasco in the negative, and that it was the enemy's, he smiled, and said: "Collingwood is doing well."

At fifty minutes past eleven, the enemy opened their fire on the commander in chief. They shewed great coolness in the commencement of the battle; for as the *Victory* approached their line, their ships lying immediately ahead of her and across her bows fired only one gun at a time, to ascertain whether she was yet within their range. This was frequently repeated by eight or nine of their ships, till at length a shot passed through the *Victory's* main topgallant sail; the hole in which being discovered by the enemy, they immediately opened their broadsides, supporting an awful and tremendous fire.

In a very short time afterwards, Mr. Scott, public secretary to the commander in chief, was killed by a cannon shot while in conversation with Captain Hardy. Lord Nelson being then near them; Captain Adair of the marines, with the assistance of a seaman, endeavoured to remove the body from his Lordship's sight: but he had already observed the fall of his secretary; and now said with anxiety, "Is that poor Scott that is gone?" and on being answered in the affirmative by Captain Adair, he replied, "Poor fellow!"

Lord Nelson and Captain Hardy walked the quarter deck in conversation for some time after this, while the enemy kept up an incessant raking fire.

A double-headed shot struck one of the parties of marines drawn up on the poop, and killed eight of them; when his Lordship, perceiving this, ordered Captain Adair to disperse his men round the ship, that they might not suffer so much from being together.

In a few minutes afterwards a shot struck the fore brace bits on the quarter deck, and passed between Lord Nelson and Captain Hardy; a splinter from the bits bruising Captain Hardy's foot, and tearing the buckle from his shoe. They both instantly stopped; and were observed by the officers on deck to survey each other with inquiring looks, each supposing the other to be wounded. His Lordship then smiled, and said: "This is too warm work, Hardy, to last long;" and declared that "through all the battles he had been in, he had never witnessed more cool courage than was displayed by the *Victory's* crew on this occasion."

The *Victory* by this time, having approached close to the enemy's van, had suffered very severely without firing a single gun: she had lost about twenty men killed, and had about thirty wounded. Her mizzen topmast, and all her studding sails and their booms on both sides were shot away; the enemy's fire being chiefly directed at her rigging, with a view to disable her before she could close with them.

At four minutes past twelve o'clock, she opened her fire, from both sides of her decks, upon the enemy; when Captain Hardy represented to his Lordship, that "it appeared impracticable to pass through the enemy's line without going on board some one of their ships."

Lord Nelson answered, "I cannot help it: it does not signify which we run on board of; go on board which you please; take your choice."

At twenty minutes past twelve, the tiller ropes being shot away: Mr. Atkinson, the master, was ordered below to get the helm put to port; which being done, the *Victory* was soon run on board the *Redoubtable* of seventy-four guns.

On coming alongside and nearly on board of her, that ship fired her broadside into the *Victory*, and immediately let down her lower deck ports; which, as has been since learnt, was done to prevent her from being boarded through them by the *Victory*'s crew. She never fired a great gun after this single broadside.

A few minutes after this, the *Téméraire* fell likewise on board of the *Redoubtable*, on the side opposite to the *Victory*; having also an enemy's ship, said to be *La Fougueux*, on board of *her* on her other side: so that the extraordinary and unprecedented circumstance occurred here, of *four* ships of the line being *on board of each other* in the heat of battle; forming as compact a tier as if they had been moored together, their heads lying all the same way. The *Téméraire*, as was just before mentioned, was between the *Redoubtable* and *La Fougueux*.

The *Redoubtable* commenced a heavy fire of musketry from the tops, which was continued for a considerable time with destructive effect to the *Victory*'s crew: her great guns however being silent, it was supposed at different times that she had surrendered; and in consequence of this opinion, the *Victory* twice ceased firing upon her by orders transmitted from the quarter deck.

At this period, scarcely a person in the *Victory* escaped unhurt who was exposed to the enemy's musketry; but there were frequent huzzas and cheers heard from between the decks, in token of the surrender of different of the enemy's ships. An incessant fire was kept up from both sides of the *Victory*: her larboard guns played upon the *Santissima Trinidada* and the *Bucentaur*; and the starboard guns of the middle and lower decks were depressed, and fired with a diminished charge of powder, and three shot each, into the *Redoubtable*. This mode of firing was adopted by Lieutenants

Williams, King, Yule, and Brown, to obviate the danger of the *Téméraire*'s suffering from the *Victory*'s shot passing through the *Redoubtable*; which must have been the case if the usual quantity of powder, and the common elevation, had been given to the guns.

A circumstance occurred in this situation which showed in a most striking manner the cool intrepidity of the officers and men stationed on the lower deck of the *Victory*. When the guns on this deck were run out, their muzzles came into contact with the *Redoubtable*'s side; and consequently at every discharge there was reason to fear that the enemy would take fire, and both the *Victory* and the *Téméraire* be involved in her flames. Here then was seen the astonishing spectacle of the fireman of each gun standing ready with a bucket full of water, which as soon as his gun was discharged he dashed into the enemy through the holes made in her side by the shot.

It was from this ship (the *Redoubtable*) that Lord Nelson received his mortal wound. About fifteen minutes past one o'clock, which was in the heat of the engagement, he was walking the middle of the quarter deck with Captain Hardy, and in the act of turning near the hatchway with his face towards the stern of the *Victory*, when the fatal ball was fired from the enemy's mizzen top; which, from the situation of the two ships (lying on board of each other), was brought just abaft, and rather below, the *Victory*'s main yard, and of course not more than fifteen yards distant from that part of the deck where his Lordship stood. The ball struck the epaulette on his left shoulder, and penetrated his chest. He fell with his face on the deck. Captain Hardy, who was on his right (the side furthest from the enemy) and [had] advanced some steps before his Lordship, on turning round, saw the serjeant major (Secker) of Marines with two seamen raising him from the deck; where he had fallen on the same spot on which, a little before, his secretary had breathed his last, with whose blood his Lordship's clothes were much soiled.

Captain Hardy expressed a hope that he was not severely wounded; to which the gallant chief replied: "They have done for me at last, Hardy."

"I hope not," answered Captain Hardy.

"Yes," replied his Lordship; "my backbone is shot through."

Captain Hardy ordered the seamen to carry the admiral to the cockpit; and now two incidents occurred strikingly characteristic of this great man, and strongly marking that energy and reflection which in his heroic mind rose superior even to the immediate consideration of his present awful condition. While the men were carrying him down the ladder from the middle deck, his Lordship observed that the tiller ropes were not yet replaced; and desired one of the midshipmen stationed there to go upon the quarter deck and remind Captain Hardy of that circumstance, and request that new ones

should be immediately rove. Having delivered this order, he took his handkerchief from his pocket and covered his face with it, that he might be conveyed to the cockpit at this crisis unnoticed by the crew.

Several wounded officers, and about forty men, were likewise carried
to the surgeon for assistance just at this time; and some others had breathed
their last during their conveyance below. Among the latter were Lieutenant
William Andrew Ram, and Mr. Whipple, captain's clerk. The surgeon had
just examined these two officers, and found that they were dead; when his
attention was arrested by several of the wounded calling to him, "Mr.
Beatty, Lord Nelson is here: Mr. Beatty, the admiral is wounded."

The surgeon now, on looking round, saw the handkerchief fall from his
Lordship's face; when the stars on his coat, which also had been covered by
it, appeared. Mr. Burke the purser, and the surgeon, ran immediately to the
assistance of his Lordship; and took him from the arms of the seamen who
had carried him below. In conveying him to one of the midshipmen's
berths, they stumbled; but recovered themselves without falling. Lord Nelson then inquired who were supporting him; and when the surgeon
informed him, his Lordship replied, "Ah, Mr. Beatty! you can do nothing
for me. I have but a short time to live: my back is shot through."

The surgeon said, "he hoped the wound was not so dangerous as his
Lordship imagined, and that he might still survive long to enjoy his glorious victory."

The Rev. Dr. Scott, who had been absent in another part of the cockpit
administering lemonade to the wounded, now came instantly to his Lordship; and in the anguish of grief wrung his hands, and said: "Alas, Beatty,
how prophetic you were!" alluding to the apprehensions expressed by the
surgeon for his Lordship's safety previous to the battle.

His Lordship was laid upon a bed, stripped of his clothes, and covered
with a sheet. While this was effecting, he said to Dr. Scott, "Doctor, I told
you so. Doctor, I am gone;" and after a short pause he added in a low voice,
"I have to leave Lady Hamilton, and my adopted daughter Horatia, as a
legacy to my country."

The surgeon then examined the wound, assuring his Lordship that he
would not put him to much pain in endeavouring to discover the course of
the ball; which he soon found had penetrated deep into the chest, and had
probably lodged in the spine. This being explained to his Lordship; he
replied, "he was confident his back was shot through." The back was then
examined externally, but without any injury being perceived; on which his
Lordship was requested by the surgeon to make him acquainted with all
his sensations. He replied, that "he felt a gush of blood every minute within
his breast: that he had no feeling in the lower part of his body: and that his

breathing was difficult, and attended with very severe pain about that part of the spine where he was confident that the ball had struck; for," said he, "I felt it break my back."

These symptoms, but more particularly the gush of blood which his Lordship complained of, together with the state of his pulse, indicated to the surgeon the hopeless situation of the case; but till after the victory was ascertained and announced to his Lordship, the true nature of his wound was concealed by the surgeon from all on board except only Captain Hardy, Dr. Scott, Mr. Burke, and Messrs. Smith and Westemburg the assistant surgeons.

The *Victory's* crew cheered whenever they observed an enemy's ship surrender. On one of these occasions, Lord Nelson anxiously inquired what was the cause of it; when Lieutenant Pasco, who lay wounded at some distance from his Lordship, raised himself up, and told him that another ship had struck, which appeared to give him much satisfaction.

He now felt an ardent thirst; and frequently called for drink, and to be fanned with paper, making use of these words: "Fan, fan!" and "Drink, drink!" This he continued to repeat, when he wished for drink or the refreshment of cool air, till a very few minutes before he expired. Lemonade, and wine and water, were given to him occasionally. He evinced great solicitude for the event of the battle, and fears for the safety of his friend Captain Hardy. Dr. Scott and Mr. Burke used every argument they could suggest, to relieve his anxiety.

Mr. Burke told him "the enemy were decisively defeated, and that he hoped his Lordship would still live to be himself the bearer of the joyful tidings to his country."

He replied, "It is nonsense, Mr. Burke, to suppose I can live: my sufferings are great, but they will all be soon over."

Dr. Scott entreated his Lordship "not to despair of living," and said "he trusted that Divine Providence would restore him once more to his dear country and friends."

"Ah, Doctor!" replied his Lordship, "it is all over; it is all over!"

Many messages were sent to Captain Hardy by the surgeon, requesting his attendance on his Lordship; who became impatient to see him, and often exclaimed: "Will no one bring Hardy to me? He must be killed: he is surely destroyed."

The Captain's aide de camp, Mr. Bulkley, now came below, and stated that "circumstances respecting the fleet required Captain Hardy's presence on deck; but that he would avail himself of the first favourable moment to visit his Lordship."

On hearing him deliver this message to the surgeon, his Lordship inquired who had brought it.

Mr. Burke answered, "It is Mr. Bulkley, my Lord."

"It is his voice," replied his Lordship: he then said to the young gentleman, "Remember me to your father."

An hour and ten minutes however, elapsed from the time of his Lordship's being wounded, before Captain Hardy's first subsequent interview with him; the particulars of which are nearly as follow.

They shook hands affectionately, and Lord Nelson said: "Well, Hardy, how goes the battle? How goes the day with us?"

"Very well, my Lord," replied Captain Hardy: "we have got twelve or fourteen of the enemy's ships in our possession; but five of their van have tacked and shew an intention of bearing down upon the *Victory.* I have therefore called two or three of our fresh ships round us, and have no doubt of giving them a drubbing."

"I hope," said his Lordship, "none of *our* ships have struck, Hardy."

"No, my Lord," replied Captain Hardy; "there is no fear of that."

Lord Nelson then said: "I am a dead man, Hardy. I am going fast: it will be all over with me soon. Come nearer to me. Pray let my dear Lady Hamilton have my hair, and all other things belonging to me." Mr. Burke was about to withdraw at the commencement of this conversation; but his Lordship, perceiving his intention, desired he would remain.

Captain Hardy observed, that "he hoped Mr. Beatty could yet hold out some prospect of life."

"Oh! no," answered his Lordship; "it is impossible. My back is shot through. Beatty will tell you so."

Captain Hardy then returned on deck, and at parting shook hands again with his revered friend and commander.

His Lordship now requested the surgeon, who had been previously absent a short time attending Mr. Rivers, to return to the wounded; and give his assistance to such of them as he could be useful to; "for," said he, "you can do nothing for me." The surgeon assured him that the assistant surgeons were doing everything that could be effected for those unfortunate men; but on his Lordship's several times repeating his injunctions to that purpose, he left him surrounded by Dr. Scott, Mr. Burke, and two of his Lordship's domestics.

After the surgeon had been absent a few minutes attending Lieutenants Peake and Reeves of the marines, who were wounded; he was called by Dr. Scott to his Lordship, who said: "Ah, Mr. Beatty! I have sent for you to say what I forgot to tell you before, that all power of motion and feeling below my breast are gone; and *you*," continued he, "very well *know* I can live but a short time." The emphatic manner in which he pronounced these last words, left no doubt in the surgeon's mind, that he adverted to the case of a man who had, some months before, received a mortal injury of the spine on board the *Victory*, and had laboured under similar privations of sense and muscular motion. The case had made a great impression on Lord Nelson: he was anxious to know the cause of such symptoms, which was accordingly explained to him; and he now appeared to apply the situation and fate of this man to himself.

The surgeon answered, "My Lord, you told me so before:" but he now examined the extremities, to ascertain the fact; when his Lordship said, "Ah, Beatty! I am too certain of it: Scott and Burke have tried it already. *You know* I am gone."

The surgeon replied: "My Lord, unhappily for our country, nothing can be done for you;" and having made this declaration he was so much affected, that he turned round and withdrew a few steps to conceal his emotions.

His Lordship said: "I know it. I feel something rising in my breast," putting his hand on his left side, "which tells me I am gone." Drink was recommended liberally, and Dr. Scott and Mr. Burke fanned him with paper.

He often exclaimed, "God be praised, I have done my duty;" and upon the surgeon's inquiring whether his pain was still very great, he declared, "it continued so very severe, that he wished he was dead. Yet," said he in a lower voice, "one would like to live a little longer, too:" and after a pause of a few minutes, he added in the same tone, "What would become of poor Lady Hamilton, if she knew my situation?"

The surgeon, finding it impossible to render his Lordship any further assistance, left him to attend Lieutenant Bligh, Messrs. Smith and Westphall, midshipmen, and some seamen, recently wounded.

Captain Hardy now came to the cockpit to see his Lordship a second time, which was after an interval of about fifty minutes from the conclusion of his first visit. Before he quitted the deck, he sent Lieutenant Hills to acquaint Admiral Collingwood with the lamentable circumstance of Lord Nelson's being wounded.

Lord Nelson and Captain Hardy shook hands again: and while the captain retained his Lordship's hand, he congratulated him even in the arms of Death on his brilliant victory; "which," he said, "was complete; though he did not know how many of the enemy were captured, as it was impossible to perceive every ship distinctly. He was certain however of fourteen or fifteen having surrendered."

His Lordship answered, "That is well, but I bargained for twenty:" and then emphatically exclaimed, "*Anchor*, Hardy, *anchor!*"

To this the captain replied: "I suppose, my Lord, Admiral Collingwood will now take upon himself the direction of affairs."

"Not while I live, I hope, Hardy!" cried the dying chief; and at that moment endeavoured ineffectually to raise himself from the bed.

"No," added he; "do *you* anchor, Hardy."

Captain Hardy then said: "Shall *we* make the signal, Sir?"

"Yes," answered his Lordship; "for if I live, I'll anchor." The energetic manner in which he uttered these his last orders to Captain Hardy, accompanied with his efforts to raise himself, evinced his determination never to resign the command while he retained the exercise of his transcendant faculties, and that he expected Captain Hardy still to carry into effect the suggestions of his exalted mind; a sense of his duty overcoming the pains of death.

He then told Captain Hardy, "he felt that in a few minutes he should be no more;" adding in a low tone, "Don't throw me overboard, Hardy."

The captain answered: "Oh! no, certainly not."

"Then," replied his Lordship, "you know what to do: and," continued he, "take care of my dear Lady Hamilton, Hardy; take care of poor Lady Hamilton. Kiss me, Hardy."

The captain now knelt down, and kissed his cheek; when his Lordship said, "Now I am satisfied. Thank God, I have done my duty."

Captain Hardy stood for a minute or two in silent contemplation: he then knelt down again and kissed his Lordship's forehead.

His Lordship said: "Who is that?"

The captain answered: "It is Hardy:" to which his Lordship replied, "God bless you, Hardy!"

After this affecting scene Captain Hardy withdrew, and returned to the quarter deck; having spent about eight minutes in this his last interview with his dying friend.

Lord Nelson now desired Mr. Chevalier, his steward, to turn him upon his right side; which being effected, his Lordship said: "I wish I had not left the deck, for I shall soon be gone." He afterwards became very low; his breathing was oppressed, and his voice faint.

He said to Dr. Scott, "Doctor, I have *not* been a *great* sinner"; and after a short pause, "*Remember,* that I leave Lady Hamilton and my daughter Horatia as a legacy to my country: and," added he, "never forget Horatia."

His thirst now increased; and he called for "Drink, drink," "Fan, fan!" and "Rub, rub!" addressing himself in the last case to Dr. Scott, who had been rubbing his Lordship's breast with his hand, from which he found some relief. These words he spoke in a very rapid manner, which rendered his articulation difficult: but he every now and then, with evident increase of pain, made a greater effort with his vocal powers, and pronounced distinctly these last words: "Thank God, I have done my duty;" and this great sentiment he continued to repeat as long as he was able to give it utterance.

His Lordship became speechless in about fifteen minutes after Captain Hardy left him. Dr. Scott and Mr. Burke, who had all along sustained the bed under his shoulders (which raised him in nearly a semi-recumbent posture, the only one that was supportable to him), forbore to disturb him by speaking to him; and when he had remained speechless about five minutes, his Lordship's steward went to the surgeon, who had been a short time occupied with the wounded in another part of the cockpit, and stated his apprehensions that his Lordship was dying.

The surgeon immediately repaired to him, and found him on the verge of dissolution. He knelt down by his side, and took up his hand; which was cold, and the pulse gone from the wrist.

On the surgeon's feeling his forehead, which was likewise cold, his Lordship opened his eyes, looked up, and shut them again.

The surgeon again left him, and returned to the wounded who required his assistance; but was not absent five minutes before the steward announced to him that "he believed his Lordship had expired." The surgeon returned, and found that the report was but too well founded: his Lordship had breathed his last, at thirty minutes past four o'clock; at which period Dr. Scott was in the act of rubbing his Lordship's breast, and Mr. Burke supporting the bed under his shoulders.

Thus died this matchless hero, after performing in a short but brilliant and well filled life, a series of naval exploits unexampled in any age of the world. None of the sons of fame ever possessed greater zeal to promote the honour and interest of his king and country; none ever served them with more devotedness and glory, or with more successful and important results. His character will for ever cast a lustre over the annals of this nation, to whose enemies his very name was a terror. In the battle off Cape St. Vincent, though then in the subordinate station of a captain, his unprecedented personal prowess will long be recorded with admiration among his profession. The shores of Aboukir and Copenhagen subsequently witnessed those stupendous achievements which struck the whole civilized world with astonishment. Still these were only preludes to the Battle of Trafalgar: in which he shone with a majesty of dignity as far surpassing even his own former renown, as that renown had already exceeded every thing else to be found in the pages of naval history; the transcendantly brightest star in a galaxy of heroes. His splendid example will operate as an everlasting impulse to the enterprising genius of the British Navy.

FROM THE TIME of his Lordship's being wounded till his death, a period of about two hours and forty-five minutes elapsed; but a knowledge of the decisive victory which was gained, he acquired of Captain Hardy within the first hour and a quarter of this period. A partial cannonade, however, was still maintained, in consequence of the enemy's running ships passing the British at different points; and the last distant guns which were fired at their van ships that were making off, were heard a minute or two before his Lordship expired.

A steady and continued fire was kept up by the *Victory*'s starboard guns on the *Redoubtable*, for about fifteen minutes after Lord Nelson was wounded: in which short period Captain Adair and about eighteen seamen and marines were killed; and Lieutenant Bligh, Mr. Palmer midshipman, and twenty seamen and marines, wounded, by the enemy's musketry alone.

The *Redoubtable* had been on fire twice, in her fore chains and on her forecastle: she had likewise succeeded in throwing a few hand grenades into the *Victory*, which set fire to some ropes and canvas on the booms. The cry of "Fire!" was now circulated throughout the ship, and even reached the cockpit, without producing the degree of sensation which might be expected on such an awful occasion: the crew soon extinguished the fire on the booms, and then immediately turned their attention to that on board the enemy; which they likewise put out by throwing buckets of water from the gangway into the enemy's chains and forecastle, thus furnishing another admirable instance of deliberate intrepidity.

At thirty minutes past one o'clock, the *Redoubtable*'s musketry having ceased, and her colours being struck; the *Victory*'s men endeavoured to get on board her: but this was found impracticable; for though the two ships were still in contact, yet the top sides or upper works of both fell in so much on their upper decks, that there was a great space (perhaps fourteen feet or more) between their gangways; and the enemy's ports being down, she could not be boarded from the *Victory*'s lower nor middle deck. Several seamen volunteered their services to Lieutenant Quilliam, to jump overboard, swim under the *Redoubtable*'s bows, and endeavour to get up there; but Captain Hardy refused to permit this. The prize, however, and the *Victory*, fell off from each other; and their separation was believed to be the effect of the concussion produced by the *Victory*'s fire, assisted by the helm of the latter being put to starboard.

Messrs. Ogilvie and Collingwood, midshipmen of the *Victory*, were sent in a small boat to take charge of the prize; which they effected. After this, the ships of the enemy's van, that had shown a disposition to attack the *Victory*, passed to windward; and fired their broadsides not only into her and the *Téméraire*, but also into the French and Spanish captured ships indiscriminately: and they were seen to back or shiver their topsails for the purpose of doing this with more precision.

The two midshipmen of the *Victory* had just boarded the *Redoubtable*, and got their men out of the boat; when a shot from the enemy's van ships that were making off cut the boat adrift. About ten minutes after taking possession of her, a midshipman came to her from the *Téméraire*; and had hardly ascended the poop, when a shot from one of those ships took off his leg. The French officers, seeing the firing continued on the prize by their own countrymen, entreated the English midshipmen to quit the deck, and accompany them below. The unfortunate midshipman of the *Téméraire* was carried to the French surgeon, who was ordered to give his immediate attendance to him in preference to his own wounded: his leg was amputated, but he died the same night.

The *Redoubtable* suffered so much from shot received between wind and water, that she sank while in tow of the *Swiftsure* on the following evening, when the gale came on; and out of a crew originally consisting of more than eight hundred men, only about a hundred and thirty were saved: but she had lost above three hundred in the battle.

It is by no means certain, though highly probable, that Lord Nelson was particularly aimed at by the enemy. There were only two Frenchmen left alive in the mizzen top of the *Redoubtable* at the time of his Lordship's being wounded, and by the hands of one of these he fell. These men continued firing at captains Hardy and Adair, Lieutenant Rotely of the marines, and some of the midshipmen on the *Victory*'s poop, for some time afterwards. At length one of them was killed by a musket ball: and on the other's then attempting to make his escape from the top down the rigging, Mr. Pollard (midshipman) fired his musket at him, and shot him in the back; when he fell dead from the shrouds, on the *Redoubtable*'s poop.

The writer of this will not attempt to depict the heartrending sorrow and melancholy gloom, which pervaded the breast and the countenance of every individual on board the *Victory* when his Lordship's death became generally known. The anguish felt by all for such a loss, rendered doubly heavy to *them*, is more easy to be conceived than described: by his lamented fall they were at once deprived of their adored commander, and their friend and patron.

The battle was fought in soundings about sixteen miles to the westward of Cape Trafalgar; and if fortunately there had been more wind in the beginning of the action, it is very probable that Lord Nelson would still have been saved to his country, and that every ship of the line composing the Combined fleets would have been either captured or destroyed: for had the *Victory* been going fast through the water, she must have dismasted the *Redoubtable,* and would of course have passed on to attack another ship; consequently his Lordship would not have been so long nor so much exposed to the enemy's musketry. From the same circumstance of there being but little wind, several of the enemy's ships made off before the rear and bad sailing ships of the British lines could come up to secure them.

The *Victory* had no musketry in her tops: as his Lordship had a strong aversion to small arms being placed there, from the danger of their setting fire to the sails; which was exemplified by the destruction of the French ship *L'Achille* in this battle. It is a species of warfare by which individuals may suffer, and now and then a commander be picked off: but it never can decide the fate of a general engagement; and a circumstance in many respects similar to that of the *Victory's* running on board of the *Redoubtable,* may not occur again in the course of centuries.

The loss sustained by the *Victory* amounted to fifty-five killed, and a hundred and two wounded; and it is highly honourable to the discipline and established regulations of the ship, that not one casualty from accident occurred on board during the engagement.

· · ·

*In 1806, Beatty was appointed physician to the Greenwich Hospital, where he remained until 1840, two years before his death. In 1807 he published* An Authentic Narrative of the Death of Lord Nelson, with the Circumstances preceding, attending, and subsequent to that Event; the Professional Report of his Lordship's Wound; and several Interesting Anecdotes. *A second edition was published the following year.*

*On October 21, 1805, Nelson effectively ended any threat of a combined French and Spanish fleet being able to spearhead Napoleon's desired invasion of Great Britain. It was, in fact, the last great fleet action of the age. From this point on, the Royal Navy controlled the seas, except for isolated instances. But on land the case was very different. As Christopher Lloyd observes in his book* Lord Cochrane, *"Before the end of 1807 the entire coastline from St. Petersburg to*

*Lisbon was under the direct or indirect control of Napoleon. That control, which culminated with the occupation of Spain by 100,000 men early in 1808, was not to last long; but at the moment it looked as if Napoleon's Continental System would succeed in bleeding Britain white" (p. 42). On the water, however, Lloyd noted, "in 1808 Collingwood could write of the Mediterranean that there was 'nothing but ourselves: it is lamentable to see what a desert the waters are become' " (p. 42).*

# WILLIAM HENRY DILLON

*An Unequal Match*

## 1807-1808

*W*hen we last heard from Midshipman William Dillon, he was *engaged in the bloody lower-deck action of the Glorious First of June. He spent much of the next eight years on the West Indies station. From 1803 to 1807, Dillon was held in captivity by the French, after being detained while under a flag of truce off Holland. Now he returns to face the morass of government and Navy bureaucracy, all the more difficult to navigate as he was unlawfully detained and thus not necessarily considered by the British to be, technically, a prisoner of war. But Dillon perseveres in rallying as much influence at the Admiralty as he possibly can, primarily through Admiral Gambier, on whose ship Dillon served at the Glorious First of June (see page 12).*

*Finally, twenty-seven years old and entering the prime of his career, he anxiously returns to action, albeit with a somewhat disadvantageous commission.*

### SEPTEMBER 1807–JANUARY 1808

MY ARRIVAL IN LONDON was a new era in my existence. I lost no time in presenting myself to the Hon. Mr. Pole, the Secretary to the Admiralty, first of all delivering to him the secret information I had received in Paris relating to a certain number of troops collected in the neighbourhood of Brest, which were intended to be landed on the coast of Ireland. Our conversation was a long one, during which I acquainted him that I had ascertained while in Paris that the French Government had obtained our private naval signals. He admitted the fact, and remarked that, when he had taken office, the private signals were kept in an outer room, open to any person who chose to enter it. Consequently they found their way to our enemies. "However," said he, "I have altered all that. They are now secure." He then desired me to call on Lord Mulgrave, the then First Lord of the Admiralty, about 12 o'clock. He would, he said, apprize his Lordship of my return to England, and ensure my being received.

I accordingly presented myself at the hour mentioned. My audience was a gracious one, but very cold. Many subjects were discussed, particularly the detention of Capt. Wright in the Temple, where he terminated his existence.[1] His Lordship positively assured me that, if our Government could have ascertained the real facts of his case, a French officer would have been similarly treated by us. But all inquiries led to nothing certain. Some years afterwards Sir Sidney Smith visited the Temple and devoted much time in trying to find out the fate of that officer, who had served under him and become his personal friend. But all his exertions failed.

His Lordship made many inquiries about Mr. Temple's escape,[2] and I stated what little I knew of it. He then assured me that he had been dismissed the Navy—the Board could not sanction such conduct. The most extraordinary thing was, after what had passed between Lord Mulgrave and me about him, he was the first person I met upon coming out of the Admiralty. He made his bow and offered his hand. In doing so he had mistaken his man, as I turned my back upon him and passed by without acknowledgment. With Lord Mulgrave I left a memorial, stating what I suffered during my captivity, and my loss of promotion. He admitted that I had very strong claims on my country. I could not help mentioning the interest my friend Gambier took in my advancement. He was then before Copenhagen in command of the British fleet. "When he returns," said I, "your Lordship will hear more of me than I can state myself." As I was retiring his Lordship invited me to dine with him on the 24th.

My next duty was to present myself at the Transport Board. The Secretary, Mr. McLeay's, reception I shall never forget. He greeted me with the warmth of an old friend. "Welcome to England," he said. "I wish you joy! We have had trouble enough about you, and I'm heartily glad to see you at last. Your trial has been a severe one. Let us hope all will be right in good time." When I was requested to attend the Board, I was very kindly

[1] John Wesley Wright of the brig-sloop Vincejo was captured May 8, 1804, and imprisoned in the Temple at Verdun where he committed suicide on October 28, 1805.
[2] One of four midshipmen who were fellows of Dillon's at Verdun, Temple broke parole and left behind a debt of £4,000.

received, Capt. Sir. Rupert George[1] of the Navy being the chairman. I was overloaded with questions, and replied to them as far as my abilities would admit. They acknowledged that my confined position at Verdun would not admit of my communicating any intelligence of consequence. They expressed a proper feeling in behalf of our unfortunate countrymen, prisoners of war and those detained in France, at the same time frankly declaring that our government had done its best to effect an exchange; but all had failed. They cordially congratulated me upon my having obtained mine, and, after a very interesting conversation relating to our political position, I retired.

[Several passages omitted. He visits his stepmother at Brompton, and meets Mr. Loveden, the member for Shaftesbury and his father's executor. He decides that Lady Dillon—and Brompton—are a little too dull and "out of the swim" for him: so he returns to his London hotel. Then in an ill moment for himself, he calls on Mr. Voller, "my old friend whose wife I had met in Boulogne," only to find him recently deceased. But "Mrs. V." insists on renewing the intimacy, and very evidently lays siege to his affections. Many of these references are erased, but it is clear that during this period he succumbed and reached an "arrangement" with the lady, whereby he was to marry her when he obtained post rank. Thereafter they spent much time in each other's company.][2]

At Lord Mulgrave's table I met many men of rank and fashion. I was seated next to Lord Palmerston, who had just commenced his political career. Sir Richard Bickerton[3] managed the naval affairs in Gambier's absence. Many questions were made to me by the company when they knew that I had just returned from Verdun. Sir Richard in particular failed not in inquisitiveness, and in conclusion remarked, "You don't appear the worse for your detention in France." I replied that I should feel sincere regret if any friend of mine underwent the same trials I had endured. He then drew in, without any further remarks.

I next applied to Lord Keith to interpose at the Admiralty in my behalf, as it was by being the bearer of his despatches that I was detained by the enemy. His Lordship instantly replied that my case gave me a claim upon the government, and I ought to be employed without the assistance of any

---

[1] Sir Rupert George, Bart., Capt. 29/11/81. One of the few officers on the "Superannuated and Retired" List.

[2] *Explanation of original editor.*

[3] This is W.H.D.'s first meeting with the man who was destined to be, perhaps, the worst enemy he ever made.

influence. I next went to the Board of Agriculture, where I was informed by Mr. Arthur Young[1] that Lord Carrington had been the principal means of getting me exchanged. His Lordship had rendered some very essential service to Sir Rupert George, the Chairman of the Transport Office, but that Board could do nothing in my favour until a proposal came from France. When my application arrived, requesting to be exchanged for Capt. Soleil, it was instantly granted. He advised me to lose no time in seeing his Lordship, who had been sincerely attached to my father. Mr. Young persuaded me to stay and dine with him, and the kind attentions I experienced from this gentleman and his family I can never forget.

When I went to Hampstead, I did not fail to call upon your worthy father[2] and mother. Nothing could exceed the warmth of their reception. Your father more than once repeated, in terms highly gratifying to me, how much he approved of my conduct towards my father. Then, alluding to the Irish estate,[3] he remarked that it had been disposed of for less than one sixteenth part of its value—not very pleasant information for me: but the deed was done, and I could not recover what was lost.

The next gentleman who expressed great anxiety to entertain me was Mr. Falconer, my friend the major's brother. The latter's case was certainly a hard one. He was on his way home from India, as aide de camp to General Sir David Baird. When captured by an enemy's privateer, the major went on board the Frenchman to be answerable for his general's person, who was allowed to remain in the Indiaman. One of our cruizers shortly afterwards recaptured the ship, and Sir David arrived safe in England. But the privateer escaped, and Falconer was sent to Verdun, where he remained many years, to the serious injury of his advancement in the Army.

Gradually I was allowed more leisure, and the sudden appearance of my old messmate Dr. Grey was a sort of relief to me, as I wanted a friend to consult. He had just left his ship, fully determined not to go to sea again. When he accompanied Capt. Brenton to England, it was understood that Grey was to go with him as his surgeon. He had done so, to the serious annoyance of his wife. Capt. Brenton, who had been appointed to the command of a fine frigate, was sent to the Mediterranean, Grey accompanying him. Brenton's ship, while watching Toulon, was one day surrounded by several of the enemy's frigates and nearly taken: but a gallant defence and clever maneuvers cleared him of the danger. That event shook Grey's

[1] The great agriculturalist, whose writings raised agriculture to the status of a science: appointed, 1793, Secretary of the new Board of Agriculture.
[2] William Mervyn Dillon.
[3] Laytown, near Drogheda.

nerves, and he succeeded in quitting the ship, to retire upon his half pay, to resume practice on shore, Mrs. Grey having a fair dowry.

I now demanded of the Transport Office whether they would sanction my claim for the lodging money which the government had authorized the officers of the Navy to draw whilst prisoners of war. In reply, they advised me to write to them officially for the said allowance. On that occasion Capt. Bowen,[1] with whom I had sailed under Ad. Sir H. Christian, being one of the commissioners, came down and kindly told me how to act, remarking that I was fully entitled to it. I accordingly sent in my application, which they forwarded to the Admiralty. In the course of a few days I received an answer refusing the lodging money! Our government had, in the first instance, after having failed in establishing a regular cartel for the exchange of prisoners, ordered the senior naval officer at Verdun to draw for lodging money, every officer being allowed so much a day according to his rank. I as a lieutenant was allowed one shilling per diem. Consequently I had nearly five years' payment due—upwards of £80! My application not being acknowledged gave me a shock, which I confess was not an agreeable one. I had hitherto formed such an favourable opinion of the government that I never would allow anyone to abuse its liberality. I had several times risked imbroiling myself in a duel when I heard illiberal words said against it. But now I could not help remarking that, if the French government had not prevented that lodging money's being distributed, I should have received it. But as my official application had been refused, our government was sanctioning the oppressive act of the enemy.[2] I in consequence again wrote to the Admiralty, pointing out in strong terms the injustice of the measure. But Grey urged me not to send it. "You are applying for employment," said he. "Take care not to give offence, or they may turn their backs on you. Make your mind up to lose the money. It is a most shabby act, but you had better submit than make them your enemies." I followed his advice, and remained silent.

From my Agent (Mr. Ommanney) I received some confidential information relating to a very fine sloop of war about to be launched, it being his opinion that if I applied I should be appointed to the command of her. I lost no time in sending in my application accordingly.

Meanwhile, I accepted an invitation from Mrs. V. to accompany her to Portsmouth, and I found myself again at that celebrated naval station. With her I visited Winchester, where I met several French officers, prisoners of

[1] Capt. James Bowen.
[2] A possible, and more charitable, explanation is that they were still regarding him, officially, as being in a category all by himself—an "illegally detained" person, and not a prisoner of war at all.

war. They were very anxious to hear my reports of Verdun, but as I could not make any flattering statements of what I had undergone there, I was not a very welcome guest. On my return to Portsmouth, I met my friend Capt. Manby, then in command of a frigate, the *Thalia*. He did all, and said all, that an officer in his position could after my unfortunate captivity, and assured me that he had represented in the strongest terms at headquarters the unjustifiable act visited upon me by the French government.

Just as we were on our return to London, Mrs. V. heard of the arrival from Sicily of the wife of the late Lord Nelson's steward to the Bronte estate, Mrs. Graeffer. She sought her out, and offered to take her to Lady Hamilton's at Merton. Mrs. V. had a son and daughter with her, also a niece. Therefore, instead of returning by mail, it was arranged that the hotel keeper should supply us with a private carriage that would hold six, which was to take us to Merton instead of London. We left Portsmouth that evening, and were the next morning, by 7 o'clock, at the place mentioned. From Lady Hamilton, although only partially known to her previous to my captivity, I experienced a hearty welcome. I examined all the curiosities of the gallant Nelson's residence, and in a couple of days returned to Town,[1] taking up my residence at Brompton.

Weeks passed on, but I heard nothing of an appointment, and my spirits began to feel the effects of disappointment. However, one satisfaction attended me. The change of scene from Verdun to England and the change of diet produced wonders in my health. I found my strength recovering daily. Port wine quite renovated me. But the arrival in town of Admiral Gambier, who was created a peer for the capturing of the Copenhagen fleet, was for me an event of the utmost consequence, and my hopes began to revive, as I had placed the fullest reliance upon his powerful influence in my favour. So soon as his Lordship had re-established himself in his official situation at the Admiralty, I called, and was received with all those expressions that convinced me of my possessing in him a friend. He invited me to dinner and presented me to Lady Gambier, who also let drop many words highly gratifying from such a virtuous and distinguished character. After I had dined, he desired me to renew my visits at breakfast, whenever I wanted his assistance, at the same time assuring me that he would take

[1] During my sojourn at Lady Hamilton's, I could not help noticing her affectionate attentions shown to Horatia, then about seven years old. She had been adopted by Lord Nelson, her maiden name supposed to be Thompson. Her real mother, I was told, would never be known. "That may be," was my reply. "But as far as I can judge from what I have witnessed, her real mother is Lady Hamilton. Her whole proceedings towards the child are those of a mother, and no mistake." My judgment in the end proved correct.[2]

[2] The ink in which this last sentence is written is that used, throughout, in the latest corrections. The rest of the note is in the same ink as the ordinary text of the Narrative.

care to let Lord Mulgrave know all about me. I could only await patiently the result of his Lordship's influence in my behalf.

The year came to a close, and I was still waiting anxiously the result of his interest: and I occasionally renewed my application at the Admiralty for employment. I went to breakfast one morning with his Lordship, who received me with his usual kindness, but I could not help noticing his extreme taciturnity. Scarcely a word escaped from his lips. Therefore, conceiving that his mind was occupied with matters of more importance than my presence, I was in the act of retiring when he desired me to wait. Lady Gambier instantly withdrew. When we were alone, the following conversation ensued.

"Well, D.," said his Lordship, "are you going to be employed?" "I hope so, my lord," I answered, "but I know nothing as yet for certain." "Have you seen Lord M.?" "Yes. His Lordship is kind in inviting me to dinner, but I would rather be left out of the dinner party, and be appointed to a command." "Have you seen the private secretary?" "I have, my lord; only a few days since. His reception was so cold that I was anxious to beat my retreat." His Lordship hesitated. "What else have you done?" he demanded. I then stated that I had drawn up a memorial which I had sent to the Board, and appealed to their Lordships for an act of justice towards me, by employing me after I had undergone so much in the cause of my country. His Lordship stopped me rather sharply. "What's that you say? Justice, did you say?" Then, holding his right hand up in the air and snapping his fingers, said, "There's justice for you at the Admiralty! I have two connections whom I have mentioned to Lord M. for employment. He has not as yet taken any notice of them. I have not yet seen your memorial, as I was not at the Board at that time. However, I shall take a look at it. But you can do nothing here without parliamentary interest. Where is your parliamentary interest?" "I have none, my Lord. I have lost all that I had by my father's death. When he was alive I was in a very different position."

His Lordship listened very patiently to all I said, but, still showing by his actions some uneasiness, he at length addressed me as follows:—"You have certainly great claims on your country. No one can deny that. I have spoken to Lord Mulgrave about you. He can not plead ignorance. What are you going to do today?" "I have nothing in view, my Lord," was my reply. "I advise you then," said his Lordship, "to go to the Secretary in my name, and tell him to let Lord M. know that I am interested in your welfare. I shall be here, and, if you are not satisfied, come and let me know." I then tendered my grateful acknowledgments to his Lordship and retired.

A few minutes after 11 o'clock, I presented myself to Capt. Moorsom,[1] Lord M.'s private secretary, and said, "I do not come to pester you on my own account. I am sent here by Lord Gambier." The instant I mentioned his Lordship's name, the secretary became quite an altered person. He rose from his seat with an anxiety that I could not help noticing, and requested me to take a chair. "I am directed by his Lordship," I said, "to call upon you and request you to explain to Lord M. his Lordship's anxiety to see me employed. Should the First Lord wish to know more about me, Lord G. is ready to answer any questions in my behalf." Capt. Moorsom opened a large book lying on his table: then, running his finger across the page, said, "By this report you are the first for employment. But the ship you have applied for is not yet ready." I could only reply that the friend who had confidentially advised me to ask for that ship intimated that she would be ready in the course of a few days; that upwards of three months had passed, and my not hearing of anything made me conclude that I was forgotten. "Moreover," said I, "younger officers than I, who have not seen half of the service that I have, are receiving appointments every day. Such a trial can not well be endured." The secretary could not say when that ship would be ready. It was therefore settled between us that he was to deliver Lord Gambier's message to the First Lord, and that I was ready to accept any other appointment which might be selected for me.

Returning to my hotel, where I had again taken up my quarters, I found an invitation from Lady Hamilton, requesting me to pass a few days at Merton, which I willingly accepted. I soon reached Lady Hamilton's, where I passed nearly a week most agreeably. Upon my return to Town, my landlord acquainted me that Capt. Moorsom had called for me the day after I had left town. I hastened to the Admiralty, it being the 18th of the month, the Queen's birthday. I was instantly received by Capt. Moorsom, who acquainted me that Lord M. had offered me the refusal of the *Childers*, brig of war.

When that vessel's name was mentioned, a sort of horror overcame me. "What," said I, "you don't mean the old *Childers* that used to run alongside of Lord Howe's ship last war, and take charge of the dispatches?" "Yes," was his reply. "Oh no," I rejoined, "I cannot accept that old worn-out craft. Only recollect, Capt. Moorsom, I am three years a commander, and am in every sense entitled to something better than that!" Much hurt at such an offer, I was in the act of retiring, having opened the door and made my bow, when the secretary called me to him. "Now, Capt. D., pause well," said he. "Recollect the interest that has been exerted for you. You have

[1] (Sir) Robert Moorsom, Capt. 22/11/90; R-Ad. 31/7/1810; V-Ad. 4/6/14; Ad. 22/7/30. C.-in-C. Chatham, 1824–27. Died, April 1835.

declared that you were prepared to take any command at a moment's notice, and proceed to any part of the world. Here is a vessel full manned and ready for sea. You have only to put yourself into a post chaise, take the command, and God knows what may happen in the next 24 hours!" Those words produced their effect. I acknowledged that I had been rather taken aback when I heard the name of the old *Childers,* but that I had recovered from the shock, and would accept the command of her. "You have no time to lose," he replied. "Capt. Innes,[1] who now commands her, is not in very good health. He has applied to be superseded, and Lord M. has pitched upon you to relieve him." In a few more words I agreed to leave town that night: then, thanking the secretary for his advice, requested him to tender my acknowledgments to Lord Mulgrave for the appointment.

I retired, and had scarcely left his room when I was accosted by one of the Admiralty messengers. "Pray, sir, is your name Dillon?" he said. "Lord Gambier wishes to see you." Thither I hastened. It was then about 2 o'clock. "Well," said his Lordship, "have you accepted the command of the *Childers?*" "I have, my lord." "Very well. I am glad of it. I was fearful you would not take her. But it is all right. It is a stepping stone to something better. You are stationed at Leith. You will go in the first place to Sheerness, where you will be ordered to Scotland. But before long I am in hopes of removing you to a superior command." With these assurances his Lordship renewed his expressions of the warmest feelings for my advancement and welfare, shaking me by the hand in confirmation of all he said. I took my leave of him.

As I passed through the hall of the Admiralty, several officers of my acquaintance accosted me in the following terms:—"Is it true that you have accepted the command of the *Childers?*" "Yes," I replied. "Then go and insure your life without loss of time. She has returned to port having thrown her guns overboard to prevent her sinking. You will never come back again!" "Very satisfactory news," I observed. "However, I shall try what I can do with her."

## JANUARY 1808–APRIL 1808

As I had promised to quit town that night, I had enough to do, not having any uniforms or anything ready. I hastened to my stepmother's, in the meantime writing a note to Mrs. V., acquainting her that I hoped to be at her house in a couple of hours. Lady D. assisted me as much as she could. I then called upon my agent and requested an advance of cash to fit me out.

[1] Thomas Innes, Cdr. 26/12/99; Capt. 21/10/1810.

Mr. Ommanney, who was in attendance, remarked in reply to my demand, "You have some property in Ireland?" My reply acquainted him that the Irish estate had been sold to pay my expenses at Verdun. "If that is the case," said he, "I can not assist you. There is a certain sum which we generally allow to officers taking a command. That will be at your disposal, but I cannot let you have more." I took a part of that sum, then made the best of my way to Mrs. V. She had ordered a tailor to be in waiting who undertook to make me a coat and waistcoat in a few hours. We then repaired to the sword cutlers, where I fitted myself with an article of that kind according to the regulations: next a cocked hat. Then I went to Wedgwood's China Establishment and bought a tray that contained four dishes with a small soup tureen in the middle. Other articles were obtained, packed up and paid for. They were to be at Sheerness next morning. I had performed wonders in the course of a few hours. We then sat down to dinner, during which, as if an inspiration had seized Mrs. V., she made up her mind to accompany me to Sheerness. Her daughter, niece and maid were to be of the party.

A travelling carriage was ordered, and by 10 o'clock it came to the door with four horses. The tailor had not kept his promise, but he declared that my coat, etc., would be at Rochester before 4 o'clock in the morning. We then started for that town accompanied by a deep fall of snow. We were too much taken up with our own affairs to attend to the brilliant illumination which everywhere appeared to our view. When we got off the pavement, and were proceeding at a rapid pace, the young ladies entertained us with some songs. However, just as we had passed the Elephant and Castle, I thought I heard a noise at the back of the carriage—something like a screw. I put my head out of the window, and to my astonishment beheld a man on the seat. His left hand had hold of the spring. With my stick I gave him a hearty thump over his knuckle which obliged him instantly to drop himself to the ground, accompanied by a partner. In their dress they had the appearance of chimney sweeps. I then called out to the postboys to stop, but it was useless. They did not, or, more properly speaking, would not hear me. Shortly afterwards, another person got up behind. However, I made him drop off—in appearance a gentleman in shoes and stockings. By 2 o'clock we were at Rochester, where we were obliged to wait till the tide would allow us to proceed to Sheerness. All my questions to the postboys ended in nothing; but I am fully persuaded that they were leagued with the fellows who got up behind. In the attempt made to wrest my portmanteau out of the back panel of the carriage a sort of large gimblet had been employed. When we stopped at the inn we saw a large hole bored by such an instrument. It had penetrated through the side of my portmanteau, which had been placed in the back seat. Had I not heard the working of the screw, it would have been carried off in a few seconds. It contained my commission appointing me to command the *Childers,* some linen and cash. At 4 o'clock the stage arrived bringing me a parcel containing my uniforms, and after that delay we proceeded to Sheerness, putting up at the inn there.

My first duty was to present myself to the port admiral, Thomas Wells, Esq. This was the officer under whom I had served in the *Defence.* Consequently I was well received by him. After the etiquette usual on such occasions, he insisted upon my immediately putting to sea. However, when he heard of my having nothing ready, and that I had quitted London the day of my appointment, he agreed to allow me two days, that indulgence being obtained with great difficulty: but I was obliged to act accordingly. He invited me to dine, then sent for Mrs. Wells and his daughters, to whom he presented me. They recognized me although we had not met for fourteen years. They were extremely affable, and I was astonished that those fine girls still remained without husbands.

I next—it being the 19th—proceeded off to the *Childers,* where Capt. Innes was waiting to receive me. My commission having been read to the crew and all the officers introduced to me, I became installed in the command of the brig. I agreed to take many articles from Capt. Innes which I thought would answer my purpose until I reached Leith, where I had directed all my luggage to be sent from London. Capt. Innes then went on shore, where we were to meet to settle other matters. I then bent my steps round the vessel, and was surprised at her diminutive dimensions. There was only one lieutenant,[1] although she was allowed two: in fact, there was no cabin fitted for a second. My inspection was not of a nature to be pleasing, but I made no remarks, not wishing anyone to suppose that I was disappointed. However, I was most seriously annoyed at all I saw. When I entered the cabin, I met the youth who was there in attendance, to whom I put some questions. This lad, anxious to please his new captain, let out a number of things that had better never have been mentioned. The cabin was very small and not very clean, which made me make some remarks on that score. "Very true, sir," said the youth. "We have been labouring heart and soul these two days to put the vessel to rights to please you." The more I saw the more I had reason to regret having accepted the command. When the officers felt themselves at liberty to offer their remarks, I found them all discontented. They could not help alluding to the throwing of the guns overboard. I made no replies, but listened patiently to all they said. After

[1] Thomas Edmonds, Lt. 28/4/1807; Ret. Cdr. 17/1/1843.

remaining on board two or three hours to ascertain the exact condition of the brig, I went on shore. In my conversations with Capt. Innes, I tried to discover the real cause of his giving up the command. He did not appear inclined to say much on the subject. He had been in the brig some time, and had made £15,000 prize money. He thought he was entitled to a larger vessel. However he assured me that, with proper management, I should take prizes, as the Norwegians and Danes had constant communications by sea, and a good look out would ensure success.

On the following day I mustered the brig's crew and exercised them at the guns—carronades, I should say. She mounted 14 of them, 12 lbers, with a crew of 63 men and boys, her proper complement being 86. The carronades, being new, were sealed, and I did all I could to inspire confidence in the men I had under command. The weather was cold, and we were visited with snow storms—not a pleasant season of the year to put to sea with an unknown crew, as it was probable that many of my regulations differed from those of the late captain. However, I had undertaken the task: therefore perseverance was my motto. I met several acquaintances among the captains. One of them, with whom I sailed in the *Prince George,* Baker,[1] commanded a fine sloop of war.[2] I had some long interesting conversations with him. He assured me that I should not be able to keep up the respectability of my station under £500 a year. "Why," said I, "I have already spent that sum in my outfit!" "Very true," he replied. "It's what we all do. And if you have not something beyond your pay the case is desperate." That literally was mine; but I did not like to tell him so. The *Childers'* pay was about £250 per annum, out of which there were many deductions, such as the agent's charges and the income tax. I confess I pondered a good deal over the position I was placed in. However, hopes of good luck buoyed me up. I met here a Capt. Sturt,[3] in command of a fine brig of war. This officer made himself known shortly afterwards by carrying off a nun from one of the convents at Madeira. This was a regular sailor's frolic.

My hours were counted, and I found there would be no peace for me until I left Sheerness. I had taken with me a fine youth of the name of Parker[4] as a naval cadet: also a mate, Mr. Knight, whom I appointed as an acting lieutenant. I was exerting myself to the utmost to make the best of a bad bargain. I had only one day more to remain at anchor, and I devoted it entirely to the brig. I had her thoroughly washed below, cleaned and

[1] John Baker, Cdr. 29/4/1802; Capt. 21/10/10. Died, March 1845.
[2] The *Kangaroo,* 18.
[3] Henry Evelyn Pitfield Sturt, commanding the *Skylark,* 16. Cdr. 29/4/1802; Capt. 21/10/10.
[4] Charles Parker, Lt. 17/9/1816.

smoked. While this operation was proceeding, I saw the smoke coming out of the seams, which indicated her crazy state. The officers pointed to many parts of the vessel, proving that she was worn out: in short, I began to be seriously impressed with the awkward situation in which I found myself. The *Childers* was in fact an inferior command to the gunbrigs under lieutenants, which mounted 18 heavier guns than those on board my craft. Turning all these matters over in my mind, being alone in my cabin whilst the crew were at dinner, I was suddenly seized with a fit of despair, and I thought it my duty to let Lord Gambier know all the difficulties I had exposed myself to in taking command of such a rotten vessel. I wrote my letter accordingly, and requested his Lordship to have me removed to a better one. I have often thought of that act since. It was, probably, lucky that I had not written the letter on shore, as if I had it would have been instantly sent to the post office. What the result would have been no one knows. But, on board the brig, I waited until the boat's crew had dined, and in the meantime I reflected upon the contents of my letter to the leading naval Lord of the Admiralty. He had acknowledged to me that he expected I would refuse the command: consequently he might be prepared for receiving my letter. However, upon more mature reflection I tore it up. I treated all the difficulties made by the officers with contempt, and finally made up my mind to brave every danger. I had not been accustomed to the management of a brig, but my own conscience led me to believe that I should succeed in my undertaking. I had not much confidence in the first lieutenant—he was very young and had not much experience—but I had a better opinion of the crew. There were some stout fellows amongst them, and my knowledge of that class of man inclined me to place reliance upon their exertions. Therefore the die was cast. I had come to the conclusion that it was more manly to trust to my fate than to make difficulties. Under these feelings my future conduct was regulated.

On the 22nd, being ready for sea, I took leave of Ad. Wells and his family. I had lent the young ladies some caricatures, which were returned: then, off to the *Childers*, and removed from the Little Nore further out. My whole thoughts were now taken up with my official duties. I had two pilots for the North Sea: they were very uncouth fellows. I slept on board for the first time. The following day, at half past two, the brig was under sail; but I cannot pass unnoticed what appeared to me an unpardonable neglect on the part of the late captain. The capstan bars were so long that they overlaid the tiller. I was all astonishment to perceive that this tiller was lashed on one side to make room for the bars to go round. Consequently, the instant the anchor was out of the ground the brig lost the use of her helm. Upon my mentioning this bad contrivance to the first lieutenant and the master, they said that they always had managed in that way. "It is a very lubberly act," I replied, "and it shall be instantly remedied." So soon as the sails were trimmed I sent for the carpenter, and ordered him to shorten the capstan bars so many inches; next, to curtail the tiller, that it might be used free of the bars. These orders were instantly executed, and everybody appeared to wonder why such a measure had not been thought of before. The safety of a vessel depends upon the motion of the rudder. So long as it remains unmanageable no one can tell what accidents may occur. This improvement for the better caused some remarks, which I could not help overhearing. It was thought that the captain knew what he was about.

In passing the *Namur*, the flag ship, at the Great Nore I received nine seamen for a passage to Yarmouth. In the evening, a fog coming on, I was obliged to anchor. The next day, Sunday, I read the Articles of War to the crew. I then acquainted them that, in so small a vessel, every precaution was necessary to prevent surprise; in consequence whereof the brig's company were never to quit the deck all together, but one watch was to be constantly on deck, and to be armed. That regulation was instantly put in force, and a number of others, the details of which I shall not dwell upon, were adopted. But I gave the crew to understand that I did not mean to be captured without a sharp defence, and every soul on board was to practice, as often as circumstances would allow, the broadsword exercise. The Marines I ordered up, inspected all their muskets, and saw them put into order fit for use. They had scarcely reported them as such when a vessel was seen nearing us. She was instantly hailed, but as the answer was not satisfactory a volley of musketry was discharged at her by the Marines of the watch—a very lucky warning, as, if the stranger had not been alarmed, he would probably have run on board of us in the fog. The vessel was an English fishing craft, and the chief received a jobation from me for not keeping a better look out. That act of mine proved to my crew that I was in earnest.

On the following afternoon the fog cleared and, the wind being fair, the brig was soon under way with studdingsails set. The crew were exercised at the guns. At dinner time one watch remained on deck till relieved by the other, having had theirs. At nightfall I was again obliged to anchor with a fog, but the next morning a fresh breeze sent it off, and by daylight we were making the best of our way towards Yarmouth. At night Lowestoft lights were seen. Shortly afterwards a lugger closed upon us. A shot was instantly fired at her, and repeated till she brought to. I sent a boat to board her. She was from Rochester bound to Yarmouth. On the afternoon of the 26th we anchored in Yarmouth Roads.

I lost no time in presenting my respects to the admiral, B. Douglas. His son, who was still at Verdun, had written to him about me, and I was most

courteously received. The supernumeraries were sent to the *Amelia,* and by
10 o'clock the next day the *Childers* was under sail, bound to Leith. At night
the weather had a threatening appearance, and as we were now more out to
sea I issued night orders. The officer of the watch was astonished that I did
not hand the square mainsail. He came to me to request that I would do so. It
had, he said, always been done before. "Then," said I, "that custom will be
changed. Should a gale of wind come on, you may furl it, but not before. If we
can't fight we must be prepared to make sail." That order, and others, were
very different from those they had been used to act under. One of the most
unpleasant duties of a captain is to train the crew of a vessel which has been
disciplined by another commander. If his regulations differ from what they
have previously been used to, it occasions unpleasant occurrences, murmurs,
and sometimes even mutiny. In this case, however, luckily for me, every one
became aware that my orders were based upon good principles, not upon
whims, and the officers and crew soon began to understand my ways.

I was anxious to be acquainted with the qualities of the *Childers.* The little experience I had of her led me to believe that she was over-masted, as
she appeared to sail better, and be more easy, under reduced canvas. I made
many enquiries relating to her guns being thrown overboard, and concluded that it was all through bad management. She was lying to in a gale
of wind, with the helm lashed alee. That old system, by which many of our
ships had been injured by getting sternway, I thought had been abandoned.
But it was not so in the *Childers,* for it was while she had sternway that the
sea came in and nearly swamped her. Therefore, to prevent her going
down, away went the guns. If I recollect rightly, those which had just been
shipped were of a lighter calibre than those thrown away, and no doubt the
brig had not so much stability on the water as formerly. Turning the officers' statements to account, I sent for all of them and pointed out the evil
consequences of lashing the helm to leeward, and forbad its being done
again. I next had the seamen and quarter masters aft, explaining to them
that, in future, the brig was to be constantly kept under command of the
helm—that is, to have headway. I threatened the steersmen with punishment if it ever came to my knowledge that the helm was lashed to leeward.
I ordered a card to be stuck on the binnacle with written instructions on it
directing the helm to be kept amidships during stormy weather. This plan,
on being followed out, proved that I was right: for, instead of laying the
vessel to in a gale of wind, I kept her under the storm staysails, always forging ahead and under control of the helm. The change for the better became
evident to all on board. The Gunner,[1] who had been nine years in the brig,

---

[1] M'Nicholl.

and who had charge of a watch at sea, was the first to notice the improvement in the ease of her motions. There was no sudden jerking, but the vessel yielded gradually to the pressure of the wind and, with the assistance of the storm staysails, went slowly through the water, to the astonishment of all the seamen who wondered that no other officer had thought of such a system before. The gunner, who proved to be a thorough good seaman, repeated over and again his regrets that this plan had not been put in practice sooner, as it would have prevented many a sail being blown away and eased the wear of the hull. All my orders, I now observed, were attended to with alacrity: it was evident the crew had confidence in their captain.

When the officers knew I had been so long detained at Verdun, they inquired if Mr. Temple was an acquaintance. When they heard my reports of that gentleman's proceedings, they were astonished, as they had formed the highest opinion of him. They had received him on board as a passenger when in the Baltic. He had, after his escape from France, visited Russia and, luckily finding his way on board the *Childers*, came to England in her. He had by his lively disposition and other attractive qualities completely captivated their good feelings towards him. However, I requested them not to bring his name again under my notice.

We were 13 days getting to Leith, during which we encountered a great deal of stormy weather. It had been my object to keep near the land, expecting by so doing to make better progress. I was right in my judgment, but the unruly pilots lost by night what I had gained by day. So soon as they knew that I was in bed, they would shape the brig's course out into the middle of the ocean. Consequently we encountered tremendously high seas: the vessel laboured woefully and shipped immense quantities of water, the leeside being constantly submerged. All this rolling about woke me, and, inquiring of the officer of the watch, I was informed that the pilot had stood away from the land. I finally put a stop to these whims. One night I went on deck to see what was going on. The vessel was rolling to an alarming extent. I was suddenly jerked from one side to the other, and fell on the cap of one of the carronade screws. The pilot who witnessed this accident, a stout lusty fellow, never came to my assistance: nor did anyone till I called out for help. I thought one of my ribs was broken, as the pain was intense. I could not keep my body upright for a long while afterwards. The crew were seized with colds and coughs: in short, the whole of us were laid up by the mismanagement of the pilots. The master was a young officer, and only acting. I therefore found myself obliged to interfere and take upon myself a responsibility not usual in such cases. The pilots kept out to sea at nights because they felt no uneasiness when at a distance from the land. But when it was near they were fidgety. The consequence of all this was that the rigging became so slack from the labouring of the vessel that I was obliged to run into Berwick Bay to set it up. Putting to sea the next day, we found the fore-topmast sprung, and I had to shift it for a sound one. Finding my arguments had no effect on these obstinate pilots, I assumed the charge myself, and gave written orders at night for the management of the brig. We soon bene-fited by the change. By keeping at a moderate distance from the shore we had smoother water, and gained ground rapidly. On our way we boarded only two vessels—English ones—nothing like an enemy being seen.

On the 9th of February we anchored in Leith Roads. Never in my life did I feel greater relief from anxiety, as every soul on board was a martyr to coughs, hoarseness and alarming colds, so severe had been the weather. When I reported my arrival to Ad. Vashon,[1] who held the naval command, and represented to him the state of the *Childers'* crew, he expressed a very proper feeling in their behalf. It was not only their case which required con-sideration, but also my own: I was completely knocked up. He assured me that time would be given for rest, etc., and that he should not think of ordering the vessel to sea till the crew had recovered from their fatigues. He also expressed his astonishment at such a useless vessel being kept in the Service. So far I had reason to be satisfied, as I now knew for certain that I should have time to fit out my brig; and I hoped to make all on board comfortable, as far as circumstances would allow. Our arrival made the fourth brig of war stationed here to cruize against the enemy. The admiral had his flag on board the *Texel*, a 64. There was a sort of depot at Leith for naval stores, but nothing in the shape of a dock yard.

Having now time to look about me, my first object was to make my cabin more comfortable. There was only room for the half of a round table in it, which was placed against the fore bulkhead. This arrangement would only admit of three, but I was determined somehow or other to find space for four. There was a stove against the after bulkhead, which I could not well do without in the winter: but it was much in the way. At last I contrived to cut away the bulkhead, making a grove to receive it. By that means I gained nearly 24 inches in length, which enabled me to fit up a small round table, with four chairs conveniently placed. I could now invite a friend or two to dine with me. I had to set all my wits to work to turn to the best account a cabin scarcely deserving the name of one. The officers were astonished at my perseverance and ingenuity in overcoming obstacles that no other cap-tain had hitherto attempted. The other brigs on the station could easily have hoisted mine in, so much superior were they in size and dimensions. They were armed with 16 32 lb. carronades and two long nines, with a crew of 120

[1] James Vashon, Capt. 12/4/82; R-Ad. 23/4/1804; V-Ad. 28/4/08; Ad. 4/6/14.

men. The names of their commanders were G. Andrews,[1] F. Baugh[2] and my old shipmate of the *Alcide,* Sanders.[3] My again meeting him was a rencontre for which I was not prepared. However, on our acquaintance being renewed, he conducted himself very properly, and a friendly intercourse was established. The four of us formed a mess at the principal inn, on the pier of Leith. There was a naval club which met occasionally in Edinburgh, which I attended once or twice. I there made the acquaintance of several naval officers of distinction, among the number Capt. George Hope,[4] who at that time was Captain of the North Sea fleet under Ad. Sir James Saumarez, and who afterwards, when a Lord of the Admiralty, became a useful friend.

As the crew were recovering from their complaints, I employed them in making such improvements as I thought necessary: but the more I examined the contents of the vessel under my command, the more I had reason to despond. The stores were in a most neglected state, and, after weighing all these defects in my mind, I thought it my duty to lay the case before the admiral. He gave strong symptoms of displeasure at having such a vessel under his flag. He ordered the master of the *Texel* to take a survey of the brig's condition. That officer in the performance of his duty gave the strongest signs of dissatisfaction—even of disgust—at all he saw, and he did not hesitate to declare that he thought the *Childers* unfit for sea service. He accordingly made his report to the admiral verbally, upon which I was directed to apply for a survey of the vessel's capabilities. I was not prepared for such a proceeding, but as the commander in chief seemed determined that something of the kind should be done, there appeared to me no backing out of the position in which I unexpectedly found myself. I thought the requesting of a survey of a vessel to which I had just been appointed might offend the Admiralty. Consequently, in my official letter, which, in the first instance was addressed to the admiral, I began by saying, "Acting under your directions, I have to report the defective state of the sloop under my command." Admiral Vashon noticed its commencement, and appeared inclined to disapprove of the sentence: but, without allowing me time to make my reply, he said, "Very well. I don't mind. I shall send it." I was considerably annoyed. The brig, everybody knew, was a worn-out craft, but I should have taken my chance in her. When I thought it my duty to represent her inefficient condition, I had not contemplated the consequences. I thought the admiral would order a supply of better stores, and

[1] George Andrews, Cdr. 29/4/1802; Capt. 22/9/09; commanding the *Ringdove,* 18.
[2] Thomas Folliott Baugh, Cdr. 29/4/1802; Capt. 21/10/10; R-Ad. (Ret.) 1/10/46; commanding the *Clio,* 18.
[3] George Sanders. Now commanding the *Bellette,* 18.
[4] (Sir) George Johnstone Hope, Cdr. 22/11/90; Capt. 13/9/93; R-Ad. 1/8/1811. Died, 1818.

direct the other defects to be made good on the spot. But when the case took the turn mentioned, I felt myself justified in placing the principal responsibility on the admiral. He was an odd-tempered man, and a stranger to me; and I felt embarrassed in my early dealings with him. However, I thought it prudent to write to Lord Gambier and explain all that had passed between the admiral and self.

Whilst employed in improving my cabin I could get no assistance from the naval depot. I was consequently obliged to buy plank and other things. The first lieutenant of the flag ship, Mr. Peake,[1] had been my shipmate in the *Alcide*. When he heard that I had been buying the articles mentioned, he hastened to the naval yard, and in strong terms pointed out to the authorities there the impropriety of making an officer in my situation purchase deal boards for his cabin. His representation produced its effect, and one of the clerks from the office came and requested me to send my bill to him. He also made a sort of apology for what had happened. I could not help reminding him that my application for a supply of the articles had been refused. I shall here state that I was obliged to buy log lines, as there were none in store, and the admiral carried his ideas of economy to such a pitch that he would not allow any to be purchased. Therefore the brig's speed through the water was reckoned at my expense.

It took three days to convey a letter from Leith to London. On the seventh day an order arrived from the Admiralty, directing that the *Childers* should be examined, whether sound or not. In the meantime all my traps had arrived from London, and I had the means of making my preparations. The admiral did not invite us often to his house. His son[2] commanded the flag ship. Mrs. Vashon appeared an amiable person, but as there was not much sociability I was left a great deal to my own resources. Capt. Sanders resided at a different inn from mine, but he came to us to dine. He had nicknamed my brig "the Half-Moon Battery," and was not backward in passing severe strictures upon her inefficiency, as the brig that he commanded—the *Bellette*—was one of the most powerful in our Navy. At one of our mess dinners he proposed that the whole of us should share prize money together: but nothing was decided. The *Childers'* defective sails were sent to the *Texel* to be repaired, and the officers from the yard were employed in examining our timbers, but as the vessel was afloat the survey could only be partial.

As time passed on, I invited my brother officers to come and dine with me. The tray which I depended on so much had not yet been used, but now was the time for displaying it. We were all seated in my cabin waiting the

---

[1] Thomas Ladd Peake, Lt. 8/5/1805; Cdr. 8/5/12; Capt. 1/3/22.
[2] James Giles Vashon, Capt. 28/5/1802.

appearance of dinner, when my steward announced that the passage leading into it was so narrow that the tray could not be brought in. Here was a
disappointment! The dishes were handed in separately. The casualty did
not interfere much with our dinner, which proved a very sociable one, and
Sanders was so anxious to see the tray that it was produced. He was so
much pleased with the construction of it that he purchased it. In a few days
he became my constant companion, and would not let me rest until I wrote
a letter to Lord Mulgrave in his behalf, reminding his Lordship of a
promise that he had made to Lord Chatham to promote him. Hitherto I
knew nothing of Sanders. At times he gave himself consequential airs,
wishing it to be understood that he possessed considerable influence. He
assumed importance from the circumstance of his commanding so fine a
vessel. However, not having much faith in this gentleman's assertions, I
demanded explanations, which proved him to be the son of a surgeon who
had for many years been attached to Lord Chatham's household. Thereat
Mr. Sanders did not rise much in my estimation. His authoritative bearing,
with other freaks, were not suited to his connexions. I had supposed him,
by his sayings and doings, to be a member of some high aristocratic family.
He was fond of the bottle, and during our rambles he had frequently
indulged in that failing. It fell to my lot to carry him home one night in a
hack carriage, but he never refunded to me my expenses therefor, or even
thanked me for my care of him. Therefore, instead of an agreeable companion, I found him a regular bore.

The builders, having terminated their examination of the *Childers'* timbers, declared them to be sound—a result no one expected. However, so it
was, and I, her captain, lost no time in completing all that was required. I
fitted a boarding netting to the brig, and had the boats, such as they were—
a cutter and jolly boat—well repaired for cutting out work. The first orders
I received were to take charge of a convoy for Gothenburg. When the merchants heard that the *Childers* had been appointed to perform that duty,
they protested against placing their property under the care of such an inefficient vessel of war, and they remonstrated. Consequently a sloop, the
*Snake*, with 32 lber. carronades, was ordered round from Sheerness to
relieve me of my charge. This was no great compliment to my brig!

In a short time all the provisions were on board, a few volunteers came
from the *Rendezvous*, and I was anxious to try my fate on the briny waves. I
hove up one anchor to be ready to start at a moment's notice. The admiral
had arranged that the four brigs should put to sea at the same time, and we,
the commanders, agreed to have a parting dinner at the inn. Here the proposal was renewed to share prize money together. Sanders made use of some

very ill-timed expressions relating to my brig, remarking that she would be taken by the smallest enemy privateer: and that, the others' vessels being so much superior to mine, the risk was not a fair one. I retorted upon Sanders, stating that, as he had been the first to moot the question of sharing, he ought to be the last to make such out-of-the-way observations. "If I am attacked," I said, "I shall not be so easily captured as you imagine. Therefore, to close the bargain with you, I will agree to share prize money with you for three months, or not at all. It is now for you to decide." In conclusion no agreement was made. The party broke up, and we repaired on board our separate vessels. I had received a clerk recommended by Mrs. V., also a steward who had been employed in her establishment. When Ad. Vashon gave me my sailing instructions, he authorized me to seek shelter against stormy weather wherever I might find it convenient, and not to expose my crew to chances of sickness. I was to cruize off Gothenburg to annoy the enemy to the best of my power. Having settled everything satisfactorily, I took my leave.

On the 10th of March, by 11 o'clock in the morning, the *Childers* was under sail, favoured with a good breeze and fine weather. So soon as we were clear of the land I exercised the seamen at the guns and the sword exercise. The boats were also put into good order, with a certain number of men fixed upon ready for boarding ships at anchor. I explained to the crew my determination to be constantly ready for action, by night or by day, directing them to keep their cutlasses and pistols in fighting condition. The next day I boarded a whaler bound to Davis Straits, but nothing of consequence occurred till the 14th when we made the land, and I saw the coast of Norway, of stupendous height, for the first time. I had suited my dress for sea service in a small vessel—a round jacket, etc. When exercising the seamen at the guns and the Marines with muskets, I appeared on deck with my sabre drawn and pistols in my belt. This proceeding seemed to be approved of by all under my command, as I noticed cheerful countenances in every direction. My orders were obeyed with alacrity and apparent good will. All these indications gave me confidence, which led me to rely on their support in the event of meeting an enemy.

It was about 1 o'clock of this day that a vessel was seen from the mast head. Sail was instantly made in chace of her. The stranger closed in with the land, by which means we lost sight of her. My dinner hour was ½ past 2 P.M. By ½ past 4 we had closed this mountainous coast and again got sight of the chace. We were now in smoother water, but the stranger disappeared among the rocks. Not thinking it prudent to stand too near to this high land, I hoisted out the cutter. Volunteers offered themselves with an animated spirit that was truly gratifying. A certain number having been selected, I gave the command of her to the master, Mr. Wilson,[1] directing him to proceed inshore and bring out the vessel. He had no sooner left the brig when more volunteers came forward, anxious to assist the cutter. Not wishing to thwart their bold intentions, I had the jolly boat lowered and soon manned, the purser[2] requesting to lead her. He evinced such determination that I complied with his wishes. All this time my dinner remained on the table. I had been so often interrupted during the chace that I had not finished the necessary meal. The two boats that had gone away contained 24 of my best men. They were soon out of sight, and the *Childers* lay to, waiting the result of their exertions.

More than an hour elapsed, and no boats were to be seen. I became anxious, as the day was closing: and this feeling was considerably increased when the man aloft on the look-out, shouted in a loud voice, "A large vessel coming towards us from under the land!" All our attentions were instantly directed to the object. Opposite to that part of the coast where I had hove to, the land trended to the north east. A long inlet extending to some distance was discerned, which the pilots informed me led to the port of Hitteroe. It was from thence that this stranger was approaching under topgallant sails. The two lusty pilots gave symptoms of extreme alarm, declaring that the enemy's vessel was a very powerful one, and that I should either be taken or sunk. I desired them to keep silence and attend to my orders: but they became so refractory that I was obliged to order them below, as their sayings made a strong impression upon the seamen.[3] I then called the crew to their guns and prepared for action.

As the stranger drew out from his apparently confined inclosure, he was still end on, and I could not see his rig. But the size of his bows indicated a vessel of some dimensions. Then, as he shaped his course towards the *Childers*, we saw the length of his hull: he was a large brig,[4] mounting nine long heavy guns upon his broadside. This was not a very agreeable visitor, and I now found myself in a most awkward position. The boats had not yet hove in sight from the NW—that is, on my right—and I was, I confess, almost at a loss how to act. If I attempted to draw further off from the land, I exposed my boats to capture. Therefore, after a few seconds of meditation, I determined to bring my opponent to action. He continued to near me, and when he was about a mile off upon my starboard bow, I fired a shot at him. At the same time up went the colours of Old England. My firing obliged him to alter his course: therefore, instead of closing nearer, he hauled off. This was

[1] William Wilson (Acting). Confirmed, 3/7/1813.
[2] A. W. H. Le Neve, 1st Warrant, 29/4/07.
[3] W.H.D. mentions their names—Drummond and Gordon—in his dispatch and praises their conduct!
[4] *It was the 20-gun brig* Lügum, *hailing from the Kingdom of Denmark and Norway.*

a most critical moment for me. When he changed his plan, which at first seemed to be one of attack, he hoisted the Danish ensign and kept aloof, whereby the advantage instantly turned in my favour: which had its effect on my crew. Fortunately for me, I had now time to make my arrangements.

But before I could make sail, to bring the enemy to action, my boats hove in sight, coming from a deep creek on our left, with a galliot in tow, under sail. Its crew, not being armed, had been unable to resist the attack of my boats, but had fled on shore, where they hurled down from the rocks huge stones. But fortunately no one had been injured by them. My crew were firing their muskets, and a similar fire was noticed from the prize, which circumstance led me to believe that my men were still contending with the Danes. However, the firing soon ceased, and the boats neared us rapidly. Yet notwithstanding these favourable appearances I was still in a very embarrassed position, because it lay in the power of the enemy to capture my boats and retake the galliot. Why the Dane did not make that exertion is no affair of mine. By his not doing so, my boats finally rejoined me, my opponent looking quietly on all the while. I now gave directions for the security of the prize, placing an officer in command of her. The boats were hoisted in, and I made sail to attack the Dane.

The day had just closed. I had therefore to beat to windward to reach him. He kept so close to the land that I could not get inshore of him. My broadsides were directed only as often as they could bear, I was obliged to shorten sail, and I could only aim at him as the flash of his guns indicated his position. Darkness now came on, which for a short while interrupted our fire. Many broadsides had been exchanged, but as yet the *Childers* had not received any injury of consequence. There was only a light air so close to the high land, and the water was as smooth as a millpond. Under these circumstances all the advantages lay with the enemy. He could see us as we were outside, but we could not see him. I therefore ceased cannonading till the moon enabled us to see what we were about. It was during this interval that we heard sounds very similar to the rowing of boats, and an impression naturally arose that the enemy was receiving men from the shore. Our quietness did not last long, for the Dane, profiting by his position, opened his fire in slow succession. One of his shots went clean through both sides of the *Childers* just above the line of flotation. Another shot lodged in the lower deck. It weighed 22 lbs. English, so that I was led to believe that he had long 18 lbers.—overwhelming odds against 12 lb. carronades. The moon at last, being at its full, shone forth in all imaginable splendour. Being now enabled to ascertain my exact position, I thought myself rather too near the land, upon an hostile coast. Judging it imprudent to expose my vessel to such unusual dangers, I directed the pilots to widen our distance, and, having placed her about three miles from the shore, I again hove to, waiting the proceedings of the Dane.

The heavens were cloudless; the stars and planets were seen in all their brilliancy. The enemy set his square mainsail, and, shaping a diagonal course, gradually increasing his distance from the land, he neared us. I was on the watch for a favourable moment to tack. I now ascertained that all the captains of the guns were on board the prize, which, in a certain way, was a loss. At about 11 o'clock I thought I had obtained the object I had been endeavouring to realise. I instantly set the courses and tacked the *Childers*. When round, I had the enemy on the lee bow. I then made a short speech to my crew, telling them that I meant to lay him on board on the weather bow and that they were all to follow me. They instantly armed themselves and patiently waited for orders. My clerk attended me carrying my sword. We were favoured with one of the finest nights I ever beheld. Every object could be seen as plainly as by daylight.

We stood on towards our opponent, and for a time all my plans bore the appearance of success. But, at the critical moment of weathering the Dane, the wind headed us two or three points. He, taking advantage of that circumstance, luffed up as close as he could, and my expectations were foiled. Instead of gaining the wind I was obliged to bear up to prevent the jib booms of the two vessels coming in contact with each other, and pass along to leeward, as near as it could be done without touching the enemy, myself directing the motions of the man at the helm.

When the two jib booms were clear of each other, I ran forward to ascertain that the steersman was acting properly. Then we poured a broadside of round and grape shot into the enemy's deck. His vessel leaning over into the wind, not one of the shot, I imagine, failed of doing mischief, and the groans of his men were distinctly heard. Then, coming aft and still directing the man at the helm, I had reached the lee side of the capstan when I was hurled down by it with such violence that I felt as if life had departed. My left arm was jammed against the edge of the lee carronade slide and my body smothered underneath the capstan. I lay in that position a few seconds till the smoke cleared away, when, my person being missed by the first lieutenant, he set to work to ascertain what had become of me. When he discovered my helpless position, with the assistance of some of the seamen he lugged me out from under the capstan, and as they were raising me from the deck my senses returned. The first words I heard were, "The captain is killed!," repeated several times. Moving my arms and opening my eyes contradicted that assertion. My clerk had received a shot in the body which killed him outright, and I was covered with his gore. Altogether I was in a shocking plight, suffering great pain in both my legs and left arm. Having been removed to the weather side, I was seated on one of the carronade slides. At that moment the Dane fired two stern guns, but they missed us. I now ordered the first lieutenant to tack and lay the enemy on board on the weather quarter, but whilst he was preparing to do so the gunner called out from below that the magazine was afloat and the brig sinking. This report was confirmed by the carpenter.[1] Consequently, renewing the action was out of the question. The enemy widened his distance by keeping on the opposite tack, and all that I could do was to close with the prize to save my crew. The enemy's last broadside killed two and wounded nine, including myself, severely.[2] When the surgeon, Mr. Allen,[3] came to my relief, I desired him to dress the wounded men first of all, then return to me. In the meantime he sent me some wine and water. When we got near the galliot we hove to. The pumps were at work and the dead were committed to the deep. Meanwhile, the Dane, standing on on the same tack, closed in with the land and we soon lost sight of him. This brought on 2 o'clock of the morning. The jolly boat was lowered, to communicate with the Prize and then to examine the damages sustained by the enemy's fire. There were eight shot between wind and water on the starboard side, seven of which penetrated the hull.

The surgeon, having dressed all the wounded, repaired to me again. I was taken down to my cabin, which I found in a wretched condition. My steward had not removed a single article from the table on which my dinner had been laid. Most of them had been smashed to atoms. I had not returned to my cabin from the moment I left it to direct the motions of the *Childers*, about 4 o'clock in the afternoon. It was afloat, and the prospect was anything but agreeable. The Surgeon found my left leg most severely contused. The right one was cut open from the knee, down the bone to the ankle, by a splinter. Had it penetrated the thickness of a wafer deeper, the bone would have been broken to pieces. My left wrist was bleeding freely and the arm below the shoulder in acute pain. Whilst he was dressing me, the first lieutenant came to report that one of the pumps was choked and the brig sinking. "Well," said I, "if that is the case I cannot help you. We must all go down together. Give me your hand, and God bless you. I have done my duty and am resigned to my fate." Whether the cool and determined manner in which I delivered these words had any effect upon the lieutenant, I know not. But he hastened on deck and in the course of a quar-

---

[1] Mason (Acting).

[2] *Killed,* Mr. Joseph Roberts, captain's clerk; Wm. James, boatswain's mate. *Wounded,* W. H. Dillon, Esq., commander, severely in both legs and left arm;———boatswain, slightly; Mr. Batterst, midshipman; Mr. Parker, Volunteer;———Allender, corporal of marines; J. Halding, seaman; D. Burke, ditto; J. Constable, Marine; J. Marshall, boy.

[3] Henry Allen, 1st Warrant, 1807.

ter of an hour returned to acquaint me that the pump had been set to rights and that there was a chance of saving the *Childers*. At that moment the water in my cabin was about six inches deep, and as clear as the sea without. The surgeon quitted me, and I attempted to get some sleep.

After a few hours the surgeon renewed his visit, and reported favourably. He expected from the severity of the contusions that an inflammation would ensue. Fortunately for me that was not the case, but he entreated me to remain quiet. The report of the injuries we had received in the action was now laid before me. Both the lower masts were struck by shot, also the bowsprit. The rigging and sails were very much cut, and several shots had struck the hull. However, by the afternoon of the 15th the damages were repaired, and the shot holes under water stopped, so that we were able to shape a course for Leith Roads. The action had lasted, with intervals, upwards of seven hours against an enemy of vastly superior force. Twenty guns were counted plainly on his deck—that is, twenty on the sides and two in the stern. When I reflected upon the conduct of the enemy, he appeared, during the whole proceeding, to have been deficient in energy, as I always attacked him. He had the advantage of the weather gage, and might at his convenience have closed upon me. But instead of doing so he allowed me to bring him to action, waiting very quietly the result. Had he, when I attempted to cross his bow from the leeward, borne down upon me, the consequences might have been most fatal to the *Childers*. I have often thought of it. His vessel, being of considerably more burden than mine, when coming in contact would probably have overpowered her, and she would have gone down. After I had poured my last broadside into him, he never altered his course, but permitted me to close with the prize and make all my arrangements without annoyance. Consequently, I beat off an enemy after a very severe contest of long duration, and bore away in triumph the vessel which he evidently intended to recapture.

In the afternoon I directed the galliot to be taken in tow. She was called the *Christina*, and had only a part of her cargo in—45 casks of fish, some iron and other materials. She did not sail well: she was accordingly taken under our stern. The damages inflicted upon my property were very serious. Three trunks containing my wearing apparel were shot through; my writing case—a very handsome one—shattered to pieces. A small pocket book containing £25 in bank notes was never recovered, but my purse with 11 guineas in it was brought to me, as well a diamond pin. Altogether my losses by the engagement could not easily be replaced. The next day I was carried on deck to breathe some fresh air. As we were proceeding towards the coast of Scotland, we passed the convoy which I had taken charge of at Leith but afterwards delivered over to the *Snake*. We exchanged the private signal with that ship. Her captain would not be liable to any annoyance from the Dane that I had engaged.

On the 18th we anchored in Leith Roads. I had dictated to the purser my official report of the action as I was in too much pain to write. When he had completed it, I sent for the officers that they might hear the statement of our proceedings. They appeared not satisfied with it, saying that I had not done myself justice, as the action was one of the hardest fought of the war, the odds being immense and that I had not sufficiently explained the enemy's vast superiority. The officers and crew repeated over and over again that the late captain never would have done anything of the kind. He would not have gone so close inshore. My only reply was that I preferred underrating the action to making a boasting report. The truth would soon be known and our exertions would be appreciated accordingly.

Not long after the *Childers* had anchored, in the forenoon, I was carried on shore and took up my quarters at the Britannia Inn on the pier of Leith, on the second floor, that I might be out of the way of all interruption. On my leaving the *Childers*, the crew gave me three hearty cheers.

My principal anxiety, now, was to learn what light my action would be viewed in by the Admiralty. The next was to recover the use of my limbs. I could not walk without crutches and my left arm was nearly useless. The following day the admiral called to see me. As I was in acute pain, he did not stay long, merely asking a few questions as to the state of the weather and the number of hours the action lasted. He then withdrew. So soon as the public became acquainted with the particulars of this engagement, all sorts of reports were in circulation—among others that the vessel I had fought was not a man of war but a privateer. Many officers of the Navy called. One in particular passed some very appropriate compliments upon my exertions, assuring me that I should receive promotion. "You command," said he, "the very worst craft in the Navy, and you have fought a vessel of vastly superior force, bringing away a prize. You are entitled to reward, and I am sure the Admiralty will place that construction upon your conduct. Promotion will be the result." I differed with him on that part relating to my advancement, as I had not captured the enemy, and told him so. "Well," he replied, "recollect what I tell you. You have performed wonders under the circumstances, and you will be noticed accordingly."

The reports to which I here allude no doubt made some impression upon Ad. Vashon as in two or three days he called again, and appeared in very ill temper. He overloaded me with questions and found fault with my report of the injury done to the rigging: in short, seemed inclined not to believe any of my statements, and refused to approve of my demand for the proper quantities of rope to replace those which had been shot away, unless I altered it. This was one of the most unpleasant official interviews I ever had in my life. I submitted patiently to all he said. I was in pain, suffering from the wounds, and therefore allowed him, without making any replies, to settle the fate of the *Childers* as he thought proper. Among other questions, he demanded in peremptory tones, "How do you know that your enemy had long 18 lbers.? The prize you have taken is not worth two pence." I told him that I saw, and very nearly touched, the guns, that the shot on board weighed 22 lbs. English, and that I would send him one. After he took his leave, I directed that one of them should be sent to his house.

On the 24th, in the morning, the surgeon had dressed my wounded limbs, it being about eight in the morning. He retired, and I set to with my razors. In the course of five minutes he returned. "What has brought you back again, Doctor?" I demanded. "I merely called to inquire whether you had received your letters from London," said he. "Not yet," was my answer. He kept pacing the room behind my chair, which made me look round, and I noticed an expression on his countenance that gave rise to an opinion of something having happened. "Will you have the goodness, Capt. Dillon," said he, "to lay your razor down?" I did so. He instantly caught hold of my right hand with considerable energy, saying,

"*I wish you joy, sir. You are a post captain!*"

· · ·

*Captain Sir William Henry Dillon (1779–1857) went on to serve at Walcheren, off Spain, and in the East Indies. He was knighted in 1835. In 1846, some thirty-eight years after he fought the* Lügum, *he became Rear-Admiral of the Blue, and, in 1853, Rear-Admiral of the Red. The miserable brig* Childers, *which had been built in 1778, was finally broken up in 1811.*

*Now we move forward to action in the Bay of Biscay, where Dillon's benefactor, Admiral Lord Gambier, commanded the Channel fleet blockading France. With the intention of uniting his Brest squadron with a squadron at Rochefort and then sailing for the West Indies, French Rear-Admiral Willaumez took advantage of a westerly gale that blew Gambier off his station to slip out of Brest with eight ships of the line. In late February, 1809, Willaumez dodged Stopford's squadron to enter the Basque Roads, and was subsequently bottled up there. Willaumez was superceded by Admiral Allemand, setting the stage for the Battle in the Aix Roads.*

*William Richardson's personal account picks up in October of 1808, as his ship is about to join the Channel fleet.*

WILLIAM RICHARDSON

*~*

# With Stopford
# in the Basque Roads
## 1808-1809

*T*his passage continues the story of William Richardson, who was
impressed into the Royal Navy while in Calcutta in 1793. In the ensuing years, Richardson has become a most useful naval hand. In 1805 he was
appointed gunner of the **Caesar**, soon to be commanded by the fighting
Admiral Sir Richard "Mad Dick" Strachan, under whom Richardson had
plenty of opportunities to exercise his guns. Strachan left the ship, however,
just before this passage picks up. Here Richardson details the events leading up to the action at Basque Roads, one of the Royal Navy's more color-
ful and dramatic actions. At this point, although Richardson doesn't
comment on it, Admiral Gambier, commander in chief of the Channel fleet,
is unpopular with his men for being a "blue lights" admiral, much given to
preachiness and less so to drawing French blood.

ON OCTOBER 30, 1808, the *Caesar* got under way, and we joined the Channel fleet off Ushant, now under the command of Lord Gambier, consisting of:
*Caledonia* (Lord Gambier, Capt. William Bedford), 120 guns; *Royal George*, 100;
*St. George*, 98; *Dreadnought*, 98; *Téméraire*, 98; *Caesar* (Capt. Charles Richardson), 80; *Achilles* (Sir Richard King), 74; *Triumph*, 74; *Dragon*, 74.

*NOVEMBER 15TH.*—A strong gale of wind came on from the westward,
which caused us all to bear up for Torbay, and while lying there our crew
got afflicted with ophthalmia; it began at the right eye and went out at the
left, and continued near a week and then left us.

*27TH.*—The wind having come to the north-east, we got under way with fleet and got off Ushant again, but next day shifted to the westward, blew a storm, and drove us back to Torbay again.

*DECEMBER 8.*—The wind got to the north-east again; got under way and got off Ushant, but the wind increasing and continuing for several days drove the fleet a long way to the westward.

On the 22nd our signal was made to proceed to Rochefort and relieve the *Gibraltar*. It blew so hard that we bore away and scudded under our foresail. Next day, in setting the close-reefed maintopsail, it still blowing hard, rain and hail, it blew to pieces; sounded frequently in eighty fathoms. A grampus has been following the ship these last twenty-four hours.

*DECEMBER 25.*—Saw Sables d'Olonne lighthouse on the French coast, and, in working up along the shore towards Rochefort, the next day at noon we saw eight sail of the enemy's merchant vessels coming down along the shore before the wind, and we put our ships about to cut them off; and now followed a specimen of our captain's abilities.

As we stood in, with the weather moderate, we fired a great many shot, which caused six of them to bring to; but the other two ran on shore among the breakers and soon went to pieces. We now lowered down the quarter and stern boats to take possession of the remaining six, but in the hurry and confusion the captain hurried them away without any arms or ammunition to defend themselves. As the ship was near the land, we wore her round with her head to the offing and maintopsail aback; as she increased her distance gradually, which a ship will do although her maintopsail be aback, the enemy perceived it, and one of them being armed with about fifty soldiers on board took her station so as to prevent our boats from boarding the others. What was to be done? Our people had no arms or ammunition, so they adopted the wisest plan, and that was to return to the ship for some. The enemy, seeing this, bore away before the wind, and off they ran, and before our boats had reached the ship they had run so far to leeward that any idea of following them was given up, and they made their escape like birds getting free from the fowler.

I never in all my life saw such confusion as was in our ship at the time: the captain was driving the people about from one place to another; one of my crew, named Andrew Gilman, in firing one of the guns, was so flurried that he did not observe a samson post[1] up behind him; the gun recoiled and killed him against it.

---

[1] *A short mast midway between the centerline and the bulwarks from which a derick is supported and stayed.*

During the time of wearing the ship a boat had been hoisted up off the booms to be got out, but was left hanging in the stay tackles and cut a fine caper during the time, swinging about from one side to the other, until some of the people lowered her down of their own accord: had Sir Richard Strachan been in the ship at the time he certainly would have gone mad. And thus ended as lubberly a piece of business as ever was heard of, and to have six merchantmen almost under the muzzle of our guns and then let them all escape, beats everything!

Next day we ran into Basque Roads, but our ships were not there; saw the French squadron lying at the Ile d'Aix; as usual they fired a great many guns, but whether they were exercising their crews, or for some victory by land, we could not tell. So we sailed out again, and met the *Aigle* frigate, who informed us that our squadron was cruising forty miles to the north-west of this place.

On the first day of this important year [1809] we joined them, consisting of the *Defiance* (Captain Hotham senior officer), with the *Donegal* and *Gibraltar*, and soon after ran into Basque Roads and there came to anchor; the *Gibraltar* shared out her provisions among us and then sailed for England. The French ships continue to fire many guns, and we suppose they are exercising their people to fire well.

*JANUARY 7.*—This morning we saw a square-rigged vessel at sea and coming in before the wind right toward us. The *Donegal* lay inside, the *Defiance* in the centre, and ours the outside ship, and we made sure of taking a prize. Our captain (I suppose to make up for his late bad conduct) ordered me to get three of the main-deck guns shotted and pointed as far ahead as possible, and then go into the magazine and be ready to supply him with powder, all which was readily done, as if something extraordinary was to be performed; but he soon made as great a blunder as before, for before the vessel got within gunshot he began to fire, and the captain of the vessel, judging from this that we were enemies, altered his course and ran her on shore near the town of St. Marie's.

The boats of the squadron, manned and armed, immediately went after her; but by the time they got near, the beach was covered with troops and they had to return without performing anything. Thus we lost another prize; and she must have been of some value, as we heard afterwards that she was a West-Indiaman. Well might the *Defiance*'s people ask ours, when alongside in a boat soon afterwards, if we were friends to the French!

*19TH.*—Foggy weather. Observed a chasse-marée near to us; hoisted French colours and decoyed her alongside, to the utter surprise of the poor

Frenchmen. Thus we got a prize at last, though of little value. In the evening saw a brig coming in, and the boats of our squadron went in pursuit of her. She ran on shore, and our people boarded, but could not get her off. Several shot were fired at them from the shore, but no harm done.

22ND.—Strong wind at south, and rain. Saw another French brig coming in, who, on discovering us, made off. In the afternoon another came in, and in passing fired three shot at her, and brought her to. She hoisted cartel colours, and proved to be the *Elizabeth* of London, with a hundred and forty of Junot's soldiers on board from Lisbon. Let her go to proceed to Rochefort, according to the Articles of Capitulation. They reported to us that the English had obtained a great victory in Spain.[1]

27TH.—Got under way with the squadron, stood out to sea, then rounded Baleines Lighthouse and came to anchor in the Breton Passage in 16½ fathoms. Next morning got under way and stood out to sea, where we met the *Indefatigable* frigate with dispatches, and were informed that Rear-Admiral Stopford was coming out to take the command, and would hoist his flag on board the *Caesar*. This news pleased us much, as we wanted a commander of such gallant abilities and knowledge.

29TH AND 30TH.—Met a convoy of victuallers, but the weather was so stormy these two days that we could get nothing out of them.

FEBRUARY 1.—Ran into Basque Roads, and there came to anchor. Five of the victuallers came in, and we got two of them alongside and cleared them of 119 tons of water. Then arrived more victuallers, and next day the *Naiad* frigate drove a brig on shore near St. Marie's laden with brandy; but the surf soon destroyed her, and our boats chased a sloop on shore laden with prunes near the Breton batteries.

The enemy's squadron fired a great many guns to-day, and had their shops dressed with colours—the English ensign undermost, and the Union downwards. What daring fellows!

15TH.—This morning we saw two men hung at the yardarm of two of the enemy's line-of-battle ships.

The *Calcutta*, formerly a British 50-gun ship, had the English ensign hung Union downwards under her bowsprit, we supposed to insult us; yet

[1] Corunna, Jan. 16, 1809. *For an account of this battle, see "When I Beheld These Men Spring from the Ground, 1809" page 234.*

they durst not venture to meet us, although they were superior in force. However, we paid them well for their audaciousness soon after. In the evening Rear-Admiral Stopford arrived in the *Amethyst* frigate.

Next morning the rear-admiral came on board and hoisted his flag on board the *Caesar*, bringing with him two lieutenants, a captain of marines, a chaplain, a secretary and his clerk, two master's mates, nine midshipmen, his coxswain and a band, and two live bullocks, which were very acceptable, as we have not tasted fresh beef this long time.

*19TH.*—Being Sabbath day, a church was rigged out and divine service performed on board the *Caesar* for the first time since I had belonged to her. The Rev. Mr. Jones, the chaplain, preached an excellent sermon. The ship's crew were very devout and attentive. The rear-admiral was on his knees at prayer time; but it was funny enough to see our captain, how fidgety he was: he neither sat nor stood, and was as unsteady as a weathercock. Some of our nobs thought that a man could not be a good seaman without swearing, but the admiral let them know the contrary. In the afternoon we saw some chasse-marées stealing along shore, and sent the boats of the squadron after them; they captured two, one laden with rye and the other with sardinian, a fish like dried herrings. The whole was shared out to the squadron and the vessels broken up for firewood, as their condemnation in England would have cost more than they were worth.

*21ST.*—The wind having come from the east, we got under way, and anchored outside of Baleines Lighthouse for fear the Brest fleet should slip out and come this way, and which they actually did, as will be seen presently. Among some prisoners taken a young man named Bordo (son of our French pilot of that name) was brought on board, and great was their joy in meeting each other again; but it did not last long, for in the evening they got drunk and fighting with each other, and the cause was that the father had married an Englishwoman. We had two more French pilots on board (both of them emigrants), one named Le Cam and the other Cameron, and although they had emigrated together they could never agree, and had separate messes. Cameron messed with me at first, but finding him a two-faced fellow I turned him off.

*23RD.*—Arrived the *Emerald* frigate from England with five live bullocks for the squadron, and exercised great guns and small arms at ten in the evening. Observed the *Amazon*, which was looking out in the north-west direction, letting off rockets, so we got the squadron under way to get near her; on meeting they told us they had seen nine sail of large ships coming along shore from the eastward, and steering for Basque Roads; we ordered her astern to inform the *Defiance* and *Donegal* of it, and to tell them to join us with all speed, and then prepared our ship for battle.

We had previously heard of a French squadron of frigates full of stores and ready to slip out of L'Orient for the West Indies, but they were block-aded by four sail of the line under Commodore Beresford; however, we thought they might have stolen out, and were coming this way to join the Rochefort squadron—we therefore crowded all sail to cut them off, and at midnight got sight of them.

It then fortunately for us fell a calm, which made us uneasy lest they should escape; but at dawn a breeze sprang up, and we steered right for them. But judge of our surprise as the daylight appeared to find they were the Brest fleet, eight sail of the line, and one of them a three-decker of 120 guns, and two of them flagships, with two frigates accompanying them! They were going to Basque Roads thinking to catch us there, but thanks to Heaven they were too late, as we were on different tacks. We continued our course and fetched into their wake, then put about and followed them; if they had begun to chase us we must have been obliged to run, for what could our three sail of the line do against such a force? But strange to say they never seemed to interrupt us; perhaps they thought we were not the ships that had been in Basque Roads this winter and were hastening along to catch them.

We made a signal to the *Naiad*, one of our frigates, to proceed with all haste to our Channel fleet and inform Lord Gambier of the French fleet being here; but before she got hull down she made the signal that another squadron of the enemy was in sight, and coming toward us, which made some on board think we were now caught at last. However, although we had the Brest fleet, the Rochefort squadron, and the others moving down on us, thus being nearly surrounded by them, yet we kept up our spirits, being determined to fight to the last rather than be taken.

As our admiral knew we could not cope with the Brest fleet, we altered our course to meet those that were coming, and as we drew near found them to be three large French frigates followed by the *Amelia* English frigate and *Dotterel* brig. We got so near that I thought it impossible for them to escape our clutches, and they, seeing their danger, ran in under the batteries of Sables d'Olonne, and there let go their anchors and prepared for battle.

As the wind was now blowing towards the land rear-admiral Stopford thought it very improper to come to anchor on a lee shore to fight, but made the signal to prepare to do it with springs on the cables; but the *Defiance*, mistaking the signal, ran in and came to anchor. As she swung round the frigates and batteries cut her severely, so that she was soon obliged to cut her cable and come out again.

Her fore-topsail yard was shot away, her sails and rigging much cut up, and two men killed and twenty-five wounded; however, all the time she was in she behaved gallantly. Hundreds of French people were seen standing on the quays looking at us as we went in, but as soon as we opened our fire they dispersed in an instant. We and the *Donegal* kept under way and as close in shore as the water would admit, and in passing on each tack fired at the frigates, and soon sent them to the bottom; we had not a man hurt, thank God, but were hit by shot from them several times; one went into the bowsprit and another through the jibboom. The *Donegal* had one killed and six wounded.

At four in the afternoon we left and went after the Brest ships, who had been in sight all this time from our mast-heads, and followed them until they came to anchor in Basque Roads; but we kept our squadron under way near the entrance, as we saw some large ships in the offing, and coming toward us. Our noble admiral is as cool and steady as if no enemy was near, and well might a good Christian know no fear.

One of our frigates—I don't know which it was, as they were changed so frequently—was stationed between us and the enemy to look out; and the latter had one of theirs for the same purpose, so they had frequently to pass each other on different tacks. British courage was severely tried, and the captain of our frigate asked permission by signal for liberty to engage the enemy; but our admiral for wise reasons would not grant it.

Next day, the ships we had seen in the offing joined us, and proved to be the squadron under the command of Commodore Beresford, consisting of the *Theseus* (Sir J. Beresford), 74 guns; *Valiant* (Capt. John Bligh), 74; *Triumph*, 74; *Revenge* (Capt. Car, or Ker), 74. They were a welcome addition to our little squadron, making us now seven sail of the line, and Sir John informed us that when the Brest fleet drove them away from blockading L'Orient, they ran close in and furled their sails, but when it came dark they set sail again, having never let go their anchors. This was a scheme to make Sir John believe they were going to remain there all night, in order to get a night's start of him, and catch us in Basque Roads before he could come to our assistance. They succeeded so far as getting the night run and no farther, and when Sir John missed them in the morning he came immediately to our assistance.

Although the enemy have now, in conjunction with the Rochefort squadron, eleven sail of the line and a 50, yet they do not think themselves safe. So they got under way to get under shelter of the batteries on the Ile d'Aix; but one of them carrying a broad pennant and named the *Jean Bart* (of 74 guns) got aground on the Palais shoal; soon after she heeled over, then filled, and became a wreck. During this time we had sent the *Indefatigable* frigate to see into the state of the three frigates we had sunk at Sables d'Olonne, and she brought us information that they were wrecks and the French were getting all the stores out of them they could get at. Their names were the *Italien, Calypso,* and *Sybille,* each of 40 guns.

Rear-admiral Stopford's letter to the Admiralty was as follows:

> H.M.S. "CAESAR."
> *February 27, 1809*
> AT ANCHOR BALEINE LIGHTHOUSE N.E. TO N. 4 MILES
> AND CHASSERON S.S.E. 10 MILES.

SIR,

YOU WILL BE PLEASED *to acquaint my Lords Commissioners of the Admiralty that on the 23rd instant, being at anchor NW of Chasseron Lighthouse, with the* Caesar, Donegal, *and* Defiance, Naiad *and* Emerald *frigates, the* Amazon *looking out to the NW, wind easterly, about 10 p.m. I observed several rockets in the NW quarter, which induced me to get under way and stand towards them; at 11 observed sails to the eastward and to which I gave chase with our squadron until daylight next morning, at which time the strange ships were standing into the Portuis Antioc (the passage to Rochefort) consisting of eight sail of the line, one of them a three-decker, and two frigates; they hoisted French colours, and conceiving them to be the squadron from Brest, I immediately dispatched the* Naiad *by signal to acquaint Lord Gambier.*

*The* Naiad, *having stood a few miles to the NW, made signal for three sail appearing suspicious. I immediately chased them with the squadron under my command, leaving the* Emerald *and* Amethyst *to watch the enemy. I soon discovered them to be three French frigates standing in for the Sables d'Olonne. I was at the same time joined by the* Amelia *and* Dotterel.

*The French frigates having anchored in a situation I thought attackable, I stood in with the* Caesar, Donegal, Defiance, *and* Amelia, *and opened our fire in passing as near as the depth of water would permit the* Caesar *and* Donegal *to go into. The* Defiance, *being of much less draught of water, anchored within half a mile of them, and in which situation, so judiciously chosen by Captain Hotham, the fire of the* Defiance *and other ships obliged two of the frigates to cut their cables and run on shore.*

*The ebb tide making and the water falling fast, obliged the* Defiance *to get under sail and all the ships to stand out, leaving all the frigates on shore. Two of them heeling much, they have been noticed closely by Captain Rodd, and by whose report of yesterday afternoon, they appeared with all their topmasts down, sails unbent and main-yards rigged for getting their guns out, and several boats clearing them. I fancy they will endeavour to get over the bar into a small pier, but I am informed by the pilots that it is scarcely practicable.*

*The batteries protecting these frigates are strong and numerous; the* Caesar *has her bowsprit cut and rigging; the* Defiance *all her masts badly wounded, two men killed and twenty-five wounded; the* Donegal *one killed and six wounded. These French frigates had been out from L'Orient but two days, and by Captain Irby's report appear to be the* Italien, Furieuse, *and* Calypso.[1]

*I am very confident they will never go to sea again. My chief object in attacking them so near a superior force of the enemy was to endeavour to draw them out and give our squadrons more time to assemble, but in this I was disappointed. I returned to* Chasseron *at sunset, and observed the enemy anchored in Basque Roads, and on the 25th I was joined by Captain Beresford in the* Theseus, *with the* Triumph, Valiant, *and* Revenge *and* Indefatigable *frigate. I therefore resumed the blockade of the enemy's ships in Basque Roads and shall continue it until further orders. The enemy's forces consist of eleven sail of the line and* Calcutta, 50, *and four frigates; the force under my command are eleven sail of the line and five frigates.*

*I have the honour to be, etc.,*
ROBERT STOPFORD.

Here was a noble turn off for Captain Hotham's mistake in anchoring by saying his ship drew less water than the others; so did the *Amelia* but did not anchor. But what seemed strange was that he did not mention any assistance from Captain Richardson, captain of the *Caesar*; the reason was, in my opinion, that he did not like him.

26TH.—Sent the *Dotterel* in chase, which took a French sloop laden with wine and brandy; the Frenchman was much surprised in finding us here, as he had been told their fleet had cleared the coast of the English. In the night a French boat came secretly alongside from the shore, with a French general and his wife in her; he told us he had fled in consequence of a duel with a French officer, whom he shot; we sent them to England in the *Dotterel*.

28TH.—Sent in the *Donegal* and *Emerald* to reconnoitre the enemy's ships more closely, and they on their return reported that the *Jean Bart's* masts were all gone and the ship full of water, with a lighter alongside to get out

---

[1] *They were, in fact, the* Italien, Calypso, *and* Sybille *as previously reported by Richardson.*

what they could save. Report says that Bonaparte has had the captain, whose name is Lebozec, tried and shot. Here the *King George* cutter arrived from England, to inform us that the Brest fleet had got out, and they were very much surprised to find that we were blockading them here. We got our squadron under way, went into Basque Roads, and anchored nearer the enemy.

*MARCH 2.*—Examined several galliards laden with brandy under licence to carry to our good citizens of London; they informed us that Austria had again declared war against France.

*7TH.*—Arrived and took command in chief, Admiral Lord Gambier in the *Caledonia*, with the *Tonnant, Bellona, Illustrious*, and several other smaller vessels, all from England; and next day arrived the *Mediator*, with a number of victuallers, and sent the *Defiance* to England to refit.

*17TH.*—This day we all shifted our anchorage and moored the ships in the form of an obtuse angle, reaching from one side the channel to the other, to stop the enemy's ships from getting in or out in the night-time. The *Caledonia* lay in the centre, the *Caesar* at one end and *Tonnant* at the other; the frigates and brigs lay in front, between us and the enemy, and the victuallers outside of all; two boats from each ship, manned and armed, rowed guard at night. We soon captured several chasse-marées, but gave the prisoners their liberty, and for which they were very thankful.

*19TH.*—Performed divine service, and when done a letter containing the thanks of the Lords Commissioners of the Admiralty to Rear-Admiral Stopford, the captains, officers and ships' companies of the squadron under his command was read, for their judicious and gallant conduct in destroying three of the enemy's frigates and afterwards blockading their fleet with an inferior force.

*APRIL 1ST.*—Observed the enemy very busy at low water on a rocky shoal named the Boyard, a long mile distant and abreast of the Ile d'Aix; and, supposing they intended to erect a battery there, the *Amelia* frigate and *Conflict* brig were sent in to annoy them; when they got as near as their depth of water would allow, they opened their fire and soon drove the enemy away in their boats; they then out boats, landed on the shoal, and upset the triangles the enemy had erected; the French fleet fired many shot at them during this gallant operation without hurting any one. Our boats (in number four) on their return saw five boats of the enemy coming after them and tossed up their oars to let them come near, but Monsieur soon altered his mind, and returned to his ships again without firing a shot.

3RD.—Arrived from England, in the *Impérieuse*, Lord Cochrane to command the fire-ships which the Lords of the Admiralty have proposed to be sent in among the enemy's ships; and a letter to that purport was posted up on board each line-of-battle ship for volunteers to man them. Numbers offered themselves on board the *Caesar*, but Mr. Jones, our flag-lieutenant, Mr. Winthorpe, acting lieutenant, and eight seamen were selected; no one was compelled to go, as the enemy by the laws of war can put any one to death who is taken belonging to a fire-ship.

5TH.—In consequence of some reproachful words uttered by Rear-Admiral Harvey against Lord Gambier, because his lordship could not grant him the command of leading in the fire-ships (as Lord Cochrane was sent here expressly by the Admiralty for that purpose), Rear Admiral Harvey was ordered to England, and there he was tried by a court-martial which dismissed him the service. He was, however, after some time reinstated.

Having got the victuallers cleared of the provisions and water, twelve of them were selected for fire-ships, and the *Mediator,* 36-gun frigate, was to be fitted for another, in order to go in ahead of the others and clear away all obstacles; eight others were expected from England, making in all twenty-one, and besides we fitted up three explosion vessels, to lead in the fire-ships and blow up first, to throw the enemy in consternation: all these ('twas thought) were sufficient to destroy the enemy's fleet. We got alongside one of the victuallers, a brig of 350 tons named the *Thomas,* and belonging to a Mr. Cowey of North Shields, and immediately began to fit her up for a fire-ship; we made narrow troughs and laid them fore and aft on the 'tween-decks and then others to cross them, and on these were laid trains of quickmatch; in the square openings of these troughs we put barrels full of combustible matter, tarred canvas hung over them fastened to the beams, and tarred shavings made out of brooms, and we cut four port-holes on each side for fire to blaze out and a rope of twisted oakum well tarred led up from each of these ports to the standing rigging and up to the mastheads; nothing could be more complete for the purpose.

We had captured lately several chasse-marées laden with resin and turpentine, which answered our purpose well, and which probably had been intended by the enemy for the same purpose against us. We placed Congreve's rockets at the yard-arms, but this was an unwise proceeding, as they were as likely to fly into our boats when escaping, after being set on fire, as into the enemy's. Having got all ready, she was hauled off and anchored near us.

My next job was to fit up a chasse-marée (lately taken) for an explosion vessel; but she rolled so much alongside as to endanger her masts being carried away against our rigging, so she was dropped astern, and hung on by a rope, and then continued to roll as much as ever; so that I had to change first one and then another of the carpenter's crew who were on board cutting the fuses, they being seasick. We stowed thirty-six barrels of gunpowder (90 lb. each) in her hold upright and heads out, on each was placed a 10 inch bomb-shell, with a short fuse in order to burst quickly.

A canvas hose well filled with prime powder was laid for a train from the barrels to a small hole cut in her quarter for the purpose, and the train was led through it to her outside, which was well fastened—a port fire which would burn twelve or fifteen minutes so as to give the people alongside in the boat who set it on fire sufficient time to escape before she exploded.

She, with two others fitted up by some of our other ships, was to go in a little before the fire-ships, run under the batteries, and then blow up, in order to put the enemy into such confusion that they might not attempt to board any of the fire-ships as they were running in. When this vessel was ready, I returned on board, it then being four in the afternoon, not having broke my fast the whole day—I had been so busily employed, and the business being so urgent, as she was expected to go in this night.

Lieutenant Davies took charge of her with the jolly-boat and crew; he and Mr. Jones, who went in with the fire-vessel, got made commanders for this business, and well they deserved it; but I, who had the sole charge of fitting them up, the most trouble, and my clothes spoiled by the stuff, did not so much as get a higher rate, which I applied for, and which from my services I thought myself entitled to: such is the encouragement that warrant officers meet with in the Navy! If an action is fought, though they have the principal duty to do in it, they are seldom mentioned in the captain's letter; whilst the purser, doctor, and boys of midshipmen are greatly applauded, though some of them were no more use in the ship at the time than old women!

The following orders were issued:

All launches and other boats of the fleet to assemble alongside of the *Caesar* and act under the orders of Rear-Admiral Stopford; ships and other vessels to be stationed as follows:

The *Pallas, Aigle* and *Unicorn* to lie near the Boyard shoal and receive the boats as they return from the fire-ships.

The *Whiting* schooner, *King George* and *Nimrod* cutters, at the Boyard to throw Congreve's rockets; the *Indefatigable* and *Foxhound* to lie near Aix to protect the *Etna* while she threw her shells into that place; the *Emerald, Dotterel, Beagle, Insolent, Conflict* and *Growler* to make a diversion on the east side of Aix; the *Lyra* to lie with lights near the Boyard side, and the *Redpole* with lights on the Aix side, a mile and a quarter from the enemy, as a direction for the explosion and fire-ships to pass between.

Lord Cochrane in the *Impérieuse* was to act as circumstances would permit, he having superintendence of the explosion and fire vessels.

The French ships of the line lay in two tiers across the passage, rather outside of Aix, as they had not room enough to lie in our *[one]* line; the frigates lay to the eastward and a great number of gunboats to the westward across the passage, and without (where the line-of-battle ships lay), they had moored a large boom, well secured with chains and anchors, to stop any vessel from entering in. Admiral Willaumez, who commanded the squadron, that we chased in the West Indies in 1806 (which was separated from us in the hurricane), and who commanded the Brest fleet that we had followed in here, has been superseded by a mighty man, if many names can make him so: he is called "Lacharie Jacques Theodore Allemand." This would have disgusted old Mr. Clark, master of the *Tromp* when I was in her: when mustering any of the people who came to join the ship, if they had two Christian names he would say, "Au, mon, I suppose you have come from some 'great family,' " then turning aside and giving a grin, would say again, "I dinna ken how these people come by twa names—it was as much as my poor father and mother could do to get me christened David."

On April 11, at half-past eight in the evening, it being very dark, and a strong tide setting with blowing weather right towards the enemy's ships, the explosion vessels set off, followed by the *Mediator* and other fire-ships. The former soon blew up with a dreadful explosion. The *Mediator* carried away the boom laid across by the enemy, and the other fire-ships followed her in, and the elements were soon in a blaze by their burning. Shells and rockets were flying about in all directions, which made a grand and most awful appearance. All hands were up that were able on board all our fleet, to behold this spectacle, and the blazing light all around gave us a good view of the enemy, and we really thought we saw some of their ships on fire. But it seems they had been prepared for this business, for as the fire-ships closed on them, they slipped or cut their cables and ran their ships on shore; and the fire-ships, after being abandoned by our people, drove with the wind and tide up mid-channel, and passed them; but we were informed by some of the prisoners taken that the *Ocean* lost near two hundred men in extricating a fire-vessel from her, and that she cut and anchored three different times.

At daybreak the following morning we saw all the enemy's ships, except two, on shore on the Palais shoal. The *Ocean* was lying with her stern on the top of the bank and her bows in the water; but next high water she, with two others, by throwing their guns and heavy stores overboard, got afloat again and ran towards Rochefort, until they stuck on the bar, and there remained until they could get more lightened.

At 2 p.m. the *Impérieuse* and some others of a light draught of water which were inside of our fleet, ran into Aix Roads and opened their fire on the *Calcutta*, and soon made her strike her colours. They then set her on fire, as she was fast aground, but it was thought she might have been got off by lightening her. The two line-of-battle ships that had not been on shore now cut their cables and ran towards Rochefort, until the bar brought them up.

The *Revenge, Valiant*, and *Etna* bomb were soon after ordered in, and began firing on the other enemy's ships that lay aground, and at five in the evening the *Varsovie, Aquilon*, and *Tonnère* surrendered, and three more fire-vessels were ordered to be got ready with all dispatch. We got the *Sisters* transport alongside for one of them, and soon fitted her up in a temporary manner for the purpose, and this same afternoon, between five and six o'clock, we got the *Caesar* under way, and with the *Theseus* and three fire-vessels ran into Aix Roads.

N.B.—In passing the Aix batteries, where our French pilots had said there were as many guns as days in the year, we could not find above thirteen guns that could be directed against us in passing; and these we thought so little of that we did not return their fire, although they fired pretty smartly at us too with shot and shells, which made the water splash against the ship's side; yet (thank God) they never hit, though the passage here is only about a mile wide. Captain Beresford of the *Theseus* had his cow put into the ship's head to be out of the way of the guns; a shot from the enemy killed it, which was the only loss received.

About seven o'clock, just as we were getting nearly out of the range of their guns, our ship took the ground and stuck fast nearly close to the Boyard. The shot and shells were flying about us at the time from Aix and Oleron, but it soon came dark, and they left off, and we had the prudence to still keep all the sails set to make them believe we were running on. However, after dark we took them all in, and as the tide fell the ship heeled much, so we started thirty tons of water overboard to help to lighten her, and ran the after guns forward to bring her more on an even keel. During this business a light was seen by the enemy through one of our port-holes, and we soon had a shot whistling across our quarterdeck. The light was quickly extinguished, and they fired no more. But this shows what a predicament we should have been in had it been daylight.

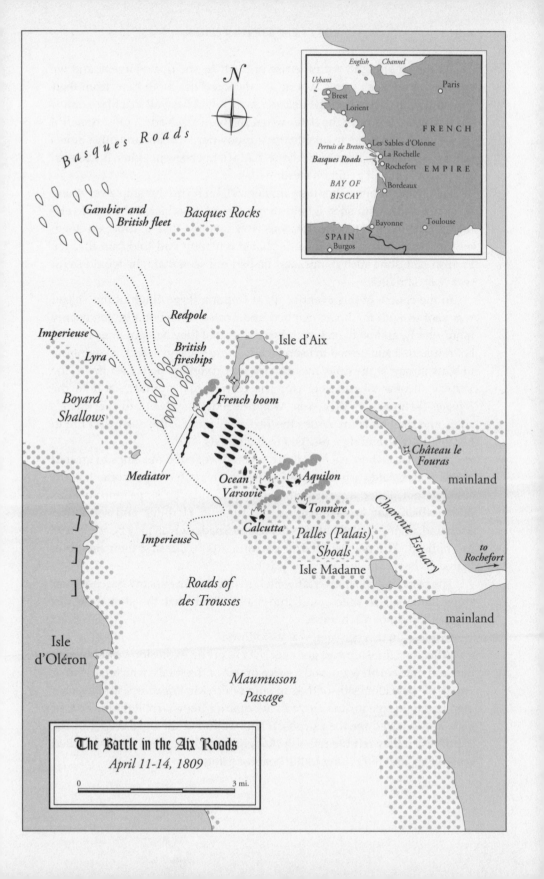

N

English Channel

Ushant

Brest

Lorient

Paris

Pertuis de Breton

**Basques Roads**

Les Sables d'Olonne

La Rochelle

Rochefort

FRENCH

EMPIRE

BAY OF
BISCAY

Bordeaux

SPAIN

Bayonne

Toulouse

Burgos

*Basques Roads*

*Gambier and
British fleet*

*Basques Rocks*

*Redpole*

*Imperieuse*

Isle d'Aix

*Lyra*

**British
fireships**

*Boyard
Shallows*

**French boom**

*Mediator*

Château le
Fouras

mainland

*Ocean
Varsovie*

*Aquilon*

*Tonnère*

*Calcutta*

*Imperieuse*

*Palles (Palais)
Shoals*

Charente Estuary

to
Rochefort

Isle Madame

*Roads of
des Trousses*

mainland

Isle
d'Oléron

*Maumusson
Passage*

### The Battle in the Aix Roads
*April 11–14, 1809*

0                                    3 mi.

At eleven at night, with the rise of the tide, she floated again, and we got her into deeper water, where we anchored her more clear from their shot and more clear from the *Calcutta*, which had been all in a blaze only a short distance from us; the latter when she blew up made a most dreadful explosion, having a great quantity of gunpowder on board and other stores which were intended for Martinique, had we not prevented her. It was said she was worth half a million sterling.

Fortunately none of her fiery timbers fell on board our ship: everything went upwards, with such a field of red fire as illuminated the whole elements. One of our French pilots was so frightened that he dropped down on the deck, and said afterwards that if anybody had told him that the English had done such things, and he had not seen them, he would say it was "one tam lie."

In the course of this eventful night Captain [John] Bligh of the *Valiant* was sent in with the boats manned and armed to reconnoitre the enemy more closely, and on his return informed us that they had got three lines of boats manned and armed to keep off any more fire-ships, and, it beginning to blow strong at the time, the attempt was given up. So we set fire to the *Varsovie*, a new 90-gun ship (for she carried that number), and to the *Aquilon* (74 guns), as they were waterlogged. They burnt to the water's edge, and then blew up. As for the *Tonnère* (74 guns), the enemy set fire to her themselves, and then escaped in their boats.

In the place where we now had anchored we found our ships to ground at low water. And early in the morning, the wind having become favourable, we got under way with the other line-of-battle ships, and left this place, which may be compared to Portsmouth Harbour, and soon after anchored among our other ships in Basque Roads, which may be compared to Spithead. The enemy fired at us from Aix in passing their line, but, thanks to Providence, not a man was hurt.

The frigates and small craft we left inside, but the enemy had got their ships lightened so much, and into shoal water, that the shot from our frigates could not reach them.

Our loss on this occasion was as follows:

When our fire-ship had got near the enemy an explosion vessel (which they did not see) blew up, and a piece of one of the shells, which had burst, struck the boat alongside of the fire-ship which Mr. Winthorpe and his four men had to escape in, and stove in her quarter (they were light four-oared gigs, and selected for the purpose), and wounded the boat-keeper in the hand. When they left the fire-ship, it being rough weather, she soon filled with water, and they clung to the boat for safety.

As the ebb tide was setting out strong they drifted out to one of our brigs, who sent her boat to save them; but two of them were gone and lost through exhaustion. Mr. Winthorpe was found in the boat quite dead, and Yankee Jack and the other were taken out of the gig nearly so, and when carried alongside the brig, Jack requested to be left in the boat until he recovered and got a little stronger, so the boat was dropped astern, and he in her.

He had not been there long before the rope broke, and being very dark, the boat soon drove out of sight, and the first landfall poor Jack made was on the French shore, where he was soon made a prisoner. We all pitied poor Jack Ellis, a good-tempered fellow, and never expected to see him again. But after the war was over, and Jack released, I met him on the Common Hard at Portsea, and was glad to see poor Jack again: he then belonged to a merchant vessel.

He told me that when he was made a prisoner he was examined strictly to know whether or not he belonged to one of the fire-ships, as by the laws of war they can put any one to death taken in them. But Jack said he belonged to one of the victuallers. They asked him then how he came to have his hand wounded, and he said it was by the boat's gunwale and ship's side as they rolled together, and by sticking to the same story (after being examined thirteen times at Rochefort and other places) he got clear, but remained a prisoner five years. When peace took place in 1814, Jack got released, returned to England, and received the whole of his pay and prize money up to that time.

Lieutenant Jones, who commanded the fire-ship, had likewise a narrow escape. One of the cabin windows had been opened for him to get into the boat, after the fuse was lighted; but the swell was so high, and the sea so rough, they durst not venture near the stern of the vessel for fear of staving the boat against the counter, and—not having a moment to spare—he jumped overboard. The boat took him up, and they all five arrived safe on board.

Lieutenant Davis, with the jolly-boat and four hands, who went in with the explosion vessel, likewise all safely returned on board.

A singular circumstance happened while we lay inside, as follows. The captain of the *Varsovie*, a prisoner, finding we were going to set his ship on fire, got permission to go on board her to get some charts, which he said he set a high value on. He went with Lord Cochrane, and sat alongside of him in the gig, and, strange to say, but actually true, a shot came from the enemy at Aix and killed the French captain on the spot, without either hurting his Lordship or any one in the gig.

Other occurrences happened, but we hardly had time to think of them, being so dangerously situated; for who could ever suppose to see four sail of the line go into Portsmouth Harbour, passing the batteries, and running up as far as the Hardway and there anchoring, and destroying part of the enemy's fleet, and then running the gauntlet out again amidst shot and shells flying about! Such was the case going into Aix Harbour. Had a gale come on from the north-west and blocked us in we should have been in a poor situation, but kind Providence favoured us in everything.

The killed and wounded in the British fleet are: Two officers and eight men killed; nine officers and twenty-six wounded, and one missing (which was Yankee Jack): total forty-six.

On the evening of April 14th the enemy succeeded in lightening the three-decker so much that with a press of sail and a high tide they got her over the bar, and she went up to Rochefort; the commodore tried hard to get the *Cassard* over, but failed; the *Etna* bomb kept throwing shells, but without any effect, as the swell made her roll so much.

Next day three more of the enemy's line-of-battle ships got over the bar and went to Rochefort; three more remained, but so far up and in the shallow water that our frigates could [not] get near enough for their shot to reach them: the *Etna*'s 13-in. mortar split, and all the shells of her 11-in. mortar were fired away, and apparently without doing any execution. Manned all the launches of the fleet to cover the three remaining fire-ships that are to be sent in to-night; but a gale came on with rain, and it was given up.

Next day, the 16th (still stormy weather), the enemy being afraid of an attack on the *Indiana* frigate, which lay aground, set her on fire, and she soon blew up.

17TH.—All the enemy's ships this day got over the bar except the *Regulus* (74 guns), which still remained aground near a place called Fouras, about four miles above the Isle of Aix; this day we released several male and female prisoners, gave them a boat, and saw them land safe at Rochelle, and hope they are thankful for their deliverance.

19TH.—By order of the commander in chief public thanks were given to Almighty God through the fleet for our success over the enemy.

28TH.—Orders arrived for the return of Lord Gambier, and we got four months of excellent provisions from the *Caledonia*, and likewise three dozen of Congreve's rockets from the *Cleveland* transport. Next day Lord Gambier sailed for England in the *Caledonia*, leaving the command to Rear-Admiral Stopford in the *Caesar*, with the *Tonnant*, *Revenge*, and *Aigle* and

*Medusa* frigates, four gun brigs, a schooner, and two cutters to watch the motions of the enemy.

Arrived the *Naiad* frigate from England, with the *Hound* and *Vesuvius* bombs; but being too late they were ordered to England again. The *Naiad* had some people on board taken out of a sinking galiot which had only left Rochefort yesterday; they informed us that Bonaparte had ordered the chief officers of his ships at Rochefort to be put under arrest, and 'twas thought some would suffer death; and that they were building two hundred gunboats with all haste to protect their coast.

A man named Wall, who called himself an American, ran away from the *Cassard,* stole a boat and got off to our squadron; he informed us that the *Tourville, Regulus,* and *Patriot* are so much disabled that they are ordered to be cut down for mortar vessels, and that the *Ocean* is in a bad state; the *Cassard* is to be docked, but the others were not very much damaged; that Captain Lacaille of the *Tourville* is to suffer two years' imprisonment, to be erased from the list of officers and degraded from the Legion of Honour, and that Captain Porteau of the *Indiana* is to be confined to his chamber three months for setting fire to his ship without orders. Captain de la Roncière of the *Tonnère* is acquitted; but John Baptist Lafon, captain of the *Calcutta,* is to be hanged at the yard-arm on board the *Ocean* for shamefully quitting his ship when in presence of the enemy. This is the fellow who had the English colours hung Union down last winter to insult us, and moreover they were hung under the bowsprit and near the privy: they generally who act in this manner are cowards.

*30TH.*—Divine service performed, and an excellent sermon was preached by the Rev. Mr. Jones, touching on several remarkable instances of divine favour which happened on several occasions on our behalf, and how the very materials the enemy were collecting to destroy us fell into our hands and acted against themselves; how the winds favoured us in going into Aix Roads, and how they shifted to bring us safe out again; these were such convincing facts that they made a great impression on the ship's company.

Next day a bowsprit with the jibboom spritsail yard and part of the knee of the head hanging to it came floating alongside, and we hoisted them on board, and to our surprise found they had belonged to the *Calcutta* when she blew up, and had come, as it were, to do homage for the insult offered on it two or three months ago, by hanging the English colours under it Union downwards. The rascals little thought at the time it would be so soon in our possession; there surely was something mysterious in this.

*MAY 12.*—A play was acted on board the *Revenge* called "All the World's a Stage," and several of us went on board to see it, the admiral among the rest, which gave much satisfaction. As for the *Caesar*, we never had diversion of any kind to cheer us up during the many weary dull nights we had passed on this station.

*24TH.*—Three very long and large boats belonging to the enemy came out from Aix Roads, and in a daring manner lay on their oars for some time nearly within gunshot, staring at us. We sent our boats manned and armed, who soon made them run, and chased them close in to Aix Roads. Five other boats came out and joined their other three; a smart fire commenced, and the shot from their batteries fell around our boats likewise. Our admiral, seeing the enemy were getting too powerful, recalled the boats, and they returned without having a man hurt.

*JUNE 5.*—This morning a heavy gale of wind and rain came on from the westward, which caused the sea to rise much; struck lower yards and topmasts; at 11 a.m. she drove with two cables out; let go the best bower and veered out another cable, which brought her up. The *Tonnant* parted from both anchors and nearly drove on shore near Rochelle, but her sheet anchor being let go brought her up; she made a signal of distress, but no assistance could be given in such stormy weather; fortunately she rode the storm out.

*10TH.*—A cartel came in from Cayenne and anchored near us; three French small craft were sent from Rochelle to take the people out of her. An American and a Maltese who came out in these vessels entered into our service, and would not return to Rochelle again: so much for Bonaparte's popularity! They told us the French ships at Rochefort were getting ready very fast and five of them would soon come down; and sure enough this same afternoon we saw three of the rascals coming down the Charente for Aix Roads. Sent our boats to assist the *Tonnant* in sweeping for her anchors, and found one.

*17TH.*—This day arrived Rear-Admiral Sotheby in the *Dreadnought* and relieved us in the command; saluted each other with thirteen guns each, distributing our provision (except one month's) to the other ships of the squadron; gave an anchor to the *Tonnant* and in the evening got under way with glad hearts for Old England.

•   •   •

*While the action at Aix Roads was politically successful and the Royal Navy further established its hegemony of the seas, it was a bitter experience for Cochrane, who had been forced by the Admiralty to command the dangerous fire-ship attack, thereby superceding officers superior to him and already on the station. This, as Cochrane knew it would, infuriated and insulted at least one, Admiral Sir Eliab Harvey, who argued vehemently with Gambier, returned to England, and was dismissed from the service. Furthermore, at a crucial stage in the attack, Gambier—the same captain who had so boldly led the British fleet into battle at the Glorious First of June—failed to send Cochrane the supporting ships of the line he needed to strike a more devastating blow upon the stranded French ships. Cochrane was made a Knight Commander of the Order of Bath for his courageous and vigorous attack; nonetheless, he aired his negative views about Gambier in public, thus tainting the victory and his reputation at the Admiralty.*

*With a little more initiative from Gambier, perhaps the Battle of Aix Roads could have been a much greater victory for the Royal Navy. But it was perceived publicly as a triumph. Britain was still riding the tide of Trafalgar. Virtually unchallenged at sea now, the Royal Navy was in a position to support land incursions on the continent by the British Army. Accordingly, troops were landed in Portugal in August of 1808, and before the end of the month Sir Arthur Wellesley (later the Duke of Wellington) had defeated the French at Vimiera, Portugal. But a politically disastrous negotiation at Cintra, which repatriated 26,000 captive French soldiers, on British ships, no less, caused Wellesley and his superiors, General Sir Harry Burrard and General Sir Hugh Dalrymple, to be recalled to England.*

*Sir John Moore now took command of the British Army on the Iberian Peninsula, moving his 35,000 men against Joseph Bonaparte, usurper of the Spanish throne. Outnumbered, Moore eventually was forced to beat a retreat to Corunna, Spain, where, in January 1809, the Navy was ready to disembark his army. Among the naval forces present was Lieutenant Basil Hall.*

BASIL HALL

~

# When I Beheld These Men
# Spring from the Ground
## 1809

*W*hen *we previously encountered Basil Hall, during the period of
peace between the two Napoleonic wars, he was a midshipman
frolicking on board the* Leander *in the waters off Bermuda. Having recently
passed for lieutenant and been appointed to the frigate* Endymion, *commanded by the Honorable Thomas Bladen Capel, Hall sailed from Spithead
to Corunna along with some two hundred transports carrying troops to
reinforce Sir John Moore's army. In this passage, Hall witnesses the brief but
fierce Battle of Corunna (January 16) on the northwest coast of Spain, where
the retreating British troops (fifteen thousand men and nine cannon) under
General Sir John Moore fight a French force of sixteen thousand men and
forty cannon under Marshal Nicolas Jean de Dieu Soult.*

AS SOON AS SIR JOHN MOORE heard of Napoleon's march from
Madrid, in the direction of Galicia, to which quarter it had been the English
general's sole object to allure his enemy, he gave orders for the retreat to
commence. This was at the beginning of the last week in December, 1808;
and as it was then proposed that the troops should fall back upon Vigo, the
transports were sent to that port from Corunna, as I have before mentioned.
The convoy were afterwards joined at Vigo by a squadron of line-of-battle
ships, under Sir Samuel Hood, to render the embarkation more secure.

On the 5th of January, 1809, however, Sir John Moore, who was then at
Herrerias, received from his engineers such reports of the unfitness of Vigo
as a place of embarkation, that he changed his line of retreat, and directed

his march upon Corunna. Orders to this effect were sent ahead to Sir David Baird, the second in command, from Sir John Moore, who, it appears, "constantly directed the movements of the rear-guard himself."[1] These orders, after reaching Sir David, were forwarded by the hands of a private dragoon, who got drunk and lost them on their way to General Fraser, who had already proceeded some distance on the road to Vigo. This trivial incident cost many lives and was the cause of much delay.[2] I know not who had charge of the original despatches sent to the admiral at Vigo; but they never came to hand. Several precious days were thus lost, before we knew that the ships would be again required at Corunna. At length, on the 9th of January, a memorandum from the commander-in-chief—a duplicate or triplicate it might be, for aught we knew—written on a drum-head, apparently in the rain, but clear, soldier-like, and to the purpose, was put into Sir Samuel Hood's hands, by an officer, half dead with fatigue and anxiety, who had found his way, on horseback, from the British head-quarters to Vigo, across the wild mountains of Galicia.

The wind blew dead in from the south, and so hard that not one of the transports could be moved. The brief despatch from the army, however, was scarcely half read through, before the signal "to weigh" was made from the *Barfleur;* and in less than half-an-hour the men-of-war were under sail, and working out to sea, under close-reefed topsails and courses. I think they all got out; and when once round the point, the wind being fair to Corunna, away they dashed, with a flowing sheet, to tell we were coming after them, as fast as we could, with our flock of three hundred transports.

On the 11th of January the wind lulled a little, and, by dint of whip and spur, we got our immense fleet fairly under weigh. By good fortune, too, we were enabled to work out of the Bay of Vigo, and afterwards to carry the wind with us all the way to Corunna, where we arrived on the morning of the 15th of January, surrounded by upwards of two hundred and fifty sail of ships. On the previous evening, the 14th of January, many of the fastest-sailing vessels of the convoy had entered the harbour of Corunna, where the squadron of men-of-war under Sir Samuel Hood had already arrived. The dismounted cavalry, the sick, some of the horses, and fifty-two pieces of artillery, were embarked during the night.

I have often since heard officers who were then with the army, in position along the ridge, just above where the battle was fought, describe the feelings with which they turned round to look at the ships crowding into

---

[1] Napier, [Sir William Francis Patrick (1785–1860), History of the War in the Peninsula *(London: 1835)]* vol. i. p. 478.
[2] Ibid. p. 479.

the harbour, under all sail, right before the wind. The sight gave fresh spirits and confidence to the soldiers, of which, poor fellows, they stood in some need; for on their first arrival at Corunna, on the 11th of January, not a single ship had made her appearance.

"As the troops approached Corunna," says General Napier, "the general's looks were directed towards the harbour; an open expanse of water painfully convinced him that to fortune at least he was no way beholden. Contrary winds detained the fleet at Vigo; and the last consuming exertion made by the army was thus rendered fruitless.

"The men," he continues, "were now put into quarters, and their leader awaited the progress of events. Three divisions occupied the town and suburbs; the reserve was posted with its left at El Burgo, and its right on the road of St. Jago de Compostella. For twelve days these hardy soldiers had covered the retreat, during which time they had traversed eighty miles of road in two marches, passed several nights under arms in the snow on the mountains, were seven times engaged with the enemy; and they now assembled at the outposts, having fewer men missing from their ranks (including those who had fallen in battle) than any other division in the army; an admirable instance of the value of good discipline, and a manifest proof of the malignant injustice with which Sir John Moore has been accused of precipitating his retreat beyond the measure of human strength."[1]

In the mean time, the enemy, treading closely on the heels of the English army, though not much less grievously fatigued, came gradually up, and, on the very day we arrived in the bay, "occupied the great ridge enclosing the British position, placing their right on the intersection of the roads leading from St. Jago and Betanzos, and their left upon a rocky eminence which overlooked both lines."[2]

Had the transports arrived a few days sooner, the whole army might have been embarked with perfect ease and safety, and thus all the objects of Sir John Moore's operations would have been accomplished. His force was decidedly too small, considering the ruined state of the Spanish troops, and other circumstances in the political history of the country, to hold out any reasonable hope of coping with the grand army of Napoleon, now directed expressly against the British. Had the admiral at Vigo received Sir John Moore's first despatch in proper time, the transports and the line-of-battle ships might undoubtedly have reached Corunna soon enough to have taken the troops on board without the loss of a single man. With a force

[1] Napier, vol. i. p. 488.
[2] Ibid. p. 492.

thus unbroken, a series of ulterior operations contemplated by Sir John Moore might then have been put in execution.

"The English general," says General Napier, "had hoped that by a quick retreat he might reach his ships unmolested, embark, and carrying his army from the narrow corner in which it was cooped, to the southern provinces, establish there a good base of operations, and renew the war under more favourable circumstances. It was by this combination of a fleet and army that the greatest assistance could be given to Spain, and the strength of England become most formidable. A few days of sailing might carry the troops to Cadiz; but six weeks' constant marching would not bring the French army from Galicia to that neighbourhood. The southern provinces had scarcely seen an enemy: they were rich and fertile; and there also was the seat of government. Sir John Moore reckoned thus, and resolved to fall down to the coast, and embark with as little loss or delay as might be."[1]

It affords a mortifying, but an instructive lesson to recollect, that this plan, so admirable in itself, and so very nearly being accomplished, was in all probability frustrated, not by any great political or military event, but by the accidental interruption of the messengers sent across the country. If the general's despatches about the removal of the fleet had arrived a few days sooner, the lives of so many brave men who died at Corunna, including their great chief, might all have been spared, while their strength and valour might afterwards have been employed on more substantial objects than fighting for the mere maintenance of the ground on which they stood.

In consequence of this delay, a battle appears to have become indispensable, or nearly so, to the safety of the army. "The late arrival of the transports, the increasing force of the enemy, and the disadvantageous nature of the ground, augmented the difficulty and danger of the embarkation so much, that several general officers proposed to the commander-in-chief that he should negotiate for leave to retire to the ships upon terms. There was little chance of such a proposal being agreed to by the enemy, and there was no reason to try. The army had suffered, but not from defeat; its situation was dangerous, but far from desperate; and the general would not consent to remove the stamp of energy and prudence which marked his retreat, by a negotiation which would have given an appearance of timidity and indecision to his previous operations, as opposite to their real character as light is to darkness. His high spirit and clear judgment revolted at the idea, and he rejected the degrading advice without hesitation."[2]

[1] Napier, vol. i. p. 475.
[2] Napier, vol. i. p. 492.

As we sailed into the harbour of Corunna, on the morning of the 15th of January, we distinctly made out with our glasses the two lines of troops; for although the ridge upon which the English were posted lay nearer to the sea, it was of such inconsiderable height, compared with that occupied by the French, that we could discover the army of the enemy mustering thick along the sky-line, and overlooking ours in a very ominous and threatening manner. Towards evening there occurred some skirmishing of a trivial nature on the right of our line, part of which we distinguished from the mast-heads of the frigate.

Several horsemen were now seen galloping up the bank which faced us till they reached the crown of the ridge, and then darting out of sight on the other side, where, from the quick firing of artillery, there appeared to be some smart work going on. By-and-bye, also, we discovered a cloud of smoke curling high into the air above both ranges of hills, just beyond the spot where the cavalry had been lost sight of. We, of course, busied ourselves in vain surmises as to what was passing in the valley beyond the ridge; for we naturally expected that a general action would spring out of this brush. To our great disappointment, however, the firing gradually subsided; and our only chance, as we then believed, of seeing a land-fight was gone.

These were the first shots we had heard fired in anger, as it is technically called, during the campaign; but the scene had likewise another and very strong interest for us, from its being placed in such contrast with all we had been seeing and hearing for the two previous months. Here, at Corunna, instead of listening to a set of boastful Spaniards, fighting with the air and vapouring from morning till night about their own prowess, we beheld the actual tug of war between Greek and Greek. The master-spirits of the earth were at last met, hand to hand, to fight it out. Nor could I help looking back to the solitude and tranquillity of the ground before me when I had last seen it. Now it was covered thickly with armed men; but only a few weeks before I had rambled over these ridges, accompanied by a single Spanish peasant, whose whole conversation turned on the facility with which his countrymen could thrust all these French out of the country. During a long morning's walk we had met only half-a-dozen people; and little did I then expect to see the time when an army of some twenty thousand British troops should hardly be able to maintain their own against these very invaders, whom it was the fashion to hold so cheap.

When the night fell, a double row of fires along the summits of the two hills pointed out, in a very striking manner, the position of the rival hosts; and although the distance was too great for us actually to hear the "hum of either army," the imagination was set finely to work to conjecture what thoughts were passing in the breast of each. The night proved very dark; and as fresh fuel was piled on the fires, they became obscured for a moment, or rose into a sudden blaze on being stirred up by the groups of soldiers, whom we saw, or fancied we saw, standing between us and the light. These gigantic figures might probably be the men stationed to feed the flames; for we may well suppose the great body of the troops on both sides were but too glad to have a full night's repose. Our soldiers, indeed, had been amply supplied, since reaching the coast, with new shoes, great-coats, and many other articles of dress, from the stores at Corunna; and were thus in a better condition than their enemies to profit by this interval of rest—to so many on both sides, the last they enjoyed on earth. Some of these exhausted warriors, we may suppose, dreamed of the next day's bat-tle; for it was probably apparent to the officers, and to the experienced amongst the men, that Soult, with whom they had already joined in many a severe fight, would never allow his old antagonists to embark in peace and quiet. It is said that people, on the eve of an action, generally dream they are killed. I have no experience to offer on the point; for, though I wit-nessed the furious contest of next day, I had no expectation at that time of being able to leave the ship. In fact, I did not sleep at all, being employed nearly the whole night in the ship's boats, embarking what are called the encumbrances of the army, consisting of the remainder of the baggage which the retreat had left them, some wounded and sick men, and a few guns and horses. In this curious assembly I observed several women, who, strange to say, had gone through the whole campaign, unbroken in spirit, and apparently not much fatigued. They even talked as if they had done no great things. We were much amused likewise by seeing an officer's servant with a huge violoncello under his charge, which he told us had accompa-nied his master all through the country from Lisbon.

It will easily be supposed that our curiosity to have a sight of the ground, and to talk with the soldiers on the field, was very great. We had small hopes, however, of being allowed to leave the ship at such a time; and I can never cease to feel grateful for the kindness of the captain, who allowed Mr. Oughton the purser, and myself, to go on shore. We were per-sonally acquainted with several of the officers in the army, whom we hoped to find on the ground; but could scarcely believe in the reality of our good fortune till we had fairly left the boat, and pushed our way through the town (which was in a shocking state of disorder), and found ourselves on the great Madrid road, which cut across the positions of both armies nearly at right angles.

As the morning turned out fine, the whole scene looked highly pic-turesque, and, though painful in many respects, it possessed an uncom-

mon degree of interest. I need hardly mention that there was none of the
show and flourish of a review to be seen here; for the soldiers lay scattered
about, wearied and dispirited, ragged in their dress, and many of them
sickly, or rather broken down in appearance, by the fatigues of this celebrated retreat. Most of their chins had been untouched by a razor for some
days, perhaps weeks, while their hands and faces, being rather less familiar with soap and water than with the smoke of their muskets and the char-
coal of their cooking fires, gave evidence enough of the want of comforts to
which the army had been so long exposed. The muskets of the troops stood
in pyramids piled along the ridge amongst the men stretched out on the
ground fast asleep—not in any very precise order, but keeping within a few
yards of one another on the summit line of the position. I observed many of
these hardy fellows lying on their backs, with their hands under their
heads, and faces half covered by what remained of a hat, becoming still
more deeply tanned in the sun. Many, however, were sitting on the grass,
or on the loose blocks of granite strewed over the ground, and gazing every
now and then in silence, with very wistful eyes towards the ships.

Along the whole line of troops, however, I observed only one or two
of the officers asleep. Generally speaking, they collected themselves into
little knots, looking about them, but seldom speaking. In fact, one of the
things which struck me most was the profound, almost melancholy silence
that prevailed amongst so many thousands of men. As our spirits were
not weighed down by any of the depressing causes which affected these
gentlemen, we talked away merrily to the officers; but, in most cases, were
disappointed to find so little animation among them. We forgot how differently from our own their lives had lately been spent. For our parts, we
had been amusing ourselves in ease and in comfort, doing everything we
could to fill our imaginations with visions of Spanish patriotism, national
sacrifices, and individual exertion, without having actually seen or heard
anything to show how frothy all this was. The army, on the other hand,
had been marching, fighting, and starving, almost without intermission,
since the day on which they landed, two months before. The Spaniards,
their nominal allies, had gone off to the right-about at the first charge of
French bayonets. The whole country through which the English troops had
retreated proved the very reverse of friendly; the season also being rigorous, the labours of the soldiers became hopeless, severe, and incessant. Was
it, therefore, surprising that what is called enthusiasm became at length an
article hardly to be found at all in the English camp?

Our morning's excursion commenced nearly at the left of the British
position, in the midst of Sir John Hope's division; then, turning to the right-
hand, we threaded our way amongst the sleeping soldiers, piled muskets,

and camp equipage, along the whole line, till the ridge upon which the army was in position gradually lost itself in the valley, just opposite a high rocky knoll, forming the extreme left of the ground similarly occupied by the French. The 95th, the well-known Rifle corps, were stationed hereabouts; and I was happy to meet an old friend alive and merry amongst the officers of this regiment. These gentlemen appeared in greater spirits than most of the others with whom we had conversed. We were surprised, indeed, to find them laughing heartily; and, upon asking the cause of their mirth, were shown a good-sized pig, which the regimental cooks were busily cutting up for a dinner ordered to be got ready in a few minutes. It seems this unfortunate grunter had been disturbed by the French pickets near the village of Elvina, just in front of the spot where the 95th were stationed. He had made good his retreat, as he thought, but fell right upon our friends the sharp-shooters, who in a trice charged and despatched him with their swords and bayonets. These merry soldiers, delighted with their good luck, pressed us much to stay and partake of their windfall; but we wished to retrace our steps along a part of the line, so as to gain the road to Corunna and return on board before sunset, as we had been ordered.

On asking them what chance there was of our seeing a battle, the officers shrugged their shoulders and said they had already had quite enough of that work. There could be no earthly advantage gained, they added, even by victory; while a reverse must inevitably be a very serious, perhaps desperate affair, at this stage of the campaign. "They had but one wish, which was to get snugly on board the ships and be carried off from such a rascally country and such a dastardly, procrastinating, pompous set of useless allies as the Spaniards."

"Nevertheless," we remarked, "you would, no doubt, make a good figure in action still, if you were put to your mettle?"

"I don't know that," said one of them; "look at the men, they are all worn out, and disheartened; if they are not sleeping, or eating whatever they can get hold of, they are gazing at the vessels and thinking only of home. Like us, indeed, they are wishing for anything but an attack from those confounded fellows over the way."

Upon this we parted; they to their welcome dinner, while we retraced our steps amongst the weary soldiers, who certainly did look in such a miserable plight that it seemed as if the enemy would have little more to do than gallop across the valley and catch them all napping.

General Napier, however, remarks, cleverly enough, in his account of this campaign, that, "although a British army may be gleaned in a retreat, it cannot be reaped:" and of this truth abundant proofs were furnished within a few minutes after the wretched appearance of the troops had drawn from us such disparaging reflections. I had but just asked the commanding officer of one of the regiments, I forget which, near the top of the position, "Whether he thought anything could possibly rouse the men up?" In reply, he said, with a very expressive smile and a slight nod of his head, implying that even then he suspected what was about to take place, "You'll see by-and-bye, sir, if the French there choose to come over."

These words had hardly been uttered, when a movement along the whole enemy's line became apparent even to our inexperienced eyes. Almost at the instant when this stir was observed, a furious cannonading opened from a battery mounting eleven guns (eight and twelve pounders), of the existence of which, I believe, no person on our side had previously the smallest suspicion, so completely, up to this moment, had it been masked. This formidable battery, which overhung the right of the English position, was so skilfully placed that it raked nearly the half of the British line, and, of course, galled the troops excessively. Had we remained to share the pic-nic with our friends of the 95th, we must have partaken, close at hand, of the first salvo of round and grape from these French guns, and, in all probability, the story of this great battle might never have fallen into naval hands.

The effect of these characteristic preparatory notes of war, thundering over the line, was extremely curious. At the first discharge from the French battery, the whole body of the British troops, from one end of the position to the other, started on their feet, snatched up their arms, and formed in line with as much regularity and apparent coolness as if they had been exercising on the parade in Hyde Park. I really could scarcely believe my eyes when I beheld these men spring from the ground, as if touched by a magic wand, full of life and vigour, though but one minute before they had all been stretched out listlessly in the sun. I have already noticed the silence which reigned over the field; now, however, there could be heard a loud hum, and occasionally a jolly shout and many a peal of laughter, along a distance of nearly a mile. In the midst of these sounds, the peculiar sharp "click-click-click" of fixing bayonets fell distinctly on the ear very ominously.

Many thousand stand of new arms had been issued to the troops from the stores at Corunna; and I could observe the men rapping the flints, tightening the screws, and tossing about their firelocks, with the air of veteran sportsmen eager to try their new pieces. The officers, who up to this moment had seemed so languid, might be seen everywhere brushing along the line, speaking to the sergeants, and making arrangements, which we did not pretend to understand. Aides-de-camp galloped past us, dropping their orders into the ears of the commanding officers of the different corps, as they moved swiftly along the position.

Not a single face could now be seen turning towards the ships, and we found it difficult to obtain an answer to any of our questions. All had become animation and cheerfulness, over minds from which, but a short time before, it seemed as if every particle of spirit had fled. There appeared to be much conversation going on, and not a little jesting amongst the men, while they braced themselves up, buckled on their knapsacks, and made various other arrangements, preparatory to the hard work they foresaw they would have to perform before the night fell. Their kits, or stock of clothes (none of them very large), being soon placed on their shoulders, the army, in a few minutes, stood perfectly ready to meet that of the enemy, whose troops, in three immense close columns, by this time were pelting rapidly down the side of the opposite heights.

I have no precise notion how many men might be in each of these square, solid masses—I think I have heard it stated at six or seven thousand. They kept themselves steadily together, looked as dark as the blackest thunder-cloud, and, I must say, their appearance, on the whole, was the most imposing and formidable thing I recollect to have seen, either before or since.

As there could be mustered on the English side only a dozen small guns, our artillery made but a feeble return to the fierce attack of the enemy's great raking battery, which continued to tear open the English ranks in dreadful style. Presently, however, the two armies became so completely intermixed in personal conflict that the enemy's cannon-shot could no longer be directed with certainty against their antagonists, without an equal chance of hitting their friends, and they ceased to fire at the troops.

When it was found, at the commencement of the action, that the English guns could make no serious impression on the heavy artillery of the battery, they had been turned upon the huge French columns, which, by this time, had reached the level space, less than a mile in width, lying between the bases of the two ranges of hills. The round and grape with which the enemy's columns were thus saluted, as they came across the valley, in some degree avenged the havoc wrought on the right, and part of the centre of our line, by the raking broadsides of the battery so often alluded to.

Mr. Oughton and I stood near the centre of the position when the battle commenced; but as the ground thereabouts was rather flat, we found it difficult to see well into the valley; we therefore climbed an abrupt rising ground on the left, on which two or three regiments were posted, as we thought, in reserve. I see no mention, however, of these corps in the accounts of the battle; and I presume they must have belonged to the main line. About half-way up this rising ground, but rather lower than the spot where these troops had been stationed, stood three English field-pieces. These guns worked away briskly at the French columns, as soon as the enemy came within range of shot, and they still fired at the rear of the three great masses, the heads of which by this time had actually mingled in the plain with the British troops in and round the village of Elvina.

The intermixture of the combatants on this day was probably rendered greater than usual in consequence of the peculiar nature of the ground. It could hardly be called a plain, for it was crossed in all directions by roads cut into the earth like deep trenches, eight or ten feet below the surface; while on the ground above lay a complete net-work of walls, hedges, and rows of olive-trees and aloes, of such intricacy, that I should imagine it nearly impossible to have formed fifty men abreast anywhere. Thus, each corn-field, or little patch of garden-ground, became the scene of a separate fight.

We were quite near enough to see the soldiers scrambling over the walls and meeting one another in these open spaces or amongst the trees; while the smoke and the flashes of musketry from the hollow roads showed that a subterranean sort of warfare was going on at the same time. To us the field of battle certainly looked as complete a scene of confusion as anything could possibly be; and I suppose it must have presented nearly a similar aspect even to the more practised observation of the commander of the destructive French battery on our right; for about the period I speak of, as I have already stated, he ceased firing at the troops and turned all his attention towards the few English field-pieces.

Heretofore we had been viewing the fray from a gentle slope, several hundred yards in front of these English guns; but so considerably below them in level, that their shot passed far over our heads. When this great flanking battery, however, set seriously about silencing the fire of our artillery, which, as I have mentioned before, kept playing away upon those parts of the French columns not yet mingled with their antagonists, our position, as mere spectators, became rather an unpleasant one. The small six-pound shot of the English field-pieces had whistled over us merrily enough; but when the heavy metal of the enemy came spinning and screaming about our ears, the story told quite differently. Some of these balls went completely over the English guns, grazed the crest of the ridge, and, falling on the high road, rolled down the other side of the hill half-way to Corunna. Several of them hit our guns and made a fine scatter amongst the artillery-men; while every shot that fell short came plump into the little hollow space where we nautical men had established ourselves, and from which we had proposed to view the battle at our ease, as if it had merely been a panoramic representation of war, instead of one of the severest struggles in which two angry nations had ever been engaged.

The purser and I now held a counsel of war, and the proverbial result of such deliberations followed. We agreed unanimously, that, under existing circumstances, a retreat was the proper measure. The French gunners, as if to quicken our prudent resolution, just at that moment pitched a shot so critically that it fell between the two amateurs and threw the dirt and stones quite over us. The feeling produced on both our minds by this broad hint was that the shot must have been aimed expressly at us; but although this was probably not the case, we took the warning in good part, and moved off towards a rising ground still farther to the left, and two or three hundred yards out of the direct line of fire.

Here we enjoyed the additional advantage of making acquaintance with the colonel and the other officers of one of the regiments of the reserve. The colonel, whose name I do not recollect, held a pocket spy-glass in his hand and very kindly described to us the nature of the different movements as they took place. By this time the centre, and a portion of the left of the English line, gradually became engaged in the valley; but the severest fighting of all appeared at the village of Elvina, which we could easily distinguish was sometimes in possession of one party, sometimes of the other. The uncertainty, indeed, of what was going on became greatly augmented by the broken nature of the ground, which, I suppose, prevented any manoeuvre on the grand scale; but this circumstance may probably have taken nothing from the fierceness of those mortal struggles, which we could discover, from time to time, in the open spaces when a puff of wind blew the smoke on one side.

The road leading into Corunna, and lying between us and the severest part of the action, passed at no great distance, and was soon covered along its whole length with wounded men; some of whom were walking alone, some supported by their comrades less severely hurt, and a good many had been placed in carts. We observed Sir David Baird led or carried off the field; but from the smoke and dust we could not exactly make out which, though I think he was walking.[1] Shortly afterwards another and a larger group passed near us, bearing along a wounded officer. It was evident from the appearance which this second party presented that some person of consequence was under their charge; and while we were trying to discover who it could possibly be that engaged so much attention, an officer rode up the hill. After he had delivered his message, he pointed to the party which had just gone by, and told us, that in the centre was carried along their brave commander-in-chief, Sir John Moore, who, a few minutes before, had been struck off his horse by a cannon-shot.

---

[1] *General Sir David Baird (1757–1829) lost his arm as the result of his wound at Corunna. This was to be his last active command, although he later served as commander in chief of Ireland.*

The command now devolved upon Sir John Hope, whom we could readily distinguish, from his being surrounded not only by his staff, but by the aides-de-camp of his two wounded senior officers.

I shall not seek to describe how greatly the interest of this scene, so new to us in all its parts, and so remarkable in itself, was heightened by these proofs of the serious nature of the conflict. The colonel of the regiment along with which we had taken up our station, had just said to us, "Well, gentlemen, I don't know how you get on at sea, but I certainly never saw on land a hotter fire than this;" when a breathless messenger came galloping up, with orders to carry his brigade as smartly as he possibly could down to the right, to support some regiments which he described as being severely pressed in that quarter. In a few minutes we found ourselves quite alone on the summit of the ridge, watching, with a painful degree of interest, the movements of our newly-made acquaintances, who trotted off, at double-quick time, right down the hill, and ere long were lost sight of in the thick of the action. So completely, indeed, were they enveloped in smoke and dust that we could only distinguish their presence by the movement in advance of the British line, which took place on the right almost immediately after their arrival.

The battle, which had commenced nearly at the foot of the English hill, had gradually, though not without several fluctuations, moved itself forward towards the French side of the valley; and the much-contested village of Elvina remained finally in our possession.

I believe I am not strictly correct in saying that this village was opposite to the right of the British army, though it was not far from that portion of the position which rested on the elevated ground. We could observe some smart fighting still farther to the right, beyond the termination of the ridge, between the English reserve and the French cavalry. But of this I can record nothing with confidence, because the scene of action lay too far off for us to see distinctly, or even to guess what they were about. I remember, however, hearing one of the officers of the regiment with whom we were conversing say that the British troops would be in an awkward scrape if the enemy should succeed in turning our right, and afterwards push themselves down the valley, so as to take up a position between Corunna and the English army. Instead of this happening, the left of the French was fortunately repulsed, and even driven considerably back, though I believe it was never fairly turned.

As the battle did not commence till between two and three o'clock in the afternoon, and was very obstinately contested on both sides, no great time was allowed, before the night set in, for those important manoeuvres which form so much of the interest of battles. All was sheer hard fighting.

The eventual advantage, however, remained manifestly on the side of the English; for it became easy to distinguish, towards the end of the day, that the struggle was carried on at a position removed considerably in advance of that on which the English had stood when first attacked. What might have been the result if the ground had been clear of hedges, ditches, walls, and deep roads, I cannot pretend to say; but it struck me at the time, when looking down with a sort of bird's-eye view on the battle, that, cut up as the ground was, there could be little communication to the right and left between the different bodies of fighting men, and consequently that each regiment or mass must have acted very much for itself; somewhat in the way ships of war manage in a general action. Cavalry, I imagine, could not have been brought into play on such ground; and, indeed, there were no horses in the battle, on our side at least, except those of the field-officers and their aides-de-camp.

What I regretted most was not seeing the French battery taken; and, from General Napier's account, it appears that if General Fraser's division had been brought into action along with the reserve at the close of the day, this purpose might have been accomplished; after which the enemy could hardly have escaped a signal overthrow.[1]

It must have cost Sir John Hope a great effort of military self-denial to have resisted such a temptation; "but, on the other hand," observes the judicious historian, "to continue the action in the dark was to tempt fortune; for the enemy were still the most numerous, and their ground was strong. The disorder the French were in offered such a favourable opportunity to get on board the ships that Sir John Hope, upon whom the command of the army had devolved, satisfied with having repulsed the attack, judged it more prudent to pursue the original plan of embarking during the night; and this operation was effected without delay, the arrangements being so complete that neither confusion nor difficulty occurred."[2]

⟞⟞

Unfortunately, we could not remain till the very last upon our elevated look-out station, from whence we had commanded so complete a view of this hard-fought field, being obliged to come down shortly after sunset, that we might get on board, if possible, before dark. We took the shortest way from the top of the hill by a little footpath, leading along a steep bank, till we gained the great Corunna high road. By this time the whole space between the field of battle and the town had become

[1] Napier, vol. i. p. 498.
[2] Ibid.

pretty well crowded with wounded men, mingled with stragglers of all kinds, wending their way, as well as they might, towards the point of embarkation.

The first person we met, on coming to the road, was an elderly officer, I think of the 50th regiment, partly supported by a private soldier, and partly leaning on his sword. We helped him to gain a seat near the door of a little cottage, which we could see had been used as a temporary hospital, from the numerous wounded, dead, and dying men stretched all round it. This situation being on the face of the hill next the town, had not been exposed to the direct fire of the enemy, while the chance of any stray shots plunging into it, over the top of the ridge, seemed not great.

The old officer's face soon turned so pale that a streak of blood flowing along his brow and cheek, though not broader than a thread, appeared as conspicuous as if it had been a line drawn on a sheet of paper. That he had received a serious wound was evident; but we had not the least idea he was dying.

"I should like the doctor to look at my head," he said; and in a minute or two the surgeon came from the cottage. He took off the officer's cap, cut away some of the hair, looked closely at the wound, and then paused.

"Well—sir—what—say—you?" asked the wounded man, whose words dropped slowly and laboriously from his lips.

"This is no time to trifle, sir," replied the surgeon, for whom a dozen miserable sufferers were calling out; "and I am sorry to tell you this wound is mortal. It is my duty to say that you have but a short time to live!"

"Indeed! I feared so," groaned the poor man. "And yet," he sighed, "I should like very much to live a little longer, if it were possible."

He spoke no more, but laid his sword on a large stone by his side, as gently as if its steel had been turned to glass, and that he was fearful of breaking it. What he meant by this action, we knew not; for he sunk dead upon the grass almost immediately afterwards.

On regaining the road, we were loudly appealed to by so many voices of men suffering from their wounds, and in despair of ever reaching the boats, that we knew not which way to turn or what to do. At first we gave our arms to those nearest us who could walk; but on these wretched men failing and others struggling to gain our assistance, it became quite evident that we should never reach the shore if we did not close our ears to these supplications. In fact, we had almost resolved, hard-hearted as it may seem, to walk along as fast as we could, without heeding the wounded and dying, when a number of artillery waggons, sent out from the city, came galloping along, with orders to glean up all the sufferers who could not readily find their way alone.

As we came nearer to Corunna, we found this precaution had already been taken, so that such of the wounded people as we now fell in with on foot (and these were many hundreds), were trudging on, I can hardly call it merrily, but with a degree of animation, which, considering the frightful predicament of many of them, was truly wonderful. Generally speaking, indeed, the soldiers displayed a great degree of fortitude. We passed a cart filled with men, none of whom uttered a complaint, though I could observe more than one stream of blood trickling on the road through the openings between the planks.

Hardly any trace of twilight remained when we entered the town; but, in consequence of orders given to illuminate the houses in the streets leading to the places of embarkation, no difficulty arose in marching the troops to the boats; an operation which, for obvious reasons, was purposely delayed till after it became quite dark.

When the action was over and the army withdrawn to the position they had occupied in the morning, every demonstration was made of an intention to retain possession of the ground. In this view, large fires were kindled along the line, and these being kept up during the whole night, effectually deceived the enemy and gave time for the different corps not only to retire at leisure in good order, but to embark almost as regularly as if nothing had happened. Such is the effect of discipline well understood. Each soldier having taken his place in the boats, was rowed on board the particular ship destined to receive him; for, it may not be uninteresting to mention, that, on visiting the field before the battle, we found the officers of each regiment in possession of the tickets, specifying the name and number of the transport in which their corps was to be embarked. Accordingly, when the troops marched into Corunna, in the middle of the night, they proceeded without any halt, straight to the shore, where they found the men-of-war's barges and launches, and the flat-bottomed boats of the transports, all ranged in order ready to receive them. As soon as it was known what regiment was approaching, a certain number of the boats were brought to the edge of the beach, when, without noise or confusion, the soldiers stepped in, and the word being given to shove off, in half-an-hour the empty boats rowed back again to the point of embarkation, having deposited these gallant freights in their respective vessels. I must say, indeed, that nothing during the whole of these memorable scenes excited my admiration more than the cheerfulness with which the harassed soldiers bore so many inevitable but trying humiliations. Their gallant bearing in the morning, when assailed by the formidable columns of the enemy, was certainly very brilliant; and still more admirable did their courage appear, when standing inactive, while their ranks were ploughed up by the

French battery. But I am not sure if their genuine stamina and merit as soldiers were not fully as much evinced in their orderly demeanour when the excitement of action was past and when the darkness rendered it easy for any man to straggle without the possibility of detection.

The embarkation of the troops had not entirely ended when the day broke on the morning of the 17th of January; and had not Corunna been a fortified place, the enemy might have rushed on, and greatly harassed, if not cut off the rear. As it was, the pickets and other detachments from the different corps left to keep the fires lighted had to scamper for it briskly enough. But the French cavalry having pushed forward at the first peep of dawn, to ascertain what was the situation of affairs, found the bird flown, the camp empty, and only a long line of well-heaped fires remaining to show the diligence of the last lingerers on the field. On galloping briskly over the ridge, they had the mortification to see the last of the retiring pickets crowding into the gates of Corunna, under cover of the guns of the fort. The walls were manned partly by the rear-guard of the British army, and partly by the Spaniards, who behaved upon this occasion with a degree of steadiness which deserves particular mention, as it was almost the only instance in which the English forces had been effectually seconded by the people they came to assist. The baffled cavalry pulled up their horses on coming within range of the grape and canister shot from the works; and thus terminated the second campaign of the great Peninsular war.

Shortly afterwards we could distinguish from the boats, as we passed to and from the shore to the transports, the heads of the enemy's columns showing themselves, one by one, over the tops of the ridge on which the English had been posted; and presently the whole of that part of the ground which faced the harbour was speckled with French troops.

As the French approached Corunna, they were not slack in bringing up those heavy guns which had harassed our position in such style the day before, and trying their efficacy on the ships. It was playing at long bowls indeed; for the point to which the guns were brought must have been more than a mile off, and, being much elevated above the sea, the balls plunged at random amongst the fleet of transports. They only excited a bustle among the merchant ships, many of which cut their cables, and, the wind being fair, they drifted out of the harbour in groups of ten or twelve. I was rowing past one transport, when the boat was hailed by a military officer. We lay upon our oars to hear what he had to say.

"I wish you would give us some help here," he cried; "we are all soldiers on board, and don't know how to get the anchor up, or how to set the sails."

"Where's the master and his crew?" we asked.

"Oh!" replied the soldier, laughing, "the scamps took to their boat upon a shot passing between the masts; and here we are, a parcel of land-lubbers, as you see, willing enough to work, shot or no shot, if you will be good enough to put us in the way."

As the ship by which we had been hailed was already full of troops, I put a midshipman and a couple of the boat's crew on board, and then proceeded with the fifty men we were embarking. Presently I saw my friends, the soldier-sailors, heaving up their anchor and making sail in very good style. The ragamuffin of a skipper joined his vessel off the port; and the midshipman returned with many thanks from the troops who had been so unhandsomely deserted.

Another transport, however, lying considerably in shore of the one which we relieved, and consequently nearer to the battery, got under weigh in the most deliberate style imaginable, made sail regularly, and, having accidentally cast the wrong way on tripping her anchor, did not wear round with her head off shore, but filled upon the larboard tack, and stood on, nearing the guns more and more every minute, and drawing all their fire upon her. After a time she tacked and sailed leisurely out to sea, actually delaying to make all sail till she was beyond the reach of shot.

Meanwhile three, if not four, of the transports lying nearest to the town of Corunna managed matters so ill that, on cutting their cables, without first having their sails properly set, they could not clear the point, and so went plump ashore, just inside a small rocky island, on which the castle of San Antonio is built, at the distance of two or three hundred yards from the walls at the north-western angle of the city. The hard granite on which Corunna stands being an overmatch for the ribs of these vessels, it very soon pierced their sides and laid them on their beam-ends. A dozen boats were employed for a full hour to remove the troops to other transports. But even these provoking ship-wrecks proved, as will be seen presently, highly useful to the purpose then in hand, the orderly embarkation of the rear-guard, and the other remaining troops, consisting of several thousand chosen men, who still kept the enemy at bay, while their comrades passed from the shore to the fleet.

A midshipman, I believe of the *Ville de Paris,* had been sent on shore with a message to Sir Samuel Hood, who superintended the embarkation of the army. On his way to the landing-place, he observed the transports alluded to bilged and deserted; and having done his errand, and being in no great hurry to return, he pulled between the castle of San Antonio and the sally-port which opens from the salient angle of the bastion, forming the extreme point of the principal works in that quarter of the citadel.

"It would be a great shame," quoth the middy, "if these vessels, wrecked though they be, should fall into the hands of the French; so I shall go on board and set fire to them."

This exploit he accordingly executed; but although there rose a considerable smoke from the wrecks during the afternoon, the flames did not burst out till about an hour or two after sunset, almost at the moment named for assembling the launches and barges of the fleet to embark the rear-guard, affording a splendid illumination, in which the soldiers marched down to the boats in companies and embarked with as much ease and celerity as if it had been noon-day: and, before breakfast-time next morning, the whole fleet of men-of-war and transports stood out to sea.

As we in the *Endymion* had the exclusive charge of the convoy of transports, it was our business to remain to the very last, to assist the ships with provisions, and otherwise to regulate the movements of the stragglers. Whilst thus engaged, and lying to, with our main-topsail to the mast, a small Spanish boat came alongside, with two or three British officers in her. On these gentlemen being invited to step up and say what they wanted, one of them begged we would inform him where the transport 139 was to be found?

"How can we possibly tell you that?" said the officer of the watch. "Don't you see the ships are scattered as far as the horizon in every direction? You had much better come on board in the mean time."

"No, sir, no," cried the officers; "we have received directions to go on board the transport 139, and her we must find."

"What is all this about?" inquired the captain of the *Endymion*; and being told of the scruples of the strangers, insisted upon their coming up. He very soon explained to them the utter impossibility, at such a moment, of finding out any particular transport amongst between three and four hundred ships, every one of which was following her own way. We found out afterwards that these gentlemen were naturally apprehensive of having it imagined they had designedly come to the frigate for better quarters. Nothing, of course, was farther from our thoughts; indeed, it was evidently the result of accident. So we sent away their little boat; and just at that moment the gun-room steward announced breakfast. We invited our new friends down and gave them a hearty meal in peace and comfort, a luxury they had not enjoyed for many a long and rugged day.

Our next care was to afford our tired warriors the much-required comforts of a razor and clean linen. We shared the party amongst us; and I was so much taken with one of these officers, Colonel de Lancey,[1] that I urged him to accept such accommodation as my cabin and wardrobe afforded. He had come to us without one stitch of clothes beyond what he then wore, and these, to say the truth, not in the best condition. Let that pass; he was as fine a fellow as ever lived, and I had much pride and pleasure in taking care of him during the passage.

We shortly became great friends; but on reaching England we parted, and I never saw him more. Of course he soon lost sight of me; but his fame rose high, and, as I often read his name in the *Gazettes* during the subsequent campaigns in the Peninsula, I looked forward with a gradually-increasing anxiety to the renewal of an acquaintance begun so auspiciously. At last I was gratified by a bright flash of hope in this matter, which went out, alas! as speedily as it came.

Not quite six years after the events here related, I came home from India in command of a sloop of war. Before entering the Channel, we fell in with a ship which gave us the first news of the battle of Waterloo, and spared us a precious copy of the Duke of Wellington's despatch. Within five minutes after landing at Portsmouth, I met a near relation of my own, which seemed a fortunate *rencontre*, for I had not received a letter from home for nearly a year, and I eagerly asked him,—

"What news of all friends?"

"I suppose," he said, "you know of your sister's marriage?"

"No, indeed! I do not! which sister?"

He told me.

"But to whom is she married?" I cried out, with intense impatience, and wondering greatly that he had not told me this at once.

"Sir William de Lancey was the person," he answered. But he spoke not in the joyous tone that befits such communications.

"God bless me!" I exclaimed, "I am delighted to hear that. I know him well; we picked him up in a boat at sea, after the battle of Corunna, and I brought him home in my cabin in the *Endymion*. I see by the despatch, giving an account of the late victory, that he was badly wounded. How is he now? I observe, by the postscript of the Duke's letter, that strong hopes are entertained of his recovery."

"Yes," said my friend, "that was reported, but could hardly have been believed. Sir William was mortally wounded and lived not quite a week after the action. The only comfort about this sad matter is that his poor

---

[1] *Colonel Sir William Howe Delancey, who was born in New York, served in the Peninsula as the Duke of Wellington's assistant, and, from 1809 to 1814, as Deputy Quartermaster General.*

wife, being near the field at the time, joined him immediately after the battle and had the melancholy satisfaction of attending her husband to the last!"

*      *      *

*Basil Hall, whose long naval career took him to the far reaches of the globe, became a prolific writer. His nine-volume work,* Fragments of Voyages and Travels *(1831–1833), included his experiences and observations regarding a wide spectrum of naval topics and was much reprinted. In 1816 he was elected a fellow of the Royal Society. He was also a fellow of the Royal Astronomical, Royal Geographical, and Geological societies. Hall died at Haslar Hospital in 1844.*

*While Lieutenant Hall was engaged on the Peninsula, in the thick of the struggle with Napoleon's forces, Lieutenant George Jackson was on the North American station, where the fighting was no less fierce, even if on a smaller scale. He proves as relentless in seeking freedom as he was in fighting for it.*

# GEORGE VERNON JACKSON

*⌇*

# "Damn 'em, Jackson, They've Spoilt My Dancing"

## 1809-1812

*T*he five sons of Navy purser George Jackson of Godshill, on the Isle of Wight, all entered the Royal Navy. Of them, three were killed and one retired a commander. George Vernon Jackson, the eldest son and the author of this narrative, is a bright and resourceful lieutenant. But his promotion to the recently taken frigate Junon, now commanded by Captain John Shortland, proves to be a dubious reward. Once again she will be confronted by superior numbers and, in the same year that she was taken by the Royal Navy, she will revert back to French ownership. Jackson's short cruise leads to an extended and peripatetic existence behind enemy lines.

### 1809

During the voyage out to Halifax I had said nothing about my hopes of promotion; and all were astonished when, soon after our arrival, Admiral Lee came on board, and after shaking hands congratulated me on my appointment as second lieutenant to one of the finest frigates in the Navy, the *Junon*, 38, Captain John Shortland. This was on 20th April 1809. I joined her during the same evening, and on the following day received an invitation to dine with the admiral and attend a ball afterwards.

This was the beginning of a great change from the hardships and uncertainties of a tarpaulin midshipman hitherto without a friend to interest himself on my behalf.

An old shipmate named Conn was third lieutenant in the *Junon;* the rest of the officers were strangers. Of the first lieutenant I have nothing to say. The marine officer, John Green, stood about six feet high, and might be compared to a switch in personal appearance. There was plenty of length but no breadth about him. I had a great regard for him, and believe the feeling was mutual, though this did not prevent us from being too often at variance. He was always going to call me out, but I always made an absurd joke of it, and declined to go out to fight a man with as much chance of hitting him as of splitting a bullet on a penknife. Poor Green, the sequel of his life proved that he was not such a difficult mark after all.[1]

Captain Shortland bore the character of an austere disciplinarian, and I felt rather nervous at the prospect of serving under him; however, I have reason to think that he took a liking to me. He was particularly celebrated as a navigator and a good seaman, and he showed preference for me in one respect, as he would allow no one to touch his chronometer but myself. This instrument was his own private property. He did not entirely depend upon my management of it when he was taking observations, but he obliged me to call over the time as it transpired.

The day before we left port an alarm was given of fire forward. I called for the drummer to beat to quarters—a foolish thing to do in those days, as it wasted time, while a word passed would have sufficed—and told the captain. It transpired that some matches had ignited somehow, but the fire was soon got under. The contents of the match-room, however, had been damaged by water, and although the damage was thought to have been rectified, it proved ere long to have been otherwise, as will shortly be seen, when occasion for their use arose.

While cruising off Guadeloupe on the afternoon of the 13th December 1809, during my watch we sighted four vessels. At first we supposed them to be Spaniards, and when the captain came on deck, he ordered me to fire and bring them to. I did so, and they obeyed the summons, and we cleared for action. We found that our enemies consisted of the two frigates *Renommée* and *Clorinde*, each with 40 guns, and the two *armées-en-flute*[2] *Loire* and *Seine*, each carrying 20 guns. From this moment until the termination of the ensuing engagement I was ignorant of what took place on deck, being on duty on the main-deck; but just as we were about to pass under the stern of the leading ship, the *Renommée*, they changed their colours and let fire a broadside. I was looking out of the port at the time. Our helm must have been put down,

---

[1] He was killed in the *Junon* while beating off a boarding party of the enemy in the action of December 13, 1809, when the *Junon* was captured by the French.—ED.

[2] Fr., *storeship.*

and as we came up into the wind the second frigate, the *Clorinde*, drew along-side of us, her bowsprit abreast of our main-mast. She manifestly did not like her position, and hauled off. The *Renommée* meantime had placed herself on our weather bow, and the *Clorinde* then resumed her old position to an inch. About this time the purser hurried up to me and said that there were no matches, and as he spoke a shot came into us and struck away an iron stanchion which stood directly between us. Once during the action I received a fearful blow across my body, caused by a poor fellow being blown into smithereens—by my side. Passing aft to my quarters I stepped over a prostrate seaman who was literally disembowelled, whom I afterwards found to be my own servant. Towards the last part of the fight, the *armée-en-flute Loire*, on board of which were some 200 French soldiers, came up as close as possible and poured volley after volley of musketry along the deck, and the *Renommée*, still on our weather bow, ran up and put her bowsprit between our main- and mizzen-mast. It was now dark. Then came a midshipman named Auchinlick, who told me that the captain was dangerously wounded, and took me to the foot of the quarter-deck ladder where he lay—not a soul near him. I approached close, and he said, "Jackson, take me down," and we carried him below directly. At the bottom of the ladder he exclaimed, "Thank you, Jackson, thank you; now encourage the men to fight bravely."

I returned to my post and saw the gunroom steward coming towards me. He said that we had struck. To satisfy myself as to the fact, I went to the quarter-deck ladder, where I was met by a salute of bayonets and the exclamation, "En bas . . ." On this I repaired as fast as I could to the captain's cabin. Poor fellow, he was lying there disabled by four severe wounds; and as I entered he turned his head and remarked with a smile, "Damn 'em, Jackson, they've spoilt my dancing[1]."

The French commodore then came on board and went to the captain. Whitehurst, one of the midshipmen and an old messmate of mine in the *Inflexible*, acted as interpreter, of whom more by-and-by. The Frenchman behaved with the utmost courtesy, requesting to know whom the captain would like with him, and offering him every attention. The captain chose myself, Auchinlick, and another midshipman named John Thompson. The latter was a brave young fellow, and I could not help being forcibly struck with his courage when, previous to the ship being taken, he was ordered to find the signal-book, which the captain had left aft. He passed amidst the shower of musket-balls to execute his commission, displaying the most

[1] *"Damn 'em, Jackson, they've spoilt my dancing."* [Later on March 6, 1811] As the 28th Regiment—now the 1st Gloucesters—were about to go into action at the storming of Barrosa Ridge, in the Peninsular War, their commanding officer, Colonel Belson, gave the order, "Fire at their legs and spoil their dancing."

consummate coolness and indifference to the risk he ran, luckily escaping without a wound. The book was ultimately found by the Frenchmen on the binnacle. Auchinlick also deserved his meed of praise for his assiduous and affectionate consideration for his captain. The scene on board during the night was a trying and miserable one. The doctor's abilities were enlisted for the dead and dying on all sides.

One poor man, a marine, was completely perforated through the jaws, and each time I passed him he called for water, but not a drop was to be found. At last I procured a bottle of porter and poured him out a glass, which he drank with grateful avidity. He died within a few hours. Whenever the captain wanted anything he sent for me, and the prayers of the wounded men were loud everywhere for water. I was stepping across a figure apparently dead on my passage from the captain's cabin once, when it suddenly raised itself and caught hold of my arm. "God bless me, Appleby,"[1] I exclaimed, "what are you doing here? Go below, man." He pointed to his wound and remarked, "It matters not where I die, Mr. Jackson; as well here as elsewhere." I insisted on his going below, and he dragged himself off and took possession of my cabin.

The doctor, Evan Evans by name, was in a most pitiable position. Besmeared up to his shoulders with blood, he was plying his instruments with untiring energy and encouraging the sufferers with kind words, but hardly able to turn for the implorations of those yet unattended to. He had no one to help him in his dreadful work, and the men would crawl about him with the bleeding forms of their messmates; while those who could amongst the wounded would clutch him with their hands and beseech him to turn to them if only to stop the blood gushing from their bodies. At times he would cry out in a way peculiar to him, "N'am of goodness me men, bear with it a bit, bear with it a bit; I'll serve you in yer turn," and then call out for his boy. "Where is my boy?" he would shout, but no boy was forthcoming, nor would he ever come again. In going the rounds I went forward in the bow of the ship, and there I soon discovered the reason of his absence from his post of duty. Excepting his legs and his arms nothing remained of him the size of an apple. He must have been bending down with his body in a horizontal position when a shot through the bow struck him straight on end, carrying away the trunk and shivering it into atoms. The last duty I performed on board was to throw the dead bodies into the sea. Our losses amounted to sixty killed and wounded.

I mentioned the captain's cabin, but he was really lying in the cabin of the first lieutenant. The latter, on being ordered by the French commodore

[1] Thomas Appleby, a midshipman.

to repair on board the *Renommée*, had been unable to remove his things, so the next in rank being ordered instead, I was made his substitute to my infinite regret.

Before taking leave of my captain, I helped him into the boat which conveyed him to one of the *"armées-en-flute,"* whither he was carried. I was accompanied by Conn and Thomas, who were likewise ordered to the *Renommée*. The other survivors were then distributed between the four French ships.

On our way we fell in with an English frigate, when all the prisoners were sent below in the hold and stowed away regardless of rank or fortune. Whilst in this confinement, sitting cramped up in a corner and scarcely capable of moving, two of my men showed a mark of attention to me which pleased me very much. They took off their neckerchiefs and tied one end of each to the battens overhead, tying the other under each arm, which then provided a sort of sling, a tolerable substitute for lying down. One of the men addressed me whilst we were in durance vile with the words, "You struck me on the head to-day, sir, with the guns." I scarcely remembered the circumstance, but he brought it more prominently forward by some additional remark, and I replied, "Yes, but what were you leaving your quarter for?" "I was going to fetch a match or something to fire the guns off with, and after all could only get some cinders from the galley." I was sorry to have punished him when I discovered this to be the fact; I had thought he was running away from his duty.

We heard a shot presently, as we thought, between the foremast and the mainmast, and our hopes rose at the thought of an action; but the English frigate, it appeared later, intending to intercept them before they could reach their destination, made a short cut to Guadeloupe. Unluckily for us, she only succeeded with the two *armées-en-flutes*. The *Renommée* now met with a mischance, and struck on the ———— Shoals, but we came across an English West Indiaman which had been captured, and the commodore settled to put us on board of her. So we were had up; and I, as senior officer, signed a declaration that we would steer south at a certain distance from Madeira before we proceeded to England. All had been arranged for us to go on board in the morning early, when, to our grief, an English frigate came in sight and altered the whole proceeding. Instead of sailing home in the West Indiaman, she was burnt without delay, and we continued prisoners without a prospect at present of release. The burning of the ship was a sufficient indication of an enemy's presence, and the English frigate kept to the windward. They little imagined what an easy prize was within their reach, as the *Renommée*, being crippled with the loss of so many guns, could have offered but small resistance. She was, however, a fast sailer, and I was amused despite my disappointment to see the ruse they adopted to keep away from the English frigate by not hauling the bowline and sheets aft. We then hastened forward to Brest and passed another English frigate at night, evidently ready for action, as all her main-deck was lighted up. But we kept dark, and it is possible that we were not observed. Twelve hours later we landed in Brest, and, after undergoing quarantine, were landed and sent to the hospital, where Whitehurst joined us. The captive officers, including the captains of merchantmen, amounted to nine in number. The commodore then called upon us and gave Conn and myself £25 apiece, and took our receipt to reimburse when we could. The act was noble and generous, as, indeed, had been all his conduct towards us since our capture. Whitehurst had also found equal comfort with the captain of the *Clorinde*.

## JANUARY 1810 TO 1811

Before we left the hospital at Brest, a Dane, the captain of a merchant vessel which was permitted to carry merchandise of a certain kind between England and France by an international understanding, came to see me on the eve of his starting for Granville, and asked me if I had not some notion of making an escape, and promised that if I could get to Granville he would do his best to carry me over to England. I mentioned Whitehurst, and he exclaimed vehemently "that he wouldn't have anything to do with him," and said that I was the only one that had treated him with any civility during our association in hospital. Whitehurst's behaviour had been quite the reverse, he said, and he'd have none of him.

As it happened, Whitehurst and I had already put our heads together and formed a plan for our escape. The captain of the *Clorinde* had given him a map of the country and a box of opium pills. And chance had chalked out our first route to Granville, the very place where the Danish captain had advised me to go.

Our short sojourn at the hospital was, considering all things, a pleasant one. Between the nine of us we managed to devise plenty of means for our amusement, and sailors are proverbially fertile in resources. All sorts of games were the order of the day, and the surveillance of our guards, though complete, was not embarrassing. At meal times we were always favoured with the society of the softer sex, who, in the profession of Mary, stood behind our chairs to watch our welfare, ordered all things to our comfort, and finally won our hearts to a man.

Whitehurst was a fine-looking fellow, standing quite 6 ft. 2 in., and apparently (I mean no scandal) an especial favourite with our fair protectresses. Thomas, the midshipman, was a lad exactly suited to carry the citadel of a lady's heart by storm—a particularly well-favoured specimen of a handsome youth. Conn and myself, disdaining the evanescent qualities of mere superficial beauty, held our proper position in the estimation of all by the force of superior rank. On leaving their charge we severally and collectively received their blessing, and with the benediction ringing in our ears, marched forth under a convoy of as many French soldiers as were men in our little band.

Whitehurst and I had sufficient penetration to observe the character of our military escort. They warmed up without reserve to those who were cheerful and unconstrained, so we kept up a continual flow of mirth along the journey and let nothing interrupt us. At the first halt after supper we proposed some mulled wine, which was produced accordingly, and shared equally with the parties without distinction. And we passed to our beds after a cheerful and perhaps rather noisy entertainment.

On the second night we halted at another inn and were all allotted rooms. We all met together as before, and the cup went round merrily, we enjoying ourselves as much as the soldiers. Whitehurst and I were to sleep together this night, so, quite casually as it were, we selected a bed nearest the window at the end of the room. We had no opportunity of conferring with the others, so counselled as well as we could between ourselves. Towards the time for turning in, Whitehurst, as if on the spur of the moment, suggested one more glass. This I resisted, warmly declaring that we had had quite enough and that it was unreasonable. He insisted and called for the wine, and set to work mixing it, taking an opportunity during the brewing of dropping some of the pills into all the glasses but our own. The soldiers were delighted and drank away unsuspectingly. Soon afterwards we prepared for rest. Half of the party repaired to a different room and left two merchant captains, Whitehurst and myself, together with our sleepy guards, to our glory. Whitehurst, unobserved, slipped into bed with his clothes on. I leisurely commenced to divest myself of mine; and the soldiers, but more actively, for they were drowsy, followed my example. They closed the shutters of the windows and barred them, and hung their knapsacks thereon, leaving their guns against the wall close by. It was not very long before they were completely overcome by their last draught and as heavy as logs.

I had not been idle in the interval but had now, thanks to sundry complicated movements under the sheet, become fully dressed again and ready for work. Whitehurst was naturally inclined to be awkward and moved about more like an elephant than a human being. Emerging from my side of the bed noiselessly, I removed the soldiers' knapsacks, unbarred the shutters, and got the window open, completing the whole of my task fortunately without a blunder. There was nothing now but to get to the ground outside, for we were in an upper room about twelve feet from the level. I went first and Whitehurst followed, coming, of course, upon his feet like the animal above-mentioned, so that I was horribly frightened lest any of the soldiers should be awakened by the disturbance of his exit; but their slumber was unbroken, I am delighted to say, and away we started as fast as our legs would carry us.

In after days I encountered one of the merchant captains who had been in the same room with us at the time of our escape. He told me that he had seen us leave and that one of the guards got up shortly afterwards, walked over to the window, closed it, and then lay down and went to sleep again. The opium had stupefied him. The merchant captain's bed-fellow had been awake also, and perceiving our escape wanted to follow, but was prevented by his companion, who knew that detection must inevitably ensue if they attempted to do likewise at that juncture.

We kept to the road until morning dawned, when we came upon what looked like a large common, or piece of waste land, on one side of which ran a ditch of sufficient depth to serve our purpose of concealment; so into it we went, and ignoring the discomfort of such an uncongenial and damp lodging, we remained therein, not venturing to raise our heads above the banks again until nightfall, when we once more took to the highroad. After a few hours' journey, guided by the map that Whitehurst had preserved, we approached a village, and hunger beginning to assert its supremacy, we debated what should be done. Whitehurst, who spoke French as well, if not better, than his native tongue, settled to go into the town and get some food. He returned with a loaf of brown bread, which was gratefully and greedily devoured; and we pushed on, nor halted again until the night had disappeared, when we made for some fields and looked up another friendly ditch, where we stretched ourselves for the day.

We had taken up our quarters not far from a gate, and to our discomfiture a man began to repair it during the morning. We kept close to the bottom of the ditch, not stirring a muscle all the time he was so unpleasantly near, and we could plainly hear him talking occasionally to himself. But this danger passed away, and right glad we were when the moment for venturing forth on our journey again arrived. Whitehurst repeated the commissariat duty at the next place through which we passed, and then we resolved to get more agreeable shelter if possible for the ensuing day.

On our road we met a man and asked him to direct us. He informed us that we were in the right course, and then asked us if we were deserters. We replied in the affirmative, and he promised to assist us, saying that he thought he could procure us horses, which he did, and we rode off, followed by a boy who beat the horses, over about the worst road I ever travelled on. The mud was over the boy's ankles: he was barefooted, and ran the whole distance behind us.

Arrived at another village, we entered an inn and asked for beds. They could give us none but had no objection to us sitting round the fire for the rest of the night. We were too glad of such a chance to hesitate a minute and so took our places with alacrity. Two maids were already nodding over the embers with their arms under their aprons; and as we had our pockets to take advantage of, we thrust our hands therein, to be as much in the fashion as practicable, and were soon in dreamland.

Towards daylight some of the customers left, and we were awakened and accommodated with their room. Our experience in the ditches had given us a fresh relish for a genuine bed, and the exertions we had made on the road prepared us for any amount of rest; therefore we gave ourselves up to a luxurious oblivion with a right goodwill, and slept so late into the hours of the ensuing day that our landlady came up to know if we were alive, or what had come to us. We ordered breakfast and despatched it in our room, after which Whitehurst sallied out for a look round.

During his absence the landlady reappeared and began to ask me some questions with great volubility. My knowledge of French was extremely limited, and I could trust myself with no confidence to any expressions in that language but the word *"Oui,"* and that I kept on using at all hazards, whenever she looked inquiringly after a speech. I must have put it in a wrong place more than once, as she testified by her manner, and what might have happened I can't say if Whitehurst had not made his appearance on the scene. She turned to him, and, as he told me, pronounced me to be English. He vociferated to the contrary, and maintained that I was purely German; but it would not do—the good woman was not born yesterday, and knew an Englishman when she saw one. At last she declared she had no desire to betray us, and if we trusted her we should be kindly treated. So Whitehurst, with my consent, made a clean breast of it. Upon this she recommended us to sign her visitors' book, putting any fictitious names we liked, and then she advised our going to St. Malo to a house where the owners, whom she knew, would do the best in their power for us.

In the evening, therefore, we resumed our flight, and were supplied by our good landlady with horses, which carried us to the place in question. Here we were conducted to a spacious room and locked in. Our meals were brought to us by a servant in regular succession next day, and at night we left again on horseback. We were told by our kind friends that we should not meet with similar attentions after we had got beyond Brittany. This intelligence was proved true at our next attempt to find a resting-place, for we were refused admission by the landlord, who declared he would not betray us: this was at Avranches. Our guide then took us to the house of two poor women, sisters, who gained their livelihood by keeping an infants' school. They found a man who engaged to take us to Granville, whither we accordingly proceeded. There I lost no time in looking up the Danish captain, whom I found in bed suffering from dropsy. He was glad to see me and renewed his former offer of assistance. I mentioned Whitehurst, and he declined to have anything to do with him. I left him and returned next evening with Whitehurst, hoping that he might mollify the Dane and induce him to alter his determination, assuring him that no offence had ever been intentionally offered, which I quite believe to be correct; but no, the Dane remained obdurate, and under no condition whatever would listen to any proposal on Whitehurst's behalf.

A ludicrous mischance happened on this occasion. A vessel full of slops was standing on a chair near the bed, and the Dane asked me if I would oblige him by emptying it out of the window. Misfortune never comes singly, they say, and an illustration of this adage was at hand. Whitehurst, in order to ingratiate himself with the captain, seized the same, rushed to the window, and without looking before him flung the contents into the street below. *"Que le diable vous emporte!"* shrieked a loud voice at the moment the act was committed, and a figure rushed into the house fresh from the untoward splashing. The mistress of the establishment, who was, it may be recorded, a very pretty woman, ran out to learn the cause of the uproar and met the furious intruder on the landing, who saluted her with the angry question, "Is it you that threw that infernal stuff out of the window just now?" With all the natural readiness of a Frenchwoman's wit, she perceived her ground at once, and assuming a most penitent mien, hoped that monsieur was not injured. He was not proof (what Frenchman is?), even under the aggravations of such an indignity, against the seductions of a pretty face; and bowing with a smile, he answered, "No hurt, madam, could proceed from so fair a hand." We learnt when he had gone that the sufferer was no less a personage than the governor of the town. Poor Whitehurst's attempt to propitiate the invalid had only augmented his aversion. He anathematised his clumsiness, and declared that such a man could only bring his friends into trouble, and he subsided into a stronger fit of contumacy than before. He still declared his wish to serve me, but of this I could no longer hear. I impressed upon his mind that to Whitehurst I was entirely indebted for having got to Granville at all, with my ignorance of the French language; but it was all to no purpose, and we took leave of each other for ever.

In this predicament we left Granville, getting over the walls of the town by means of a rope, and retraced our steps to the schoolmistresses at Avranches. We stopped at a farmhouse before it dawned, and as well as we could in the dark we took a survey of the place. There was a hayloft open above some buildings, and we contrived to get up into it. We found it a capacious loft, half-filled with trusses of straw loosely packed. Between these we crawled, and got as far to the rear as possible. A dog was chained in the chambers below and scented out our intrusion at once. The noise he made gave us some apprehension, especially as he continued barking furiously till the whole household at the farm was astir. They did not appear to discover the cause of his excitement, and he therefore got a correction pretty often. Worse than the dog, however, was the sudden advent of a girl, who commenced peering about amongst the sheaves for eggs; however, she confined her search to a safe distance from us, and finally left, singing to herself, without a suspicion of our presence.

We remained as usual, shunning the face of man at daylight, and when all was quiet, again descended and pushed on to Avranches, where we arrived in the forenoon. We did not so much fear travelling by day through the town as through the country. In the former we were not likely to be much noticed. The two old ladies received us again with pleasure, and I believe were really glad to see us. They turned us into the same room and sent for the guide who had taken charge of us before. We had been without food for thirty-six hours this trip. We were assured by our friends that our safety had been more than once committed by them into the hands of some patron saint selected by them, and to render the goodwill of his saintship more certain they had sold a pair of stockings we had left behind, and honestly recompensed the treasury of the Church with the proceeds.

As early as we could manage to do so, we took leave of our kind friends, God bless them, and set off on horseback for Caen in Normandy. Our guide provided us with a new friend in Normandy, by trade a baker, who proved faithful in all things. He took us to a neighbour who lived in the suburbs and placed us under his protection. This step was a politic one on his part. The second man had a son who was a prisoner in England, and he would aid our escape if possible in the hope that we might be of service to him in a corresponding way by exerting ourselves on behalf of the son. Here we lived in strict and often painful seclusion for nearly fourteen months. Twice only during this long seclusion did I venture out. The first occasion was to see Napoleon enter the town, and in the concourse of eager spectators there was little probability of my coming to grief. The other opportunity occurred at the instance of a priest, the only brother of our hostess, an Abbé Martin, somewhat distinguished in his generation, who obtained a passage for us on board a drogher[1] bound for Dieppe. The captain of this vessel took us as a mere speculation in the hope that if his boat were captured by any English cruiser he might be released on our account.

Our good genius was absent, and no English vessel was even seen. We returned perforce with the captain and resumed our old life.

Whitehurst had an advantage over me: he could leave the house with less risk, from his perfect knowledge of the French tongue. It had been a scheme of mine for a considerable period to secure a boat from the shore one night and make boldly across the Channel for England. I fretted in this constrainment and was ready for any resource that could be devised for escape; but Whitehurst opposed me, and the worthy padre shook his head when it was mentioned. I was out-voted. Nevertheless, as month after month rolled by and brought no improvement in our condition, my plan was at last reluctantly adopted. Whitehurst made a preliminary examination of the coast and the position and number of the boats. He ascertained one important and very satisfactory piece of information—namely, that no men were allowed to sleep on board any of the vessels or boats. The news of itself was sufficient encouragement to our enterprise. We had to wait until the wind and tide had become jointly auspicious, and then we sallied forth under cover of the darkness with a sheet for a sail and began our excursion. After a nine-mile walk we arrived at the beach and saw a boat not far from the shore, so we stripped to our shirts and trousers and swam out to it. It was flat-bottomed and about twelve feet long. The painter was cut and we moved off, and shortly after came alongside a good-sized fishing craft. This took my fancy, and I suggested an immediate change. Whitehurst, by constitution an objector, refused to entertain my proposal. Another, nearly as favourable to our needs, came in view, and I resumed my solicitation without avail. Then a third "all cut and dried" for our very purpose. Mast and sails all ready for a start. This I could not stand, so with a growl and an oath at Whitehurst for his pains, I pulled a hard stroke that brought us into contact with the coveted prize. We had hardly touched the boat's side when, to our dismay, up jumped half a dozen Frenchmen. We pulled away for our lives. There was a spanking breeze from the south, and we hoisted our sheet and sped away as fast as a flat-bottomed boat under difficulties could go. Our sail was a lamentable resource, and took her through the water not much faster than we could have rowed. We still had the oars at liberty, as the spars for the sail were lying in the boat when we took her, so I took them in hand, and Whitehurst steered. We were quite in sight when morning broke, and had the satisfaction of seeing the boat we

---

[1] A slow cargo vessel.

had disturbed get away and follow in pursuit. It was only a question of a few hours; at about eleven o'clock they were close on our heels, and a few moments later I was being hauled into the fishing boat under a salute of as many fists as could get at me. The captain of her came to my rescue, and ordered them to desist, and I was passed aft. Whitehurst came after the saving clause had been introduced by the captain, and so was allowed to go aboard peacefully. It was late in the afternoon when we landed, and a crowd of people received us on the shore. We were led up to a respectable-looking house just as we were, with our wet shirts and trousers on, anything but a reviving spectacle. The first question put to us on getting ashore again was, "Where are your clothes?" Our reply explained a mystery which had hung over a heap of clothes discovered that morning early, unclaimed, by the edge of the sea.

Whitehurst was placed at the head of a table presided over by a functionary, when the apartment rapidly filled to excess, all anxious to have a stare at that fine-looking man. When our nationality was revealed it seemed to cause some regret at our misfortunes, the women especially showing great sympathy. What with one thing and another, in the crush I was gradually squeezed into a corner, where I awaited my turn. Whitehurst being asked in the course of examination whom his companion was, and having replied, *"Lieutenant de Vaisseau,"* all eyes were directed to myself, and the women now began in earnest to bestir themselves into more active demonstrations of kind feeling. One of them got a needle and thread, and applied herself on the spot to the rents in my shirt, while another devoted herself in a like manner to anything else you may like to mention. Our discarded garments from the "sea-beach shore" were brought to light, and ere we left the room of justice our appearance was quite *à la mode*.

The examination concluded, we were removed to prison at Caen, and there taken before the governor, where, to our almost irrepressible joy, we found the padre. I was ordered to appear first, and the padre was called upon to interpret. The ordeal was a stiff and unpleasant one. I refused to admit that I knew the names of any of the places at which we had stayed or the names of those who had given us assistance. This put the governor at last out of patience, and he made the padre ask me, "Do you mean to say that you are the second lieutenant of an English frigate, and that you do not know any of the places in France at which you have stayed during the last fourteen or fifteen months?" I maintained an obstinate denial, and the padre evidently put a word in to my credit, as I was presently dismissed without further criticism. Whitehurst must have come in for a double share of interview, as the governor kept him a very long while in his presence.

Our stay here was not prolonged, and short as it was we managed to conciliate our keeper, because he despatched us from Caen as "English prisoners" *en fenille de route,* and not as "deserters," which would have subjected us to the inconvenience of chains. We were ordered to the prison at Verdun, the questionable celebrity of which had reached us already.

## 1811

On the following day our long march commenced. Owing to our lengthy confinement we had become bad walkers, and could scarcely keep up with the convicts who formed the companions of our march. Indeed by the time we had reached our first halt, Whitehurst and I were completely done up.

There was no inn this time for accommodation, but a square unsightly building containing one door and one window, the latter defying all hope. There was only one room for convicts and the rest of us, twelve in number, but plenty of space and very little straw. Two sides were boarded like a guard-house for the purpose of sleeping on; the floor was composed of stoneflags; a large round tub devoted to sanitary purposes stood in one corner. One principal feature in the place contributed in no small degree to our felicity. The boards provided for our repose were almost concealed under a cloak of vermin of the vilest description. This prevented us, tired as we were, from entertaining any idea of sleep, and so we determined to remain standing. But nature was not to be superseded. I began to fail in my strength, and finally was obliged to declare to Whitehurst that vermin or no vermin I must lie down, and down I went. I was aroused by Whitehurst after a slight rest. "For goodness sake, Jackson," he said, "get up, you're literally swarming with lice." Up I jumped and tried to shake off the pests, while the convicts, enjoying our misery, laughed and joked heartily. They were not so dainty in their tastes and seemed to care nothing for these filthy hosts.

In the morning we were brought round to the front of the prison and supplied with large kids of soup and a horn and a wooden spoon for each. The latter, however, happened to be short in number, and we were glad to obtain for ourselves in any way we could some of this slush, which really was fitter for pigs than men. At the time we partook of this *soupe* as though it were a luxury, so keenly do hardships and deprivation whet the appetite. This meal being over, the gendarmes marshalled us, and we began another weary march.

We continued thus, marching from prison to prison, until we reached ——, where we received a pleasant surprise at finding ourselves at last in a jail which was the very picture of cleanliness. Our joy met with a repulse, however, because we were left to ourselves, Whitehurst and I, for such a weary length of time that we began to fear that we had been forgotten, and hunger now made us feel the neglect more acutely. There was nothing in our cell of any description, with the exception of what we stood in. The jailor eventually came, and food and other things followed: everything corresponding with the place and being delightfully clean. We were an exception to the prevailing rule, I grieve to say, having still about our persons many a living memorial of our late prison experiences.

It sounds revolting and nasty to an English ear to describe such a condition, but do what we would we found it impossible to keep the enemy under. Every fold and crease in our garments boasted a colony of those hideous little crawlers; and what we expelled during the day when we had an opportunity, was repaid sevenfold during the night. We could obtain no change of clothes and had to make the best of it. Here at least we might do execution with some prospect of success so long as we were permitted to remain, and we commenced a crusade without delay.

A few days' rest at ———— and our prospects darkened. More dirty prisons awaited us; and in one where we were incarcerated for a week, another kind of plague revealed itself. Instead of lice, we had to war against a larger and more elastic foe. The room alloted to us and the others was capacious, full of dirty beds, and alive with fleas. Variety may be charming, but I confess I shrank from the contact of those ravenous little vampires, and would have almost preferred the infliction to which we had already become habituated.

Whitehurst was as loath as myself to encounter them, but necessity deprived us of any choice in the matter, so we braced up our energies to fresh herculean tasks. In the morning we easily procured brooms and a bucket and access to a pump, when to the amazement of our fellow-prisoners, who appeared in succession resentful, bewildered, and finally tickled beyond endurance, we doused about the water and rubbed and scrubbed until we almost flooded the apartment. We repeated this for three mornings, and succeeded in getting a night's uninterrupted rest before we left, our idle companions deriving an unappreciated benefit from our labours.

This idea of cleanliness was quite an abstract one with them, and nothing contributed more to excite their mirth than the daily practice observed by Whitehurst and myself of alternately pumping cold water over each other. A Russian amongst them afforded a slight exception to the rest, and was more averse to dirt; he was an amusing fellow, and would scrape off his living tormentors whenever we were on the eve of quitting a prison and solemnly dedicate them to the next occupier.

The masters of the prisons were as indulgent as their limited powers would permit them to be. The custom of waiting in ranks for the turn of the spoon, when articles of this description were scarce, was an ordeal as unpleasant as any to which we were subjected; and on some occasions it was positively insupportable—the spoon bearing unmistakable signs of its transit through a dozen abominable stages.

The soup was always brought out into the middle of the yard, contained in a great kid or tub, and the rush made at it resembled the conduct of a pack of hounds rather than a gang of human beings. I never see a number of hungry pigs being fed now, but the spectacle recalls to my mind the scene in the prison yard. Fastidious persons suffering from delicate stomachs would derive a salutary cure after a few months' experience such as we encountered. The vicissitudes of our march from Caen to Verdun were extended over a period of two months, the length of our detention at the intermediate prisons varying with circumstances.

Towards the conclusion of our journey I suffered acutely on one occasion from exhaustion and implored the gendarmes to let me sit down for a few minutes. They peremptorily refused. I then asked to be allowed to get something to drink as we passed a public-house, with the same result. On reaching the next prison I fairly sank to the ground and gave myself entirely up, careless what they might do. After some considerable trouble I was taken within, and the gendarme then came to me and said that he did not intend any unkindness in refusing to let me rest on the road, but he knew only too well that when a prisoner in a similar condition was allowed to halt, it was next to impossible to get him to move again.

At the bureau at Verdun the authorities at first refused to acknowledge me as an officer at all; and well they might refuse, for my personal appearance betokened anything but a respectable caste; my boots were toeless and had not enjoyed contact with a brush for eighteen months. My trousers, despite the friendly offices of the women at Caen, had broken into instalments, and my shirt was a curiosity. My coat was a model of good ventilation, and my hair, which curled over my head, had forgotten the application of any other comb save what nature permitted me to adapt in my fingers.

Upon being satisfied at last of my respectability, I was committed to the citadel, where I was put into a comfortable room and treated as became my rank.

I had not been here for more than two or three days when I remarked that certain fellow-prisoners were chalking out a plan of escape. I therefore resolved to keep my weather eye upon them without exciting suspicion. My room was in a part of the building appropriated to officers of higher rank than that held by my fellow-prisoners who were in the conspiracy. In fact I had the most fortunate situation that was possible. It had struck me as being peculiar that on several occasions I had found more than one of the parties dodging about the vicinity of my compartment; and once on return- ing there I must have unexpectedly given an alarm, as a fellow bolted sud- denly from a door which stood opposite to mine in the corridor, and in his hurry omitted to close it fast. I then took the liberty of looking, and to my astonishment discovered the whole plot. They had removed the stones from the wall on one side of the room and made an opening of quite two feet square—which led to another chamber where there was a little den with a curiously devised window.

The place had originally been a convent, and it struck me that the cell to which I allude must have been adapted for the solitary confinement of the nuns. The window that pierced the massive wall described in its course the segment of a circle, so that the light from without was reflected but scantily into the cell. Beyond the curve of the arch it was impossible to see. The aperture, however, was of sufficient dimensions to allow the forced pas- sage of a slight figure. So this is your game, I mentally ejaculated. Satisfied on this point, I retraced my steps, secured the door, and sought the open air. Whilst strolling about, one of the prisoners, Devonshire, a midshipman, came close to me and observed, "I think it will be a fine night?" I replied I thought it would be, and added, "And when do you go?" He affected not to understand me, but I continued more unequivocally, "I know of your intentions to escape and the means to which you have resorted for accom- plishing your purpose, but let me advise you not to go so frequently to the place of your rendezvous, to be more careful when you do go, and to be quick in your movements."

He was now fully convinced of my acquaintance with the scheme afloat; and I proposed to profit by it also but not at the risk of compromis- ing their success. He listened to my proposal and said he would go and refer it to his companions. He came back with a unanimous offer for me to join them in leaving together—which I joyfully accepted. There were three concerned—viz., Devonshire, Gordon, and Street. I made a fourth. Their plan had been dexterously conceived, but so far rather clumsily executed, because, had suspicion not been asleep among the officials, they must have noticed the constant visits of the confederates to a part of the establishment in which these had no business; and had they repaired thither to ascertain the reason, there was nothing in the world to prevent their seeing the breach in the wall.

Being the eldest and the senior in rank, I took the lead, and as my room was so contiguous to the principal scene of operations, I could give very material assistance in hastening the crisis. This soon arrived. We had repeated consultations in my room; for now it was manifest that I had picked up a friend or two amongst my fellow-prisoners, and it was only natural they should spend a great deal of time with me.

From my window we could look into a fine garden, where a noble pear-tree reared its branches above the central wall. Directly under the window was a sentry's beat, over which one of those inconvenient gentlemen passed day and night. It was absolutely necessary, therefore, to make our plans as perfect as possible to evade his vigilance at the onset, as one end of his beat went painfully close to the spot upon which we should descend upon emerging from this prison. It was therefore agreed that the selected night should be a dark one; that we should be furnished with a strong rope of twisted sheets and strong pegs; that a midshipman who was unwilling to share the risk of our exploit but yet agreeable to lending us a hand, should sit at my open window, from which the light was thrown across the sentry's path, and play certain airs upon a flute to apprise us when the sentry was close or distant; that Gordon should then descend first; and that as soon as each one reached the ground he should, accordingly as the musician admonished, either remain immovable until the tune changed, or dart quickly across his track into the gloom beyond.

Our stations at the pear-tree were allotted and, if the darkness served, the night appointed.

The hour came when I had been about seven days at Verdun, and was all that could be desired. We were highly favoured, as, in addition to a darkness rivalling the shades of Erebus, a light wind, strong enough to scatter the leaves and make a noise, sprang up. On gaining the cycloidal window, Gordon's courage, he being very juvenile, failed him, and he expressed a fear of being able to push himself through the confined space which constituted our means of egress. Thereupon Devonshire interposed and insisted on leading the way. He soon effected the desired passage. But it still remained for him to get safely into the garden without alarming the sentry. The flute began its piping melody, and the wished-for tune came wafted on the breeze. Now, however, the slower air succeeded, and we held our breaths. Anon the desired note recurred, and we knew that Devonshire's retreat was assured. One by one the rest of us followed. This was the most anxious part of the programme, and we performed it without a fault.

Now for the tree. Gordon took the start and his position on the wall, and we placed ourselves on the branches in a perpendicular line beneath him. The top of the wall was covered with tiles, and a portion of them had to be removed before we could fix the pegs and rope for our descent into the moat. We were still disagreeably near the sentry, and caution was the order of the night. Gordon carefully removed one tile at a time, which was handed down from one to another and deposited gently at the foot of the tree. This done, with but a few interruptions, we fixed the rope, and found ourselves on the safe side of the enemy.

I now resigned myself to the safe guidance of my companions, as they were well acquainted with the geography of the locality, two of them having been prisoners at Verdun for some years. We soon got out of the moat and then made for the town, where an English midshipman was on the *qui vive* expecting us. He was at liberty on his parole and joined us before we had gone far. To his house we first repaired and remained the night. In the interval he provided us with another sanctuary in the house of a German count, where we went in the morning. We were received very graciously and put into his bedroom, where he directed us to lock the door and not open it again on any account except to himself. He had not left us long when somebody tried the door—evidently a woman by her tread. One of our number, at the moment quite oblivious to the caution, jumped up to undo the lock, but we restrained him, and the person departed. She returned, however, in a few minutes, and the same fellow through some unaccountable impulse of madness or folly gained his end this time, and before any one could interpose, let in the applicant. The woman's astonishment may be supposed at seeing her master's room occupied by four questionable-looking strangers, and without saying a word she beat a retreat.

The count's surprise and annoyance was great on hearing of this insane *contretemps*, but he ordered us at once to betake ourselves through a trap-door overhead into a little cupola or look-out above the room, just large enough to hold us packed like sardines. Whatever had induced Street to act so foolhardily neither he nor any one else could explain. He was sorry for it afterwards, but the thing was done. We were left in the cupola without anything to eat or drink until night, when we disentangled ourselves and were taken to the house of a neighbour, and conducted into a large unoccupied loft—which had never been finished. It was next to the kitchen, into which we could plainly see through the seams of the partition. Here we were left to beguile ourselves as well as we could for the remainder of the day. Presently there appeared on the same scene a man and a woman, who quickly took their departure on finding themselves in the presence of strangers. This little incident gave us some apprehension, and when our friend appeared again we mentioned it to him. He shared our fears and counselled a speedy retreat to another place of refuge. We then repaired to a house where an English lieutenant on parole was lodging. On being acquainted with our wishes he came out and told us that, with every disposition to assist us, it was not in his power to take more than one of the party under his care. "You are all strangers to me, gentlemen," he continued, "but I hear there is a lieutenant among you, and I would fain select the man to serve who is of my own rank and position in the service." It was hereupon resolved that I should accept his offer, as the smaller the party became the better. We shook hands for the last time and separated.

Two of the number, Street and Gordon, I afterwards heard, had reached the seashore and ventured out by themselves in a small boat and were drowned. Long after the above events Devonshire and myself met one day by accident in the streets of London. He had escaped from France about the same time as I had, he having been fully under the impression that I was dead.

My new protector recommended me to go into the bath and amuse myself there as long as I liked—a bit of advice very necessary. My patience was not taxed much this time. The lieutenant reappeared with my old messmate Conn, who was also on parole. By them it was arranged that I should follow them at a certain distance to the abode of Thomas—like Conn a prisoner at large. But first of all he presented me with a cap that had a gold tassel. They then set out and stopped at the house, which they entered; but here an unfortunate mistake occurred. Mr. Thomas did not live in that house, they were told, but next door. Some little delay had taken place, and I was now close to their heels when they emerged and passed on to the next door. Here again they were equally disappointed, and were assured that Mr. Thomas did live in the house they had just left, but in the upper part of it. Back we went.

These desultory movements attracted the attention of an old pensioner, who communicated his observations to a gendarme; and on hearing some heavy footsteps in the rear I had just time to conceal myself behind a glass door with a curtain across it, when my friends were accosted very civilly by the official and asked if "Mr. Jackson was there?" A woman was occupied in the room, and divining how matters stood attracted my notice, and pointed under the bed. The gendarme accepted their answer and quitted the house. Nevertheless it was thought expedient to put me elsewhere as quickly as possible. So I was called out upon the landing and handed over to a little old woman who held a key in her hand, with which she motioned me to follow her. I did so, and we got to a door which she opened, and pushing me through she locked it behind her and ran away downstairs with the key.

Woman's wit for ever, said I to myself, and I made for a huge pile of brush-wood faggots filling one end of the room. They were promiscuously heaped together, and I found no difficulty in effecting a passage through them to the farthest corner, where I pulled them about to conceal any opening I had made. Here I crouched down to await the future.

I had not been too prompt in thus installing myself. The door was opened presently and perhaps a dozen men entered. They gabbled away as only Frenchmen can, and then they made an attack upon the faggots. The pile was pretty thick or I should have suffered more than once from the points of their swords, which they thrust in here and there. One active gentleman got a well-pointed stake which he propelled through the heap, and it hit the wall disagreeably close to where I lay doubled. This apparently satisfied him, as he exclaimed in French, "He is not there." Despite the critical aspect of affairs I could not help remarking in my mind, "What a lie."

I was immensely relieved when the sound of their voices and footsteps assured me of their retreat; but the relief was not permanent. They came back even in stronger numbers than before, and began a fresh inquisition upon the faggots. Fortune certainly favoured me under these ordeals, or I should have, beyond a doubt, been pinked most uncomfortably. Again I rejoiced to hear sounds of their departure. Only one remained, and then, whilst I was speculating on his motives for lagging, all my new-born hopes were scattered beyond redemption by hearing him declare that if I was anywhere in the house I was in the faggots, and he would not go until he had searched every bundle. Confound your perseverance I almost said, as the abominable old foe began to carry out his promise. I have already alluded to the cap I wore. When the gendarme had taken away most of the faggots, and had left relatively a few sticks between us, his eye suddenly caught the glitter of the gold tassel. It was all up with me: he tore down the topmost faggot and revealed your humble servant, with anything but an easy assurance displayed on his countenance.

"*Ah vous . . .*" he cried; for the particular expression denoted by a blank there is an authority in one of Sterne's narratives which may or may not be familiar to my reader. In reply to this salutation I crawled out, and submitted myself a third time a reluctant captive. An investigation at the bureau, of course, impended, and I was presented formally to the authorities as a fugitive prisoner. Captain F. W. Fane of the English Navy was then awaiting his papers of permission to return to England. He had commanded the *Cambrian,* and now the fact that he had treated some French prisoners with great kindness having come to the knowledge of the emperor, the latter had ordered his release, and he was now on the point of leaving the French country for his own. He witnessed my introduction and the company in which it was made. I made known the details of my case to him, whereupon he promised to inform a personal friend of mine at the Admiralty of my position. I am sorry to relate that he forgot to redeem this pledge. All remembrance of the poor lieutenant whom he had left in bondage in a foreign land became dissipated in the excitement and joy of recovering his own release.

The French general examined me himself, and was anxious to ascertain how I had descended the wall of the convent. "By my hands," I replied. This assertion he could not believe, of course, as my hands bore no marks of the friction usually sustained in such undertakings. A great many other questions were applied, to most of which I answered evasively. At the termination of these I felt dry and parched, and asked for a glass of water. I was refused somewhat abruptly, and the general turned to the gendarme, directing him in almost the same tone of voice to take me to his—the general's—wife, and bid her give me the best bottle of wine in his cellar. I asked for my parole, promising that if I received it I should respect it; but this he explained was out of his powers to grant.

In the course of this process a tin case was brought into the room, which invested me with anything but favourable anticipations; for Whitehurst had repeatedly terrified me with the prospect of compulsory confession elicited by those means which, of all things, I most dreaded—namely, the thumb-screws. However, there was nothing to terrible as this in store. I was merely handcuffed and led away along the ramparts of the town to the Porte Chaussée—a prison situated over the gates of the town.

## 1811–1812

On arrival at my new prison I found there were three occupants, one of them being a music-master. I suspected one of the other two of being a spy, but he called himself a captain in the English Army, an old joke even in those days. Nevertheless it was largely due to the kind assistance of this friend, whom I was now misjudging, that I was enabled subsequently to make good my escape from France, as will be explained later. The third occupant was a lieutenant in the East Indian Service, and bore a despicable character. This much for my associates—so far I stuck to the music-master. While at Porte Chaussée I became acquainted with a military lieutenant outside, named George Beamish, who tendered me his good offices in attempting to escape. He visited me frequently, always bringing with him a piece of line. I was to let him know when I was prepared for action, and began my designs at once. In the planks above our heads I detected an unsound corner, and by standing on the shoulder of a companion, who in his turn was elevated upon the bed, I established a hole there one evening through which I squeezed and then fastened the line to the parapet. This having been accomplished, I went back to help the others. It was then understood that each should wait until the others had ascended, and then slip down the parapet in order. I first assisted up the East Indian and then the "military captain," who, being stout and awkward, made a great noise getting through the hole. This scared the East Indian, who, in complete defiance of the previous arrangement, rushed to the rope and let himself down into the embrace of a gendarme. The stout party, ignorant of his companion's mishap, quickly emulated his example, but not being an expert in the art of gymnastics, he let the rope slide through his fingers and fell heavily to the ground, breaking his thigh in the fall.

The gendarmes were now gathered round the spot, and in the confusion the East Indian seized a favourable opportunity and eluded his captor, getting clear away to the appointed place where Beamish was expecting us, from whom he derived the benefit intended for me. Seeing the game up, I made for the room again and was snug under the bedclothes when the jailor opened the door. Appearances are deceptive. So thought the jailor, I presume, for he approached the bed and drew off the sheets, of course discovering me habited for a journey. "Ah," he exclaimed, "I knew you had a hand in it; I was sure that nobody thought of breaking out unless you put it into their heads."

This little affair brought the lieutenant of the gendarmes down about the middle of the night, perhaps called from the enjoyment of a pleasant party, as he was in anything but a mild humour. I was the main object of his strictures, and he spared no pains to convince me of his displeasure. He said, "You have given us all a great deal of trouble, Mr Jackson; I have already doubled the sentries on your account, and now I must add fresh precautions. I have therefore given them strict injunctions, should you repeat to-night's experiment, to fire at you without hesitation, and I leave it entirely at the discretion of the jailor to place you or not in the black hole."

"And I, sir," I retorted, "beg to inform you that I have not had my parole, and despite all your threats I am determined to escape if I can—whether your sentries fire or not."

The jailor didn't presume upon his authority, but allowed me to go quickly to bed. The only penalty I suffered after all was being called upon to pay for the damage done to the rotten planks. A fresh accession to our small circle in the prison of Porte Chaussée was soon made by new-comers in two relays. On arrival of the second batch we were put under orders for Bitche[1].

This intelligence instilled fresh energy into me, and after dinner, on the day when it was received, I stood up and addressed them in my room as follows—they were six in number: "Gentlemen, we are all of us bound for Bitche; there is a prospect of escape if you like to take advantage of it." A man named L'Estrange[2], a lieutenant of the 71st Foot, immediately exclaimed, "I will." I then requested the music-master to play on the piano which one of the prisoners was allowed to keep in the room, and to select the loudest piece he could choose. All hands then proceeded at my instigation to make a rope out of the sheets. It was rapidly done, and each wound a portion of it round his body beneath his clothes.

The prisoners in the adjoining room were indulging in a somewhat boisterous mirth, and so between them and the piano, upon which our friend was doing most laudable execution, we had plenty of noise.

The rope disposed of, we rang for the jailor and supplied him with the usual reason for allowing us to leave the room. We gained by this means access into the next compartment, where I had previously scented out another spot in the planks above; and we would be left here until we chose to summon the jailor to reconduct us to our own quarters, not so conveniently appointed. I arrested the conviviality for a moment to introduce the subject in contemplation, and it was gladly accepted *nem. con.* I then begged them to continue their jollification, and to sing and shout as if nothing was in the wind.

---

[1] *Bitche, Bîche, or Bitsch* is a town in Lorraine. The citadel is built upon a rock 250 feet above the town. There had been an old castle here, on the site of which Vauban had later constructed a fortress. After the capture of the town by the French in 1624, the defence works were destroyed prior to restoring it to Lorraine.

In 1740 the fortress was repaired, and proved impregnable in all the succeeding campaigns. Even in the Franco-Prussian War of 1870, though closely invested by the Germans, it held out until the end. A deep well within the fort is sufficient to keep the garrison supplied. A good deal of the fortification has been made by excavating the actual rock. There is a tale that Louis XIV, on being informed as to the cost of these works, asked if the fort had been built and paved with bullion.

In the Napoleonic wars, Bitche, besides being the special receptacle for deserters and others who had been accused of grave military crimes, was found to be a convenient and fairly secure place of detention for recalcitrant British prisoners of war, that is to say, those who would not give their parole, and who had made or were suspected of being about to make attempts to escape. Other British officers than Jackson and L'Estrange did actually succeed in getting away from Bitche; some of them, incredible as it may seem, by negotiating the ramparts, though at least one of such attempts ended in the death of the fugitive (Sub-Lieutenant John Essel).

[2] *Edward L'Estrange* was a lieutenant in the 71st Foot. After separating from Jackson at Verdun, he succeeded in reaching Bordeaux, where he took a boat and got on board the *Hanni-*

To prevent surprise I asked a doctor who was present, a very timid man, to watch the gratings in the door, and when the jailor or his wife approached to pop out his head and call for a jug of beer. This post he accepted, and I set to. The plank was started in a few minutes, and I was shoving away with all my heart, when I heard sundry smothered remarks on all sides, such as "Hush, hush, Jackson——." I, not dreaming of danger, merely turned my head for a moment, when lo, the poor cowardly doctor had bolted, and the jailor's wife was calmly watching my proceedings from the deserted gratings. Down I dropped like a stone from my eminence, and tried hard to look unconcerned, with very lame results I am afraid. The jailor came and restored us to our proper places, and the question arose what should be done with the ten ropes and how account for the missing sheets, as we were to start in the morning.

The ropes were ultimately packed into two of the midshipmen's bags, and I undertook to manage about the sheets.

The jailor took his inventory before we left, and I explained that the sheets had been sent on an emergency to the washerwoman, but as it was not probable she would return them when she knew of our departure, I honourably offered to pay for them. This honest conduct on my part raised me considerably in the estimation of the jailor, who was perfectly contented with the arrangement and took quite an affecting leave of me.

A new system was adopted for our security on the road in the march now impending, and one not at all favourable to our ideas of pleasant locomotion. We were handcuffed in pairs, and a long chain run through all the irons—thus ensuring close quarters to all. Some of the handcuffs were small and exceedingly painful. Mine were of this character, and I suffered severely.

Our journey to Bitche was accomplished in seven days. The aspect of the place was not inviting. The prison has been described as like a ship bottom upwards in a saucer. Our new quarters were good enough, considering all things. We were packed sixteen into one room with three beds, under which the fuel was stocked. During the first night a midshipman

---

bal, 74, Captain Sir Michael Seymour, who immediately wrote a strong letter in his favour to headquarters. On his arrival in England, three months after Lieutenant Jackson, he was received at the Horse Guards by the Duke of York in the most gracious manner, and was allotted three years retrospective rank as captain with indulgences, and in two years attained his majority. This treatment is in marked contrast with that meted out to Lieutenant Jackson, who had no one of consequence to take an interest in his career. Jackson, on arrival at Portsmouth, at once reported himself to the Port Admiral. However, he had not the satisfaction of being greeted with even a word of approbation. Nor, on repairing to the Admiralty, could he obtain either an interview with the First Lord, or the slightest notice from any one in authority.

named H. Leworthy, a tall powerful young fellow, possessing also good qualities of mind as well as of body, was my bedfellow. When he awoke in the morning he began to attack me, saying, "Hallo, Jackson, have you been bunging up my eyes in your sleep? What on earth is wrong with my face?" A general cry of "bugs" was now raised. Every one was more or less affected by their visitation except me. This time, marvellous to say, for I was generally marked out as a signal victim to misfortune, I had unwittingly defied the enemy. How it was I can't explain, because poor Leworthy was a mass of bites, and unable to see for them. We had been expecting this evil sooner or later as a sort of necessary sequence to our vermin troubles.

After an interval we were better accommodated. I had a room to myself and belonged to a mess of eight persons, all of whom were tacitly resolved to make our connections as pleasant as possible. We were divided from the other half of our fellow-prisoners by mutual consent, on account of a quarrel which had arisen between us and a man named C——, who had played me a dirty trick soon after our arrival at the prison. It was the habit of those who could afford it to hire furniture from some dealer in the town, to replace that supplied by the authorities; and I sent for what articles I required as soon as a room had been placed at my service. Amongst the things was a French bedstead, and on its way to my quarters it was levied upon by Mr. C—— for his own use, and in spite of all representation he persisted in keeping possession of it. When this came to my ears I accused him of committing a mean, ungentlemanly action; and this caused no small indignation to himself and his friends. Upon this disagreement we split ourselves into different communities.

Some merchant captains, several midshipmen, an elderly gentleman— a *détenu*—named Throgmorton, a Mr Melville and myself constituted our mess.

Almost from the moment of our entrance I commenced to prepare for my escape. Economy was my first consideration, and in pursuit of it I made every sacrifice consistent with propriety. I wore the coarsest and commonest things and purchased nothing I could by reasonable means do without. My prison allowance was fifty francs a month, £2, 1s. 8d., and upon this I managed to live, independently of my English pay, which it was my object to save for an emergency. In drawing my quarterly bill I almost lost one-third of it in the exchange, which was, however, refunded to me eventually by the English government.

Our occupations and amusements at Bitche were limited to those of the most primitive nature. No gambling was tolerated amongst us; our principal recreations were out of doors, where we practised athletic and other games such as lay in our power to promote.

Bitche had been used as a prison for the lower class of English prisoners, but most of them had been removed before we had been sent there, and only sufficient left to perform the duties of servants. These were placed in the *souterraines*, where they reigned supreme and legislated for their community upon principles of their own, administering reward and punishment to all who deserved one or the other—but woe betide the offender whoever and whatever he might be. He was allowed no money, and was kicked, cuffed, or tossed in the blanket as the contingency required. The latter system of retribution was that most frequently adopted and most dreaded. The rank of a man was of no avail as soon as he appeared in the *souterraines*, and if any one with a voice amongst the men owed the visitor a grudge, master or no master, the latter was sure to pay the penalty. A man named Spillier was the presiding genius of this place, and to him were referred all questions of arbitration. When any remarkable act of justice was on the eve of consummation, he usually apprised me of the event. And if I felt inclined, as I am sorry to say I always was, to witness the spectacle, I repaired forthwith to the scene under his convoy. There was a lieutenant at Bitche who was an especial object of aversion to the underground community, and they never were so anxious to get a man into their power as they were to catch him. He was of an exclusive overbearing disposition, and in some way or other had raised their ire; but he was far too knowing to trespass on their limits, and so avoided their vengeance.

All through the winter I had my eye on a future plan of escape which I communicated to Mr. Throgmorton, inviting him to join me in the attempt. He, however, declined, and I then spoke to Lieutenant L'Estrange, and reminded him of an old understanding between us that if either had a practical view of escaping he should tell the other of it; and I had observed that he was in concert with two others in a design which I felt convinced would prove fruitless. He was surprised that I knew anything about it, but, like the plot at Verdun, it would have been manifest to any one who took the trouble to look at him.

I now submitted my scheme for his approval and offered to take him into league, as he could speak French and I could not. He was not able to decide at once, as he was pledged to a general in the British Army, a prisoner on parole at Verdun, in agreement for standing each other's bail. He therefore wrote, and received a reply that the general gave him back his parole; so he was at liberty to act upon his own bottom.

My plan was greatly accelerated by an old acquaintance who had lately turned up in the person of the fellow who had broken his thigh at Verdun. I am considerably indebted to his ingenuity for my escape from Bitche. He cajoled the guards into selling to him some of their old clothes and equip-

ment on the most plausible pretences; and so adroitly did he transact the
business that none of them had the smallest apprehension of his real purpose. He obtained a cloak, a cocked hat, a cap and a greatcoat, and a large
water-pitcher; and these were all we required with a little self-possession
and management to effect our purpose.

During the latter end of February we intended to carry the project into
execution. When the time came L'Estrange and I duly rigged ourselves out
as became the occasion. He took the cocked hat and cloak, I, the more humble suit and the water-pot. It was then about half-past seven. Until eight the
prisoners were allowed to visit the yard, and we went through a very ordinary form of leaving our room at that time. As we were descending the
stairs we encountered Leworthy anathematising the sentry below because
he would not let him pass according to custom. As his eye met mine he
spared the obdurate official any further abuse, and laying hold of me in a
playful manner shouted, "Hullo, Jackson, my boy, what are you up to?"
"Hush, old fellow," I said, *sotte voce*, "don't be a fool, and let go that infernal grip of yours." He caught at my meaning and intention at once, and
seizing me by both hands said, "God bless you, old fellow—I wish I had
your luck." L'Estrange and I then gained the yard.

We had planned that I should take the lead until we gained a spot
where we should be challenged. I therefore struck off boldly armed with
my friendly water-jar, and passed No. 1 sentinel unmolested. Of course he
would not trouble a comrade going to fetch water, and when L'Estrange
followed with an easy and familiar air, his cocked hat looming above, it
was not probable that the soldier would question the right of a French officer to go where he pleased. Nos. 2 and 3 and 4 were passed with similar
success, and we were now at the entrance to a covered way that intercepted
our purpose to get past the guard-room. Here L'Estrange was to precede
me in order that he might answer the sentry's challenge in a good accent. I
entered already, and was half-way through when I stopped for him to pass
on, but looking round I found him standing still at the end. "Come on," I
cried in as loud a whisper as I could, but he only replied, "I can't," and
when I went back to him I found he could hardly move for laughing. This
set me off. He was quite hysterical. We proceeded at length, and received
the challenge—"*Qui vive?*" I waited for L'Estrange to reply "*Ami*," but he
never made a sound. The challenge was repeated more vigorously still:
L'Estrange held his peace. On the impulse of the moment I gave the word
myself, for there was no other alternative left or they would have been
down on us. For once in my life I must have spoken French like a native, as
the sentry passed us on. L'Estrange still followed, and we made down the
slope which carried us to the covered bomb-proof passage, and left another

danger behind us. The most ticklish moment was at hand. I advanced to the gate, but the sentry put his arm before me, and I thought we were lost, when L'Estrange boldly approached, spoke a word or two to the sentry, who released me, and we were free. About two or three hundred yards from the gate we passed close to the sergeant of the guard, who in the darkness gave us no heed.

The snow was now falling. All the better for us. We put our best foot foremost and rushed on in concert. We reached Sarreguemines about four o'clock. I was now in another guise, having discarded the friendly coat and cap, which I deposited in a ditch, where it must have soon been covered with snow. I appeared as a gentleman in full French costume, which I had lately procured direct from Paris, feeling sure that an imposing appearance would be more useful to me than the wretched one I had hitherto been compelled to present in like undertakings. My coat was a well-cut snuff-coloured one, buff-coloured waistcoat, pepper-and-salt breeks, and white top-boots. A man followed us, but vanished on seeing L'Estrange's cocked hat.

We pushed through Sorbey and applied for admission at a public-house; we were taken in and shown to a large room containing two beds, covered with what I took to be huge bundles. L'Estrange jumped into bed without much premeditation, but I hesitated and sat on a chair looking dismal. There did not appear to be any sheets or blankets—nothing but that uncouth ugly lump of a thing.

"Jump into bed, man," said L'Estrange.

"But what's the use?" I remarked. "I am cold and tired, and there is nothing to make me warm."

"What? Get under this quilt like me."

"Quilt," I ejaculated, "call that a quilt?"

"Try it," he resumed; and I did so sulkily, and oh, the joy, my grief was turned to ecstasy—it was an eider-down quilt and as warm as could be. I had never seen such a thing in my life before.

After a capital sleep I got up and asked the landlord for horses to Metz. After breakfast we started, with an attendant on a third horse, there being two feet of snow on the ground. We had not gone far when we reached the crown of a hill and noticed a gendarme escorting an English prisoner to Verdun. This brought us to a halt; however, we put confidence in the guide, telling him that we wished to avoid the party. He at once "twigged," and consented to follow out our views; and taking a sharp turn out of the road, he led us by a short cut to Metz. My horse was not in any trim for a long journey, and fell on his knees again and again.

On our arrival at Metz, we dismissed our guide with the horses and sought an hotel. We played our parts as travelling gentlemen and procured a voiture to Etain, a place not far from Verdun. When close to Verdun we separated, and L'Estrange, being dressed in the uniform of a French officer, walked up to the gates of the town and entered with a military baggage waggon. Not having a parole ticket I was inadmissible, and therefore remained outside depending upon L'Estrange's good offices with my friends at Verdun. Every officer on parole, when he leaves the town, deposits his ticket with the gate-keeper and reclaims it on return.

I hung dodging about the walls, and not long after L'Estrange's disappearance I saw two wholesome-looking figures approach from the town. I divined them to be Englishmen at once, and when they came near accosted them. They were such, and without telling them of my position, I merely asked them if they would carry a message for me into Verdun to a friend named Conn, and say that someone was waiting for him outside. The answer I promptly received was: "Take the message yourself," and they walked off. "Well, you're a couple of ungracious beasts," I grumbled to myself as they left me, and I began to cudgel my brains as to what should be done next, when I observed that they had returned and were coming back towards me. I was in no humour to come into collision with such bears, and was on the point of avoiding them when one of the two advanced and said, "Was it a meeting, sir, you desired me to promote with Mr. Conn?" Catching at his meaning I disavowed any such intention, and added that, if I was not wrong in thinking that I spoke to two English gentlemen, I would acquaint them with the reason of my former request. They directly informed me of their respective names and rank. One was a major and the other a doctor in the English Army. Upon hearing this I explained that I was a lieutenant in the English Navy just escaped from Bitche, and that having no parole ticket, I was unable to get into Verdun where my friend and former messmate was at present living, and I wished to appraise him of my neighbourhood. They redeemed their former conduct by executing my commission without further hesitation, and reappeared soon after with Conn, who was surprised and delighted to see me. We had a long chat together and arranged to meet again at night, when I was to be at a certain spot under the walls, and Conn and some friends of his would be above with a rope to hand me up. At dusk we separated, and to be secure against surprise I looked out some chance place of concealment until the time appointed for the meeting. I soon found the stunted remains of an old hedge on the common, that grew from a slight elevation, formerly, I suppose, some boundary line on a bank: behind this I lay safely concealed from all stragglers.

At the proper time I cautiously made the spot selected, where I hugged the wall with both ears open to the slightest sound. After some anxious waiting my name was pronounced in a loud whisper, twice. I answered likewise, and felt along the wall for the rope, which I soon secured. When I tested it and found all fast, I began to ascend monkey-fashion hand over hand, but I had scarcely reached half-way when I discovered the rope itself being hauled upwards. Determined not to let go, I clung savagely to it, and up I went until my hands came into contact with the edge of the parapet, with the result that the skin of my knuckles and the backs of my hands was badly lacerated. A strong grip was then made on my collar, and I was soon standing in the presence of Conn and his confederates, two fine young fellows in the English Army named Beamish. Smarting from the injuries to my hands, I ungratefully muttered as soon as I had recovered breath, "What a damned lubberly trick to haul me up that way." "Lubberly or not," answered one of the Beamishes, "you ought to consider yourself devilish lucky to get up at all." And so I did when I reflected a second, and I thanked them warmly for the good turn they had done me. Only I afterwards wished that they had been a little less zealous in the enterprise and allowed me to scale the wall in a more orthodox manner, for my hands were a frightful sight, and even to this day the marks of the midnight adventure are apparent upon them.

Conn took me direct to some quarters in the town, where I was stored away in a room next to the kitchen. I remained here about a fortnight, during which time L'Estrange came to see me. He paid his share of our late expenses, and told me that his friends, amongst them a Lord and a Baronet, had advised him not to proceed any farther with me, as they considered my ideas of escape too romantic.

## FEBRUARY, MARCH, APRIL 1812

L'Estrange's secession placed me in a dilemma; but I found a new friend in J. Carslake, who was a perfect stranger to me. He was a lieutenant in the Navy, and he procured for me a passport as a Swiss clockmaker. Furthermore, he made arrangements with a man to take me a certain distance from Verdun.

When preparations had been completed I took leave of my protectors and accompanied my guide, who lowered me from the wall by means of a rope which he had brought. It had already been concerted between us that on reaching the ground I should speedily seek the shelter of a large avenue which led up to one of the entrances of the town, and that when I saw a man standing with a white handkerchief in his hand I should join him and follow his instructions. A curious coincidence now happened, which would have undone me but for a lucky bit of judgment on my part. I had entered the avenue and walked hardly one hundred yards, when I saw an individual with a white handkerchief in his hand. It occurred to me that my supposed ally was disagreeably close to the gates of the town. Thinking this suspicious, I pushed on a while pretending not to notice him. It was well I did so, for some way ahead of this person stood another also holding a white handkerchief. I had no scruples this time, but in passing uttered a word which he answered, as previously agreed upon, and we pursued our way to his cart. In this vehicle we proceeded through the whole night.

The next morning at about breakfast-time we stopped at an inn. My guardian angel put up at a public-house where there were about one dozen gendarmes. He coolly ordered breakfast, said something to me that only required a nod of the head, said something to one of the gendarmes in a manner that all might hear him, then went out to his horse, and in due time came into his meal. It is said that "Fortune favours the brave," for it was evident that not one of the gendarmes were aware that there was a culprit and an enemy so near to their elbows. It is true they were very busy getting ready their accoutrements and appeared to be much pressed for time.

In proceeding we passed several regiments bound for Russia. A marshal and two outriders came up, and my friend could not get out of the way for the first outrider, and the second struck the horse in the eye, which no doubt made the unfortunate animal a blinker for the rest of his life.

At Chalons he took a place for me in the diligence for Paris. When I entered it I found to my horror it was occupied by seven officers, five of them decorated with the Legion of Honour. The one by whose side I sat was a colonel; and a lady at the further end of the carriage said something to him which I could see related to me, and for which he rebuked her. When we stopped he asked me if I would join them in a bottle of wine, suggesting that if I changed places with a person who was sitting by the side of the driver, I should be more comfortable. I gladly took the hint, but found that I had changed from the frying-pan into the fire, for the guard asked me what countryman I was. I answered "Swiss." "What canton?" On my naming Berne, he exclaimed, "Ah, my own," but he had penetration enough to see that I was not disposed to talk, and did not trouble me more.

We went on to Paris. When landing in the yard, the lady, a very pretty woman, came to me and in the kindest manner said, "If she could be of any service to me, she would render it with the greatest pleasure." I felt her kindness much, but my object was to go ahead; and I secured a place in the diligence for Caen, and took a voiture to drive about Paris to beguile the time, taking care to change my coachman once or twice.

I started for Caen next morning, taking my seat by the guard. I kept my handkerchief to my mouth, hoping that my neighbours would believe me to be tormented with toothache. At the dinner-time who should sit alongside of me but the great man before whom I had been taken with White-hurst. He said, "Will any gentleman join me with a bottle of burgundy?" I saw that he had been eyeing me, so that I thought it best to put a good face on the matter, and signified my readiness to do so. We then left the room, and a gendarme came in and demanded to see our passports. I gave him mine—"Grieme, watchmaker"—was the name on my passport, and he went out with it. That I enjoyed my meal much in his absence cannot be supposed. However, he did not keep me long in suspense, for he soon returned and handed me my passport as well as the rest. Dinner over and the diligence ready, nothing occurred to interrupt our journey to Caen.

Arrived there, I went out at once to my old friend and made arrange-ments for getting on to the seaside. At the end of the week he brought me intelligence that he had found a man that would take me in until a fair wind offered. On the day when we were to leave Caen, I was attacked with ear-ache. However, that did not alter the hour—nine o'clock—when he punctu-ally made his appearance. Heavy rain had set in just before we started and fell in torrents during the whole of our nine-mile walk. Of course we were wet through before we had accomplished one. It would not have signified, perhaps, if I had not been obliged to stop at the corner of a wall toward the end of our journey, where I had to wait for half an hour in the bitter cold wind. The night was pitch dark and I dare not move, as my conductor had strictly enjoined silence. On his return he brought a man with him and duly handed me over to him, and I took leave of my sound-hearted friend.

My new acquaintance bade me follow him, and we went to a house with a sort of a stable directly opposite it, in which was his horse. Above was a loft just high enough in the centre for me to stand up. It was half-full of straw, to which he pointed, signifying that it was my home, and that I must make the best of it. Then he wished me good-night and took away the lantern. There was I in agony with the earache, which soon doubled, for as my clothes dried on me so did the pain increase in the other ear, and there I was for a fortnight. I could not hear a word, and I was in a state of utter wretchedness; while the discharge from my ears was so offensive that my hostess could scarcely bear to come near me. I thought I could not last long; and they were in a stew as to how to dispose of my body when dead.

However, at the end of three weeks I heard a bell, and in a few days, with plenty of food, became myself again in strength. One day the landlady asked me to let her bring her daughter, as she had never seen an English-man, and at my next meal she made her appearance. A very pretty girl about fifteen or sixteen years of age came to me, as I sat on the straw, and presented her cheek for me to kiss, and twice turned it so that I had three; and she expressed much the same sentiment as her brother had done before.

Their astonishment was great that an Englishman could be so good-looking, as I was the first they had ever seen. The compliment was equivocal.

At last the hour arrived when the father and son came to me about ten o'clock at night, and helped me to launch a flat boat, and gave me a pole with which I poled my way to a fishing-boat at anchor, and in "quarter less no time" I had cut her cable and was a free man on the ocean. I got an oar out, put her head the right way, and away she drifted. Of course, being in the dark, I had to feel for everything, so that it was some time before I could step the foremast and lash a light spar over the bows; but it was done in time to get out of sight of the land when daylight dawned.

As the day opened the wind lessened, and nearly all that day—Sunday—was a calm, so I had nothing to do but calculate my chances. One doubt was whether the rickety old thing I had got into would bear a sea. It was an old patched-up boat with a rudder belonging to some craft twice her size, and it took me four hours before I could ship it, although calm, it being so heavy that I could scarcely lift it. As to getting the mainmast up, it was quite out of the question. Towards evening the wind sprang up again from the south, and I gently glided over the silent waves, with the full moon shining surrounded with the largest halo I have ever seen; and as I had nothing else to occupy my mind, I speculated as to whether it might prognosticate a storm or fine weather. I put up an oar and made the top-sail fast to it to act as a mainsail, and then fixed the main yard-arm as far out over the quarter as I could rig it. Thus I contrived to get my small vessel to move over the water. Of course, through the night I steered by the North star, and in the forenoon of Monday I saw the Isle of Wight, and in the afternoon I could see I was approaching a convoy. As I neared them I put my black handkerchief up on an oar. On seeing a man-of-war brig—the *Mutine*—I stood towards her, and they soon recognised me, and to my delight I saw them draw towards me.

We soon closed off the Owers, and she ran alongside of me in a very pretty style, threw a rope into me, and two or three midshipmen ran down, laid hold of me, and helped me up the side. Of course, I bowed to the captain and stated who I was. The officers of the gun-room invited me down to take some refreshment, and the purser, Mr Morgan, lent me a clean shirt. The captain questioned me very much about the coast, and promised me that he would take back the boat, as it evidently belonged to a poor man, though I heard afterwards he put her on the beach somewhere on the coast of Sussex. Being near a little gun brig going into Portsmouth, he put me on board her with the lieutenant in command.

I went to the admiral's office, where I was introduced to the flag lieutenant—a very kindhearted old fellow, who saw that I was much fatigued, and said he knew my brother, and told me that if I would go over to the George Inn and get a good night's rest, he would have my brother there by nine o'clock the next morning. About that time I was handed into the presence of two admirals, one resigning, Sir Roger Curtis, the other, Sir Richard Bickerton, taking office. Neither of these important functionaries deigned to notice me. The flag lieutenant asked them if they had any commands for this gentleman, to which he received from each the curt answer, "No," and he beckoned me to go out with him. He then told me that my brother had arrived, and on emerging from the admiral's office, he discovered my brother, saying to him at the instant, "There, Jackson, that's what I've brought you."

My brother was greatly affected at this unexpected meeting. He had been summoned by the flag lieutenant that morning to appear at the admiral's office, without being informed for what purpose, and as he had made up his mind that something unpleasant was afloat, the deception was all the more powerful. He had considered me dead long since, as it turned out that Captain Fane to whom I had entrusted a message for my surviving parent—my mother—had forgotten to deliver it.

I now lost no time in going home to join my mother, and here I reaped in the embraces of a kind and rejoicing parent a full reward for the toils and hardships of the last few painful years of my life.

. . .

*Quite remarkably, Jackson experienced little animosity while a fugitive in France. In fact, he recounts many instances of kindness, even admiration, behind enemy lines. For the two frigates that treated Captain Shortland's Junon so roughly, however, no succor was available. They received payment in kind by the Royal Navy. On May 20, 1811, the* Renommée *was taken along with the frigate* Néréide *off Madagascar, while* Renommée's *consort, the* Clorinde, *fled in ignominy, abandoning her mates to a squadron of four British frigates. (The* Renommée *was taken in to the Royal Navy and renamed the* Java; *she surrendered to the USS* Constitution *in 1812.)*

*While Jackson relentlessly pursued escape on the continent, James Durand, an American sailor, embarked on a lengthy and unexpected cruise of his own. His account shows the grim reality of Britain's frequently wanton practice of impressment, a condition that exacerbated the growing animosity felt between the United States and Britain and that, in part, led to the War of 1812. On another level, it is a tale that exhibits once again the resilience and resourcefulness of an able-bodied seaman, no matter his nationality.*

# JAMES DURAND

## The Woodwind Is Mightier than the Sword

### 1809-1812

*B orn in Connecticut in 1786, James Durand turned to the sea follow-*
*ing a five-year apprenticeship as a farmer. He entered the United*
*States Navy in 1804 and served on board the* John Adams *and the* Constitution *in the Mediterranean. At the beginning of this passage, he is*
*serving on board a Swedish merchant brig that is about to sail from Ply-*
*mouth, England. HMS* Narcissus, *the crew of which so rudely interrupts*
*Durand's repose, is a fifth rate of thirty-two guns built in 1801.*

AT LENGTH we were ordered out to sea. The men wished for a little pleasure on shore before we sailed and asked the captain for permission.

"I have no objections," he said, "but there is a very hot press on shore
and you'll all do better to stay on board."

This caution had no effect on the plans of the men and they accordingly
went. I was afraid of the press and stayed on board.

While they were away, about 11 o'clock at night, there came along side
a boat belonging to the *Narcissus* frigate. They boarded our brig and they
came below where I was asleep. With much abuse, they hauled me out of
my bed, not suffering me to even put on or take anything except my
trowsers.

In this miserable condition, I was taken on board their ship but did not
think to be detained there for a term of seven years. Had I known my destiny that night, I would have instantly committed the horrid crime of self-
murder. In this sorrowful condition I spent the night. At day light, I found

my way on deck and soon after heard the word given to un-moor the ship and get her ready for sea.

At this, I was overcome by grief. I ran below and tried to procure some paper, pen and ink from the members of the crew, offering any price. I was able to offer money, as I had concealed some of my savings by tying the coins in a handkerchief about my neck. The robbers who took my money from my belt did not find this horde. However, no member of the crew durst sell me pen, ink nor paper, as they guessed my intention of writing for aid to escape from a hateful service.

There came along side a boat with stuff to sell. For a shilling, I procured a sheet of paper on which I wrote a letter to the captain of the brig. I desired him to break open my chest and take out my protection and indenture and send them on board as quick as possible. I hired the boat to take this message to him immediately. The message boat made all possible speed; she had a mile and one-half to go, yet she went with such rapidity that in one hour and one-half after, the captain was on board with my indenture and protection.

The lieutenant of the *Narcissus* said he could do nothing about clearing me, but told the captain of the brig that if he (the captain) would go ashore and see the captain of the frigate, he would direct him where to find him.

There is an island to pass between the spot where we lay on the frigate and the town. It is called Drake's Island. It was my bad fortune that the captain of the brig carrying my protection and indenture passed on one side of this isle in the message boat, while the captain of the *Narcissus* passed it on the other side. Therefore they missed each other and my last chance of regaining my liberty was gone. As soon as our captain arrived on the *Narcissus*, he weighed anchor and put out to sea. I never saw the captain of the brig again.

In this unfortunate manner, I was dragged on board a British man-of-war, August 21, 1809. Despair so complete seized my mind, that I lost all relish for the world. For the first twelve days thereafter, my entire victualing would not have amounted to the one ration as it was allowed us.

I lost, as I left behind me on the brig, more than 50 pounds sterling, a chest full of excellent and well-chosen clothes. Only lately I had quitted the service of the U. States' after enduring everything. The thought of serving with the British fleet touched every nerve with distress and almost deprived me of reason. I had been eight years from home and I began to despair of ever seeing that place again.

After I had been on board a few days, the captain called me to the quarter deck and asked me if I would enter. He said that if I would, he would give me five pounds.

I utterly refused, telling him I was an American. I also said I would not do duty if I could help it.

"If you will not work I'll flog you until you're glad to set about it," said the captain. "Go below, for I won't hear another word out of you."

Below decks, I found twelve more Americans who had been previously impressed. One of them told me that, when he refused to obey an order, the captain had given him four dozen lashes. "Therefore," said he to me, "I advise you to do as you are bid."

I thought this excellent advice and I went to work and made myself as contented as possible. I concluded I would write to the American consul when we came to port again.

We voyaged to France and lay to off the port of Nantz. Near us lay the *Shannon*, on which I was detained a prisoner when they took the American brig as a prize. Some of the *Shannon*'s crew told me I had better have stayed with them.[1]

"Our captain is twice as clever as the captain of the *Narcissus*," they said.

"Yes," I replied, "I'd give the devil one if he'd take the other."

At length, I was noticed by our captain and put in the gig boat. Our allowance for food was so small that I began to lose flesh. One night the gig boat was ordered to go thirty miles from the ship under cover of the darkness, to a place called Horse Island. This lies about four miles from the main land. A great many small boats come out there to pass it by, and our purpose was to capture them.

The island was uninhabited except for five wild horses we saw there. We had only two days provisions with us and, as we stayed there five days, we were forced to shoot one of the horses for food. Neither did we durst make much fire, through fear of being seen from the main land and being surprised and captured. However we made a little fire that just scorched the outside of the meat, which we ate with a great relish, notwithstanding that we had no salt to put on it.

We returned to the frigate after the fifth day on the island. We were not put on duty the morning we returned, which we considered a great favor. The next day again, we were sent off in the same boat, to try if our luck would be better.

This time we took five prizes and brought them to the frigate. They were full of stores and supplies for General Napoleon. They were small craft, called "chamois," of five to 25 tons burden.

[1] *In 1807, Durand was on board an American merchant brig that ran the British blockade of France. As the brig was leaving Belle Isle, France, bound for the West Indies, she was taken by the British frigate Shannon.*

Our captain, considering my forwardness in taking and securing these boats, gave me better usage than I had previously received.[1] We lay off Nantz for six months, then returned to Plymouth. At once I wrote to our consul at London, but I have since then been informed that my letters as well as those of other impressed Americans, were intercepted. Even the petitions which the consul made were little noticed and many a sailor brought himself to an untimely end through despair, in consequence of this cruelty and oppression which is called British courage and justice.

We were informed that the French fleet had escaped from Brest. We were ordered to Barbadoes with despatches to inform Admiral [Sir Alexander] Cochrane of their escape.

## IN THE WEST INDIES AGAIN
## AS A BRITISH SAILOR

On our way we captured a French merchantman which was bound for Martinico. These are the particulars of it. Eighteen days out from Brest, early one morning, we espied a sail upon our weather, standing with the wind in her starboard quarter. She was about two leagues distant, with her studding sails set. We gave chase, but since we had the wind directly aft, we hauled our wind on the starboard tack and took in our leeward studding sails.

Soon after we came within gun shot. We gave her a bow shot to the windward, to bring her to, but she still stood on her course. Then we hauled a little to the wind and gave her several shots until at length we shot

---

[1] British Navy officers seemed to hold a high opinion of Americans as fighting men. Frequent comments are made, although sometimes in a sneering tone, of the capabilities of the Yankees as fighters and navigators. But Michael Scott ("Tom Cringle's Log"—*Blackwood's Magazine*, 1829–1830) gave an estimate which is worth repeating.

Scott, born in Glasgow in 1789, lived in Jamaica, the West Indies, for many years. He was a careful observer and shrewd commentator upon men and events between 1806 and 1817. "More of contemporary life can be learned from Scott than from all the official papers and documents of the time" (Adams).

"I don't like Americans," Scott said. "I never did and I never shall. I have seldom met an American gentleman, in the large and complete sense of the term. I have no wish to eat with them, drink with them, deal or consort with them in any way. But let me tell the whole truth— *nor to fight with them*, were it not for the laurels to be acquired by overcoming an enemy so brave, determined, alert and in every way so worthy of one's steel as they have always proved.

"In the field, or grappling in mortal combat on the blood-slippery quarter deck of an enemy's vessel, a British soldier or sailor is the bravest of the brave. No soldier or sailor of any country, *saving and excepting always those damned Yankees*, can stand against them."

*(The italics and punctuation do not appear in the original.)*

away her main-top-mast, at which she hove to. When we came within pistol shot, we put out our boat and brought her crew on board. She was a brig, richly laden with cordage and provisions and mounting one 21-pounder.

We put 18 men and a lieutenant on board her and ordered her to the Barbadoes. On the 25th day we arrived there ahead of our prize. We tarried but two hours, having learned that Martinico had surrendered to His Majesty's forces. We sailed for that port where we found the fleet riding out the bay of Port Royal. We delivered the despatches to the admiral and watered ship.

Next the *Narcissus* was ordered to cruise to the windward, keeping out a sharp look for the French fleet which had escaped from Brest. On the third day, we discovered a French corvette making in for the island. We kept to the leeward of her for three days sailing, but when another sail came between her and the island, we were able to come within reach of shot.

Upwards of 100 shots were exchanged, before she struck her colors to us. She was a national corvette, mounting 22 guns. We put a prize master on board and sent her to St. Pierre. In the course of 12 days' cruise, we had but one man killed and we made four prizes.

Then we returned to port to make ready to take part in an expedition against the Saints, a small island lying about five leagues to the westward of Guadaloupe. From thence we were to proceed to Barbadoes to take in troops destined for the operation against the island.

We took transport ships under our convoy. They had 2,000 troops on board them, which force was to make the attack. We were obliged to land the men in flat bottomed boats, under cover of our cannon. We did this in the space of two hours.

One of our light vessels was sent up to keep the fort in play until the land attack could be formed. Our men took two mortar pieces on shore and planted them. While we were busy at this, three French sail of the line and two of their frigates slipped out and escaped us.

Then our land party under General Walter made a noble assault in every part of the island. They resisted us for ten hours then retired to the forts for safety. We kept up the siege for five days.

## WOUNDED BY A FRENCH SHOT

I was one of a party which, on the fifth morning, was making a breast works and platform on which we were to plant some more mortars. While working there, an 18-pound shot from them struck the planking next me and a splinter of it broke my leg just below the calf. I was taken to the surgeon's tent, where a temporary dressing was put on, then was sent to the cock-pit on board the *Narcissus*, where I underwent a more careful dressing of my hurt.

The following night, the forts surrendered. I never knew the conditions of the surrender. The British lost, in killed and wounded, more than 300 men. The islanders' loss was said to be more than 700. The wounded were all taken on board and after a common attendance with our own people, were received as prisoners of war.

I was allowed to be confined in a cot as the condition of my leg would not permit me to make use of a hammock. All I could do was to ruminate on the various incidents of my life and there was nothing to prevent these reflections but the pain of my leg. Therefore, like Hamlet, I reasoned with myself. I had been in the service of the British for more than a year and if I continued seven more, I decided I would see my limbs scattered all over the globe and like the wages promised me by the U. States' service, it would get me nothing material.

"If I kill or am killed," said I to myself, "who is there to benefit except King George?"

> The world's a stately bark—
> On dangerous seas
> To be boarded at your peril,

said I, with the poet.

In the meantime, we victualed, watered and got ready for sea in the harbor of Port Royal. Here they had some talk of sending me on shore; but through fear of my escape, they changed their minds and continued me on board.

We cruised for three weeks and made several attacks on a French frigate of superior metal, but as the weather was boisterous, we could not board her. On the last attempt, we were parted by a heavy gale just as the sun went down. In the morning the French frigate had either gone down in the storm or made her escape.

They did us so much damage with their shot between wind and water and with balls which carried a part of our rigging away that we were obliged to go into port to repair the damages.

During this battle, I lay on my cot in an extraordinary uneasyness, wishing to fight rather than to have our colors strike but more because of bravado and pride than because of any self interest in the outcome. But the thought of lying there still while there was so much thunder overhead was, at the same time, insupportable to me. Had not the surgeon's attendants kept me in, I would have stood at my gun and served it.

However, after the affray was over, when the surgeon examined all the wounded, he found my leg still inflamed. He conceived that all was not right. Therefore he measured and found my injured leg one inch shorter than the other. As a result, I was forced to bear the painful operation of having it broken all over again and newly set. In this condition I was slowly recovering for 60 days before I could be called a "tight sailor" as the saying is, or fit for duty.

Next we were ordered to England, after we had picked up two officers at St. Thomas who were being returned. We arrived in Plymouth July 17, 1810. Here we waited for six or seven weeks for repairs. I was not allowed to go on shore nor to converse with boats that came alongside. I was then put at the business of sail making.

Next we were sent to France to cruise off L'Orient. We found a French brig and schooner lying in Coneall Bay. The brig mounted 14 guns and had 150 men on board. Accordingly, we attempted to cut them out of the bay with our ship's boats. Five boats and fifty men were selected for this purpose.

We rowed five miles with the tide and came up near the French sail about 8 o'clock in the evening. They hailed us.

"Are you coming to pay us a visit?" they asked.

"Yes," was our answer and we gave them three cheers.

"Come along, we're ready," said they.

Our boats took their station, one on each quarter. The master's boat was in the center. We attempted to board the brig, but we met with every resistance, as they were fully prewarned against our attack.

As we came along side I attempted to board her by seizing hold of a small cannon whose muzzle protruded through an open port. Finding it impossible to get a footing at this point, I stepped back. I had no sooner done so than she discharged her whole contents at our boat.

Then I attempted to board her by seizing hold of the netting, but I was met by two of their men armed with boarding pikes. I drew a pistol and killed one of them on the spot. I could not reload, as I must keep one hand in the netting, so I killed the other with my second pistol. Then I attempted to board her, sword in hand, but was severely wounded in my leg.

After a while, I grew weak from the loss of blood and fell back into our boat. Two of our boats were destroyed, ten men killed and fifteen wounded. We retreated.

While they were rowing us away, a shot hit the stern of our boat. She took in water very fast and we would all have been drowned there, had not one of the men plugged the hole with the head of a dead man who had been killed at the discharge of the cannon.

With other wounded, I was sent to the hospital at Plymouth, where I was cared for 31 days. I applied for my discharge but it was refused me. My reputation for courage in a fight prevented my being discharged, as it gained me interest from the officers, so that they would not suffer me to go.[1]

The captain was transferred to another ship and Captain Almyer took command. By his direction, I joined the musicians thinking it easier to play an instrument in the ship's band than to do ship's duty. There was a first rate instructor and for three weeks while we chased French privateers, my chief work was blowing on a flute. Gradually I gained some proficiency at it.

The captain now purchased new instruments equal to a full band. I learned the claronet. Even this did not occupy my mind and I longed to return to my own home and my own country. One day, I asked for permission to go ashore. Captain Almyer refused me.

"For," said he, "you will escape and will be caught and flogged through the fleet."

Nevertheless, I resolved to escape but the guards were so plenty that I had no chance to put my design into execution. Then the fleet sailed for Spain. There were the frigates *Amazon, Dryad, Arathusa* and *Narcissus*. We took on board some Spanish troops whom we carried to St. Antony and landed them there in spite of the French who had possession of the place. However there was later a battle in which the French general was killed with a great many of his men, but for all that, they chased the Spanish troops up into the mountains and forced us back on the ships.

The *Amazon*, a Spanish frigate and our *Narcissus* were ordered to Corunna. The wind was ahead, so we put into Vevarrow Bay for the night. The Spanish frigate anchored ahead of us. In the night a great wind arose and she dragged her anchors. Then she drifted on our bow. Our rigging was tangled and her fore-yards, our fore-mast and main-mast all came down on the deck together. Then she dropped astern of us and ran foul of a Spanish brig, whose cable parted. They both ran ashore and only 18 men from their crews of 750 men were saved. This was Nov. 21st, 1811.

On our ship, two men were killed and eighteen injured by the falling of the masts. In the morning, the crew of the *Amazon* came aboard us to help repair the damage. We worked for four days and then put to sea, to go to Plymouth to refit.

---

[1] Durand was not the only American prisoner who was found "too good to be discharged."

"The British were keen to impress American sailors, who proved themselves the best seamen in the King's Navy. For that reason the British were loath to abandon their practice of search and seizure" (Lossing).

A tremendous storm came up. The wind tore our sails to pieces. With every surf, we expected to go to the bottom, as our stern was shattered by the falling masts. She took in a great deal of water, and for days the wind blew the most violently I have ever experienced in many years service. Through God's mercy we were spared. So we put into Plymouth dock to repair.

## A TRIP ON SHORE
## AFTER THREE YEARS' IMPRESSMENT

When a ship undergoes a careful repairing, it is customary to take off her deck, pull her down to the keel and build her up with new timbers. In such a case, it takes three to four months to refit. If the captain has any influence with the Admiralty, he is allowed to retain his hands, instead of recruiting anew. To save them for him, they are sent aboard a hulk for quarters until the ship is again ready for sea. This was the case with us. Our stores, guns and supplies were taken out of the *Narcissus*, and we went aboard a hulk while they repaired her.

I had now been three years in the service, and I thought it high time to go on shore. I asked the captain for permission, and he said I might, if I would give him my promise not to make my escape. So I went with the musicians who had orders to watch me, although I did not know it at the time. I stayed on shore for 24 hours, enjoying every kind of diversion I thought proper, and then I returned to the hulk.

At that place, ships are built with great expedition. I saw a 74 gun ship launched from the stocks on June 21, 1812 and the same day hauled from her ways into a dry dock. On the 22nd, carpenters were employed coppering her bottom, on the 23rd, she came out of dock and was beside a sheer hulk where she took in her masts and bowsprit. Next she was hauled to the hulk where she was to be rigged. On the 24th, the shrouds were put over her mast-head and the dead eyes turned in, the lower rigging rattled down, fore and aft, her bowsprit shrouds and bob-stays put on, all three top masts pointed through and made ready for swaying away before 12 o'clock. Hands were then piped to dinner and turned up at 1 o'clock. The top masts were swayed, their rigging set up, the fore-castle men rigged, their jib and flying-jib boom after guard, the spanker boom sent up, the fore and main yard and top-sail yards were sent up.

While some of the men were bending the fore and main sail, the fore, main and mizzen-top sails were bent; main-top-mast and middle and top-gallant stay sails bent; jib and spanker bent; mizzen-stay-sail, top sails, top gallant halyards rove, fore and main braces rove; likewise all the running rigging that was necessary. All this was done by sun set. On the 25th, one-half the ship's company was employed on one side of the ship taking on guns, while the other half, on the other side, the larboard, were taking in provisions, stores and water.

On the 26th, she was complete and ready for sea and on the 28th, of the same month, she joined the Channel fleet. To explain the manner in which they rig a ship so quickly, the reader will understand that the rigging is already fitted in the dock yard, before the ship is launched. All they have to do is put it in a lighter, bring it alongside and put it in its place.

I must here make mention of our crew which our captain was so loath to part with; he applied to the Admiralty and got a grant to keep them in the temporary hulk for three months, expecting that his ship would be over-hauled and ready to sail at the end of that time. However, the ship carpenters found her hull so rotten that she was obliged to undergo six months repairs. The crew was accordingly drafted.

It is a courtesy that is always extended to captains to allow them to keep their own boat's crew. When our crew was drafted away, the captain chose to keep the band instead. So we were sent aboard the *St. Salvadore,* a guard ship, to await his pleasure. Now she had been a Spanish ship of 120 guns which the British had captured. She had on board 1,750 men, including prisoners. Here we were to tarry, I mean the band, until our captain was ready for sea. I went on board this ship March 7, 1812, and left her February 19, 1813.

•  •  •

*On June 18, 1812, war broke out between the United States and Britain. Durand complained bitterly about the unfair treatment of American sailors serving in the Royal Navy during the war. Against his will, he served through 1815 and even saw service in American waters. In his memoir, he reported that he was threatened with hanging, put in irons, and kept on water and maggoty bread for refusing to take part on the attack on Stonington, Connecticut.*

# Part IV

## The Napoleonic War, Continued, and the War of 1812

SAMUEL LEECH

*⟅⟆*

# HMS *Macedonian* vs. USS *United States*

## 1812

*T*he war between Britain and the United States was not one of great
*fleet actions. In fact, the fledgling U.S. Navy had no fleet of line-of-
battle ships. In that sense, King George III's Royal Navy, perhaps the most
dominant naval force in history, was forced to fight down a level and on relatively equal terms. While the big ships of the Royal Navy blockaded the
U.S. coast unchallenged, it was Britain's frigates that would do the high-
profile fighting. The U.S. Navy did have powerfully built, heavy frigates.
At first, the proud, fighting frigate captains of the British Navy did not
realize or would not acknowledge that they were simply outgunned by the
large U.S. frigates.*

*Samuel Leech, R.N., fought in the brutal October 25, 1812, battle between
the 38-gun HMS* Macedonian, *commanded by Captain John Surman Carden,
and the 44-gun USS* United States, *Commodore Stephen Decatur. Leech's valuable account of this classic mismatch is one of the most telling of a naval action
of the time. It lacks the characteristic reserve of the period. His honest introspec-
tion and grim detail paint a darker, more realistic picture than is normally
the case.*

AT PLYMOUTH we heard some vague rumors of a declaration of war
against America. More than this, we could not learn, since the utmost care
was taken to prevent our being fully informed. The reason of this secrecy
was, probably, because we had several Americans in our crew, most of
whom were pressed men, as before stated. These men, had they been cer-

tain that war had broken out, would have given themselves up as prisoners of war, and claimed exemption from that unjust service, which compelled them to act with the enemies of their country. This was a privilege which the magnanimity of our officers ought to have offered them. They had already perpetrated a grievous wrong upon them in impressing them; it was adding cruelty to injustice to compel their service in a war against their own nation. But the difficulty with naval officers is, that they do not treat with a sailor as with a *man*. They know what is fitting between each other as officers; but they treat their crews on another principle; they are apt to look at them as pieces of living mechanism, born to serve, to obey their orders, and administer to their wishes without complaint. This is alike a bad morality and a bad philosophy. There is often more real manhood in the forecastle than in the ward-room; and until the common sailor is treated *as a man,* until every feeling of human nature is conceded to him in naval discipline—perfect, rational subordination will never be attained in ships of war, or in merchant vessels. It is needless to tell of the intellectual degradation of the mass of seamen. "A man's a man for a' that;" and it is this very system of discipline, this treating them as automatons, which keeps them degraded. When will human nature put more confidence in itself?

Leaving Plymouth, we next anchored, for a brief space, at Torbay, a small port in the British Channel. We were ordered thence to convoy a huge East India merchant vessel, much larger than our frigate and having five hundred troops on board, bound to the East Indies with money to pay the troops stationed there. We set sail in a tremendous gale of wind. Both ships stopped two days at Madeira to take in wine and a few other articles. After leaving this island, we kept her company two days more; and then, according to orders, having wished her success, we left her to pursue her voyage, while we returned to finish our cruise.

Though without any positive information, we now felt pretty certain that our government was at war with America. Among other things, our captain appeared more anxious than usual; he was on deck almost all the time; the "look-out" aloft was more rigidly observed; and every little while the cry of "Mast-head there!" arrested our attention.

It is customary in men of war to keep men at the fore and main mast-heads, whose duty it is to give notice of every new object that may appear. They are stationed in the royal yards, if they are up, but if not, on the top-gallant yards: at night a look-out is kept on the fore yard only.

Thus we passed several days; the captain running up and down and constantly hailing the man at the mast-head: early in the morning he began his charge "to keep a good look-out," and continued to repeat it until night.

Indeed, he seemed almost crazy with some pressing anxiety. The men felt there was something anticipated, of which they were ignorant; and had the captain heard all their remarks upon his conduct, he would not have felt very highly flattered. Still, everything went on as usual; the day was spent in the ordinary duties of man-of-war life, and the evening in telling stories of things most rare and wonderful; for your genuine old tar is an adept in spinning yarns, and some of them, in respect to variety and length, might safely aspire to a place beside the great magician of the north, Sir Walter Scott, or any of those prolific heads that now bring forth such abundance of fiction to feed a greedy public, who read as eagerly as our men used to listen. To this yarn-spinning was added the most humorous singing, sometimes dashed with a streak of the pathetic, which I assure my readers was most touching; especially one very plaintive melody, with a chorus beginning with,

> *"Now if our ship should be cast away,*
> *It would be our lot to see old England no more,"*

which made rather a melancholy impression on my boyish mind, and gave rise to a sort of presentiment that the *Macedonian* would never return home again; a presentiment which had its fulfilment in a manner totally unexpected to us all. The presence of a shark for several days, with its attendant pilot fish, tended to strengthen this prevalent idea.

The Sabbath came, and it brought with it a stiff breeze. We usually made a sort of holiday of this sacred day. After breakfast it was common to muster the entire crew on the spar deck, dressed as the fancy of the captain might dictate; sometimes in blue jackets and white trowsers, or blue jackets and blue trowsers; at other times in blue jackets, scarlet vests, and blue or white trowsers with our bright anchor buttons glancing in the sun, and our black, glossy hats, ornamented with black ribbons, and with the name of our ship painted on them. After muster, we frequently had church service read by the captain; the rest of the day was devoted to idleness. But we were destined to spend the Sabbath, just introduced to the reader, in a very different manner.

We had scarcely finished breakfast, before the man at the mast-head shouted, "Sail ho!"

The captain rushed upon deck, exclaiming, "Mast-head there!"

"Sir!"

"Where away is the sail?"

The precise answer to this question I do not recollect, but the captain proceeded to ask, "What does she look like?"

"A square-rigged vessel, sir," was the reply of the look-out.

After a few minutes, the captain shouted again, "Mast-head there!"

"Sir!"

"What does she look like?"

"A large ship, sir, standing toward us!"

By this time, most of the crew were on deck, eagerly straining their eyes to obtain a glimpse of the approaching ship and murmuring their opinions to each other on her probable character. Then came the voice of the captain, shouting, "Keep silence, fore and aft!" Silence being secured, he hailed the look-out, who, to his question of "What does she look like?" replied, "A large frigate, bearing down upon us, sir!"

A whisper ran along the crew that the stranger ship was a Yankee frigate. The thought was confirmed by the command of "All hands clear the ship for action, ahoy!" The drum and fife beat to quarters; bulk-heads were knocked away; the guns were released from their confinement; the whole dread paraphernalia of battle was produced; and after the lapse of a few minutes of hurry and confusion, every man and boy was at his post, ready to do his best service for his country, except the band, who, claiming exemption from the affray, safely stowed themselves away in the cable tier. We had only one sick man on the list, and he, at the cry of battle, hurried from his cot, feeble as he was, to take his post of danger. A few of the junior midshipmen were stationed below, on the berth deck, with orders, given in our hearing, to shoot any man who attempted to run from his quarters.

Our men were all in good spirits; though they did not scruple to express the wish that the coming foe was a Frenchman rather than a Yankee. We had been told, by the Americans on board, that frigates in the American service carried more and heavier metal than ours. This, together with our consciousness of superiority over the French at sea, led us to a preference for a French antagonist.

The Americans among our number felt quite disconcerted at the necessity which compelled them to fight against their own countrymen. One of them, named John Card, as brave a seaman as ever trod a plank, ventured to present himself to the captain, as a prisoner, frankly declaring his objections to fight. That officer, very ungenerously, ordered him to his quarters, threatening to shoot him if he made the request again. Poor fellow! He obeyed the unjust command and was killed by a shot from his own countrymen. This fact is more disgraceful to the captain of the *Macedonian* than even the loss of his ship. It was a gross and a palpable violation of the rights of man.

As the approaching ship showed American colors, all doubt of her character was at an end. "We must fight her," was the conviction of every breast. Every possible arrangement that could insure success was accordingly made. The guns were shotted; the matches lighted; for, although our guns were all furnished with first-rate locks they were also provided with matches, attached by lanyards, in case the lock should miss fire. A lieutenant then passed through the ship, directing the marines and boarders, who were furnished with pikes, cutlasses, and pistols, how to proceed if it should be necessary to board the enemy. He was followed by the captain, who exhorted the men to fidelity and courage, urging upon their consideration the well-known motto of the brave Nelson, "England expects every man to do his duty." In addition to all these preparations on deck, some men were stationed in the tops with small-arms, whose duty it was to attend to trimming the sails and to use their muskets, provided we came to close action. There were others also below, called sail trimmers, to assist in working the ship should it be necessary to shift her position during the battle.

My station was at the fifth gun on the main deck. It was my duty to supply my gun with powder, a boy being appointed to each gun in the ship on the side we engaged, for this purpose. A woollen screen was placed before the entrance to the magazine, with a hole in it, through which the cartridges were passed to the boys; we received them there, and covering them with our jackets, hurried to our respective guns. These precautions are observed to prevent the powder taking fire before it reaches the gun.

Thus we all stood, awaiting orders, in motionless suspense. At last we fired three guns from the larboard side of the main deck; this was followed by the command, "Cease firing; you are throwing away your shot!"

Then came the order to "wear ship," and prepare to attack the enemy with our starboard guns. Soon after this I heard a firing from some other quarter, which I at first supposed to be a discharge from our quarter deck guns; though it proved to be the roar of the enemy's cannon.

A strange noise, such as I had never heard before, next arrested my attention; it sounded like the tearing of sails, just over our heads. This I soon ascertained to be the wind of the enemy's shot. The firing, after a few minutes' cessation, recommenced. The roaring of cannon could now be heard from all parts of our trembling ship, and, mingling as it did with that of our foes, it made a most hideous noise. By-and-by I heard the shot strike the sides of our ship; the whole scene grew indescribably confused and horrible; it was like some awfully tremendous thunder-storm, whose deafening roar is attended by incessant streaks of lightning, carrying death in every flash and strewing the ground with the victims of its wrath: only, in our case, the scene was rendered more horrible than that, by the presence of torrents of blood which dyed our decks.

Though the recital may be painful, yet, as it will reveal the horrors of war and show at what a fearful price a victory is won or lost, I will present the reader with things as they met my eye during the progress of this dreadful fight. I was busily supplying my gun with powder, when I saw blood suddenly fly from the arm of a man stationed at our gun. I saw nothing strike him; the effect alone was visible; in an instant, the third lieutenant tied his handkerchief round the wounded arm, and sent the groaning wretch below to the surgeon.

The cries of the wounded now rang through all parts of the ship. These were carried to the cockpit as fast as they fell, while those more fortunate men, who were killed outright, were immediately thrown overboard. As I was stationed but a short distance from the main hatchway, I could catch a glance at all who were carried below. A glance was all I could indulge in, for the boys belonging to the guns next to mine were wounded in the early part of the action, and I had to spring with all my might to keep three or four guns supplied with cartridges. I saw two of these lads fall nearly together. One of them was struck in the leg by a large shot; he had to suffer amputation above the wound. The other had a grape or canister shot sent through his ancle. A stout Yorkshireman lifted him in his arms and hurried him to the cockpit. He had his foot cut off, and was thus made lame for life. Two of the boys stationed on the quarter deck were killed. They were both Portuguese. A man, who saw one of them killed, afterwards told me that his powder caught fire and burnt the flesh almost off his face. In this pitiable situation, the agonized boy lifted up both hands, as if imploring relief, when a passing shot instantly cut him in two.

I was an eye-witness to a sight equally revolting. A man named Aldrich had one of his hands cut off by a shot, and almost at the same moment he received another shot, which tore open his bowels in a terrible manner. As he fell, two or three men caught him in their arms, and, as he could not live, threw him overboard.

One of the officers in my division also fell in my sight. He was a noble-hearted fellow, named Nan Kivell. A grape or canister shot struck him near the heart: exclaiming, "Oh! my God!" he fell, and was carried below, where he shortly after died.

Mr. Hope, our first lieutenant, was also slightly wounded by a grummet, or small iron ring, probably torn from a hammock clew by a shot. He went below, shouting to the men to fight on. Having had his wound dressed, he came up again, shouting to us at the top of his voice, and bidding us fight with all our might. There was not a man in the ship but would have rejoiced had he been in the place of our master's mate, the unfortunate Nan Kivell.

The battle went on. Our men kept cheering with all their might. I cheered with them, though I confess I scarcely knew for what. Certainly there was nothing very inspiriting in the aspect of things where I was stationed. So terrible had been the work of destruction round us, it was termed the slaughter-house. Not only had we had several boys and men killed or wounded, but several of the guns were disabled. The one I belonged to had a piece of the muzzle knocked out; and when the ship rolled, it struck a beam of the upper deck with such force as to become jammed and fixed in that position. A twenty-four-pound shot had also passed through the screen of the magazine, immediately over the orifice through which we passed our powder. The schoolmaster received a death wound. The brave boatswain, who came from the sick bay to the din of battle, was fastening a stopper on a back-stay which had been shot away, when his head was smashed to pieces by a cannon-ball; another man, going to complete the unfinished task, was also struck down. Another of our midshipmen also received a severe wound. The unfortunate ward-room steward, who, the reader will recollect, attempted to cut his throat on a former occasion, was killed. A fellow named John, who, for some petty offence, had been sent on board as a punishment, was carried past me, wounded. I distinctly heard the large blood-drops fall pat, pat, pat, on the deck; his wounds were mortal. Even a poor goat, kept by the officers for her milk, did not escape the general carnage; her hind legs were shot off, and poor Nan was thrown overboard.

Such was the terrible scene, amid which we kept on our shouting and firing. Our men fought like tigers. Some of them pulled off their jackets, others their jackets and vests; while some, still more determined, had taken off their shirts, and, with nothing but a handkerchief tied round the waistbands of their trowsers, fought like heroes. Jack Sadler, whom the reader will recollect, was one of these. I also observed a boy, named Cooper, stationed at a gun some distance from the magazine. He came to and fro on the full run and appeared to be as "merry as a cricket." The third lieutenant cheered him along, occasionally, by saying, "Well done, my boy, you are worth your weight in gold."

I have often been asked what were my feelings during this fight. I felt pretty much as I suppose every one does at such a time. That men are without thought when they stand amid the dying and the dead is too absurd an idea to be entertained a moment. We all appeared cheerful, but I know that many a serious thought ran through my mind: still, what could we do but keep up a semblance, at least, of animation? To run from our quarters would have been certain death from the hands of our own officers; to give way to gloom, or to show fear, would do no good, and might brand us with the name of cowards, and ensure certain defeat. Our only true philosophy, therefore, was to make the best of our situation by fighting bravely and cheerfully. I thought a great deal, however, of the other world; every groan, every falling man, told me that the next instant I might be before the Judge of all the earth. For this, I felt unprepared; but being without any particular knowledge of religious truth, I satisfied myself by repeating again and again the Lord's prayer and promising that if spared I would be more attentive to religious duties than ever before. This promise I had no doubt, at the time, of keeping; but I have learned since that it is easier to make promises amidst the roar of the battle's thunder, or in the horrors of ship-wreck, than to keep them when danger is absent and safety smiles upon our path.

While these thoughts secretly agitated my bosom, the din of battle continued. Grape and canister shot were pouring through our port-holes like leaden rain, carrying death in their trail. The large shot came against the ship's side like iron hail, shaking her to the very keel, or passing through her timbers and scattering terrific splinters, which did a more appalling work than even their own death-giving blows. The reader may form an idea of the effect of grape and canister, when he is told that grape shot is formed by seven or eight balls confined to an iron and tied in a cloth. These balls are scattered by the explosion of the powder. Canister shot is made by filling a powder canister with balls, each as large as two or three musket balls; these also scatter with direful effect when discharged. What then with splinters, cannon balls, grape and canister poured incessantly upon us, the reader may be assured that the work of death went on in a manner which must have been satisfactory even to the King of Terrors himself.

Suddenly, the rattling of the iron hail ceased. We were ordered to cease firing. A profound silence ensued, broken only by the stifled groans of the brave sufferers below. It was soon ascertained that the enemy had shot ahead to repair damages, for she was not so disabled but she could sail without difficulty; while we were so cut up that we lay utterly helpless. Our head braces were shot away; the fore and main top-masts were gone; the mizzen mast hung over the stern, having carried several men over in its fall: we were in the state of a complete wreck.

A council was now held among the officers on the quarter deck. Our condition was perilous in the extreme: victory or escape was alike hopeless. Our ship was disabled; many of our men were killed, and many more wounded. The enemy would without doubt bear down upon us in a few moments, and, as she could now choose her own position, would without doubt rake us fore and aft. Any further resistance was therefore folly. So, in spite of the hot-brained lieutenant, Mr. Hope, who advised them not to strike, but to sink alongside, it was determined to strike our bunting. This was done by the hands of a brave fellow named Watson, whose saddened brow told how severely it pained his lion heart to do it. To me it was a pleasing sight, for I had seen fighting enough for one Sabbath; more than I wished to see again on a week day. His Britannic Majesty's frigate *Macedonian* was now the prize of the American frigate *United States*.

Before detailing the subsequent occurrences in my history, I will present the curious reader with a copy of Captain Carden's letter to the government, describing this action. It will serve to show how he excused himself for his defeat, as well as throw some light on those parts of the contest which were invisible to me at my station. My mother presented me with this document on my return to England. She had received it from Lord Churchill and had carefully preserved it for twenty years.

*"Admiralty Office,*
*Dec. 29, 1812.*

*"Copy of a letter from Captain John Surman Carden, late commander of His Majesty's ship the* Macedonian, *to John Wilson Croker, Esq., dated on board the American ship* United States, *at sea, the 28th October, 1812:—*

*"Sir: It is with the deepest regret, I have to acquaint you, for the information of my Lords Commissioners of the Admiralty, that His Majesty's late ship* Macedonian *was captured on the 25th instant, by the United States ship* United States, *Commodore Decatur commander. The detail is as follows:*

*"A short time after daylight, steering NW by W, with the wind from the southward, in latitude 29° N, and longitude 29° 30' W, in the execution of their Lordships' orders, a sail was seen on the lee beam, which I immediately stood for, and made her out to be a large frigate, under American colors. At nine o'clock I closed with her, and she commenced the action, which we returned; but from the enemy keeping two points off the wind, I was not enabled to get as close to her as I could have wished. After an hour's action, the enemy backed and came to the wind, and I was then enabled to bring her to close battle. In this situation I soon found the enemy's force too superior to expect success, unless some very fortunate chance occurred in our favor; and with this hope I continued the battle to two hours and ten minutes; when, having the mizzen mast shot away by the board, topmasts shot away by the caps, main yard shot in pieces, lower masts badly wounded, lower rigging all cut to pieces, a small proportion only of the fore-sail left to the foreyard, all the guns on the quarter deck and forecastle disabled but two, and filled with wreck, two also on the main deck disabled, and several shot between wind and water, a*

*very great proportion of the crew killed and wounded, and the enemy compara-
tively in good order, who had now shot ahead and was about to place himself in a
raking position, without our being enabled to return the fire, being a perfect wreck
and unmanageable log; I deemed it prudent, though a painful extremity, to surrender His Majesty's ship; nor was this dreadful alternative resorted to till every
hope of success was removed, even beyond the reach of chance; nor till, I trust their
Lordships will be aware, every effort had been made against the enemy by myself,
and my brave officers and men, nor should she have been surrendered whilst a man
lived on board, had she been manageable. I am sorry to say our loss is very severe;
I find by this day's muster, thirty-six killed, three of whom lingered a short time
after the battle; thirty-six severely wounded, many of whom cannot recover, and
thirty-two slightly wounded, who may all do well; total, one hundred and four.*

*"The truly noble and animating conduct of my officers, and the steady bravery
of my crew, to the last moment of the battle, must ever render them dear to their
country.*

*"My first lieutenant, David Hope, was severely wounded in the head, towards
the close of the battle, and taken below; but was soon again on deck, displaying that
greatness of mind and exertion, which, though it may be equalled, can never be
excelled. The third lieutenant, John Bulford, was also wounded, but not obliged to
quit his quarters; second lieutenant, Samuel Mottley, and he deserves my highest
acknowledgments. The cool and steady conduct of Mr. Walker, the master, was
very great during the battle, as also that of Lieutenants Wilson and Magill, of the
Marines.*

*"On being taken on board the enemy's ship, I ceased to wonder at the result of
the battle. The* United States *is built with the scantling[1] of a 74-gun ship, mounting thirty long 24-pounders (English ship-guns) on her main deck, and twenty-
two 42-pounders, carronades, with two long 24-pounders, on her quarter deck and
forecastle, howitzer guns in her tops, and a travelling carronade on her upper deck,
with a complement of four hundred and seventy-eight picked men.*

*"The enemy has suffered much in masts, rigging, and hull, above and below
water. Her loss in killed and wounded I am not aware of; but I know a lieutenant
and six men have been thrown overboard.*

*JNO. S. CARDEN*

*"To J. W. CROKER, Esq., Admiralty."*

Lord Churchill sent the above letter, with a list of the killed and
wounded annexed, to inform my mother that the name of her son was not

---

[1] *The dimensions of the structural parts of a vessel regarded collectively.*

among the number. The act shows how much he could sympathize with a mother's feelings.

⚊

I NOW WENT below, to see how matters appeared there. The first object I met was a man bearing a limb, which had just been detached from some suffering wretch. Pursuing my way to the ward-room, I necessarily passed through the steerage, which was strewed with the wounded: it was a sad spectacle, made more appalling by the groans and cries which rent the air. Some were groaning, others were swearing most bitterly, a few were praying, while those last arrived were begging most piteously to have their wounds dressed next. The surgeon and his mate were smeared with blood from head to foot: they looked more like butchers than doctors. Having so many patients, they had once shifted their quarters from the cockpit to the steerage; they now removed to the ward-room, and the long table, round which the officers had sat over many a merry feast, was soon covered with the bleeding forms of maimed and mutilated seamen.

While looking round the ward-room, I heard a noise above, occasioned by the arrival of the boats from the conquering frigate. Very soon a lieutenant, I think his name was Nicholson, came into the ward-room and said to the busy surgeon, "How do you do, doctor?"

"I have enough to do," replied he, shaking his head thoughtfully; "you have made wretched work for us!" These officers were not strangers to each other, for the reader will recollect that the commanders and officers of these two frigates had exchanged visits when we were lying at Norfolk some months before.

I now set to work to render all the aid in my power to the sufferers. Our carpenter, named Reed, had his leg cut off. I helped to carry him to the after ward-room; but he soon breathed out his life there, and then I assisted in throwing his mangled remains overboard. We got out the cots as fast as possible; for most of them were stretched out on the gory deck. One poor fellow, who lay with a broken thigh, begged me to give him water. I gave him some. He looked unutterable gratitude, drank, and died. It was with exceeding difficulty I moved through the steerage, it was so covered with mangled men and so slippery with streams of blood. There was a poor boy there crying as if his heart would break. He had been servant to the bold boatswain, whose head was dashed to pieces. Poor boy! he felt that he had lost a friend. I tried to comfort him by reminding him that he ought to be thankful for having escaped death himself.

Here, also, I met one of my messmates, who showed the utmost joy at seeing me alive, for, he said, he had heard that I was killed. He was looking up his messmates, which he said was always done by sailors. We found two of our mess wounded. One was the Swede, Logholm, who fell overboard, as mentioned in a former chapter, and was nearly lost. We held him while the surgeon cut off his leg above the knee. The task was most painful to behold, the surgeon using his knife and saw on human flesh and bones as freely as the butcher at the shambles does on the carcass of the beast! Our other messmate suffered still more than the Swede; he was sadly mutilated about the legs and thighs with splinters. Such scenes of suffering as I saw in that ward-room, I hope never to witness again. Could the civilized world behold them as they were, and as they often are, infinitely worse than on that occasion, it seems to me they would forever put down the barbarous practices of war, by universal consent.

Most of our officers and men were taken on board the victor ship. I was left, with a few others, to take care of the wounded. My master, the sailing-master, was also among the officers, who continued in their ship. Most of the men who remained were unfit for any service, having broken into the spirit-room and made themselves drunk; some of them broke into the purser's room and helped themselves to clothing; while others, by previous agreement, took possession of their dead messmates' property. For my own part, I was content to help myself to a little of the officers' provisions, which did me more good than could be obtained from rum. What was worse than all, however, was the folly of the sailors in giving spirit to their wounded messmates, since it only served to aggravate their distress.

Among the wounded was a brave fellow named Wells. After the surgeon had amputated and dressed his arm, he walked about in fine spirits, as if he had received only a slight injury. Indeed, while under the operation, he manifested a similar heroism—observing to the surgeon, "I have lost my arm in the service of my country; but I don't mind it, doctor, it's the fortune of war." Cheerful and gay as he was, he soon died. His companions gave him rum; he was attacked by fever and died. Thus his messmates actually killed him with kindness.

We had all sorts of dispositions and temperaments among our crew. To me it was a matter of great interest to watch their various manifestations. Some who had lost their messmates appeared to care nothing about it, while others were grieving with all the tenderness of women. Of these was the survivor of two seamen who had formerly been soldiers in the same regiment; he bemoaned the loss of his comrade with expressions of profoundest grief. There were, also, two boatswain's mates, named Adams and Brown, who had been messmates for several years in the same ship.

Brown was killed, or so wounded that he died soon after the battle. It was really a touching spectacle to see the rough, hardy features of the brave old sailor streaming with tears, as he picked out the dead body of his friend from among the wounded and gently carried it to the ship's side, saying to the inanimate form he bore, "O Bill, we have sailed together in a number of ships, we have been in many gales and some battles, but this is the worst day I have seen! We must now part!" Here he dropped the body into the deep, and then, a fresh torrent of tears streaming over his weather-beaten face, he added, "I can do no more for you. Farewell! God be with you!" Here was an instance of genuine friendship, worth more than the heartless professions of thousands, who, in the fancied superiority of their elevated position in the social circle, will deign nothing but a silly sneer at this record of a sailor's grief.

The circumstance was rather a singular one, that in both the contending frigates the second boatswain's mate bore the name of William Brown, and that they both were killed; yet such was the fact.

The great number of the wounded kept our surgeon and his mate busily employed at their horrid work until late at night; and it was a long time before they had much leisure. I remember passing round the ship the day after the battle. Coming to a hammock, I found some one in it apparently asleep. I spoke; he made no answer. I looked into the hammock; he was dead. My messmates coming up, we threw the corpse overboard; that was no time for useless ceremony. The man had probably crawled to his hammock the day before, and, not being perceived in the general distress, bled to death! O War! who can reveal thy miseries!

When the crew of the *United States* first boarded our frigate to take possession of her as their prize, our men, heated with the fury of the battle, exasperated with the sight of their dead and wounded shipmates, and rendered furious by the rum they had obtained from the spirit-room, felt and exhibited some disposition to fight their captors. But after the confusion had subsided and part of our men were snugly stowed away in the American ship, and the remainder found themselves kindly used in their own, the utmost good feeling began to prevail. We took hold and cleansed the ship, using hot vinegar to take out the scent of the blood that had dyed the white of our planks with crimson. We also took hold and aided in fitting our disabled frigate for her voyage. This being accomplished, both ships sailed in company toward the American coast.

I soon felt myself perfectly at home with the American seamen; so much so that I chose to mess with them. My shipmates also participated in similar feelings in both ships. All idea that we had been trying to shoot out each other's brains so shortly before seemed forgotten. We eat together, drank together, joked, sung, laughed, told yarns; in short, a perfect union of ideas, feelings, and purposes seemed to exist among all hands.

A corresponding state of unanimity existed, I was told, among the officers. Commodore Decatur showed himself to be a gentleman as well as a hero in his treatment of the officers of the *Macedonian*. When Captain Carden offered his sword to the commodore, remarking, as he did so, "I am an undone man. I am the first British naval officer that has struck his flag to an American": the noble commodore either refused to receive the sword or immediately returned it, smiling as he said, "You are mistaken, sir; your *Guerriere* has been taken by us, and the flag of a frigate was struck before yours." This somewhat revived the spirits of the old captain; but, no doubt, he still felt his soul stung with shame and mortification at the loss of his ship. Participating as he did in the haughty spirit of the British aristocracy, it was natural for him to feel galled and wounded to the quick, in the position of a conquered man.

We were now making the best of our way to America. Notwithstanding the patched-up condition of the *Macedonian*, she was far superior, in a sailing capacity, to her conqueror. The *United States* had always been a dull sailer, and had been christened by the name of the Old Wagon. Whenever a boat came alongside of our frigate and the boatswain's mate was ordered to "pipe away" the boat's crew, he used to sound his shrill call on the whistle and bawl out, "Away, *Wagoners*, away," instead of "away, *United States* men, away." This piece of pleasantry used to be rebuked by the officers, but in a manner that showed they enjoyed the joke. They usually replied, "Boatswain's mate, you rascal, pipe away *United States* men, not Wagoners. We have no wagoners on board of a ship." Still, in spite of rebuke, the joke went on, until it grew stale by repetition. One thing was made certain however by the sailing qualities of the *Macedonian*; which was, that if we had been disposed to escape from our foe before the action, we could have done so with all imaginable ease. This however, would have justly exposed us to disgrace, while our capture did not. There was every reason why the *United States* should beat us. She was larger in size, heavier in metal, more numerous in men, and stronger built than the *Macedonian*. Another fact in her favor was that our captain at first mistook her for the *Essex*, which carried short carronades, hence he engaged her at long shot at first; for, as we had the weather gage, we could take what position we pleased. But this maneuver only wasted our shot and gave her the advantage, as she actually carried larger metal than we did. When we came to close action, the shot from the *United States* went "through and through" our ship, while ours struck her sides and fell harmlessly into the water. This is to be accounted for both by the superiority of the metal and of the ship. Her guns

were heavier and her sides thicker than ours. Some have said that her sides
were stuffed with cork. Of this, however, I am not certain. Her superiority,
both in number of men and guns, may easily be seen by the following sta-
tistics. We carried forty-nine guns; long eighteen-pounders on the main
deck, and thirty-two-pound carronades on the quarter deck and forecastle.
Our whole number of hands, including officers, men and boys, was three
hundred. The *United States* carried four hundred and fifty men and fifty-
four guns: long twenty-four-pounders on the main deck, and forty-two-
pound carronades on the quarter deck and forecastle. So that in actual force
she was immensely our superior.

To these should be added the consideration that the men in the two
ships fought under the influence of different motives. Many of our hands
were in the service against their will; some of them were Americans,
wrongfully impressed and inwardly hoping for defeat: while nearly every
man in our ship sympathized with the great principle for which the American nation so nobly contended in the war of 1812. What that was, I suppose all my readers understand. The British, at war with France, had
denied the Americans the right to trade thither. She had impressed American seamen and forcibly compelled their service in her navy; she had violated the American flag by insolently searching their vessels for her
runaway seamen. Free trade and sailors' rights, therefore, were the objects
contended for by the Americans. With these objects our *men* could but sympathize, whatever our officers might do.

On the other hand, the crew of our opponent had all shipped *voluntar-
ily* for the term of two years only (most of our men were shipped for life).
They understood what they fought for; they were better used in the service.
What wonder, then, that victory adorned the brows of the American commander? To have been defeated under such circumstances would have
been a source of lasting infamy to any naval officer in the world. In the matter of fighting, I think there is but little difference in either nation. Place
them in action under equal circumstances and motives, and who could pre-
dict which would be victor? Unite them together, they would subject the
whole world. So close are the alliances of blood, however, between
England and America, that it is to be earnestly desired, they may never
meet in mortal strife again. If either will fight, which is to be deprecated as
a crime and a folly, let it choose an enemy less connected by the sacred ties
of consanguinity.

Our voyage was one of considerable excitement. The seas swarmed
with British cruisers, and it was extremely doubtful whether the *United
States* would elude their grasp and reach the protection of an American
port with her prize. I hoped most sincerely to avoid them, as did most of

my old shipmates; in this we agreed with our captors, who wisely desired to dispose of one conquest before they attempted another. Our former officers, of course, were anxious for the sight of a British flag. But we saw none, and, after a prosperous voyage from the scene of conflict, we heard the welcome cry of "Land ho!" The *United States* entered the port of New London; but, owing to a sudden shift of the wind, the *Macedonian* had to lay off and on for several hours. Had an English cruiser found us in this situation, we should have been easily recovered; and, as it was extremely probable we should fall in with one, I felt quite uneasy, until, after several hours, we made out to run into the pretty harbor of Newport. We fired a salute as we came to an anchor, which was promptly returned by the people on shore.

With a few exceptions, our wounded men were in a fair way to recover by the time we reached Newport. The last of them, who died of their wounds on board, was buried just before we got in. His name was Thomas Whittaker; he had been badly wounded by splinters. While he lived, he endured excessive torture. At last his sufferings rendered him crazy, in which sad state he died. He was sewed up in his hammock by his messmates and carried on a grating to the larboard bow port. There Mr. Archer, a midshipman of the *Macedonian*, read the beautiful burial service of the church of England. When he came to that most touching passage, "we commit the body of our brother to the deep," the grating was elevated, and, amid the most profound silence, the body fell heavily into the waters. As it dropped into the deep, a sigh escaped from many a friendly bosom, and an air of passing melancholy shrouded many a face with sadness. Old recollections were busy there, calling up the losses of the battle; but it was only momentary. The men brushed away their tears, muttered "It's no use to fret," and things once more wore their wonted aspect.

At Newport our wounded were carried on shore. Our former officers also left us here. When my master, Mr. Walker, took his leave of me, he appeared deeply affected. Imprinting a kiss on my cheek, the tears started from his eyes, and he bade me adieu. I have not seen him since.

• • •

*While the* Macedonian *suffered around 104 killed and wounded, the* United States *had only a dozen killed or wounded. Decatur had fought well, and his much sturdier ship had protected her crew. The prize eventually sailed from Newport, Rhode Island, to New York, where Leech, a resourceful sort, made money giving tours of her while describing the battle. Leech went on to serve in the United States Navy.*

*Along with the losses of the* Guerriere *(August 19, 1812) and the* Java *(December 29, 1812) to the USS* Constitution, *the capture of the* Macedonian *was shocking news to the British, whose experience so far had dictated that any Royal Navy frigate should defeat any frigate of any other nation. The Royal Navy had other problems as well. Hundreds of pesky American privateers, defying the British blockade of the American coast, took to the North Atlantic and Caribbean waters to troll for British merchantmen. Though they rarely attacked British warships, they could be amazingly brazen in British waters. U.S. privateers managed to take more than a thousand merchant vessels, although many of them were retaken on their way into United States ports for condemnation.*

GEORGE LITTLE

*⌒*

# An Unjustifiable and
# Outrageous Pursuit
## 1812-1813

*Despite the frequent unfairness and cruelty of naval life, the rigorous rules
and severe punishments for transgressing them ultimately brought a certain respectableness and pride to the service, especially in "happy" ships, governed
by fair and competent commanders. Serving one's country augmented that pride.
Privateering, on the other hand, was considered by many as an activity only a
notch more respectable than piracy, and very frequently resembled it.*

*In this passage, a young merchant seaman unlucky at business, George Little,
originally from Massachusetts, finds himself compelled to ship on board a privateer at the outbreak of hostilities between Britain and the United States. During
its wartime cruises, the privateer* Paul Jones, *on which Little eventually ends up,
was captained by J. Hazzard and later A. Taylor. Carrying a complement of 120
men and pierced for seventeen guns, she was originally woefully underarmed.
With a show of men in the rigging and cut-off masts painted black to resemble
cannon (along with three real ones), she bluffed a fourteen-gun British merchantman into submission and thus equipped herself for future battles, of which she
would see many.*

I SAILED on my sixth voyage, and arrived safely in Buenos Ayres. After
having been there a few days, another vessel arrived from Rio, having persons on board with powers to attach my vessel and cargo. I soon learned
that the house at Rio in whose employment I sailed had failed for a large
amount, and that these persons were their creditors. I was now left without
a vessel, and, fearing that I should lose the funds placed in their hands, lost

no time in getting back to Rio; and when there, I found the condition of the house even worse than I had anticipated; for all my two years' hard earnings were gone, with the exception of about five hundred dollars.

With this small sum I took passage in the ship *Scioto*, bound for Baltimore. I was induced to do this because little doubt was then entertained that there would be a war between the United States and England, and I was anxious to get home, if possible, before it was declared. We were fortunate enough to arrive in safety, although the war had been actually declared fifteen days before we got inside of the Capes of Virginia. When we arrived in Baltimore, I found the most active preparations were in progress to prosecute the war. A number of privateers were fitting out; and every where the American flag might be seen flying, denoting the places of rendezvous; in a word, the most intense excitement prevailed throughout the city, and the position of a man was not at all enviable if it were ascertained that he was in any degree favorably disposed towards the British. It happened to fall to my lot to be an eye-witness to the unpleasant affair of tarring and feathering a certain Mr. T., and also to the demolishing of the Federal Republican printing-office by the mob.

Once more I returned to Boston to see my friends, whom I found pretty much in the same situation as when I left them. Two years had made but little alteration, except that my sister was married, and my father, being aged, had retired from the Navy, and taken up his residence in Marshfield. Every persuasion was now used to induce me to change my vocation, backed by the strong reasoning that the war would destroy commerce, and that no alternative would be left for seamen but the unhallowed pursuit of privateering. These arguments had great weight, and I began to think seriously of entering into some business on shore; but then most insuperable difficulties arose in my mind as to the nature of the business I should pursue. My means were limited, quite too much so to enter into the mercantile line; and the only branch of it with which I was acquainted being the "commission," another obstacle presented itself, which was to fix upon an eligible location. These difficulties, however, soon vanished, for a wealthy relative offered me the use of his credit, and a young friend with whom I was acquainted, having just returned from the south, informed me that there was a fine opening in Richmond, Virginia; whereupon we immediately entered into a mutual arrangement to establish a commission-house in that place. The necessary preparations were made, and we started for the south.

To my great surprise and mortification, however, when we reached Norfolk, I ascertained that my partner was without funds; neither had he the expectation of receiving any. This changed the current of my fortunes altogether. I was deceived by him; consequently all intercourse was broken off between us. As my prospects were now blasted, in reference to establishing myself in business on shore, I resolved once more to embark on my favorite element, and try my luck there again. Here too, in Norfolk, all was bustle and excitement—drums beating, colors flying, soldiers enlisting, men shipping in the States' service, and many privateers fitting out,—creating such a scene of confusion as I had never before witnessed.

Young, and of an ardent temperament, I could not look upon all these stirring movements an unmoved spectator; accordingly, I entered on board the *George Washington* privateer, in the capacity of first lieutenant. She mounted one twelve-pounder on a pivot and two long nines, with a complement of eighty men. She was in all respects a beautiful schooner, of the most exact symmetrical proportions, about one hundred and twenty tons' burden, and said to be as swift as any thing that floated the ocean. In reference to this enterprise, I must confess, in my cooler moments, that I had some qualms: to be sure, here was an opportunity of making a fortune; but then it was counterbalanced by the possibility of getting my head knocked off, or a chance of being thrown into prison for two or three years: however, I had gone too far to recede, and I determined to make the best of it. Accordingly, I placed what little funds I had in the hands of Mr. G., of Norfolk, and repaired on board of the privateer, with my dunnage contained in a small trunk and clothes-bag. On the morning of July 20th, 1812, the officers and crew being all on board, weighed anchor, made sail, and stood down the river, with the stars and stripes floating in the breeze, and was saluted with a tremendous cheering from the shore. I now was on board of a description of craft with which I was entirely unacquainted; I had, therefore, much to learn. The lieutenants and prize-masters, however, were a set of clever fellows; but the captain was a rough, uncouth sort of a chap and appeared to me to be fit for little else than fighting and plunder. The crew were a motley set indeed, composed of all nations; they appeared to have been scraped together from the lowest dens of wretchedness and vice, and only wanted a leader to induce them to any acts of daring and desperation. Our destination, in the first place, was to cruise on the Spanish main to intercept the English traders between the West India Islands and the ports on the main. This cruising ground was chosen because, in case of need, we might run into Carthagena to refit and water. When we had run down as far as Lynnhaven Bay, information was received from a pilot-boat that the British frigate *Belvidere* was cruising off the Capes. This induced our captain to put to sea with the wind from the southward, as the privateer's best sailing was on a wind.

On the morning of 22d of July, got under way from Lynnhaven Bay, and stood to sea. At 9 A.M., when about 10 miles outside of Cape Henry lighthouse, a sail was discovered directly in the wind's eye of us, bearing down under a press of canvass. Soon ascertaining she was a frigate, supposed to be the *Belvidere,* we stood on upon a wind until she came within short gunshot. Our foresail was now brailed up and the topsail lowered on the cap; at the same time, the frigate took in all her light sails and hauled up her courses. As the privateer lay nearer the wind than the frigate, the latter soon dropped in our wake, and when within half-gunshot, we being under cover of her guns, she furled her top-gallant sails; at the same moment we hauled aft the fore sheet, hoisted away the topsail, and tacked. By this maneuver the frigate was under our lee. We took her fire, and continued to make short boards, and in one hour were out of the reach of her guns, without receiving any damage. This was our first adventure, and we hailed it as a good omen. The crew were all in high spirits, because the frigate was considered to be as fast as any thing on our coast at that time, and, furthermore, the captain had not only gained the confidence of the crew by this daring maneuver, but we found we could rely upon our heels for safety.

Nothing material occurred until we got into the Mona passage, when we fell in with the *Black Joke* privateer, of New York; and being unable to ascertain her character, in consequence of a thick fog, we came into collision and exchanged a few shots, before we found out we both wore the same national colors. This vessel was a sloop of not very prepossessing appearance; but as she had obtained some celebrity for sailing in smooth water, having previously been an Albany packet, she was fitted out as a privateer. In a sea-way, however, being very short, she could not make much more head-way than a tub. It was agreed, between the respective captains of the two vessels, to cruise in company, and in the event of a separation, to make a rendezvous at Carthagena. We soon ascertained that our craft would sail nearly two knots to the *Black Joke*'s one, and it may well be supposed that our company-keeping was of short duration. In two days after parting with her, the long-wished-for cry of "Sail ho!" was sung out from the mast-head. Made all sail in chase. When within short gunshot, let her have our midship gun, when she immediately rounded to, took in sail, hoisted English colors, and seemed to be preparing to make a gallant defence. In this we were not mistaken, for as we ranged up, she opened a brisk cannonading upon us. I now witnessed the daring intrepidity of Captain S.; for, while the brig was pouring a destructive fire into us, with the greatest coolness he observed to the crew, "That vessel, my lads, must be ours in ten minutes after I run this craft under her lee quarter." By this time we had sheered up under her stern, and received the fire of her stern-chasers, which did us no other damage than cutting away some of our ropes and making wind-holes through the sails. It was the work of a moment; the schooner luffed up under the lee of the brig, and, with almost the rapidity of thought, we were made fast to her main chains. "Boarders away!" shouted Capt. S. We clambered up the sides of the brig, and dropped on board of her like so many locusts, not, however, till two of our lads were run through with boarding-pikes. The enemy made a brave defence, but were soon overpowered by superior numbers, and the captain of the brig was mortally wounded. In twenty minutes after we got along-side, the stars and stripes were waving triumphantly over the British flag. In this affair, we had two killed and seven slightly wounded, besides hav-ing some of our rigging cut away, and sails somewhat riddled. The brig was from Jamaica, bound to the Gulf of Maracaibo[1], her cargo consisted of sugar, fruit, &c. She was two hundred tons' burden, mounted six six-pounders, with a complement of fifteen men, all told. She was manned with a prize-master and crew, and ordered to any port in the United States wherever she could get in.

This affair very much disgusted me with privateering, especially when I saw so much loss of life, and beheld a band of ruthless desperadoes—for such I must call our crew—robbing and plundering a few defenceless beings, who were pursuing both a lawful and peaceable calling. It induced me to form a resolve that I would relinquish what, to my mind, appeared to be an unjustifiable and outrageous pursuit; for I could not then help believing that no conscientious man could be engaged in privateering, and certainly there was no honor to be gained by it. The second lieutenant came to the same determination as myself; and both of us most cordially despised our commander, because it was with his permission that those most outrageous scenes of robbing and plundering were committed on board of the brig. After repairing damages, &c., we steered away for Carthagena to fill up the water-casks and provision the privateer, so that we might extend the cruise.

IN A FEW days we arrived at our destination, without falling in with any other vessel; and, on entering the port, we found our comrade, the *Black Joke* privateer, which had arrived a day or two previously. Carthagena lies in the parallel of 10° 26′ north, and 75° 38′ west longitude; the harbor is good, with an easy entrance; the city is strongly fortified by extensive and commanding fortifications and batteries, and I should suppose, if well gar-risoned and manned, they would be perfectly able to repel any force which might be brought to bear against them. It was well known, at this time, that

[1] *In modern-day Venezuela.*

all the provinces of Spain had shaken off their allegiance to the mother country and declared themselves independent. Carthagena, the most prominent of the provinces, was a place of considerable commerce; and about this time, a few men-of-war and a number of privateers were fitted out there. The Carthagenian flag now presented a chance of gain to the cupidity of the avaricious and desperate, among whom was our commander, Capt. S. As soon, therefore, as we had filled up our water, &c., a proposition was made by him, to the second lieutenant and myself, to cruise under both flags, the American and Carthagenian, and this to be kept a profound secret from the crew, until we had sailed from port. Of course we rejected the proposition with disdain and told him the consequence of such a measure, in the event of being taken by a man-of-war of any nation—that it was piracy to all intents and purposes, according to the law of nations. We refused to go out in the privateer if he persisted in this most nefarious act, and we heard no more of it while we lay in port.

In a few days we were ready for sea and sailed in company with our companion, her force being rather more than ours, but the vessel very inferior, as stated before, in point of sailing. While together, we captured several small British schooners, the cargoes of which, together with some specie, were divided between the two privateers. Into one of the prizes we put all the prisoners, gave them plenty of water and provisions, and let them pursue their course: the remainder of the prizes were burned. We then parted company, and, being short of water, ran in towards the land, in order to ascertain if any could be procured. In approaching the shore, the wind died away to a perfect calm, and, at 4 P.M., a small schooner was seen in shore of us. As we had not steerage way upon our craft, of course it would be impossible to ascertain her character before dark; it was, therefore, determined by our commander to board her with the boats, under cover of the night. This was a dangerous service, but there was no backing out. Volunteers being called for, I stepped forward; and very soon, a sufficient number of men to man two boats offered their services to back me. Every disposition was made for the attack. The men were strongly armed, oars muffled, and a grappling placed in each boat. The bearings of the strange sail were taken, and night came on perfectly clear and cloudless. I took command of the expedition, the second lieutenant having charge of one boat. The arrangement was to keep close together, until we got sight of the vessel; the second lieutenant was to board on the bow and I on the quarter. We proceeded in the most profound silence; nothing was heard, save now and then a slight splash of the oars in the water, and before we obtained sight of the vessel I had sufficient time to reflect on this most perilous enterprise.

My reflections were not of the most pleasant character, and I found myself inwardly shrinking, when I was aroused by the voice of the bow-man, saying, "There she is, sir, two points on the starboard bow." There she lay, sure enough, with every sail hoisted, and a light was distinctly seen, as we supposed, from her deck, it being too high for the cabin-windows. We now held a consultation and saw no good reason to change the disposition of attack, except that we agreed to board simultaneously. It may be well to observe here that any number of men on a vessel's deck, in the night, have double the advantage to repel boarders, because they may secrete themselves in such a position as to fall upon an enemy unawares, and thereby cut them off with little difficulty. Being fully aware of this, I ordered the men as soon as we gained the deck of the schooner—proceed with great caution—and keep close together, till every hazard of the enter-prise was ascertained. The boats now separated and pulled for their respective stations, observing the most profound silence. When we had reached within a few yards of the schooner, we lay upon our oars for some moments, but could neither hear nor see any thing. We then pulled away cheerily, and the next minute were under her counter, and grappled to her; every man leaped on the deck without opposition. The other boat boarded nearly at the same moment, and we proceeded in a body, with great cau-tion, to examine the decks. A large fire was in the caboose, and we soon ascertained that her deck was entirely deserted, and that she neither had any boat on deck, nor to her stern. We then proceeded to examine the cabin, leaving an armed force on deck. The cabin, like the deck, being deserted, the mystery was easily unravelled. Probably concluding that we should board them under cover of the night, they, no doubt, as soon as it was dark, took to their boats and deserted the vessel. On the floor of the cabin was a part of an English ensign and some papers, which showed that she belonged to Jamaica. The little cargo on board consisted of Jamaica rum, sugar, fruit, &c.

The breeze now springing up, and the privateer showing lights, we were enabled to get alongside of her in a couple of hours. A prize-master and crew were put on board, with orders to keep company. During the night, we ran along shore, and, in the morning, took on board the privateer the greater part of the prize's cargo.

Being close in shore in the afternoon, we descried a settlement of huts; and, supposing that water might be obtained there, the two vessels were run in and anchored about two miles distant from the beach. A proposition was made to me, by Capt. S., to get the water-casks on board the prize schooner, and, as she drew a light draught of water, I was to run her in and anchor her near the beach, taking with me the two boats and twenty men.

I observed to Capt. S. that this was probably an Indian settlement, and it was well known that all the Indian tribes on the coast of Rio de La Hache were exceedingly ferocious, and said to be cannibals; and it was also well known that whoever fell into their hands never escaped with their lives; so that it was necessary, before any attempt was made to land, that some of the Indians should be decoyed on board and detained as hostages for our safety. At the conclusion of this statement, a very illiberal allusion was thrown out by Capt. S. and some doubts expressed in reference to my courage; he remarking that if I was afraid to undertake the expedition, he would go himself. This was enough for me; I immediately resolved to proceed, if I sacrificed my life in the attempt. The next morning, twenty water-casks were put on board the prize, together with the two boats and twenty men, well armed with muskets, pistols, and cutlasses, with a supply of ammunition; I repaired on board, got the prize under way, ran in, and anchored about one hundred yards from the beach. The boats were got in readiness, and the men were well armed, and the water-casks slung, ready to proceed on shore. I had examined my own pistols narrowly that morning and had put them in complete order, and, as I believed, had taken every precaution for our future operations, so as to prevent surprise.

There were about a dozen ill-constructed huts, or wigwams; but no spot of grass or shrub was visible to the eye, with the exception of, here and there, the trunk of an old tree. One solitary Indian was seen stalking on the beach, and the whole scene presented the most wild and savage appearance, and, to my mind, augured very unfavorably. We pulled in with the casks in tow, seven men being in each boat; when within a short distance of the beach, the boats' heads were put to seaward, when the Indian came abreast of us. Addressing him in Spanish, I inquired if water could be procured, to which he replied in the affirmative. I then displayed to his view some gewgaws and trinkets, at which he appeared perfectly delighted, and, with many signs and gestures, invited me on shore. Thrusting my pistols into my belt and buckling on my cartridge-box, I gave orders to the boats' crews that in case they discovered any thing like treachery or surprise after I had gotten on shore, to cut the water-casks adrift and make the best of their way on board the prize. As soon as I had jumped on shore, I inquired if there were any live stock, such as fowls, &c., to be had. Pointing to a hut about thirty yards from the boats, he said that the stock was there and invited me to go and see it. I hesitated, suspecting some treachery; however, after repeating my order to the boats' crews, I proceeded with the Indian, and when within about half a dozen yards of the hut, at a preconcerted signal (as I supposed), as if by magic, at least one hundred Indians rushed out, with the rapidity of thought. I was knocked down, stripped of all my clothing except an inside flannel shirt, tied hand and foot, and then taken and secured to the trunk of a large tree, surrounded by about twenty squaws, as a guard, who, with the exception of two or three, bore a most wild and hideous look in their appearance. The capture of the boats' crews was simultaneous with my own, they being so much surprised and confounded at the stratagem of the Indians that they had not the power, or presence of mind, to pull off.

After they had secured our men, a number of them jumped into the boats, pulled off, and captured the prize, without meeting with any resistance from those on board, they being only six in number. Her cable was then cut, and she was run on the beach, when they proceeded to dismantle her, by cutting the sails from the bolt-ropes and taking out what little cargo there was, consisting of Jamaica rum, sugar, &c. This being done, they led ropes on shore from the schooner, when about one hundred of them hauled her up nearly high and dry.

By this time the privateer had seen our disaster, stood boldly in, and anchored within less than gunshot of the beach; they then very foolishly opened a brisk cannonade, but every shot was spent in vain. This exasperated the Indians, and particularly the one who had taken possession of my pistols. Casting my eye around, I saw him creeping towards me with one pistol presented, and when about five yards off, he pulled the trigger. But as Providence had, no doubt, ordered it, the pistol snapped; at the same moment a shot from the privateer fell a few yards from us, when the Indian rose upon his feet, cocked the pistol, and fired it at the privateer; turning round with a most savage yell, he threw the pistol with great violence, which grazed my head, and then with a large stick beat and cut me until I was perfectly senseless. This was about 10 o'clock, and I did not recover my consciousness until, as I supposed, about 4 o'clock in the afternoon. I perceived there were four squaws sitting around me, one of whom, from her appearance (having on many gewgaws and trinkets), was the wife of a chief. As soon as she discovered signs of returning consciousness, she presented me with a gourd, the contents of which appeared to be Indian meal mixed with water; she first drank, and then gave it to me, and I can safely aver that I never drank any beverage, before or since, which produced such relief.

Night was now coming on; the privateer had got under way; and was standing off and on with a flag of truce flying at her mast-head. The treacherous Indian with whom I had first conversed came, and, with a malignant smile, gave me the dreadful intelligence that at 12 o'clock that night we were to be roasted and eaten.

Accordingly, at sunset I was unloosed and conducted by a band of about half a dozen savages to the spot, where I found the remainder of our men firmly secured by having their hands tied behind them, their legs lashed together, and each man fastened to a stake that had been driven into the ground for that purpose. There was no possibility to elude the vigilance of these miscreants. As soon as night shut in, a large quantity of brushwood was piled around us, and nothing now was wanting but the fire to complete this horrible tragedy. The same malicious savage approached us once more, and with the deepest malignity taunted us with our coming fate. Having some knowledge of the Indian character, I summoned up all the fortitude of which I was capable, and in terms of defiance told him that twenty Indians would be sacrificed for each one of us sacrificed by him. I knew very well that it would not do to exhibit any signs of fear or cowardice; and, having heard much of the cupidity of the Indian character, I offered the savage a large ransom if he would use his influence to procure our release. Here the conversation was abruptly broken off by a most hideous yell from the whole tribe, occasioned by their having taken large draughts of the rum, which now began to operate very sensibly upon them; and, as it will be seen, operated very much to our advantage. This thirst for rum caused them to relax their vigilance, and we were left alone to pursue our reflections, which were not of the most enviable or pleasant character. A thousand melancholy thoughts rushed over my mind. Here I was, and, in all probability, in a few hours I should be in eternity, and my death one of the most horrible description. "O," thought I, "how many were the entreaties and arguments used by my friends to deter me from pursuing an avocation so full of hazard and peril! If I had taken their advice and acceded to their solicitations, in all probability I should at this time have been in the enjoyment of much happiness." I was aroused from this reverie by the most direful screams from the united voices of the whole tribe, they having drunk largely of the rum, and become so much intoxicated that a general fight ensued. Many of them lay stretched on the ground with tomahawks deeply implanted in their skulls; and many others, as the common phrase is, were "dead drunk." This was an exceedingly fortunate circumstance for us. With their senses benumbed, of course they had forgotten their avowal to roast us, or, it may be, the Indian to whom I proposed ransom had conferred with the others, and they no doubt agreed to spare our lives until the morning. It was a night, however, of pain and terror, as well as of the most anxious suspense; and when the morning dawn broke upon my vision, I felt an indescribable emotion of gratitude, as I had fully made up in my mind, the night previous, that long before this time I should have been sleeping the sleep of death. It was a pitiable sight, when the morning light broke forth, to see twenty human beings stripped naked, with their bodies cut and lacerated and the blood issuing from their wounds; with their hands and feet tied and their bodies fastened to stakes, with brushwood piled around them, expecting every moment to be their last. My feelings on this occasion can be better imagined than described; suffice it to say that I had given up all hopes of escape and gloomily resigned myself to death. When the fumes of the liquor had in some degree worn off from the benumbed senses of the savages, they arose and approached us, and, for the first time, the wily Indian informed me that the tribe had agreed to ransom us. They then cast off the lashings from our bodies and feet, and, with our hands still secured, drove us before them to the beach. Then another difficulty arose; the privateer was out of sight, and the Indians became furious. To satiate their hellish malice, they obliged us to run on the beach, while they let fly their poisoned arrows after us. For my own part, my limbs were so benumbed that I could scarcely walk, and I firmly resolved to stand still and take the worst of it, which was the best plan I could have adopted; for, when they perceived that I exhibited no signs of fear, not a single arrow was discharged at me. Fortunately, before they grew weary of this sport, to my great joy the privateer hove in sight. She stood boldly in, with the flag of truce flying, and the savages consented to let one man of their own choosing go off in the boat to procure the stipulated ransom. The boat returned loaded with articles of various descriptions, and two of our men were released. The boat kept plying to and from the privateer, bringing with them such articles as they demanded, until all were released except myself. Here it may be proper to observe, that the mulatto man who had been selected by the Indians performed all this duty himself, not one of the privateer's crew daring to hazard their lives with him in the boat. I then was left alone, and for my release they required a double ransom. I began now seriously to think that they intended to detain me altogether. My mulatto friend, however, pledged himself that he would never leave me.

Again, for the last time, he sculled the boat off. She quickly returned, with a larger amount of articles than previously. It was a moment of the deepest anxiety, for there had now arrived from the interior another tribe, apparently superior in point of numbers and elated with the booty which had been obtained. They demanded a share and expressed a determination to detain me for a larger ransom. These demands were refused, and a conflict ensued of the most frightful and terrific character. Tomahawks, knives, and arrows were used indiscriminately, and many an Indian fell in that bloody contest. The tomahawks were thrown with the swiftness of arrows, and were generally buried in the skull or the breast; and whenever two came in contact, with the famous "Indian hug," the strife was soon over with either one or the other, by one plunging the deadly knife up to the hilt in the body of his opponent; nor were the poisoned arrows of less swift execution, for, wherever they struck, the wretched victim was quickly in eternity. I shall never forget the frightful barbarity of that hour; although years have elapsed since its occurrence, still the whole scene in imagination is before me—the savage yell of the warwhoop, and the direful screams of the squaws, still ring afresh in my ears. In the height of this conflict, a tall Indian chief, who, I knew, belonged to the same tribe with the young squaw who gave me the drink, came down to the beach where I was. The boat had been discharged and was lying with her head off. At a signal given by the squaw to the chief, he caught me up in his arms with as much ease as if I had been a child, waded to the boat, threw me in, and then, with a most expressive gesture, urged us off. Fortunately, there were two oars in the boat, and, feeble as I was, I threw all the remaining strength I had to the oar. It was the last effort, as life or death hung upon the next fifteen minutes. Disappointed of a share of the booty, the savages were frantic with rage, especially when they saw I had eluded their grasp. Rushing to the beach, about a dozen threw themselves into the other boat, which had been captured, and pulled after us; but fortunately, in their hurry they had forgotten the muskets, and being unacquainted with the method of rowing, of course they made but little progress, which enabled us to increase our distance.

The privateer, having narrowly watched all these movements, and seeing our imminent danger, stood boldly on toward the beach, and in the next five minutes she lay between us and the Indians, discharging a heavy fire of musketry among them. Such was the high excitement of my feelings, that I scarcely recollected how I gained the privateer's deck. But I was saved, nevertheless, though I was weak with the loss of blood and savage treatment—my limbs benumbed and body scorched with the piercing rays of the sun—the whole scene rushing through my mind with the celerity of electricity! It unmanned and quite overpowered me; I fainted and fell senseless on the deck.

THE USUAL restoratives and care were administered, and I soon recovered from the effects of my capture. Some of the others were not so fortunate; two of them especially were cut in a shocking manner, and the others were so dreadfully beaten and mangled by clubs that the greatest care was necessary to save their lives. My dislike for the captain had very much increased since that unhappy, disastrous affair; it would not have occurred if he had taken my advice, as his illiberality and the hints he threw out in reference to my courage were the causes of my suffering and the sad result of the enterprise. I determined, therefore, in conjunction with the second lieutenant, to leave the privateer as soon as we arrived in Carthagena, to which port we were now bound. We soon had a good pretext for putting this determination into execution; for, two days after the affair with the Indians, we fell in with a Spanish schooner, and, for the first time since leaving Carthagena, a commission and flag of the latter place were produced by Captain S. Under this commission and flag he captured the schooner, being deaf to every remonstrance that was made to him by us. The prize was manned and ordered to Carthagena, where she arrived two days after our entrance into that port. The second lieutenant and myself immediately demanded our discharge, and share of prize money, which were granted, when we received eighteen hundred dollars each, as our part of the captures. With these funds we purchased a fine coppered schooner, and succeeded in getting a freight and passengers for New Orleans. In about a week we sailed and bade adieu to the privateer and her unprincipled commander, who would at any time sacrifice honor and honesty and expose himself to the ignominious death of a pirate for sordid gain.

We arrived at New Orleans, after a passage of eleven days, without accident or interruption. Here all was excitement, as the news of the capture of the *Guerriere* frigate by the *Constitution* had just been received. Three large privateers were fitting out, from the commanders of which very tempting offers were thrown out to enter on board; but I had enough of privateering and considered it at that time a most unjustifiable mode of warfare; and, although I could not obtain business for our vessel, and the probability was that nothing would offer for some time, I resolved to remain on shore rather than to engage again in that nefarious calling.

New Orleans, at that period, was swayed by French and Spanish influence. The manners and customs of these people universally prevailed; consequently, presented to a mind trained under the strict regulation of moral precepts, the greatest degree of repugnance; and although, in my travels, I had frequently been among these people in South America, and, of course, had become acquainted, in some degree, with their habits, yet I could never reconcile the strongly-marked deviations from those principles of virtue and piety so prevalent in the other states and cities of North America. The consequence was that I soon became weary, and, as we could find no employment for our vessel, I embraced a most advantageous offer as first officer of a letter of marque, bound to Bourdeaux. No time was lost in settling the business of the schooner with my friend, and as he had also procured a berth, we gave a power of attorney to a merchant of high respectability, to act for us during our absence.

On the 8th October, 1812, the letter of marque being ready for sea, with the crew, &c., all on board, we cast off from the "Levee," dropped down the river, and on the 12th went out of the "north-east pass," and discharged our pilot. This vessel was a schooner of three hundred tons' burden, Baltimore-built, and of the most beautiful symmetrical proportions; she mounted ten guns, with a crew consisting of thirty men. Our commander was a native of New Orleans, a good seaman, possessing at the same time great affability of manners and great decision of character. The second officer was an old American seaman, rough in his exterior, yet, at the same time, frank, open, and generous, with a frame and constitution that seemed to defy the hardships of a sea life. The crew were a fine set of able seamen, and in such a craft I promised myself as much comfort as could be expected apart from the danger of capture and the perils of the sea.

Nothing material transpired until we reached the Maranilla Reef, when, on the morning of the 21st, we fell in with an English frigate. Fortunately for us, we were to the windward, or she would have crippled us, being within gun-shot. All sail was made on the schooner; the chase continued throughout the whole day; and at sunset we had not gained in distance more than one mile; the reason of this, however, was owing to a strong breeze which obliged us to "reef down," the frigate carrying topgallantsails during the whole day. When night set in, under its cover we altered our course and eluded the vigilance of the enemy, for in the morning nothing was to be seen from the mast-head. This was the first chase; and, although I had great confidence in the judgment and ability of Captain N. as a schooner-sailer, yet I had not so much in the sailing of the schooner; but was informed by the captain that her best play was before the wind. It was not long before we had a fair trial of her speed in that way; for on the 25th, at 8 in the morning, we fell in with an English sloop-of-war, about two miles to the windward. As there was no possibility of escaping her on a wind, it blowing a strong breeze at the time, we kept away right before the wind, so as to bring the sails of the sloop-of-war all on one mast; in this way, we beat her easily without setting our squaresail. In this, the second chase, our confidence in the speed of the schooner became very much strengthened.

The weather now became boisterous, with almost continual westerly gales, and it might be said that we were literally under water one half of the time. It was a rare thing, even with a moderate breeze, to see a dry spot on our decks when under a press of canvass, and it was often the same thing below; but, more especially, the condition of the forecastle was such that the men had usually to "turn in wet, and turn out smoking."

We were now reaching up toward the Grand Banks, and, as that was the usual track for outward-bound vessels, we expected to fall in with cruisers; and, consequently, kept a good look-out. In this we were not mistaken; for on the 5th of November, while scudding under a reefed foresail in a westerly gale, we fell in with an English seventy-four, about a mile ahead of us, lying to on the starboard tack. In order to get clear of her, it was necessary to haul up, the schooner holding a better wind than the seventy-four; the latter soon dropped to leeward; but another difficulty now arose; a frigate was seen broad upon the weather quarter, bearing down for us, under a press of canvass. It was evident that our situation was a critical one; for, if we bore away before the wind, we must necessarily close in with the seventy-four, and receive her fire; so the only alternative, therefore, left us was to keep away four points, and, if possible, pass to the windward of the seventy-four. Setting every rag of canvass that the schooner would bear, careening her lee gunwales to the water, she became now so laborsome that it was necessary to throw the lee guns overboard. This service was immediately performed; and to our no small satisfaction she bounded over the tremendous sea with ease, and her speed was sensibly increased. It was not certain, however, that we could pass to windward of the seventy-four,—at least, it was not probable that we should pass her out of gun-shot; and, to increase our troubles at this juncture, another sail was made on our starboard bow, standing for us on the larboard tack. No alternative was now left us, but to cross the bows of the seventy-four, and take the chance of her fire. It was the work of a few minutes, as we had closed in with her, and it became evident that we should not pass more than half gun-shot off. The seventy-four, perceiving our predicament, kept away; but it was too late; she was now on our quarter. We received her fire without damage, and in the next ten minutes had a reefed squaresail set, and our noble craft was running off at the rate of twelve knots. It became now a stern-chase, for already had the vessel to windward, which proved to be a sloop-of-war, kept away, and under a press of canvass was bearing down upon our beam. This was a hard chase, for we soon altered the bearings of the frigate and seventy-four; but it was not until sunset that we brought the sloop-of-war in our wake, about two miles' distance astern. The next morning, the gale had increased, and the sea had risen to such a height that scudding became dangerous; it was, therefore, determined to bring the schooner up to the wind. No evolution on board of a vessel, especially in a sharp schooner, is fraught with so much hazard as bringing her to the wind in a heavy gale. The greatest care is necessary by watching the rolling seas, which are generally three in number, after which it is proportionally smooth for a few seconds; occasionally, in these intervals, the wind lulls;

advantage must then be taken, such sail as the vessel will bear must be set and well secured, and then she should be brought to the wind by easing her helm to leeward. This was done with our craft in a seaman-like manner; a balanced-reefed foresail was set, the sheet bowsed taut aft, and a tackle hooked on to the clew, and it bowsed nearly amidships with the helm two and a half points to leeward. She rode in this way nearly head to the sea, forging ahead two knots, and not making more than two and a half points lee-way. This was the first time that I had seen a craft of this description hove to, and I was perfectly astonished; for she rode as easy and safely as if she had been in a harbor; this easy motion, however, was owing, in a good degree, to the management of Captain N. In the hands of one who does not understand managing a craft of this description, they are the most uncomfortable, as well as uneasy, vessels that float the ocean.

The gale lasted twelve hours, after which it moderated, and we bore away to the eastward; the wind continued blowing until the 9th of November, when we entered the famous Bay of Biscay. The weather now became moderate, with a smooth sea, and we were all elated with the prospect of reaching our port of destination in safety. We were the more confirmed in this hope, because, at the close of the day on the 13th of November, we were within half a day's sail of Bourdeaux, and fully expected, with a moderate breeze, to make Cordovan lighthouse early next morning. Alas! how soon are the brightest prospects frustrated! At sunset that evening, it fell away calm, and nothing was to be seen from the mast-head; not a breath of air or "cat's paw" was felt during the whole of the night. The conversation which I had with Jack Evans, in the ship *Dromo,* on the night previous to the action, was irresistibly brought to my recollection. It was a night similar to this; and, although it might have been a superstitious feeling, yet I could not shake it off, and a secret foreboding agitated my mind, and kept it in a state of the deepest anxiety and suspense. When the morning dawn broke forth, conviction came, and suspense was at an end; for there lay a ship and two brigs, with English ensigns flying at their peaks. Flight was now impossible, for it was a dead calm; and resistance was entirely useless, for we lay at the mercy of their whole broadsides. Our ensign was hoisted, but we well knew, to our great mortification, it must soon be hauled down in unresisting humility.

The ship first opened her battery upon us, followed by one of the brigs. The rest is soon told. The American ensign was struck, and in twenty minutes they had possession of this valuable vessel and cargo. So strong was my presentiment of some coming disaster that I had taken the precaution during the night to sew up in a flannel shirt all the money I had, consisting of seventeen doubloons, and then put it on. It was well I did so, for these vessels proved to be three Guernsey privateers. The ship mounted eighteen guns, with seventy men; the two brigs each mounted fourteen guns, with fifty men. After getting possession of the schooner, they robbed us of almost every thing they could lay their hands upon. Our crew were distributed among the three vessels; the captain, myself, and two men, were put on board the ship. The schooner was manned and ordered to the Island of Guernsey; after which the privateers separated to cruise on different stations. The destination of the ship, from what I understood, was to cruise on the coasts of Spain and Portugal. The captain and myself received good treatment; for, after we had reported to the captain of the privateer the loss of our clothing, he ordered a search to be made for them, and all were recovered, as they happened to be on board of the ship. They were very much elated with their success and assured us that the first licensed ship they fell in with, we should be released.

Three days after our capture, while standing on a wind, the cry of "Sail ho!" was heard from the mast-head, bearing on the lee beam. The ship was kept off, until the strange sail could be clearly made out. It proved to be a large rakish-looking schooner, evidently American by the set of her masts, cut of the sails, and color of the canvass. It was immediately suggested to us by the captain of the ship that there was another fine prize, and I was requested to look at her with the glass. I soon discovered that she was a man-of-war of some description and intimated as much to him; he was soon confirmed in this opinion, for the strange sail kept her wind and manifested no disposition to get out of the way. When the ship had gotten within two miles of the schooner, she hauled her wind and made every preparation for action.

Both vessels were under a press of canvass, standing on a wind on the larboard tack; but the schooner, lying a point higher than the ship, gained up to windward; and although she did not forge ahead quite so fast as the ship, yet she was not more than a mile and a half astern, exactly in the wake of the ship, at sunset. Night came on; and under its cover the course of the ship was altered, in order, if possible, to elude the one in pursuit. I now perceived that all on board were very much alarmed, especially the captain. The crew, for the most part, were a set of raw greenhorns, and the captain well knew that no dependence could be placed in them. At 10 o'clock, the wind dying away to a perfect calm, all hands were at their quarters, and the strictest look-out was kept. Our vessel now made sure that they had gotten clear of the schooner, for the night was very dark and cloudy; but, to their great surprise, at half past ten, there she was, not more than two musket-shots off. It was a night of deep suspense to all, and especially to us. The captain of the ship was aware that the schooner would not engage in the night; consequently every advantage was taken of the wind to get clear of her, but it was all in vain. At daylight, in the morning, the schooner was about a mile astern; the ship at this time was under a cloud of sail, but it was soon perceived that the enemy came up with her.

Capt. N. and myself were now ordered below, when a running fight commenced, the ship discharging her stern-chasers in quick succession, and the schooner discharging her forward division, which cut away the stern boat and part of her starboard quarter. In half an hour the contest was decided, most of the ship's crew having deserted their quarters; the British flag was hauled down, and she became a prize to the *Paul Jones* privateer, of New York, mounting eighteen guns, with a complement of one hundred and twenty men. The boats immediately came from the privateer, and the crew of the ship was sent on board the schooner. Now, a scene of plunder and robbery was perpetrated, by the privateer's crew, which beggars all description; every article of clothing and stores, which they could lay their hands upon, were taken without any ceremony. The crew were a perfect set of desperadoes and outlaws, whom the officers could neither restrain nor command. Capt. N. and myself were now conveyed to the privateer without our clothes, for we had shared the like fate with the crew of the ship, by having our trunks broken open and robbed of all their contents.

The excitement being over, a prize-master and crew were put on board of the ship, and she was ordered to the United States. Capt. N. prevailed with the captain of the privateer to let him proceed in her; but all the arguments I could make use of, to accompany him, were fruitless; so I concluded to make the best of a bad bargain, and was induced, by the persuasions of the captain and the prospect of gain held out to me, to enter as prize-master. The next cruising ground was in the neighborhood of the Western Islands, to which, with all possible despatch, we repaired.

It may not be out of place here to present the reader with a sketch of the characters of the men with whom I was now associated. Capt. T., a man of about thirty-five years of age, was a gentleman in his manners, yet impatient of contradiction; bold and fearless; generally acted with great precipitation, and, consequently, without the exercise of much judgment. Mr. B., the 1st lieutenant, was an educated man, a good seaman, cool and intrepid, and was strongly marked with the protuberance of cause and effect. Mr. J., the 2d lieutenant, was about thirty years of age, an active seaman, with limited education, but was a smart and enterprising officer. Mr. G., the 3d lieutenant, was a young man who did not seem to be designed for the perils of war or the hardships of a sea life; he was amiable, but being limited in his knowledge of seamanship, had very little confidence in himself. I understood, however, that his courage was undoubted. Mr. W., the sailing-master, was about fifty years of age, had formerly been captain of a West Indiaman out of Connecticut, a tolerably good seaman and navigator; but he was a low, mean-spirited chap, a kind of anomaly, possessing none of those noble and generous qualities which characterize a sailor—avaricious to the last degree, and would resort to the meanest acts to acquire gain. The prize-masters, six in number (including myself), were a set of jolly fellows, and believed themselves to be superior in rank and talent to any on board except the captain, because they concluded that they would be installed into the office of commander before the cruise was up. Mr. C., lieutenant of marines, was neither soldier nor sailor, had been a sort of country lawyer, and would rather sit down to a good dinner than face an enemy. In going through the drill exercise, he might appropriately be called "Captain Bunker," of the privateer. The surgeon very much resembled, to my imagination, the apothecary of Shakspeare; he was somewhat advanced in years, and had, in the days of his youth, read physic in a doctor's office, and listened to some half-dozen lectures in a medical college, and was then dubbed M.D., and let off with a diploma, lancet, and pill-box to practise upon a credulous public. He had obtained some little celebrity by the amputation of a limb; but as he could not subsist upon fame exclusively, being well nigh starved to death for want of practice, he resolved (to use his own expression) to sink or swim by plunging into the turbulent scenes of war. His usual remedy to a sick sailor was a pint of salt water, because, he said, other medicines were too costly to be lavished on a common sailor, and because, he added, it was a safe and easy remedy, always at hand, and cost nothing. On one occasion, the doctor unfortunately fell from the gangway rail on the deck and hurt himself very seriously; a wag of a sailor hove a bucket over the side, and drew up some water, and immediately presented the poor surgeon with a tin-pot full, swearing it was the best medicine that could be given for a wound or fractured limb, "because," he added, with a broad grin, "it is safe and easy and costs nothing."

And now for the crew; but here description fails. The English language is too poor adequately to do them justice. Imagine to yourself, reader, a company of eighty men, selected from the very *élite* and respectable portions of the lowest sinks located in the "Five Points," "Hook," and other places of like celebrity in New York. Here they were, a motley crew of loafers, highbinders, butcher boys, &c. &c. To be sure, there was, now and then, a good and true-hearted sailor among them; but, "like angels' visits, they were few and far between." As it may well be supposed, long confinement with such a company as above described could not be an enviable situation to a man of taste; but the continual hurry-scurry, uproar, and excitement, on board of a privateer, leave but a short time for reflection; and furthermore, being creatures of imitation, we soon become insensibly conformed to the daily habits of surrounding associations. This was my case; for, although my better judgment taught me to despise this mode of warfare—at best, in my opinion, it is only a systematic method to plunder unoffending men—yet I soon became in some degree reconciled to my situation.

ON THE MORNING of the 21st of November, the privateer had reached her cruising ground, and on the afternoon of the same day, made the Island of Terceira, one of the group of the Azores, or Western Islands. The third day after cruising around those islands, a small English brig, bound to Fayal, was captured without resistance; she was manned and ordered to the United States. On the afternoon of the same day, we took a small English schooner bound to Terceira, the island being then in sight. We released our prisoners, and putting them all on board this vessel, they steered away for the island. From the captain of the small schooner, we obtained information that the Lisbon and Mediterranean fleets of merchantmen, under a strong convoy, had sailed from England. We lost no time, therefore, after ridding ourselves of the prisoners, to get on the Lisbon station, so that, if possible, we might intercept some of the fleet. A few days, with a strong westerly breeze, brought us up to our cruising ground. Three days thereafter, we fell in with a large British brig, and, after a sharp action of forty minutes, succeeded in capturing her. She was from Cork, bound to Cadiz, with a rich and valuable cargo, consisting of Irish cut glass, linens, &c. She was manned and ordered to the United States, where she safely arrived, and the vessel and cargo sold for nearly four hundred thousand dollars. This was the richest prize taken during the cruise, and caused the most extravagant expressions of joy among the crew; but the cruise was not yet up. Entertaining serious doubts as to the privateer's sailing, I was under the impression that a smart-sailing man-of-war with any chance would capture us, for she could not compete with the letter-of-marque which I was last on board of, in point of sailing. The next day after the capture of the brig, a large sail was made, broad off on the starboard bow. We soon came up with the chase, and she proved to be an American ship bound to Lisbon. Captain T., suspecting that she was sailing under a British license, made the most diligent search for it, but for a long time without effect. At length, however, the anchors were unstocked, and, to our great satisfaction, we found the license concealed between the upper and lower parts of the anchor-stock. Of course, this settled her business; she was a good prize, and we despatched her to the

United States—all of the crew, except the officers, entering on board the privateer.

At daylight in the morning, December 4th, we fell in with the combined Lisbon and Mediterranean fleets: they were far to leeward to us; consequently we had the advantage of choosing our position, and harassing them under cover of the night; but we soon perceived Captain T.'s intention was to run into the midst of the fleet in the daytime. Against this mode of procedure every officer on board remonstrated loudly; the captain, however, was obstinate; the privateer ran down amidst the fleet, hauled up alongside of a large ship, and engaged her at pistol-shot distance. Signals were now made by all the fleet for an enemy. The convoy, being in the van, quickly perceived what was going on, and a frigate and sloop-of-war were seen bearing down upon us under a press of canvass. No other alternative was left but to run. The wind being moderate, the privateer was kept before it, dropping the frigate, but the sloop-of-war gained upon us, and it seemed to be almost certain that she would bring us to an action; but when within gun-shot, she let drive her bow-chasers. By the impediment attendant upon her firing, together with her yawing to bring her guns to bear, the privateer gained about a quarter of a mile. By running the guns forward and aft, the schooner was put in proper trim; and it soon became evident that we were rapidly leaving the chase astern. After running us about six hours directly to leeward of the fleet, the enemy hauled her wind and gave up further pursuit. This unfortunate, headstrong adventure on the part of Captain T. was the cause of destroying all confidence in him. If he had taken advice and kept a proper position to the windward, no doubt, under cover of the night, we might have captured two or three of the fleet and thus completed our cruise. But, as it was, we ran into the most imminent danger without the least probability of capturing a single vessel.

A day or two after, a large ship was made to the windward, having a main top-gallantsail set, and her fore and mizzen top-gallantmasts down. As we closed in with her, some bales of cotton were seen lashed on the quarter. I was sent aloft with the glass to watch her movements, and soon ascertained that she was a man-of-war in disguise, and reported my conjecture to the captain, who made light of it at first; but his tune, however, soon changed when he saw her bear up, and in fifteen minutes she was under a cloud of canvass in pursuit of us. The wind was blowing fresh on shore, and as we had seen the land that morning, we knew that we were not more than forty miles distant from it. It was now about 3 o'clock in the afternoon. It appeared to be the object of the frigate, in case we outsailed her, to run us ashore. This was the hardest chase we had during the whole time I was on board; no difference was perceptible in the sailing of the two vessels. We were running at the rate of eleven knots per hour; consequently, in four hours, with the same speed, we should be high and dry ashore. The days, however, being short at this season of the year, our main hope was to elude the enemy when night came on. At sunset the land was full in sight, distant about twenty miles; and as we were running directly for it, in two hours we should either be a prize or a wreck, unless we could evade him by some stratagem. The greatest anxiety and excitement reigned throughout the privateer. The crew were packing up their traps, and the officers manifested the deepest suspense: fortunately, the weather was cloudy; and, as night shut in intensely dark, our only chance was to profit by it. The lights were now all put out and profound silence enjoined. The frigate, on account of the darkness, could not be seen. The privateer was luffed to on the starboard tack, every sail lowered, and nothing was to be seen except her hull and poles. In about ten minutes, the frigate appeared, under a cloud of canvass, about two hundred yards from us, flying away to leeward like a race-horse. We now hauled on a wind to the eastward, and saw no more of the frigate. Captain T. decided to make a dash into the Irish Channel to intercept the West India fleet, which was destined to sail in a few days, having made their rendezvous at Cork. We obtained this information from the captured brig. A few days not only brought us to our station, but it also terminated our cruise, as will be seen in the sequel.

On the morning of December 14th, it blowing fresh from the southwest, with thick, foggy weather, we were in the midst of the West India fleet before we saw them, they having sailed from Cork the day previous. No better opportunity could be wished for, to make captures, than the one before us; the fog would sometimes clear up, and then shut in thick, so that we could select any vessel we chose. Hauling alongside of a fine large brig, we boarded and captured her in ten minutes. A prize-master and crew were put on board of her, with orders to remain with the fleet until night, and then make the best of their way to any port in the United States. As I had succeeded in boarding and capturing this vessel with only the assistance of five men, I was promised the finest ship in the fleet by Captain T. The promise was somewhat premature, the fulfilment rather problematical. As the fog cleared up, we selected a large ship, and I of course got ready, and picked my prize crew, to take possession of her without further ado. The fog now set in so thick that no object was visible five yards' distance, and when it lifted, there lay a frigate on our starboard bow, not more than a musket-shot off. She quickly saw us; but being on different tacks, she stood on until she got under our larboard quarter, then tacked, and gave us a taste of her forward division, which did us no other damage than to cut away two of the lee main-shrouds. In half an hour, it was clearly ascertained that we outsailed the frigate on a wind. Captain T. now held a council with the officers and proposed to bear up before the wind, as that was the privateer's best sailing quality—adding that no doubt could be entertained but that we could beat the frigate before a wind, and in the end, by thus maneuvering, we should save our prize. The strongest objections were urged to this proposal, especially by the first lieutenant, who declared it to be his opinion that, if the privateer was kept away, we should be a prize in thirty minutes. All opinions and remonstrances were entirely thrown away upon the captain. Every sail was got ready, the helm put up, and in a few minutes she was under a cloud of canvass before the wind. It was not long before Captain T. saw his egregious error; for it will be evident to every seaman that we were now running nearly in a line to meet the frigate. The latter, quickly perceiving our mistake, kept her wind, and as there was no time now to be lost with us, the helm was put down, and the privateer brought to the wind; in the act of doing which, she gave us another division of her eighteen-pounders, which cut away the fore-gaff, the slings of the fore-yard, and riddled our lower sails, and, to add to the difficulty, our unfortunate maneuver gave the frigate the weather-gage of us—the principal sail, too, had become useless from the loss of the gaff. The next discharge from the frigate cut away the main-topman lift. There being a heavy sea on at the time, the main-boom got command of the quarter deck, and carried away the bulwarks from the tafferel to the gangway. The frigate now overhauled us without any difficulty and opened a most murderous fire, with the marines. We were unable to haul down our colors, from the fact of the topman-lift having been shot away. Seven men killed and fifteen wounded lay on our decks; and notwithstanding the frigate must have perceived that we were so much cut up that we had no command of the privateer and that she lay like a log upon the water, nevertheless, she poured into us her quarter deck carronades, which, striking us a-midships, nearly cut our craft in halves. It was about four hours from the time we fell in with the frigate until the time of our capture, and in about one hour after, all of our crew were snugly stowed away on board of the frigate.

The prisoners were shoved down into the cable tiers; but the officers, seven in number, were politely treated with the soft side of a plank against the ward-room bulk-head. We were robbed of nearly all our clothing, and as roughly used as if we had been pirates. The prize was manned, and ordered into Plymouth, where, to our great satisfaction, she never arrived, having sunk off the Land's End. The crew, however, were saved in the boats.

The next morning the cry of "Sail ho!" was heard from the frigate's mast-head; in three hours she was up with the vessel, and, to our great mortification, it proved to be the prize brig we had taken from the fleet. When possession was taken of her, the prize-master and nearly the whole crew were found drunk. It appeared they did not make sail on the vessel during the night, and, on being interrogated, the prize-master was entirely ignorant of the position of the brig. Great exultation was now manifested by the officers of the frigate, and, to use their own expression, they had now taken the "*Paul Jones* and his mate."

In fifty hours the frigate was at an anchor in Plymouth harbor, and we were all put on board of a prison-ship, with the exception of the captain, first lieutenant and surgeon, who were entitled to parole. Here we found already three hundred and fifty American prisoners, who were crammed away on the two decks of an old condemned seventy-four, fitted up for that purpose and strongly guarded. We remained in this ship four weeks, during which time the number of American prisoners was augmented to six hundred; it became necessary, therefore, in view of this daily increase, to send the prisoners to depots allotted for that purpose. Accordingly, several drafts were ordered to Stapleton, near Bristol, a distance of one hundred and thirty miles. It fell to my lot to be one of the number composing these drafts, and I was not a little pleased, for I considered that any prison would be preferable to the unwholesome air, and close confinement, of a ship into which five hundred human souls were crammed.

* * *

*Perhaps Little's adventures are a bit too singular to satisfy historians; certain dates he cites do not correspond with dates in the log of the* Paul Jones. *But his account gives a good idea of the chaotic nature and constant perils of the privateering life. According to his narrative, Little was later removed to the infamous prisoner-of-war camp Dartmoor, where he remained until the end of the war. Afterward, he was unable to claim his prize money earned while on board the* Paul Jones *because the prize agent had apparently defrauded his clients and failed.*

*Whether or not they made the individuals involved rich (it was rare, you can be sure), privateers did make merchants poorer. Among the five hundred American privateers, some mere desperadoes as Little indicates, the bolder took prizes in the Irish Sea and off the mouth of the Thames. In all, they took in excess of one thousand British merchant ships during the War of 1812. That and the resulting soaring maritime insurance rates crippled British merchants and created a general atmosphere of discontent with the war.*

*Meanwhile, as we saw in the battle between the* Macedonian *and the* United States, *the Royal Navy had bigger fish to fry. Although the* Constitution's *and*

United States's *victories at sea were setbacks for the Royal Navy, her defeated captains could at least take consolation in the fact that in both cases these heavy frigates were damaged enough that they were forced to return to home waters for refitting. The* Macedonian *thus prevented the* United States *from molesting the East India convoy. The* Java *forced the* Constitution *and her consort, the sloop* Hornet, *to abandon their plans to cruise in the Pacific, where they could have created much havoc among the British whalers and merchants.*

*While it lost some high-profile battles, the Royal Navy effectively limited the amount of damage the upstart United States Navy could inflict. But one warship escaped the Royal Navy's long arms, at least for a while. Commanded by Captain David Porter, the small but powerful frigate* Essex, *which had been ordered to the Pacific along with the* Constitution *and* Hornet, *carried on with her mission.*

# DAVID PORTER

# A Yankee Cruiser
# in the South Pacific

## 1813

*Commanding the frigate* Essex, *armed with forty 32-pounder car-*
*ronades and six long 12-pounders, Captain David Porter rounded*
*the Horn in early 1813, becoming the first warship of the U.S. Navy to*
*cruise in the Pacific. (A thirteen-year-old midshipman and the captain's*
*adopted son, the future admiral David Farragut, was also on board.) Arriv-*
*ing at Valparaiso on March 14, 1813, Porter is momentarily the most pow-*
*erful force in the South Pacific. Still, the shifting politics of the Spanish*
*American states and the inevitable arrival of British warships make his*
*position tenuous.*

ON THE MORNING of the 25th, at daylight, we discovered a sail to the
northeast, which we gave chase and soon came up with. She proved to be
the American whale-ship *Charles*, Captain Gardner, belonging to Nan-
tucket, about four months from Lima, where she had been sent for adjudication by a privateer belonging to that port, and was liberated after paying
costs. Captain Gardner informed me, that, two days before, he had been in
company with the American whale-ships *Walker* and *Barclay*, near the port
of Coquimbo; that he had been chased and fired at by a Spanish and an
English ship; and that he saw them take possession of both the *Walker* and
*Barclay*. I consequently crowded all sail, in company with the *Charles*, for
Coquimbo, with an expectation of falling in with them. At eight o'clock
descried a sail to the northward, to which I gave chase, and at meridian we

345

were near enough to discover her to be a ship of war, disguised as a whaler, with whale-boats on her quarters. She shortly afterwards hoisted the Spanish flag, when we showed English colours, and fired a gun to leeward, which she shortly returned, and run down for us. The *Charles*, agreeably to directions I had previously given Captain Gardner, hoisted an English jack over the American ensign; the Spaniard, when at the distance of a mile, fired a shot at us which passed our bow. I immediately, from her appearance and the description I had received of her, knew her to be one of the picaroons that had been for a long time harassing our commerce, and felt so exasperated at his firing a shot, that I was almost tempted to pour a broadside into him; but reflecting that we were under British colours and that the insult was not intended for the American flag, I contented myself with firing a few shot over him to bring him down. Shortly afterwards, a boat was lowered down from her, and sent to the *Essex:* but perceiving her crew to be armed, I directed her to return immediately to the ship, with orders for her to run down under our lee, and for her commander to repair on board with his papers, and to apologize for firing a shot at us. She soon returned with the second lieutenant, who brought her commission and stated that the captain was too unwell to leave his ship.

She proved to be the Peruvian privateer *Nereyda,* of fifteen guns. The lieutenant informed me that they were cruising for American vessels and had captured the *Barclay* and *Walker* in the port of Coquimbo, but that the British letter of marque *Nimrod,* Captain Perry, had driven their people from on board the *Walker* and taken possession of her; that they were in search of the *Nimrod,* to endeavour to recover their prize; that seeing us, with the *Charles* in company, they had supposed us to be the vessels they were in search of, and this had been the cause of their firing a shot. He stated that the Peruvians were the allies of Great Britain; that he had always respected the British flag; and that his sole object was the capture of American vessels; that he had been out four months and had only met the aforesaid vessels; and that the crew of the *Barclay,* and the captain and part of the crew of the *Walker,* were now detained as prisoners on board the *Nereyda.*

I informed him that I wished to see the captain of the *Walker* and one of the prisoners from the *Barclay;* and informed him that if his captain was too unwell to come on board, it would be necessary for the first lieutenant to repair on board and make the apology required. On this, he despatched his boat to the *Nereyda,* which returned with Captain West, of the *Walker,* and one of the crew of the *Barclay,* as well as the first lieutenant of the *Nereyda.* On taking Captain West into the cabin and assuring him that he was on board an American frigate, he informed me that he, as well as the rest of the Americans on board the *Nereyda,* amounting to twenty-three, had been plundered of every thing; that the Spaniards had not assigned any other motives for the capture of the vessels than that they were Americans; that both his ship and the *Barclay* were employed solely in the whale-fishery and not concerned in any mercantile pursuit whatever; that both ships had full cargoes of oil, were about returning to America, and had put into Coquimbo for refreshments; and that the first intelligence they had received of the war was at the time of their capture.

The *Nereyda* was now under the muzzle of our guns, and I directed the American flag to be hoisted, and fired two shot over her, when she struck her colours. I then sent Lieutenant Downes to take possession of her, with directions to send all the Spaniards on board the *Essex*; and as I had reason to expect that the *Nimrod* and the other ships were somewhere in our neighbourhood, I stood in shore with a view of looking into Tongue Bay and Coquimbo, sending Lieutenant M'Knight to take charge of the *Nereyda* for the night. Next morning had all her guns, ammunition and small arms thrown overboard, as well as all her light sails. What surprised us very much was that all the shot of this vessel, round, bar, and star-shot, were made of copper; and I have since been informed that this metal is in such abundance, and so cheap in Peru and Chili, as to be held in very little estimation, there being no comparison between the value of that and iron. Wanting a few nails while at Valparaiso, I found they could not be procured for less than one dollar per pound. But it seemed equally curious that, although copper was in such abundance, and brass guns are so far preferable to iron, yet all the guns of this vessel, except one, were cast of the latter metal, differing in this respect from the customs of every other part of the world. After I had completely dismantled her, leaving her only her topsails and courses to take her back to Callao, which is the port of Lima, I liberated all the Americans from on board of her, sent back all the Spaniards, and directed her commander to proceed to Lima with the following letter to the viceroy.

*UNITED STATES FRIGATE* ESSEX, *AT SEA,*
*March 26, 1813.*

YOUR EXCELLENCY,

*I have this day met with the ship* Nereyda, *mounting fifteen guns, bearing your excellency's patent, and sailing under the Spanish flag.*

*On examination of said ship, I found on board her, as prisoners, the officers and crews of two vessels belonging to the United States of America, employed solely in the whale-fishery of those seas, captured by her, and sent for Lima after being plundered of boats, cordage, provisions, clothing, and various other articles; and was*

**A Yankee Cruiser in the South Pacific**

0         2000 mi.

NORTH AMERICA

Philadelphia

Bermuda

NORTH ATLANTIC OCEAN

Azores

Canary Is.

NORTH PACIFIC OCEAN

Caribbean Sea

Cape Verde Is.

Porto Praya

Chatham I.
James I.
Galápagos Is.

Guayaquil
Tumbez
Payta

SOUTH AMERICA

Nuka Hiva (Nooaheevah)

Marquesas Is.

C. Ajugia
Is. Lobos
I. San Lorenzo
I. San Gallan

Callao-Lima

Bahia

AMERICA

Rio de Janeiro

SOUTH ATLANTIC OCEAN

C. Frio

SOUTH PACIFIC OCEAN

Tongue Bay
Essex vs Phoebe
Concepcion
Mocha I.
I. de Chiloe

Coquimbo

Valparaiso

St. Catherine I.

Buenos Aires

R. Plate

Tierra del Fuego

Cape Horn

Staten I.

---

informed by her officers that they were cruising, as the allies of Great Britain, to capture and send in for adjudication all American vessels they should meet with, alleging, at the same time, that they had not your excellency's authority for such proceedings.

I have, therefore, to preserve the good understanding which should ever exist between the government of the United States and the provinces of Spanish America, determined to prevent in future such vexatious and piratical conduct; and with this view have deprived the Nereyda of the means of doing the American commerce any farther injury for the present, and have sent her to Lima in order that her commander may meet with such punishment from your excellency as his offence may deserve.

I have the honour to be, with the highest respect and consideration, your excellency's obedient humble servant,

(Signed)                D. PORTER.

His excellency the viceroy of Peru, Lima.

I then left the *Nereyda* and looked into Tongue Bay; but perceiving no vessels, I stood on for Coquimbo and at sundown arrived within five miles of some small rocks called the Chinques, which lay off the mouth of the bay. I then caused one of the whale-boats to be manned (both of which I had taken from the *Nereyda*, as they belonged to the captured ships) and sent her in with Lieutenant Downes and Captain West to reconnoitre the harbour, lying off and on with the ship until they returned, which was not until eleven o'clock that night. I had fixed on signals, by which Lieutenant Downes was to inform me whether the ships were in the port, as well as such by which the boat could find the *Essex:* the latter were observed from the shore; for immediately after we had made them, several alarm guns were fired from the battery, which consisted, as I was informed, of six guns, without platform or breastwork. The boat had entered the harbour and gone all around it, and had approached so near the shore and battery as to hear the people talking, without being discovered. Finding that the *Nimrod* was not at this place, I thought it probable that she had proceeded with a view of intercepting the *Barclay* on her way to Lima; and this I was the more strongly induced to believe, as the captain of that ship had stated his determination of taking the *Barclay* from the Spaniards, alleging that, as she had not been engaged in any contraband or illicit trade, they had no right to capture her and that the Peruvian government would certainly liberate her on her arrival at Callao, by which means he should be cheated out of a prize. I therefore determined to lose no time in endeavouring to get to the northward, on the coast of Peru, where I hoped to arrive in time not only to frustrate the views of the captain of the *Nimrod*, but to recapture the *Barclay* and the *Walker.* I considered the capture of the *Nimrod* of the greatest importance to our national interests in those seas, and while there was a chance of effecting this object, provided it did not interfere too much with my other views, I thought the pursuit of her should not be abandoned. To Captains Gardner and West I intimated my intentions, advising the former to run into Coquimbo, and there demand for his vessel the protection of government. The latter I advised to proceed with all expedition to St. Jago and lay his claim for damages before the government.

I gave the Americans whom I had liberated from the *Nereyda* their choice, either to remain in the *Essex* or be landed at Coquimbo. Nine of them preferred remaining; the remainder, with Captain West, were put on board the *Charles*, who made sail in for the harbour, and I steered to the northwest with all the sail we could crowd.

Prior to leaving Captains Gardner and West, I requested them to give me a list of all the whale-ships, both English and American, that they could recollect and were certain of being now in this sea. They both agreed that the Gallipagos was the most likely place to find them, and confirmed in every particular the account given by Captain Worth. The list they gave me was as follows:

### AMERICAN SHIPS ON THE COAST OF PERU AND CHILI.

| Ship | Captain |
| --- | --- |
| Fame | Coffin |
| Lion | Clarke |
| John and James | Clasby |
| John Jay | Coffin |
| Criterion | Clark |
| Samuel | Coleman |
| Sterling | Swain |
| Henry | Gardner |
| William Penn | W. Gardner |
| President | Folger |
| Sukey | Macey |
| Perseverando | Paddock |
| Monticello | Coffin |
| Atlas | Joy |
| Gardner | Ray |
| Chili | Gardner |
| Lima | Swain |
| Renown | Barnard |
| George | Worth |
| Charles | Gardner |
| Barclay | Randall |
| Walker | West |
| Thomas | Whipple, (doubtful) |

### BRITISH SHIPS ON THE COAST OF PERU AND CHILI.

| Ship | Captain |
| --- | --- |
| Nimrod | Perry, no figure head |
| Perseverance | King, a figure head |
| Seringapatam | Stivers, a figure head |
| Carleton | Allero, a figure head |
| Catharine | Folger, a figure head |
| Thames | Bomon |

| | |
|---|---|
| *Greenwich* | ——— |
| *Montezuma* | Baxter |
| *Rose* | Monroe, has a poop |
| *Sirius* | Has a figure head, is a low ship |

These were all the vessels the names of which they could at the moment recollect; but they assured me that the number of British whalers now on the coast of Chili and Peru did not amount to less than twenty, all fine ships of not less than four hundred tons burthen; and that their cargoes in England would be worth two hundred thousand dollars each, which, agreeable to this estimate, would be upwards of four millions of British property now exposed to us; for I did not conceive that their whole force united would be a match for the *Essex*. Besides the capture and destruction of those vessels, I had another object in view, of no less importance, which was the protection of the American whale-ships; and if I should only succeed in driving the British from the ocean and leaving it free for our own vessels, I conceive that I shall have rendered an essential service to my country, and that the effecting this object alone would be a sufficient compensation for the hardships and dangers we have experienced, and be considered a justification for departing from the letter of my instructions. That I can effect this, no doubts exist, provided the *Standard*[1] has left Lima; and this it is necessary I should be informed of before I make my attack on the Gallipagos, for I have knowledge of letters having been written to Lima by an active English merchant (perhaps an agent of the British government) residing at Valparaiso. They were sent by the ships which sailed four days before us; but as they had the reputation of being bad sailers, and calculating some on Spanish indolence, and much on our own activity and industry, I am in hopes of looking into Lima before they can arrive there; and shall so disguise the ship that she cannot be known there from any description that the aforesaid letters may contain. Until information respecting the *Standard* can be obtained, all my proceedings must be governed by views toward that vessel, she being the only vessel of war the British have in those seas, and I can have but little apprehension of being pursued by any from the Atlantic for some months, or at least until I have time to do them much injury. Although information had been sent from Buenos Ayres to Valparaiso of my being on the coast of Brazils, and this information had reached Valparaiso two weeks before my arrival, yet they could not have had an idea of my intention of coming into this sea, as it was unknown to every person but myself until after passing

[1] *The* Standard *was a British third-rate built in 1782.*

the River of Plate. The same mail that brought intelligence of my being on the coast of Brazils, also gave an account of an action having been fought off Bahia between the American frigate *Constitution* and the British frigate *Java* of forty-four guns, in which the latter was sunk; also of the capture of her convoy; and of some small place on the coast of Africa having been laid under contribution by the squadron under the command of Commodore Rodgers. It was also stated that the *Wasp*, an American sloop of war, had captured a British sloop of war after a hard-fought action, but had afterwards been captured by a frigate; and that the *Constitution* was repairing her damages at St. Salvador, where the British admiral ([Vice-Admiral Sir Manley] Dixon) had proceeded, with a determination of destroying her. This news of the operations of our little navy makes us pant for an opportunity of doing something ourselves. We have, however, a wide field for enterprise before us and shall shortly enter on the scene of action; and although, perhaps, we shall neither have an opportunity of laying towns under contribution, nor sinking frigates, still we hope to render a service to our country no less essential, to wit: the protection of our commerce, and the destruction of that of the enemy.

On the 28th I made all sail to the northward, and on the 3d of April made the high lands of Nasia, on the coast of Peru. The interval between these two periods was not marked by any extraordinary occurrence. We were employed in taking all advantages of the winds in getting to the northward, and in disguising our ship, which was done by painting her in such a manner as to conceal her real force and exhibiting in its stead the appearance of painted guns, &c.; also by giving her the appearance of having a poop and otherwise so altering her as to make her look like a Spanish merchant vessel. The winds were constantly fair; the weather remarkably clear, fine, and temperate; the sea smooth; and every thing favourable for making such little repairs and alterations as the ship required.

Immediately on passing the tropic, we met with flying-fish: this is the first we met with since we left the coast of Brazil.

At six o'clock of the 28th, we were abreast the island of Sangallan, or St. Gallan, when I hauled off to the northwest, with a view of crossing the track of vessels bound to Callao. On the morning of the 29th, to the great joy of all on board, we discovered three sail standing in for the harbour, two to windward and one to leeward. I consequently made all sail for the port to cut them off, and, as I approached the headmost vessel, she seemed to answer the description I had received of the *Barclay*. As she was nearest to the port, I determined to turn all my attention to her and to use every effort to prevent her getting in: but as she approached the island of St. Lorenzo, which lies off the port of Callao, I began to despair of succeeding.

I however directed all the light sails to be wet, in order to make them hold wind the better, and prepared my boats to send in to bring her out of the harbour, if she should succeed in getting past the island. As I approached St. Lorenzo, I discovered that she would be becalmed so soon as she doubled the point of the island, as she eventually was. We were, at the moment of her turning the point, at the distance of two miles and a half from her, but shot in with the breeze to within one hundred yards of her, then lowered the boats down and sent on board to tow her out, which was not effected without considerable labour, in consequence of an indraught. As we were but a short distance from the shipping in the harbour, and perceiving the two Spanish vessels had not arrived from Valparaiso, I hoisted English colours on board the *Essex* and directed the officer of the captured vessel (which proved to be the *Barclay*) to hoist English colours over the American. The vessels in port, which were numerous, now hoisted their colours, which were all Spanish except one British flag hoisted on board an armed ship, which did not answer the description of the *Nimrod*.

The other strange vessels continued standing in; one of them had the appearance of a coasting brig, the other a fine looking ship; and we were induced to believe her the *Nimrod* from the description we had received of that vessel. I therefore took a position to prevent her passing the point, when she hauled her wind to go between the island and main, where there is a passage for ships of large burthen, but shortly afterwards bore up, under a press of sail, to run by us, and on his near approach I perceived it to be one of the Spanish vessels that had sailed from Valparaiso before us. I felt satisfied that we had so altered the vessel that they could not know us; besides, how was it possible that they could expect to find the *Essex* off Callao, when they left her at Valparaiso, beginning to take in provisions and water?

On her getting into the calms under the lee of the island, I despatched a boat to get the news from her, but recalled her on seeing the guard-boat go on board. I now sent for the captain of the *Barclay* (Randall), informed him he was at liberty to act as he thought proper with respect to his ship, and that, although his crew had entered with me, they might return to the *Barclay*, if they were disposed to do so. But as they expressed their determination not to return to that ship, the captain informed me he was entirely at a loss what course to pursue and asked my advice. I at the moment felt as much embarrassment as he; for he was without hands, except two or three who were down with the scurvy, having been constantly at sea for seven months without refreshments. No port on the coast of Peru could afford him a shelter, as our destruction of the armament of the *Nereyda*, in consequence of the capture of the *Barclay*, would render the condemnation of that vessel highly probable, if she should again be in the power of the Peruvians; and if

the remainder of his crew were all healthy, they would not be strong enough
to take her to Valparaiso or any other port of Chili, even if there was nothing
to be apprehended from capture by British and Peruvian vessels. I however
concluded to give him all the protection in my power, and advised him to
remain by me, offering to put on board hands enough to work his vessel,
and promised not to leave him until I had put him in a place of safety. With
this promise he appeared much pleased and offered his services to me in
any way he could prove useful, giving me assurances that he could take me
where the British whale-vessels most frequented, advising me, by all means,
to proceed to the islands of Gallipagos, keeping at the distance of from thirty
to fifty leagues from the land, and on my way looking into Payta. He confirmed, in every respect, the information respecting the British whalers that
I had formerly received, and assured me that there were many other vessels
of that description, and others engaged in contraband trade, now on the
coast; he had no doubt we could find as many as we could conveniently
man, among the islands, as well as the American vessels they might have
captured. After putting on board the *Barclay* Midshipman Cowan and eight
men, and fixing on Payta and the Gallipagos as the places of rendezvous in
case of separation, also furnishing him with suitable signals and giving him
instructions to steer such courses as would enable us to spread over as much
ground as possible in our track, I shaped my course to the WNW, to run
between the rocks of Pelado and the Hormigas, which lies about thirty miles
from Callao.

The town of Callao is the seaport of Lima, from which the latter is distant about three leagues. Callao is an open road-stead; but as the wind here
always blows from the southward, and never with violence, and as it is
well sheltered from this quarter by the projecting capes, and by the island
of St. Lorenzo, it is considered in this sea as one of the safest harbours for
vessels. In this place all the trade of Peru centres; it is apparently well fortified by batteries on shore and is said to be well protected, in addition to
those, by a formidable flotilla of gunboats. The calms which appear to prevail in the bay seem to render this mode of defence very proper; and if this
is the case, it must be very dangerous for hostile vessels to venture beyond
the island of St. Lorenzo. Off the point of St. Lorenzo is a very suitable station for a vessel blockading Callao, as she can there, in consequence of the
calms, prevent every vessel from going in, as she can run in and have the
breeze at the distance of half gun-shot of them, after they have doubled
the point, and while they are perfectly becalmed; in this situation, exposed
to her guns, the boats can take possession and tow them out.

While we lay to here, I observed the sea filled with small red specks,
and supposed at first that some hog had been killed on board and that part

of the blood was floating along side; but on a close examination I perceived them to have at times a very quick motion, and on directing some of them to be caught in a bucket, discovered them to be young craw-fish, of different sizes, but generally from one inch in length to one tenth that size. The ocean appeared filled with them; and from the immense number of birds that kept about this spot, I am induced to believe that no small number of them were daily devoured. They did not appear to be governed by any general laws, each one pursuing his own course, and shifting for himself; no two appearing in the same direction; and it is probable that, as soon as they left the egg, each one began to seek his own subsistence. Two of them were put into a bottle of sea-water, and on some crumbs of bread being thrown in, they seized and devoured them very ravenously.

About this time I concluded to change the water in which the fish had been put, that was pumped out of the cask off Cape Horn. To this period it had been very lively; but perceiving the water to have a yellow tinge, and feeling apprehensive that it might undergo fermentation, from the food which had at different times been thrown in, I supposed that pure water would be better than that in which it had been so long confined, but concluded it best to produce a gradual change. With this view I put into the bottle about one gill of the water we had taken on board at Valparaiso. The water in the bottle gradually assumed a milky appearance, and next morning I found the fish dead and floating on the surface. This confirmed suspicions we had before entertained of the bad qualities of this water. Doctor Miller, who was in a very low state of health and had been so ever since he joined the *Essex*, complained of its producing costiveness. I also, and many others, experienced the same effect; it has a disagreeable, brackish taste, and it is with great difficulty it can be made to mix with soap.

On the evening of the 4th, James Spafford, the gunner's mate, who had been so unfortunately wounded by accident at Mocha, departed this life, regretted by every officer and man in the ship.[1] He had distinguished himself by his moral and correct conduct under my command, and I had intended promoting him to a better situation, so soon as circumstances would admit.

After this the body of Spafford was committed to the deep, according to the funeral ceremonies of the church.

We, as I before observed, steered to the WNW, and at two P.M. on the 6th, the man at the mast-head cried out a sail; but on standing toward it, in a short time discovered it to be the Rock of Pelado, bearing NE by N. We

---

[1] *James Spafford was accidentally shot by a fellow, near-sighted officer at dusk on the island of Mocha as the men were shooting wild horses for meat.*

soon gave up the chase and stood on our course, as I was anxious to get an offing to fall in with the track of whalers, as, from the best information I could collect on this subject, on this part of the coast they keep at the distance of from thirty to fifty leagues.

At half past three, a sail was discovered from the mast-head, bearing W NW, and we immediately made all sail in chase of her, the *Barclay* making every exertion to keep up with us; but by sundown we had run her out of sight astern. At seven o'clock we brought the chase to. She proved to be a Spanish brig from Callao, bound to Conception, but had taken in a load of salt at Oucho, a place a short distance to the north of Callao. The captain and supercargo of this vessel both came on board, and supposing the *Essex* to be an English vessel, were disposed to give us every information in their power; and, what was of the utmost importance to us, they informed me that an English frigate had been for some time expected at Callao from Cadiz, for the purpose of taking in money; and that the money which was to compose her cargo was nearly all collected. He also informed me that an English armed ship had put in there in distress a few days since, having sprung a-leak; that two English whale-ships had, within a few days, sailed from thence; that they had been sent in for adjudication by the corsairs of Peru, and on examination had been liberated. On inquiry respecting the disposition of the government of Peru towards those of the United States and Great Britain, they informed me that the latter was held in high repute, and its vessels treated with great civility, in consequence of being the allies of Spain; but that the former were held in very little estimation; and that, although war had not actually taken place between Spain and the United States, it was momentarily expected, and every preparation was made in Peru to meet it; that the Americans were notorious violators of their revenue laws (*grandes contrabandistas*) and neither received nor expected much civility; however, it was the policy of the government of Peru to hold out ideas and the appearance of a strict neutrality, and therefore British vessels were not allowed to dispose of their prizes at Callao. The supercargo of this vessel appeared to be a man of considerable intelligence; and when I inquired where was the most suitable place to proceed to give protection to British vessels and annoy those of the United States, he advised me to go to leeward, observing that the Gallipagos Islands were much frequented by the British whale-ships, and between that and the latitude of the Lobos Islands, I should most likely find many Americans, as the sea thereabouts was full of them. The *Barclay* was now a great distance astern; but as we ran to the northward under easy sail after leaving the Spaniard, and made flashes at intervals, she was enabled to join us by midnight.

At daylight in the morning, we stretched away to the westward, leaving the *Barclay* to steer to the northward, and spread to such a distance as just to see her signals, and closed again at night. This course we pursued until our arrival off Cape Ajugia, where we arrived on the morning of the 10th, and in the course of our run saw but two vessels, only one of which we spoke, knowing them to be Spaniards. She was a small brig from Guyaquil, bound to the southward, and could give us no information whatever. In our run we passed near to the islands of Lobos de la Mare, and Lobos de la Terre; they are two small islands, situated some distance from the continent, and at the distance of five leagues from each other, bearing NNW and SSE; they appear to be perfectly destitute of vegetation and serve as a residence to an immense number of birds, with which the hills were covered. There can be no doubt that an abundance of seals may be caught on them, as in passing we were surrounded with them, one of which we struck with the harpoon. The sea was here also covered with pelicans and various other aquatic birds, feeding on the schools of small fish, which were to be seen in great numbers, constantly pursued by seals, bonetas, and porpoises; and such as attempted to escape their ravenous jaws by jumping out of the water were immediately snapped up by the innumerable swarms of birds that were hovering over them.

On our arrival off Ajugia, we had another opportunity of witnessing a similar scene; and as the water was perfectly smooth and the winds light, we were enabled to examine it more minutely. We discovered the sea boiling violently in many places, and wherever this was the case, vast numbers of seals, large fish, and birds were apparently in pursuit of small fish. On approaching one of these places, the water had so much the appearance of having been put into action by violent currents, opposed by sunken rocks, that I felt some uneasiness and directed the helm to be put a-weather to avoid it; however, the next one had the same appearance and was equally attended by fish. I therefore steered close to it and saw that in the centre of the agitated spot (which bore the appearance of water boiling in a pot) were myriads of small fish, collected together, and appeared as though it were impossible for them to escape from this violent whirlpool, which was so powerful as to affect considerably the steerage of the ship. Whether this boiling of the water was occasioned by the vast numbers of seals and large fish which kept constantly darting in among the small fry, which were drawn as it were to a focus, I will not pretend to say. It is possible, however, that whales, or some fish perhaps nearly as large as whales, which did not show themselves above the surface, might also have been concerned in the pursuit and occasioned the agitation that so much surprised us; for I cannot think it possible that the seals and bonetas, numerous as they were, could have produced so violent a commotion.

A breeze springing up, we stood away for Payta, with a view of looking into that port, and at sunset were in sight of the island of Lobos, which lies a short distance to the southward, where we hove to for the *Barclay* to come up, as we had nearly run her out of sight; and, after speaking her, stretched off under easy sail, and at two o'clock in the morning made sail in shore. The weather at sunrise was hazy and prevented us for some time from seeing the saddle of Payta, which is a remarkably irregular mountain to the south of Payta, and when once seen cannot be mistaken, the highest part making something like a saddle, and running away to a low point to the northward, which is the point forming the harbour of Payta. As we stood in shore we discovered two small sail coming out, and as we approached them were at a loss to know what to make of them; but at last discovered them to be rafts or catamarans, steering by the wind, having each six men to work them. I had at first believed them to be fishing rafts from Payta, but was surprised they should have ventured so great a distance from the land, as we were, when we spoke them, about seven leagues off shore, and was induced, from their strange appearance, to visit them.

On going along side, I learnt, to my astonishment, that they were from Guyaquil, with cargoes of cocoa, bound to Guacho, a port to leeward of Lima, and had already been out thirty days. They were destitute of water and had no other provisions on board than a few rotten plantains. We, however, perceived a number of fish bones and pieces of fish scattered about the rafts, which induced us to believe that they were enabled to catch an abundance of fish, which no doubt follow them to get the small barnacles and grass with which the logs were plentifully supplied. Nothing can exceed the miserable construction of these floats. Eight logs of from twenty-five to thirty feet in length, with the bark scarcely taken off, and three pieces lashed across with a kind of grass rope, to form the floor; each side is formed of two logs, laid one on another, and the deck is composed of rough logs laid crosswise, and projecting from four to six feet beyond the sides, and all lashed (though very insecurely) together. Forward and aft are some pieces of board from three to four feet in length, stuck down between the logs forming the floor, and serving as a substitute for a keel. A mast is stepped in between the logs of the floor, and, instead of partners, secured by a lashing from side to side, and having the additional security of a stay and a shroud, which is shifted always to the weather side, and to this is hoisted a large lug-sail made of cotton. Their ground tackling consists of some bark, twisted in the form of a rope, which serves as a cable, and a large stone with a stick lashed to it, of about eighteen inches long, for a stock, serves as an anchor; she is steered by a paddle, carries her cargo on the logs forming the deck, and has as a substitute for a caboose, a small quantity of dirt thrown on the logs that project beyond the sides forward. The crews appear equally as miserable in their appearance as the machine they navigate; and it excited no little surprise in our minds when we were informed that the navigation from Guyaquil to Lima, a distance of about six hundred miles, against a constant head wind and frequently rapid current, should be very common with those rafts. This passage takes them two months; and there can be no stronger proof of the mildness of this ocean, so justly, in this part, deserving the name of the Pacific, than the fact, that the loss of those vessels, frail as they are, is very uncommon. Nor can there be a more convincing instance of the unenlightened state of the people of this part of the world than that they should continue the use of such barbarous vessels, when the fastest sailing vessels are so necessary; where materials for building them are so abundant; and where the state of the climate will admit of vessels of such construction as best suits their purpose, without any apprehensions of danger from the violence of the sea. But so far are they behind hand in civilization and intelligence with the rest of the world that the appearance of all the vessels built on the Spanish coast of the Pacific (except the few built at Guyaquil) bespeaks the extreme ignorance of the constructor as well as the navigator. There are established at Guyaquil some European constructors, who have built large vessels that have been justly admired in Europe and other parts of the world; but nothing, except the catamarans, can be more clumsy in their appearance, and apparently more unsuitable to the navigation of this ocean, than the miserable vessels employed in the coasting trade of Peru.

The two catamarans above mentioned had looked into the harbour of Payta and were consequently enabled to give me all the intelligence I required. They informed me there were no vessels lying there except two or three small coasting vessels; and as there was now no necessity for showing ourselves before that place, I shaped my course for the Gallipagos Islands, directing the *Barclay* to steer WNW by compass, in order that we might fall in with the latitude to the eastward of them, intimating to her commander that I should, from time to time, so vary from this course as to look over as much ground in our way as possible. This method we put in practice until we made Chatham Island, which was on the morning of the 17th. During our run we had no opportunity of correcting our dead reckoning by lunar observations, nor have we had a chance of ascertaining the rate of the chronometer since leaving St. Catharines. We were enabled to discover by our latitude that we had a current of fifteen miles per twenty-four hours, setting to the northward; and from the violent ripples we frequently met with, were induced to believe that its rate was much greater, and concluded it to set also westerly. On our making the land, found we had, since taking our departure from Payta, been set two degrees a-head of our reckoning. We employed ourselves during our passage in getting the magazine in good order for service, as we had been led to expect some resistance from the heavy armed letters of marque that we hoped to meet among the Gallipagos, employed in the whale-fishery. Having understood that calms were very prevalent there, we prepared our boats in the best manner for attacking them, selecting crews for them in addition to their oarsmen; and laid down plans of attack, and established signals for them. The whole, amounting to seven boats, carrying seventy men, were placed under the command of Lieutenant Downes.

I discovered that we should meet with great delays from the prevalence of calms; and as I could form no plans for future operations until my arrival at the general rendezvous of the whalers, I considered it adviseable to put the crew on two quarts of water per day. This reduction was now severely felt, as the weather was extremely hot; but all seemed reconciled to bear every privation without a murmur. The health of the crew had improved in a remarkable manner since leaving Valparaiso, and at this time we had but two men on the sick list, one affected by chronic debility, the other by a pain in the muscles of the neck, but neither disabled from coming to their quarters. Doctor Miller, the surgeon of the ship, a very infirm man, who was in a deep consumption when he joined the ship, and whose health had not improved on board her, requested permission to go with his servant on board the *Barclay*, and there remain, as he believed that a change of water, pure air, and greater tranquillity would render his situation more tolerable. As the extreme debility of the gentleman prevented him from doing his duty on board, and as he was constantly complaining of his sufferings from the confined air of this ship, I was happy he had fallen on an expedient to render his existence more supportable and took the first opportunity of sending him on board the *Barclay*, where he soon found himself more comfortably situated than amidst the noise and confusion of a man of war, for which his low state of health entirely unsuited him.

AT DAY-LIGHT ON the morning of the 29th [*of April*], I was roused from my cot, where I passed a sleepless and anxious night, by the cry of "*Sail ho!*" "*Sail ho!*" which was re-echoed through the ship, and in a moment all hands were on deck. The strange sail proved to be a large ship, bearing west, to which we gave chase; and in an hour afterwards we discovered two others, bearing southwest, equally large in their appearance. I had no doubts of their being British whale-ships; and as I was certain that toward mid-day, as usual, it would fall calm, I felt confident we should succeed in taking the whole of them. I continued my pursuit of the first discovered vessel, and at nine o'clock spoke her under British colours. She proved to be the British whale-ship *Montezuma*, Captain Baxter, with one thousand four hundred barrels of spermaceti oil. I invited the captain on board; and while he was in my cabin, giving me such information as was in his power respecting the other whale-ships about the Gallipagos, I took his crew on board the *Essex*, put an officer and crew in the *Montezuma*, and continued in pursuit of the other vessels, which made all exertions to get from us. At eleven A.M., according to my expectation, it fell calm; we were then at the distance of eight miles from them. I had reason, from the information obtained, to believe them to be the British armed whale-ships *Georgiana*, of six eighteen-pounders, and the *Policy*, of ten six-pounders, the one having on board thirty-five, and the other twenty-six men; but that they were British ships, there could not be a doubt, and we were determined to have them at all hazards. Thick and hazy weather is prevalent here, and, as there was every indication of it, I was fearful that, in the event of a breeze, one or the other of them might make its escape from us, as I had understood that they were reputed fast sailers. I therefore thought it adviseable to attempt them in our boats, and with this view had them prepared for the purpose, and in a few minutes they departed in two divisions.

Lieutenant Downes, in the whale-boat, commanded the first division, consisting of the third cutter, Lieutenant M'Knight, jolly-boat, Sailing-Master Cowell, and second cutter, Midshipman Isaacs; and Lieutenant Wilmer, in the pinnace, commanding the second division, consisting of the 1st cutter, Lieutenant Wilson, and gig, Lieutenant Gamble of the marines. The heavy-rowing boats occasioned considerable delay to the whole, as I had given the most positive orders that the boats should be brought into action all together, and that no officer should take advantage of the fleetness of his boat to proceed ahead of the rest, believing that some of them, from their extreme anxiety to join with the enemy, might be so imprudent as to do so. At two o'clock, the boats were about a mile from the vessels (which were about a quarter of a mile apart), when they hoisted English colours, and fired several guns. The boats now formed in one division and pulled for the largest ship, which as they approached, kept her guns trained on them. The signal was made for boarding; and, when Lieutenant Downes arrived within a few yards of her gangway and directed them to surrender, the colours were hauled down. They now proceeded for the other vessel, after leaving an officer and some men on board, and as soon as she was hailed, she followed the example of the first by striking her colours. Shortly after-

wards a breeze sprung up, the prizes bore down for us, and we welcomed
the safe return of our shipmates with three hearty cheers. The captured vessels proved to be, as I had expected, the *Georgiana*, captain Pitts, of two hundred and eighty tons, and the *Policy*, of two hundred and seventy-five tons;
and these three vessels, which we had taken with so little trouble, were estimated to be worth in England upwards of half a million of dollars. The ease
with which the last vessels were taken by our open boats gave us but a poor
opinion of British valour; and the satisfaction which the possession of these
valuable vessels gave us made us forget for a moment the hardships of Cape
Horn and the time we had spent without seeing an enemy. It also afforded
us a useful lesson, as it convinced us we ought not to despair of success
under any circumstances, however unfortunate they may appear; and that,
although the patient and persevering may for a time meet with disappoint-
ments, fortune will at length most commonly make amends. Slight mur-
murings had on one or two occasions been heard from some of the crew,
occasioned by our want of success heretofore, and with a view of prevent-
ing it in future, I considered it adviseable to inculcate this maxim by the following note:

*SAILORS AND MARINES,*
   *Fortune has at length smiled on us, because we deserved her smiles, and the
first time she enabled us to display* free trade and sailors' rights, *assisted by your
good conduct, she put in our possession near half a million of the enemy's property.*
   *Continue to be zealous, enterprising, and patient, and we will yet render the
name of the* Essex *as terrible to the enemy as that of any other vessel before we
return to the United States. My plans shall be made known to you at a suitable
period.*

(Signed)          *D. PORTER.*
                 *April 30, 1813.*

The possession of these vessels, besides the great satisfaction it produced, was attended by another advantage of no less importance, as it
relieved all our wants except one, to wit, the want of water. From them we
obtained an abundant supply of cordage, canvas, paints, tar, and every
other article necessary for the ship, of all of which she stood in great need,
as our slender stock brought from America had now become worn out and
useless. Besides the articles necessary for the ship, we became supplied
with a stock of provisions, of a quality and quantity that removed all apprehensions of our suffering for the want of them for many months, as those

vessels, when they sailed from England, were provided with provisions and stores for upwards of three years, and had not yet consumed half their stock. All were of the best quality; and were it only for the supplying our immediate wants the prizes were of the greatest importance to us. We found on board of them, also, wherewith to furnish our crew with several delicious meals. They had been in at James' Island and had supplied themselves abundantly with those extraordinary animals the tortoises of the Gallipagos, which properly deserve the name of the elephant tortoise. Many of them were of a size to weigh upwards of three hundred weight; and nothing, perhaps, can be more disagreeable or clumsy than they are in their external appearance. Their motion resembles strongly that of the elephant; their steps slow, regular, and heavy; they carry their body about a foot from the ground, and their legs and feet bear no slight resemblance to the animal to which I have likened them; their neck is from eighteen inches to two feet in length, and very slender; their head is proportioned to it and strongly resembles that of a serpent. But, hideous and disgusting as is their appearance, no animal can possibly afford a more wholesome, luscious, and delicate food than they do; the finest green turtle is no more to be compared to them in point of excellence than the coarsest beef is to the finest veal; and after once tasting the Gallipagos tortoises, every other animal food fell greatly in our estimation. These animals are so fat as to require neither butter nor lard to cook them, and this fat does not possess that cloying quality common to that of most other animals. When tried out, it furnishes an oil superior in taste to that of the olive. The meat of this animal is the easiest of digestion, and a quantity of it, exceeding that of any other food, can be eaten without experiencing the slightest inconvenience. But what seems the most extraordinary in this animal, is the length of time that it can exist without food; for I have been well assured, that they have been piled away among the casks in the hold of a ship, where they have been kept eighteen months, and when killed at the expiration of that time, were found to have suffered no diminution in fatness or excellence. They carry with them a constant supply of water, in a bag at the root of the neck, which contains about two gallons; and on tasting that found in those we killed on board, it proved perfectly fresh and sweet. They are very restless when exposed to the light and heat of the sun, but will lie in the dark from one year's end to the other without moving. In the day-time, they appear remarkably quick-sighted and timid, drawing their head into their shell on the slightest motion of any object; but they are entirely destitute of hearing, as the loudest noise, even the firing of a gun, does not seem to alarm them in the slightest degree, and at night, or in the dark, they appear perfectly blind. After our tasting the flesh of those animals, we regretted that numbers of them had been thrown overboard by the crews of the vessels before their capture, to clear them for action. A few days afterwards, at daylight in the morning, we were so fortunate as to find ourselves surrounded by about fifty of them, which were picked up and brought on board, as they had been lying in the same place where they had been thrown over, incapable of any exertion in that element, except that of stretching out their long necks.

I had merely placed a temporary crew on board the prizes, but took the first opportunity to make a more permanent arrangement, putting Midshipman Odenheimer in charge of the *Montezuma*, and Midshipman Cowan of the *Policy*, giving them the necessary directions for clearing their decks of the lumber of oil casks and other articles, to bend all their light sails, and reave their running rigging, which had all been unbent and unrove, as unnecessary while fishing, and to preserve them from injury. I also furnished them with the necessary signals and appointed the island of Plata, and the bay of Tumbez, as rendezvous in case of separation, directing them to use the utmost economy in the expenditure of their provisions, stores, and water, ordering all hands to be put on the same allowance as the crew of the *Essex*.

On examining the *Georgiana*, I found her not only a noble ship but well calculated for a cruiser, as she sailed well, had been built for the service of the British East-India Company, and had been employed as a packet until this voyage. I therefore determined to equip and arm her completely, and mounted on her the ten guns of the *Policy*, making her whole number now sixteen, to which were added two swivels and a number of heavy blunderbusses mounted on swivels, as well as all the muskets, pistols, cutlasses, and other military equipments we could find on board the other vessels. By these means rendering her as formidable, in point of armament, as any of the British letters of marque I could hear of in this ocean. But this I did not undertake until I was well satisfied she could be well manned without reducing too much my own crew. A number of seamen captured in the prizes had already proffered their services to us; and on inquiry I found many of them to be Americans. They volunteered their services in equipping the *Georgiana* and freeing her from much of the lumber on board, consisting of empty casks and other cumbrous articles, which were sent on board the other prizes. The heavy brick-work and large iron boilers used for trying out the oil were taken down to give more room on her decks and relieve her from the great weight, which was found greatly to improve her sailing. The command of this vessel, now completely equipped for war, I gave to Lieutenant Downes, with a crew consisting of thirty-six of our own men and five of the men who had entered from prizes, making her number altogether forty-one men. The remainder I kept on board the *Essex*, whose crew now amounted to two hundred and sixty-four men, including officers, and those on board the *Barclay*. I appointed Midshipman Haddaway as acting lieutenant on board the *Georgiana* and sent Mr. Miller (my former gunner) there to do duty, as well as Kingsbury as boatswain and two quarter-masters. The equipping and manning of this vessel also enabled me to make some promotions on board my own ship from some of the most deserving of my crew, to fill up the vacancies occasioned by the petty officers sent on board her. We now considered the sloop of war *Georgiana*, as she was styled, no trifling augmentation of our own force. But, taken in another view, she was of the utmost importance to our safety; for, in the event of any accident happening to the *Essex*, a circumstance to which she was every moment liable, while cruising in a sea with which we were little acquainted, we could calculate on relief from the *Georgiana*. Added to this, she doubled the chance of annoying the enemy, and might serve as an excellent decoy, as we were particularly careful not to change in the slightest degree her appearance as a whaler. On the 8th she hoisted the American ensign and pendant, and saluted the *Essex* with seventeen guns, which was returned by our crew with three cheers.

The light baffling winds and strong westerly currents prevented me now from laying any plans for my future operations; my whole attention was turned to getting up to the islands again, as I had intelligence of several other British vessels being in the neighbourhood and expected there; among others the *Perseverance*, the *Rose*, and the *New Zealand*, three fine vessels with nearly full cargoes. I felt anxious to get into port to recruit my stock of water and wood, the only articles we now stood in want of, as was the case with my prizes, which were all short of water. But I was desirous of looking once more into Banks' Bay, where I confidently expected, on a change of current, to make as many prizes as I could conveniently man.

The weather being remarkably pleasant, I took advantage of it to put our rigging in order, by overhauling and tarring it, and painting the ship inside. As we had been enabled to procure an abundance of small spars, planks, timber, and nails, I set the carpenters to work, making many repairs, which we had not heretofore been enabled to do for the want of the necessary materials; for although we had had it in our power to supply ourselves at Valparaiso, I did not procure them there, confidently believing that the enemy would, in due time, furnish us with what we wanted.

Doctor Miller, about this time, became dissatisfied with his new situation on board the *Barclay*, and expressed a desire to remove to the *Policy*, where the accommodations, he had understood, were equal to those of the *Barclay*. To this wish I assented; as the captain of the *Policy* was in very low health, I had been induced to let him remain on board his ship. As he was a man of considerable loquacity, and some intelligence, I believed that the doctor would find himself agreeably situated, if it were possible to make him so, as to comfort and society.

• • •

*Porter cruised the Galápagos Islands from April 17 to October 3, 1813, taking a dozen prizes. After repairing ship and reprovisioning in the Marquesas Islands, he returned to the coast of South America in January of 1814. His cruise continues in the next passage.*

# DAVID PORTER

# Showdown at Valparaiso
## 1814

*With his captured prize* Atlantic, *rechristened the* Essex Junior, *Captain Porter, commanding the* Essex, *entered the bay at Valparaiso, the principal seaport of Chile, ostensibly a neutral nation. Heretofore unchallenged, his profitable days in the South Pacific were about to end. In this passage, the proud captain narrates his bitter engagement with HMS* Phoebe, *commanded by Captain James Hillyar, and HMS* Cherub, *Captain Thomas Tucker.*

ON THE 3D OF FEBRUARY I anchored in the bay of Valparaiso, exchanged salutes with the battery, went on shore to pay my respects to the governor, and the next day received his visit under a salute. The governor was accompanied by his wife and several of his officers.

The *Essex Junior* was directed to cruise off the port, to intercept the enemy's merchant vessels and to apprise me of the appearance of any of his ships of war. In the mean time, every effort was made to get the *Essex* ready for sea, while my crew were allowed by turns to go ashore on liberty. The attention and hospitality of the people of Valparaiso seemed to increase; and not having had an opportunity to return their civilities on my former visit, I took advantage of the present occasion to supply the omission. On the evening of the seventh, I invited the officers of the government, their families, and all the other respectable inhabitants, to an entertainment on board the *Essex*. To give Lt. Downes an opportunity to participate in these gayeties, I directed him to anchor his vessel, but so as to save a full view of the sea.

The dancing continued until midnight; after which Lt. Downes repaired to his vessel, got her under way, and proceeded to sea. We had not yet taken down the awnings, flags, &c. which we usually employed on these occasions for the decorations of ships of war, nor got clear of the confusion which so large a company naturally occasioned, before the *Essex Junior* made a signal for two enemy's ships in sight. At this time, one half of my crew were on shore; but, having established a signal for them to repair on board, I caused a gun to be fired, and after directing the ship to be prepared for action, repaired on board the *Essex Junior*, and went out to reconnoitre. Both vessels had the appearance of frigates. Upon this I directed Lt. Downes to run into port and take a position where we could mutually defend each other.

On my return to the *Essex*, at half past seven, one hour and a half only after the enemy came in sight, I found the ship completely prepared for action, and every man on board, and at his post. We had now only to act on the defensive. At eight o'clock the two ships came into the harbour; the frigate, which proved to be the *Phoebe*, Captain Hillyar, ranging up alongside of the *Essex*, and between her and the *Essex Junior*, within a few yards of the former. The *Phoebe* was fully prepared for action.

Captain Hillyar very politely inquired after my health; to which inquiry I returned the usual compliment. And here it may be proper to observe that Captain Hillyar and myself had been acquainted in the Mediterranean. While his family resided at Gibraltar, I was in the habit of visiting them frequently, and had spent many pleasant hours in their company. For Captain Hillyar and his family I entertained the highest respect; and among the American officers generally, no officer of the British navy was so great a favourite as Captain Hillyar. The former paid to his family greater attentions than to any other persons similarly situated; and on the other hand, were always received with the like in return. On one occasion, during the absence of Captain Hillyar, they placed themselves under the protection of Commodore Rodgers and came in his ship from Malta to Gibraltar; where Mrs. Hillyar joined her husband. But, to proceed with my narrative:

Finding the *Phoebe* was approaching nearer than prudence or a strict neutrality would justify me in permitting, I observed to Captain Hillyar that my ship was perfectly prepared for action, but that I should only act on the defensive. He immediately answered, as he leaned over the quarter, in a careless and indifferent manner: "O, Sir, I have no intention of getting on board of you." I told him again, if he did fall on board of me, there would be much bloodshed. He repeated his assurances, with the same *nonchalance*, that such was not his intention. Finding, however, that he luffed up so as to cause his ship to take aback, whereby her jib-boom came across my forecastle, I immediately called all hands to board the enemy, directing them, if the ships' hulls touched, to spring upon the deck of the *Phoebe*. At this moment, not a gun from the *Phoebe* could be brought to bear on either the *Essex* or *Essex Junior*, while her bow was exposed to the raking fire of the one, and her stern to that of the other. Her consort, which proved to be the *Cherub*, of 28 guns, was too far off to leeward to afford any assistance.

It is quite impossible for me to describe the consternation on board the *Phoebe*, when they saw every officer and man of the *Essex* armed with a cutlass and a brace of pistols, ready to jump on board. They had been informed by the boat of an English ship in port that the *Essex* was in great confusion from the entertainment and that the greater part of her crew were on shore. On witnessing this unexpected preparation for his reception, Captain Hillyar raised both his hands and protested with the utmost vehemence that he had no intention of getting on board of me; that it was altogether an accident that his ship had been taken aback; that he was exceedingly sorry she had been placed in that situation; and that he had no hostile intention in doing so.

The *Phoebe* was at this moment completely at my mercy. I could have destroyed her in fifteen minutes. The temptation was great; and the equivocal appearance of this near approach of the enemy might have justified my attacking him on the plea of self-defence. But I was disarmed by these assurances of Captain Hillyar; and accordingly, hailing lieut. Downes, told him not to commence hostilities without my orders, as it was my intention to allow Captain Hillyar to extricate himself from his disagreeable situation. The *Phoebe* accordingly separated from the *Essex*, drifted by my ships, constantly exposed to their raking fire; and after getting clear of them, anchored on the eastern side of the harbour, within reach of her long eighteen-pounders, but beyond the range of my carronades. The *Cherub* anchored within pistol-shot of my larboard bow, and, upon this, I ordered the *Essex Junior* to take a position that would place the *Cherub* between her fire and that of the *Essex:* an arrangement that gave great umbrage to her commander, Captain Tucker.

On going ashore, there was a general expression of astonishment among the officers of the government, and the people of Valparaiso, at my forbearance in not taking advantage of the opportunity which had thus presented itself for destroying the enemy. My reply was that I had always respected the neutrality of their port and should scrupulously continue to do so. Nor, although subsequent events have proved that Captain Hillyar was incapable of a similar forbearance, have I ever regretted for a single moment that I permitted him to escape, when, either by accident or design, he had placed himself entirely at my mercy. At no time, during the engagement which took place afterwards, or since, would I have changed situations or feelings with that officer.

Captain Hillyar and Captain Tucker, the day after their arrival, paid me a visit at the house of Mr. Blanco, where I generally staid while on shore. Their visit was soon returned, and a friendly intimacy established, not only between the commanders and myself, but the officers and boats' crews of the respective ships. No one, to have judged from appearances, would have supposed us to have been at war, our conduct towards each other bore so much the appearance of a friendly alliance. At our first interview, I took occasion to tell Captain Hillyar, it was very important that I should know of him whether he intended to respect the neutrality of the port. He replied, with much emphasis and earnestness: "*You* have paid so much respect to the neutrality of the port that I feel myself bound in honour to respect it." I told him, the assurance was sufficient, and that it would place me more at ease, since I should now no longer feel it necessary to be always prepared for action.

In the course of this conversation, I adverted to a flag he had hoisted, containing the following motto: "God and country; British sailors best rights; traitors offend both;" and asked him the object of it. He said it was in reply to my motto of "free trade and sailors' rights," which gave great offence to the British navy—whenever I hoisted that flag, he should not fail to hoist the other. I told him, my flag was intended solely for the purpose of pleasing ourselves and not to insult the feelings of others; that his, on the contrary, was considered as highly insulting in the light of an offset against ours; and that, if he continued to hoist it, I should not fail to retort on him. The next day, this flag being hoisted, I displayed one bearing the motto of "God, our country, and Liberty—tyrants offend them." Three cheers followed on the part of the crew of the *Phoebe*, which were returned from my ship. The thing was taken in good part by Captain Hillyar; we talked freely and good humouredly of the object of his coming to that sea; the long hunt he had after me, and of my views in coming to Valparaiso. He asked me what I intended to do with my prizes; when I was going to sea; and various other inquiries were put and answered. I told him, whenever he sent away the *Cherub*, I should go to sea; that it would depend upon him altogether when I departed; that, having thus met him, I should seek an opportunity of testing the force of the two ships. I added that the *Essex* being smaller than the *Phoebe*, I did not feel that I should be justified to my country for losing my ship if I gave him a challenge; but if he would challenge me, and send away the *Cherub*, I would have no hesitation in fighting him.

To these and similar observations, Captain Hillyar would reply that the results of naval actions were very uncertain: they depended on many contingencies—and the loss of a mast or a spar often turned the fate of the day. He observed that notwithstanding the inferiority of my ship, still, if I could come to close quarters with her carronades, I should no doubt do great execution. On the whole, therefore, he should trust to circumstances to bring us together, as he was not disposed to yield the advantage of a superior force, which would effectually blockade me until other ships arrived, and at all events, prevent my doing any further injury to the commerce of Britain. As regarded my prizes, I informed him, they were only incumbrances to me, and I should take them to sea and destroy them the first opportunity. He told me I dared not do it while he was in sight. I replied, "we shall see."

Finding Captain Hillyar determined to yield none of the advantages of his superior force and being informed there were other ships bound into the Pacific Ocean in pursuit of me, I secretly resolved to take every means of provoking him to a contest with his single ship. The *Cherub* being quite near to the *Essex*, the respective crews occasionally amused themselves with singing songs, selecting those most appropriate to their situation and feelings. Some of these were of their own composition. The songs from the *Cherub* were better sung, but those of the *Essex* were more witty and more to the point. The national tune of "Yankee Doodle" was the vehicle through which the crew of the *Essex*, in full chorus, conveyed their nautical sarcasms; while "the sweet little cherub that sits up aloft" was generally selected by their rivals. These things were not only tolerated but encouraged by the officers through the whole of the first watch of the calm, delightful nights of Chili; much to the amusement of the people of Valparaiso, and the frequent annoyance of the crew of the *Cherub*. At length, Captain Hillyar requested me to put a stop to this practice, and I informed him, I certainly should not do so, while the singing continued on board the *Cherub*.

About this time, one of my prisoners made his escape, by jumping overboard from the *Essex Junior*. A boat put off from the *Cherub* to pick him up; and notwithstanding every effort on our part, he was carried on board the *Cherub*. This affair led to the following correspondence between Captain Hillyar and myself, in which the reader will perceive some little asperity, and the first which had showed itself since our meeting. I felt that Captain Hillyar had violated his pledge in permitting the rescue of this man, and could not forbear placing it in its true light. The reason of my not demanding his restoration must be obvious to all when it is considered how advantageous such a precedent would be to me, predisposed as the British sailors are to desert at every opportunity.

His Britannic Majesty's ship PHOEBE, Valparaiso,
9th Feb. 1814

Sir,

By an Englishman picked up by one of his majesty's sloop Cherub's boats, in a drowning state, Captain Tucker has been informed, that nine of our countrymen are suffering the miseries of close confinement, on board the American ship of war under your orders; and that the calamity of imprisonment is aggravated by their being kept in irons. As this mode of treatment is so contrary to any I have ever witnessed, during a very long servitude, as well as the usages of honourable warfare, may I beg (if the statement is just) that you will do me the favour to interest yourself in their behalf.

I HAVE THE HONOUR TO BE, &c.
(Signed)             JAMES HILLYAR.

U. S. Frigate ESSEX, Valparaiso,
10th Feb. 1814.

Sir,

I HAVE the honour to acknowledge the receipt of your letter of yesterday. The information you have received from the prisoner who made his escape from my armed prize, and who was assisted in effecting it by the boat and crew of his majesty's ship Cherub, is correct as respects the situation of the remaining prisoners of war on board the Essex Junior, as well as those in the Frigate I have the honour to command.

When at the Island of Nooaheevah, my prisoners, while on their parole of honour, made a most diabolical attempt to possess themselves of my prize by means of poison, with a view of making their escape. I detected and secured them; and when I no longer apprehended further danger, I liberated them. Since my arrival here, I have again found it necessary to secure them, and those on board my prize have been confined two days.

I have not perhaps had as long a servitude as Captain Hillyar; nor was it necessary I should, to learn honour and humanity. I deem it only necessary to say, that, of the many prisoners who have fallen into my hands since hostilities commenced between the United States and Great Britain, none have been confined but for my own security; or otherwise punished but when they deserved it.

I HAVE THE HONOUR TO BE, &c.
(Signed)             D. PORTER.

Our next meeting on shore, after this correspondence, was, however, very cordial. I made a proposition to put all my prisoners on board one of my prizes, without a cargo, and send her to England, with a passport, to secure her from capture; there to take in an equal number of American prisoners, and proceed with them to the United States. Captain Hillyar expressed some doubts of the propriety of this course, and adverted to a similar arrangement with the captain of the sloop of war *Alert*, captured by me, sent to St. John's, Newfoundland, with my prisoners, and thence to the United States, with an equal number of Americans. He wished, if possible, to see the correspondence respecting this arrangement.

In the course of this conversation, he mentioned the stories related to him by the man who made his escape from the *Essex Junior*, respecting my treatment of prisoners. Some of these were of the most extravagant and malicious kind; and if true, rendered me unworthy of my country. They had made an impression on the minds of the British officers, much to my disadvantage, and were calculated to operate greatly to the injury of the American prisoners that might hereafter fall into their hands. I felt it therefore due to my country and countrymen, as well as to my own honour, that the thing should be perfectly explained and understood. I accordingly wrote him the following letter, and received a reply—both of which I shall lay before the reader.

*U. S. Frigate Essex, Valparaiso,*
*23d Feb. 1814.*

Sir,

 *As you have expressed some doubts respecting the correctness of an arrangement proposed by me for the disposal of the prisoners of war on board the ships under my command—and as those doubts were occasioned by a communication made by Admiral Duckworth to the secretary of the Navy of the United States, of which you had not a perfect recollection, I have done myself the honour to transmit a copy of a letter from the department, containing an extract from the aforesaid communication, by which you will be enabled to judge whether the objections made by the admiral can be here applied.*

 *I also do myself the honour to send you the copy of a letter from the admiral to myself, as well as several other communications of a private nature, and beg you to restore the originals after you have perused and (if you think them of sufficient importance) taken a copy of them. I have been induced to do this from a wish to remove certain impressions which have been made on the public mind, highly prejudicial to the character of an American officer, and I assure you, although I have endeavoured to perform, and shall continue to do, my duty to my country to the utmost of my abilities, I disdain a mean and dishonourable act, whatever advantages may result from it. It has been my study to alleviate the miseries of war, and I have been rewarded in most instances with the basest ingratitude.*

British boats, with British subjects on board, daily pass and repass between the shore and the ships under your command, when far beyond the jurisdiction of this port. It has frequently been in my power to cut them off; but I have not done so, under the persuasion that American boats, under similar circumstances, would be permitted by you to pass unmolested. I beg you to inform me, whether my opinion is correct?

I HAVE THE HONOUR TO BE, &C.
(Signed)                    D. PORTER.

Captain James Hillyar, &c. &c.


H. B. M. SHIP PHOEBE, OFF VALPARAISO,
24th Feb. 1814.

SIR,

I HAVE the honour to acknowledge the receipt of your favour of yesterday, with its enclosures, and I beg you will accept my thanks for the trouble you have taken. The copy of Sir John Duckworth's letter, and the extracts accompanying it, confirm me in my opinion that the cases are too nearly similar to justify my acceding to your proposition of sending one of your prizes as a cartel; and the British government would certainly disapprove of the act.

The letters from your prisoners must be highly gratifying to your personal feelings—and I hope the individuals who have benefited by your humane attentions, will feel themselves bound in honour to rescue your character from every unjust and illiberal aspersion.

I certainly could have no objection to American boats passing in the way British do to us under similar circumstances. They have all the governor's permission.

I must now appeal to your humanity; repeat to you how anxious I am for the sufferings of my countrymen, at present your prisoners—and express my request that you will liberate them here, as the only expedient I can think of. If you accede to it, I pledge myself that they shall not be permitted to serve on board any of his majesty's ships, under my orders; and I will write immediately to the British government, that an equal number of Americans may be restored to their country.

I have availed myself of your permission to copy some of the papers and have taken the names of those who have acknowledged your goodness to them. The liberal minded will always do you justice—and a much higher reward awaits the performance of every Christian duty to an afflicted fellow-creature.

I HAVE THE HONOUR TO BE, &C.
(Signed)                    JAMES HILLYAR.

David Porter, Esq. &c. &c.

It will be understood, from the foregoing letters, that the *Phoebe* and *Cherub* had gone to cruise off the port. The circumstance that hastened their going to sea was as follows: A signal from the Spanish Telegraph, on the hill, announced a sail in the offing. The morning being calm, I ordered the *Essex Junior* to get under way, and go in pursuit, towing her with the boats of the *Essex*. After reconnoitering the vessel, which proved to be a store ship of the enemy, the *Phoebe* and *Cherub* got under way, and made all sail to cut off the *Essex Junior* from the harbour, which they were near effecting, but for the timely aid of the *Essex*'s boats, which again brought her safe to her old anchorage.

On the 25th of February, I sent a flag of truce on board the *Phoebe*, with the following note:

U. S. FRIGATE ESSEX, VALPARAISO,
*25th Feb. 1814.*

SIR,

*I HAVE the honour to acknowledge the receipt of your letter of yesterday, and agreeably to your request and assurances, immediately liberated on parole the British prisoners who were on board the vessels under my command. Their obligation, as well as a certificate of their liberation, are herewith enclosed.*

*My feelings have been greatly roused by the scandalous reports which have been circulated respecting my conduct. Yet I hope I shall always have sufficient control over myself to prevent any change in my conduct towards those whom the fortune of war may place in my power; for, though such a change might be just, it would not be generous. I fear I have done injury to my country, and my fellow-citizens, by the practice of liberating British subjects who have fallen into my hands before they were exchanged. But the purity of my intentions was evident to Admiral Duckworth, and so long as my country does not disapprove of this mode, I hope I may be the means of averting some of those evils incident to captivity.*

I HAVE THE HONOUR TO BE, &C.

(Signed)                              D. PORTER.

*Captain James Hillyar, &c. &c.*

H. B. M. SHIP PHOEBE, OFF VALPARAISO,
*26th Feb. 1814.*

SIR,

*I RECEIVED your letter announcing the liberation of my countrymen, as well as the accompanying obligation and certificate, and shall immediately transmit copies of the letter to the British government. I beg you will do me the honour to accept my sincere thanks for your attention to my request, and remain, with sentiments of respect and consideration, Sir,*

YOUR OBEDIENT SERVANT,

(Signed)          JAMES HILLYAR.

*David Porter, Esq. &c. &c.*

About this time, I thought it adviseable to know the sailing of my ship, and that of the enemy. I therefore chose a favourable opportunity, when the British vessels were to leeward, and unable to cut me off, to get under way, and let them chase me. I soon ascertained that the *Essex* had greatly the advantage, and consequently believed I could, at almost any time, make my escape from them. I did not like, however, to abandon the hope of bringing the *Phoebe* to action; and notwithstanding my own impatience to depart, I determined to keep it under control while I endeavoured to provoke my adversary to combat.

On the afternoon of the day on which the last letter was written, it being calm and the two British ships far in the offing, I towed one of my prizes, the *Hector*, to sea; and, when within the reach of their guns, set fire to her, and made my escape from them, notwithstanding every effort on their part, to cut me off. This insult had the desired effect. On the afternoon of the 27th, the *Cherub* was about two or three miles to leeward of the port, and the *Phoebe* was seen standing in for the harbour. At 5 o'clock she hove about, a short distance from me, with her head off shore, shortened sail, fired a gun to windward, and hoisted the flag containing the motto intended as an answer to mine. As every man on board my ship considered this a challenge, I did not hesitate a moment to accept of it as such. I immediately hoisted my motto, fired a gun, and got under way. The *Phoebe* now stood off shore and made sail. I followed her—increased sail—and was closing with her very fast, when, to my astonishment, she bore up before the wind, and ran down for her consort. My indignation was roused at this conduct, and I directed two shot to be fired ahead of her, to bring her to; but she continued on her course. I consequently hauled my wind and returned into port. When the *Phoebe* had joined her consort, both gave chase to me and after I had anchored, came gallantly into the harbour together.

I confess I felt exceedingly indignant at this conduct of Captain Hillyar and so expressed myself on shore, among the inhabitants. Certain of these expressions were communicated to the British residents in Valparaiso, and by them to Captain Hillyar. This state of affairs gave rise to another kind of annoyance. The *Cherub* was now too far off to hear the songs of the *Essex;*

but still feeling sore at some taunts of my crew, on the score of the late challenge, addressed some letters to them, of a very insulting character, which were brought to me. They informed me they had answered them. I thought this a fair opportunity of rousing Captain Hillyar to offer battle again in earnest. I accordingly wrote the following letter with this express object.

U. S. FRIGATE ESSEX, VALPARAISO,
14th March, 1814

SIR,

THE two enclosed papers have been handed to me by my ship's company and were delivered to one of my seamen by a British prisoner on parole, as coming from your ship. One of my seamen has also assured me that the crew of an English ship now in port have showed him a letter bearing your signature, holding forth encouragement to my people for deserting the cause in which they are now engaged. The style of the two papers is a sufficient evidence that they were not written by a common sailor. But, although I have received the most positive assurances respecting the letter, my knowledge of the character of Captain Hillyar will not permit me to believe him capable of so base an expedient to effect the object of his cruise— notwithstanding the circumstances, and alleged object of the Phoebe's flag might induce a suspicion. It appears that my ship's company have made some reply to the first of these papers; and it is highly probable that it was couched in the ordinary language of sailors. The most insulting epithets have been applied to them, and in the most public manner. I have not therefore thought it proper to restrain that indignation my people have felt, in common with myself, at such proceedings. Their character, as well as my own, has been misunderstood; and if it is believed that we have wished to shake the loyalty of your seamen, I can positively assure you our intentions have been equally misunderstood. It is not necessary for us to resort to so pitiful an expedient—and were it necessary, I should spurn it. My men are equally prepared with myself to do our duty: they have given me innumerable proofs of their readiness at all times to die in support of their country's cause: they have my unlimited confidence—I have theirs.

I HAVE THE HONOUR TO BE, &C.

(Signed)          D. PORTER.

Captain James Hillyar, &c. &c.

To this letter Captain Hillyar returned a temperate reply, disclaiming in the strongest terms the conduct I had attributed to him; retorting the charge of his people being the aggressors in this paper war; charging my men with blasphemy; and finally hinting at various reports he had lately heard to my disadvantage, but which he wished not to believe. Some other letters passed between us; of which both the originals and copies were lost in my capture. The crews of the hostile ships also continued to carry on the war, in poetry and prose: and some of the poetical effusions of our opponents were so highly meritorious as to cause a suspicion of their being the production of Captain Hillyar himself.

On the 16th of March, twelve days before my capture, the first lieutenant of the *Phoebe* came on board the *Essex,* under a flag of truce, and stated that he had a message from Captain Hillyar. Presuming it was another challenge, I required the presence of some of my officers, to which he consented. When they were assembled, I asked the purport of his message. He then stated, that Captain Hillyar had been informed, I had said that he acted in a cowardly manner by running away from the *Essex* after challenging her, but could not believe the report, and had sent him on board to ascertain the truth. I told him I had said so and still thought so. He then stated, that Captain Hillyar had entrusted him to tell me that his firing a gun and hoisting the flag, was not intended as a challenge, but as a signal to the *Cherub.* I replied that Captain Hillyar had informed me the motto of the flag was intended for my ship and that there was not a man, woman, or child in Valparaiso that did not think it a challenge. He still repeated that Captain Hillyar had desired him to assure me it was not a challenge.

I told him in reply that I had considered it one, but was bound to believe Captain Hillyar, if he said it was not. I added that, however it might be intended, I should always consider it a challenge, whenever he chose to send away the *Cherub,* and perform a similar maneuver—and, under that impression, act precisely as I had done before. Again the officer assured me of the mistake; adding that Captain Hillyar was a religious man, and did not approve of sending challenges.

I shall now close this part of my narrative by laying before my readers two certificates, one from the only officer now alive who was present at the foregoing conversation between Lt. Ingraham and myself. I would appeal to the candour of Lt. Ingraham himself had he not been killed in the subsequent action.

"On Sunday *the 27th February, 1814, at 5 P.M. the* Phoebe *ran close in with the harbour, hoisted an English ensign, bearing the motto, "God and our country; British sailors' best rights; traitors offend them;" and fired a gun to windward. The sloop of war was about two and a half miles to leeward. The* Essex *immediately got under way, hoisted a flag bearing the motto, "God, our country, and liberty; tyrants offend them;" and fired a gun to windward. The Phoebe hove to, until the Essex was within gun-shot, when she bore up and ran down for the sloop. Two shot were fired across her bows to bring her to, but without effect. After chasing her as far as was prudent, Captain Porter observed that their conduct was cowardly and dishonourable and returned into port, where we came to anchor.*

(Signed)

JOHN DOWNES,
WM. ODENHEIM,
EDWARD BARNWELL,
RICHARD K. HOFFMAN,
JOHN K. SHAW,
M. W. BARTOWE,
ALEXR. MONTGOMERY,
GEO. W. ISAACS,
S. L. DUZENBERY.

"ON *the 10th of March, 1814, Lt. Ingraham, first of the* Phoebe, *came on board the* Essex, *under a flag of truce, having a letter from Commodore Hillyar to Captain Porter. Lt. Ingraham informed Captain Porter that Commodore Hillyar had heard Captain P. had called him a coward for running away from the* Essex *and begged to know if it was the case. Captain Porter informed him that, considering the circumstance of the challenge and the conduct of the* Phoebe *in bearing up, he believed any thing he could have said on the occasion justifiable. Lt. Ingraham assured Captain Porter that no challenge was intended and that the gun was fired by accident. Captain P. said he supposed it to be a challenge at the time and had accepted it; and that he should accept another if given by the* Phoebe; *observing,* "it cannot be expected that I would take upon myself the responsibility of challenging a 36-gun frigate, with a frigate of 32 guns; as my country would censure me should I prove unsuccessful; but the difference of force will not prevent my accepting a challenge given by Captain Hillyar.*

*The* Phoebe *and* Cherub, *ever after, kept close together, and showed a determination of not risking an action unless they could both engage the* Essex."

(Signed)          JOHN DOWNES.

These are the most important circumstances which preceded the capture of the *Essex,* in the bay of Valparaiso; the particulars of which are related in the following letter to the secretary of the Navy:

COPY OF A LETTER FROM CAPTAIN PORTER TO THE SECRETARY OF THE NAVY.

Essex Junior, July 3d, 1814, at sea.

SIR,

I have done myself the honour to address you, repeatedly, since I left the Delaware; but have scarcely a hope that one of my letters has reached you, and therefore, consider it necessary to give you a brief history of my proceedings since that period.

I sailed from the Delaware on the 27th of October, 1812, and repaired, with all diligence (agreeably to the instructions of Commodore Bainbridge[1]), to Port Praya, Fernando de Noronho, and Cape Frio, arriving at each place on the day appointed to meet him. On my passage from Port Praya to Fernando de Noronho, I captured his Britannic majesty's packet Nocton—and after taking out about eleven thousand pounds sterling in specie, sent her under command of Lieutenant Finch for America. I cruised off Rio de Janeiro, and about Cape Frio, until the 12th January, 1813, hearing frequently of the commodore by vessels from Bahia. I here captured one schooner with hides and tallow; I sent her into Rio. The Montague, the admiral's ship, being in pursuit of me, my provisions now getting short, and finding it necessary to look out for a supply to enable me to meet the commodore by the first of April, off St. Helena, I proceeded to the island of St. Catherine's (the last place of rendezvous on the coast of Brazil) as the most likely to supply my wants, and, at the same time, afford me that intelligence necessary to enable me to elude the British ships of war on the coast, and expected there. I here could procure only wood, water, and rum, and a few bags of flour; and hearing of the commodore's action with the Java, the capture of the Hornet by the Montague, and of a considerable augmentation of the British force on the coast, several being in pursuit of me, I found it necessary to get to sea as soon as possible. I now, agreeably to the commodore's plan, stretched to the southward, scouring the coast as far as Rio de la Plata. I heard that Buenos Ayres was in a state of starvation and could not supply our wants; and that the government of Montevideo was very inimical to us. The commodore's instructions now left it completely discretionary with me what course to pursue, and I determined on following that which had not only met his approbation, but the approbation of the then secretary of the Navy. I accordingly shaped my course for the Pacific; and after suffering greatly from short allowance of provisions, and heavy gales off Cape Horn, (for which my ship and men were ill provided) I arrived at Valparaiso on the 14th of March, 1813. I here took in as much jerked beef and other provisions as my ship would conveniently stow and ran down

---

[1] Commodore William Bainbridge, on board the Constitution, was in charge of the squadron consisting of the Constitution, the Essex, and the Hornet, dispatched to the South Pacific.

*the coast of Chili and Peru. In this track I fell in with a Peruvian corsair, which had on board twenty-four Americans as prisoners, the crews of two whale ships, which she had taken on the coast of Chili. The captain informed me that, as allies of Great Britain, they would capture all they should meet with in expectation of a war between Spain and the United States. I consequently threw all his guns and ammunition into the sea, liberated the Americans, and wrote a respectful letter to the viceroy, explaining the cause of my proceedings, which I delivered to her Captain. I then proceeded for Lima and recaptured one of the vessels as she was entering the port. From thence I shaped my course for the Gallipagos islands, where I cruised from the 17th April until the 3d October, 1813. During this time I touched only once on the coast of America, which was for the purpose of procuring a supply of fresh water, as none is to be found among those islands, which are perhaps the most barren and desolate of any known.*

*While among this group, I captured the following British ships, employed chiefly in the spermaceti whale fishery, viz:*

### LETTERS OF MARQUE.

|                  | tons. | men. | guns. | pierced for |
|------------------|-------|------|-------|-------------|
| Montezuma        | 270   | 21   | 2     |             |
| Policy           | 175   | 26   | 10    | 18          |
| Georgiana        | 280   | 25   | 6     | 18          |
| Greenwich        | 338   | 25   | 10    | 20          |
| Atlantic         | 355   | 24   | 8     | 20          |
| Rose             | 220   | 21   | 8     | 20          |
| Hector           | 270   | 25   | 11    | 20          |
| Catharine        | 270   | 29   | 8     | 18          |
| Seringapatam     | 357   | 31   | 14    | 26          |
| Charlton         | 274   | 21   | 10    | 18          |
| New Zealander    | 259   | 23   | 8     | 18          |
| Sir A. Hammond   | 301   | 31   | 12    | 18          |
|                  | 3369  | 302  | 107   |             |

*As some of those ships were captured by boats, and others by prizes, my officers and men had several opportunities of showing their gallantry.*

The Rose *and* Charlton *were given up to the prisoners: the* Hector, Catharine, *and* Montezuma. *I sent to Valparaiso, where they were laid up. The* Policy, Georgiana, *and* New Zealander *I sent for America; the* Greenwich *I* kept as a store ship, to contain the stores of my other prizes, necessary for us; and the Atlantic, now called the Essex Junior, I equipped with twenty guns, and gave the command of her to Lieutenant Downes.

Lieutenant Downes had convoyed the prizes to Valparaiso, and on his return, brought letters, informing me that a squadron under the command of Commodore James Hillyar, consisting of the frigate Phoebe of thirty-six guns, had sailed on the 6th July for this sea.—The Racoon and Cherub had been seeking me for some time on the coast of Brazil, and on their return from their cruise, joined the squadron sent in search of me to the Pacific. My ship, as it may be supposed, after being near a year at sea, required some repairs to put her in a state to meet them, which I determined to do, and bring them to action, if I could meet them on nearly equal terms. I proceeded, now, in company with the remainder of my prizes, to the island of Nooaheevah, or Madison's island, lying in the Washington group, discovered by a Captain Ingraham of Boston. Here I caulked and completely overhauled my ship, made for her a new set of water casks, her old ones being entirely decayed, and took on board from my prizes, provisions and stores for upwards of four months, and sailed for the coast of Chili on the 12th December, 1813. Previous to sailing, I secured the Seringapatam, Greenwich, and Sir Andrew Hammond, under the guns of a battery, which I had erected for their protection. After taking possession of this fine island for the United States and establishing the most friendly intercourse with the natives, I left them under charge of Lieutenant Gamble of the Marines, with twenty-one men, with orders to repair to Valparaiso after a certain period.

I arrived on the coast of Chili on the 12th January, 1814; looked into Conception and Valparaiso, found at both places only three English vessels, and learned that the squadron which sailed from Rio de Janeiro for that sea had not been heard of since their departure, and were supposed to be lost in endeavouring to double Cape Horn.

I had completely broken up the British navigation in the Pacific; the vessels which had not been captured by me, were laid up, and dared not venture out. I had afforded the most ample protection to our own vessels, which were, on my arrival, very numerous and unprotected.—The valuable whale fishery there, is entirely destroyed, and the actual injury we have done them may be estimated at two and a half millions of dollars, independent of the expenses of the vessels in search of me. They have supplied me amply with sails, cordage, cables, anchors, provisions, medicines, and stores of every description—and the slops on board them have furnished clothing for the seamen. We had, in fact, lived on the enemy since I had been in that sea; every prize having proved a well found store ship for me. I had not yet been under the necessity of drawing bills on the department for any object, and had been enabled to make considerable advances to my officers and crew on account of pay.

*For the unexampled time we had kept the sea, my crew had continued remarkably healthy; I had but one case of the scurvy, and had lost only the following men by death. viz:—*

*John S. Cowan, lieutenant,*
*Robert Miller, surgeon,*
*Levi Holmes, [ordinary] seaman,*
*Edward Sweeny, do.*
*Samuel Groce, seaman,*
*James Spafford, gunner's mate,*
*Benjamin Geers,* ⎫
                          ⎬ *qr. gunners,*
*John Rodgers,* ⎭
*Andrew Mahan, corporal of marines,*
*Lewis Price, private marine.*

*I had done all the injury that could be done to the British commerce in the Pacific, and still hoped to signalize my cruise by something more splendid before leaving that sea. I thought it not improbable that Commodore Hillyar might have kept his arrival secret, and believing that he would seek me at Valparaiso, as the most likely place to find me, I determined to cruise about that place, and should I fail of meeting him, hoped to be compensated by the capture of some merchant ships, said to be expected from England.*

*The* Phoebe, *agreeably to my expectations, came to seek me at Valparaiso, where I was anchored with the* Essex, *my armed prize the* Essex *Junior, under the command of Lieutenant Downes, on the look-out off the harbour. But, contrary to the course I thought he would pursue, Commodore Hillyar brought with him the* Cherub *sloop of war, mounting twenty-eight guns, eighteen thirty-two pound carronades, eight twenty-fours, and two long nines on the quarter deck and forecastle, and a complement of a hundred and eighty men. The force of the* Phoebe *is as follows: thirty long eighteen-pounders, sixteen thirty-two pound carronades, one howitzer, and six three-pounders in the tops, in all fifty-three guns, and a complement of three hundred and twenty men; making a force of eighty-one guns and five hundred men—in addition to which, they took on board the crew of an English letter of marque lying in port. Both ships had picked crews, and were sent into the Pacific in company with the* Racoon *of twenty-two guns, and a store-ship of twenty guns, for the express purpose of seeking the* Essex, *and were prepared with flags bearing the motto, "God and country; British sailors' best rights; traitors offend both." This was intended as a reply to my motto, "Free trade and sailors' rights," under the erroneous impression that my crew were chiefly Englishmen, or to counteract its effect on their own crews.—The force of the* Essex *was forty-six* guns, forty thirty-two pound carronades, and six long twelves, and her crew, which had been much reduced by prizes, amounted only to two hundred and fifty-five men. The Essex Junior, which was intended chiefly as a store-ship, mounted twenty guns, ten eighteen-pound carronades, and ten short sixes, with only sixty men on board. In reply to their motto, I wrote at my mizen—"God, our Country, and Liberty; tyrants offend them."

On getting their provisions on board, they went off the port for the purpose of blockading me, where they cruised for near six weeks; during which time I endeavoured to provoke a challenge, and frequently, but ineffectually, to bring the Phoebe alone to action, first with both my ships, and afterwards with my single ship, with both crews on board. I was several times under way, and ascertained that I had greatly the advantage in point of sailing, and once succeeded in closing within gun shot of the Phoebe, and commenced a fire on her, when she ran down for the Cherub, which was two and a half miles to leeward. This excited some surprise and expressions of indignation, as previous to my getting under way, she hove too off the port, hoisted her motto flag, and fired a gun to windward. Commodore Hillyar seemed determined to avoid a contest with me on nearly equal terms, and from his extreme prudence in keeping both his ships ever after constantly within hail of each other, there were no hopes of any advantages to my country from a longer stay in port. I therefore determined to put to sea the first opportunity which should offer; and I was the more strongly induced to do so, as I had gained certain intelligence that the Tagus, rated thirty-eight, and two other frigates, had sailed for that sea in pursuit of me. I had also reason to expect the arrival of the Racoon from the NW coast of America, where she had been sent for the purpose of destroying our fur establishment on the Columbia.

A rendezvous was appointed for the Essex Junior, and every arrangement made for sailing, and I intended to let them chase me off, to give the Essex Junior an opportunity of escaping. On the 28th of March, the day after this determination was formed, the wind came on to blow fresh from the southward, when I parted my larboard cable and dragged my starboard anchor directly out to sea. Not a moment was to be lost in getting sail on the ship. The enemy were close in with the point forming the west side of the bay; but on opening them I saw a prospect of passing to windward, when I took in my top-gallant sails, which were set over single reefed top-sails, and braced up for this purpose. But on rounding the point a heavy squall struck the ship and carried away her main-top-mast, precipitating the men who were aloft into the sea, who were drowned. Both ships now gave chase to me, and I endeavoured in my disabled state to regain the port; but finding I could not recover the common anchorage, I ran close into a small bay, about three quarters of a mile to leeward of the battery, on the east side of the harbour, and let go my anchor within pistol shot of the shore, where I intended to repair my damages as soon as possible. The enemy continued to approach, showing an evident intention of attacking us, *regardless of the neutrality of the place where I was anchored. The caution observed in their approach to the attack of the crippled* Essex *was truly ridiculous, as was their display of their motto flags, and the number of jacks at their mast heads. I, with as much expedition as circumstances would admit, got my ship ready for action, and endeavoured to get a spring on my cable, but had not succeeded when the enemy, at fifty-four minutes after three P.M. made his attack, the* Phoebe *placing herself under my stern, and the* Cherub *on my starboard bow. But the* Cherub *soon finding her situation a hot one, bore up and ran under my stern also, where both ships kept up a hot raking fire. I had got three long twelve-pounders out at the stern ports, which were worked with so much bravery and skill, that in half an hour we so disabled both as to compel them to haul off to repair damages.*

*In the course of this firing, I had by the great exertions of Mr. Edward Barnewall the acting sailing master, assisted by Mr. Linscott the boatswain, succeeded in getting springs on our cables three different times—but the fire of the enemy was so excessive, that before we could get our broadside to bear, they were shot away, and thus rendered useless to us. My ship had received many injuries, and several men had been killed and wounded—but my brave officers and men, notwithstanding the unfavourable circumstances under which we were brought to action, and the powerful force opposed to us, were nowise discouraged—all appeared determined to defend their ship to the last extremity, and to die, in preference to a shameful surrender.*

*Our gaff, with the ensign and motto flag at the mizzen, had been shot away— but* FREE TRADE AND SAILORS' RIGHTS *continued to fly at the fore.—Our ensign was replaced by another—and to guard against a similar event, an ensign was made fast in the mizzen rigging, and several jacks were hoisted in different parts of the ship. The enemy soon repaired his damages for a fresh attack; he now placed himself, with both his ships, on my starboard quarter, out of the reach of my carronades, and where my stern guns could not be brought to bear; he there kept up a most galling fire, which it was out of my power to return, when I saw no prospect of injuring him without getting under way and becoming the assailant. My top-sail sheets and halliards were all shot away, as well as the jib and fore-top-mast-stay-sail-halliards. The only rope not cut was the flying-jib-halliards; and that being the only sail I could set, I caused it to be hoisted, my cable to be cut, and ran down on both ships, with an intention of laying the* Phoebe *on board.*

*The firing on both sides was now tremendous; I had let fall my fore-top-sail and fore-sail, but the want of tacks and sheets had rendered them almost useless to us. Yet we were enabled for a short time to close with the enemy; and although our decks were now strewed with dead, and our cock-pit filled with wounded, although our ship had been several times on fire and was rendered a perfect wreck, we were still encouraged to hope to save her, from the circumstance of the* Cherub *being compelled to haul off. She did not return to close action again, although she apparently had it in her power to do so, but kept up a distant firing with her long guns.*

*The* Phoebe, *from our disabled state, was enabled, however, by edging off, to choose the distance which best suited her long guns, and kept up a tremendous fire on us, which mowed down my brave companions by the dozen. Many of my guns had been rendered useless by the enemy's shot, and many of them had their whole crews destroyed. We manned them again from those which were disabled, and one gun in particular was three times manned—fifteen men were slain at it in the action. But, strange as it may appear, the captain of it escaped with only a slight wound.*

*Finding that the enemy had it in his power to choose his distance, I now gave up all hopes of closing with him, and as the wind, for the moment, seemed to favour the design, I determined to endeavour to run her on shore, land my men and destroy her. Every thing seemed to favour my wishes. We had approached the shore within musket shot, and I had no doubt of succeeding, when, in an instant, the wind shifted from the land (as is very common in this port in the latter part of the day) and payed our head down on the* Phoebe, *where we were again exposed to a dreadful raking fire. My ship was now totally unmanageable; yet, as her head was toward the enemy, and he to leeward of me, I still hoped to be able to board him. At this moment lieutenant commandant Downes came on board to receive my orders, under the impression that I should soon be a prisoner. He could be of no use to me in the then wretched state of the* Essex; *and finding (from the enemy's putting his helm up) that my last attempt at boarding would not succeed, I directed him, after he had been about ten minutes on board, to return to his own ship, to be prepared for defending and destroying her in case of an attack. He took with him several of my wounded, leaving three of his boats crew on board to make room for them.*

*The slaughter on board my ship had now become horrible, the enemy continuing to rake us, and we unable to bring a gun to bear. I therefore directed a hawser to be bent to the sheet anchor, and the anchor to be cut from the bows to bring her head round: this succeeded. We again got our broadside to bear, and as the enemy was much crippled and unable to hold his own, I have no doubt he would soon have drifted out of gun shot before he discovered we had anchored, had not the hawser unfortunately parted. My ship had taken fire several times during the action, but alarmingly so forward and aft; at this moment, the flames were bursting up each hatchway, and no hopes were entertained of saving her; our distance from the shore did not exceed three-quarters of a mile, and I hoped many of my brave crew would be able to save themselves, should the ship blow up, as I was informed the fire was near the magazine, and the explosion of a large quantity of powder below served to increase the horrors of our situation—our boats were destroyed by the enemy's shot; I, therefore, directed those who could swim to jump overboard and endeavour to gain the shore. Some reached it—some were taken by the enemy, and some perished in the attempt; but most preferred sharing with me the fate of the ship. We, who remained, now turned our attention wholly to extinguishing the flames; and when we had succeeded, went again to our guns, where the firing was kept up for some minutes, but the crew had by this time become so weakened that they all declared to me the impossibility of making further resistance and entreated me to surrender my ship to save the wounded, as all further attempt at opposition must prove ineffectual, almost every gun being disabled by the destruction of their crews.*

*I now sent for the officers of divisions to consult them; but what was my surprise to find only acting Lieutenant Stephen Decatur M'Knight remaining, who confirmed the report respecting the condition of the guns on the gun-deck—those on the spar deck were not in a better state. Lieutenant Wilmer, after fighting most gallantly throughout the action, had been knocked overboard by a splinter while getting the sheet anchor from the bows, and was drowned. Acting Lieutenant John G. Cowell had lost a leg; Mr. Edward Barnewall, acting sailing master, had been carried below after receiving two wounds, one in the breast and one in the face; and acting Lieutenant William H. Odenheimer had been knocked overboard from the quarter an instant before, and did not regain the ship until after the surrender. I was informed that the cock-pit, the steerage, the ward-room and the birth-deck, could contain no more wounded; that the wounded were killed while the surgeons were dressing them, and that, unless something was speedily done to prevent it, the ship would soon sink from the number of shot holes in her bottom. And, on sending for the carpenter, he informed me that all his crew had been killed or wounded, and that he had been once over the side to stop the leaks, when his slings had been shot away, and it was with difficulty he was saved from drowning.*

*The enemy, from the smoothness of the water, and the impossibility of our reaching him with our carronades, and the little apprehension that was excited by our fire, which had now become much slackened, was enabled to take aim at us as at a target; his shot never missed our hull, and my ship was cut up in a manner which was, perhaps, never before witnessed—in fine, I saw no hopes of saving her, and at twenty minutes after six* P.M. *gave the painful order to strike the colours. Seventy-five men, including officers were all that remained of my whole crew, after the action, capable of doing duty, and many of them severely wounded, some of whom have since died.* The enemy still continued his fire, *and my brave, though unfortunate companions, were still falling about me. I directed an opposite gun to be fired to show them we intended no further resistance;* but they did not desist; four men were killed at my side, and others in different parts of the ship. *I now believed he intended to show us no quarter, and that it would be as well to die with my flag flying as struck, and was on the point of again hoisting it, when about* ten minutes after hauling the colours down he ceased firing!

*I cannot speak in sufficiently high terms of the conduct of those engaged for such an unparalleled length of time (under such circumstances) with me in the arduous and unequal contest—Let it suffice to say that more bravery, skill, patriotism, and zeal were never displayed on any occasion. Every one seemed determined to die in defence of their much loved country's cause, and nothing but views to*

*humanity could ever have reconciled them to the surrender of the ship; they remem-*
*bered their wounded and helpless shipmates below. To acting Lieutenants M'Knight*
*and Odenheimer I feel much indebted for their great exertions and bravery through-*
*out the action, in fighting and encouraging the men at their divisions, for the dex-*
*terous management of the long guns, and for their promptness in re-manning their*
*guns as their crews were slaughtered. The conduct of that brave and heroic officer,*
*acting Lieutenant John G. Cowell, who lost his leg in the latter part of the action,*
*excited the admiration of everyman in the ship, and after being wounded, would not*
*consent to be taken below, until loss of blood rendered him insensible. Mr. Edward*
*Barnewall acting sailing-master, whose activity and courage were equally conspic-*
*uous, returned on deck after his first wound, and remained after receiving his sec-*
*ond until fainting with loss of blood.—Mr. Samuel B. Johnson, who had joined me*
*the day before, and acted as marine officer, conducted himself with great bravery and*
*exerted himself in assisting at the long guns; the musketry after the first half hour*
*being useless, from our great distance.*

*Mr. M. W. Bostwick, whom I had appointed acting purser of the* Essex Junior,
*and who was on board my ship, did the duties of aid, in a manner which reflects on*
*him the highest honour, and Midshipmen Isaacs, Farragut, and Ogden, as well as*
*acting Midshipmen James Terry, James R. Lyman, and Samuel Duzenbury, and*
*Master's Mate William Pierce, exerted themselves in the performance of their*
*respective duties, and gave an earnest of their value to the service; the three first are*
*too young to recommend for promotion.—The latter I beg leave to recommend for*
*confirmation, as well as the acting lieutenants, and Messrs. Barnewall, Johnson,*
*and Bostwick.*

*We have been unfortunate, but not disgraced—the defence of the* Essex *has not*
*been less honourable to her officers and crew than the capture of an equal force; and*
*I now consider my situation less unpleasant than that of Commodore Hillyar, who,*
*in violation of every principle of honour and generosity, and regardless of the rights*
*of nations, attacked the* Essex *in her crippled state, within pistol shot of a neutral*
*shore—when, for six weeks, I had daily offered him fair and honourable combat, on*
*terms greatly to his advantage. The blood of the slain must be on his head, and he*
*has yet to reconcile his conduct to heaven, to his conscience, and to the world.—*
*The annexed extract of a letter from Commodore Hillyar, which was written previ-*
*ously to his returning me my sword, will show his opinion of our conduct.*

*My loss has been dreadfully severe, fifty-eight killed, or have since died of their*
*wounds, and among them Lieutenant Cowell; thirty-nine were severely wounded,*
*twenty-seven slightly, and thirty-one are missing—making in all one hundred and*
*fifty-four, killed, wounded, and missing, a list of whose names is annexed.*

*The professional knowledge of Dr. Richard Hoffman, acting surgeon, and Dr.*
*Alexander Montgomery, acting surgeon's mate, added to the assiduity and the*
*benevolent attentions and assistance of Mr. D. P. Adams, the chaplain, saved the*

*lives of many of the wounded—those gentlemen have been indefatigable in their attentions to them; the two first I beg leave to recommend for confirmation, and the latter to the notice of the department.*

*I must, in justification of myself, observe that with our six twelve-pounders only we fought this action, our carronades being almost useless.*

*The loss in killed and wounded has been great with the enemy; among the former is the first lieutenant of the* Phoebe, *and of the latter, Captain Tucker of the* Cherub, *whose wounds are severe. Both the* Essex *and* Phoebe *were in a sinking state, and it was with difficulty they could be kept afloat until they anchored in Valparaiso next morning. The shattered state of the* Essex *will, I believe, prevent her ever reaching England, and I also think it will be out of their power to repair the damages of the* Phoebe *so as to enable her to double Cape Horn. All the masts and yards of the* Phoebe *and* Cherub *are badly crippled, and their hulls much cut up; the former had eighteen twelve-pound shot through her below her water line, some three feet under water. Nothing but the smoothness of the water saved both the* Phoebe *and* Essex.

*I hope, sir, that our conduct may prove satisfactory to our country, and that it will testify it by obtaining our speedy exchange, that we may again have it in our power to prove our zeal.*

*Commodore Hillyar (I am informed) has thought proper to state to his government that the action only lasted forty-five minutes; should he have done so, the motive may be easily discovered—but the thousands of disinterested witnesses who covered the surrounding hills, can testify that we fought his ships near two hours and a half; upwards of fifty broadsides were fired by the enemy, agreeably to their own accounts, and upwards of seventy-five by ours: except the few minutes they were repairing damages, the firing was incessant.*

*Soon after my capture, I entered into an agreement with Commodore Hillyar to disarm my prize, the* Essex Junior, *and proceed with the survivors of my officers and crew to the United States, taking with me her officers and crew. He consented to grant her a passport to secure her from recapture. The ship was small, and we knew we had much to suffer, yet we hoped soon to reach our country in safety, that we might again have it in our power to serve it. This arrangement was attended with no additional expense, as she was abundantly supplied with provisions and stores for the voyage.*

*In justice to Commodore Hillyar, I must observe, that (although I can never be reconciled to the manner of his attack on the* Essex, *or to his conduct before the action) he has, since our capture, shown the greatest humanity to my wounded (whom he permitted me to land, on condition that the United States should bear their expenses), and has endeavoured as much as lay in his power to alleviate the distresses of war, by the most generous and delicate deportment towards myself, my officers, and crew. He gave orders that the property of every person should be* respected; which orders, however, were not so strictly attended to as might have been expected; besides being deprived of books, charts, &c. &c. both myself and officers lost many articles of our clothing, some to a considerable amount. I should not have considered this last circumstance of sufficient importance to notice, did it not mark a striking difference between the navy of Great-Britain, and that of the United States, highly creditable to the latter.

By the arrival of the Tagus a few days after my capture, I was informed that besides the ships which had arrived in the Pacific in pursuit of me, and those still expected, others were sent to cruize for me in the China seas, off New Zealand, Timor, and New Holland, and that another frigate was sent to the river La Plata.

To possess the Essex, it has cost the British government near six millions of dollars, and yet, sir, her capture was owing entirely to accident; and if we consider the expedition with which naval contests are now decided, the action is a dishonour to them. Had they brought their ships boldly into action with a force so very superior, and having the choice of position, they should either have captured or destroyed us in one-fourth of the time they were about it.

During the action, our consul general, Mr. Poinsett, called on the governor of Valparaiso and requested that the batteries might protect the Essex. This request was refused, but he promised that if she should succeed in fighting her way to the common anchorage, he would send an officer to the British commander and request him to cease firing, but declined using force under any circumstances; and there is no doubt a perfect understanding existed between them. This conduct, added to the assistance given to the British and their friendly reception after the action, and the strong bias of the faction which govern Chili in favour of the English, as well as their hostility to the Americans, induced Mr. Poinsett to leave that country. Under such circumstances, I did not conceive it would be proper for me to claim the restoration of my ship, confident that the claim would be made by my government to more effect. Finding some difficulty in the sale of my prizes, I had taken the Hector and Catharine to sea and burnt them with their cargoes.

I exchanged Lieutenant M'Knight, Mr. Adams, and Mr. Lyman, and eleven seamen for a part of the crew of the Sir Andrew Hammond and sailed from Valparaiso on the 27th April, where the enemy were still patching up their ships to put them in a state for proceeding to Rio de Janeiro, previous to going to England.

Annexed is a list of the remains of my crew to be exchanged, as also a copy of the correspondence between Commodore Hillyar and myself on that subject. I also send you a list of the prisoners I have taken during my cruise, amounting to three hundred and forty-three.

I HAVE THE HONOUR TO BE, &c.

(Signed)                    D. PORTER.

The honourable Secretary of the Navy of the U.S. Washington.

*P.S. To give you a correct idea of the state of the* Essex *at the time of her sur-render, I send you the boatswain's and carpenter's report of damages; I also send you a report of the divisions.*

It will be perceived by the foregoing narrative that every means was resorted to on my part to provoke the enemy to offer battle with his single ship, but without effect. For this I do not blame Captain Hillyar, since the interests of his country ought to have been, and undoubtedly were, paramount to every other consideration, on this occasion. The reader, however, will judge for himself, whether Captain Hillyar's attack on the *Essex,* then in a crippled state, and within the limits of a neutrality, which he had pledged himself to respect, was, setting aside the question of legality, either brave or magnanimous.

It was my intention to have explained the alteration in the conduct of the Chilian government towards myself, evinced in denying me a right to the protection accorded me by the laws of nations. But this would swell my narrative beyond the limits I had prescribed myself. The explanation may be found in those changes which have been so common in that country, torn by different factions, and in the meanness of that spirit, which takes part ever with the strongest. When I commanded the most powerful force in the Pacific, all were willing to serve me: but when Captain Hillyar appeared, with one still stronger, it became the great object to conciliate his friendship by evincing hostility to me. It will be recollected, by those conversant with the history of the Chilian Revolution, that my particular friends the Carreras were stripped of power and thrown into prison, the government of Chili being usurped by their most inveterate enemies. Added to all this, Captain Hillyar was acting in the character of mediator between the viceroy of Peru and the officers of the Chilian government; in which capacity, he at length caused the country to be delivered up to the royal troops, under a promise of a general and free pardon to those then in possession of power. For this service, Captain Hillyar was made an Hidalgo, and honoured with a conspicuous place in a religious procession, commemorative of the occasion, where he wore the habit of a friar and bore in his hand a waxen candle.

Soon after the capture of the *Essex,* I was sent on board the *Phoebe,* by the officer who took possession of the *Essex.* I had no cause to complain of my treatment while there. Captain Hillyar's conduct was delicate and respectful. The instant of anchoring in Valparaiso, I was allowed to go on shore on parole, and the same privilege granted to my officers, as well as those of my crew who were wounded. The rest were placed under guard, on board a Spanish merchant ship, hired by Captain Hillyar for that purpose.

Under present circumstances, I could not expect any civilities from those in authority at Valparaiso. But the neglect of the governor and his officers was fully compensated by the kind attentions of the good citizens. When my wounded companions were brought on shore, they were borne to the place selected by me for a hospital, by the kind Chilians. The ladies of Valparaiso took upon themselves the task of providing for their necessities and administering to the alleviation of their sufferings. At all times, women of the most respectable appearance attended at the hospital, who tendered their services gratuitously, to take care of the wounded. Without their aid, I have no doubt, many would have died, who now live to thank them. For myself, I shall never forget their gentle humanity; and if it should not be in my power to return it, I bequeath the remembrance as a legacy of gratitude to be repaid by my country.

After providing every thing in my power for the comfort of my wounded companions, I made a visit to the capital of Chili. I shall pass over the events of this journey, and hasten to a conclusion. On referring to the correspondence between myself and Captain Hillyar, in the appendix, it will be seen there was an arrangement made for disarming the *Essex Junior*, and converting her into a cartel; which I considered highly advantageous, as it ensured the safety of a prize. This case was similar to that of the *Alert*, to which Captain Hillyar had objected on a former occasion. His motives for acceding to such an arrangement at this time were probably founded in some apprehensions with respect to my crew, and the probable danger of trusting them on board of the *Phoebe*, which carried a large quantity of specie on freight to England.

The remainder of my brave crew were accordingly embarked in the *Essex Junior*; and on taking leave of Captain Hillyar, after acknowledging his attentions, I seized the opportunity to tell him that though I should take every occasion to do him free justice in that respect, I should nevertheless be equally plain in making known his conduct in attacking me in the manner he had done. The tears came into his eyes, and, grasping my hand, he replied, "My dear Porter, you know not the responsibility that hung over me, with respect to your ship. Perhaps my life depended on my taking her." I asked no explanation at that time, and he gave none. He still has it in his power, however, to clear up the affair to the world; and if he can show that the responsibility rests on his government, I shall do him justice, with more pleasure than I now impeach his conduct. Until then, the stigma rests on him.

On leaving Valparaiso, every effort was made to reach home in time to fit out ships to proceed to the British channel, for the purpose of intercepting the *Phoebe* and her prize; and, favoured by the wind, of which we took every advantage, we arrived off Sandy Hook in seventy-three days. Here we fell in with the *Saturn*, a British ship of war, commanded by Captain Nash, who treated me, in the first instance, with great civility; examined the papers of the *Essex Junior*; furnished me with late newspapers; and sent me some oranges—at the same time making offers of his services. The boarding officer endorsed my passport and permitted the ship to proceed. She stood on in the same tack with the *Saturn*; and about two hours afterwards was again brought to—the papers examined, and the ship's hold overhauled by a boat's crew and officer. I expressed my astonishment at such proceedings; and was informed that Captain Nash had his motives. It was added that Captain Hillyar had no authority to make such arrangements; that the pass-port must go on board the *Saturn* again and the *Essex Junior* be detained. I insisted, that the smallest detention would be a violation of the contract on the part of the British and declared I should consider myself a prisoner to Captain Nash and no longer on my parole. I then offered my sword; assur-ing the officer, I delivered it with the same feelings I surrendered it to Cap-tain Hillyar. He declined receiving it; went on board the *Saturn*; and returned with the information that Captain Nash directed the *Essex Junior* to remain all night under the lee of the *Saturn*. I then said—I am your prisoner; I do not consider myself any longer bound by my contract with Captain Hillyar, which has thus been violated, and shall act accordingly.

At 7 the next morning, the wind being light from the southward, and the ships about thirty or forty miles off the eastern part of Long Island, within about musket shot of each other, I determined to attempt my escape. There appeared no disposition on the part of the enemy to liberate the *Essex Junior*, and I felt myself justified in this measure. A boat was accordingly lowered down, manned and armed; and I left with Lieut. Downes the fol-lowing message for Capt. Nash: "that Captain Porter was now satisfied, that most British officers were not only destitute of honour, but regardless of the honour of each other; that he was armed and prepared to defend himself against his boats, if sent in pursuit of him; and that he must be met, if met at all, as an enemy." I now pulled off from the ship, keeping the *Essex Junior* in a direct line between my boat and the *Saturn*, and got nearly gun shot from her before they discovered me. At that instant, a fresh breeze sprang up, and the *Saturn* made all sail after us. Fortunately, however, a thick fog came on, upon which I changed my course, and entirely eluded further pursuit. During the fog, I heard a firing; and on its clearing up, saw the *Saturn* in chase of the *Essex Junior*; which vessel was soon brought to. After rowing and sailing about sixty miles, I at last succeeded, with much difficulty and hazard, in reaching the town of Babylon, on Long Island, where, being strongly suspected of being a British officer, I was closely interrogated; and, my story appearing rather extraordinary, was not credited. But on showing my commission, all doubts were removed, and from that moment, all united in affording me the most liberal hospitality.

On my arrival by land at New York, the reception given me by the inhabitants, as well as by those of every other place through which I passed, it becomes not me to record. It is sufficient to say, it has made an impression on my mind, never to be effaced.

The *Essex Junior,* after being detained the whole of the day following my escape, and ransacked for money; her crew mustered on deck, under pretence of detecting deserters; her officers insulted and treated with shameful outrage; was at length dismissed and arrived next day at New-York, where she was condemned and sold. In the language I used at that time and subsequently, with regard to the character and conduct of British naval officers, some persons have found great cause of offence. For my full justification, I rest on the foregoing narrative, with the documents by which it is supported. Years have passed away since I first made these assertions; but they have brought with them no experience but what confirms my first impressions.

My escape from unjustifiable detention by the captain of the *Saturn,* was asserted to be a breach of parole; and I have the most undeniable evidence that Admiral Cochrane mustered the officers of his fleet, on his quarter deck, declaring to them that I was out of the pale of honour, and must be treated accordingly. The correspondence between the agents of the two governments, in the Appendix to this volume, will show, by Admiral Cochrane's own distinct admission, that his government, on being made fully acquainted with the circumstances, declared me "discharged from my parole and as free to serve in any capacity as if I had never been made prisoner." Yet, notwithstanding all this, care has been taken to keep up the impression that I remain still under this imputation of a breach of parole, by withholding, on all occasions, the public recantation of a charge publicly made and—unanswerably refuted.

•  •  •

*In 1815 Captain Porter was named to the Board of Navy Commissioners. He would later serve as commander in chief of the Mexican Navy against Spain. President Andrew Jackson employed him in diplomatic capacities in the Mediterranean before his death in 1843.*

# WILLIAM BOWERS

## We Discussed a Bottle
## of Chateau Margot Together

### 1812-1815

*F*ollowing *a tour in the West Indies, Lieutenant William Bowers joined the 10-gun brig HMS* Helicon *in 1810 for a cruise off the Scilly Islands, a stretch of water he would come to know well during the next five years. With the outbreak of the American war, "we began to tire of our hard weather, and limited station," notes Bowers. "Now and then, however, we contrived to stretch a point by getting into the wake of some smart sailing runner from Guernsey or Jersey, which by a long chase brought us into the stream of Nantes or Bordeaux. It was only necessary to keep out of the way of senior officers, and not to be caught poaching on their domains"* (Naval Adventures During Thirty-Five Years' Service, *vol. 1, p. 259).*

WE HAD NOW CAPTURED or destroyed six privateers, besides other vessels of the enemy; this perhaps had some weight with the powers, as, on putting into Plymouth to refit, our worthy commander at length received the promotion he had so long merited, and he left us accompanied by the regret and good wishes of all on board. He was superseded in the command by the youngest son of a distinguished flag officer, who, having been all his time in large ships, at first seemed by no means to congratulate himself on his appointment to the "little bum-boat" as he called her, and used frequently to rally me on the pride I seemed to take in her; but when he got accustomed to her, his opinion of her became as favourable as my own.

Not long after, we returned to our old station west of Scilly, in company with the W——, one of the crack American prize schooners, a beautiful vessel, which the dock-yard wiseacres, however, had done their best to spoil by twice reducing her masts and cramping her with bulk heads and wood work below, so that, though built expressly for fast sailing, as her model denoted, we could at all times work round her. From this, and a deficiency of skill and activity in her commander, an officer who, not having been employed for twenty years, knew not how to handle her—we lost several good prizes. One day when he was about five miles to windward, a large ship came down before the wind and passed him within hail without heaving-to. She was at first steering west by north, but, observing her gradually alter her course, as if to avoid us, I made known my suspicions to the captain, who was at first inclined to let her pass, and obtained his permission to board her. A few shot brought her down; I was already in the boat, but out of sight to leeward, and as soon as she passed within hail, saying she was bound to Newfoundland, I was alongside before any one on board were well aware of the movement, and, springing on deck, found two sailors overhauling a pocket-book, which I instantly seized, and found it contained two American protections or certificates of naturalization. On asking for the captain, a dirty-looking fellow with ear-rings, in the costume of a pig-driver, and with hands the colour of soot, presented himself with a roll of greasy papers. I asked him what privateer he belonged to; he coolly answered, "The *True-Blooded Yankee*."[1] The ship in fact was a valuable West Indiaman, the salvage of which subsequently furnished us with something to carry on the war in Plymouth, and make a cruise or two to Ivybridge.[2] She had been captured two days before, on her way from Bristol to Cork, to join the convoy. Two young men were found locked up in one of the cabins—one, the nephew of the mayor of the former place; these expressing a desire to pay their respects to our captain, I took them on board, and on their return they insisted on loading the boat with some of the good things with which the ship abounded, which they requested us to accept in the name of their friends.

About the beginning of July we received orders to proceed to the longitude of 12° west, to join our old consort the *Reindeer*; this was very agreeable to us all, as we had not only more than once cruised together before, but had always admired the spirit and activity evinced by the management

[1] *This, as my professional readers are aware, was a well-known privateer that made no little havoc among our trade about this time. The* True-Blooded Yankee *was one of the most famous American privateers. She was owned by an American living in Paris and operated out of French ports. On one thirty-seven-day cruise in 1814, she took twenty-seven ships off the coasts of Ireland and Scotland, destroyed seven more in a Scottish harbor, and took possession of an island off the Irish coast for nearly a week.*

[2] *Ivybridge is a town up the Erme River, west of Plymouth.*

of this ill-fated vessel, and the officerlike and gentlemanly bearing of her truly noble commander, Captain Manners, with whom I had the pleasure of being on the most intimate terms. We had frequently discussed together the best way of dealing with our disproportioned American foes, to which one or both were liable every hour to be opposed. His favourite idea always was, "Yard-arm, and yard-arm, three broadsides double-shotted, and board."—Poor fellow! he little thought the opportunity of essaying the experiment was so near. Approaching our ground, we fell in with the *Achates,* Captain Langhorn, and the following day discovered the wreck of a vessel's mast and rigging floating in the water. This at first created no sensation, supposing it to have belonged to some unfortunate foundered trader, one of those numerous instances of unnavigable craft, so little seaworthy, that no one will underwrite them, but which nevertheless are permitted to sacrifice the lives and property of thousands.

Our feelings may be imagined, when, on sending a boat to examine the wreck, the evidence afforded by the grape-shot sticking in the mast, the marks and dimensions of the main cap, the sails, and rigging, left no doubt of the *Reindeer*'s fate.[1] The main-mast appeared to have been burnt off by the copper in the wake of the main boom. Everything denoted that the strife had been sanguinary, and the catastrophe recent; whoever had been the antagonist, he had found tough work. We steered away to the west-

---

[1] The following are the particulars of this action received from one of the survivors: "The enemy (the *Wasp,* American corvette) was discovered on our lee bow about ten A.M. *[on June 28, 1814]* standing towards us. Little preparation was necessary: brother Jonathan had already cured us of that overweening conceit and false security, which long and uninterrupted success had given us, and we were always ready. Finding she would pass to windward, we tacked, and by hard sweeping soon gained a position that would enable us to keep the weather-gauge, when we put about again, and stood towards her. The American now tacked, and stood away from us. By hard sweeping, however, we gained a position on his weather quarter, and from a gun placed on the forecastle, at which Captain Manners attended himself, galled the enemy considerably, killing and wounding several of his men. This advantage was however but temporary; they were silently preparing a deadly return. Luffing athwart our bows, he poured in a deadly broadside, which mowed down our men like grass. The two vessels were now nearly alongside of each other, the carnage was dreadful. Poor Manners, badly wounded in both legs, was carried on the poop, where he remained on his knees, his left elbow on the larboard round-house, and waving his sword in his right to encourage his men, until a musket shot through the head from the enemy's main-top deprived this talented and gallant young officer of existence and spared him the pain of lowering his country's flag to her foe. The action was continued, and the first lieutenant and master being both badly wounded, the gunner, in the absence of the second lieutenant, left at Cork, was called up from the magazine to take the command, but not making his appearance in time, the action was continued by the captain's clerk. In this condition, with seventy out of a crew of one hundred and nine killed and wounded, and the brig a perfect wreck, so as to be unmanageable, we were compelled to strike."

It is unnecessary to comment on this action, and its deplorable results, which, against such an overwhelming disparity of force, ought to have been foreseen. The *Reindeer* mounted

ward, keeping a sharp look-out, and, impotent as our endeavours might prove, fervently prayed for the opportunity of avenging our unfortunate companions. At the end of a week we returned to the spot, where we now found the wreck of the fore-mast.

Not long after, in company with the *Scylla*, eighteen, about two hundred miles west of Scilly, we descried a large ship under a heavy press of sail, steering about W by N. She was painted black, showed no guns or colours, other than a small white flag at the fore-mast, which, with the manner she shortened sail, and backed her main-top sail, keeping the fore-sail and jib on her, after we had whipped a few shot across her bows, impressed us with the idea of her being a merchantman. I proceeded to board her, and on pulling up in her wake, was struck with her breadth of beam, and the warlike cut of her canvass. When close up on her quarter, I hailed her, and was given to understand she was the United States ship *John Adams*, having on board the American Envoy from the Texel, bearing the proposals for peace, and with an Admiralty passport. The captain at the same time invited me on board, pledging his word of honour, that I should not be detained. On this I pulled up and mounted the side. To my astonishment, as I was about to step on deck, I found the whole crew at their guns prepared for action, the matches burning, and the man with the train tackle falls in hands ready for running out the guns. This corresponded so little with the peaceable declaration I had just received, that, not choosing to risk my own honour and the fate of the two vessels, I instantly jumped into the boat, and returned to report what I had seen. By this time the *Scylla* was on her weather quarter, and her commander, a fine veteran of the old school, being senior officer, I reported to him what I had seen. He replied,

---

eighteen twenty-four pounders, and had one hundred and nine men. The *Wasp*, twenty six 32-pounders, and upwards of two hundred men; these were for the most part English seamen, who, having no other alternative than victory or an ignominious death, would, like the crew of the *Essex*, combat with the almost supernatural energy of despair. For this among other national benefits, we are indebted to the sages who some time before had turned adrift all our old men-of-war's men, of eleven years standing, to seek their fortunes wheresoever they might list. Captured in our merchant ships, these ill-used men, indignant at their treatment, and having to choose between a prison or comfortable quarters, good wages, and other inducements, would not long hesitate. This policy deprived us of nine of our best men, all petty officers, and well affected to the service. Might it not have been better to have offered them an extra bounty and allowed them to volunteer for those cruisers most likely to fall in with our powerful adversaries? What might not poor Lambert have done with three hundred such as these? It is said, that previously to his sailing, he wrote to the Admiralty, requesting a survey of his crew, and reporting their inefficient state. He was answered by a certain *ci-devant* secretary, that "if he had any disinclination to go to India in the *Java*, some one should be found to supersede him." [*The* Java *was taken by the USS* Constitution *on December 29, 1812.*] Well might old Admiral O——, when asked how it was the Yankees were walking off with our frigates? exclaim with honest indignation, "Look at your Admiralty, what are they composed of?"

"Bear a hand on board your ship; tell W—— to keep his jib-boom on my taffrail, and we will soon see who he is." A few minutes after, both brigs ranged up on his weather beam, as close as we could without danger of falling on board, and with a voice like the roaring of a lion old Darby then hailed, ordering him to send an officer with his passport. This was complied with, and all being found correct, I returned with the American first lieutenant, a fine young fellow, and was received very ceremoniously.

On entering the cabin I was introduced to the envoy, Mr. Dallas[1]; refreshment was offered, and I am almost ashamed to say refused; however, a young man may sometimes be excused if, influenced by a national sentiment, and in the hurry of the moment, he should overlook those nice shades of conduct, which should guide him according to time, place, and circumstance. A mutually courteous bearing between individuals of hostile nations, thus thrown together, certainly tends "to smooth war's wrinkled front," the ordinary evils of which are enough for suffering humanity, without carrying the brand to the social board. The American captain expressed himself hurt at the cavalier and imperious manner in which he was hailed by the English commodore, as he styled him. I assured him nothing offensive was intended, but that it was his natural manner, being a plain rough seaman. This ship had been a frigate, now razée, and mounting twenty forty-two pounders, and two long twelves, with a crew of three hundred men.

The downfall of Napoleon, and the consequent turn which affairs had taken in Europe, having now left us but one enemy to contend with, we continued on our old station, keenly looking out for, and expecting every day to come to the scratch with some of our "Yankee cousins," who were making great havoc among our merchant-ships, but never could get scent of any of them. We had by this time weathered out four years on this trying service, and, as little was now to be done, began anxiously to wish for a change. At length Buonaparte returned from Elba, and in the beginning of April we were sent to Nantes, with the Prince Regent's proclamation, promising protection to all vessels navigating under the white or Bourbon flag. The merchants of this large city were so well pleased with this intelligence, that they sent on board about two hundred dozen of their choice wines, for the admiral, Sir Henry Hotham, and ourselves. Fifteen months after, when the battle of Waterloo, and the surrender on board the *Bellerophon*, had finally sealed the emperor's fate, we were again sent to the same place with the news. On this occasion the purser, doctor, and myself accompanied the captain to the city, and were received by the mayor and authorities with marked respect and attention. The former, being too much

[1] *George M. Dallas (1792-1864), later vice president of the United States under James K. Polk.*

occupied with his municipal duties to be much with us, consigned us to the care of his brother-in-law, who entertained us at the Hotel de France, where we had an excellent dinner, and in the evening, accompanied us to the theatre. Between the play and farce we adjourned to the coffee-house attached to the latter, and were sipping our punch, when the hussar officers entered, apparently in a state of intoxication, and in the greatest excitement. On seeing us, one of them exclaimed, "*Voilà! les b——s Anglois, les pirates!*" with other insulting language. I was for resenting the injury instanter, by sending a bottle at his head, and was with some difficulty prevailed on by my companions to take no notice of the affront, which, under all the circumstances of our situation, was undoubtedly the most prudent course. Our respectable host, aware of the effervescing feeling of the military, who were entirely opposed to the political opinions of the commercial part of the community, and expressed the most rancourous hatred of every thing English—appeared very uneasy. Our hero, having apostrophized us in some of the choicest rhetorical flowers of La Halle, appropriately finished by filling a paper biscuit-bag with wind, putting it behind one of our chairs, and, stamping on it, which made it explode like a pistol; then drawing his sword, he flourished it over his head. I never found it more difficult to repress my indignation. We now rose to leave the room, and, loitering behind the others, I fixed myself in the middle of the saloon, opposite to our Bobadil, and fixing on him a look which could not well be misinterpreted—for I knew not a word of the language—drew my sword half way out of the scabbard. The effect was magical; he cowered from my gaze, all his heroics seemed in an instant to have evaporated, and in a minute he was taken out of the room as peaceable as a lamb by a gendarme, and placed under arrest by order of his colonel.

During our final cruise in the bay, in the month of February, I had a very narrow escape. One afternoon, on a bitter cold day, we fell in with the wreck of a schooner abandoned by her crew. On going in the boat to examine her, I found her floating on her broadside, half full of water, her sails all blown away. On her deck were a few pieces of salt provisions, two trunks, and some other articles. By a rope, which hung over the side and was quite fagged out, we were led to conclude that her boat had gone down under her counter, and the crew had probably perished. A starved cat in her last agonies was stretched on the cabin floor. In the hold was a quantity of salt, and, floating in all directions, a number of broken fruit-boxes. About one hundred cases of oranges and lemons, and some bales of figs, were in good preservation. The flag of Oldenburg was in her rigging, and by her papers we judged she was from St. Ubes [*Setúbal, Portugal*]. I sent the boat back with two cases of oranges, advising the captain to hoist the cutter out, clear her of all that was worth taking, and let her go. The boat returned with orders to endeavour to pump her out, and put her in sailing order, for which purpose I received a reinforcement of the boatswain and twelve men. Her pumps were hoisted on deck, cleared, and with copper strainers over their heels put down again, and placed in ballast-baskets. With these, and a well formed in the main hatchway for baling, we soon freed her, set her on her keel, and fitting her with some of our storm stay-sails, put a mid-shipman with a few men on board, took her in tow, and made sail for Scilly.

A heavy swell from a previous westerly gale got still higher as the wind freshened in the night. At daybreak I perceived her heeling very much to leeward, and I requested permission to go on board, to see how matters really were. I was desired to wait until after breakfast, when I reminded the captain of it again. Again procrastination was the order of the day. "When the lower deck was cleared I might go." I felt uneasy; the breeze was fresh-ening, and the sea rapidly getting up. About ten A.M. the jolly-boat was lowered, and with the boatswain and fourteen men I went on board. I immediately perceived she was settling fast in the water, and sent the men's hammocks and bags with the midshipman, whom I desired to say that she could not swim long. The boat returned with orders to cast her off and leave her. Unluckily the stream cable, by which she had been towed, was so jammed with the strain, that some time was lost in obeying the order; at length we attempted to cut it with our knives, but, before this could be done, seeing her going down, I ordered every man into the boat, and was in the act of shoving off, when I found three of them missing.

I jumped on board again, and was urging them to lose no time, when she suddenly lurched to port, fell on her broadside, her mast heads in the water, and nearly sunk the boat, which had got entangled with her main-mast head and crosstrees. We meanwhile secured ourselves as well as we could in what had been the weather rigging, every moment expecting to share the fate of the boat and crew, which, if she went down, appeared inevitable. When the former at length got clear, I gave the boatswain the necessary orders for extricating us from our perilous situation; this was scarcely done, when she settled gradually for a few seconds, and then as quick as lightning sunk to rise no more. The world of waters closed over our heads; it was an awful moment. How far I was carried down, or how long under water, I do not know: when I emerged, I felt as if about to burst. My leather hat, forced down over my eyes by the pressure of the water, at first prevented me from seeing; and, when this was a little arranged, all I could perceive was an empty orange-case, which I ineffectually attempted to reach: clogged with a pair of heavy boots, and my winter dress saturated with water, I in vain struggled towards it—a mountain-sea was running, which, just as I thought it within my reach, came and carried it further from me. At length I saw a glimpse of a hat waving, and immediately after, as the sea lifted, the boat, with the boatswain standing abaft. She was, however, so crowded, that they could scarcely keep her head to the sea; and, although only a few yards distant, I was so exhausted, that I could only just keep my head above water. My legs were beginning to sink; my sight was getting dim; at every breath I was swallowing the brine, and was suffering the last horrors of a protracted death by drowning, when my hand was seized by a marine in the bow of the boat, and I was saved. The carpenter's mate and the captain of the top, the latter a good swimmer, were also saved, but a third companion in danger was seen no more. I was put to bed, and by proper treatment brought about again, but my health had received a severe shock, and I remained for some time languid and spiritless.

One morning at daylight, about ten days after, we perceived a large ship, apparently steering for Bourdeaux; we instantly gave chase, and in ten hours came up with, and took possession of her; she proved to be an American from Charlestown [*Charleston, South Carolina*], bound to Bourdeaux with cotton, cocoa, and rice; we sent her into Plymouth, and she turned up a noble prize. It is astonishing how this operated on my impaired health; I seemed suddenly to have taken a new lease of existence.

•   •   •

At length we were at peace with all the world, our exertions were no longer needed, we were ordered to Hamoaze and were paid off all standing, with scarce sufficient time, with the assistance of our acquaintance, to sweat out the fifty dozen of wine, presented to us by our liberal friends, the merchants of Nantes.

Scarcely was the pendant hauled down, when I received an appointment to the Y—— brig of eighteen guns, fitting at Woolwich for the North Sea station, and I joined her in September 1815. Not being allowed to open a rendezvous for the entry of seamen, the greater part of my time was passed in the neighbourhood of Tower Hill, and the purlieus of Wapping, with now and then a trip to the Brickhelms, Epping Forest, and other places, whither our tars had retired to rusticate, and where, with the characteristic improvidence of real sailors, they were "spending like asses" that pay and prize-money which "they had earned like horses." While the cash lasted, to say nothing of the general antipathy to the service, there was little inclination for employment. But, by dint of coaxing—for Jack, if humoured, is easily managed—and a liberal supply of "heavy wet," I succeeded in getting the vessel tolerably well manned.

At the latter end of September, we sailed for Shields, where we remained nearly four months to keep the colliers in order. During this interval, our men, taking advantage of the captain's disinclination to punishment, became quite disorderly, and, availing themselves of our proximity to the shore, before we sailed, the greater part of them deserted. In consequence of this we returned to Sheerness, to complete our compliment; and I, once more enacting the part of Sergeant Kite, was sent up to London to enter men. This, as on a former occasion, cost me about thirty pounds in treating, and redeeming Jack's traps "out of chancery,"[1] for which I never received a farthing's compensation, while the officers of larger ships employed on this service had a liberal allowance. Except on the principle that "the weakest goes to the wall," I know of no reason why this, as well as many other invidious distinctions made between large and small craft, should have place.

Once more manned, we sailed in April on a cruise to the North Sea, against the smugglers, and were not long before we sent some hundreds of tubs to the custom-house. Our captain, who had made but little prize-money during the war, hoped now to bring up the lee-way, or get promoted for working up the unfortunate contrabandiers; with this view we had procured at Dover, a sailing galley, about thirty-six feet long, by eight broad, built on the plan of some lieutenant of the impress at Folkstone, a complete coffin. The most arduous period of the war, when surrounded with enemies, and the strictest vigilance was necessary, was nothing to this harassing service. Day and night there was no rest for a soul on board; every floating thing was taken for a smuggler and chased, boarded, and submitted to the most rigorous search. I soon got sick of this sort of employment; and, the galley being equipped as a tender, I was very glad to get the command of her, receiving an order to cruise eight days off Flushing, and then join the ship at or off the Hock of Holland. With a midshipman, twelve seamen, and two marines, riflemen, I set out in search of adventures. I had been ordered "rigorously to blockade the port," and could not help smiling on contrasting the present with my former service on the same spot in the P——, seventy-four, when, in many a heavy gale, with three cables ahead, we had been pitching bows under on the seventeen fathom bank; West Cappel church or lighthouse dipping in the horizon, with seventeen sail of the line "blockading the Dutch fleet." The day was fine when I quitted the brig, and I stood close in and reconnoitred my ground, anchoring in the evening on Steer Bank in eight fathoms, West Cappel in sight to the eastward. About two A.M. the wind got up, and soon freshening into a gale, the boat became very uneasy. I tried her in every way, but could not make her lay-to with-out shipping so much water that we could scarcely keep her free, all hands baling.

[1] Pawn.

The weather became worse, and our situation alarming. I consulted with the quarter-master, and it was deemed necessary to bear up for shelter, but where? Dangerous sands lay between us and the shore, I did not know the channels, and the rain and sea prevented us from seeing the buoys. The lead was kept going, and a man was placed at the fore-mast head to look out for the Dumloo Channel; nought however was perceptible but the sea breaking in all directions. "One wide water all around us, all above but one black sky."

I had a chart in my hand, but the wind and rain, which poured down in torrents, prevented me from using it. All depended upon a sharp look-out and good steerage. I had reason to fear I had missed the channel, and death appeared inevitable. All at once, to our great joy, however, a buoy is seen on the starboard bow; immediately after another Hurra! In two minutes more we are in smooth water between the banks, and shortly after anchored in the five-fathom channel close to the beach, with the north-west bastion, and one of the churches of Flushing in sight, congratulating each other on our narrow escape. Unbending the foresail, we spread it over the main-boom as a covering from the rain, made a fire in our hanging stove, and, splicing the main brace, in five minutes all our dangers were forgotten in our present security. The gale continued, the rain still poured down upon us in spite of the awning, which afforded but a partial shelter, but we huddled round our stove and beguiled the night with telling long "yarns." Daylight brought us better weather; we returned to our cruising ground, and our term of service being expired, rejoined the ship to the great satisfaction of the captain and crew, who had been very apprehensive for our safety. We took several boats with their cargoes, but our success by no means inspired the same feeling that the capture of the enemies of our country had done. The poor fellows always told a piteous tale of their own, and the distress of their wives and families, who would now be ruined by their detention.

In the month of July I applied to be superseded; this was immediately complied with, and I found myself, for the first time in my life, on shore "Lord of myself," and with sufficient of the sinews of war to carry it on for some time. Having seen the lions of London, I essayed the air of Cheltenham, then took a trip to Brighton, and hence crossed over to Paris, the *agrémens* [*agréments*, pleasures] of which detained me five months. The wounds the national sentiment had sustained by the reverses at Waterloo, and the occupation of la grande Cité, still fresh, were galled and kept open by the supercilious arrogance, the pride, and ostentation of many of our unbending countrymen, who, bringing with them all the deep-rooted prejudices springing from ignorance and conceit, which it has so long been the invidious policy of our oligarchy to foster among us, made no attempt to conceal their own imagined superiority and the contempt in which they held every other nation. This, among a high-spirited people, blinded by similar mistaken prepossessions, could not but lead to frequent collision; and quarrels and duels (in which many of both parties fell) were the order of the day. For my own part, my English notions of men and things having been more than once revised by early travel and experience, any false ideas I might have formed of our neighbours were easily corrected. Those who, like the learned Smellfungus,[1] see every thing through the jaundiced or distorted medium of spleen, journey with a predetermination to be satisfied with nothing, make comparisons, and, for want of understanding, taste, or discrimination, find "nothing so good as at home," will always do well to save the expenses of locomotion, by stopping at home and remaining contented within their own narrow circle, among the people and things which alone they are capable of appreciating, and not lowering their own or their country's pretensions in the eyes of foreigners.

I passed a very agreeable time among this light-hearted, vivacious, and really good-tempered people. The only unpleasantness I experienced occurred at Havre, on my return. I was one day dining at Justan's *table d'hôte* in that town, when some gentlemen recently arrived by the diligence were discussing the circumstances of the battle of Waterloo, and the loss of so many of our officers on that sanguinary day. This led to some remarks from an officer-like Frenchman, at the table in a military undress, who, as usual, gasconaded so vehemently on the superior skill of his countrymen in the use of the sword, at the same time contemning the deficiency of our officers in science, that I could not help correcting his notions, evidently preconceived in an ignorance at least of one side of the question, and endeavoured to show him that, in a thousand instances, our seamen, with no other training than that acquired on the forecastle at single stick (generally as an amusement), when wielding the ship's cutlass on similar principles, somehow or other always contrived to drive their adversaries like sheep before them, whatever the science of the latter might be. As usual on such occasions, the argument waxed warm. Both, like

> *"Men convinced against their will*
> *Were of the same opinion still."*

Moreover I felt excited, and an unlucky reminiscence of the unmerited and dastardly insult received at Nantes coming across my mind, I lost my cen-

---

[1] *Smellfungus was Sterne's name for Smollett, so earned for the unforgiving and discontented tone of his* Travels Through France and Italy *(1766).*

tre, and could not help saying somewhat intemperately, "Only rouse me in a good cause and give me a ship's cutlass, and I don't care a d——n for any Frenchman that exists." On this, with an urbanity and moderation that reproached me, he explained to me that it was by no means his intention to cast any reflection on the bravery of a class of men whose prowess he had not only witnessed, but personally experienced, having been cut down by a British officer at Badajos. The cloth was removed, the party broke up, and I was left alone with a stranger, who, complimenting me on the manner I had supported the national reputation, announced himself as the brother-in-law of the Hon. C. B. of our Navy. We discussed a bottle of Chateau Margot together, and I was going down stairs, when I saw my quondam *[former]* friend, the officer, making towards me. I really thought he was about to test my skill as an *escrimeur [fencer]*, and was well pleased to accept his challenge—more in accordance with my inclinations—to sip my coffee with him. He was a fine fellow, had seen much service, and like all others of his class was devoted to l'Empereur.

# Notes on the Texts

### "In the King's Service, 1793–1794," and
### "With Stopford in the Basque Roads, 1808–1809"

*A Mariner of England: An Account of William Richardson from Cabin Boy in the Merchant Service to Warrant Officer in the Royal Navy [1780 to 1819] as Told by Himself,* ed. Colonel Spencer Childers, C.B., R.E., was published in 1908 by John Murray of London. "In the King's Service" is part (pp. 100–11) of chap. 5 of the original; "With Stopford in the Basque Roads" is part (pp. 228–57, with some omissions) of chap. 10. The chapter titles and text used in *Every Man Will Do His Duty* are from the 1908 edition.

### "Commence the Work of Destruction: The Glorious First of June, 1794," and "An Unequal Match, 1807–1808"

These two passages were excerpted from *A Narrative of My Adventures (1790–1839),* by Sir William Henry Dillon, K.C.H., Vice-Admiral of the Red, edited by Michael A. Lewis, C.B.E., M.A., F.S.A., F.R.Hist.S., for the Navy Records Society and published in two volumes as *Dillon's Narrative: Vol. 1, 1790–1802* (Navy Records Society, vol. 93, 1953) and *Dillon's Narrative: Vol. 2, 1802–1839* (Navy Records Society, vol. 97, 1956). "Commence the Work of Destruction, 1794," originally appeared in vol. 1, chap. 3, "The Revolutionary War: 'The First of June,' April 1794–December 1794" (aet. 13½–14½)." "An Unequal Match, 1808," originally appeared in vol. 2, chap. 10, "Post Captain: September 1807–April 1808 (aet. 27–27½)." The annotations are those of Michael Lewis.

In his introduction to *Dillon's Narrative,* Lewis writes:

The trouble with the sea-novelists as a group is that they tend to "typify" their characters. There is a suspicious family likeness between all Captains, all First Lieutenants, all Midshipmen, all Warrant Officers. Dillon has none of this weakness. There is no reason why he should, because all his characters are so plainly real people drawn from life; and life does not reproduce such straight similarities, even when it places men in similar environments. It is for this reason more than any other that this Narrative of Dillon's is probably the finest naval-social document of his period yet discovered. (vol. 1, p. xxxi)

## "The Noted Pimp of Lisbon and an Unwanted Promotion in Bull Bay, 1794"

This passage appears as "Gorgon, 44," pp. 155–71, in *Recollections of James Anthony Gardner, Commander R.N. (1775–1814)*, ed. Sir R. Vesey Hamilton, G.C.B., Admiral, and John Knox Laughton, M.A., D.Litt., for the Navy Records Society, 1906.

In his introduction to a later edition, entitled *Above and Under Hatches* (London: Batchworth Press, 1955), editor Christopher Lloyd writes,

Compared with other naval memoirs of the period, it may be said that Gardner's are by far the most racy and colourful. . . . He had an eye for detail and a natural turn of phrase which any professional novelist might envy. He is, in fact, the literary counterpart of Rowlandson, and in the literature of the sea he stands in the first rank. These recollections have been the favorite reading of members of the Navy Records Society since they were first printed for the Society in 1906. . . . (p. xv)

*Ed. note:* This chapter has been substantially rearranged for this volume. Gardner tended to deliver a quick and dry summary of the movements of his ship and then to follow that with a series of anecdotes and observations. Here, for readability, the anecdotes and observations have been inserted into their respective places of occurence during the *Gorgon*'s voyage.

## "For the Good of My Own Soul, 1795," and "Mad Dickey's Amusement, 1798–1800"

These two chapters are excerpted from *The Nagle Journal: Diary of the Life of Jacob Nagle, Sailor, from the Year 1775 to 1841* (New York: Weidenfeld and Nicolson, 1988). The former is part of a chapter entitled "Run to India" (pp. 182–90), and the latter is the chapter entitled "Prizemaster of HMS Netley" (pp. 218–44). The diary is edited and annotated by John C. Dann. Nagle's spelling and grammar appear as they do in his original diary; all bracketed notations are Dann's. Both passages are reprinted by the permission of John C. Dann.

### "They Would as Soon Have Faced the Devil Himself as Nelson, 1796"

This passage originally appeared as "Nelson at Bastia," by An Old Agamemnon [and also signed M.C.] in *United Service Journal*, Feb. 1841, no. 147: 212–18.

### "The Battle of Cape St. Vincent, 1797"

This passage was taken from the second edition of *A Narrative of the Battle of St. Vincent; with Anecdotes of Nelson, Before and After that Battle*, by Colonel Drinkwater Bethune, F.S.A. (London: Saunders and Otley, 2d ed., 1840). Courtesy of the Naval War College.

### "The Fortune of War, 1799"

This passage is taken from *A Master Mariner: Being the Life and Adventures of Captain Robert William Eastwick*, ed. Herbert Compton (London: T. Fisher Unwin, and New York: Macmillan, 1891). It originally appeared as chapter 7 (pp. 130–51).

### "The Audacious Cruise of the *Speedy*, 1800–1801"

This passage originally appeared as "Cruise of the 'Speedy,' " chap. 5, in *The Autobiography of a Seaman*, by Thomas, Tenth Earl of Dundonald, G.C.B., Admiral of the Red, Rear-Admiral of the Fleet, Marquess of Maranham, etc. (London: Richard Bentley and Son, 1890), pp. 38–54.

Cochrane's action served as the historical basis for much of Patrick O'Brian's first Aubrey-Maturin novel, *Master and Commander*.

### "Bermuda in the Peace, 1802–1803," and "When I Beheld These Men Spring from the Ground, 1809"

*The Midshipman: Being the Autobiographical Sketches of His Own Early Career, from Fragments of Voyages and Travels*, by Captain Basil Hall, R.N., F.R.S. (London: Bell and Daldy and Sampson Low, Son, and Co., 1865). *Fragments of Voyages and Travels* was originally published in three volumes between 1831 and 1833 and was frequently reprinted. In "Bermuda in the Peace, 1802–1803," the passage here entitled "A Whale of an Adventure" was originally "Bermuda in the Peace" (pp. 50–63). The section here entitled "History of Shakings, the Middies' Cur" was originally "Midshipmen's Pranks—History of Shakings" (pp. 64–78).

The passage entitled "When I Beheld These Men Spring from the Ground, 1809," comes from chaps. 24 and 25 of the original (pp. 262–95).

### "The Battle of Trafalgar, 1805"

This passage was originally published in *Nautical Economy* by Jack Nastyface in 1836. The author's real name, which he concealed for fear of reprisal, was William Robinson. The book later appeared as *Jack Nastyface: Memoirs of a Seaman* (Hove, East Sussex: Wayland Ltd., 1973).

### "The Death of Lord Nelson, 1805"

This passage was taken from *The Death of Lord Nelson, 21 Oct. 1805*, 2d ed., by William Beatty, M.D.; ed. and originally published by Edward Arber, F.S.A., 1807. (Birmingham: War Library, 1894).

In his preface to *The Death of Lord Nelson*, Arber writes,

This little book . . . is valuable not only for giving us the fullest and most authoritative account in existence of Lord Nelson's death; but also for much interesting information respecting his life, from one who knew him well. Especially would we note that "He possessed such a wonderful activity of mind as even prevented him from taking ordinary repose, seldom enjoying two hours of uninterrupted sleep; and on several occasions he did not quit the deck during the whole night."

### " 'Damn 'em, Jackson, They've Spoilt My Dancing,' 1809–1812"

This passage originally appeared in chaps. 7, 8, 9, 10, and 11 (pp. 138–219) of *The Perilous Adventures and Vicissitudes of a Naval Officer, 1801–1812; Being Part of the Memoirs of Admiral George Vernon Jackson (1787–1876)*, ed. Harold Burrows, C.B.E., F.R.C.S. (Edinburgh and London: William Blackwood and Sons Ltd., 1927).

In his introduction to *The Perilous Adventures*, Burrows suggests that he believes Jackson was the prototype for Captain Frederick Marryat's fictional character Peter Simple.

### "The Woodwind Is Mightier than the Sword, 1809–1812"

This passage was taken from the chapter "Impressed into the British Navy," in *James Durand: An Able Seaman of 1812, His Adventures on "Old Ironsides" and as an Impressed Sailor in the British Navy,* ed. George S. Brooks (New Haven: Yale University Press, 1926), pp. 47–64. *The Life and Adventures of James R. Durand, During a Period of Fifteen Years, From 1801 to 1816: In Which Time He Was Impressed on Board the British Fleet, and Held in Detestable Bondage for More Than Seven Years; Including an Account of a Voyage to the Mediterranean,* "Written by Himself," was originally published by E. Peck & Co., of Rochester, New York, in 1820.

### "HMS *Macedonian* vs. USS *United States,* 1812"

This passage is from *Thirty Years from Home or A Voice from the Main Deck,* 15th ed., by Samuel Leech (Boston: Tappen, Whittemore and Mason, 1843), pp. 122–53. Leech spent six years in the British and American navies. He was captured in the British frigate *Macedonian,* and afterward entered the American Navy. Later he was then taken in the United States brig *Syren* by the British ship *Medway.*

### "An Unjustifiable and Outrageous Pursuit, 1812–1813"

*Life on the Ocean; or, Twenty Years at Sea: Being the Personal Adventures of the Author,* by George Little, was first published in 1843. The sections reprinted here, chaps. 17, 18, 19, and part of 20, were taken from the 3d ed., (Boston: Waite, Pierce, 1845).

Little was released from Dartmoor prison at the end of the war. Later, his days as a merchant captain sailing from Baltimore were cut short by blindness. He became increasingly committed to temperance and Christianity, and the publication of his memoirs, *Life on the Ocean,* was at least in part to champion these causes.

### "A Yankee Cruiser in the South Pacific, 1813," and "Showdown at Valparaiso, 1814"

These passages were taken from *Journal of a Cruise Made to the Pacific Ocean by Captain David Porter in the Unites States Frigate Essex, in the Years 1812, 1813, and 1814,* 2 vols., 2d ed. (New York: Wiley and Halsted, 1822). "A Yankee Cruiser in the South Pacific, 1813," is from vol. 1, chap. 5, "Run Down the Coast of Chile and Peru; Arrive at the Galapagos Islands," pp. 108–26, and chap. 6, "The Gallipagos Islands; Prizes," pp. 148–54. "Showdown at Valparaiso, 1814," is from vol. 2, chap. 18, "Events at Valparaiso, Previous to the Capture of the Essex," pp. 143–77.

## "We Discussed a Bottle of
## Chateau Margot Together, 1812–1815"

This passage originally appeared as chap. 12 of *Naval Adventures During Thirty-Five Years' Service*, vol. 1, by Lieutenant W. Bowers, R.N. (London: Richard Bentley, 1833), pp. 272–302.

# Selected Bibliography

Chandler, David G. *Dictionary of the Napoleonic Wars*. New York: Simon & Schuster, 1993.

Clowes, William Laird. *The Royal Navy*, vols. 4 and 5. London: Sampson Low, Marston and Company, 1899–1890.

Davies, David. *Fighting Ships: Ships of the Line, 1793–1815*. London: Constable, 1996.

Falconer, W. A. *A New Universal Dictionary of the Marine*. Modernized and enlarged by William Burney. London: 1815. (Reprint. London: Macdonald and Jane's, 1974.)

Harvey, A. D. *English Literature and the Great War with France: An Anthology and Commentary*. London: Nold Jonson Books, 1981.

Hattendorf, John B., et al, eds. *British Naval Documents, 1204–1960*. London: Navy Records Society, 1993.

Heinl, Robert Debs, Jr. *Dictionary of Military and Naval Quotations*. Annapolis: United States Naval Institute, 1966.

Henderson, James, CBE. *The Frigates: An account of the lesser warships of the wars from 1793 to 1815*. New York: Dodd, Mead, 1970.

Hill, Richard. *The Oxford Illustrated History of the Royal Navy*. Oxford and New York: Oxford University Press, 1995.

King, Dean, with John B. Hattendorf. *Harbors and High Seas: An Atlas and Geographical Guide to the Aubrey-Maturin Novels of Patrick O'Brian*. New York: Henry Holt, 1996.

——— and J. Worth Estes. *A Sea of Words: A Lexicon and Companion for Patrick O'Brian's Seafaring Tales*. New York: Henry Holt, 1995.

Lloyd, Christopher. *Captain Marryat and the Old Navy*. London: Longmans, Green, 1939.

———. *Lord Cochrane: Seaman—Radical—Liberator: A Life of Thomas, Lord Cochrane, 10th Earl of Dundonald*. London: Longmans, Green, 1947.

Long, David F. *Nothing Too Daring: A Biography of Commodore David Porter, 1780–1843*. Annapolis: United States Naval Institute, 1970.

Maclay, Edgar Stanton. *A History of American Privateers.* New York: 1899. (Reprint. New York: Burt Franklin, 1968.)

Manning, Captain T. D., and Commander C. F. Walker. *British Warship Names.* London: Putnam, 1959.

Pivka, Otto von. *Navies of the Napoleonic Era.* Newton Abbot: David & Charles, 1980.

Price, Anthony. *The Eyes of the Fleet: A Popular History of Frigates and Frigate Captains 1793–1815.* London: Hutchinson, 1990.

Steel, David. *Steel's Naval Chronologist of the War.* London: C. & W. Galabin. (Reprint. London: Cornmarket Press, 1969.)

Werstein, Irving. *The Cruise of the Essex: An Incident from the War of 1812.* Philadelphia: Macrae Smith, 1969.

# Index

*Achates*, HMS, 397

*Achille, L'* (French ship), 183

*Achilles*, HMS, 213

Adair, Captain, 172, 181, 182

*Adamant*, HMS, 109*n*

Adams, D. P., 388, 390

Adams, Mate, 314

*Agamemnon*, HMS, 55

*Aigle* (French ship), 215, 224, 230

Ajugia, Cape, 357

*Alcide*, HMS, 30, 33, 54–55, 202, 203

Aldrich, Mr., 308

*Alert*, HMS, 33, 38, 373, 392

*Alexander*, HMS, 38

Allemand, Adm. Lacharie Jacques Theodore, 212, 225

Allen, Mr. Henry, 209

Allen, Vice-Counsel, 94, 94*n*, 95, 97–100

Almyer, Captain, 297

*Amazon*, HMS, 217, 220, 297

*Amelia*, HMS, 199, 218, 220, 221, 222

*America*, HMS, 36, 38

American privateers, 319, 320–44, 395–96

American Revolution, xxvii

American seamen, 37, 45

   impressment of, 290–99, 303–4

American ships, on coast of Peru and Chili, 350

*Amethyst*, HMS, 217, 220

*Amitié, L'* (French ship), 129

Andrews, Capt. George, 202

*Apollo*, HMS, 46*n*

Appleby, Thomas, 258

*Aquilon* (French ship), 226, 228

*Arathusa*, HMS, 297

Archer, Mr., 318

*Arethusa*, HMS, 9

*Argo* (merchant vessel), 13

"Arthur O'Bradley" (song), 42

Atkinson, Mr., 173

*Atlantic* (British whale-ship, *later* Essex Junior), 367, 382

Auchinlick, Midshipman, 257, 258

*Audacious*, HMS, 16

"Audacious Cruise of the *Speedy*, The" (Cochrane), 120–36

Austria, declares war on France, 222

*Authentic Narrative of the Death of Lord Nelson* (Beatty), 183

*Ave Maria* (Spanish ship), 132

Avranches, France, 265

Azores (Western Islands), 339

*Babet* (French ship), 10

Bainbridge, Comm. William, 380, 380*n*

Baird, Gen. Sir David, 188, 235, 245, 245*n*

Baker, John, 196

Ball, Captain, 109

Bandy (ship's cook), 8

Barbadoes, 294

*Barclay* (American whale-ship), 345, 346, 349, 352–54, 356–60, 365

*Barfleur*, HMS, 73, 77, 79, 120, 235

Barnwell (Barnewall), Edward, 379, 385, 387, 388

Barrère de Vieuzac, 31*n*

Barrosa Ridge, 257*n*

Bartowe, M. W., 379

Basque Roads action, xxvii, 213, 215, 216, 218–21

Bastia, Corsica, 54–63, 123

Batavian Republic (Netherlands), 44, 156

Battle in the Aix Roads, 212, 226–33
  map, 227

Battle of Blenheim (1704), 58*n*, 80

Battle of Camperdown (1797), 87

Battle of Cape St. Vincent (1797), xxiv, xxv, xxvi, 64–87, 169, 180
  map, 74–75

Battle of Copenhagen (1801), 169

Battle of Corunna (1809), xxiv, xxv, xxvii, 216*n*, 234–54

Battle of Malplaquet (1709), 58*n*

Battle of Oudenarde (1708), 58*n*

Battle of Rammiles (1706), 58*n*

Battle of the Nile (1798), 119, 169

Battle of Trafalgar (1805), 18*n*, xxiv, 156, 159–68, 233
  and death of Nelson, 169–84
  map, 163
  Nelson's signal for, xxiii, 161, 161*n*, 171

Battle of Vimiera, Portugal, 233

Battle of Waterloo, 253, 405

Baugh, Capt. Thomas Folliott, 202

Baxter, Captain, 361

Bay of Bengal action, xxv, 108, 109–19

Bay of Biscay, 212, 335

*Beagle*, HMS, 225

Beamish, Lieut. George, 276–77

Beamish brothers, 285

Beatty, William, xxvi, 168, 169–84

Beaulieu La Loup, Captain, 111

Bedford, Capt. William, 213

Beecher, Lieut., 18, 24–25

*Belle Caroline, La* (French brig), 131

*Bellette*, HMS, 203

*Bellona*, HMS, 222

Belson, Colonel, 257*n*

*Belvidere*, HMS, 322, 323

Bentham, Gen. Samuel, 88*n*

Bentinck, Capt. George William, 30, 30*n*

Beresford, Commodore, 218, 219, 226

Beresford, Sir J., 219

Berkeley, Adm. Sir George Cranfield, 28, 28*n*

"Bermuda in the Peace" (Hall), 139–56

Bermuda Islands, 142, 234

Berry, Lieutenant, 77, 82

*Berwick*, HMS, 36

Bethune, Drinkwater, xxv, xxvi, 64–87

Bickerton, Sir Richard, 187, 289

*Bien Aimé*, HMS, 3–5, 8

Bitche citadel, 278–84, 278*n*

*Black Eyed Susan*, HMS, 91

*Black Joke* (air), 39

*Black Joke* (American privateer), 323

Blackwood, Captain, 170, 171

*Blanche*, HMS, 53, 88, 89, 91

Blanco, Mr., 370

*Blenheim*, HMS, 28*n*, 71, 73

Bligh, Capt. John, 219, 228

Bligh, Lieutenant, 178, 181

Bombay, India, 7–8

Bonaparte, Joseph, 233

Bond, Capt. Francis, 87–94, 90*n*, 98–100, 102–7

*Bonne Citoyenne, La*, HMS, 69, 71

Bordo (prisoner), 217

Bostwick, M. W., 388

Bowen, Capt. James, 189

Bowers, Lieut. William, 395–406

Boycott, Lieutenant, 27

Brenton, Captain, 30*n*, 188

Brest, France, 260

Bridport, Baron, 18*n*. See also Alexander Hood

Britain
  declares war on France (1803), 156
  Napoleon's desire to invade, 183
  Spain declares war on (1804), 156
  and War of 1812, 299

*Britannia*, HMS, 76, 79

British Fleet, 12*n*, 16
  Mediterranean Fleet, 55
  ships on the coast of Peru and Chili (list), 350–51, 381
  and Trafalgar, 18*n*
  See also Channel Fleet

Brown, Lieutenant, 174

Brown, Mate William, 314–15

*Brunswick*, HMS, 27, 27*n*, 51

"Bryan O'Lynn" (comic song), 42–43

*Bucentaur* (Spanish ship), 170, 173

Buchan, Mr., 106

Bulford, Lieut. John, 312

Bulkley, Mr., 176, 177

Burgh, General de, 57, 60, 63

Burke, Mr., 175, 176–77, 178, 180

Burley, Mr., 50

Burrard, Gen. Sir Harry, 233

Cadiz, Spain, 35, 36
  bombardment of, 87
*Caesar*, HMS, 16, 19, 213, 216, 217, 220–24, 226, 230, 232
*Calcutta* (French ship), 216–17, 221, 226, 228, 231
Calder, Capt. Robert, 70, 85, 86, 159
*Caledonia*, HMS, 213, 222, 230
Callao, Peru, 354–55
*Calypso* (French ship), 220, 221
*Cambrian*, HMS, 142, 275
Cameron (French pilot), 217
Cape Finister, 105–6
Capel, Thomas Bladen, 234
*Captain*, HMS, 54, 55, 69, 73, 76–83, 82*n*
Car (Ker), Captain, 219
Card, John, 306
Carden, Capt. John Surman, 303, 311–12, 316
Carreras, 391
Carrington, Lord, 188
Carslake, Lieutenant J., 285
Cartagena, Spain, 324–25
*Carysfort*, HMS, 13*n*
*Cassard* (French ship), 230, 231
*Castor*, HMS, 13, 28
*Catharine*, HMS, 381, 390
Cazy, Squire, 95
*Cerberus*, HMS, 46*n*
*Chance*, HMS, 118
Channel Fleet, 299
  and Basque Roads, 213, 218
  and blockade of France, 212
  and French Revolutionary War, 10
  and Glorious First, 11–13, 13*n*, 14, 17–20
Chantrell, Lieut. Billy, 35, 37, 40
*Charles* (American whale-ship), 345–46, 349
*Charlton*, HMS, 381
Chatham, Lord, 204
Chatham Island, 359–60
Chatterton, George, 52*n*
*Cherub*, HMS, 367, 369–79, 382–85, 389
Chesapeake action (1781), 12*n*
Chevalier, Mr., 179
*Childers*, HMS, 192–93, 195–97, 199, 200, 201–12
Chilean Revolution, 391
Chili (Chile), coast of, 350–51, 354, 381, 391
Christian, Adm. Sir H., 189
*Christina* (Danish galliot), 210
Churchill, Lord, 311, 312
Cintra negotiations, 233
Clark, Mr., 225
*Cleveland*, HMS, 230
*Clorinde* (French ship), 256–57, 260, 289

Cochrane, Adm. Sir Alexander, xxv, xxvi, 120, 223, 225, 229, 232–33, 293, 394
Cochrane, Hon. Archibald, 136
Cochrane, Lieut. Thomas, 119, 120–36
Cockburn, Captain, 56, 65, 66–67
Collingwood, Admiral Lord, 8, 161, 164, 171, 172, 178, 179, 184
Collingwood, Captain, 76, 77
Collingwood, Midshipman, 182
*Colossus*, HMS, 71, 72, 76
Combined Fleets, 170, 183
Comenia River fort, 97
"Commence the Work of Destruction" (Dillon), 12–32
*Commerce de Marseilles* (French ship), 33, 33*n*
Committee of Thirty (Corsica), 59
*Concord*, HMS, 9
*Conflict*, HMS, 222, 225
Conn, Lieutenant, 256, 259–61, 274, 284, 285
Consitt, Seaman, 26, 30*n*
*Constitution* (French privateer), 123
*Constitution*, USS, 289, 290, 332, 343, 344, 352, 380*n*
Cook, Capt. James, 111, 111*n*
Cook (Cooke), Capt. Edward (of *La Sybille*), 111, 111*n*, 116, 117, 117*n*, 118
Cooke, Captain (of *Mornington*), 110, 111, 112, 114, 118
Cooper, Boy, 309
Coral reefs, 143–44, 145, 146
Cordova, Adm. Don José de, 63, 66, 73
Cornwallis, Adm. Sir William, 4, 7, 8, 9, 10, 18*n*
Cornwallis, Lord, Charles, 1st Marquis, 4
Corsica, 54, 56–63
Corunna, Spain, 156, 233, 234. *See also* Battle of Corunna
Cosby, Vice-Admiral P., 33, 34
Covington, Gunner, 89
Cowan, Lieut. John S., 383
Cowan, Midshipman, 354, 364
Cowell, John G., 361, 387, 388
Cowey, Mr., 223
Croker, John Wilson, 311
Crump, Mr., 36
*Culloden*, HMS, 71, 72, 73, 80
Culverhouse, Lieutenant, 65, 68, 69
Curtis, Sir Roger (*later* Baronet), 29, 29*n*, 289

"Daddy" (midshipman), 151–55
*Daedalus*, HMS, 108*n*, 109
Dallas, George M., 399, 399*n*
Dalrymple, Gen. Sir Hugh, 233

"Damn 'em, Jackson, They've Spoilt My Dancing" (Jackson), 255–89
Danish, 169, 206–8
Dann, John, xxvi
Davies, Lieutenant, 224
Davis, Captain, 112, 117, 118
Davis, Lieutenant, 229
"Death of Lord Nelson, The" (Beatty), 169
Decatur, Comm. Stephen, 303, 311, 316, 318, 387
*Defence*, HMS, xxvi, 195, 12–32
*Defiance*, HMS, 215, 218–19, 220, 221, 222
Delancey, Col. Sir William Howe, 253–54, 253n
Demerara, 156
*Demourisque* (merchant ship), 14
Devonshire, Midshipman, 271, 272, 274
*Diadem*, HMS, 56, 58, 73, 77
Dickson (Dixon), Lieut. John, 27, 27n
Diego Garcia Island, 4–5
Dillon, Lady, 187
Dillon, Sir John Joseph, xxvi
Dillon, Sir William Henry, xxv–xxvi, xxvii, 12–32, 185–212
Dillon, William Mervyn, 188
Discipline
   and cat-'o-nine-tails, 159
   and impressed Americans, 292
   and mast-head, 153
   and swearing, 7
*Discovery*, HMS, 111
Dixon, Admiral, 352
Donalson, Boatswain, 89
*Donegal*, HMS, 215, 218, 219, 220, 221
*Dotterel*, HMS, 218, 220, 221, 225
Douglas, Mr., 111, 116
Douglas, Admiral B., 198–99
Douglas, Sir Andrew, 30
Downes, Lieut. John, 347, 349, 360, 361, 364, 367–68, 369, 379, 382, 383, 386, 393
*Dragon*, HMS, 213
Drake's Island, 291
*Dreadnought*, HMS, 213, 232
*Dromo* (American ship), 335
*Dryad*, HMS, 297
Dubosc, Captain, 40
Ducker, Boatswain, 37–38, 42
Duckworth, Adm. Sir John, 373, 375
Duncan, Admiral, 87
Duncan, Mr., 34
*Dunciad, The*, 38n
Durand, James, xxvii, 289, 290–99
Duzenbery, Samuel L., 379, 388

East India Company, 44, 45, 47n, 48, 48n, 117n, 118, 344, 364
Eastwick, Robert, xxv, xxvi, 107, 108–19
*Ecce Homo* (Spanish ship), 129
Edgar, Lieutenant, 34, 40, 42
Edmonds, Lieut. Thomas, 195n
*Egmont*, HMS, 54, 58, 76
*Egyptienne, L'* (French privateer), 91
Ehrman, John, 47n
Elba Island, 56
*Elizabeth* (British ship), 216
Elliot, Mr., 30, 30n
Elliot, Sir Gilbert, 54, 56n, 57, 59–60, 63–70, 80, 81, 83, 84, 86, 87
Ellis, Jack, 229
*Emerald*, HMS, 217, 220, 221, 225
Emmet, Tom, 8
*Endeavour*, HMS, 110, 116, 117, 118
*Endymion*, HMS, 234, 252
*Engageant* (French ship), 10
*Eole, L'* (French ship), 30
*Esperance, L'* (schooner), 93, 94
Essel, Sub-Lieut. John, 278n
*Essex*, USS, 316, 344–66, 368, 388, 398n
   action with *Phoebe*, xxv, 368–80, 383–91
*Essex Junior*, USS, 367, 368, 372, 373, 375, 380, 382, 383, 384, 388, 389, 392, 393, 394
*Etna*, HMS, 225, 226, 230
*Euryalus*, HMS, 169, 170
Evans, Dr. Evan, 258
Evans, Jack, 335
*Excellent*, HMS, 73, 76, 77

Falconer, Major, 188
Fane, Captain F. W., 275–76, 289
Farragut, Adm. David, 345, 388
Finch, Lieutenant, 380
Fitzpatrick, Boatswain, 27
*Flora*, HMS, 9
Flying Squadron, Howe's, 13n, 15
*Forte, La* (French frigate), 107, 108, 117n
   action with *La Sybille*, xxv, xxvi, 111–19
"For the Good of My Own Soul" (Nagle), 45–53
"Fortune of War, The" (Eastwick), 108–19
*Fougueux, La* (French ship), 173
*Foxhound*, HMS, 224
*Fragments of Voyages and Travels* (Hall), 254
France
   behind enemy lines in, 259–89
   Britain declares war on, 1803, 156
   peace with Spain in 1795, 44
Franco-Prussian War of 1870, 278n
Fraser, General, 235, 247

Frederick, Captain, 73
French Fleet, 86, 169
  and Battle of Trafalgar, 162, 165–66
  Brest Fleet, 63
  Brest Fleet, and Basque Roads, 218–23
  and Glorious First of June, 15–22, 23
  and Revolutionary War, 11, 13, 14–15
French National Convention, 15, 31*n*
French prisons, xxvi, 268–73
  at Bitch, 276–81
  escapes, 273–76, 278–79, 281–82
French privateers
  in Bay of Bengal, 108
  in Mediterranean, 123–26
  off Spain and Portugal, 91–92, 103–4
French Revolutionary War (1793–1802), xxiv,
  xxvii, 9–11, 34*n*
Fugleman, 5, 28, 28*n*
*Furieuse* (French ship), 221

Gallipagos Islands, 356, 359, 360–61, 363–64,
  366
Gambier, Captain (*later* Admiral Lord), 12,
  17–18, 20, 21, 27–30, 185, 186, 190–92,
  193, 197, 203, 212, 213, 218, 220, 222, 223,
  230, 233
Gambier, Lady, 190, 191
Gamble, Lieutenant, 361, 382
*Gamo, El* (Spanish ship), 120, 128, 134–36
Gardner, Captain, 345, 346, 349
Gardner, James Anthony, xxv, xxvi, 33–44
Gardner, Midshipman, 32
Gardner, Sir Alan (*later* Baron), 18, 18*n*
Garlies, George, Viscount, 69, 80, 80*n*, 81, 86
Geers, Benjamin, 383
*Généreaux* (French ship), 119, 120, 121, 139
Genoa, Italy, 122
George, Capt. Sir Rupert, 187, 187*n*, 188
George III, King of England, 83, 303
*George Washington* (American privateer),
  322
*Georgiana* (British whale-ship), 361, 362, 364,
  365, 381
Gibraltar, 64, 66
*Gibraltar*, HMS, 214
Gill, Mr., 101
Gilman, Andrew, 214
Glorious First of June (1794), xxiv, xxvi,
  xxvii, 11–32
  map, 23
*Glory* (French ship), 18
*Goliah*, HMS, 76
Goodall, Mr., 45, 48, 49–51, 52
Gordon, Midshipman, 271, 272–74

*Gorgon*, HMS, 32, 33, 38, 41–43, 48, 50, 52,
  52*n*, 53, 88
Graeffer, Mrs., 190
Granville, France, 264–65
*Gratuities to the Relations of Officers and Others
  Killed in Action*, xxxvii
Graves, Adm. Thomas, 12, 12*n*
Gray, Alexander, 46*n*, 53*n*
Gray, Lieutenant, 109*n*
Green, John, 256, 256*n*
*Greenwich* (British whale-ship), 381–82
Grey, Dr., 188–89
Grimes, William, 101
Groce, Samuel, 383
*Growler*, HMS, 225
*Guerrier*, HMS, 318, 332
Guns, 18
  filling with powder, 14
  loading, 22, 22*n*, 26
Guthrie, Dr., 134
Guyaquil, Peru, 358–59

Hacker, Jerry, 39–40
Haddaway, Midshipman, 365
Halifax, Canada, 140
Hall, Basil, xxv, xxvii, 139–56, 233, 234–54
Hamilton, Captain Sir C., 38
Hamilton, Lady, 169, 175, 177–79, 190, 190*n*,
  192
*Hannibal*, HMS, 278–79*n*
*Hanoverian London* (Rude), 52*n*
Hardy, Captain, 169, 171–78, 180, 181–82
Hardy, Lieutenant, 64, 65–66, 68, 69
Hardyman, Lieutenant, 116–17, 119
Harvey, Rear-Adm. Sir Eliab, 223
Havre-de-Grâce, Le (Haverdegrass), 89–91
Hawtayne, Mr., 27
*Hazard*, HMS, 46*n*
Hazzard, Captain J., 320
*Hector*, HMS, 381, 390
*Helicon*, HMS, 395
Hills, Lieutenant, 178
Hillyar, Capt. James, 367, 368–79, 382, 383,
  384, 388–93
*Hind*, HMS, 120
"HMS *Macedonian* vs. USS *United States*"
  (Leech), 303–19
Hoche, General, 63
Hoffman, Richard K., 379
Holmes, Gun Captain, 24
Holmes, Levi, 383
Hood, Adm. Sir Alexander, Baron Bridport,
  18, 18*n*, 118
Hood, Sir Samuel, 94*n*, 234, 235, 251

Hope, Capt. Sir George Johnstone, 202
Hope, Lieut. David, 308, 311, 312
Hope, Sir John, 240, 246, 247
*Hornet* (American sloop), 344, 380
Horse Island, 292
Hotham, Adm. Sir Henry, 53, 54, 215, 220, 221, 399
*Hound*, HMS, 231
Howe, Admiral Lord, 11–13, 13n, 15, 16–17, 19–20, 21, 28, 29, 29n, 32

*Illustrious*, HMS, 222
*Impérieuse*, HMS, 223, 225, 226
Impressment, xxvi, 7, 10
   of American sailors by Britain, 289–99
   in England, 3, 44, 45, 46, 47, 48–52
*Inconstant*, HMS, 108
*Indefatigable*, HMS, 216, 220, 224
*Indiana* (French ship), 230, 231
Indian Ocean, 107
*Indomptable, L'* (French ship), 17, 19
*Inflexible*, HMS, 257
Ingraham, Lieutenant, 378, 379, 382
Innes, Capt. Thomas, 193, 195, 196
*Insolent*, HMS, 225
"In the King's Service" (Richardson), 3–22
*Intrépide* (French privateer), 121
*Intrepid*, HMS, 9
*Invincible*, HMS, 29, 41
Irish invasion attempt (1796), 63
*Irresistible*, HMS, 71, 73, 77, 78, 82
Isaacs, George W., 361, 379, 388
*Italien* (French ship), 220, 221

Jackson, George Vernon, 254, 255–89
Jackson, President Andrew, 394
*Java*, HMS (formerly *Renomée*), 289, 318, 343, 344, 352, 380, 398n
*Jean Bart* (French ship), 219–20, 221
Jennings, Midshipman, 35
Jervis, Adm. Sir John, Earl St. Vincent, 54, 55, 56, 62, 66–77, 82–85, 82n, 84n–85n, 87, 94n
*John Adams*, USS, 290, 398
Johnson, Captain, 118
Johnson, Samuel B., 388
Jones, Lieutenant, 223, 224, 229
Jones, Rev. Mr., 217, 231
*Junon*, HMS, 255–57, 289

Keith, Admiral Lord, 119, 120, 122–23, 126, 187–88
Ker (Car), Captain, 219
King, Lieutenant, 174

King, Lieut. Sir Richard, 3, 4, 213
*King George*, HMS, 222, 224
Kingsbury, Boatswain, 365
Kivell Nan, 308, 309
Knight, Mr., 196

Lacaille, Captain, 231
Lafon, Capt. John Baptist, 231
Laforey, Captain F., 13n
Lagos Bay, 84, 84n, 85
Langhorn, Captain, 397
*Leander*, HMS, 139–40, 145, 146, 147, 155, 234
Lebozec, Captain, 222
Le Cam, French pilot, 217
Lee, Admiral, 255
Lee, John, 24
Leech, Samuel, xxvii, 303–19
*Légère, La* (French cutter), 100
Leghorn Roads (Livorno), 56, 129n
Le Neve, A. W. H., 206
L'Estrange, Lieutenant, 278, 278n–79n, 281–85
*Leviathan*, HMS, 171
Leworthy, H., 280, 282
Lightroom, 14, 14n
Lindsay, Captain, 71
Linois, Admiral, 136
Linscott, Mr., 385
Lisbon, Portugal, 36–38, 99, 106
Little, George, xxv, xxvi, 320–44
*Lively*, HMS, 64, 69–72, 77, 80n, 81, 83, 84, 85–86
*Liza, La* (Spanish ship), 127
Lloyd, Christopher, xxvi, 183–84
Lobos islands, 357, 358
Logholm, Mr., 314
*Loire* (French ship), 256, 257
Longford, Lord, 30
*Lord Cochrane* (Lloyd), 183–84
Lossing, 297n
*Lougen* (*Lügum*, Danish brig), 206–8, 206n, 212
Lovedon, Mr., 187
Lyman, James R., 388, 390
Lynes, Mr., 101
*Lyra*, HMS, 225

McBride, Rear-Admiral, 13
*Macedonian*, HMS, 343, 344
   action with USS *United States* (1812), xxiv, 303–19
McGuire, Lieutenant, 30
Macguire, Pat, 61–62
Mackerel, Mr., 110, 111, 115
M'Knight, Lieutenant, 347, 361, 387, 388, 390

McLeay, Mr., 186
M'Nicholl, Gunner, 199–200
"Mad Dickey's Amusement" (Nagle), 88–107
Madison's island (Nooaheevah), 382
Mahan, 31*n*
Mahan, Andrew, 383
Major, Mr., 116
Malabar coast, 6
Malta, 129–30
Manby, Captain, 190
*Manerva* (French-built ship), 93
Manly, Captain, 46*n*
Manners, Captain, 397, 397*n*
Mantua, siege of, 56
*Margretta*, HMS, 46*n*
*Marlborough*, HMS, 28
Marlborough, John, Duke of, 58, 58*n*
Martin, Abbé, 265–66
Martin, Capt. Byam, 38
Martin, Captain G., 78, 82
Martinico, 294
Massena, 122–23
Mauritius Islands, 4–5
*Mediator*, HMS, 222, 223, 225
Mediterranean
    British control of, 184
    cruise of 1801, xxv
*Medusa*, HMS, 231
*Melampus*, HMS, 9
*Meleager*, HMS, 56
Melville, Mr., 280
Menzies, Archibald, 57–58, 59
Merchant ships
    effects of wars on, xxv, 344
    and French Revolutionary War, 13–14
    smuggling by, 35–36
Miller, Captain R. W., 77, 81
Miller, Doctor, 355, 360, 365–66
Miller, Dr. Robert, 383
Miller, Gunner, 365
*Minerva*, HMS, 3–7, 9, 10, 11
*Minerve*, HMS, 64–69, 71, 76, 78, 79
*Minotaur*, HMS, 126
Mitchell, Sir Andrew, 139, 156
*Modeste*, HMS, 33, 38
Montagu, Rear Adm. George, 13, 13*n*, 15*n*
*Montague*, HMS, 380
*Montezuma* (British whale-ship), 361, 364, 381
Montgomery, Dr. Alexander, 379, 388
Moore, Captain, 118
Moore, Gen. Sir John, 233, 234–35, 236–37, 245
Moorsom, Capt. Robert, 159, 192

Morard de Galles, Vice-Admiral, 63
Morgan, Mr., 288
*Mornington*, HMS, 110, 116, 118
Mornington, Lord, 112, 117, 118
Mottley, Lieut. Samuel, 312
Mulgrave, Lord, 186, 187, 191–93, 204
Murray, Captain, 76
*Mutine*, HMS, 126, 288

Nagle, Jacob, xxv, xxvi, xxvii, 44, 45–53, 87, 88–107
Nagle, Mrs. Jacob, 49–51, 52
*Naiad*, HMS, 169, 216, 218, 220, 231
*Namur*, HMS, 76, 79, 198
Napier, Gen. Sir William Francis Patrick, xxv, 235*n*, 236, 237, 241, 247
Napoleon Bonaparte, 47, 54, 55, 156, 183, 184, 222, 231, 234, 236, 265, 399
Napoleonic War (1803–1815), xxiv–xxv, 156
*Narcissus*, HMS, 290–91, 294, 295, 297, 298
Nash, Captain, 393
Nastyface, Jack. *See* William Robinson
National Bank of England, 86
*Nautical Economy* (Robinson/Nastyface), 168
*Naval Chronicle* (1799), xxxvii
*Naval Chronologist of the War* (Steel), 87
Navy Record Society, British, xxvi
Nelson, Adm. Lord Horatio (*formerly* Captain), xxv, 123, 139, 156, 190
    and Battle of Cape St. Vincent, 65–69, 71, 73, 77, 78, 81, 82, 82*n*, 87
    and Battle of Trafalgar, xxiii, 159, 160, 161
    Bethune on, 64
    death of, at Trafalgar, 162, 169–84
    distinctions and honors, 55, 83–84, 87
    and evacuation of Bastia, Corsica, 54–60, 63
    made Colonel of Marines, 55
    and Malta, 119
    motto of, 307
    and ordinary seamen, xxiii–xxiv
    and rebellion of *Blanche*, 53
Nelson, Horatia (adopted daughter), 175, 179, 190*n*
Nelson, Lady, 87
Nepean, Evan, 90*n*
*Néréie* (French ship), 289
*Nereyda* (Peruvian privateer), 346–49, 353
*Netley*, HMS, 87, 88, 88*n*, 93, 95, 97, 98, 100–105, 106
New Orleans, United States, 332
*New Zealand* (British ship), 365, 381
Nicholson, Lieutenant, 313

Nielly, Rear-Admiral, 15n
Niger, HMS, 71, 79
Nimrod, HMS, 224, 346, 347, 349, 353
Nocton, HMS, 380
North Rock, Bermuda, 143–44, 147
"Noted Pimp of Lisbon and an Unwanted Promotion in Bull Bay, The" (Gardner), 33–44
Nymph (American brig), 98

Ocean, HMS, 225–26, 231
Odenheimer, William H., 364, 379, 387–88
Ogden, Midshipman, 388
Ogilvie, Mr., 182
Ommanney, Mr., 189, 194
Orion, HMS, 17, 71, 73, 76
Osterley (British ship), 111
Oughton, Mr., 239, 243, 244–45

Pakenham, Capt. Thomas, 29, 29n, 30
Pallas, HMS, 224
Palmer, Mr., 181
Palmerston, Lord, 187
Parker, Lieutenant, 135
Parker, Lieut. Charles, 196
Parker, Rear-Admiral, 73, 87
Parry, Sir William Edward, 140, 147
Pasco, Lieutenant, 172, 176
Pasley, Rear-Admiral, 16
Patriot (French ship), 231
Paul Jones (American privateer), 320, 337–43
Payta, 358, 359
Peace of Amiens (1802), 136, 139
Peake, Lieutenant, 177
Peake, Lieut. Thomas Ladd, 203
Pearl (French ship), 33, 38
Pearson, Lieutenant, 77, 82
Pellew, Sir Edward (Lord Exmouth), 9
Peninsular War, xxv, 257n
Perrée, Rear-Admiral, 119
Perrey, Captain, 346
Perseverance (British ship), 365
Peru, coast of, 350–51, 352, 353–54, 356, 381
Phaeton, HMS, 30
Phoebe, HMS, 169, 382
   action with USS Essex, xxv, 367, 368–79, 383–86, 389–92
Pierce, William, 388
Pitmans, Mr., 49, 52n
Pitts, Captain, 362
Plane Island, 127
Plymouth, England, 298
Poinsett, Mr. Consul General, 390
Pole, Secretary to the Admiralty, 185–86

Policy (British whale-ship), 361, 362, 364, 365, 381
Poliphemus, HMS, 46n
Pollard, Mr., 182
Polly, John, 22–24
Pomone (French ship), 10
Poplar, England, 47, 47n
Porteau, Captain, 231
Porte Chaussée prison, 276–78
Porter, Capt. David, xxv, 344, 345–94
Porto Port, Portugal, 91–96, 98, 99, 101, 102, 104
Portugal, coast of, 87
   privateers off, 91–97
Portuguese, 6
Preneuse, La (French privateer), 108, 109, 109n
Price, Lewis, 383
Prince George, HMS, 71, 73, 196
Pringle, Capt. Thomas, 30, 30n
Privateering, xxv
   American, 319, 320–44, 395–96
   and Bay of Bengal, 108–11
   and coast of Portugal, 91–92, 102–7
   English, 102, 105
   French, 91–92, 103–4, 108, 123–26
   and Mediterranean, 123–26
   Spanish, 92, 95–96, 102, 128–36
Prompte, HMS, 10, 11
Prudente, La (French privateer), 108–9, 108n

Queen, HMS, 18, 27, 31
Queen Charlotte, HMS, 16, 28
Quiberon Bay invasion, 44, 47n
Quilliam, Lieutenant, 181

Racoon, HMS, 382, 383, 384
Rainier, Comm. Peter, 13, 13n
Ram, Lieut. William Andrew, 175
Randall, Captain, 353
Recovery (British ship), 117
Redoubtable (French ship), 173, 174, 181–82, 183
Redpole, HMS, 225
Reed (carpenter), 313
Reeves, Lieutenant, 177
Regulus (French ship), 230, 231
Reindeer, HMS, 396, 397, 397n–98n
Renaudin, Captain, 31n
Rendezvous, HMS, 204
Renommée (French ship, later Java), 256–57, 259–60, 289
Resolution (British ship), 111
Revenge, HMS, 159, 219, 226, 230, 231–32

*Revolutionnaire* (French ship), 16, 16*n*
*Reyna Luisa, La* (Spanish packet), 106
Richardson, Capt, Charles, 213, 221
Richardson, William, xxvii, 3–11, 213–33
Rio de La Hache Indians, 327–31
Ritchie, seaman, 26
Rivers, Mr., 177
Robinson, Lieutenant, 4, 7
Robinson, William (Jack Nastyface), xxiv,
  xxvi, 159–68
Rodd, Captain, 220
Rodgers, Commodore, 368
Rodgers, John, 383
Rodney, Comm. John, 38
*Romulus*, HMS, 66
Roncière, Captain de la, 231
*Rose* (British merchant ship), 45–47, 46*n*, 53*n*,
  365, 381
Rotely, Lieutenant, 182
*Royal George*, HMS, 18, 213
Royal Navy, British, xxv, xxvii, 54, 107, 303,
  319
*Royal Sovereign*, HMS, 26, 161, 170, 171–72
*Royal William*, HMS, 10, 41
Rude, George, 52*n*

Sadler, Jack, 309
*St. Anna*, 171–72
*St. Fiorenzo* (French ship), 33, 38
*St. George*, HMS, 55, 213
St. George's Island, 142, 147
St. Lorenzo Island, 352–53, 354
St. Lucia, 156
*St. Salvadore*, HMS, 299
*Salamine*, HMS, 126
*Salvador del Mondo* (Spanish ship), 78
Sanders, Capt. George, 202, 202*n*, 203, 204–5
*San Josef* (Spanish ship), 78, 82
*San Nicolas* (Spanish ship), 77, 78, 82
*Sanspareil* (French ship), 28
*Santa Sabinga* (Spanish frigate), 69
*Santissima Trinidad* (Spanish ship), 73, 79, 85,
  170, 173
*San Ysidro* (Spanish ship), 78
*Saturn*, HMS, 393, 394
Saumarez, Adm. Sir James, 202
Sawyer, Capt. Charles, 53
Schomberg, 33*n*
Scilly Isles, 41, 41*n*, 395
*Scioto* (American ship), 321
Scott, Dr., 170, 175, 176, 177, 178, 179–80
Scott, Michael, 293*n*
Scott (public secretary), 170, 172
*Scylla*, HMS, 398–99

Seamen
  clothing, 4, 10
  dancing, 7
  discipline of, xxiii–xxiv, 6–7, 152–53
  drinking, 8
  food for, 20, 40
  grievances of, xxv
  loyalty of, xxiv
  rat infestations and, 52, 52*n*
  scurvy and, 10
  treatment of, by British, 304, 317
  vantage points of, xxv–xxvi
Secker, Serjeant Major, 174
*Seine, La* (French ship), 14, 256
*Señora de Gratia* (Genoese ship), 129
Sercey, Rear-Adm. Marquis de, 111, 118
*Seringapatam* (American ship), 382
Seymour, Capt. Sir Michael, 279*n*
Shakings (dog), 148–52
*Shannon*, HMS, 292, 292*n*
Shaw, John K., 379
Shortland, Capt. John, 255, 256, 257, 258–59,
  289
Shovell, Sir Clowdsiley, 41, 41*n*
"Showdown at Valparaiso" (Porter), 367–94
*Sir Andrew Hammond* (American ship), 382,
  390
*Sirius*, HMS, 169
*Sisters*, HMS, 226
Smith, Assistant Surgeon, 176, 178
Smith, Mr., 53
Smith, Sir Sidney, 186
Smollett, Tobias, 405*n*
Smuggling, 35–36
Smyth, John Greatrise, 53*n*
*Snake*, HMS, 204, 210
Soleil, Captain, 188
Sotheby, Rear-Admiral, 232
Soult, Marshal Nicolas Jean de Dieu, 234,
  239
South Pacific
  cruise of 1812–1814, xxv, 345–66
  map, 348
Spafford, James, 355, 355*n*, 383
Spain, 56, 56*n*, 87, 128–29
  declares war on Britain, 156
  Napoleon's occupation of, 184
Spanish Coast, 132–33
Spanish Grand Fleet, 63, 64–69, 86
  and Battle of Cape St. Vincent, 70–80, 84*n*,
    85, 169
  and Battle of Trafalgar, 162, 164, 167–68
Spanish Main, xxv, 127, 322
Spanish privateers, 92, 95–96, 102, 128–36

*Speedy*, HMS, 119, 120–36
   map of cruise, 124–25
Spiller, Mr., 281
Spithead, England, 41
*Standard* (British ship), 351
Steel, 87
Sterne, Laurence, 275, 405*n*
Stopford, Rear-Adm. Robert, 212, 216, 217, 218, 220–21, 222, 224, 230, 231
Strachan (Strawen), Sir Richard, 10, 89, 90, 213, 215
Street, Midshipman, 271, 273, 274
Sturt, Capt. Henry Evelyn Pitfield, 196
*Suffolk*, HMS, 13, 74
*Surprize*, HMS, 118
Sutton, Capt. John, 58
*Swallow* (packet), 4
Sweeny, Edward, 383
*Swiftsure*, HMS, 182
*Sybille, La* (French ship), 220, 221*n*
*Sybille, La*, HMS
   action with *La Forte*, xxv, xxvi, 111–19, 117*n*

*Tagus*, HMS, 384, 390
Tagus River, 99, 102
Taylor, Captain, 10
Taylor, Captain A., 320, 340, 341, 342
*Téméraire*, HMS, 171, 173, 174, 182, 213
Temple, Midshipman, 186, 186*n*, 200
Teneriff Island, 87
Terceira Island, 339
*Terrible* (Spanish ship), 65, 66
Terry, James, 388
*Texel*, HMS, 201, 202, 203
*Thalia*, HMS, 190
*Theseus*, HMS, 219, 226
"They Would as Soon Have Faced the Devil Himself as Nelson" (M.C.), 54–63
*Thomas*, HMS, 223
Thomas, Midshipman, 259, 261, 274
Thompson, John (Jack), 60
Thompson, Midshipman John, 257–58
Thompson, Vice-Admiral, 79, 87
Throgmorton, Mr., 280, 281
*Tigat, Le*, 88
Tobago, 156
"Toe-the-line matches," 152
Tomlinson, Seaman, 36
*Tonnant*, HMS, 222, 230, 232
*Tonnère* (French ship), 226, 228, 231
*Topaze* (French ship), 33, 38
Torres, Capt. Don Francisco de, 135
*Tourville* (French ship), 231
Tower of London, 50*n*

Townsend, Old Jack, 61–62
Towry, Capt. George Henry, 56
*Travels Through France and Italy* (Smollett), 405*n*
*Tremendous*, HMS, 109*n*
*Triumph*, HMS, 213, 219
Trogoff, Rear-Adm. Comte de, 33
*Tromp*, HMS, 225
Troubridge, Capt. Sir Thomas, 13*n*, 28, 28*n*, 72, 73
*True-Blooded Yankee* (American privateer), 396*n*
Tucker, Capt. Thomas, 367, 369, 370, 389
Tunis Bay, 131
Turtles, 5–8
Twysden, Lieutenant, 18, 21, 22, 28
*Tyrannicide, Le* (French ship), 17, 19
Tyrrell, Capt. Edward, 50–52, 50*n*

"Unequal Match, An" (Dillon), 185–212
*Unicorn*, HMS, 224
United States
   and French Revolutionary War, 15
   War of 1812, 299
   *See also* American privateers; American seamen; American ships
U.S. Navy, xxvii, 290
*United States*, USS, xxvii, 343, 344
   action with *Macedonian* (1812), xxiv, 303–19
"Unjustifiable and Outrageous Pursuit, An" (Little), 320–44
Ushant Island, 13

*Valiant*, HMS, 30, 219, 226, 228
Valparaiso, Chile, 345, 353, 354, 367–94
Van Stabel, Rear-Admiral, 15*n*
*Varsovie* (French ship), 226, 228, 229
Vashon, Adm. James, 201, 202–3, 204, 205, 211–12
Vashon, Capt. James Giles, 203
Vashon, Mr., 116
Vashon, Mrs., 203
*Vengeur* (French ship), 27*n*, 31, 31*n*
*Vesuvius*, HMS, 231
Viana, Portugal, 95, 96, 97, 102, 103
*Victory*, HMS, 41, 70, 72, 73, 76–77, 79, 81, 84, 168, 169–74, 176, 177, 181–83
Vigo, Portugal, 91, 92, 94–96, 94*n*, 95*n*, 98, 100, 103, 234–35, 236
Villaret-Joyeuse, Rear-Admiral, 11
*Ville de Paris*, HMS, 251
Villeneuve, Admiral, 156, 170
Voller, Mr., 187
Voller, Mrs., 187, 189, 190, 193, 194

Waldegrave, Vice-Admiral W., 77
*Walker* (American whale-ship), 345, 346, 349
Walker, Mr., 312, 318
Wall, Sailor, 231
Wallis, Capt. James, 33, 34, 35, 38, 40, 41, 42, 43
Walter, General, 294
War of 1812 (1812–1815), xxiv, 289, 299, 303–19, 321–44, 345
War of the Spanish Succession (1707), 41*n*, 58*n*
Warren, Sir John Borlase, 9
*Wasp*, USS, 352, 397, 398*n*
Watson, Mr., 311
Webster, Master, 27
"We Discussed a Bottle of Chateau Margot Together" (Bowers), 395–406
Wellesley, Sir Arthur (*later* Duke of Wellington), 233, 253
Wells, Adm. Thomas, 195, 197
Wells, Mr., 314
Wells, Mrs., 195
West, Captain, 346–47, 349
West, John, 24, 28, 32
Westemburg, Assistant Surgeon, 176
West Indies, 156, 185
Westphall, Mr., 178
Whales, 145–47
"When I Beheld These Men Spring from the Ground" (Hall), 234–54

Whipple, Mr., 175
Whitby, Captain, 6–7, 10
Whitehurst, Midshipman, 257, 260–70, 276
White Swan tavern, 48–49, 48*n*
*Whiting*, HMS, 224
Whittaker, Thomas, 318
Willaumez, Rear-Admiral, 212, 225
Williams, Lieutenant, 174
Wilmer, Lieutenant, 361, 387
Wilson, Lieutenant, 361
Wilson, Mr. William, 206
Winthorpe, Lieutenant, 223, 228–29
"With Stopford in the Basque Roads" (Richardson), 213–33
*Wohlfort* (Dutch ship), 92
Wolfe, General, 117
"Woodwind is Mightier than the Swore, The" (Durand), 290–99
Wright, Capt. John Wesley, 186, 186*n*

"Yankee Cruiser in the South Pacific, A" (Porter), 345–66
*Yarmouth*, HMS, 118
York, Duke of, 279*n*
Young, Arthur, 188, 188*n*
Young, Mr., 35
Young, Mrs., 35
Yule, Lieutenant, 174

*Zealous*, HMS, 55